STRATEGIES FOR MANAGING BEHAVIOR PROBLEMS IN THE CLASSROOM

Third Edition

Mary Margaret Kerr

University of Pittsburgh

C. Michael Nelson

University of Kentucky

Merrill,
an imprint of Prentice Hall

Upper Saddle River, New Jersey   Columbus, Ohio

LIBRARY OF CONGRESS CATALOGING-IN-PUBLICATION DATA

Kerr, Mary Margaret.
   Strategies for managing behavior problems in the classroom / Mary
Margaret Kerr, C. Michael Nelson. --3rd. ed.
    p. cm.
Includes bibliographical references and index.
ISBN 0-02-363527-4
    1. Classroom management 2. Behavior disorders in children.
3. Behavior modification. 4. School discipline. I. Nelson, C.
Michael (Charles Michael). II. Title
LB3013.K47 1998
  371.5'3–dc21

97-15169
CIP

Cover art: David Stevens/West Central High School, Columbus, Ohio FCB MR/DD
Editor: Ann Castel Davis
Production Editor: Linda Hillis Bayma
Production Coordination, Illustrations, Text Designer: Custom Editorial Productions, Inc.
Photo Coordinators: Nancy Harre Ritz and Kecia Cornelius
Design Coordinator: Julia Zonneveld Van Hook
Cover Designer: Russ Maselli
Production Manager: Patricia A. Tonneman
Director of Marketing: Kevin Flanagan
Marketing Manager: Suzanne Stanton
Advertising/Marketing Coordinator: Julie Shough

This book was set in New Baskerville by Custom Editorial Productions, Inc., and was printed and bound by Quebecor Printing/Book Press. The cover was printed by Phoenix Color Corp.

© 1998 by Prentice-Hall, Inc.
Simon & Schuster/A Viacom Company
Upper Saddle River, New Jersey 07458

Earlier editions © 1989 by Macmillan Publishing Company and © 1983 by Merrill Publishing Company.

Photo credits: Scott Cunningham/Merrill, pp. 35, 67, 191, 323, 385; Jean Greenwald/Merrill, p. 227; Larry Hamill/Merrill, p. 3; Kenneth Kerr, p. 297; Gail Meese/Merrill, p. 265; Anne Vega/Merrill, p. 107; Tom Watson/Merrill, p. 151; Todd Yarrington/Merrill, p. 341.

Printed in the United States of America

10 9 8 7 6 5 4 3

ISBN : 0-02-363527-4

Prentice-Hall International (UK) Limited, *London*
Prentice-Hall of Australia Pty. Limited, *Sydney*
Prentice-Hall of Canada, Inc., *Toronto*
Prentice-Hall Hispanoamericana, S. A., *Mexico*
Prentice-Hall of India Private Limited, *New Delhi*
Prentice-Hall of Japan, Inc., *Tokyo*
Simon & Schuster Asia Pte. Ltd., *Singapore*
Editora Prentice-Hall do Brasil, Ltda., *Rio de Janeiro*

Children are our immortality.
—*Alfred North Whitehead*

We dedicate this book to our children:

Cristina and Rob
Jean and Jeff

PREFACE

Since the second edition of *Strategies for Managing Behavior Problems in the Classroom* was published, public and professional concerns about students with challenging behavior have increased alarmingly. America's schools are facing a crisis in dealing with violent and aggressive behavior, including pupils bringing weapons to school, assaults by students against other children and teachers, defiant and disruptive behaviors, and many other problems, suggesting that, for an increasing number of students, traditional approaches to discipline and behavior management are not effective. Numerous school districts are adopting a policy of "zero tolerance" with regard to undesired pupil behavior, which has resulted in large numbers of students, including preschoolers, being suspended and expelled.

At the same time, national reports indicate that special education programs for the segment of the school population identified as having serious emotional disturbance (SED) or emotional and behavioral disabilities (EBD)[1] have not been effective. Status and outcome reports indicate poor academic achievement, high rates of grade retention, the lowest rate of high school graduation of any group of students with disabilities, and extremely poor post-school adjustment. Furthermore, identified students are educated in the most restrictive settings and experience the lowest rates of planned inclusion.[2]

These issues continue to prevail in spite of the articulation of national educational policies and goals that focus more than ever on recognizing and addressing the mental health needs of children (i.e., Education 2000). Educational reform has been a major agenda in many states. Unfortunately, the traditional approach to dealing with serious behavior problems in schools—harsh, reactive interventions applied piecemeal and too late—continues to prevail. More and more students are being excluded from schools because of undesired behavior, which results in the transference of these problems to other child-serving agencies, such as those in mental health, child welfare, and juvenile justice. These systems likewise are being overwhelmed by the sheer number of children needing services, as well as by their own set of poor outcomes (e.g., high rates of psychiatric hospitalization, out-of-home placement, and incarceration). Professionals in all of these disciplines are recognizing that EBD is a severe disability that often cannot be adequately addressed within a single system or in one location. Accordingly, in many locations, systems of care initiatives, which strive to provide coordinated,

---

[1]These terms are considered to be synonymous: The SED category continues to be used in the federal definition of this disability group, despite preference for the term EBD voiced by professional groups and families.

[2]Because students with EBD are the most underidentified special education population, the majority are found in general education classrooms, but in many instances neither they, nor their teachers, receive any special support services.

intensive services to these children and their families in their local communities, are being developed. However, even within these initiatives, services often are applied well after the child's and family's needs have reached crisis proportions. Nonetheless, evaluation reports indicate that it is possible to meet the diverse and complex needs of these children and their families without resorting to expensive and ineffective programs that remove the child and attempt to treat her out of her natural context.

If these were the only events to report, there would be little use in producing a third edition of this text. Fortunately, much has been accomplished in recent years with regard to appropriate and effective intervention for students with challenging behavior. Significant advances have been made in intervention technology, particularly that based on applied behavior analysis, including new strategies for the assessment of behavior that enable practitioners to identify the functions of aberrant behavior and use this information for intervention planning. Specific interventions based on this research include effective behavioral support, precorrection, and behavioral momentum. In addition, important strides have been made in instructional methodology, including the accelerating role of technology for professional training and support, curriculum development and application at the classroom level, and innovations at the system level, including dissemination of intervention resources, communication among professionals, and the development and evaluation of interventions. The professional literature about understanding and helping students with difficult behavior also has mushroomed. Since the publication of our second edition, four new journals have been introduced: *Behavior Modification, The Journal of Behavioral Education, The Journal of Emotional and Behavioral Disorders,* and *The Journal of Emotional and Behavioral Problems.* Many existing journals have published special issues on violent and aggressive behavior in schools, and new literature is developing on the creation of safe, effective, and supportive school environments for all students and staff.

Another set of advances concerns students with or at risk of EBD. These include systematic screening to identify pupils who are at risk, who then may be provided critical early intervention services. This screening methodology currently is available at the preschool and elementary levels. For students who have been identified as having EBD, innovations in educational and treatment strategies are increasingly used, such as wraparound planning, collaborative team teaching in general education classrooms, and the inclusion of social skills instruction as an integral part of the curriculum. As educators have become more involved in systems of care for this population, their collaboration with other providers and with families has increased, which has resulted in improved support for both the student and the classroom teacher. The Office of Special Education and Rehabilitation Services in the U.S. Department of Education has sponsored a National Agenda for Achieving Better Results for Children and Youth with Serious Emotional Disturbance, which has focused attention on seven strategic targets: (1) expanding positive learning opportunities and results, (2) strengthening school and community capacity, (3) valuing and addressing diversity, (4) collaborating with families, (5) promoting appropriate assessment, (6) providing ongoing skill development and support, and (7) creating comprehensive and collaborative systems. Facilitating the achievement of this agenda must become a priority of all educators.

New in This Edition

The third edition of *Strategies for Managing Behavior Problems in the Classroom* addresses school-based interventions in the context of a system of care, not just for those pupils who have been identified as having EBD, but for all students with troubled or troubling behavior.

The features of this new edition include a greater emphasis on

◆ The total ecology of the student and his family, taking into account children's needs across multiple life domains and employing expanded assessment procedures to identify and incorporate environmental influences on behavior to design more proactive, positive interventions.

◆ Collaboration with other disciplines, agencies, and families in designing more effective services and interventions in the educational system, as well as better coordination of treatments across settings and life domains, thereby facilitating more awareness and consistency among treatment providers.

Organization of the Text

As in the previous editions, this text is organized in three sections. Part I provides background information from the professional literature regarding assessment and intervention methodology. Part II presents specific intervention strategies organized according to broad categories of problem behavior. Part III deals with issues involving the generalization of intervention effects and the role of professional educators in the context of a system of care. Many chapters include new case studies that illustrate the concepts and interventions presented.

Acknowledgments

Many persons have contributed to the development of this text. Although we cannot name all of those whose ideas, suggestions, and criticisms are reflected in these pages, we hope that our friends and colleagues will recognize their influences on this volume.

We do wish, however, to acknowledge specific persons who devoted much of their time and energy in the development and production of this work. We wish to thank the reviewers of this edition: Marion S. Boss, University of Toledo; Sandra Cohen, University of Virginia; Martha J. Meyer, Valdosta State College; Mary W. Schmidt, East Carolina University; and Mary M. Jensen Wilber, Western Illinois University.

We also thank our many family members, friends, and colleagues, specifically Jamey Covaleski, Susan Lounsbury Crone, Lucille Eber, Steve Forness, Mary Anne Frederick, Heather Gill, Dee Hill, MeShelda Jackson, Kristina Johnson, Jim Kauffman, Mary Ellen Kohlman, Leslie Laird, Deborah Lambert, John Lloyd, Nicholas Long, Mary Newell, Joan Paynter-Bandy, Bruce Perrone, Lewis Polsgrove, Robert Rutherford, Richard Shores, Jennifer Stachnick, George Sugai, Hill Walker, Kristen Warren, and Shawna Wilson.

Finally, our special thanks go to our editor, Ann Davis, and her assistant, Pat Grogg, as well as the production and marketing staff at Prentice Hall.

MMK
CMN

CONTENTS

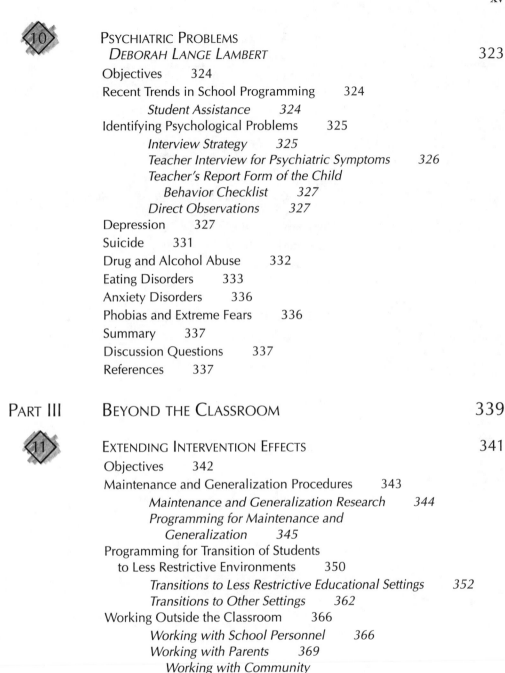

FOUNDATIONS OF EFFECTIVE BEHAVIOR MANAGEMENT

IDENTIFYING AND SERVING STUDENTS WITH BEHAVIORAL PROBLEMS

OUTLINE

Objectives

Behavior Disorders or Problem Behaviors?

Identifying Students with Behavioral Disorders

The Continuum of Behavioral Problems and Educational Services

Summary

Discussion Questions

References

OBJECTIVES

After completing this chapter, you should be able to

◆ Indicate what a definition of behavioral disorders should accomplish and indicate some weaknesses of current definitions.
◆ Compare traditional identification procedures with more recent approaches for identifying students with behavioral disorders.
◆ Discuss prereferral intervention strategies and the role of teacher assistance teams.
◆ Describe the process of determining pupil eligibility for special education services, including the assessment data that should be collected and the decisions that should be made.
◆ Describe the continuum of educational services available for students with behavior problems and indicate when special education becomes involved.
◆ Give a rationale for systematic screening, identification, and prereferral intervention services as part of comprehensive educational programming for students who exhibit problem behaviors.

Aggressive, disruptive, noncompliant, socially inadequate, stereotypic, or withdrawn behaviors constitute a difficult set of problems for educators. Among the many questions raised in reference to pupils exhibiting these behaviors are the following:

◆ Should these pupils be formally identified as having an emotional or behavioral disorder (EBD)[1] and served in special education programs, or should they remain in regular programs and be treated as disciplinary problems?
◆ To be served by special education, must these pupils display significant deficits in academic performance in addition to behavior problems?

◆ Can the needs of students identified as having EBD be addressed in mainstream educational settings, or do they require services in self-contained special classes or even more restrictive settings?
◆ Are there two groups of students; those who are emotionally disturbed and those who are behaviorally disordered? If so, do they have different educational needs? Is the former group "mentally ill" and is the latter group socially maladjusted or simply "naughty"?
◆ Regardless of their educational placements, what approaches to managing these pupils' behavior problems are most effective? What skills and resources are needed to accomplish desired behavior changes?

The Education of the Handicapped Act of 1975 (PL 94–142) is a major accomplishment in

---

[1]The classification used for this population in the Individuals with Disability Education Act (PL 101–476) is seriously emotionally disturbed (SED). However, many professionals and organizations have lobbied for a change in both the terminology and definition.

terms of guaranteeing appropriate educational experiences for children and youth with disabilities. However, pupils whose educational performance is impaired by their behavior problems have not benefited greatly from this legislation; compared with a very conservative prevalence estimate of 2 percent of the school-age population, less than 1 percent are receiving special education across the nation (U. S. Department of Education, 1994). Koyanagi and Gaines (1993) estimate that fewer than one in three children with EBD receive the services they need. Moreover, little evidence exists that schools are dealing effectively with the behavior problems of students not identified as having EBD.

Subsequent amendments to the Education of the Handicapped Act (i.e., PL 99–457, PL 101–436) substantially expand the scope of the 1975 legislation. Current provisions include these:

◆ Increased funding incentives for states that provide services to preschool children with disabilities (ages 3 to 5).
◆ Greater emphasis on programs that improve the transition of students with disabilities to adult life.
◆ A call for early intervention services to infants and toddlers (birth to age 2) with disabilities and their families.
◆ A change in the wording used to describe persons with disabilities so that it emphasizes the person before the disability.

In the most recent amendment, students with serious emotional disturbance (SED; this is the term used in the federal definition) were prioritized for special research studies. The Federal government brought up the issue of whether children with attention deficit hyperactive disorder (ADHD) should be considered for special education classification. Currently, the rights of this population, as well as other students with disabilities not considered eligible for services under the Individuals with Disabilities Education Act (IDEA) of 1990, are protected under Section 504 of the Vocational Rehabilitation Act of 1973. This regulation requires that all individuals with a disability that substantially limits one or more life activities receive

an education comparable to that of their typical peers through an accommodation plan.

In 1990 the Americans with Disabilities Act (ADA; PL 101–336) also was passed. It addresses all types of discrimination against persons with physical or mental disabilities, primarily with regard to employment.

Unfortunately, to date the effects of this legislation on children and youth with EBD have not been profound or positive. This population continues to be the most underidentified and underserved of all special education categories (Eber & Nelson, 1994). In addition, outcomes for students with EBD have been consistently dismal, including these:

◆ Higher percentages of students with EBD are placed on homebound instruction and in residential, hospital, and other restrictive settings than any other group of students with disabilities (Koyanagi & Gaines, 1993)
◆ Students with EBD fail more courses and are retained in grade more often than students with any other disabilities. Only 42 percent of this population earn a high school diploma compared with 50 percent of all students with disabilities and 76 percent of youth in the general population (Chesapeake Institute, 1994).
◆ Only about 18 percent of youth identified with EBD go to college or vocational schools as compared to 22 percent of all students with disabilities (McLaughlin, Leone, Warren, & Schofield, 1994).
◆ Students with EBD have difficulty maintaining jobs; about 75 percent of these students were employed at the time they left school, but only 44 percent still had jobs three to five years later (McLaughlin et al., 1994).
◆ Using even low criteria for "successful" adjustment to adulthood, fewer than 25 percent of both graduates and dropouts of programs for students with EBD were judged to be successful three years after their class exited high school (Carson, Sitlington, & Frank, 1995).
◆ About 20 percent of all youth identified as having EBD have been arrested while in school; 58 percent are arrested within five

years of leaving school. Of students with EBD who drop out of school, 73 percent are arrested within five years of leaving school (Chesapeake Institute, 1994).

◆ African Americans and males are significantly overrepresented in special education programs for students with EBD compared to proportions in the general school-age population (Chesapeake Institute, 1994).

This text presents methods to successfully remediate the behavior problems of students across the range of educational certification and settings. The strategies presented have been researched carefully and proven effective with student populations ranging from those with severe and profound developmental disabilities to those with no disabilities, from preschool children to adults. Educators in a variety of professional roles (regular and special classroom teachers, consultants, psychologists, guidance counselors, and administrators) as well as other professionals and parents have applied these methods. This is not to suggest that effectively managing behavior problems is easy or that it can be done by untrained persons without supervision. On the contrary, it involves a complex technology and careful decision making. Moreover, the needs of children and youth with EBD greatly exceed the service delivery capacity of the educational system (or any human services system). Therefore, if educational programs and interventions are to succeed, they must occur in the context of an integrated system of services offered by numerous agencies and occurring with (rather than to) the child and his family. Children and youth experiencing significant emotional and behavioral problems require a variety of services that flexibly "wrap around" their needs in numerous settings, including the home, community, and (when appropriate) the workplace in addition to the school (Clark, Schaefer, Burchard, & Welkowitz, 1992). Such integrated **systems of care** (Stroul & Friedman, 1986) are being established in many communities and several states (Epstein, Quinn, Nelson, Polsgrove, & Cumblad, 1993).

Unfortunately, with few exceptions (e.g., Alaska, Kentucky, North Carolina, and Vermont),

the educational system is the only agency with a state-wide legal mandate to provide services for children and youth identified as having EBD. This mandate has imposed enormous burdens on the human and financial resources of school districts required to offer appropriate educational and related services to students identified as having EBD. In fact, in the opinion of many professionals (e.g., Kauffman, 1993; Nelson, 1992; Nelson, Rutherford, Center, & Walker, 1992; Skiba & Grizzle, 1991), the mandate to provide services, in the context of the *Honig v. Doe* decision (56 S. Ct. 27, 1988), has been a significant disincentive to identifying and serving students with EBD. (Chapter 12 presents a more in-depth discussion of the issues involving education's role in the delivery of integrated services for children and youth with EBD.)

Preceding the development of a system of care models for children and youth with EBD, the technology of applied behavior analysis has yielded important insights and strategies for the assessment of and interventions for students with EBD. For more than 30 years, applied behavior analysts have contributed research that has led to more effective interventions for children and their families affected by this disability (Baer, Wolf, & Risley, 1987). This technology provides an overriding structure for analyzing and altering maladaptive behaviors and forms the basis of intervention strategies described in this text. Applied behavioral analysis has proven effective across individuals, settings, and time when applied in a knowledgable and consistent manner by skilled practitioners (see Nelson & Rutherford, 1988).

This body of research has led to the inescapable conclusion that the systematic analysis of behavior, child, and setting variables and appropriate decision making based on these factors are essential to effective treatment of children with problem behaviors. These assessments and decisions concern student behavior and environmental characteristics that affect their behavior. This chapter describes assessment procedures used to identify and classify those students whose behavior interferes with their educational progress, as well as the early intervention strategies designed to avoid the necessity of special education classification.

Chapter 2 deals with assessment for intervention planning. The focus of Chapter 3 is assessment for monitoring and facilitating student progress; that of Chapter 4 is assessment for selecting and evaluating interventions. The selection of interventions, part of the assessment/decision-making process, also is described in Chapter 4. Chapter 5 presents considerations and strategies for effective classroom behavior management. In the present chapter, we address the broad question of which students should be considered, for education purposes, as having an emotional or behavioral disability. We also present an overview of special education for students with EBD—specifically, who they are, how they are identified, and what services are available to them in school programs.

BEHAVIOR DISORDERS OR PROBLEM BEHAVIORS?

Algozzine, Ruhl, and Ramsey (1991) identified two major assessment purposes related to behavioral disorders: to determine eligibility for services and to plan treatment programs. The focus of this chapter is eligibility—specifically, determining whether students with problem behaviors should be classified as having a disability and placed in special education or not classified and retained in the regular education program. Chapters 2 through 4 discuss assessment for treatment planning (i.e., deciding what academic and social behaviors to target for intervention, determining whether interventions are effective, and matching interventions to students and setting characteristics).

An initial decision that you already have made, or are contemplating, is whether to work with children or youth who exhibit problem behaviors. As you know, such pupils may be classified by a variety of terms from *emotionally disturbed* or *behaviorally disordered* to *autistic* or *psychotic;* from *juvenile delinquent* or *socially maladjusted* to *discipline problem*. These students may or may not display behaviors characteristic of their classification to a greater extent than do "typical" children. Often these terms are given for administrative convenience to facilitate a student's removal from or placement in a particular classroom or program.

Table 1.1 Combinations of Terms*

Column A	Column B
Emotional	Disturbance
Behavioral	Disorder
Social	Maladjustment
Personal	Conflicted
	Impaired

*Note: These terms are expressed in the language currently preferred; that is, they identify the condition that the person may exhibit. Therefore, the phrase, "a child with," should be assumed to precede the term.
Source: Adapted from Kauffman, J. M. (1993). *Characteristics of emotional and behavioral disorders of children and youth* (5th ed.). Copyright 1993 by Prentice Hall. Used with permission.

The variety of terms applied to students exhibiting EBD is due to federal legislation, which requires only that states adopt classifications and definitions to identify students whose characteristics and needs are like those identified in the federal definition of SED. Table 1.1 illustrates the possible combinations of terms used to describe these students. All such terms should be considered synonymous; many professionals prefer *behavioral disorders,* because it is less stigmatizing and more accurately describes the socialization difficulties of these children and youth (see Kauffman, 1993). The National Mental Health and Special Education Coalition chose the term *emotional or behavioral disorders* because it indicates that the children to whom it refers may exhibit disorders of emotion or behavior or both (Forness & Knitzer, 1992).

All teachers, whether in special or regular education, must deal with students exhibiting problem behavior. Pupils with EBD are no more homogeneous than are children classified any other way. Furthermore, classifying a student as having a "learning disability," "mental retardation," or even "gifted" does not guarantee that behavior problems may not exist. Our focus, therefore, is on techniques for dealing with students with problem behaviors rather than on students considered "emotionally and behaviorally disordered" or "seriously emotionally disturbed." We believe that such a focus will better serve your pupils' interests and will make you a better practitioner.

We also believe that thinking of working with students with specific behavior problems rather than with a group of pupils described as having an emotional disturbance, for example, will lessen your anxiety. If you perceive that such children may be more like so-called normal students than they are different and that their classifications may reflect the system's intolerance for their deviation more than their alleged psychopathology, you will be a better advocate for maintaining them in, or returning them to, less restrictive environments.

Nevertheless, IDEA requires that pupils provided special education services because of their behavior deviations be defined so that the programs serving them can receive state and federal funds. This law defines students with SED as those who exhibit one or more of the following characteristics that adversely affect educational performance over a long period of time and to a marked degree:

1. An inability to learn that cannot be explained by intellectual, sensory, or health factors.
2. An inability to build or maintain satisfactory interpersonal relationships with peers and teachers.
3. Inappropriate types of behavior or feelings under normal circumstances.
4. A general pervasive mood of unhappiness or depression.
5. A tendency to develop physical symptoms or fears associated with personal or school problems.

The term *SED* includes children with schizophrenia or autism.[2] It does not include children with social maladjustment unless they are determined also to have a serious emotional disturbance (45 C.F.R. 121a.5[b][8][1978]).

Authorities in the field of behavioral disorders (e.g., Bower, 1982; Gresham, 1985; Kauffman, 1987) have widely criticized this definition as being vague,

contradictory, confusing, arbitrary, and impractical. For example, what constitutes a "long period of time," "to a marked degree," or "adversely affects educational performance"? Or, for that matter, what do "inability" and "pervasive" mean? Professionals have attacked the exclusion of those with social maladjustment as being arbitrary and meaningless (Nelson et al., 1992; Skiba & Grizzle, 1991). The inclusion of children with schizophrenia or autism is seen as redundant with the preceding five characteristics (Kauffman, 1987). The definition's basic weakness is that it fails to provide a rational or objective basis for discriminating between students with EBD and those without such a disability.

The Council for Children with Behavioral Disorders (CCBD), the major professional organization for special educators serving students with EBD, issued a position paper criticizing the federal definition and current identification practices (CCBD, 1987). In 1991 the Delegate Assembly of the Council for Exceptional Children (CEC) approved a revised definition and category for the population currently identified as having SED (see Table 1.2). The Definition Task Force of the Mental Health and Special Education Coalition proposed this definition, which the CEC Advocacy and Governmental Relations Committee modified. Although the proposed definition includes some redundant phrasing (e.g., inclusion of schizophrenia, affective disorders, anxiety disorders, or other sustained disturbances of conduct, attention, or adjustment), it does not contain a clause that excludes pupils exhibiting social maladjustment. However, until Congress passes into law this new category and definition, the population of students with behavioral disabilities will continue to be categorized and defined as seriously emotionally disturbed.

As indicated previously, IDEA permits states to adopt their own definitions of this population as long as state definitions identify an equivalent group of pupils. However, so much variety exists among states' definition and identification procedures that whether students are identified as having EBD for special education services is, to some extent, contingent on their state of residence (CCBD, 1987).

---

[2]The National Society for Autistic Citizens successfully lobbied to have autism moved from the category of seriously emotionally disturbed to other health impaired because the belief that it is a condition with a biological etiology. Under IDEA, it now is a separate disability category.

Table 1.2 Proposed New U.S. Federal Label and Definition

Emotional or Behavioral Disorder (EBD) refers to a condition in which an individual's behavioral or emotional responses in school are so different from his generally accepted, age-appropriate, ethnic, or cultural norms that they adversely affect educational performance in such areas as self-care, social relationships, personal adjustment, academic progress, classroom behavior, or work adjustment.

◆ EBD is more than a transient, expected response to stressors in the child's or youth's environment and will persist even with individualized interventions, such as feedback to the individual, consultation with parents or families, and/or modifications of the educational environment.

◆ The eligibility decision must be based on multiple sources of data about the individual's behavioral or emotional functioning. He must exhibit EBD in at least two different settings, at least one of which is school related.

◆ EBD can coexist with other handicapping conditions, as defined elsewhere in this law.

◆ This category may include children or youth with schizophrenia, affective disorders, anxiety disorders, or with other sustained disturbances of conduct, attention, or adjustment.

The test of any definition of EBD is whether it is useful in distinguishing between those pupils who need special education services and those who do not. In other words, a definition should assist in identification. Gerry (1984) states that a student must meet three criteria to qualify for special education on the basis of having a behavioral disorder: (1) the disorder must constitute a condition (i.e., a relatively persistent pattern of behavior, as opposed to a transient or situational problem), (2) the condition must have an adverse effect on the student's educational performance or progress so that (3) special education and related services are required. Nevertheless, simply meeting these criteria will not eliminate the subjectivity of a definition. Gresham (1985) indicates that a useful definition should (1) specify the excesses, deficits, or situational inappropriateness of behavior in operational terms, (2) specify the objective features of a behavior and its dimensions (e.g., frequency, duration, intensity), (3) specify the behavioral system through which the excesses and deficits are expressed (e.g., cognitive verbal, overt motoric, physiological emotional), (4) demonstrate the occurrence of the behavior across situations and over time, (5) establish that multiple methods of assessment agree on the occurrence of the behavior, and (6) establish that the behavior continues at an unacceptable level subsequent to school-based

intervention. Similar criteria have been incorporated into some state definitions and identification procedures (e.g., Kentucky: Kentucky EBD Task Force, 1992; Oregon: Waksman & Jones, 1985).

For the purposes of this text, the issue is not whether a pupil should be identified as having EBD and served through special education but whether an intervention strategy needs to be designed. Unfortunately, in many cases, students not identified as having EBD receive no services or inadequate ones because schools tend to lack effective strategies for helping pupils without disabilities who exhibit behavior problems. The effectiveness of such traditional disciplinary practices as corporal punishment, suspension, and expulsion has not been proven for the majority of students with which they are used. Therefore, the dilemma is whether to identify the student as having EBD, which has potentially negative social and educational consequences (i. e., stigmatization, separation from behaviorally typical peers and from the regular academic program), or not to identify in the hope that the student's problem behaviors can be remediated by using resources available in the regular education program. Procedures for identifying and serving students exhibiting behavior problems within the regular education program have been improved through systematic screening and prereferral intervention services. These procedures are discussed in the following section.

IDENTIFYING STUDENTS WITH EBD

Procedures to identify students with EBD may be described in three stages: (1) screening to determine which are at risk for behavioral disorders, (2) implementing prereferral intervention strategies within the regular education program (with appropriate documentation of the effects of these modifications on student performance), and (3) using more intensive assessments to determine whether the student should be certified as eligible for special education services because of EBD (Algozzine et al., 1991). A multidisciplinary team of individuals performs these comprehensive assessments and decides whether to classify the student as having EBD, determines the nature and extent of the services to be provided, and implements the service plan.

Screening

Systematic school-wide screening procedures routinely are applied to detect other disabilities (e.g., sensory, psychomotor, physical, learning, and cognitive disabilities); screening for EBD typically amounts to a referral to a special education program administrator from the regular classroom teacher. Once referred, teacher-nominated students are very likely to be certified by a multidisciplinary team as having EBD, especially if they exhibit externalizing (acting-out) behavior patterns. On the other hand, students manifesting internalizing (withdrawn, depressed) behavior patterns tend not to be referred and therefore are not identified because they are less bothersome to classroom teachers (Walker & Fabre, 1987). Assessment instruments typically include an individualized intelligence scale, norm-referenced achievement tests, standardized behavior rating scales, direct observations, and a test of perceptual-motor skills. Less frequently, personality or projective tests are administered, although their poor reliability and validity render them suspect for diagnosing behavioral disorders (Waksman & Jones, 1985). In any case, as Walker and Fabre (1987) observed, research suggests that the behavioral characteristics and performance deficits of referred and nonreferred pupils are quite similar and that assessment data typically have little impact on certification decisions.

Recent improvements in screening and identification procedures have made this process more objective and systematic. For example, the state of Iowa has adopted a comprehensive assessment model for students exhibiting behavior problems (Wood, Smith, & Grimes, 1985). Other states also are developing systematic procedures for screening and identifying such pupils and providing services for them. Figure 1.1 presents a checklist from a technical assistance paper developed by Waksman and Jones (1985) to facilitate identifying students with SED in Oregon and providing services to them. This checklist provides operational guidelines for applying Oregon's definition (which closely resembles the definition the federal law uses) to determine whether a student should be considered to have SED for special education purposes. The items pertaining to the pupil's behavior document that the problems are severe (i.e., occur to a "marked degree"). A "long period of time" is defined as six months (note the exception in the case of dangerous behavior), and "adverse effects on educational performance" are documented either through academic performance markedly below capacity or through deficiencies in social skills. Finally, note the requirement that attempts to solve the problem by documenting consultative intervention in the regular program. Wood et al. (1985) and CCBD (1987) also recommend using multiple sources of data for identifying and documenting efforts to modify the student's behavior in regular education settings. The CCBD, Iowa, and Oregon all urge that multidisciplinary teams be used to make special education eligibility decisions.

Students' school records are a rich source of screening information. Walker and his colleagues (Walker, Block-Pedego, Todis, & Severson, 1991) developed the *School Archival Records Search*, a systematic protocol for compiling and analyzing such school records data as attendance and grade promotion patterns, office referrals, health history, and anecdotal comments.

Figure 1.1   Suggested SED Evaluation Checklist

	Yes	No

1. At least two of the following five apply.
  a. The student is rated at or above the ninety-eighth percentile on two different acceptable problem rating scales (or similarly named subscales by two or more current teachers.
  b. The student is rated at or above the ninety-eighth percentile on two different acceptable problem-behavior rating scales (or similarly named subscales) by her current teacher and by at least one previous year's teacher.
  c. The student is rated at or above the ninety-eighth percentile on two different acceptable problem-behavior rating scales (or similarly named subscales) by one or more parents or guardians.
  d. The student is currently displaying behavior that is endangering her life or seriously endangering the safety of others.
  e. The student's observable school or classroom problem behavior is documented to be more severe than approximately 98 percent of her peers.
 	
All of these apply:
 	
2. Behavior management consultation has been provided to the classroom teacher(s) over a period of at least four weeks by a behavioral specialist, and documentation indicates that specifically prescribed and consistently employed classroom management interventions have not reduced the inappropriate behavior within acceptable limits suggested by these eligibility criteria.
3. The problem behaviors have been exhibited for over six months. This may be waived if the child is endangering her life or seriously endangering the safety of others.
  Waived: _____ Yes _____ No
4. No recent acute stressor or isolated traumatic event in the child's environment (e.g., divorce or death in the family, loss of property) can adequately explain the problem behavior.
5. No medical problem or health impairment can adequately explain the problem behavior pattern.
6. An inappropriate educational program cannot adequately explain the problem behavior pattern.
7. Culturally different norms or expectations cannot adequately explain the problem behavior pattern.
8. The child is either
  a. performing markedly below her academic potential on acceptable academic tests or school report cards (_____ Yes _____ No), or
  b. severely deficient in social skills or social competence (_____ Yes _____ No).
9. Direct observation by a school psychologist or behavior specialist has documented that either
  a. the student is displaying problem behaviors at a high frequency (_____ Yes _____ No), or
  b. the student is displaying low-frequency behaviors that grossly deviate from acceptable social norms (_____ Yes _____ No).		

Source: Waksman, S., & Jones, V. (1985, August). A suggested procedure for the identification and provision of services to seriously emotionally disturbed students. *Technical assistance papers: A series on PL 94-142 and related Oregon laws.* Portland, OR: Department of Education.

Although such procedures make identifying students who exhibit EBD more objective and accountable, they do not remove the bias that exists when identification is based on teacher referral. As Gerber and Semmel (1984) observed, referral-driven identification procedures place the regular classroom teacher in the role of a gatekeeper who determines which students will be considered for special education services. We already have noted that the referral process is biased toward students with externalizing behavior problems. Also, some

pupils are referred because their teachers are simply less tolerant of disruptive behavior.

However, systematic screening techniques for these at-risk children have been developed for use in the elementary schools (McConaughy & Achenbach, 1989; Walker & Severson, 1990). Recently, screening strategies for elementary pupils have been revised for use in identifying children of preschool age at risk of school failure because of emotional and behavioral problems (Feil & Becker, 1993; Feil, Severson, & Walker, 1994;

Sinclair, Del'Homme, & Gonzalez, 1993). The capability of conducting systematic screening, coupled with early intervention that impacts the child and her home, presents a significant opportunity to prevent the development of intractable EBD.

Walker and Severson (1990) developed a school-wide standardized screening and identification procedure that reduces the bias inherent in teacher referral-driven screening procedures by using a series of progressively more precise and rigorous assessments, or gates. At the first gate, classroom teachers systematically evaluate all pupils in their classes in terms of whether they are at risk for either internalizing or externalizing behavioral disorders. This brief procedure results in a rank-ordered list of up to ten students in each group. The second gate involves teachers rating the three highest ranked students in each group on two short scales. Those pupils whose ratings exceed local norms advance to the third gate, which consists of two sets of observations by a trained observer in a classroom and an unstructured play situation. These data are compared to age- and sex-appropriate norms. In the second and most resource-intensive part of the third gate, a range of standardized tests and diagnostic procedures relevant to a certification decision may be administered. A similar screening procedure now is available for screening at the preschool level (Feil et al., 1994; Feil, Walker, & Severson; Walker, Severson, & Feil, 1995).

The advantages of this procedure include the systematic and routine screening of all students to determine their potential need for special education services, the equal consideration given to pupils exhibiting withdrawn (internalizing) and externalizing behavior, and the use of standardized and locally normed procedures. Furthermore, this procedure provides several points at which prereferral intervention strategies may be applied. Prereferral interventions consist of systematic modifications in the student's regular education program, including altering the instructional setting, academic curriculum, or behavior management system. These changes are planned and supervised by regular education personnel, and the data collected regarding their effects may be one of the criteria for determining the

student's eligibility for special education (Gresham, 1985). Systematic screening for EBD has been implemented in a number of school districts and some states (e.g., Kentucky).

Prereferral Intervention

Interventions at this level should consist of program modifications that are relatively easy to implement by the regular classroom teacher. Interventions that are too complex or time consuming will not be properly applied by busy teachers responsible for 25 to 30 other pupils. However, some of the most effective interventions are also the most straightforward. Clearly explaining expectations, modifying instructions, providing peer assistance, changing seating arrangements, removing obstacles to desired behavior, having students monitor their behavior, and providing feedback or praise for desired performances are strategies familiar to most regular educators. Figure 1.2 is a form used to document prereferral intervention strategies and their effects. It indicates a substantial range of available regular classroom interventions, which may be used singly or in combination.

The difference between an informal tactic and a prereferral intervention strategy is that the latter should be applied and evaluated systematically. To ensure this, it is desirable to create building-based teacher assistance teams as a resource for teachers experiencing difficulty with specific pupils (Chalfant, Pysh, & Moultrie, 1979; McGlothlin, 1981; Phillips & McCullough, 1992). Teacher assistance teams typically are composed of regular education teachers, support staff (e.g., school counselor, psychologist), and a special educator. The core team of three to five members is available to all school staff to provide immediate crisis intervention, short-term consultation, continuous support, information, resources, or training (Phillips & McCullough, 1992). For example, if a student is screened as being at risk for EBD or if a teacher (or parent) expresses a concern, the team may respond by assisting the teacher in assessing the problem and implementing a systematic program modification. The team may act in a consultative capacity until the problem is solved or until it is determined that more intensive action is needed

Figure 1.2   Alternative Regular Classroom Interventions

Please check the various educational strategies that have been employed in attempts to enable the student to overcome the suspected problem(s) in the regular classroom and WRITE in the space provided the student's performance after the application of the strategies.

Instructional Modification
1. Provided structured routine. _____
2. Provided a place with limited visual and auditory distraction. _____
3. Changed seat if auditory or visual problems were suspected. _____
4. Gave abbreviated assignments. _____
5. Provided clear, concise directions (verbally or orally)._____
   _____
6. Matched assignments with ability; taught at instructional level, not frustration level. _____
   _____

Academic Strategies
7. What learning aids have you used (e.g., language master, games, stencils)? _____
   Describe their effect on the student. _____
   _____
8. What modalities were used in the approach to reading and math (e.g., visual, auditory, tactile, kinesthetic)? _____
   _____
   Describe their effect on the student. _____
   _____

Responsivity to Learning
9. Describe the student's attitude toward learning (e.g., gives up easily, perseveres). _____
10. Describe the parent's participation in this student's educational process (e.g., degrees of interest, time spent with child, standard of excellence). _____
   _____
11. How does the student view her ability to be successful in accomplishing school work (academic and nonacademic)? _____

Behavior Management Strategies
12. Ignored inappropriate behavior. _____
13. Reinforced appropriate behavior. _____
14. Increased positive statements. _____
15. Gave extra privileges and responsibilities as a reward for completed assignments. _____
   _____
16. Used time out area. _____
17. Eliminated privilege. _____
18. Used modeling. _____
19. Established specific goals for student—one at a time. _____
20. Charted good behavior. _____
21. Provided student with chart of progress. _____
22. Set up contracts with consistent follow through. _____
23. Provided successful experiences. _____
24. Held parent conferences for home reinforcement. _____

Classroom Interaction
Describe your interaction with this student. _____
_____
Describe this student's interaction with you. _____
_____
Describe this student's interaction with her peers. _____
Describe her peers' interaction with her. _____
Describe her interactions with other staff members in the building (e.g., lunch aides, custodians, music teacher).
_____
_____

Source: Adapted from National Association of School Psychologists. (1986). *Intervention assistance teams: A model for building level instructional problem solving.* Washington, DC: Author.

Figure 1.3   Request for Assistance Form

Date _____

Student's Name _____ Grade Level _____ D.O.B._____
Class/Cluster/Subject _____ Teacher _____ Bldg. _____

I. Describe the problem in specific terms: _____
_____
_____
_____

The following checklists may also be of assistance:

1. ___ Disruptive	7. ___ Distractible	12. ___ Poor study habits
2. ___ Poor attendance	8. ___ Slow rate of work	13. ___ Lacks initiative
3. ___ Off task	9. ___ Cannot follow oral	14. ___ Lack of participation
4. ___ Disorganized	directions	15. ___ Hyperactive
5. ___ Doesn't complete	10. ___ Cannot follow	16. ___ Inconsistent
assignments	written directions	17. ___ Poor peer relationship
6. ___ Poor attitude	11. ___ Poor retention	18. ___ Works below grade level

II. What modifications or adjustments have you made to remediate the problem? _____
_____

What instructional material changes have you made? _____
_____

Have you involved the parents? ___ Yes ___ No
Have you reviewed the student's cumulative record folder? ___ Yes ___ No

FOR CONFERENCE USE ONLY

III. Date of Planning Conference _____ Observer _____
Recommended Strategies and Changes _____
_____

Implementation Period _____ Review Conference Date _____
Plan Approved by _____   _____
                              Teacher   Principal

_____   _____   _____
            Observer   Other   Other
IV. Measurable or Observable Changes During the Implementation Period
_____
_____

Modification Has Provided Satisfactory Progress _____
Multifactored Evaluation Will Be Requested _____

(Use other side if additional space is needed in any area.)

Source: National Association of School Psychologists. (1986). *Intervention assistance teams: A model for building level instructional problem solving.* Washington, DC: Author.

(e.g., a referral for special education evaluation). Figure 1.3 is a form included in a document compiled by the National Association of School Psychologists (1986) to help schools develop teacher assistance team models. This form is used to request team assistance with a problem student. Note that the teacher is requested to provide information concerning specification of the problem and prior efforts to solve it. The team uses the lower half of the form in designing and evaluating systematic interventions.

There are no hard-and-fast rules concerning the duration of prereferral interventions, but 20 to 40 school days (i.e., one to two months) constitutes an adequate period for determining whether the problem can be managed without more formal procedures. To avoid the tendency to turn prereferral interventions over to special services personnel, ownership of both the problem and intervention plans should be vested in the regular education program. Therefore, we recommend that teacher assistance teams be composed of staff identified with the regular education program. Specialized staff (e.g., special education teachers, school psychologists) may serve as ancillary team members on specific cases. Schools should seek in-service staff training before adopting a consultative prereferral intervention model.

Prereferral interventions are important for two reasons: first, they emphasize making attempts to solve students' behavior problems using resources available in the regular education program before considering special education referrals. Second, the results of such interventions provide assessment information useful for those making decisions about pupils' eligibility for services and determining what services are needed. School-wide screening and prereferral intervention procedures, if systematically applied and evaluated, make determining who does and does not have a behavioral disorder more objective and accountable, and they will make available services to students who have behavior problems, not just those who are certified as having EBD. For more information about prereferral interventions and teacher assistance teams, consult Chalfant et al. (1979), Fuchs et al. (1990), Phillips and McCullough (1992), and Sugai and Tindal (1993).

Certification

This stage initiates formal consideration of the student's eligibility for special education services. The question of whether a student is manifesting a condition that constitutes a disability is a serious matter. Therefore, IDEA requires that the student's parents be notified of the school's intent to assess the child and give their approval. Parents also should be active participants throughout the assessment and decision-making processes, including decisions regarding the child's educational placement and the **individualized educational plan** (IEP). These due process safeguards protect students' and parents' rights, including the right to have an independent assessment of their child and to request a hearing in the event that they disagree with the decision of the multidisciplinary team.

As mentioned previously, traditional assessment for identifying behavioral disorders consists of administering a battery of psychoeducational instruments, including an individual intelligence scale, norm- and criterion-referenced measures of achievement, instruments that assess perceptual-motor skills, and, less frequently, measures of personality characteristics. Data from these instruments may be supplemented with teacher or parent interviews, direct observation of the pupil, and anecdotal information from school records. Most of the responsibility for this stage of the classification process falls on school psychologists. However, as Gresham (1985) observes, school psychologists are more comfortable and competent in assessing mental retardation and learning disabilities than behavioral disorders.

Mental Health Assessment   Many school districts do not have staff psychologists to perform assessments for the purpose of classifying pupils. These districts must rely on other agencies or professionals (e.g., mental health clinics, psychologists or psychiatrists in private practice) to conduct these evaluations. Mental health professionals use an assessment model that is considerably different from models useful for educational purposes. One of the chief differences is that the mental health assessment model is based on identifying emotional or cognitive pathology that is presumed to underlie the student's behavior problems. Until recently, this **medical model** dominated other approaches to the assessment of behavioral disorders. It is still widely used by mental health practitioners and school districts in some states.

The classification decisions resulting from mental health assessment often result in diagnostic labels that come from the *Diagnostic and Statistical Manual,* Fourth Edition (*DSM-IV*), published by the American Psychiatric Association (1994). The *DSM-IV* classifies psychological disorders along five axes or dimensions. Axis I consists of the major pattern of symptoms, or clinical disorders, that the student exhibits; Axis II describes personality disorders; Axis III addresses general medical conditions; Axis IV describes psychosocial factors that impose stress on the individual; and Axis V considers the pupil's level of adaptive functioning over the past year. A diagnosis may or may not be made on every axis, depending on the student and how much information the evaluator has about the case. However, a principal diagnosis, using the categories and accompanying diagnostic codes for Axis I and/or II, always is made. The Axis I or II categories for disorders usually first diagnosed in infancy, childhood, and adolescence are grouped into ten classes, as follows (American Psychiatric Association, 1994, pp. 13–14):

Mental Retardation

Mild Mental Retardation

Moderate Mental Retardation

Severe Mental Retardation

Profound Mental Retardation

Mental Retardation: Severity Unspecified

Learning Disorders

Reading Disorder

Mathematics Disorder

Disorder of Written Expression

Learning Disorder Not Otherwise Specified (NOS)

Motor Skill Disorder

Developmental Coordination Disorder

Communication Disorders

Expressive Language Disorder

Mixed Receptive-Expressive Language Disorder

Phonological Disorder

Stuttering

Communication Disorder NOS

Pervasive Developmental Disorders

Autistic Disorder

Rett's Disorder

Childhood Disintegrative Disorder

Asperger's Disorder

Pervasive Developmental Disorder NOS

Attention-Deficit and Disruptive Behavior Disorders

Attention-Deficit/Hyperactivity Disorder

Combined Type

Predominantly Inattentive Type

Predominantly Hyperactive-Impulsive Type

Attention-Deficit/Hyperactivity Disorder NOS

Conduct Disorder (*Specify type:* Childhood-Onset Type/Adolescent-Onset Type)

Oppositional Defiant Disorder

Disruptive Behavior Disorder NOS

Feeding and Eating Disorders of Infancy or Early Childhood

Pica

Rumination Disorder

Feeding Disorder of Infancy or Early Childhood

Tic Disorders

Tourette's Disorder

Chronic Motor or Vocal Tic Disorder

Transient Tic Disorder (*Specify if:* Single Episode/Recurrent)

Tic Disorder NOS

Elimination Disorders

Encopresis

With Constipation and Overflow Incontinence

Without Constipation and Overflow Incontinence

Enuresis (Not Due to a General Medical Condition) (*Specify type:* Nocturnal Only/Diurnal Only/Nocturnal and Diurnal)

Other Disorders of Infancy, Childhood, or Adolescence

Separation Anxiety Disorder (*Specify if:* Early Onset)

Selective Mutism

Reactive Attachment Disorder of Infancy or Early Childhood (*Specify type:* Inhibited Type/Disinhibited Type)

Table 1.3 DSM IV Diagnostic Criteria for Autistic Disorder

A. A total of six (or more) items from (1), (2), and (3), with at least two from (1), and one from each (2) and (3).

    (1). Qualitative impairment in social interaction, as manifested by at least two of the following:
        (a). Marked impairment in the use of multiple nonverbal behaviors such as eye-to-eye gaze, facial expression, body postures, and gestures to regulate social interaction
        (b). Failure to develop peer relationships appropriate to developmental level
        (c). Lack of spontaneous seeking to share enjoyment, interests, or achievements with other people (e.g., by a lack of showing, bringing, or pointing out objects of interest)
        (d). Lack of social or emotional reciprocity

    (2). Qualitative impairments in communication as manifested by at least one of the following:
        (a). Delay in, or total lack of, the development of spoken language (not accompanied by an attempt to compensate through alternative modes of communication such as gesture or mime)
        (b). In individuals with adequate speech, marked impairment in the ability to initiate or sustain a conversation with others
        (c). Lack of varied, spontaneous make-believe play or social imitative play appropriate to developmental level

    (3). Restricted repetitive and stereotyped patterns of behavior, interests, and activities, as manifested by at least one of the following:
        (a). Encompassing preoccupation with one or more stereotyped and restricted patterns of interest that is abnormal either in intensity or focus
        (b). Apparently inflexible adherence to specific, nonfunctional routines or rituals
        (c). Stereotyped and repetitive motor mannerisms (e.g., hand- or finger-flapping or twisting, or complex whole-body movements)
        (d). Persistent preoccupation with parts of objects

B. Delays or abnormal functioning in at least one of the following areas, with onset prior to age 3 years: (1) social interaction, (2) language as used in social communication, or (3) symbolic or imaginative play.

C. The disturbance is not better accounted for by Rett's Disorder or Childhood Disintegrative Disorder

Source: American Psychiatric Association. (1994). *Diagnostic and statistical manual of mental disorders* (4th ed.), 70–71. Copyright American Psychiatric Association, Washington, DC. Used with permission.

Stereotypic Movement Disorder (*Specify if:* With Self-Injurious Behavior)

Disorder of Infancy, Childhood, or Adolescence NOS

More specific diagnoses are made within these categories and subcategories for individual cases. For example, Table 1.3 lists the diagnostic criteria for autistic disorder.

Children also may be assigned an Axis I or II diagnosis from one of the other categories included in the system (e.g., school phobia, classified as one of the anxiety disorders; anorexia nervosa, which is one of the eating disorders). As the preceding example suggests, the *DSM-IV* approach to assessment is descriptive in that the diagnosis is based on a pattern, or **syndrome,** of behavior. It also is clinical because portions of the diagnosis are based on judgments and inferences made from the presenting symptoms (e.g., "failure to

develop peer relationships appropriate to developmental level"). *DSM-IV* notes that the categories are not mutually exclusive, that children often have problems not subsumed within a single diagnostic category, and that many behavior problems do not warrant diagnostic classification. To these cautions we must reiterate our previous observation that students who have other disabilities also may exhibit EBD. Moreover, traditional diagnostic procedures usually occur in the clinician's office where the verbal reports of the client and others (e.g., parents) must be used instead of direct behavioral observation. This affects the reliability of the diagnosis (i.e., two clinicians may not arrive at the same diagnostic assessment because each receives a different report or interprets the same information differently). In some cases the diagnosis is applied to internal processes or **constructs** (theoretical constructions of traits or attributes, e.g., separation anxiety disorder).

The validity of these constructs (i.e., the extent to which the construct really exists) also may be questionable.

The limitations of the mental health diagnostic and classification system have been widely discussed (see Kauffman, 1993). In fact, Algozzine et al. (1991) indicated that "applying nonschool-based models or psychological perspectives to educational decisions may be the single most damaging practice in the field of (E)BD today" (p. 7). Perhaps the major weakness of this approach stems from its reliance on a disease analogy, that is, on the assumption that psychological disorders are analogous to disease processes that exist within the individual. The addition of Axis IV (psychosocial stressors) classification notwithstanding, *DSM-IV* diagnoses tend to attribute the causes of behavior disorders to conditions within the individual. This is in contrast to the practice we prefer, which is to view disordered behavior as the outcome of interactions between characteristics of the individual and the environmental settings in which behavior occurs (Polsgrove, 1987).

The first step in traditional mental health assessments begins with a referral that includes a statement of the presenting problems or the reason for referral. As suggested earlier, the reason for referring a student has been shown to bias the outcome of assessment. In one study, for example, pupils referred for behavior problems were more often assessed as being emotionally disturbed than pupils who were referred for academic difficulties (Ysseldyke & Algozzine, 1982). The study was based on a computer simulation, but we believe that the same bias operates in the real world as well, resulting in a better than average possibility that a student referred for mental health assessment will be assigned a category. Ysseldyke and Algozzine (1982) suggested that when referring a student for assessment, the first steps should be to clarify the nature of the referral problem and to articulate the decision that must be made (e.g., whether the student should be enrolled in a special class for children with EBD). Such clarification reduces the likelihood that the diagnostician will miss the real problem or that inappropriate assessment procedures will be used when the decision is made.

The next step is to conduct the assessment. The procedure followed depends on the discipline of the evaluator (psychiatrist, psychologist, social worker), the evaluator's skills, and the diagnostic tools available. Many diagnosticians conduct structured or unstructured interviews with the student, the student's parents, or others (e.g., classroom teachers). In some cases, standardized assessment procedures or instruments also may be used. These may include individually administered intelligence tests, personality tests, tests of interest or preference, behavior rating scales, or self-concept inventories. Table 1.4 lists a number of such tests that may be used. It is important to recognize that many of the instruments, especially those using projective techniques (in which the client "projects" his personality through responses to ambiguous stimuli, such as ink blots or pictures), offer poor reliability and validity as well as inadequate norms (Salvia & Ysseldyke, 1995). The inadequacy and educational irrelevance of personality tests, as well as the threat of legal sanction arising from decisions based on their results, have led to increasing reliance on more objective procedures (Salvia & Ysseldyke, 1995).

Nevertheless, clinical assessment procedures that result in a diagnostic mental health classification are still employed for children and youth. Despite their weaknesses (tests that are often static, subjective, narrow in scope, and inferential), a good diagnostic evaluation can be helpful, especially if the outcomes include multidisciplinary planning and follow-up activities. We have chosen to organize this text in terms of educationally relevant behavioral categories rather than the *DSM-IV* categories; therefore, you may need to ignore psychiatric categories or translate them into more useful terms. The term *emotional disturbance* or *behavioral disorder* is sufficient to qualify pupils for special education. Once more, we stress that classifying students is not necessary to work with them.

School-Based Assessment   A more functional process for determining whether students should be considered as exhibiting EBD consists of building on the information gathered from systematic screening and prereferral intervention procedures through comprehensive assessments directed by school personnel. This process begins with a referral for formal evaluation and involves compiling information from attempts to manage the problem at the prereferral level, as well as systematic

Table 1.4 Formal Measures of Classroom Behavior and Related Concerns

Name (Authors)	Ages or Grades
Classroom Behavior and Social-Emotional Development	
Behavior Evaluation Scale-2 (McCarney & Leigh, 1990)	Gr. K–12
Behavior Rating Profile (2nd ed.) (Brown & Hammill, 1990)	Gr. 1–12 and Ages 6–6 to 18–6
Burk's Behavior Rating Scales (Burks, 1977)	Gr. 1–9
Child Behavior Rating Scale (Cassell, 1962)	Gr. K–3
Comprehensive Behavior Rating Scale for Children (Neeper, Lahey, & Frick, 1990)	Ages 6 to 14
Devereux Behavior Rating Scales-School Form (Naglieri, LeBuffe, & Pfeiffer, 1993)	Ages 5 to 18
Mooney Problem Check Lists (Mooney & Gordon, 1950)	Gr. 7–12 and college
Revised Behavior Problem Checklist (Quay & Peterson, 1987)	Gr. K–8 regular class, Gr. K–12 special class
School Behavior Checklist (Miller, 1977)	Ages 4 to 13
School Social Skills Rating Scale (Brown, Black, & Downs, 1984)	School ages
Social-Emotional Dimension Scale (Hutton & Roberts, 1986)	Ages 5–6 to 18–5
Social Skills Rating System (Gresham & Elliott, 1990)	Ages 3–0 to 4–11 and Gr. K–12
Test of Early Socioemotional Development (Hresko & Brown, 1984)	Ages 3–0 to 7–11
Walker Problem Behavior Identification Checklist, Revised (Walker, 1983)	Ages 2 to 5 and Gr. K–6
Walker-McConnell Scale of Social Competence and School Adjustment (Walker & McConnell, 1988)	Gr. K–6
Attention Disorders and Hyperactivity	
Attention Deficit Disorders Evaluation Scale (McCarney, 1989a, 1989b)	Ages 4–6 to 21
Children's Attention and Adjustment Survey (Lambert, Hartsough, & Sandoval, 1990)	Gr. K–5
Conners' Teacher Rating Scales (Conners, 1969b, 1978b)	Long Form, Ages 4 to 12; Short Form, Ages 3 to 17
Conners' Parent Rating Scales (Conners, 1970, 1978a)	Long Form, Ages 6 to 14; Short Form, Ages 3 to 17
Self-Concept	
Coopersmith Self-Esteem Inventories (Coopersmith, 1981)	Ages 8 to adult
Culture-Free Self-Esteem Inventories (2nd ed.) (Battle, 1992)	Gr. 2–9 and Ages 16 to 65
Multidimensional Self-Concept Scale (Bracken, 1992)	Gr. 5–12
Piers-Harris Children's Self-Concept Scale (Piers & Harris, 1984)	Gr. 4–12
Dimensions of Self-Concept (Michael, Smith, & Michael, 1984)	Gr. 4–12 and college
Self-Esteem Index (Brown & Alexander, 1991)	Ages 8–0 to 18–11
Student Self-Concept Scale (Gresham, Elliott, & Evans-Fernandez, 1992)	Gr. 3–12
Tennessee Self-Concept Scale (Fitts & Roid, 1988)	Age 12 and above
Peer Acceptance	
Behavior Rating Profile (2nd ed.) (Brown & Hammill, 1990)	Gr. 1–12 and Ages 6–6 to 18–6
Peer Attitudes Toward the Handicapped Scale (Bagley & Greene, 1981)	Gr. 4–8
Test of Early Socioemotional Development (Hresko & Brown, 1984)	Ages 3–0 to 7–11
School Interests and Attitudes	
Estes Attitude Scales (Estes, Estes, Richards, & Roettger, 1981)	Gr. 2–12
Quality of School Life Scale (Epstein, 1976)	Gr. 4–12
School Interest Inventory (Cottle, 1966)	Gr. 7–12
Woodcock-Johnson Psycho-Educational Battery, Part Three, Tests of Interest (Woodcock & Johnson, 1977)	Ages 3 to 80+

Source: McLoughlin, J. A., & Lewis, R. B. (1994). *Assessing special students* (4th ed.). Upper Saddle River, NJ: Prentice Hall. Copyright 1994.

assessments by school staff and other professionals. Table 1.5, which is based on Kentucky's assessment procedures, summarizes the process. The compilation of prereferral screening and intervention data may include documentation such as that included in Oregon's evaluation checklist (Figure 1.1). This documentation should demonstrate that (1) problem behaviors are perceived as extreme by more than one observer across more than one setting; (2) prereferral interventions have been attempted and have failed; (3) the problem has existed over a reasonably long period of time (except in the case of behavior that poses a hazard to life or safety); (4) the problem cannot be explained by factors such as temporary stress, medical problems, inappropriate educational programming, or cultural differences; (5) the pupil has deficits in academic performance or social skills; and (6) the problem behaviors occur at a high rate or deviate markedly from acceptable norms.

Intelligence tests have very limited utility for assessing behavior problems. However, an *intellectual assessment* can document that the problem is not due to cognitive impairment. (If the student has some degree of mental disability, it should be documented that specific programming related to this condition has not solved the student's behavior problems.) It is important to realize that students may exhibit both cognitive disabilities *and* behavior problems or EBD. Therefore, schools should be able to bring the needed services to the pupil in the current school placement rather than moving the student to another program unless it is decided that the latter is more appropriate. Changes in school placement require invoking due process, as well as reassessment and decision making by the multidisciplinary team established to supervise the pupil's educational program, and thus cannot be made quickly or easily. Taking services to the student is more expedient and less disruptive and so is the preferred strategy.

The *academic assessment* may be accomplished through a variety of procedures, including individually administered norm-referenced achievement tests, curriculum-based assessments, analysis of classroom work samples and data regarding academic progress, and direct observation of time on task. Several sources of academic data should be provided to rule out the possibility that conclusions are based on inadequate samples of student performance.

Academic assessment is important for two reasons. First, in most states, the EBD diagnosis can be made only if educational performance is adversely affected. Second, behavior problems and academic difficulties often are functionally related. Students who are frustrated by academic tasks and expectations that are beyond their current skill levels may act out or withdraw to avoid such tasks or to express their feelings. Conversely, problem behaviors may interfere with academic learning because they are incompatible with academic performance or because they result in disciplinary actions that cause pupils to be removed from the instructional setting.

The *social competence assessment* is likely to reveal social skills deficits in students considered for EBD classification because failure to establish satisfactory social relationships is a defining characteristic. Therefore, it is important that skills related to social interactions with peers and adults be assessed. Recall that in some states (e.g., Kentucky, Oregon), social skill deficits carry as much weight as academic deficiencies when identifying pupils with EBD. Social competence is a general domain referring to summative evaluative judgments regarding the adequacy of a student's performance on social tasks by an informed social agent (Walker & McConnell, 1988). Gresham and Reschly (1987) indicated that social competence is composed of two subdomains: adaptive behavior and specific social skills. Measures of adaptive behavior typically assess general independent functioning, including physical development, self-direction, personal responsibility, economic or vocational skills, and functional academic skills (Walker & McConnell, 1988). The *American Association of Mental Deficiency (AAMD) Adaptive Behavior Scale,* School Edition (Lambert, Windmiller, Tharinger, & Cole, 1981) or the *Vineland Adaptive Behavior Scale* (Sparrow, Balla, & Cicchetti, 1985) are appropriate measures of adaptive behavior. The format of these scales consists of ratings completed through interviews with persons familiar with the pupil's functioning or development in relevant settings. Social skills are the specific strategies one uses to respond to social living tasks (Walker & McConnell, 1988). Several social skills assessment instruments have been developed, among them the *Social Behavior Assessment* (Stephens, 1979), the *Teacher Ratings of Social Skills* (Clark, Gresham, & Elliott, 1985), the *Social Skills Rating System* (Gresham & Elliott, 1990), and *The Walker-McConnell Scale of Social Competence and School Adjustment: A Social Skills Rating Scale for*

Table 1.5 Pupil Identification Assessment Process

I. Compilation of Screening and Prereferral Data Documentation that student's problem behaviors occur more frequently or more intensely than nonreferred peers, that such behaviors have occurred for a long period of time, and that they have not been solved through systematic management in the regular education setting

Acceptable procedures
- Standardized behavior ratings completed by two or more teachers, or by teachers and parents
- Direct observation data (including data on nondeviant peer)
- Evidence that problems have occurred for a prolonged period
- Evidence that problems are not due to temporary stress or to curriculum or cultural factors
- Evidence that interventions in regular program have been systematically implemented and have not been effective
- Verification by school personnel that behavior is dangerous to student or to others

II. Intellectual Assessment
Documentation that behavior is not due to impaired cognitive functioning, or if cognitive deficits are present, that appropriate programming has not solved behavior problems

Acceptable procedures
- Acceptable individual measure of intelligence or aptitude, administered by qualified examiner

III. Academic Assessment
Documentation that academic performance or progress has not been satisfactory for a period of time

Acceptable procedures
- Individually administered norm-referenced measures of academic achievement
- Group-administered achievement tests *and* written analysis of classroom products and documentation of classroom academic progress
- Curriculum-based or criterion-referenced assessments documenting progress across curriculum
- Direct observation of academic time on task
- Samples of classroom work across time and tasks

IV. Social Competence Assessment
Documentation that student is deficient in social skills or that social status is seriously affected

Acceptable procedures
- Administration of approved standardized social skills inventories or checklists
- Administration of adaptive behavior scales
- Administration of sociometric scales or procedures
- Direct observation in unstructured social setting (include peer comparison data)

V. Social, Developmental, and School History
Documentation that problem is not due to any previously undiscovered factors or cultural differences

Acceptable procedures
- Interviews with parents or guardians, referring teacher, other teachers, student
- Review of student's cumulative school records

VI. Medical Evaluation
Documentation that problem is not due to health factors

Acceptable procedures
- Medical screening by physician, school nurse, or physician's assistant
- Comprehensive medical evaluation if student fails to pass screening

Teachers (Walker & McConnell, 1988). As their names suggest, these instruments consist of rating scale items completed by persons who are familiar with the student's functioning.[3] Alternate procedures for assessing social competence include sociometrics and direct observations of the pupil's behavior in unstructured social situations.

The direct observation of social behavior is an important assessment tool for pupils being considered for special education services. It provides an opportunity to analyze the student's behavior in the immediate social context, enabling the assessor to identify excess and deficit problem behaviors and adaptive behavior patterns, as well as the antecedents and consequences of specific behaviors. Potential biases associated with personal judgment are reduced when using direct observation procedures. Behavioral observation strategies are described in Chapter 3.

Additional data may be collected about social, developmental, and school history through interviews with the student's caregivers, the referring teacher, other teachers, and the student. A thorough search of the pupil's cumulative school records should be conducted to assess such variables as attendance, health history, discipline reports, and previous screenings or referrals for special education evaluation.[4] Concurrently, a medical evaluation should be performed to rule out possible health factors. Students who do not pass this screening should be referred for a comprehensive medical examination.

It is also important to assess the extent to which cultural differences may contribute to behavior problems in school. Although membership in a racially or ethnically different cultural group should not be a reason to overlook a student's maladaptive behavior, school personnel must be sensitive to the effects of cultural attitudes and customs on behavior. Students from families with low income and those who belong to a racial minority, especially African American males, are overrepresented in special education programs for pupils with EBD (Chin & Hughes, 1987; McIntyre, 1992; Peterson & Ishii-Jordan, 1993). Culturally different students may exhibit patterns of language and social behavior that conflict with the normative standards and expectations of the school. Moreover, pupils' awareness of their deviation from school norms regarding dress, extracurricular activities, and financial status may cause them to withdraw from or rebel against persons exemplifying these norms. Cultural stereotypes also may affect the expectations and reactions of other pupils and school staff, which can intensify difficulties involving cultural issues. Therefore, in assessing culturally different students, evaluators should attempt to determine the function that "deviant" behaviors may serve for the student (e.g., "playing the dozens," avoiding direct eye contact) with reference to her cultural group before concluding that such behavior patterns are maladaptive. When culturally appropriate behaviors conflict with staff or peer expectations, assessors should be open to the conclusions that the expectations are in error and that intervention should address expectations in addition to (or instead of) the student's behavior.

Cultural differences should be considered during prereferral screening and during identification, of course. In fact, sensitivity to cultural factors underlying presumed behavior problems may be even more important at this level, because culturally related behavior patterns and stereotypes may trigger a sequence of events that lead to certification and identification of pupils with EBD. Algozzine, Christenson, and Ysseldyke (1982) demonstrated that initiation of special education referrals is likely to result in special education certification. They surveyed a national sample of state directors of special education and found that 92 percent of students referred for psychoeducational evaluation were actually tested, and 73 percent of those evaluated were declared eligible for special education.

---

[3]Standardized instruments and informal procedures for assessing student behavior and social status are described in Chapter 2.

[4]The *School Archival Records Search* (Walker et al., 1991) has been developed to facilitate the systematic search of school records for pertinent information.

McIntyre (1995) developed an instrument to assist in evaluating the influence of culture on behavior and learning. Intended for use in the pre-referral and/or referral process, the *McIntyre Assessment of Culture (MAC)* contains a student information form, a parent/home information form, and a behavior checklist. The information derived from these sources is analyzed to determine whether the behaviors of concern to educators have a cultural bias.

Thus, an adequate assessment of students referred for possible classification as EBD is comprehensive and complex. However, the seriousness of the decision being considered justifies this detailed evaluation process. Also, this process is multidisciplinary; no single professional is qualified to perform all of these assessments. It is appropriate and desirable to involve professionals in other roles within the school as well as outside the schools in gathering and analyzing assessment data. However, it is important that a staff member or a team of staff from the pupil's school compile and analyze the assessment data and present it to the persons who will make the certification decision.

Classification

The decision to classify a pupil as having EBD is too important to be made on the basis of limited information or by persons not familiar with all facets of the student's personality and environment. Thus, IDEA requires that eligibility decisions be made by a team of persons, which must include the parents or guardians (if they are not available, a parent surrogate may be appointed), the referring teacher, a school administrator, the special education teacher, and a person able to interpret the results of the diagnostic procedures. Other individuals should be included as necessary. This group may be called a **child study team** or the *special education admission and release committee*. The team determines whether the assessment information supports the need for special education certification, makes decisions regarding the most appropriate educational program and placement, and evaluates the student's progress and the effectiveness of the educational services provided.

The validity of the classification decisions made by child study teams has been questioned, however. Potter, Ysseldyke, and Regan (1983) gave a large group of school professionals assessment information on a hypothetical student that reflected performance in the average range for the student's age and grade placement. They indicated that the student had been referred for special education and asked the professionals whether they believed the pupil was eligible for it. Of these professionals, 51 percent declared the student eligible for special education services. This study verifies that assessment data often are not used in making certification decisions (Walker & Fabre, 1987). The procedures we described in the previous sections should help to remedy this problem; however, decisions involving the judgments of persons inescapably are subjective. Careful analysis and review are needed to make this decision.

The decision to certify that a student has EBD actually consists of a set of decisions. If the child study team decides that the pupil is eligible for services, it must determine which services are needed and in what settings they should be provided. In the past these decisions were guided by the limited range of services available in schools. Often the only alternatives were special academic instruction or behavior management in a self-contained special classroom or resource room. The availability of an increased range of special education and support services reduces the team's dependency on placing students in restrictive educational settings to provide them with needed services. Thus, the team may determine that a pupil needs systematic behavior management, highly structured academic instruction, and social-skills training. However, because the school has adopted a policy of **inclusion** supported by such staff resources as teacher assistance teams or consulting teacher services as well as a social skills teaching curriculum, these services can be provided without changing the student's current educational placement. Even in schools without a wide range of services, decisions regarding what services pupils need should precede and be separate from decisions about where students will access them (i.e., where they will be placed).

The integration of students with EBD into educational settings with their peers who are not disabled is a laudable goal with numerous advocates in the special education profession. They base their arguments on the observations that segregated special class programs can be stigmatizing and ineffective, that a two-track educational system (regular and special) is inefficient, and that both disabled and typical pupils benefit from integrated placement (Gartner & Lipsky, 1987; Reynolds, 1991; Stainback & Stainback, 1984). They also claim that regular education teachers, with appropriate support services, can deal effectively with children who are difficult to teach.

On a philosophical level, these arguments are incontrovertible. However, the feasibility of providing all the appropriate educational services to effectively meet the needs of children with EBD in regular classroom settings has been questioned (Braaten, Kauffman, Braaten, Polsgrove, & Nelson, 1988; Council for Children with Behavioral Disorders, 1989; Kauffman, Lloyd, Astuto, & Hallahan, 1995). Children with EBD, particularly those with externalizing behaviors, can be extremely challenging under the most carefully controlled circumstances (i.e., small, highly structured classrooms with specially trained teachers and aides). The larger number of students in regular classrooms, teachers' lack of sophisticated training in classroom management procedures, and the unavailability of adequate technical assistance to classroom teachers make the full inclusion of many pupils with behavioral disabilities implausible. Meadows, Neel, Scott, and Parker (1994) compared the educational programming for students with EBD who were placed in mainstream versus segregated programs. They found that "placement in general education settings represented a major reduction, if not complete cessation, of [individually differentiated] programming" (p. 170).

To compound these problems, children with serious behavioral disorders do not interact well with their peers, who do not accept them (Nelson, 1988). Moreover, the regular class curriculum often falls short of meeting the needs of pupils who are behind their age mates both academically and socially. Many students with mild disabilities (those who are closest to their nondisabled peers in terms of functional levels), especially those with EBD, drop out or are "elbowed out" of school by the time they reach adolescence (Edgar, 1987).

Yell (1995) analyzed legal issues related to inclusion. He concluded that

> The courts have indicated that there are two primary grounds for removing a student from the general education classroom: If the child does not benefit educationally (considering both academic and nonacademic benefits) and if the student disrupts the learning environment or adversely affects the education of other students. In these instances the most appropriate and least restrictive setting will not be the regular education classroom (p. 188).

The implication of this position for students whose behavior results in either of these two outcomes is that they are not likely to be considered eligible for inclusive educational programs. Thus, students with externalizing behavior patterns who are identified as EBD will experience difficulty being appropriately served in mainstream educational settings.

The basic dilemma is whether to redouble efforts to integrate these pupils into regular academic programs (which may not meet their needs) or to educate them in segregated environments, in which they miss many of the curricular and extracurricular opportunities available in the mainstream and in which they are likely to remain throughout their public school years. Unfortunately, the dilemma has no ready solution. The most promising approach may be to continue improving and expanding the range of educational and related services across the entire continuum of educational settings in which children and youth with behavior problems are found (Kauffman & Hallahan, 1995; Kauffman et al., 1995).

Finally, we advocate that when students are certified as being eligible for special education, criteria for their *decertification* be set. This means that the child study team should specify the goals and objectives for the pupil's special education program (which is required by law) and indicate that when these are met, the student should be declared as no longer exhibiting a disability and should be returned to regular education, with appropriate support services. (The decision to retain the pupil in special education also should be justified through a comprehensive re-evaluation and should be made by the student's child study team.) This strategy would reduce the tendency to leave pupils in special education for the rest of their school careers.

Table 1.6 summarizes the eligibility decision-making process from screening through decertifying and returning pupils to the regular program. For a complete, step-by-step guide to the assessment of behavioral disorders, see the *Iowa Assessment Model* (Wood et al., 1985) or *Kentucky's Emotional-Behavioral Disability Technical Assistance Manual* (Kentucky EBD Task Force, 1992).

THE CONTINUUM OF BEHAVIORAL PROBLEMS AND EDUCATIONAL SERVICES

The range of problem behaviors encountered in schools can be described in many ways. For practical reasons, this range generally is matched to a continuum of special education interventions: the more severe the problem behavior, the more restrictive the special education program (the further removed from the educational mainstream). In the past, special education interventions have been "place oriented" (Reynolds & Birch, 1977), that is, confined to special places such as self-contained classrooms or resource rooms. This orientation has created an expectation that pupils who are referred for special education will be removed from the regular program

Table 1.6 Eligibility Decisions

Question	Action
I. Screening	
A. Is student "at risk"?	A. Administer screening procedure, activate teacher assistance team
B. Can student be helped through regular program?	B. Modify or adapt regular program
II. Identification	
A. Has student benefited from adaptations made in regular program?	A. Evaluate effects of regular education interventions
B. Is additional support or service needed?	B. Implement consultative intervention
C. Should student be identified as behaviorally disordered?	C. Conduct assessment; hold staffing
III. Certification	
A. Should student be referred for EBD services?	A. Conduct child study team meeting
B. What services are needed?	B. Develop individualized education plan (IEP)
C. Where should services be provided?	C. Identify least restrictive settings for pupil
D. What expectations must the pupil meet to return to the regular classroom?	D. Specify criteria for decertification
IV. Program Evaluation	
A. Is the program working?	A. Implement formative and summative evaluation procedures
V. Decertification	
A. Is special education no longer needed?	A. Evaluate progress against exit criteria, conduct exit child study team meeting

and treated in some "special" place with a "special" set of methods. Nowhere is this expectation more prevalent than in the area of EBD. Students who are unruly, aggressive, disrespectful, threatening, or just "weird" are aversive to regular classroom teachers; many such teachers report that they are unable to manage such students effectively (Lloyd & Kauffman, 1995). Others use punishment and coercive tactics in attempting to cope with undesired student behavior (Shores, Gunter, & Jack, 1993). For years, special education has served these students in segregated pull-out programs, thereby reinforcing the expectations that pupils with behavior problems cannot be taught in the mainstream and that regular educators are not responsible for their management.

Unfortunately, this refer-and-remove pattern reinforces the assumption that it is the referred pupil who "owns" the problem. Seldom is it acknowledged that inappropriate expectations, curriculum, or teaching methods may contribute to the behavioral disorder. Thus, the referring teacher emerges from this process without a problem and with a reinforced attitude that the problem was entirely the student's fault. The referred child, on the other hand, comes out of this process stigmatized by a label and transferred to a "special" environment to be "treated" and, perhaps, never returned to the educational mainstream.

Fortunately, the emphasis on place-oriented services is giving way to a philosophy of providing a continuum of services brought to the pupils and their teachers. For example, Colorado has adopted an approach to educational programming for students with behavioral disorders based on these students' needs (Cessna, 1993). Oregon's suggested continuum of behavior management services is presented in Table 1.7. Note that the first three steps in this continuum involve procedures and resources provided in the regular classroom. A change in educational placement (from regular to special) is not considered until step 4.

An outgrowth of this new philosophy of moving services to the student instead of moving the student to the services attempts to design services that "wrap around" the pupil's needs. The

Table 1.7 Continuum of Services for Managing Student Behavior

Step	Responsibility	Procedure	Resources
1	Classroom teacher	Regular classroom placement	The teacher utilizes instructional and classroom management methods that include posted classroom rules and consequences for behavior.
2	Classroom teacher and school staff	Regular classroom placement and referral to school resources	This involves advice and support from colleagues, involvement of the school support staff, or student referral to a systematic school discipline system.
3	Classroom teacher, school staff, and district staff	Regular classroom placement and request for district resources	The district provides consultation resources such as a special education school psychologist or behavior specialist.
4	Classroom teacher, school staff, and district staff	Request for special education evaluation and eligibility decision. Placement in a special building, program, or regular classroom.	The multidisciplinary team determines eligibility, the IEP team determines the placement and programming, and the special education staff provides and coordinates services.
5	School staff, special education, district staff, and community resources	Placement within district resources and referral to community resources	District and community resources.

Source: Waksman, S., & Jones, V. (1985, August). A suggested procedure for the identification and provision of services to seriously emotionally disturbed students. *Technical assistance papers: A series on PL 94–142 and related Oregon laws.* Portland, OR: Department of Education.

wraparound approach is based on providing support and interventions that build on strengths within the student as well as the ecological settings in which the student functions. A variety of services within the school building (as well as from the community) is blended into a comprehensive service plan that brings interventions to the student rather than moving the student to settings where these services customarily are provided. Consistent with the philosophy we have just advocated, wraparound services are determined by student needs rather than by educational placement. In addition, these interventions are based on the identification and assessment of strengths in both the student and settings, rather than on the mere elimination of identified deficits. The major components of school-based wraparound services are listed in Table 1.8 (Eber, 1995). Wraparound service delivery is described in more detail in subsequent chapters.

We stress repeatedly throughout this text that problem behaviors occur without regard for a student's educational placement or labels. Thus, pupils who have been certified and placed in programs for other categories of disabilities are as likely to require intervention services as are students in regular programs or in programs for pupils with EBD. Regular and special education administrators should view behavior problems as indicating a need for services, not a need to change a student's educational placement. The latter requires considerably more elaborate and time-consuming activities, which are likely to disrupt the student's program, with no guarantee that the new placement will benefit the pupil more than the old one did.

Figure 1.4 describes the continuum of services to students who have been certified as having EBD. In contrast to Table 1.7, this continuum puts more emphasis on placement. Levels I and II include pupils identified as EBD who are in regular classes without consultative assistance to the regular classroom teacher (Level I) or with consultative assistance (Level II). Subsequent levels indicate more restrictive placements, including placement outside the public school setting.

When special education placement is deemed necessary, the level in the continuum that is **least restrictive** for the student must be determined. Least restrictive placement is *not* synonymous with the regular classroom. The educational environment that imposes the fewest obstacles to the pupil's optimal social and academic functioning depends on that student's individual needs. We believe this decision cannot be made without a comprehensive and thorough assessment of the pupil and total environment.

If the pupil is causing a management problem in one setting, a consultation with the teacher regarding effective management strategies may be sufficient (i.e., Level II services). If the pupil's behavior problems occur across more settings (e.g., all classes, on the playground, in the lunchroom, on the bus) or if the pupil exhibits academic difficulties needing special remedial methods, a more restrictive placement such as a resource room or self-contained special class, might be considered (i.e., Level III or IV). In our view, severe and widespread

Table 1.8   Some Major Elements of School-Based Wraparound Care

- Is responsive to the needs of the individual student and her family
- Provides strength/support not deficits/fix orientation
- Delivers flexibly in terms of time, quantity, and approach
- Is typical of age/culture/environment
- Is comprehensive for all domains and entire school day
- Integrates formal school services with informal school-based supports
- Is unconditional
- Ensures that resources are delivered on the basis of need rather than program or setting definitions
- Analyzes school or special education operations on the basis of the single student

Figure 1.4 Continuum of
Services for Children and
Youth with EBD

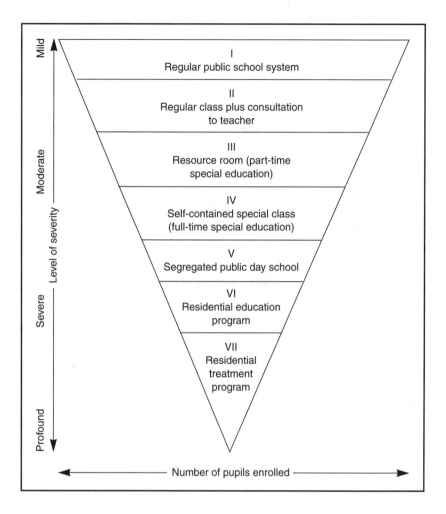

behavior problems or serious communication difficulties should be present before placement in more restrictive settings (i.e., Levels V, VI, and VII) is considered.

Placements that eliminate students' opportunity for contact with the typical school environment should be avoided if possible. The only advantage afforded students in these placements is more intensive programming by a qualified team. For example, segregated day schools may offer psychologists, social workers, and other mental health professionals who assist in designing a consistent and therapeutic program. Some pupils need this degree of structure and support. Still others require a 24-hour structured program such as that in a residential school. The last level,

a residential treatment program, is available for children and youth who require a psychiatrically oriented treatment program that may include medical treatment and intensive psychotherapy.

Figure 1.4 suggests that more students, with less severe behavior problems, are at the upper levels of the continuum. This observation holds true for students who have not been certified as having EBD; however, as the U. S. Department of Education (1994) reported, 20 percent of all students with EBD are served in separate facilities (compared with 5 percent of all students with disabilities), 30 percent of all homebound students are identified as having EBD, 37 percent are educated in self-contained special classes, and 28 percent are placed in resource rooms. In contrast, of the overall population of students with disabilities, 68 percent receive most of their education in regular classes. Thus, it appears that, in general, schools are reluctant to identify students with EBD, and, if they do, they prefer to remove them as far as possible from the mainstream. The assumption that pupils certified with EBD are placed in more restrictive settings because their behavior problems are more severe is intriguing but essentially is untestable because judgments of the severity of behavior problems are subjective. Even with standardized rating scales and direct observation, behavioral disorders cannot be quantified along a continuum, as is the case with IQ and achievement test scores.

Again, the least restrictive placement depends on the individual student, and we urge that special education be conceptualized as a continuum of services, with consideration given to more restrictive educational placements only after interventions have been tried unsuccessfully in less restrictive settings. We also recommend that the behavioral requirements of educational settings be assessed and that those competencies be targeted for instruction in more restrictive placements so that the curriculum is functional and promotes student progress to less restrictive educational settings. Procedures for assessing the behavioral expectations of less restrictive environments have been developed (see Walker & Rankin, 1983) and are described in Chapter 11.

As a professional working with problem behavior, you may function anywhere within this continuum, from a consultant working with regular classroom teachers to a teacher in a residential psychiatric hospital. The methods presented in this book have been applied effectively in all of these settings. Although the focus of our discussion is the classroom, the techniques and procedures described may be used elsewhere: in the lunchroom, library, gym, playground, home, and neighborhood. Often you will find that you must generalize your classroom procedures to these settings because students with behavior problems experience their greatest difficulty there. Then, too, unless you want to be the exclusive caregiver for your students with EBD for the entire school day, you must teach others to implement your curriculum and behavior management procedures. Not only do your pupils need to learn to cope with the larger environment but also the environment (other school staff, parents, other children) must learn how to cope with them.

Finally, to change problem behavior—to teach pupils and their caregivers to use new and better skills in their total environment—you must systematically implement strategies to ensure that these skills are generalized and maintained in other settings (Rutherford & Nelson, 1988). What has been accomplished when you have taught a student to accept your correction of his or her behavior or not to steal in your classroom if the student blows up when corrected in algebra class or steals money from a purse at home? Working with pupils exhibiting behavioral disorders requires that you spend a good deal of time outside your classroom. In Chapter 11 we offer techniques and suggestions for working effectively in other settings.

The concepts and strategies presented in this chapter currently are not in widespread use in many school programs. In addition, their implementation may depend on school policies developed by boards of education and administrators. Therefore, you may feel powerless to use these models in your role. Nevertheless, we have presented these concepts and strategies because, far from being futuristic ideals, they are part of a currently developing technology for serving pupils who have behavior problems. In the following chapters you will learn some of this technology, as well as guidelines for judging when and where to apply it. We hope that the skills you acquire will help you to function more effectively in your professional role and to advocate for more effective services for students whose behavior reduces their chances of succeeding in the educational system.

SUMMARY

Assessing students exhibiting behavior problems is a complex and technical process that leads to decisions about student classification and intervention procedures. This chapter has focused on assessment to identify and certify pupils with EBD for special education services. Unfortunately, numerous subjective and political factors typically have influenced the identification of students with EBD. The result is that this population is among the most underserved of all groups of pupils with disabilities. Even more unfortunately, the regular education system has inadequately served students at risk for EBD but who fail to meet definitional criteria for special education. These problems currently are being addressed by developing systematic screening and identification procedures, prereferral interventions, and using systematic assessment data to match pupil needs with a continuum of educational services.

DISCUSSION QUESTIONS

1. Why is identifying students who are disabled by their behavior more difficult than other populations of students with disabilities? How does this affect prevalence estimates?
2. How does assessment for classification purposes differ from assessment for treatment planning? What instruments and procedures would you include in an "ideal" classification system?
3. Would you advocate identifying and certifying students with EBD to provide them with educational services, or would you favor serving them through systematic interventions in regular programs? Support your position.
4. Children and youth with EBD continue to be served in residential treatment programs outside of local school districts. How does this affect the likelihood that students can successfully reintegrate into the educational mainstream?

REFERENCES

Algozzine, B., Christenson, S., & Ysseldyke, J. (1982). Probabilities associated with the referral to placement process. *Teacher Education and Special Education, 5,* 19–23.

Algozzine, B., Ruhl, K., & Ramsey, R. (1991). *Behaviorally disordered? Assessment for identification and instruction.* Reston, VA: Council for Exceptional Children.

American Psychiatric Association. (1994). *Diagnostic and statistical manual to mental disorders* (4th ed.). Washington, DC: Author.

Apter, S. J. (1982). *Troubled children: Troubled systems.* New York: Pergamon Press.

Baer, D. M., Wolf, M. M., & Risley, T. R. (1987). Some still-current dimensions of applied behavior analysis. *Journal of Applied Behavior Analysis, 20,* 313–327.

Bagley, M. T., & Greene, J. F. (1981). *Peer attitudes toward the handicapped scale.* Austin, TX: PRO-ED.

Battle, J. (1992). *Culture-free self-esteem inventories* (2nd ed.). Austin, TX: PRO-ED.

Bower, E. M. (1982). Defining emotional disturbance: Public policy and research. *Psychology in the Schools, 19,* 55–60.

Braaten, S., Kauffman, J. M., Braaten, B., Polsgrove, L., & Nelson, C. M. (1988). The regular education initiative: Patent medicine for behavioral disorders? *Exceptional Children, 55,* 21–27.

Bracken, B. A. (1992). *Multidimensional self concept scale.* Austin, TX: PRO-ED.

Brown, L., & Alexander, J. (1991). *Self-esteem index.* Austin, TX: PRO-ED.

Brown, L., & Hammill, D. D. (1990). *Behavior rating profile* (2nd ed.) Austin, TX: PRO-ED.

Brown, L. J., Black, D. D., & Downs, J. C. (1984). *School social skills rating scale.* East Aurora, NY: Slosson Educational Publications.

Burks, H. F. (1977). *Burks' behavior rating scales.* Los Angeles, CA: Western Psychological Services.

Carson, R. R., Sitlington, P. C., & Frank, A. R. (1995). Young adulthood for individuals with behavior disorders: What does it hold? *Behavioral Disorders, 20,* 127–135.

Cassell, R. H. (1962). *The child behavior rating scale.* Los Angeles, CA: Western Psychological Services.

Cessna, K. K. (Ed.). (1993). *Instructionally differentiated programming: A needs-based approach for students with behavior disorders.* Denver: Colorado Department of Education.

Chalfant, J. C., Pysh, M., & Moultrie, R. (1979). Teacher assistance teams: A model for within-building problem solving. *Learning Disabilities Quarterly, 2,* 85–96.

Chesapeake Institute. (1994, September). National agenda for achieving better results for children and youth with serious emotional disturbance. Washington, DC: Department of Education, Office of Special Education and Rehabilitative Services, Office of Special Education Programs.

Chin, P., & Hughes, S. (1987). Representation of minority students in special education classes. *Remedial and Special Education, 8*(4), 41–46.

Clarke, R. T., Schaefer, M., Burchard, J. D., & Welkowitz, J. W. (1992). Wrapping community-based mental health services. *Journal of Child and Family Studies, 1,* 241–261.

Clark, L., Gresham, F. M., & Elliott, S. N. (1985). Development and validation of a social skills measure: The TROSS-C. *Journal of Psychoeducational Assessment, 4,* 347–356.

Conners, C. K. (1969). *Conners' teacher rating scales* (long form). San Antonio, TX: Psychological Corporation (distributor).

Conners, C. K. (1970). *Conners' parent rating scales* (long form). San Antonio, TX: Psychological Corporation (distributor).

Conners, C. K. (1978). *Conners' parent rating scales* (short form). San Antonio, TX: Psychological Corporation (distributor).

Conners, C. K. (1978). *Conners' teacher rating scales* (short form). San Antonio, TX: Psychological Corporation (distributor).

Coopersmith, S. (1981). *Coopersmith self-esteem inventories.* Palo Alto, CA: Consulting Psychologists Press.

Cottle, W. C. (1966). *School interest inventory.* Chicago, IL: Riverside.

Council for Children with Behavioral Disorders. (1987). Position paper on definition and identification of students with behavioral disorders. *Behavioral Disorders, 13,* 9–19.

Council for Children with Behavioral Disorders. (1989). Position statement on the regular education initiative. *Behavioral Disorders, 14,* 201–207.

Eber, L. (1995, April). *LASDE EBD network training developing school-based wraparound plan.* LaGrange, IL: LaGrange Area Department of Special Education.

Eber, L., & Nelson, C. M. (1994, November). Compendium digest: Special education and related services for students with serious emotional disturbance. Prepared for the National Disabilities Council, pursuant to the reauthorization of IDEA.

Edgar, E. B. (1987). Secondary programs in special education: Are many of them justifiable? *Exceptional Children, 35,* 5–22.

Epstein, J. L. (1976). *Quality of school life scale.* Chicago, IL: Riverside.

Epstein, M. H., Quinn, K., Nelson, C. M., Polsgrove, L., & Cumblad, C. (1993). Serving students with emotional and behavioral disorders through a comprehensive community-based approach. *OSERS News in Print, 5*(3), 19–23.

Estes, T. H., Estes, J. J., Richards, H. C., & Roettger, D. (1981). *Estes attitude scales.* Austin, TX: PRO-ED.

Feil, E. G., & Becker, W. C. (1993). Investigation of a multiple-gated screening system for preschool behavior problems. *Behavioral Disorders, 19,* 44–53.

Feil, E. G., Severson, H. H., & Walker, H. M. (1994). Early screening project (ESP): Identifying preschool children with adjustment problems. *The Oregon Conference Monograph, 6,* 177–183.

Feil, E. G., Walker, H. M., & Severson, H. H. (1995). The Early Screening Project for young children with behavior problems. *Journal of Emotional and Behavioral Disorders, 3,* 194–204.

Fitts, W. H., & Roid, G. H. (1988). *Tennessee self-concept scale.* Los Angeles, CA: Western Psychological Services.

Forness, S. R., & Knitzer, J. (1992). A new proposed definition and terminology to replace "serious emotional disturbance" in the Individuals with Disability Education Act. *School Psychology Review, 21,* 12–20.

Fuchs, D., Fuchs, L., & Bahr, M. W. (1990). Mainstream assistance teams: A scientific basis for the art of consultation. *Exceptional Children, 57,* 128–139.

Gartner, A., & Lipsky, D. K. (1987). Beyond special education: Toward a quality system for all students. *Harvard Educational Review, 57,* 367–395.

Gerber, M., & Semmel, M. (1984). Teacher as imperfect test: Reconceptualizing the referral process. *Educational Psychologist, 19,* 137–148.

Gerry, M. (1984). Expert witness deposition from Lavon *v.* Turlington. Class action lawsuit settled in State of Florida.

Gough, H. (1969). *California Psychological Inventory.* Palo Alto: Consulting Psychologists Press.

Gresham, F. M. (1985). Behavior disorders assessment: Conceptual, definitional, and practical considerations. *School Psychology Review, 14,* 495–509.

Gresham, F. M., & Elliot, S. N. (1990). *Social skills rating system.* Circle Pines, MN: American Guidance Service.

Gresham, F. M., Elliot, S. N., & Evans-Fernandez, S. (1992). *Student self-concept scale.* Circle Pines, MN: American Guidance Service.

Gresham, F. M., & Reschly, D. (1987). Issues in the conceptualization, classification, and assessment of social skills in the mildly handicapped. In T. Kratchowill (Ed.), *Advances in school psychology* (Vol. 6, pp. 203–264). Hillsdale, NJ: Lawrence Erlbaum Associates.

Honig v. Doe, 56 S. Ct. 27 (1988).

Hresko, W. P., & Brown, L. (1984). *Test of early socioemotional development.* Austin, TX: PRO-ED.

Huntze, S. (1985). A position paper of the Council for Children with Behavioral Disorders. *Behavorial Disorders, 10,* 167–174.

Hutton, J. B., & Roberts, T. G. (1986). *Social-emotional dimension scale.* Austin, TX: PRO-ED.

Kauffman, J. M. (1987). Forward: Social policy issues in special education and related services for emotionally disturbed children and youth. In N. Haring (Ed.), *Measuring and managing behavior disorders* (pp. x–xx). Seattle: University of Washington Press.

Kauffman, J. M. (1993). *Characteristics of emotional and behavioral disorders of children and youth* (5th ed.). Upper Saddle River, NJ: Merrill/Prentice Hall.

Kauffman, J. M., & Hallahan, D. P. (Eds.). (1995). *The illusion of full inclusion: A comprehensive critique of a current special education bandwagon.* Austin, TX: Pro-Ed.

Kauffman, J. M., Lloyd, J. W., Astuto, T. A., & Hallahan, D. P. (1995). *Issues in the educational placement of students with emotional or behavioral disorders.* Hillsdale, NJ: Lawrence Erlbaum Associates.

Kentucky EBD Task Force. (1992). *Emotional-behavioral disability technical assistance manual.* Frankfort, KY: Kentucky Department of Education.

Koyanagi, C., & Gaines, S. (1993). *All systems failure: An examination of the results of neglecting the needs of children with serious emotional disturbance.* Alexandria, VA: National Mental Health Association.

Lambert, N., Hartsough, C., & Sandoval, J. (1990). *Children's attention and adjustment survey.* Circle Pines, MN: American Guidance Service.

Lambert, N., Windmiller, M., Tharinger, D., & Cole, L. (1981). *AAMD Adaptive Behavior Scale* (school edition). Monterey, CA: Publishers Test Service.

Lloyd, J. W., & Kauffman, J. M. (1995). What less restrictive placements require of teachers. In J. M. Kauffman, J. W. Lloyd, D. P. Hallahan, & T. A. Astuto (Eds.), *Issues in educational placement: Students with emotional and behavioral disorders* (pp. 317–334). Hillsdale, NJ: Lawrence Erlbaum Associates.

McCarney, S. B. (1989a). *Attention deficit disorders evaluation scale, Home version.* Columbia, MO: Hawthorne Educational Services.

McCarney, S. B. (1989b). *Attention deficit disorders evaluation scale, School version.* Columbia, MO: Hawthorne Educational Services.

McCarney, S. B., & Leigh, J. E. (1990). *Behavior evaluation scale-2.* Columbia, MO: Hawthorne Educational Services.

McConaughy, S. M., & Achenbach, T. M. (1989). Empirically based assessment of severe emotional disturbance. *Journal of School Psychology, 27,* 91–117.

McGlothlin, J. E. (1981). The school consultation committee: An approach to implementing a teacher consultation model. *Behavioral Disorders, 6,* 101–107.

McIntyre, T. (1992). A primer on cultural diversity for educators. *Multicultural Forum, 1*(2), 13–16.

McIntyre, T. (1995). *The McIntyre Assessment of Culture.* Columbia, MO: Hawthorne Educational Services.

McLaughlin, M. J., Leone, P. E., Warren, S. H., & Schofield, P. F. (1994). *Doing things differently: Issues and options for creating comprehensive school linked services for children and youth with emotional or behavioral disorders.* College Park, MD: University of Maryland and Westat, Inc.

McLoughlin, J. A., & Lewis, R. B. (1994). *Assessing special students* (4th ed.). Upper Saddle River, NJ: Merrill/Prentice Hall.

Meadows, N. B., Neel, R. S., Scott, C. M., & Parker, G. (1994). Academic performance, social competence, and mainstream accommodations: A look at mainstreamed and nonmainstreamed students with serious behavioral disorders. *Behavioral Disorders, 19,* 170–180.

Michael, W. B., Smith, R. A., & Michael, J. J. (1984). *Dimensions of self-concept.* San Diego, CA: EdITS.

Miller, L. C. (1977). *School behavior checklist.* Los Angeles, CA: Western Psychological Services.

Mooney, R. L., & Gordon, L. V. (1950). *The Mooney problem check lists* (rev. ed.). San Antonio, TX: Psychological Corporation.

Naglieri, J. A., LeBuffe, P. A., & Pfeiffer, S. I. (1993). *Devereux behavior rating scales—School form.* San Antonio, TX: Psychological Corporation.

National Association of School Psychologists (1986). *Intervention assistance teams: A model for building level instructional problem solving.* Washington, DC: Author.

Neeper, R., Lahey, B. B., & Frick, P. J. (1990). *Comprehensive behavior rating scale for children.* San Antonio, TX: Psychological Corporation.

Nelson, C. M. (1988). Social skills training for handicapped students. *Teaching Exceptional Children, 20*(4), 19–23.

Nelson, C. M. (1992). Searching for meaning in the behavior of antisocial pupils, public school administrators, and lawmakers. *School Psychology Review, 21,* 35–39.

Nelson, C. M., & Rutherford, R. B., Jr. (1988). Behavioral interventions with behaviorally disordered students. In M. C. Wang, H. J. Walberg, & M. C. Reynolds (Eds.), *The handbook of special education: Research and practice* (Vol. 2, pp. 125–153). Oxford, England: Pergamon.

Nelson, C. M., Rutherford, R. B., Center, D., & Walker, H. M. (1992). Do public schools have an obligation to serve troubled children and youth? *Exceptional Children, 57,* 406–415.

Peterson, R. L., & Ishii-Jordan, S. (Eds.). (1993). *Multicultural issues in the education of behaviorally disordered youth.* Cambridge, MA: Brookline Books.

Phillips, V., & McCullough, L. L. (1992). *Student/staff support teams.* Longmont, CO: Sopris West.

Piers, E. V., & Harris, D. (1984). *The Piers-Harris children's self-concept scale: Revised manual.* Los Angeles, CA: Western Psychological Services.

Polsgrove, L. (1987). Assessment of children's social and behavioral problems. In W. H. Berdine & S. A. Meyer (Eds.), *Assessment in special education* (pp. 141–180). Boston: Little, Brown.

Potter, M. L., Ysseldyke, J. E., & Regan, R. R. (1983). Eligibility and classification decisions in educational settings: Issuing "passports" in a state of confusion. *Contemporary Educational Psychology, 8,* 146–157.

Quay, H. C., & Peterson, D. R. (1987). *Revised behavior problem checklist.* Coral Gables, FL: University of Miami.

Reynolds, M. C. (1991). Classification and labeling. In J. W. Lloyd, A. C. Repp, & N. N. Singh (Eds.), *The regular education initiative: Alternative perspectives on concepts, issues, and models* (pp. 29–41). Sycamore, IL: Sycamore Publishing Co.

Reynolds, M. C., & Birch, J. W. (1977). *Teaching exceptional children in all America's schools.* Reston, VA: Council for Exceptional Children.

Rutherford, R. B., Jr., & Nelson, C. M. (1988). Generalization and maintenance of treatment effects. In J. C. Witt, E. N. Elliott, & F. M. Gresham (Eds.), *Handbook of behavior therapy in education* (pp. 227–324). New York: Plenum.

Salvia, J., & Ysseldyke, J. E. (1995). *Assessment in special and remedial education* (6th ed.). Boston: Houghton Mifflin.

Shores, R. E., Gunter, P. L., & Jack, S. L. (1993). Classroom management strategies: Are they setting events for coercion? *Behavioral Disorders, 18,* 92–102.

Sinclair, E., Del'Homme, M., & Gonzalez, M. (1993). Systematic screening for preschool behavioral disorders. *Behavioral Disorders, 18,* 177–188.

Skiba, R., & Grizzle, K. (1991). The social maladjustment exclusion: Issues of definition and assessment. *School Psychology Review, 20,* 577–595.

Sparrow, S. S., Balla, D. A., & Cicchetti, D.V. (1985). *Vineland Adaptive Behavior Scale.* Circle Pines, MN: American Guidance Service.

Rating Scale. Devon, PA: The Devereux Foundation Press.

Stainback, W., & Stainback, S. (1984). A rationale for the merger of special and regular education. *Exceptional Children, 51,* 102–111.

Stephens, T. M. (1979). *Social behavior assessment.* Columbus, OH: Cedars Press.

Stroul, B. A., & Friedman, R. A. (1986). *A system of care for severely emotionally disturbed children and youth.* Washington, DC: CASSP Technical Assistance Center, Georgetown University Child Development Center.

Sugai, G. M., & Tindal, G. A. (1993). *Effective school consultation: an interactive approach.* Pacific Grove, CA: Brooks/Cole.

U. S. Department of Education. (1994). *Sixteenth annual report to Congress on the implementation of the Individuals with Disability Education Act.* Washington, DC: U.S. Department of Education, Office of Special Education and Rehabilitative Services.

Waksman, S., & Jones, V. (1985, August). A suggested procedure for the identification of and provision of services to seriously emotionally disturbed students. *Technical assistance papers: A series on PL 94–142 and related Oregon laws.* Portland: Oregon Department of Education.

Walker, H. (1983). *Walker Problem Behavior Identification Checklist. (Revised).* Los Angeles: Western Psychological Services.

Walker, H. M., Block-Pedego, A., Todis, B., & Severson, H. (1991). T*he School Archival Records Search.* Longmount, CO: Sopris West.

Walker, H. M., & Fabre, T. R. (1987). Assessment of behavior disorders in the school setting: Issues, problems and strategies revisited. In N. Haring (Ed.), *Measuring and managing behavior disorders* (pp. 198–243). Seattle: University of Washington Press.

Walker, H. M., & McConnell, S. R. (1988). *The Walker-McConnell Scale of Social Competence and School Adjustment: A Social Skills Rating Scale for Teachers.* Austin, TX: PRO-ED.

Walker, H. M., & Rankin, R. (1983). Assessing the behavioral expectations and demands of less restrictive settings. *School Psychology Digest, 12,* 274–284.

Walker, H. M., & Severson, H. (1990). *Systematic Screening for Behavioral Disorders.* Longmont, CO: Sopris West.

Walker, H. M., Severson, H., & Feil, E. G. (1995). *Early screening project: A proven child-find process.* Longmount, CO: Sopris West.

Wood, F. H., Smith, C. R., & Grimes, J. (Eds.). (1985). *The Iowa assessment model in behavioral disorders: A training manual.* Des Moines, IA: Department of Public Instruction.

Woodcock, R. W., & Johnson, M. B. (1977). *Woodcock-Johnson psycho-educational battery.* Chicago, IL: Riverside.

Yell, M. L. (1995). *Clyde K. and Sheila K. v. Puyallup School District:* The courts, inclusion, and students with behavioral disorders. *Behavioral Disorders, 20,* 179–189.

Ysseldyke, J. E., & Algozzine, B. (1982). *Critical issues in special and remedial education.* Boston: Houghton Mifflin.

2

ASSESSMENT FOR INTERVENTION PLANNING

OUTLINE

OBJECTIVES

After completing this chapter, you should be able to

◆ Describe the purposes and outcomes of the behavioral-ecological assessment process.
◆ Indicate the difficulties of evaluating discrepancies between social behaviors and standards and describe some procedures for assessing these discrepancies.
◆ Describe assessment decisions based on the model in Figure 2.1 given information about target behaviors.
◆ Explain how the following influence the selection of social behavior targets: the communicative function, the fair pair rule, the criterion of ultimate functioning, and the criterion of functioning in the next environment.
◆ Write terminal intervention objectives and analyze these objectives by breaking them down into three to five task steps, given descriptions of target behaviors.

In Chapter 1 we described two sets of assessment decisions: those regarding students' eligibility for special education services and those involving their educational treatment, which include what to teach and how to teach (Algozzine, Ruhl, & Ramsey, 1991). This chapter concerns assessment for the purpose of planning educational interventions directed at pupils' social behaviors (i.e., what to teach). At this point we assume that you have made placement decisions and are concerned with assessments for the purpose of identifying and evaluating behaviors for intervention. In other words, the assessment decisions discussed here are those you make as an intervention agent, whether you are a classroom teacher, a school counselor or psychologist, or some other support person in the school setting. We begin by describing the process of behavioral-ecological assessment (Polsgrove, 1987), then present a systematic model for assessing social behavior that leads to intervention planning decisions. This model encompasses a range of instruments and procedures, including norm- and criterion-referenced assessment scales, direct observation procedures, interviews, and sociometric techniques for selecting and analyzing targeted social behaviors. We conclude with a discussion of the outcomes of treatment planning assessment—namely, intervention goals and objectives—as well as how to task-analyze terminal objectives for intervention. The case study at the end of the chapter illustrates a portion of an IEP concerning social behaviors. Chapters 3 and 4 extend the assessment process, including monitoring students' progress through intervention programs, evaluating these programs, making data-based decisions, and selecting intervention strategies.

Although we describe assessment in terms of two distinct sets of decisions—those involving educational classification and those concerned with intervention—we are not suggesting that these processes are separate or unrelated. On the contrary, they are closely linked. For example, in conducting systematic school-wide screening procedures, teacher assistance teams or school-based specialists will plan prereferral interventions. The results of these interventions provide another set of assessment data that includes the pupil's response to the intervention, the characteristics of the intervention strategy (e.g., specific components, how complex, how intensive), and the resources needed to deliver a successful intervention. These data may be used by appropriate school personnel (e.g., teacher assistance teams, assessment or behavioral specialists) to make subsequent decisions, such as whether to continue a prereferral intervention, adjust it, replace it with a more intensive strategy, or refer the student for formal special education evaluation. Assessments for classification and for treatment planning also involve many of the same instruments and procedures, such as rating scales, checklists, and behavioral observations. Thus, we view the assessment process as a continuum of procedures and decisions, each assessment providing information for subsequent decisions and each decision influencing interventions that follow. Assessment may begin at a general level with a question: "Which students are at risk for emotional or behavioral disorders?" It becomes much more specific when you ask such questions as "What intervention will maintain the student in a regular education program?" or "What factors are influencing the student's aggressive behavior?"

Intervention planning requires data from various levels of assessment in order to tailor strategies to the characteristics of the students to which they are to be applied, the persons applying them, and the settings in which they are used. The purposes of these assessments are to verify that a problem exists and that it warrants intervention; to analyze the problem in terms of which behaviors

are occurring, where they occur, and which characteristics compose these environmental settings (which persons, expectations, degrees of structure, etc.); and to develop hypotheses about the factors that may cause or contribute to the problem, as well as about the potential intervention strategies that address the relevant characteristics. These hypotheses then are tested by systematically implementing interventions and monitoring their effects (Wehby, 1994).

THE ASSESSMENT PROCESS

Behavioral-ecological assessment is the evaluation of observable student behaviors across the range of environmental settings in which they occur. As indicated in the previous chapter, traditional mental health assessment focuses on internal processes that are assumed to underlie overt behavior patterns. In contrast, behavioral assessment focuses upon the objective analysis of the overt behavior itself, which minimizes inferences about underlying conditions. Tests that measure personality constructs, attitudes, and feelings typically are not used in behavioral assessment. Because behaviors occur in a variety of settings (e.g., home, school, community), and because the behaviors that occur in one setting may not happen in others, it is important to assess student behaviors across various settings. A single ecological setting actually is comprised of many subsettings. For example, the school setting consists of classrooms, offices, a lunchroom, a gymnasium, hallways, a bus waiting area, a playground, and so forth. Even students placed in self-contained classrooms function in many settings, each of which differs in terms of other persons, behavioral expectations, the degree of structure, and the interactions likely to occur. The concept of behavioral-ecological assessment emphasizes the need to conduct behavioral assessments in the ecological settings relevant to planning and implementing effective interventions. Polsgrove (1987) articulated the goals of behavioral-ecological assessment as identifying specific interpersonal and environmental variables within each setting that influence behavior, analyzing the behavioral expectations of various settings, and comparing expectations and the pupil's behavior across settings. These analyses provide a comprehensive picture of the student's behavior in a range of places and among a variety of persons. They also reveal differences in expectations, structure, and social interaction patterns that characterize these settings. Table 2.1 presents guidelines for assessing behavior across the settings in which the student functions. The procedures used to obtain assessment data include interviews, checklists, rating scales, sociometric devices, and direct observations.

Thus, behavioral-ecological assessment procedures address the range of behaviors and settings that characterize each student's total environment. Such broad assessments are particularly useful in identifying potential target behaviors, where they occur, both immediate and remote environmental factors that influence their occurrence, and other variables that potentially may contribute to intervention planning. Within and across these ecological settings, increasingly specific and precise assessments are conducted to identify, analyze, and monitor the behaviors targeted for intervention. The decisions made by intervention agents guide this process as those persons evaluate the student's behavior relative to the characteristics of the ecological settings in which the student functions. Following is a discussion of a decision model for assessing specific social behaviors.

A Model for the Assessment of Social Behavior

Assessment of behavior problems essentially is a process of collecting information and making decisions based on this information. The decision-making process that guides intervention planning is described in Figure 2.1. The assessment procedures and instruments used in collecting the data for making initial intervention decisions are described in the following sections.

Does a Problem Exist?

Your initial assessment task is to evaluate pupils' social behaviors across the settings in which they are expected to perform. Data from behavioral-ecological assessment procedures will suggest which student behaviors are problems in which settings relative to the expectations for social behavior in those different settings. As Howell, Fox, and Morehead (1993) point out, a problem exists if there is a discrepancy between student behavior and a standard. In other words, someone must use his own judgment and decide that there is a discrepancy and that it is serious enough to justify intervention. In the case of academic behaviors, making judgments about discrepancies between standards and behaviors is relatively straightforward and objective (e.g., the student is getting less than 50 percent correct on her assignment in language arts). However, standards for social behavior are based on the expectations

Table 2.1 Guidelines for Ecological Assessment

Information to Be Obtained	Potential Sources of Information
1. What are the pupil's major environmental settings and reference groups?	1. Pupil, parents, other teachers, peers.
2. Who are the significant persons in these settings?	2. Pupil, parents, other teachers, peers, direct observation.
3. What behaviors occur in these settings? (List both desired and undesired behaviors.)	3. Parents, other teachers, peers, direct observation.
4. (For settings in which problem behavior occurs) Who sees the behavior as a problem?	4. Significant others in the setting.
5. What behaviors are expected in the setting?	5. Significant others in the setting.
6. How does the pupil's behavior differ from these expectations?	6. Significant others in the setting.

Figure 2.1 Assessment Model

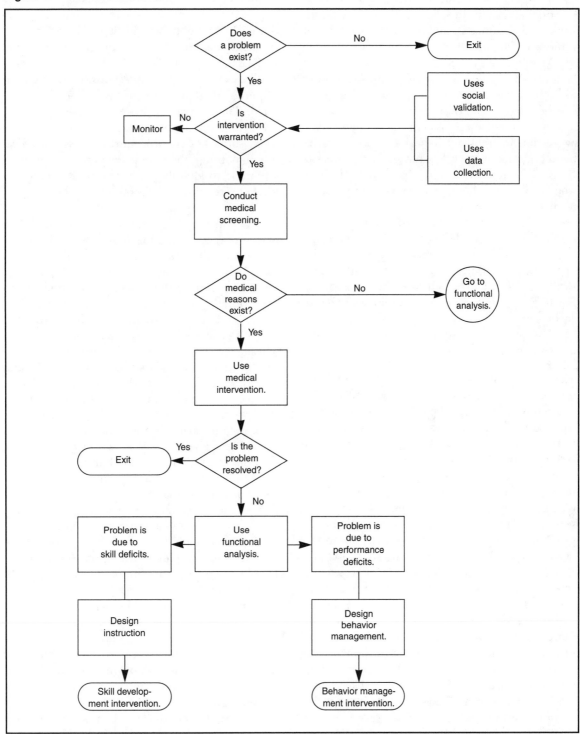

of other persons, and such expectations are both personal and subjective. For example, Mrs. Smith believes that pupils should not talk to each other while working; therefore she expects students to speak only when called upon. But Ms. Peterson believes that pupils should talk to each other while working; therefore she expects some level of noise in her classroom.

In the case of a serious behavior problem (e.g., aggression, stereotypic behavior), discrepancies between standards and behavior are more obvious. Students with severe disabilities or those who display "psychotic" behaviors clearly depart from expectations for "normal" behavior. However, judgments about the seriousness of less extreme behavior problems are more difficult due to the absence of instruments and procedures for measuring behavioral standards and student performance accurately relative to these standards. Fortunately, the assessment technology needed to accomplish such measurement is being developed and there are a few procedures that may be used for this purpose.

Methods of Assessment   Screening procedures are used to determine whether a problem exists. The procedures used should be relatively brief and efficient so that persons in each relevant setting will be inclined to cooperate. Alternately, screening assessments may be conducted by persons who are familiar with the student's performance across most or all of the relevant settings. The school-wide screening procedures discussed in Chapter 1 serve the purpose of establishing whether a problem exists, but currently these are not widely used. The traditional method of screening students for behavioral problems is through teacher referral. You will recall that referral-driven identification procedures are unreliable and biased against students who are socially withdrawn. The more systematic and reliable procedures for identifying students with behavioral problems described in Chapter 1 also may be used to determine the existence of a significant discrepancy between behavior and expectations, irrespective of whether the student is being considered for special education. The methods we describe here

include checklists and rating scales, teacher rankings, self-report measures, and sociometric procedures. In addition, we describe procedures designed to measure teacher expectations and pupil social skills. Screening for intervention planning addresses the following questions: Is intervention required? If so, in which settings should it be applied? The assessment procedures used to answer these questions are likely to involve more time and more sophisticated procedures across more ecological settings than those required for general screening to identify pupils at risk. However, this level of screening focuses on a limited number of students, and the importance of the decisions to be made justifies the greater expenditure of time and resources needed for these assessments.

Checklists and *rating scales* generally use information supplied by a significant other (e.g., teacher, parent, sibling, peer) to produce a picture of a target child's behavior. A checklist merely asks the responder to indicate whether she has observed specific behaviors at any time. These behaviors are selected from a list of behaviors. A rating scale gives the rater a set of items and asks him to evaluate these items with respect to a particular student in terms of how frequently they occur. Less commonly, the rater responds to each item in terms of how much it characterizes the student's behavior (e.g., is very characteristic of the student; is not at all characteristic). Typically, ratings are presented in a Likert or similar numeric scale format.

Sometimes you may be asked to rate how often a student engages in a particular behavior (never, rarely, occasionally, often, very frequently). If you are asked to complete a rating scale as part of a formal screening program, be sure that you have had enough experience with the child to provide valid responses. Remember, screening is not a fine-tuned stage in the assessment process.

Behavior rating scales may be *standardized*, meaning that tests were administered to a number of persons and, on the basis of their responses, norms and criteria for discriminating between groups were established (e.g., a conduct problem/not a conduct problem). Some of the better-known standardized rating scales include

the *Revised Behavior Problem Checklist* (Quay & Peterson, 1983), the *Walker Problem Behavior Identification Checklist* (WPBIC) (Walker, 1983), and the *Behavior Rating Profile* (Brown & Hammill, 1983).
Others are listed in Table 1.3. Figure 2.2 presents a
sample of items from WPBIC. Rating scales also
may be informal and nonstandardized, such as the
instrument shown in Figure 2.3. The format
shown here has the advantage of rating a group of
students on the same sheet, thereby permitting
comparisons. Rating scales may contain items that
assess undesired or maladaptive behaviors, desired
or adaptive behaviors, or both. Many rating scales
are available commercially, and we suggest that
you study their items, reliability, validity, norms,
and recommended uses in order to identify those
that are likely to be most appropriate and useful
for your purposes (see McMahon, 1984).

To make the assessment of **teacher expectations** less subjective, Walker and Rankin (1980)
developed a standardized rating scale format, the
*SBS Inventory of Teacher Social Behavior Standards
and Expectations.* It asks teachers to rate the importance of adaptive behaviors (e.g., child takes

turns, uses free time appropriately) and their own
tolerance for maladaptive pupil behaviors (e.g.,
child whines, has tantrums, uses obscene language) in terms of how these affect their willingness to work with the students in their classrooms.
This instrument also is a component of the *Assessment for Integration into Mainstream Settings* system
(AIMS) (Walker, 1986), which is used to identify
the minimal skill requirements of mainstream settings, to prepare the student to meet these requirements, and to assess the pupil's adjustment
following mainstream placement. The other instruments in the AIMS system include the *SBS
Correlates Checklist,* which asks teachers to check
behaviors that would cause them to oppose placement of the student in their classes or for which
they would require technical assistance in order
to accept the placement; a criterion-referenced
rating scale to assess the pupil's behavioral status
on the SBS items that the teacher has indicated
either as important classroom skills or unacceptable behaviors; and two interval observational
coding systems for observing the target student's
behavior in academic and free-play situations.

Figure 2.2 Sample Items from the *Walker Problem Behavior Identification Checklist* (1983)

	Scale				
	1	2	3	4	5
20. Has nervous tics: muscle-twitching, eye-blinking, nail-biting, hand-wringing............					.3
21. Habitually rejects the school experience through actions or comments..................	.1				
22. Has enuresis (wets bed)..					.1
23. Utters nonsense syllables and/or babbles to himself....................................				.4	
24. Continually seeks attention..			.1		
25. Comments that nobody likes him..				.2	
26. Repeats one idea, thought, or activity over and over.................................				.4	
27. Has temper tantrums..	.2				
28. Refers to himself as dumb, stupid, or incapable......................................				.3	
29. Does not engage in group activities..		.2			
30. When teased or irritated by other children, takes out his frustration(s) on another, inappropriate person or thing..	.2				

Directions: The rater identifies those statements that describe the student and circles the number in the column corresponding to these statements. The circled values in each column are then added to yield a score for each of the five scales. The scales are Acting Out (column 1), Withdrawal (column 2), Distractibility (column 3), Disturbed Peer Relations (column 4), and Immaturity (column 5).

Figure 2.3   Teaching Rating Form

Students	Child has close friends.	Child is frequently chosen by classmates to play on a team, study together, etc.	Child spends most of recess time playing with others.	Child volunteers for classroom "jobs."	Child answers appropriately when the teacher asks questions of the group.	Child follows most teacher instructions independently or with minimal assistance.	Child brings materials and ideas to school for inclusion or class discussions and projects.	Child initiates conversations with the teacher.	Child completes most assignments within allotted time.	Child's academic performance is about right or better than expected for his grade level.	Child regularly follows classroom rules of conduct.	Child checks over most work papers before submitting them.	Child's statements about school are usually positive.	Child attends school regularly.	Child has no known major health problems.
1.															
2.															
3.															
4.															
5.															
6.															
7.															
8.															
9.															
10.															
11.															
12.															

Teacher _____ Interviewer _____ School _____

Grade _____ Date _____ Time _____

Sample items from the AIMS system are presented in Figure 2.4; we describe the AIMS system in greater detail in Chapter 11.

Teacher rankings on the basis of social criteria (e.g., frequency of peer verbal interactions) have been shown to be a reliable and valid method of identifying pupils who are not socially responsive (Walker, Severson, & Haring, 1986). Figure 2.5 illustrates one such ranking procedure. The teacher initially ranks all students in the class, divides them into two groups according to the behavior pattern being considered (e.g., most and least talkative), and finally ranks all pupils according to the criterion (Hops & Greenwood, 1981). The systematic

school-wide screening procedure (Walker & Severson, 1990) described in Chapter 1 includes this ranking procedure. Teacher rankings offer a quick way to establish the relative standing of pupils in the group with respect to a criterion.

Another format for problem identification screening is a **self-report.** As the name implies, this type of instrument requires that students describe their own behavior in response to a number of questions or statements. For young students or nonreaders the questions may be read orally with subsequent directions for students to color in a response area, to circle a happy or sad face, or to sort pictures into groups

Figure 2.4 Sample Items and Rating Formats from the SBS Inventory and Correlates Checklist

SBS Inventory			
Section I	Critical	Desirable	Unimportant
___ Child responds to requests and directions promptly.	( )	( )	( )
___ Child completes tasks within prescribed time limits.	( )	( )	( )
Section II	Unacceptable	Tolerated	Acceptable
___ Child disturbs or disrupts the activities of others.	( )	( )	( )
___ Child is physically aggressive with others (e.g., hits, bites, chokes, holds).	( )	( )	( )

Section III*

In the line space to the left of the Section I (critical) items, indicate whether:
(a) You would insist that the child have mastered the skill or competency *prior* to entry into your class, or
(b) Following entry, you would accept responsibility for developing the skill/competency, but you would expect technical assistance in the process of doing so, or
(c) Following entry, you would accept responsibility for developing the skill/competency and would not require technical assistance.

Similarly, for Section II (unacceptable) items, indicate whether:
(a) The child must be within normal limits on the social behavior in question *prior* to entry into your class, or
(b) Following entry, you will take responsibility for moving the child to within normal limits on the social behavior but only with technical assistance provided, or
(c) Following entry, you will take responsibility for moving the child to within normal limits on the social behavior and would not require technical assistance.

*Please indicate your answer by placing an *a, b,* or *c* in the space to the left of the item.

SBS Correlates Checklist

Child has severely dysfluent speech and/or impaired language.	___
Child is enuretic, (e.g., has inadequate bladder control).	___
Child requires specialized and/or adapted instructional materials to progress academically.	___

Source: Walker, H. M. (1986). The AIMS (*Assessment for Integration into Mainstream Settings*) assessment system: Rationale, instruments, procedures, and outcomes. *Journal of Clinical Child Psychology, 15* (1), 55–63. Used with permission.

Figure 2.5   Student Ranking Form

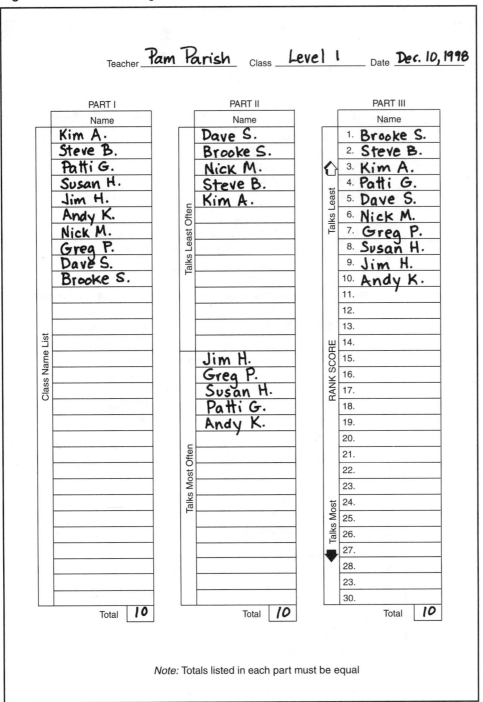

Source: Hops, H., & Greenwood, C. R. (1981). Social skills deficits. In E. J. Msh and L. G. Terdal (Eds.), *Behavioral assessment of childhood disorders.* New York: Guilford Press, 359. Used with permission.

(Finch & Rodgers, 1984). Self-report instruments have been designed to assess a variety of general (e.g., locus of control) and specific (e.g., anger, depression) constructs. Self-reports provide useful information, but they should be supplemented with data from other sources, such as behavioral ratings and observations (Finch & Rodgers, 1984).

Although **sociometric procedures** may not be considered traditional screening devices, they nevertheless can play an important role in identifying students at risk for social behavior problems (Hops & Lewin, 1984). Sociometric measures have been shown to be valuable predictors of later social behavior problems such as dropping out of school (Ullmann, 1952) and delinquency (Roff, Sells, & Golden, 1972). Before using a sociometric procedure in your classroom, check with your supervisor to determine what, if any, parental permissions are required in order for students to participate in this process. In general, a sociometric procedure requires that students describe one another according to a predesignated set of criteria. For example, students might be asked to name their best friends or to list classmates they do not like. In this type of peer nomination, a student makes an acceptance or rejection choice about a selected number of peers. Because peer acceptance and rejection appear to be independent dimensions, both positive (e.g., "With whom would you most like to go to a movie?") and negative (e.g., "With whom would you least like to go to a movie?"), social preferences should be obtained from peers (Hops & Lewin, 1984). Asking students to make negative nominations raises ethical questions that should be weighed before using this procedure. Students' sociometric ratings of peers should be kept confidential.

Another drawback of peer nomination sociometric procedures is that students who are socially isolated never may be nominated at all. A sociometric procedure that does not have these limitations is the *peer-rating method*. A teacher using this method asks a student to rate each of his classroom peers according to a scale. For example, a young child might be asked to circle a numeral from one to five to indicate how much she likes a particular peer. Faces depicting expressions ranging from frowns to smiles might accompany the numeral to make the directions more clear. Each child in the classroom thus earns a score: the average of his ratings from her peers. Another procedure for young children is to show each child pictures of peers and ask her to rate that peer (Bower & Lambert, 1961).

Sociometric techniques are limited by their relatively high cost in teacher time, especially for younger pupils. Also, because elementary schools are adopting more flexible scheduling, which means that pupils move from class to class more often, making it difficult to establish a stable reference group (e.g., a homeroom) for nominations or ratings.

Instruments that measure student social skills are relatively new additions to behavioral ecological assessment technology. The *Social Behavior Assessment* (SBA) (Stephens, 1981) is a teacher rating scale of 136 social skills grouped into four behavioral domains (environmental behaviors, interpersonal behaviors, self-related behaviors, and task-related behaviors). The *Social Skills Rating System* (SSRS) (Gresham & Elliott, 1990) consists of three rating scales: one for parents to complete, one for teachers, and one self-report format for the pupil. The SSRS include a version for elementary-age pupils and one for junior and senior high school students. Unlike the SBA, it is standardized on a national sample. The *Walker-McConnell Scale of Social Competence and School Adjustment* (Walker & McConnell, 1988) consists of 43 positively worded items describing social skills. The Walker Scale contains three subscales. Subscale I, Teacher Preferred Social Behavior, includes 16 items measuring peer-related social behaviors that are highly valued by teachers (e.g., shows sympathy for others, controls temper). Subscale II, Peer Preferred Social Behavior, consists of 17 items that assess peer-related social behaviors valued by the peer group (e.g., makes friends easily with other children, plays games and activities at recess skillfully). The 10 items in Subscale III, School Adjustment Behavior, measure adaptive social-behavioral competencies that are highly valued by teachers in classroom settings (e.g., displays independent study skills, listens carefully to teacher directions and instructions for assignments).

In addition to these methods, direct observation and interviewing may be used to establish that a problem exists. (Because these procedures are more specific and may require more time to administer, we have described them in the section dealing with the analysis of problem behaviors.) Recall from the discussion of behavioral-ecological assessment that it is important to assess student behavior across several settings and to obtain data from multiple sources in order to get a valid and comprehensive picture of pupils' behavioral assets and liabilities.

Pinpointing Target Behaviors In completing an assessment, you will have determined the student's eligibility for special education services (if this is an issue), identified problem behavior areas, identified his behavioral strengths, and determined the settings in which desired and undesired behaviors occur. Now you are ready to select and define the student behaviors you would consider for intervention. **Pinpointing** refers to the specification of behaviors to be modified or taught. Behavior pinpoints may include those to be decreased (e.g., refusal to complete assignments, tantrums, self-injurious behavior) or increased (e.g., completion of assignments, making appropriate requests of peers, keeping hands to self). Both classes of pinpoints are referred to as **target behaviors** if they are observable, measurable, and definable so that two persons can agree on their occurrence or nonoccurrence. A criterion then can be set for a desired level of performance. It is extremely important to pinpoint target behaviors to be increased, rather than those to be decreased, whenever possible. The tendency to identify those to be decreased leads to an emphasis on aversive consequences that creates an unpleasant atmosphere for both students and teachers. Intervention strategies should emphasize teaching appropriate and useful social skills. A positive focus also is much more palatable to parents and other professionals, and it is a good model for other educators. Moreover, excessive reliance on aversive control has influenced several professional organizations (e.g., The Association

for the Severely Handicapped, The Association for Retarded Citizens) to establish policies severely limiting the use of punishment procedures. It also has led to criticism of special education programs for students with EBD as relying excessively on a "curriculum of control" (Knitzer, Steinberg, & Fleisch, 1990), in which great emphasis is placed on behavior management at the expense of functional academic instruction. If your objective is to reduce undesired target behaviors, we recommend that you follow the **fair pair rule** (White & Haring, 1980); that is, simultaneously identify a desired social behavior to replace the behavior to be reduced (e.g., target an increase in appropriate social initiations to peers in combination with a reduction in verbal or physical aggression). Ideally, the replacement behavior should serve the same function for the student as the undesired behavior (e.g., to obtain something the child wants; see Chapter 4).

It also is important to pinpoint behaviors to be increased that are adaptive, desirable, and contribute to the development of social competence (McConnell, 1987). Unfortunately, research indicates that the behaviors educators target for intervention tend to lack social relevance. Black (1985; cited in Gresham & Reschly, 1988) had teachers rate pupil behaviors as to importance. The ten highest rated behaviors corresponded to what Hersh and Walker (1983) described as the model behavioral profile: compliance with teacher expectations and acceptable academic performance. Although such targets appear desirable, it is necessary to ask whether compliance and academic achievement are the only critical target behaviors for a given pupil and whether changes in these behaviors are important to students, their caregivers, and significant others. These questions have been a major concern of educators working with students exhibiting moderate and severe developmental disabilities. Brown, Nietupski, and Hamre-Nietupski (1976) developed an approach to curriculum design based on the **criterion of ultimate functioning,** which refers to the functional skills needed by adults to participate freely in community environments (e.g., interviewing for a job). Although this criterion may seem to lack relevance for younger

Table 2.2 Examples of Target Behavior Definitions

General Statement	Target Behavior
1. Kim does not comply with teacher requests.	1. When given a direction by the teacher, Kim fails to exhibit the topography of behavior described in the direction within 5 seconds.
2. Andy is hyperactive.	2. Andy is out of his seat more than one time in 10 minutes.
3. Fred cannot ride the school bus appropriately.	3. Fred is out of his assigned seat on the bus.
4. Betsy is aggressive.	4. Betsy hits, kicks, pushes, and calls other children names during recess.
5. Billy is withdrawn.	5. Billy initiates less than one interaction with a peer in any given 10-minute free-play period.

pupils or for those who do not exhibit severe developmental disabilities, you may find it useful to think in terms of the **criterion of functioning in the next environment** (Vincent et al., 1980) when pinpointing behaviors to increase. This means identifying the skill requirements and expectations of less restrictive environments (e.g., a regular classroom, playground, school club) and teaching these in order to increase pupils' chances of successful participation. For example, a student may need to learn how to participate in class discussions before she can be mainstreamed into a regular social studies class.

We have indicated that behavioral pinpoints should be observable, measurable, and definable so that persons can agree regarding their occurrence. These characteristics describe an **operational definition** of target behaviors. Sometimes you will be working from the verbal descriptions of behavior provided by others or from statements contained in behavior checklists. Also, you will be writing behavioral objectives based on definitions of behaviors. For these reasons, it is important that your definitions be observable and precise. Table 2.2 provides examples of target behavior definitions derived from general statements. Study these operational definitions and practice writing some of your own in order to gain competency in this skill.

Is Intervention Warranted?

The procedures we have just described will provide a wealth of information about pupil behaviors and setting characteristics that are useful in documenting a problem. However, keep in mind that in most schools, awareness of student behavior problems reaches assessors and supervisors much more informally, perhaps through a conversation in the teachers' lounge or through a referral by a classroom teacher. Also, if you are the teacher of the student in question, simply recognizing that the pupil's behavior is a concern constitutes problem identification.[1] No matter how the problem is brought to the attention of the person or persons responsible for making decisions about interventions, the next step is to analyze the behavior and the settings in which the student functions in order to decide whether intervention is warranted. For example, one teacher may regard students who are noisy and boisterous or who violate his standards for order and routine as having serious problems that require intervention, but other staff members may view the same behavior in other settings as typical. We are not suggesting that students who act out in only one classroom should not be considered candidates for intervention; we mean only that persons' standards and tolerance for pupil behavior are subjective and vary from setting to setting or from one occasion to another. Also, because students with behavioral problems seldom display only one undesired behavior or lack only one appropriate social skill, it is necessary to decide which behaviors to act upon first. As Figure

---

[1]Remember that informal procedures fail to identify most socially withdrawn pupils and result in identifying students who act out too late for many less intrusive and reactive strategies to be effective.

2.1 indicates, social validation and direct observation procedures will help you evaluate the discrepancy between pupil behavior and standards. With this information, you can determine whether intervention is justified and which behaviors should receive priority for intervention.

Social Validation of Problem Behaviors Social validation (Wolf, 1978) is a strategy for evaluating whether significant persons agree that a problem is serious enough to require intervention.[2] Several procedures can be used to validate the existence and severity of a behavior problem. The most obvious is simply to ask other persons who have daily contact with the student whether the identified target behaviors are serious problems. If systematic screening procedures such as those described in Chapter 1 have been used, the data from various sources and instruments can be compared in order to see whether the same problems occur in multiple settings and in the presence of several persons. This is not a complex process but it provides some assurance that a student is not singled out for intervention because one person has unreasonable standards for behavior.

Checklists and rating scales also may be administered across persons and settings to socially validate the perception of a problem. Another strategy is to collect direct observation data on peers in the same setting. The validity of a nominated problem behavior can be established by comparing rates of targeted behavior between peers (who have not been identified as exhibiting excessive rates of the problem behavior) and the target student.

Another facet of social validation is consideration of whether the student's behavior is nondeviant with respect to the standards of his cultural reference group. The overrepresentation of culturally different learners in classes for children with disabilities, including programs for students

with EBD, may be explained partially by teachers' lack of sensitivity to culturally based behavior (McIntyre, 1996). Therefore, it should be determined that the problem behavior is not typical for the student's cultural group. Assessment procedures that may provide this information include interviews with the target student or her caregivers, in combination with rating scales, checklists, and direct observation of behavior across settings. *The McIntyre Assessment of Culture (MAC)* (McIntyre, 1995) may be helpful in discriminating between behavior that is culturally normative and that which is not. This scale consists of three parts. A Student Information Form is used to gather demographic and life history events regarding the student. The Parent/Home Information Form guides interviewers in gathering information regarding familial, cultural, and linguistic influences on the student. The Behavior Checklist is used by teachers and other professionals to rate the frequency or intensity of various student behaviors. These ratings then are analyzed to determine whether the behaviors have a cultural basis.

Collection of Observational Data in Natural Settings Another procedure for assessing the severity of problem behavior is to observe the student in those settings in which the target behavior occurs. Direct observation formats include a functional analysis (see pages 52–57), event recording, and interval recording procedures that measure single or multiple behaviors of one or more pupils (see Chapter 3). Direct observation data will tell you little about the need for intervention, however, unless the target behavior is dangerous or intolerable at any level, or unless you have some indication of what level of the behavior the setting will tolerate. For example, even a single instance of physical aggression during a classroom work period is likely to be intolerable, but what about off-task, out-of-seat, or noncompliant behavior? Almost all students display some undesirable social behaviors, as well as some deficits in appropriate social skills. Pupils who are identified as having EBD usually are distinguished from those who are not by excesses or

---

[2]Social validation also encompasses the acceptability of intervention procedures and goals to professionals and caregivers as well as their satisfaction with the results of interventions (Wolf, 1978). The latter two facets of social validation are discussed in Chapters 4 and 5.

Figure 2.6 Target Student and Peer Comparison Observational Data

Behavior Observation Record

Recorder B. Hogg
Child Frank
Date 2/16/98
Circumstance Study Period
Length of time observed 15 min.

+ = Behavior observed at least once during interval.
− = Behavior not observed during interval.

																TOTAL
Target Child																
Noise	−	+	+	−	−	−	+	+	−	+	−	+	−	+	+	8
Out of place	−	−	+	+	−	−	+	+	−	+	−	−	−	−	−	5
Off-task	−	+	+	+	+	−	+	+	+	−	+	+	+	+	+	12
Physical contact	−	−	+	−	−	−	−	−	−	+	−	−	−	−	−	2
Other: Calling out for teacher	−	−	−	+	−	−	+	−	−	−	+	−	−	−	+	4
Peer																
Noise	+	−	+	−	−	+	+	−	+	−	+	+	−	+	+	9
Out of place	−	−	−	−	−	−	−	−	−	−	−	−	−	−	−	0
Off-task	−	−	+	−	−	+	−	−	+	−	−	−	−	+	+	5
Physical contact	−	−	−	−	−	−	−	−	−	−	−	−	−	−	−	0
Other	−	−	−	−	−	−	−	−	−	−	−	−	−	−	−	0

Note: Each square represents one minute of observation.

Source: Deno, S., & Mirkin, P. (1978). *Data-based program modification.* Reston, VA: Council for Exceptional Children. Used with permission.

deficits in the *frequency* or *rate* at which they exhibit such behaviors rather than by differences in the *kinds* of behaviors they exhibit. It is possible that the teacher simply notices the designated student's disruptive behavior more than he notices the same behavior in others. One way to assess the discrepancy between the target student's behavior and the standard for that behavior in the classroom is to simultaneously observe the target pupil and a peer whom the teacher designates as nondeviant for the target behavior (Walker & Fabre, 1987). Comparing the frequencies of the behavior exhibited by the two students will help you assess the relative severity of the target behavior. Figure 2.6 displays a sheet of interval data collected on a target student and a selected peer. Note that on some behaviors the target student was much like his behaviorally acceptable peer.

Ranking Target Behaviors   If students were in only one setting for the entire school day or presented only one behavior to be changed, setting priorities for intervention would be easy. However, pupils with behavioral problems, whether or not they are identified as having a disability, usually exhibit several or many problem behaviors in a variety of settings. Not every problem can be addressed simultaneously. Therefore, the persons responsible for the student's education and welfare must agree upon a set of priorities for changes in the student's behavior. In school settings a forum for this decision-making activity is provided in the evaluation and the individual education program conferences (i.e., child study team meetings) required by IDEA. In other treatment agencies (e.g, residential treatment programs), habilitation planning conferences or case conferences are held for the same purpose. It may be difficult to achieve group consensus regarding which of the student's behaviors should be addressed first. Behaviors that are intervention priorities can be identified by asking such questions as the following (Wolery, Bailey, & Sugai, 1988):

1. Does the behavior cause injury to the student or others?
2. Does the behavior interfere with the student's or other pupils' learning?
3. Does the behavior present a safety risk to the student or to others?
4. Is the behavior age-appropriate or likely to be transient?
5. Does the behavior occur at frequencies similar to that of peers' behavior?
6. Is the behavior due to skill deficits in other areas?
7. Does the behavior cause others to avoid interacting with the student?

Other high-priority target behaviors include self-help skills (e.g., dressing, feeding, toileting, identifying environmental dangers), behaviors that restrict access to less restrictive environments (e.g., aggression, noncompliance, defiance), and "survival" skills or information (e.g., following directions, staying on task, bringing required materials to class).

One way to achieve consensus on which targeted social behaviors are priorities for intervention is to ask persons who have frequent contact with the student to develop a rank-ordered list of these behaviors. The average of their rankings provides a basis for deciding which behaviors should receive top priority. Figure 2.7 shows a form used to list and rank target behaviors of a student whose teacher has requested consultation services. Each person who works with this pupil may be asked to rank the target behaviors, and the average of their rankings may be used to determine the priority of each target.

Are There Medical Reasons for the Problem Behavior?

A student who lacks functional communicative skills may be unable to tell you that she is striking her head because she has an earache. Or a pupil whose listlessness, lethargy, and inattention to tasks interfere with his educational performance may be unaware that he has diabetes. Mild or potentially serious medical problems may underlie student behavior problems and educators should not assume that managing the environment is the only effective way to control behavior. Particularly if an undesired behavior pattern has a sudden onset, and if behavioral-ecological assessment procedures reveal no apparent environmental factors that affect its occurrence, you should ask the parents if they have observed any recent changes in their child's behavior, and whether the child has had a recent physical examination. In any case, it may be wise to ask the school nurse or health practitioner to conduct a brief medical screening (with parental permission). If the screening reveals any indicators of potential health problems, ask the parents to obtain a medical examination and indicate the suspected medical cause

Figure 2.7 Priority-Ranking Form

Directions: Ask each person concerned with student to complete a form. Items may be listed by the consultant or each person may generate her own list.

Referee ___*Ricky*___ Age/Grade ___*9 / Gr. 3*___ Date ___*9/12/98*___

Name of person completing this form ___*Ms. B. / Classroom Teacher*___

Specify those goal (terminal) behaviors that you would most like to see attained through program modification.

Academic *Acceptable Level of Performance*

Rank		
1	*Reading*	*1 yr. below grade level*
3	*Spelling*	*75% correct*
4	*Math*	*75% correct*
5	*Handwriting*	*faster and legible*

Social

2	*Noise*	*none*
2	*Fights*	*none*

After you complete your list, rank order the list in terms of those most requiring immediate attention.

Source: Deno, S., & Mirkin, P. (1978). *Data-based program modification.* Reston, VA: Council for Exceptional Children, 71. Used with permission.

of the problem. If the parents approve, you may contact the examining physician to explain the behaviors of concern.

If there is an underlying health problem, the next step is appropriate medical intervention. While the pupil is receiving treatment, continue to observe the behaviors of concern and note any changes. Be aware that in cases of long-standing medical problems, successful medical treatment may not solve the problem immediately. For example, if the student has missed out on instruction in important skills, or if the undesired behavior originally caused by his health problem has been reinforced (e.g., he has been able to avoid undesired tasks), solving his physical problem may not alleviate the corresponding behavior pattern. Thus, whether or not medical explanations have been ruled out, you may need to proceed to a functional analysis of behavior.

Performing a Functional Analysis

A **functional analysis** of behavior involves assessing student behavior in the context of environmental variables that occur before, during, and after the target behavior. This entails careful observation in the immediate environment in which the behavior occurs, as well as gathering information regarding events that are more distant. The skill requirements and behavioral tolerances of other current or potential environments in which the pupil might function also should be considered. Procedures to be used include direct observation, interviews and rating scales, and assessments of current and potential future environmental expectations and skill demands.

Direct Observation Human behavior occurs in environmental contexts that contain a variety of stimuli. Some of these stimuli influence behavior directly or indirectly. It is helpful to know precisely which stimuli affect behavior and which do not. Environmental variables should be analyzed systematically to sort out those that potentially influence what the student does. Direct observation may enable you to identify variables that affect student behavior. An antecedent-behavior-consequence (A-B-C) analysis is a direct observation format that organizes events into those that are present or take place immediately before a behavioral event and those that occur immediately afterward. Some of the antecedent stimuli that may affect pupil behavior include *environmental*

obstacles that prevent the student from performing as desired (e.g., she may be in a location where you cannot see her when she needs to ask for your assistance). Certain **setting events,** such as the student's experiences over a weekend, the time of day, classroom environment, or transition periods, may set the occasion for some behaviors. Other antecedent events such as the *task* the student is expected to perform, the *other persons present,* or the *instructions* provided to the student may be important. On the other hand, stimuli that occur subsequent to the pupil's behavior may prove to be consequences that influence that behavior. For example, does the student receive social attention, praise, or criticism following specific behaviors? Does his behavior result in avoiding or escaping task demands? Does his behavior enable him to obtain things he otherwise does not get?

An A-B-C analysis involves carefully observing and recording events that occur immediately before the target pupil's behavior, the behavior itself, and the events that take place immediately afterward. Figure 2.8 illustrates an A-B-C analysis. Note that the observer logs the time and describes the immediate antecedents, the student's response, and the consequences in the sequence in which they occur. An analysis of recurring antecedent and consequent events provides some clues as to which of these stimuli potentially influence behavior. Can you identify some of these events in the example? An A-B-C analysis is only useful for observing students individually; it would become too unwieldly used with several pupils at the same time. Also, it is not something you can do during direct instruction. However, you can organize the informal observations you make about specific incidents into an A-B-C format at a later time.

Touchette, MacDonald, and Langer (1985) devised a format that enables observers to monitor targeted behaviors across extended periods of time. This procedure, called a **scatter plot,** is a system for rating behavior in time intervals. This format is presented in Figure 2.9. Each day is represented by a vertical column divided into

Figure 2.8 Sample A-B-C Record

	Student *Raymond*	Date *Oct. 29, 1998*
	Observer *Dianne McInerney*	Time *2:15 - 2:25*
	Behavior *Talking out during class discussion, off task* Activity *Social Studies*	

Antecedent	Behavior	Consequence
Teacher says, "Everyone please get out your Social Studies notebook and pencil."	Raymond asks student next to him, "What did she say?"	Teacher says, "No talking."
Teacher asks Tommy to name the capital of Alabama.	Raymond shouts out, "Montgomery."	Tommy yells, "Shut up, Raymond."
Teacher says, "Please, Raymond, sit quietly until it is your turn."	Raymond yells, "What did I do?"	Teacher says, "Raymond, be quiet."
Teacher asks, "Which state has the largest population? Raymond, can you answer?"	Raymond says, "Uh? I didn't do anything!"	Class laughs.
Teacher asks, "Alice, which state is nicknamed the Keystone State?"	Raymond calls out, "I know. It's Pennsylvania."	Teacher says, "Raymond, I've had enough. Put your head down on your desk."

Source: McInerney, D. (1986). Personal communication.

thirty-minute blocks of time. During each interval, the observer indicates whether the behavior occurred by filling in the cell representing the day and time. Symbols may be used to indicate whether the behavior occurred at a high rate (e.g., a completely filled cell) or at a low rate (e.g., a slash). A blank grid indicates that the behavior did not occur. Although a scatter plot does not indicate the actual frequency with which a target behavior occurs, it does reveal patterns over time and settings. Therefore, this procedure may be used to identify relationships between problem behaviors and time of day, the presence or absence of certain persons, a physical or social setting, a particular activity, and so forth. (Touchette et al., 1985).

Figure 2.9 Scatter plot grid with a key at the top to indicate response frequencies corresponding to filled, slashed, and open boxes. Each location on the grid identifies a unique time interval on a given day.

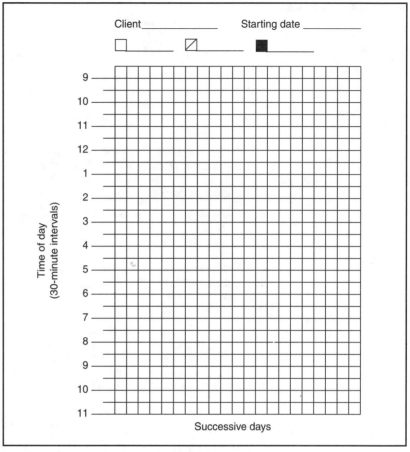

Source: Touchette, P. E., MacDonald, R. F., & Langer, S. N. (1985) A scatter plot for identifying stimulus control of problem behavior. *Journal of Applied Behavior Analysis 18,* 343–351. Used with permission.

Interviews Not all stimuli that influence student behavior occur immediately before or after a behavior. Moreover, other important information, such as the skills pupils need to gain access to less restrictive environments or the events taking place at home that affect pupils' school behaviors, cannot be obtained through an A-B-C analysis. Behavioral interviews are a useful assessment tool for obtaining assessment data from both children and adults. The interview should be structured to elicit specific information about the behaviors that occur, the settings in which they take place, and the antecedent and consequent conditions associated with these behaviors, including the social behavior of other persons (Conroy & Fox, 1994). An interview may be used

to gather information about concerns and goals, identify factors that maintain or occasion problem behaviors, obtain historical information, and identify reinforcers (Gross, 1984). Information from two or more sources can be compared to evaluate the reliability of informants or to obtain individual perceptions of behaviors and environmental events across ecological settings. For example, Kern, Childs, Dunlap, Clarke, and Falk (1994) developed a student-assisted functional assessment interview that provides information from the student's perspective regarding expectations, curricula, and other variables in the school setting, as well as her perceptions about her target behaviors. Lewis, Scott, and Sugai (1994) designed a teacher-based interview format that

Figure 2.10 Anecdotal
Interview Recording Form

Teacher _____

Consultant _____

Date _____

Student(s) _____

1. Can you describe for me in your own words what the problem behavior seems to be?

2. Could you be a little more specific? For example, when you say that the student disrupts the class, what exactly does she do?

3. Now I'm getting the picture. Tell me, does this behavior take place every day (period)?

4. (If no) Would you say it happens every week? Every other week?

5. Can you identify anything that seems to happen before this behavior?

6. Is there a pattern regarding when the behavior occurs (e.g., more often on Mondays, after lunch, during writing period)?

7. Let's try to figure out what the student gains from this behavior. Can you recall what happens to the student (that is, what do you do) after this behavior occurs?

8. Have you been able to notice what other students in the room do when this behavior takes place?

9. Is there anything else you can tell me about this behavior or this student?

provides information from the teacher's perspective regarding the student's problem behaviors and the circumstances under which they occur as well as those under which they do not occur.

Figure 2.10 is a general interview format for identifying and analyzing target behaviors. Note that the questions are open ended (they do not limit answers by requiring only one-word responses or by asking the respondent to hypothesize as to why the pupil's behavior occurs) and that they include probes for following up on previous answers. Consult Gross (1984) or Polsgrove (1987) for more information on conducting behavioral interviews. Additional interview formats are presented in subsequent chapters.

Other Strategies for Performing a Functional Analysis Researchers and educators have come to recognize that multiple and interacting variables make significant contributions to student behavior. Fortunately, new tools are being developed to assist in the important task of identifying these variables and their relationship to pupil behavior. For example, Kern et al. (1994) and O'Neill, Horner, Albin, Storey, and Sprague (1990) developed practical guides for the compilation of functional analysis data. In Chapter 8 we offer a behavior incident log that allows practitioners to summarize information related to behavioral crises after the fact. However, performing an adequate functional analysis is neither quick nor simple. The purpose of a functional analysis is to generate hypotheses regarding which variables may influence the student's behavior. As Wehby (1994) pointed out, up to ten hours of assessment time may be needed to assess functioning in all the areas required for a functional analysis of a student's behavior.

Analysis of data obtained through the methods described above may reveal that some undesired student behaviors serve a **communicative function.** The student may exhibit some maladaptive behaviors because he lacks a more effective means of communicating his needs or of obtaining reinforcement. Although much of the research concerning the communicative function of behavior has been conducted with persons with severe and profound disabilities, recent applications have extended to students with behavioral problems, including EBD (Dunlap et al., 1993; Lewis & Sugai, 1996; Wehby, 1994; Wehby, Symons, & Shores, 1995). Donnellan, Mirenda, Mesaros, and Fassbender (1984) suggested that persons with severe developmental disabilities may exhibit maladaptive behaviors because they serve such communicative

functions as requesting attention, interactions, or items; expressing protests, refusals, or desire to terminate an event; making declarations or comments; or noninteractive functions that have personal meaning. Carr and Durand (1985) demonstrated that children with developmental disabilities who received functional communication training reduced their rates of maladaptive behavior that had previously been their means of sending messages.

As recent research demonstrates (see Shores, Wehby, & Jack, in press), the undesired behavior of students with more extensive behavioral repertoires than those with severe disabilities also may serve a communicative function. For example, the student who displays disruptive behavior during certain classroom activities resulting in her being removed from the classroom, may be trying to tell someone that the work is too difficult. In this case, providing remedial instruction or adjusting the level of task difficulty is a more appropriate response than punishing the student's undesired behavior (or reinforcing it by removing her from the classroom). Thus, knowledge about recurring antecedent-response-consequence relationships is important for intervention planning. However, as Shores et al. (in press) observe, the extensive social behavioral repertoires of many students who exhibit behavioral disorders, as well as the complexity of their social interactions with peers and adults, renders the task of establishing functional relationships between their behavior and environmental variables extremely difficult.

Assessing the Skill Requirements of Current and Future Environments We previously indicated that information about the skills needed to succeed in current and future school settings is important assessment data. This also is true of skills needed in other environments in which students function currently or will be expected to function at some future time (e.g., community and work settings). Behavioral interviews, direct observation, and the AIMS system are three methods that can be used to obtain these data. Information regarding these skill requirements is important for two reasons. First, the absence of these skills may prevent pupils' access to these settings. For instance, if a student lacks the skills needed to buy a theater ticket, he may be prevented from attending a movie. Similarly, an adolescent who cannot initiate a telephone conversation is restricted from an important source of social learning and reinforcement. Second, desired social skills may serve as targeted **replacement behaviors** to be strengthened as undesired maladaptive behaviors are reduced (Gast & Wolery, 1986).

Evans and Meyer (1985) suggested a five-step process for assessing discrepancies between environmental expectations and student behavior. In step 1, the teacher lists some least restrictive settings in which the pupil presently can function (e.g., home room, regular physical education class). Next, she lists some future least restrictive environments in which the student *could* function (e.g., school cafeteria, school bus, playground, regular classrooms). In step 3, the teacher lists those skills the student *currently* has that allow her to participate in current settings (e.g., follows teachers' directions, participates in games and sports). Skills that the pupil *currently does not have* but that would allow him to participate in future least restrictive settings (e.g., appropriate table manners, conversational skills, appropriate verbal responses to peer initiations, controlling temper) are listed in step 4. Step 5 involves a discrepancy analysis. The teacher enters first the skills that typical students will perform in those settings listed as future least restrictive (e.g., share toys, take turns, use appropriate table manners, initiate and respond to peers). If the target student can perform the skill, the teacher enters a plus beside that skill. A minus is recorded if he cannot perform the skill. For those skills the student cannot perform, the teacher lists the behaviors that he exhibits (e.g., cries, has tantrums, eats with fingers). Thus, Evans and Meyer's (1985) procedure not only provides information about the skills that are needed in current and future environments, but it also evaluates the pupil's status for these skills as well as any undesired behaviors that should be reduced to increase his chances of succeeding in these settings.

Outcomes of a Functional Analysis   As we indicated previously, the purpose of conducting functional analyses of student behavior is to generate hypotheses regarding the environmental variables that may influence targeted student behaviors. Functional analysis research suggests that undesired behavior may be the result of social skills deficits, positive or negative reinforcement, environmental deficits, or deficits in the cognitive processing of social stimuli (Wehby, 1994). Careful data collection in the settings in which the behavior occurs as well as from significant other persons and settings, may reveal antecedent and consequent events, in addition to more remote setting events, that appear functionally related to the student's behavior. This information forms the basis of **assessment-based** (Lewis & Sugai, 1996) or **curriculum-based** (Kern et al., 1994) **interventions,** which involve the systematic manipulation of the hypothesized functional variables while monitoring the effects of these changes on student behavior. These assessment procedures are contributing to the development of an emerging technology of **effective behavior support** (Horner, O'Neill, & Flannery, 1993; Sugai, 1995). Effective behavior support addresses the communicative function of problem behaviors and focuses on strategies for strengthening functionally equivalent replacement behaviors. At the same time strategies are employed to ensure that the problem behavior will not serve these purposes well. The state of California requires that all students identified as having EBD be given an effective behavior support plan (Wright, Gurman, California Association of School Psychologists/Diagnostic Center, and the Southern California Positive Intervention Task Force, 1994). Effective behavior support is described in more detail in Chapter 4.

Is the Behavior Problem the Result of Skill or Performance Deficits?

A fundamental distinction between hypothesized relationships of functional stimuli to problem behavior is whether the target behavior reflects a deficit in skills or in motivational factors (Howell, Fox, & Morehead, 1993).

For example, if the student lacks the skills necessary to gain peer attention appropriately, he may use undesired behavior to produce this effect. On the other hand, perhaps reinforcement contingencies in the setting are such that the student gains reinforcement through maladaptive behavior. To examine this issue, we recommend that attention be shifted to the student's desired behavior, what he *should* be doing instead of engaging in the maladaptive behavior. If the desired behavior is one the pupil cannot do (i.e., perhaps she lacks the necessary information or component skills), the appropriate intervention is instruction in these skill areas. Attempting to change the student's motivation to perform the skill through arranging positive or aversive consequences will be ineffective unless accompanied by relevant skill instruction. On the other hand, if the skill is something the student can perform (i.e., she has done it before or does it in other settings), the problem is due to a performance deficit. A performance deficit may be caused by a lack of motivation or of opportunity to perform as desired (i.e., environmental deficits). In this case, the appropriate intervention consists of providing opportunities for the student to perform or removing obstacles to desired performance and reinforcing the desired behavior when it occurs, while at the same time reducing undesired behaviors by removing reinforcement or applying consequences. Thus, knowing whether targeted behavioral excesses and deficits are the result of skill or performance deficits is an important factor in selecting alternate intervention procedures. Intervention decisions regarding strategies for responding to undesired behavior when it occurs are discussed in Chapter 4.

It is important to be sensitive to the possibility that pupils may be deficient in social skills. Often, teachers assume that undesired student behavior reflects the pupil's decision to misbehave. However, the student who lacks appropriate social behavior does not have a choice because alternative social behaviors are missing from his repertoire. As Howell et al. (1993) emphasized, students should be taught the social skills they lack rather than just receiving behavior management interventions to control their maladaptive behavior. When targeting undesired social behaviors for intervention, remember to consider the communicative function the behavior serves. Identify and teach a desired replacement behavior that serves the desired communicative function, or is a skill the student will find useful in a current or future ecological setting.

Kaplan, McCollum-Gahley, and Howell (1988) argued that **curriculum-based assessment** (CBA) procedures represent the best practice for both academic and social skills and involve assessing pupils' status with regard to specific curriculum content and objectives. While published social skills curricula are becoming more available, they are not widely accepted and used, which limits the use of CBA with social skills instruction. This results in a tendency to confuse classroom control problems with social skills deficits: teachers wait for a pupil to misbehave and then respond with a behavior management (i.e., control) intervention, when in fact the student's behavior is a direct outcome of his lack of particular social skills (e.g., he responds to being teased with physical aggression). Several excellent social skills curriculum packages have been developed (see Chapter 10), and some (e.g., the ACCEPTS Program, Walker et al., 1983) included CBA scales. Examine several social skills curricula and ask your school district to purchase one or more of them for your program. If you do not have access to these curricula, Kaplan et. al. (1988) suggested a task-analytic approach to social skills assessment, which involves evaluating the pupil with respect to prerequisite and specific subskills of appropriate social behaviors (see below and Chapter 7).

INTERVENTION OBJECTIVES AND TASK ANALYSIS

The beginning point of intervention, whether it consists of skill instruction or behavior management, is to write **behavioral objectives** that describe the behavior to be achieved following intervention. A well-written behavioral objective specifies in observable and measurable terms the **terminal behavior** the student is to demonstrate,

Table 2.3 Acceptable and Unacceptable Instructional Objectives

Instructional Objectives	*Acceptable?*	*Reason (If Unacceptable)*
1. Arnold will behave in gym class.	No	Behavior and criteria not specified
2. Given a 45-minute study hall, Sally will remain on task 90 percent of the time.	No	On-task behavior not specified; impossible to assess "90 percent of the time"
3. Yen-Su will interact with her peers with no hitting, kicking, biting, pushing, or verbal taunting for 30-minute lunch periods for five consecutive days.	Yes	
4. Washington will be punctual in arriving at school for 15 consecutive days.	No	"Punctual" not defined
5. When given a task request, Tanya will begin the task within 10 seconds without saying "I can't."	Yes	
6. Karen will refrain from biting or scratching herself for any given one hour period.	No	Conditions not specified (i.e., instruction, prompts, or supervision to be provided during the hour)
7. Yolonda will not take any drugs during school for 20 consecutive days.	No	Impossible to monitor drug intake accurately
8. When approached by a peer, Philip will emit an appropriate greeting response (make eye contact, extend his right hand, smile, shake hands, and say "hello") on 10 of 10 trials.	Yes	

the **conditions** under which the behavior should occur, and the **criteria** for acceptable performance (Mager, 1962). Table 2.3 contains examples of acceptable and unacceptable terminal instructional objectives.

Maheady, Harper, Mallette, & Sacca (1989) analyzed the IEP objectives of students who exhibit social behavior problems. They determined that the objectives for these students, who were certified as having EBD, reflected a preponderance of academic targets and few social behavioral objectives. The written social objectives tended to target behaviors related to the completion of academic tasks, such as staying on task, completing work, and turning in assignments on time. It has been our experience that many written objectives for social behaviors are inappropriate not because the teacher could not specify the behavior in observable and measurable terms but because the conditions or criteria for the objective are meaningless ("90 percent of the time"), are not matched to the skill ("Tony will demonstrate that he understands the classroom rules by coming to class on time"), or are not matched to the intervention strategy used ("Given immediate positive

consequences for completing her math assignments, Renee will remain on-task for 80 percent of five consecutive math periods"). With practice and feedback, you will become proficient at writing good instructional objectives for social skills. As Mager (1962) noted, if your objectives are written precisely, there may be little more you need to do, other than provide appropriate materials or learning trials.

Terminal behavioral objectives indicate relatively long-range desired outcomes of intervention strategies. The student may have none or some of the skills she needs to perform the desired behavior. Once you have written the objective, it is important to know whether she can perform all necessary components of the terminal behavior, because this information will affect the strategies you will use to get her there. The best way to assess the skills pupils need in order to perform a particular task (or to engage in a desired social behavior) is to perform a **task analysis.** Essentially, task analysis is a fine-grained assessment of a task; that is, the task is broken down into sequential component steps. The number of components depends on the complexity of the task and the entry skills of the pupil (the skills the pupil brings to the task).

Analyzing academic or motor tasks is relatively simple. For example, most teachers are familiar with the component steps involved in solving two-place addition problems. Social skills are more difficult to analyze by task, however. One reason is that many social behaviors are performed without obvious, discrete steps. Another reason is that most persons are not accustomed to analyzing social skills systematically. Organize task steps according to one or a combination of the following:

1. A change in response criterion (e.g., a systematic increase in length of time engaged in desired play behavior across days or trials).
2. A progression through a sequence of discrete skills (e.g., learning social greeting responses).
3. A change in response topography (e.g., controlling one's temper by substituting verbal for physical reactions, such as counting to ten silently).

Once you have constructed a task sequence, assess the pupil with respect to the component steps. The evaluation will help you determine where to begin instruction and how to revise your sequence if needed. The steps included in your program can be written as instructional objectives and matched to teaching methods and materials. This then constitutes your intervention plan for a target behavior. Describe it in general terms on the student's IEP and develop it more specifically in your weekly and daily lesson plans. Your plan is not inflexible; it should be adjusted and revised as indicated by your continued assessment of the student's progress. The following chapter describes this phase of monitoring progress.

SUMMARY

Assessment for intervention planning is a decision-making process involving multiple sources of information and assessment strategies. To guide this process, we have presented a model that uses behavioral assessment procedures across and within the ecological settings in which the student functions. It is important to assess both pupil and setting variables. The outcomes of behavioral-ecological assessments include information about the following (Polsgrove, 1987):

1. The variety and severity of the student's problem behaviors across various settings.
2. The significant persons in these settings who object to the pupil's behavior and why they object to it.
3. The discrepancies between the student's behavior and the expectations that significant others have for behavior.
4. The differences among the behavioral expectations of persons in various settings.
5. Persons who are more or less effective in managing the pupil's behavior.
6. The cultural norms in these settings and the differences among settings in terms of norms and values.
7. The specific antecedents and consequences associated with problem behavior in each setting in which it occurs.
8. The sources of support for problem behavior in each setting.

If student behavior problems are few, relatively mild, or confined to one or two settings, the assessments needed to generate such information are not too involved. However, if the converse is true, the assessment burden is proportionately greater. This is one reason multidisciplinary assessment involving several professionals is recommended for students who may be disabled by their behavior.

Assessment information is used to identify both adaptive and maladaptive target behaviors, to decide which behaviors to address first, and to decide whether the intervention should be instructional or motivational. The steps preceding intervention consist of writing terminal behavioral objectives and breaking these down according to a task analysis based on the behavior's characteristics and the desired changes that can be accomplished.

CASE STUDY

AN IEP FOR IMPROVING SOCIAL INTERACTIONS

Susan was identified in the first grade as a socially isolated child. The teacher first noticed that Susan was different from the other students when she failed to interact with anyone during recess. The teacher's attempts to introduce Susan to the other children and to have her participate in classroom games were unsuccessful. During a parent-teacher conference, the teacher shared this problem with the parents, who stated that Susan had only one playmate with whom she would play in the afternoons. During academic activities, Susan worked hard and almost always finished her assignments. Still, she did not speak up during classroom discussions or volunteer for special jobs in the classroom. She seemed especially fond of the gerbils, however, and occasionally played with them. When a child approached Susan to play, Susan would leave immediately.

The problem continued in the second grade, so Susan's teacher tried a peer-mediated procedure. Because the teacher had never observed Susan playing with classroom toys, she did not know whether Susan actually possessed play skills. Because Susan typically played alone, her parents could not confirm that she possessed the skills to play cooperatively with toys such as play telephones or blocks. She preferred to do puzzles or color by herself at home as well as at school. Therefore, the teacher selected a short-term peer imitation program to assist Susan in learning basic play skills. The IEP shown in Figures 2.11 and 2.12 was written by Susan's teacher and a consultant.

Susan's teacher chose a friendly female classmate to assist in the peer-imitation training. The teacher then selected three of the most popular toys in the classroom and asked the peer trainer to demonstrate for Susan how to use the toys. She conducted the peer-imitation training sessions for one week, assisting Susan in participating with the other child. Then the teacher determined that Susan had the skills to use these toys but simply had been reluctant to play with them. At this point she decided to use the peer-mediated social initiation procedure with Susan, asking the same child to serve as the peer trainer. Using the same three toys, the peer trainer made initiations toward Susan in a quiet area of the classroom each day for fifteen minutes. This intervention lasted for three weeks, and the teacher maintained simple records of Susan's progress during these sessions. By observing the students playing together twice a week, the teacher could record the number of times Susan responded to her peer trainer's initiation to play. She also recorded which toys Susan enjoyed.

After three weeks of this intervention, Susan's teacher decided to introduce three new toys to Susan. The peer trainer used the new toys for an additional week. At this point the teacher decided to bring in two new playmates who would take turns carrying out the peer-initiation procedures. This particular intervention lasted for two weeks, after which the teacher made a decision to involve Susan with the classroom group since she now had three playmates with whom she played comfortably for fifteen minutes each day.

To involve the entire classroom group, the teacher set up a group goal-setting and feedback procedure. Susan's goal was simple: to play with one of her friends during recess. In maintaining this simple goal the teacher was ensuring that Susan could participate successfully in the group goal-setting and feedback while playing with the same friends with whom she had established some rapport. Other members of the classroom group had goals either related to academic or social skills. The group goal-setting and feedback procedure was maintained for the rest of the school year. The only modifications in Susan's goal were to expand the number of friends with whom she played and to introduce some nonplay social interactions.

To maintain the effects of the peer-mediated procedure outside of school, Susan's teacher met with Susan's parents and explained the procedure very simply. She suggested they attempt the same procedure with Susan's friend in the neighborhood. Susan's teacher hoped Susan would be introduced to various new toys and to other children in her neighborhood in the same sequence that new activities and friends had been introduced to her at school.

Figure 2.11 Individual Education Program: Total Service Plan

Child's Name ___Susan Thurman___

School ___Rosebank Elementary School___

Date of Program Entry ___9/7/98___

Prioritized Long-Term Goals

1. Susan will participate successfully in group goal setting and feedback activities.

2. Susan will play with friends.

3. Susan will socially interact with friends in a nonplaying context.

Short-Term Objectives	Specific Educational and Support Services	Person(s) Responsible	Percentage of Opportunities	Beginning and Ending Date	Review Date
1. Susan will imitate Alicia.	Teacher will reinforce Susan for playing with peers.	Teacher and the student Alicia	90% (during recess)	9/15/98–11/5/98	6/10/99
2. Susan will play blocks with Alicia during recess.	Teacher will prompt and reinforce Alicia and classmate for interacting with Susan.		90% (of offers)	9/15/98–11/5/98	
3. Susan will use the free play area and play 10 minutes with a classmate.	Cooperative toys will be available for recess and free play.	Classroom peers and teacher	100% (ten consecutive minutes)	9/15/98–11/5/98	

Percent of Time in Regular Classroom

100%

Placement Recommendation

Summary of Present Levels of Performance

Susan was identified as an isolate child, never interacting during recess times. Susan completed assignments, but never played with others afterwards.

Committee Members Present

Anne Thompson, Principal

Melissa Rutter, School Consultant

Bonnie Edwards, Teacher

Mark & Jamie Thurman, Parents

Dates of Meeting ___11/2/98; 12/5/98___

Figure 2.12 Individual Education Program: Individual Intervention Plan

Child's Name ____Susan Thurman____

School ____Rosebank Elementary School____

Date of Program Entry ____9/7/98____

Goal Statement ____To increase social skills.____

Short-Term Objective ____When told to play building blocks or to share blocks with Alicia, Susan will comply for 10 minutes during free play.____

Task Analysis/ Instructional Sequence	Criteria for Mastery	Strategies and/or Techniques	Materials and/or Resources	Start Date	End Date	Comments
1. Teacher will talk to Alicia, saying, "Try your best to get Susan to play blocks with you."	Spend 10–20 min./day until Alicia can initiate 80% 1 wk/peer imitation training.	Prompting & reinforcement by teacher & Alicia. Susan will be praised for playing & will be hugged by teacher & rewarded. Recording of toys Susan enjoyed.	Cooperative play toys: building blocks, dolls, & ball.	9/15	10/5	If program is successful with building blocks, Susan will be introduced to other toys and other peers besides Alicia. Eventually, a group goal setting and feedback will be used for Susan and entire class.
2. Role-play activity with Alicia. Train Alicia to initiate, verbally and gesturally, toward Susan.	Use different toys 80% for 2 consecutive days.					
3. Carry out role play with building blocks, then dolls, and then a ball.	80% daily.					
4. Have Alicia initiate toward Susan with building blocks.						
5. When told to play, Susan should share blocks during recess with Alicia.	10 minutes of playing together.					
6. Susan will repeat sequence, this time with dolls (new toys will be introduced once a week for two weeks).	2 weeks, 10 minutes a day with Alicia or another peer.	Teacher prompting & reinforcement.	Dolls	11/8	12/8	If the program is successful, Susan's parents and neighborhood friends will be involved. Other toys will continue to be introduced.
7. Susan will repeat sequence with ball. (Susan can return to play with blocks.) During this period she will at least be introduced to new toys.		Peer prompting & social reinforcement.	Ball	1/5	1/5	
8. Teacher will involve other classmates. Children will take turns using same procedure described on IEP.				10/15	6/10	

DISCUSSION QUESTIONS

1. A student has been referred to you because his behavior is a concern to school staff. How would you design a strategy to assess both the pupil's behavior and the expectations of the settings in which he functions?

2. For the situation described in Question 1, indicate several alternate instruments and procedures you could use to assess the pupil's behavior and setting expectations. What would you use as a criterion for deciding whether intervention is needed? Where should intervention be applied?

3. What procedures are used in performing a functional analysis? How does a functional analysis affect intervention decisions?

4. If you were asked to assist a teacher in designing an intervention to reduce a student's physical aggression, what questions would you ask in order to identify target behaviors? What procedures would you use to identify behaviors with which to replace the pupil's aggression?

5. What is a behavioral objective for reducing physical aggression? Write one and analyze it into three to five sequential tasks.

REFERENCES

Algozzine, B., Ruhl, K., & Ramsey, R. (1991). *Behaviorally disordered? Assessment for identification and instruction.* Reston, VA: Council for Exceptional Children.

Black, F. (1985). Social skills assessment for mainstreamed handicapped students: The disciminative efficiency of the Teacher Ratings of Social Skills. Unpublished doctoral dissertation, Louisana State University.

Bower, E. M., & Lambert, N. M. (1961). *Inschool screening of children with emotional handicaps.* Sacramento, CA: California State Department of Education.

Brown, L. L., & Hammill, D. D. (1983). *The Behavior Rating Profile—teacher rating scale.* Austin, TX: Pro-Ed.

Brown, L., Nietupski, J., & Hamre-Nietupski, S. (1976). The criterion of ultimate functioning and public school services for severely handicapped students. In A. Thomas (Ed.), *Hey, don't forget about me: Education's investment in the severely, profoundly, and multiply handicapped* (pp. 2–15). Reston, VA: Council for Exceptional Children.

Carr, E. G., & Durand, M. (1985). Reducing behavior problems through functional communication training. *Journal of Applied Behavior Analysis, 18,* 111–126.

Conroy, M. A., & Fox, J. J. (1994). Setting events and challenging behaviors in the classroom: Incorporating contextual factors into effective intervention plans. *Preventing School Failure, 38*(3), 29–34.

Deno, S. L., & Mirkin, P. K. (1978). *Data-based program modification: A manual.* Reston, VA: Council for Exceptional Children.

Donnellan, A. M., Mirenda, P. L., Mesaros, R. A., & Fassbender, L. L. (1984). Analyzing the communicative functions of aberrant behavior. *Journal of the Association of the Severely Handicapped, 9,* 201–212.

Dunlap, G., Kern. L., dePerczel, M., Clarke, S., Wilson, D., Childs, K. E., White, R., & Falk, G. D. (1993). Functional analysis of classroom variables for students with emotional and behavioral disorders. *Behavioral Disorders, 18,* 275–291.

Evans, I. M., & Meyer, L. H. (1985). *An educative approach to behavior problems: A practical decision model for interventions with severely handicapped learners.* Baltimore, MD: P. H. Brookes.

Executive Committee of the Council for Children with Behavioral Disorders. (1989). White paper on best assessment practices for students with behavioral disorders: Accommodation to cultural diversity and individual differences. *Behavioral Disorders, 14,* 263–278.

Finch, A. J., Jr., & Rodgers, T. R. (1984). Self-report instruments. In T. H. Ollendick & M. Hersen (Eds.), *Child behavior assessment: Principles and procedures* (pp. 106–123). New York: Pergamon Press.

Gast, D. L., & Wolery, M. (1986). Severe maladaptive behaviors. In M. E. Snell (Ed.), *Systematic instruction of the moderately and severely handicapped* (3rd ed.) (pp. 300–322). Upper Saddle River, NJ: Merrill/Prentice Hall.

Gresham, F. M., & Elliott, S. N. (1990). *Social Skills Rating System.* Circle Pines, MN: American Guidance Service.

Gresham, F. M., & Reschly, D. J. (1988). Issues in the conceptualization, classification, and assessment of social skills in the mildly handicapped. In T. R. Kratochwill (Ed.), *Advances in school psychology,* (Vol. 6, pp. 203–247). Hillsdale, NJ: Lawrence Erlbaum Associates.

Gross, A. M. (1984). Behavioral interviewing. In T. H. Ollendick & M. Hersen (Eds.), *Child behavioral assessment: Principles and procedures* (pp. 61–79). New York: Pergamon Press.

Hersh, R. H., & Walker, H. M. (1983). Great expectations: Making schools effective for all students. *Policy Studies Review, 2,* 147–188.

Hops, H., & Greenwood, C. R. (1981). Social skills deficits. In E. J. Mash & L. G. Terdal (Eds.), *Behavioral assessment of childhood disorders* (pp. 347–396). New York: Guilford Press.

Hops, H., & Lewin, L. (1984). Peer sociometric forms. In T. H. Ollendick & M. Hersen (Eds.), *Child behavioral assessment: Principles and procedures* (pp. 124–147). New York: Pergamon Press.

Horner, R. H., O'Neill, R. E., & Flannery, K. B. (1993). Effective behavior support plans. In M. E. Snell (Ed.). *Instruction of students with severe disabilities* (4th ed.)(pp. 184–214). Upper Saddle River, NJ: Merrill/Prentice Hall.

Howell, K. W., Fox, S. L., & Morehead, M. K. (1993). *Curriculum-based evaluation: Teaching and decision making* (2nd ed.). Pacific Grove, CA: Brooks/Cole.

Kaplan, J. S., McCollum-Gahley, J. M., & Howell, K. W. (1988). Direct assessment of social skills. In R. B. Rutherford Jr., C. M. Nelson, & S. R. Forness (Eds.), *Bases of severe behavioral disorders in children and youth* (pp. 143-162). San Diego: College Hill Press.

Kern, L., Childs, K. E., Dunlap, G., Clarke, S., & Falk, G. D. (1994). Using assessment-based curricular intervention to improve the classroom behavior of a student with emotional and behavioral challanges. *Journal of Applied Behavior Analysis, 27,* 7–19.

Knitzer, J., Steinberg, Z., & Fleisch, B. (1990). *At the schoolhouse door: An examination of programs and policies for children with behavioral and emotional problems.* New York: Bank Street College of Education.

Lewis, T., Scott, T., & Sugai, G. (1994). The problem behavior questionnaire: A teacher based instrument to develop functional hypotheses of problem behavior in general education classrooms. *Diagnostique, 19*(2–3), 59–78.

Lewis, T. J., & Sugai, G. (1996). Descriptive and experimental analysis of teacher and peer attention and the use of assessment-based intervention to improve pro-social behavior. *Journal of Behavioral Education, 6,* 7–24.

Mager, R. F. (1962). *Preparing instructional objectives.* Palo Alto, CA: Fearon Press.

Maheady, L., Harper, G. F., Mallette, B., & Sacca, M. K. (1989, September). Opportunity to learn prosocial behavior: Its potential role in the assessment and instruction of behavior disordered students. Paper presented at the CEC/CCBD Topical Conference on Behaviorally Disordered Youth, Charlotte, North Carolina.

McConnell, S. R. (1987). Entrapment effects and the generalization and maintenance of social skills training for elementary school students with behavioral disorders. *Behavioral Disorders, 12,* 252–263.

McIntyre, T. (1996). Guidelines for providing appropriate services to culturally diverse students with emotional and behavioral disorders. *Behavioral Disorders, 21,* 137–144.

McIntyre, T. (1995). *The McIntyre assessment of culture.* Columbia, MO: Hawthorne Educational Services.

McMahon, R. J. (1984). Behavioral checklists and rating scales. In T. H. Ollendick & M. Hersen (Eds.), *Child behavioral assessment: Principles and procedures* (pp. 80–105). New York: Pergamon Press.

O'Neill, R. E., Horner, R. H., Albin, R. W., Storey, K., & Sprague, J. R. (1990). *Functional analysis of problem behavior: A practical assessment guide.* Sycamore, IL: Sycamore Publishing Co.

Polsgrove, L. (1987). Assessment of children's social and behavioral problems. In W. H. Berdine & S. A. Meyer (Eds.), *Assessment in special education* (pp. 141–180). Boston: Little, Brown.

Quay, H. C., & Peterson, D. R. (1983). *Interim manual for the revised Behavior Problem Checklist.* Coral Gables, FL: University of Miami.

Roff, J. E., Sells, S. B., & Golden, M. M. (1972). *Social adjustment and personality development in children.* Minneapolis: The University of Minnesota.

Shores, R. E., Wehby, J. H., & Jack, S. L. (in press). Analyzing behavior in classrooms. In A. C. Repp & R. H. Horner (Eds.), *Functional analysis of problem behavior: From effective assessment to effective support.* Baltimore, MD: Paul H. Brookes.

Stephens, T. M. (1981). *Technical information: Social behavior assessment.* Columbus, OH: Cedars Press.

Sugai, G. (1995, June). Pro-active classroom management. Workshop presented at the Springfield School Improvement Conference, Springfield, OR.

Touchette, P. E., MacDonald, R. F., & Langer, S. N. (1985). A scatter plot for identifying stimulus control of problem behavior. *Journal of Applied Behavior Analysis, 18,* 343–351.

Ullman, C. A. (1952). *Identification of maladjusted school children.* Public Health Monograph No. 7. Washington, DC: Federal Security Agency.

Vincent, L. J., Salisbury, C., Walter, G., Brown, P., Gruenewald, L. J., & Powers, M. (1980). Program evaluation and curriculum development in early childhood/special education: Criterion of the next environment. In W. Sailor, B. Wilcox, & L. Brown (Eds.) *Methods of instruction for severely handicapped students* (pp. 303–328). Baltimore: Paul H. Brookes.

Walker, H. M. (1983). *Walker problem behavior identification checklist.* Los Angeles: Western Psychological Services.

Walker, H. M. (1986). The AIMS (Assessments for Intregration into Mainstream Settings) assessment system: Rationale, instruments, procedures, and outcomes. *Journal of Clinical Child Psychology, 15* (1), 55–63.

Walker, H. M., & Fabre, T. R. (1987). Assessment of behavior disorders in the school setting: Issues, problems and strategies revisited. In N. G. Haring (Ed.), *Assessing and managing behavior disabilities* (pp. 198–243). Seattle: University of Washington Press.

Walker, H. M., & McConnell, S. R. (1988). *The Walker-McConnell scale of social competence and school adjustment: A social skills rating scale for teachers.* Austin, TX: PRO-ED.

Walker, H., McConnell, S., Holmes, D., Todis, B., Walker, J., & Golden, N. (1983). *The Walker social skills curriculum: The ACCEPTS program.* Austin, TX: PRO-ED.

Walker, H. M., & Rankin, R. (1980). *The SBS inventory of teacher social behavior standards and expectations.* Eugene, OR: SBS Project, University of Oregon.

Walker, H. M., & Severson, H. (1990). *Systematic screening for behavioral disorders.* Longmont, CO: Sopris West.

Walker, H. M., Severson, H., & Haring, N. (1986). Standardized screening and identification of behavior disordered pupils in the elementary age range: Rationale, procedures and guidelines. Eugene, OR: University of Oregon.

Wehby, J. H. (1994). Issues in the assessment of aggressive behavior. *Preventing School Failure, 38*(3), 24–28.

Wehby, J. H., Symons, F. J., & Shores, R. E. (1995). A descriptive analysis of aggressive behavior in classrooms for children with emotional and behavioral disorders. *Behavioral Disorders, 20,* 87–105.

White, O. R., & Haring, N. G. (1980). *Exceptional teaching* (2nd. ed.). Columbus, OH: Merrill.

Wolery, M., Bailey, D., & Sugai, G. (1988). *Effective teaching: Principles and procedures of applied behavior analysis with exceptional children.* Boston: Allyn & Bacon.

Wolf, M. M. (1978). Social validity: The case for subjective measurement or how applied behavior analysis is finding its heart. *Journal of Applied Behavior Analysis, 11,* 203–214.

Wright, D. B., Gurman, H. B., California Association of School Psychologists/Diagnostic Center, & Southern California Positive Intervention Task Force (1994). *Positive intervention for serious behavior problems.* Sacramento, CA: Resources in Special Education.

3

CLASSROOM
MEASUREMENT OF
STUDENT PROGRESS

OUTLINE

OBJECTIVES

After completing this chapter, you should be able to

◆ Given descriptions of target behaviors, select alternate measurement strategies that take into consideration the characteristics of the behavior, the setting, constraints on data collection, and the person collecting the data.
◆ Explain and illustrate the following measurement strategies so that a parent or paraprofessional could use them: permanent product recording, event recording, trials to criterion recording, duration and response latency recording, interval recording, and time sampling.
◆ Given two or more target behaviors, or given more than one student exhibiting targeted behaviors, design an appropriate recording strategy.
◆ Given event or interval data collected simultaneously by two observers, select the appropriate reliability formula and calculate interobserver agreement correctly.
◆ Summarize and graph or chart data using techniques appropriate for the data.

In the previous chapters, we discussed assessment strategies and procedures that guide screening, identification, and assessment planning. If you follow the assessment sequence that we have been describing, you should be able to determine which students are in need of social behavior interventions and which behaviors you are going to target for intervention (i.e., what to teach). This chapter presents strategies and techniques for measuring and summarizing student progress. It serves as an important bridge to Chapter 4, which presents strategies for selecting and evaluating interventions on the basis of your measures of student performance, as well as guidelines for selecting the most appropriate intervention procedures. Thus, the precise and systematic monitoring of student progress provides data upon which to base decisions regarding instructional and behavior management interventions.

Evaluating intervention programs involves many complex decisions: Should you continue with an intervention, discard it, or modify it? Is the pupil ready to move on to more complex skills or to less restrictive settings, or does she need more training at her current skill level and in the present setting? To make good decisions, you must have useful data. In behavior change programs involving powerful methods that can be misapplied, student progress must not be evaluated subjectively or casually. As White (1986) explained, "to be responsive to the pupil's needs the teacher must be a student of the pupil's behavior, carefully analyzing how that behavior changes from day to day and adjusting the instructional plan as necessary to facilitate continued learning" (p. 522). Careful monitoring is a critical element of your role as an intervention agent.

To be an effective teacher—that is, to ensure that your students are progressing as rapidly as their capacities and present educational technology allow—you need a system for monitoring their progress on a frequent and regular basis. Because your daily planning depends upon the information you obtain from such monitoring, you are, in effect, conducting ongoing assessments of your students throughout the school year. The data you obtain serve as a basis for evaluating pupil growth, for locating flaws or deficiencies in your instructional or management programs, and for evaluating the effects of program modifications. You can also improve your use of pupil data by implementing **data decision rules,** teacher-determined guidelines for responding to patterns in student performance. Data decision rules are developed by the teacher to facilitate the efficient and effective evaluation of instructional and behavior management programs. You will find guidelines for developing data decision rules in Chapter 4.

Some special educators may be able to function adequately without using systematic procedures such as those described in this text. Continuous data collection for the purpose of monitoring and evaluating student progress is one of the most time consuming of these procedures. Because most public school and educational agencies do not require teachers to collect data continuously, it is the first set of skills lost from a beginning teacher's repertoire. Nevertheless, effective teachers constantly monitor, evaluate, and revise their instructional and behavior management programs. Consequently, they are more sensitive to the instructional needs of their pupils, and they are accountable to students, supervisors, and parents for the methods they use. If you want to be an effective teacher, you must expect to spend much time and effort collecting student performance data and planning and implementing systematic interventions. The result will be greater pride in your own skill as a teacher, the recognition of fellow professionals, and more rapid progress by your

students. Fuchs and Fuchs (1986) found that students whose programs are systematically monitored and adjusted through ongoing data-based evaluation procedures make greater gains than students whose programs are not monitored systematically or formatively evaluated.

We begin this chapter with an overview of measurement procedures, including common objections to data collection, frequent pitfalls of monitoring student performance, and the use of measurement in IEPs. Next, we present measurement considerations, followed by step-by-step procedures for data collection, reliability assessment, and summarizing and visually displaying data. A number of alternate strategies are described and illustrated.

OVERVIEW OF CLASSROOM MEASUREMENT

Teacher Objections to Systematic Data Collection

Educators and supervisors lament the tendency of classroom teachers to avoid data collection, despite the emphasis placed on this function in preservice training. The most common objections are presented below, and alternative remedial strategies are mentioned. These strategies are described in greater detail later in this chapter.

"I Don't Have Enough Time to Collect Data—I Have to Teach." Walton (1985) surveyed regular and special education teachers regarding their data collection practices. Approximately 76 percent reported not having enough time during the day to carry out data collection. This objection suggests a basic misunderstanding of the role of data collection. Frequently, it is seen as impractical or as a useless activity required by an administrator or bureaucrat. We understand why many teachers hold this attitude. School districts and state and federal agencies require teachers to gather and report such data as daily attendance, which students will be eating the school's hot lunch, who will be taking the early (or late) bus home, and so on, in addition to periodic surveys, questionnaires, and lists. Because these data have little application to what the teacher does, it is no wonder that practitioners develop a repugnance for data collection in general.

Still, teachers are notorious data collectors. Their gradebooks are full of checkmarks showing assignments turned in, scores on daily or weekly tests, counts of disciplinary actions, and so forth. Unfortunately, these data are used infrequently as a basis for evaluating pupils or programs. One solution to the problem of time constraints on data collection is to make sure the data you keep are data you will use. This does not include IQ scores, test profiles, who owes you milk money, and the like. It does include daily reading or math performance rates, spelling test scores, rates of targeted social behaviors, number of disciplinary actions, and student progress toward individual behavioral objectives. As a rule of thumb, you should carefully decide what to measure; then measure it as precisely as you can.

Another solution is to simplify your data collection. Later we describe several alternate strategies. These include using data probes, time samples, and scatter plots instead of continuous measurement, as well as auto-graphing. You also may train someone else to observe and record data, such as an aide, a fellow teacher or other staff person, another pupil, or the student whose behavior is being measured. (See page 76 for guidelines for training observers.)

"Collecting Data Doesn't Help Me Teach."   Nearly 45 percent of teachers surveyed by Walton (1985) reported that data collection procedures were of little help or only somewhat helpful to their teaching responsibilities. This objection also suggests that the teacher is not gathering useful data, that is, data that can be used to make educational decisions and upon which to base program adjustments. In response to this objection, we offer this guideline: If you do not use the data frequently, do not collect it. (Note: This guideline does not apply to data you are required to collect by your agency.) On the other hand, failure to gather data you should use is inexcusable. As Kauffman (1993) emphasizes:

The teaching profession is dedicated to the task of changing behavior—changing behavior demonstrably for the better. What can one say, then, of educational practice that does not include reliable and forthright measurement of the behavior change induced by the teacher's methodology? I believe this: It is indefensible. (pp. 491–492)

If your data are not useful to you, perhaps you need to select measures that are more sensitive to what you are trying to accomplish. A common mistake is to measure the results of behavior instead of the behavior itself. For example, if you are trying to increase a pupil's use of specific social skills, do not record the number of points he earns for appropriate social behaviors each day. Instead, directly record the frequency with which these skills are exhibited.

Systematic data collection can: assist in instructional decision making; provide feedback on the effectivess of instructional and behavioral management programs; create a concrete method of ensuring accountability; offer a common basis for discussion among parents, teachers, other professionals, and students; provide reinforcement for parents, teachers, and students; and increase student performance (Cooke, Heward, Test, Spooner, & Courson, 1991; Fuchs & Fuchs, 1986; Lund, Schnaps, & Bijou, 1983). We hope you will appreciate the value of data collection by the time you complete this text.

"I Don't Get Any Support or Reinforcement for Data Collection."   Obviously, if you do not gather data, you cannot expect to be reinforced for doing so. However, many teachers enter their profession with an earnest desire to use systematic teaching and measurement procedures, and a year later their teaching is guided by guesses and hunches. Frankly, there are no explicit reinforcement contingencies for data-based instruction in most schools. Neither your salary nor your effectiveness, as measured by most parents or administrators, depends on the objective documentation of student progress. Therefore, to maintain such a complex and sometimes difficult task, you will need to "recruit" reinforcement (Stokes and Baer, 1977). One way is to share your data with those to whom you report student progress. Parents should be more receptive to graphs or charts detailing their child's progress in, for example, learning a functional speaking vocabulary than they would be to a letter grade in language arts. Administrators too can learn to view your performance in the school by progress made toward individual student objectives. (We feel this perception would be an immense help to public education in general.) So, share your student data with everyone with whom you communicate. Show them what you are trying to do and how you are trying to measure and evaluate progress. Solicit their assistance in solving your measurement problems. In addition to getting valuable feedback and support, you are more likely to gain other teachers' cooperation with data-collection activities such as beginning to record student performances in their own classrooms.

Common Pitfalls of Data Collection

In addition to recruiting reinforcement for data-based instruction from others, you also must minimize the cost to yourself in terms of time and effort. Here are a few teacher behaviors that tend to make data collection less relevant and more aversive.

1. *Trying to collect data about everything.* As Scott and Goetz (1980) point out, some teachers collect data seemingly for its own sake. Gast and Gast (1981) suggest that the question "To what practical end can the data be used?" be employed as a guideline for describing how much data are needed and how often it should be collected. And, as we said earlier, there is little purpose in gathering data to which you do not respond. So if you intend to do something about a behavior, even if your intention is only to monitor it, record it. If you have no such design, ignore it. Some behaviors will have to be ignored simply because they are not a top priority for immediate intervention. For example, if the student's IEP committee has ranked his physical aggression and name-calling as priority targets, and his occasional out-of-seat behavior as a much lower priority, you will probably want to devote

more effort to monitoring the first two behaviors and let the third go until later. You may wish to conduct periodic measurement probes (see page 78) of lower-priority targets in order to verify that there are no abrupt changes in their rates.

If you follow the rule of collecting only those data you can use in decision-making, you also may find that you can consolidate some data. For example, if you are concerned with general classroom disruptions and have no desire to respond differently to specific behaviors in this category, such as out-of-seat or talking out, count the number of disruptions rather than the number of times out-of-seat and the number of talkouts.

2. *Collecting data on nonessential behaviors.* The points we mentioned above obviously apply here also. If you rank objectives and target behaviors, if you consolidate measures of behaviors, if you gather only those data to which you will respond, you should be able to cut down on this problem significantly. It does not hurt to ask, "Do I need this?" every time you review data sheets and displays. Our emphasis on using data to make frequent program adjustments applies to your data-collection procedures as well. Remember, your recording strategy also is part of your program.

3. *Recording the results of behavior.* Whereas academic performances result in a permanent product that is a reasonably sensitive measure of the behaviors that produced it, social behaviors leave no such record. Behavioral indexes such as teacher rating or point earnings are affected by variables other than the pupil's behavior (e.g., the teacher's mood) and therefore are inaccurate measures of actual behavior. These data are convenient, and they perhaps provide a rough estimate of student progress, but they are not a sufficient base for making specific educational decisions. Further, the time and effort used in obtaining and summarizing these data can be spent more productively in more precise recording. For example, some teachers monitor classroom behavior by charting daily token earnings. Token earnings may be affected by factors other than the behaviors the teacher wishes to measure (e.g., the teacher may award more tokens to a pupil during the process of shaping a complex new behavior). Such indirect measures are not as sensitive to changes in behaviors as are more direct approaches. Therefore, instead of counting the number of tokens earned, it is preferrable to count the behaviors that earn tokens (completing assignments, following directions). Finally, if your students are interested in such information as their daily point earnings, teach *them* to record and chart these data.

Teachers are not always present to observe and record student behavior when it occurs. Further, some behaviors (e.g., stealing, verbal threats) are less frequent when an authority figure is around. However, sometimes these behaviors do have measurable effects on the environment. For example, the number of items stolen, papers torn, marks made on furniture, or objects damaged represent **permanent products** that can be counted accurately. These results of behavior are not based on teachers' subjective evaluations of pupils' responses, and so they are more reliable indicators of the behaviors that produced them.

The increased use of alternative assessment procedures, particularly student **portfolios,** has led many practitioners to incorporate data from such procedures as rating scales, informal criterion-referenced assessments, and curriculum-based measurement of progress in social skills curricula. We will describe some of the uses of portfolios in monitoring student progress in a later section.

4. *Not responding to the data collected.* If you follow our suggestions thus far, you should have little difficulty avoiding this pitfall. Still, it is wise to review periodically all student programs with your supervisor or colleagues to ensure that you are gathering important data, that your data-collection procedures are appropriate, and that you are making the best use of these data. A number of teachers may be interested in informal biweekly meetings to talk about programs and review data.

A major reason teachers fail to use the data they collect is that the data are not summarized graphically. This process takes time and frequently is put off until it is too dated to be useful (Fabry & Cone, 1980). Teachers' gradebooks or planbooks often are full of data regarding academic performances and social behaviors. However, these data are not arranged so as to show change over time. Graphing or charting organizes these data to show such changes and is critical to making program adjustments based on student performance (Fabry & Cone, 1980). More efficient techniques have been devised, some of which combine the functions of data recording and graphing or charting (e.g., Fabry & Cone, 1980; Nelson, Gast, & Trout, 1979). We illustrate these procedures later in this chapter.

Finally, because monitoring of pinpointed social behaviors occurs repeatedly over time and covers a relatively narrow range of behaviors, you should select your monitoring points carefully. Just as a physician knows where to find a pulse that tells important things about a patient, so too should you measure a few behaviors that describe the student adequately and that are sensitive to the changes you are attempting to achieve. You should neither measure too much nor too little, nor should you monitor behaviors that are not directly related to the changes you want. That's like searching for a pulse in the wrong place—the data will tell you nothing.

The Role of Program Monitoring and Evaluation in IEPs

The IDEA mandates that the total service plan for a pupil's education be reviewed at least annually. However, as White and Haring (1980) point out, an annual review of goals and objectives is far too infrequent for any child, especially one who has a great deal of catching up to do. Annual, semiannual, or quarterly reassessments relative to the goals and objectives stated in a pupil's IEP are **static measures,** that is, they provide a report of progress at a single point in time. In addition to the potential inaccuracy or unreliability of static measures, they are not made often enough to allow the teacher to make timely program decisions or precise program adjustments.

That educational decisions (e.g., to change a pupil's grade placement) frequently are made on the basis of such static measures is no excuse for perpetuating these practices in your classroom. As Gast & Gast (1981) stated:

To go beyond perfunctory "paper compliance" with the static assessment of a child's progress annually, it is necessary to evaluate and measure the efficacy of a child's program on a frequent and regular basis. The pretest/posttest methods of determining pupil performance are only the peripheral ends of a continuum of evaluating and monitoring individual education plans. Systematic procedures that result in formative data, from which decisions of program maintenance and modification can be made, are imperative if the IEP is to be a truly functional tool for assuring appropriate education for exceptional children. (p. 3)

The following sections present a number of measurement principles and techniques. As you read, you may find yourself thinking, "I can't do all this!" You will be quite right. The measurement principles and strategies presented here describe an ideal situation, one that can be achieved only when sufficient resources are available. Our goal is for you to understand these principles and procedures well enough to make intelligent compromises about fitting these methods to your teaching situation. For example, if you are a beginning teacher, we suggest that you attempt some systematic data collection (e.g., on your top-ranked academic or social behavior targets). As you gain skill and confidence, you can increase the amount and sophistication of your data collection. Furthermore, it is not necessary to do everything we suggest in order to be an effective teacher. Experienced educators develop their own decision-making strategies. (You will notice that the chapter case studies do not follow all of our guidelines regarding data collection.) As you gain more experience, you will develop your own strategies, many of them perhaps less formal than those we describe. Nevertheless, we hope you will strive for the principles presented here and will find the measurement strategies useful in your efforts to be a systematic and effective teacher.

MONITORING STUDENT PROGRESS

Progress monitoring involves four basic steps, several of which we already have highlighted: selecting a measurement strategy and procedures; recording data; assessing reliability; and summarizing the data for analysis. In this section, we describe and illustrate procedures for accomplishing each of these steps.

Selecting a Measurement Strategy

This step includes several components: determining what aspects of student behavior to measure, selecting an appropriate recording procedure, and deciding what data to collect. We mention these separately, but in practice, you probably will evaluate these components simultaneously.

Deciding what to measure requires that you must first know what properties of behavior can be measured. Obviously, human behavior does not have the dimensions of a physical object; therefore, it cannot be measured in terms of height, weight, volume, or mass. However, behavior does have properties that can be observed and reliably measured. The first of these is *frequency* or *rate*, which refers to how often a behavior occurs in a period of time. For example, you can measure the number of times a child hits, self-stimulates, or is out-of-seat in an hour. Second, behavior may be described or measured in terms of its *duration:* the length of time out of seat, the duration of temper tantrums, and so forth. Third, the *latency*, or time between the presentation of a prompt, or verbal instruction, and the initiation of a response, may be observed. Behavior also may be measured in terms of *intensity*, which includes its frequency and its duration: for example, recording the number and the length of a pupil's temper tantrums. Finally, behavior sometimes is measured in terms of its *magnitude*, or force, although this is difficult to do objectively without laboratory apparatus. The decision of which of these properties to measure depends upon which is best suited to the pupil, the situation, and the changes you want. For instance, if your target is a student's temper tantrums, you may consider whether tantrums are best characterized in terms of their frequency or their duration, and then, whether your goal is to lessen the number of tantrums or their length of occurrence or both (i.e., intensity).

The selection of a measurement strategy therefore partly is based on the characteristics of the behavior being emitted and how you want it to change. To increase fluency, measure rate. To reduce time, measure duration. However, another important consideration is convenience. Although you may want to reduce the duration of out-of-seat behavior, for instance, keeping track of it with a stopwatch is highly inconvenient, unless you have nothing else to do. We suggest alternative strategies for such problems later.

Thus, you have several decisions to make regarding the choice of the behaviors you will measure and attempt to change. The range of these **dependent measures** is described in Table 3.1. Study it carefully to determine which option best suits your purposes and situation.

If you are not accustomed to observing behavior systematically, it is easy to make mistakes that adversely affect the data you collect. Because unreliable data increase the probability of bad decisions, it is imperative that your procedures be as sensitive and precise as possible. To help you accomplish this goal, we offer the following guidelines.

1. *Select a direct and sensitive measurement strategy.* Consider several factors before deciding upon a measurement strategy: What constraints does the observation setting place on measurement and recording? What is it about the behavior observed that you want to change? How do you want the behavior to change? Remember, you should measure behavior directly (i.e., measure the behavior itself, not the results of the behavior). For example, many persons monitor their eating by measuring their weight. They are dismayed if decreases in eating are not accompanied by immediate reductions in their weight. This may occur because weight also is affected by other factors, such as fluid retention or muscle mass. (See our previous discussion of indirect measures.)

Direct measures of behavior are more sensitive to the effects of your instructional and management programs. Therefore, the data are more useful to you in analyzing and "fine tuning" your program. The more experience you acquire with observation and recording techniques, the easier it will become to tailor measurement strategies to the behaviors you want to monitor. The major

exception to measuring behavior directly is permanent products. Written responses on worksheets, number of objects stolen, and so forth, are indirect measures of the behaviors contributing to responses, but they are also more convenient, and unless it is possible for students to cheat on every written assignment or items reported as stolen were simply misplaced, there generally is only one way to produce the outcome that is measured.

2. *Observe and record daily for as long as possible.* A busy teacher decided to monitor a pupil's fighting during the first thirty minutes of school. She was dismayed that her baseline data showed zero fights, even though the student had been in several that week. Fighting occurred rather infrequently, and her observation sample was too brief to capture it. Therefore, the behavior "escaped." Unless the behaviors you want to monitor occur fairly often across all settings and times, you should plan to observe or have others record the events long enough to obtain an adequate sample. This is important particularly with regard to social behaviors that are not limited to certain settings or antecedent stimuli. Usually, by the time you decide a behavior warrants measurement, you will have a fairly good idea of when and where it occurs, and can design your measurement strategy accordingly.

Longer observation and recording periods yield more accurate samples of behavior and provide a better check of your intervention program. In addition, you will be able to check for generalization of behavior changes across settings or time. If the behavior is discrete, not constant, and apparent when it occurs (e.g., tantrums and physical aggression), you should be able to observe and record several times during the day. On the other hand, if it is more subtle or continuous (e.g., stereotypic behavior, off-task), you may be able to use one of the momentary time-sampling techniques described below that permit you to sample behaviors across the day.

There are no hard and fast guidelines for determining the optimal length for observation periods. Generally, you should adjust the interval to the "typical" rate at which the behavior occurs; that is, you should get a representative sample.

Table 3.1 Summary of Dependent Measures

Dependent Measure	Definition	Considerations
1. Number	Simple count of the number of times a behavior or event occurs	1.1 Requires constant time across observational periods when response opportunities are not controlled
		1.2 Requires constant number of trials across sessions/days with teacher-paced instruction
2. Percent	Number of occurrences divided by the total number of opportunities for the behavior to occur multiplied by 100	2.1 Equalizes unequal number of opportunities to respond across sessions/days
		2.2 Easily understood
		2.3 Frequently used measure for accuracy
		2.4 Efficient means for summarizing large numbers of responses
		2.5 No reference to the time over which behavior was observed
		2.6 Generally, should be used only when there are 20 or more opportunities to respond
3. Rate	Number of occurrences divided by the number of time units (minutes or hours)	3.1 Converts behavior counts to a constant scale when opportunities to respond or observation time varies across sessions/days
		3.2 Reveals response proficiency as well as accuracy
		3.3 Reported as responses per minute or responses per hour
		3.4 Appropriate for behaviors measured under conditions in which opportunities to respond are not controlled
		3.5 Cumbersome to use with behaviors measured under teacher-paced conditions
4. Duration (total)	Amount of time behavior occurs during an observation period	4.1 Expressed as the percentage of time engaged in behavior
		4.2 Does not yield information about frequency or mean duration per occurrence
5. Duration per occurrence	Amount of time engaged in each episode of the behavior	5.1 Yields behavior frequency: mean duration per occurrence and total duration information
6. Latency	Elapsed time from the presentation of the discriminative stimulus (S^D) and the initiation of the behavior	6.1 Appropriate measure with compliance problem behaviors (long response latency)
		6.2 May yield information regarding high error rate when there is a short response latency
7. Magnitude	Response strength or force	7.1 Direct measure requires automated-quantitative instrumentation
		7.2 Indirect measure of magnitude possible by measuring effect response has on environment
8. Trials to criterion	Number of trials counted to reach criterion for each behavior	8.1 Yields information on concept formation (learning-to-learn phenomenon)
		8.2 Post hoc summary measure

Source: Tawney, J. W., & Gast, D. L. (1984). *Single subject research in special education.* Upper Saddle River, NJ: Merrill/Prentice Hall. Used with permission.

Infrequent target behavior requires longer observation periods. On the other hand, briefer time samples are possible for more frequent behaviors, provided they represent the rate of occurrence accurately. Ask yourself, "Do these data reflect the behavior as I evaluate it?" If the answer is "No," adjust your recording period (or re-evaluate your subjective assessment of the behavior).

Although daily measurement provides the best data base for making intervention decisions, research supports the conclusion that twice-weekly monitoring of student academic performance is as adequate as daily monitoring in terms of promoting academic achievement (Fuchs, 1986). However, priority social behaviors should be monitored daily during the initial phases of intervention (i.e., when programs are being tested and revised). Less frequent measurement probes may be taken when students have advanced to maintenance or generalization phases.

3. *Observe and record behavior where it occurs.* The teacher we mentioned who monitored her student's fighting for thirty minutes daily also violated this guideline. Obviously, your measures of behavior are not going to be valid if your observation periods do not coincide with the times or activities during which the behavior occurs. Thus, if fighting occurs only during lunch or recess, observe in the lunchroom or playground instead of the study hall. And, as we stated earlier, if the behavior does not occur in your presence, find someone who is present when it happens and train him to monitor it. Given proper training and supervision, peers are reliable observers of behavior (Fowler, 1986). Also, do not overlook other school staff: the janitor, cafeteria workers, aides, and so forth. The following guidelines are suggested for training others to observe behavior systematically and reliably. It is very important that you train observers well, if you are going to base decisions on the data they collect.

◆ Develop a specific, observable definition of the behavior(s) to be observed. Include all instances (what is counted as an occurrence) and noninstances (what is not counted as an occurrence). Review this with the observer.

◆ Explain recording sheets and apparatus to the observer. Teach the observer to use the recording equipment (e.g., wrist counter, stopwatch) as well as the recording procedures (response codes, interval data sheets, etc.). Go over these procedures several times.

◆ Ask the observer to practice data collection. At first, you may label the behavior and have the observer record it according to your procedure. Later, you may role-play the behavior while the observer records, or use a videotape to simulate an actual situation. Be sure to stop immediately to answer questions or correct mistakes.

◆ Ask the observer to collect data in the actual situation with you (or another qualified observer) present to provide assistance.

◆ Ask the observer to collect data while a more experienced observer simultaneously observes and records. Assess the reliability of the novice's data, answer questions, correct errors, and so forth. Continue reliability checks until interobserver agreement (see pages 89–90) is 80 to 90 percent. Do not use any of the data until this has been achieved!

◆ The observer is now ready to begin formal data collection. Continue frequent reliability checks (e.g., once a week, depending on the frequency of data collection). If reliability falls below 80 percent, stop formal data collection and retrain this observer.

Unless there are no reliable differences in the level of the behavior across settings or activities, you should observe and record in the same setting, activity, or time period each day. Not only will this result in more comparable data, it also will be easier for you to remember to monitor specific performances.

4. *Keep observation time relatively constant.* If you are maintaining a frequency count of behavior, your data will be affected by the length of time you observe. For instance, there is twice as much opportunity to commit physical aggression in 60 minutes as in thirty minutes. If your observation period is not controlled, your data may reflect variations in the opportunity to respond rather than in the response itself. If you are unable to observe for the same amount of time each session or day, use a rate or a percent of time recording procedure (discussed later) to control for these variations. Rate data are useful particularly because they permit comparison of measures taken across different settings or for varying lengths of time.

5. *Once a behavior is defined, observe and record only responses meeting that definition.* One of us supervised a teacher who was working on a preschool child's self-injurious behavior. The teacher was counting the number of times the child slapped herself in the head or bit her fingers. The teacher reported that intervention was successful, and our observations in the classroom confirmed this. However we could see very little change in the data. Our questioning revealed that the teacher's definition of self-injurious behavior gradually had shifted from slaps and bites to touches and mouthings.

This change in response definition is called **observer drift** (Gelfand & Hartmann, 1984), and there are two solutions. The first is to decide on what constitutes the behavior. Thus, self-injurious behavior could be defined as slaps to the face or head, bites to the fingers or hands that result in an audible sound and perhaps skin reddening. Noninstances would include covering the face with hands, twisting hair with fingers, and so forth. The latter would not be counted as instances of self-injurious behavior. The best way to discriminate instances from noninstances when developing behavioral definitions is to observe the child continuously for a period of time, writing down every response as well as antecedents and consequences. This initial A-B-C analysis will not only help you establish all the forms of the behavior you will be observing, it will also help identify associated environmental variables (see Chapter 2).

Sometimes, as in the case of self-injurious behavior, behavior definitions encompass several different but related responses. These are called **response classes,** of which there are two types. A **functional response class** consists of behaviors that have the same effect on the environment. Self-injurious behavior belongs in this category, because although there are many forms of self-injurious behavior (striking, biting, scratching, or pinching oneself), they all have the same result:

pain or injury. Disruptive behaviors (see Chapter 6) also constitute a separate functional response class, as does attention-seeking and door-slamming. On the other hand, behaviors belonging to a **topographic response class** are related in terms of their form or the movements comprising the response (Gelfand & Hartmann, 1984). For example, hand-raising, out-of-seat, and headweaving may be described in terms of a set of physical movements, all of which may not be emitted in any given instance. Some response classes may involve both functional and topographic descriptions (e.g., bullying). Knowing how to group behaviors into response classes is useful if you want to consolidate data on behaviors for which you are going to develop comprehensive programs, as, for example, when a student exhibits a variety of disruptive classroom behaviors.

The second solution is to conduct periodic reliability checks. These are especially helpful if after each reliability session the observers discuss their agreements and disagreements. It still is possible that **consensual observer drift** (Gelfand & Hartmann, 1984) will occur. This amounts to both observers gradually changing their response definitions as they become accustomed to the behavior, and is more likely to occur if some element of subjectivity is involved in scoring response instances or noninstances. The best way to avoid consensual observer drift is to avoid using subjective response criteria and to retrain observers frequently (Gelfand & Hartmann, 1984).

6. *Monitor only as many behaviors in as many settings as you can manage.* There is little purpose in observing and recording so many behaviors that you have no time left for instruction or you confuse yourself and your students. Likewise, the purpose of data collection is lost if you have more data than you can act upon. Cooper (1981) suggested that the more severe the pupil's educational problem, the more behaviors should be monitored. Teachers of students with mild disabilities should monitor all responses to direct (planned academic) instruction, whereas teachers of students with severe and profound disabilities should monitor all student responses to planned academic instruction and those during social activities.

Cooper also provides several practical suggestions for initiating data-based instruction:

◆ Begin observing one or two behaviors of one student. Gradually expand observations of the same behavior to include another student, a third, and so on. Experiment with different measurement strategies (duration, time sample, interval) to find those that are most useful, sensitive, and direct for a particular setting.
◆ Measure behavior for the shortest time possible to get an adequate sample (i.e., without occurrences of behavior "escaping" measurement).
◆ Use other persons, especially students, to observe, to record, and to collect observer agreement information.
◆ Ask persons who are skilled in recording and graphing behavior to help you analyze your measurement strategies.

You will find it possible to monitor a larger number of behaviors if you adjust your data-collection procedures to the behavior you are recording. All behavior does not need to be monitored constantly, such as when you are evaluating the maintenance or generalization of a previously taught skill. In such cases, you might employ periodic (weekly or biweekly) **measurement probes.** For example, you may observe a student once a week to see whether he continues to play appropriately with others during recess. Data probes also are useful for general monitoring (e.g., spot-checking pupils' on-task behavior) and for monitoring programs in which

student progress is slow. Table 3.2 summarizes guidelines for adjusting the frequency of measurement to student and program characteristics.

7. *If you are observing in a setting other than your own classroom or school building, follow established procedures.* Each institution, residential facility, or school district has its own policies regarding visitors. Although we cannot prepare you for every situation, we have summarized general guidelines. These procedures are important if you are to obtain accurate data without offending anyone.

Do obtain permission to observe the student. Consult the building or program administrator and the teacher. Some agencies require parental consent. Check with the teacher or supervisor to find out if this is the case.

Do sign in and out when entering and leaving the building.

Do talk with the teacher beforehand about the purpose of your observations, what to tell the class about your visits, and the extent of your class participation.

Do enter and leave the classroom unobtrusively, ideally during a normal break in the routine.

Do avoid being conspicuous. Sit where you can see the pupil and monitor the behavior you want to observe but out of the student's direct line of vision.

Don't interact or make eye contact with any of the students or the teacher during your observations. If a student insists on getting your attention, indicate that you are not allowed to talk and redirect her attention.

Table 3.2   Guidelines for Adjusting Frequency of Monitoring

Student or Program Characteristics	Monitoring Strategy
Rapid student progress or progress through small-step sequence	Session-by-session recording (one or more per day)
Daily progress or fluctuation in student behavior, daily program adjustments	Daily recording
Slow rate of student progress	Data probes (biweekly, weekly)
General monitoring of behavior. Less frequent program adjustments	Data probes (biweekly, weekly)
Evaluating maintenance or generalizing previously mastered programs or steps	Data probes (biweekly, weekly, monthly)

Table 3.3 Considerations in Selecting a Measurement Strategy

1. Definition of the behavior target	Movement/function/both?
2. Characteristics of target behavior	Frequency/duration/latency/intensity? Individual/group? High rate/low rate?
3. Goal of intervention	Change rate/duration/latency/intensity?
4. Observation situation	Your class/another class? Group/one to one? Teacher giving lesson/individual seatwork/recess or free time/lunch/other?
5. Person doing observation	Trained observer/untrained observer? Adult/child?
6. Time available for observation	All day/one period/portion of several periods/portion of one period?
7. Equipment available for measurement	Automatic recorder/cumulative recorder/multiple event recorder/wrist counter/timing device/pad and pencil?
8. Accuracy	High/medium/low? Interobserver agreement critical/not critical? Reliability observers trained/untrained?
9. Audience for whom data are intended	Professionals/parents/students?

Don't participate in classroom activities.

Don't begin systematic observations until the pupils have become accustomed to your presence.

Do thank the teacher for allowing you to observe and share your data with the teacher if you can do so without disrupting the classroom.

Recording Strategies

Advances in the technology of behavior measurement have resulted in a variety of alternatives for recording. The alternatives you select depend on a number of factors, some of which are presented in Table 3.3. Your answers to the questions posed in this table will help determine which recording procedure you should use. For example, if you must observe while you are involved in direct instruction with pupils other than or in addition to the target student, you would likely choose a sampling technique or train someone other than yourself to observe and record. Following is a discussion of alternative approaches for recording behavior.

Permanent Products   If your measurement strategy is based on permanent products, your choices of recording techniques are fairly straightforward. You may obtain numerical counts, rate or percent, or record the number of instructional trials required for the student to reach the criterion (see page 80). Your choice will be based upon some of the considerations listed in Table 3.3: Does the student not attempt work, or is the work inaccurate? Will you be recording student

responses in a one-to-one instructional situation, in which you are presenting discrete learning trials? Do you want to increase the pupil's response speed, accuracy, or both? Will you be giving daily or weekly probes over the objective you are attempting to reach? Will the student monitor and record the target behavior himself? Will you use a peer observer? Permanent product recording is useful primarily for monitoring academic behaviors that result in written student responses, although, as we suggested earlier, some social behaviors may have results that can be measured as permanent products. Also, you can use audio or video recordings as permanent products of social behaviors (Tawney & Gast, 1984). Permanent products are useful documentation for inclusion in student portfolios. Consult Cooper (1981), Deno and Mirkin (1978), or White and Haring (1980) for information about permanent product recording strategies.

To measure behaviors that do not result in a permanent product (e.g., most human social behavior), you must rely upon observational recording techniques. A variety of these are available or you may adapt or design a recording procedure suited to your own situation. We briefly describe and illustrate several approaches, and other examples appear in Chapters 6 through 10.

Event Recording   If you have defined target behaviors specifically and objectively, recording their frequency is relatively easy. Event recording is the method of choice for most behaviors that are brief and discrete (i.e., have a definite beginning and end and are best characterized in terms of their frequency rather than their duration). In some cases, a simple numerical count will be sufficient, but it generally is better to record the time period in which the behavior occurred or keep observation time constant to permit comparison across observation sessions. If recording sessions vary in length, you may convert event data to rate by dividing the numerical count by the time observed (e.g., Katy was out of her seat seven times in thirty minutes. Rate = 7/30 or .23 times per minute). This will permit comparison of your data across unequal observation periods.

Event recording may be accomplished with a paper and pencil or you may use one of several devices pictured in Figure 3.1. Although sophisticated recording instruments are available, a variety of inexpensive devices are equally useful for recording event data. For example, you can attach a piece of masking tape to a clipboard, watchband, or pencil, and mark on it whenever a target behavior occurs. Transfer coins or paper clips from one pocket to another or to a container whenever a target behavior occurs. Golf counters, knitting counters, button counters, and even digital stopwatches or wristwatches can be purchased at department stores for under ten dollars.

Trials to Criterion Recording When you are providing skill instruction through **discrete learning trials** (i.e., presenting a fixed number of trials that consist of a specific instruction or model, the pupil's response, and a subsequent teacher response), or when you are otherwise controlling the student's opportunities to respond (e.g., through teacher-paced instructions), it is useful to record data concerning each trial. Figure 3.2 shows a discrete trial-recording format for teaching a pupil to take time-outs in the classroom. Note that the teacher has set ten trials per training session and that the criterion for moving to the next level of response duration is specified on the recording sheet. Trials to criterion data sheets may be attached

to a separate clipboard for each student. Trials to criterion is an appropriate measurement strategy for monitoring progress through a task-analysis sequence (as in Figure 3.2), or for measuring skill generalization (Tawney & Gast, 1984).

Duration Recording If the length or the latency of a response is its major characteristic or the one you most want to change, duration recording may be the best method. For example, a student may have a low frequency of out-of-seat behavior but each episode may last several minutes, or a student may be extremely slow in following directions or in joining group activities.

Response duration or latency may be monitored by any watch or clock with a second hand or second counter, but a stopwatch is best. By starting and stopping a stopwatch without resetting it, you may record cumulative time out-of-seat or off-task across several instances. Although a total duration recording procedure is more convenient, it is less descriptive than duration per occurrence because the latter keeps track of each event and its duration. Both of these procedures are easier to use if the observer is not occupied with direct instruction or classroom management.

Response latency is measured by starting the timer when a cue (verbal instruction, visual signal, etc.) is presented and by stopping the timer when the pupil complies with the request (e.g., "Take your seat"). Although teachers generally want to decrease latency, as when a student does not comply with teacher requests or instructions, sometimes it is desirable to increase latencies, as when students respond impulsively and thereby increase errors (Tawney & Gast, 1984).

Interval Recording Even with a stopwatch, duration recording tends to be unreliable and awkward. Interval recording is a versatile technique for recording both discrete and continuous responses. It requires your full attention for observing and recording, but you can observe several behaviors or pupils simultaneously. Interval recording also may be the most practical strategy if a response occurs too frequently for each instance to be counted (e.g., hand flapping or

Figure 3.1 Manual Recording Devices

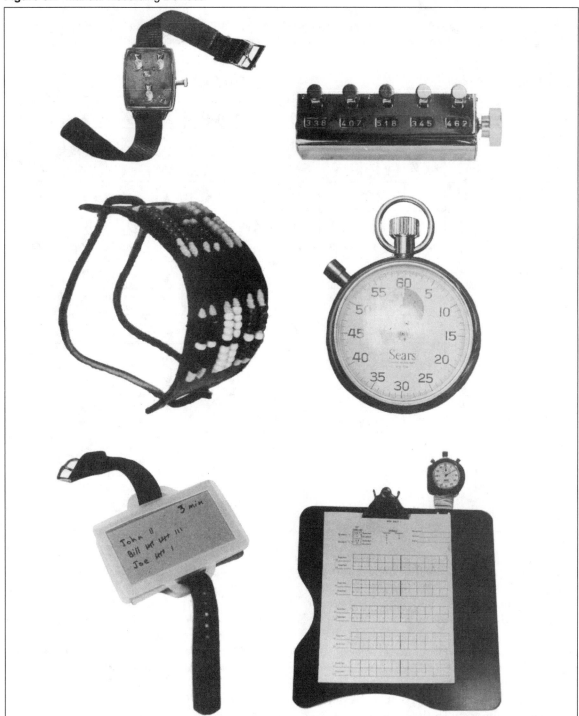

Figure 3.2   Trials to Criterion Data Sheet

Objective: When instructed to "show me the time-out position," Robert will demonstrate the correct time-out position (sitting or standing) for 30 seconds. *Criterion:* 8 of 10 consecutive correct trials for two consecutive sessions.

Duration	Session	Trials									
		1	2	3	4	5	6	7	8	9	10
	1	O	XP	XP	O	XP	XP	X	X	X	X
5 seconds	2	XP	O	XP	XP	X	X	X	X	X	X
	3	XP	XP	X	X	X	X	X	X	X	X
	4	X	X	X	X	X	X	X	X	X	X
	1	O	O	OP	OP	XP	XP	OP	OP	XP	XP
	2	XP	XP	OP	OP	X	X	O	O	XP	XP
15 seconds	3	X	X	X	O	XP	XP	X	X	X	X
	4	O	XP	X	X	X	X	X	X	X	X
	5	X	X	X	X	X	X	X	X	X	X
	1	XP	XP	O	XP	X	X	X	X	X	X
	2	O	O	XP	X	X	X	X	X	X	X
30 seconds	3	X	X	X	X	X	X	X	X	X	X
	4	X	X	X	X	X	X	X	X	X	X

Scoring Key: X = correct
             O = incorrect
             XP = correct prompted (verbal)
             OP = incorrect prompted (verbal)

other stereotypic behaviors). When using this technique, break the observation period down into small intervals of equal length (ten, fifteen, or thirty seconds) and observe whether the behavior occurs or does not occur in any given interval. Gelfand and Hartmann (1984) recommended that the size of the interval be at least as long as the average duration of a single response but short enough so that two complete responses normally cannot occur in the same interval. You may count a behavior as occurring according to a proportion of the interval during which it took place (e.g., 50 percent or more of the interval) or if the behavior occurred at all during the interval (Gelfand & Hartmann, 1984). The latter procedure is easier and more reliable. When observing several behaviors simultaneously, it may be easier to observe for one interval and use the next to record your observations (ten seconds to observe, ten seconds to record, etc.). It also

Figure 3.3 Sample Interval Recording Form

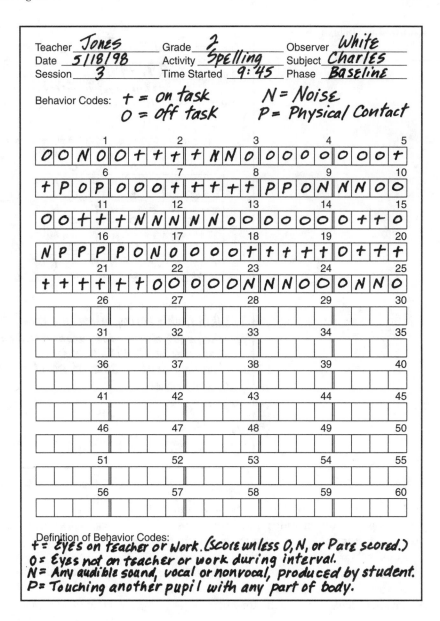

Teacher **Jones** Grade **2** Observer **White**
Date **5/18/98** Activity **Spelling** Subject **Charles**
Session **3** Time Started **9:45** Phase **Baseline**

Behavior Codes: **+ = on task   N = Noise**
O = off task   P = Physical Contact

	1			2			3			4			5	
O	O	N	O	O	+	+	+	+	N	N	O	O	O	O
	6			7			8			9			10	
O	O	O	+				O	O	O				+	

Definition of Behavior Codes:
+ = Eyes on teacher or work. (Score unless O, N, or P are scored.)
O = Eyes not on teacher or work during interval.
N = Any audible sound, vocal or nonvocal, produced by student.
P = Touching another pupil with any part of body.

is possible to arrange your recording sheet to allow more time for observing than for recording (e.g., fifteen seconds to observe followed by five seconds to record, or three observation and recording intervals per minute). Figure 3.3 shows interval data collected in fifteen-second blocks. Another option for coding more than one behavior is to preprint recording sheets with the behavior codes written in each interval, as in Figure 3.4. The observer indicates a behavior's occurrence by drawing a slash through the appropriate code. Subsequent chapters contain other examples of interval recording.

In addition to being versatile, interval recording does not require sophisticated equipment. A clipboard and a stopwatch or watch with a sweep

Figure 3.4 Interval
Recording Form

Observer **Dianne McInerney** Student(s) **John**

Date **Oct. 29, 1998** Activity **Science**

Behavior Code(s) **T= talking out, O= out of seat / N= not attending** Time **10:45 – 10:50**

	10 secs.	20 secs.	30 secs.	40 secs.	50 secs.	60 secs.
1	T, O	N	T, O	N	T, O	N	T, O	N	T, O	N	T, O	N
2	T, O	N	T, O	N	T, O	N	T, O	N	T, O	N	T, O	N
3	T, O	N	T, O	N	T, O	N	T, O	N	T, O	N	T, O	N
4	T, O	N	T, O	N	T, O	N	T, O	N	T, O	N	T, O	N
5	T, O	N	T, O	N	T, O	N	T, O	N	T, O	N	T, O	N

Definition of Behavior Codes

T= talking, whispering, or making vocalizations without permission
N= looking out the window, around the room, out into the hall, or sitting with eyes closed
O = leaving seat or seated position during lesson

Total % of Intervals

T= 16.6%
N= 26.6%
O= 13.3%

second hand are all you need.[1] Because interval recording does not provide a measure of absolute frequency, it is not appropriate to report the total number of target behaviors that occurred in a given observation period. Instead, report the percentage of the intervals in which you observed the behavior. Calculate this by the formula:

$$\frac{\text{Number of intervals in which behavior occurred}}{\text{Total number of intervals}} \times 100 = \text{Percent of occurrence}$$

With a little practice, you will become proficient in collecting interval data.

The *scatter plot* (Touchette et al., 1985) described in Chapter 2 is a compromise between rating and interval-scale measurement. Once each interval (e.g., thirty minutes) or instructional period, the practitioner enters a code indicating her estimation of the strength of the target behavior for that interval. However, convenience comes at the price of accuracy, because the scatter plot yields a summary estimate of the behavior rather than an indication of whether it occurred in a much briefer time period.

---

[1] However, to increase the reliability of interval recording, use a device to signal the beginning and end of an observation interval. For example, beeps or verbal signals ("fifty seconds . . . one minute . . . ten seconds") may be recorded on an audiotape and replayed via an earphone for the observer to use while recording. Calculators that signal time intervals also may be used for this purpose. The audible signal they produce may distract students, however, and therefore these devices should be used when the observer is separated from the group (e.g., in an observation room), or with an earpiece so the sound can be detected only by the observer.

Time Sampling If you do not have a block of time to devote to observing and recording, if you want to sample behaviors across an extended time period or across settings, or if you are monitoring a number of pupils or behaviors, a time sampling technique may suit your needs. **Time sampling** is similar to interval recording, but the intervals are much longer (one to twenty minutes), less frequent, and may be variable. There are many variations to this approach. For example, you may take a five-minute sample out of every hour, or take one momentary sample every five minutes, or sample behavior on a variable interval schedule. If you employ a **momentary time sampling procedure,** rate the occurrence or nonoccurrence of the target behavior immediately following a specified interval of time (Cooper, 1981). In this case, it is advisable to use a kitchen or wristwatch timer to signal when to observe. Set the timer for the desired interval and when it rings, record whether the behavior is occurring (remember to reset the timer after recording). Kubany and Slogett (1973) developed a recording form to use in conjunction with a timer set for variable schedules averaging four, eight, or sixteen minutes (see Figure 3.5). The advantage of a variable observation schedule is the unpredictability of each interval. Students may be aware of the behavior being observed, but cannot predict each interval and change their behavior when the timer is due to ring. This strategy is particularly useful for measuring the behavior of a group of pupils relative to classroom rules, for example. When the timer rings, you can check which pupils are on task, in-seat, and so forth. A similiar procedure is PLACHECK (Hall, 1973), which involves recording which students are engaged in a particular activity at the end of specified intervals. Pupils also may be trained to take momentary time sample data.

Observing and Recording Multiple Behaviors of Students

As some of the examples we have presented indicate, event, interval, and time sampling formats can be adapted to monitor several behaviors simultaneously. Sometimes researchers measure a number of behaviors at the same time, but we do not recommend that you attempt such complex recording systems without appropriate training. Teachers usually can observe and record up to four behaviors accurately by using appropriately constructed interval recording formats. There are occasions when you may want to monitor two students who are exhibiting the same behaviors or when you may want to collect simultaneous data on the target pupil's behavior and that of selected peers, either as a basis for comparison with the target pupil or for setting a criterion level (see Chapter 2). One way to accomplish this using an interval format is to observe and record one student's behavior for ten seconds. Then observe and record the second pupil's, and so on, until you have sampled the behavior of all pupils you wish to observe. Observe pupils in the same sequence (Jim, then Vernon, then Carol, then Yolanda, etc.) during any single observation session but vary the sequence from session to session to avoid unintentional bias. Kubany and Sloggett's (1973) variable-interval procedure or Hall's (1973) PLACHECK strategy may be used if you are observing the same behavior for each student. Figure 3.6 shows an interval recording form developed for this purpose. When recording more than one behavior or the behavior of more than one student, be careful not to make your data-collection task too great. The advantages of having more data may be erased by the problem of low reliability. When attempting new or complex recording procedures, practice collecting data with a reliable observer until you reach 80 to 90 percent agreement. Remember to recheck your reliability frequently.

Student Portfolios

Educational reform efforts that call for increasing literacy and academic achievement among school-age children have posed a dilemma for professionals working with students with disabilities. Should these pupils be required to take standardized tests along with their typical peers, and should their scores be averaged in with those of their school or district? One response that does not place students or schools at a disadvantage is to develop alternative assessment and reporting strategies. Student portfolios are a viable

Figure 3.5 Variable Interval Recording Form

Target Behavior *On task (✓)*　　Date *5/18/98*

Schedule *VI 4 min.*　　　　　Student *Rob*

　　　　　　　　　　　　　　　Teacher *Jones*

　　　　　　　　　　　　　　　Starting time *8:40*

　　　　　　　　　　　　　　　Activity *Language Arts*

VI Schedule (in minutes)

Comments	Four		Eight	Sixteen
	2	✓	12	12
	5	—	2	8
	7	✓	10	28
	1	✓	4	2
	3	✓	6	24
	6	—	14	6
	4	✓	8	24
	6	—	2	6
	4	—	10	30
	1	✓	14	12
	2	✓	8	16
	5	✓	10	4
Came in from fire drill	3	—	6	8
	7	—	4	30
	2	—	12	28
	1	✓	4	6
	7	—	12	24
	3	✓	14	16
	4	—	2	12
	5	✓	6	2

Scoring Key: ✓ = on-task
— = off-task

Source: Kubany, E. S., & Slogett, B. B. (1973). Coding procedure for teachers. *Journal of Applied Behavior Analysis, 6,* 330–334. Used with permission.

alternative. A student portfolio contains information systematically compiled from relevant curricular domains that documents student change and growth over time (Swicegood, 1994). Therefore, portfolios offer a means of monitoring student progress across curricula and ecological settings.

Table 3.4 suggests the types of information you may enter into student portfolios.

Portfolios are developed through a team process, involving all who participate in delivering services listed on the student's IEP. The student should assume increasing responsibility

Figure 3.6 Interval Recording Form for Monitoring Four Students

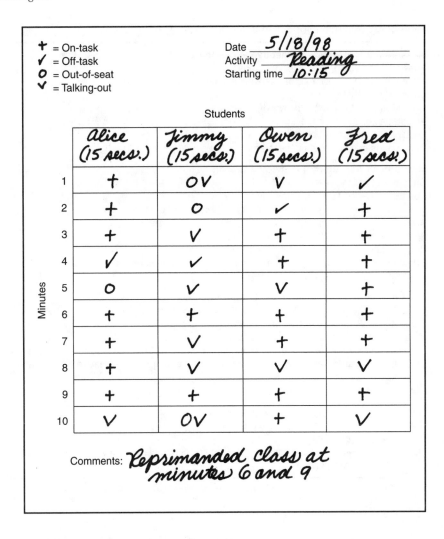

| + = On-task
✓ = Off-task
O = Out-of-seat
V = Talking-out | | Date _5/18/98_
Activity _Reading_
Starting time _10:15_ | | |

Students

Minutes	Alice (15 secs.)	Jimmy (15 secs.)	Owen (15 secs.)	Fred (15 secs.)
1	+	OV	V	✓
2	+	O	✓	+
3	+	V	+	+
4	✓	✓	+	+
5	O	V	V	+
6	+	+	+	+
7	+	V	+	+
8	+	V	V	V
9	+	+	+	+
10	V	OV	+	V

Comments: *Reprimanded class at minutes 6 and 9*

for managing his portfolio, and it should be reviewed and updated frequently by the student, his parents, and relevant professionals. Make the shift to portfolio assessment carefully and allow sufficient time for students, parents, and staff to learn to use them properly (Swicegood, 1994). See the following sources for more information about portfolio assessment:

Belanoff, P., & Dickson, M. (Eds.). (1991). *Portfolios: Process and product.* Portsmouth, NH: Heinemann.

Graves, D. H., & Sunstein, B. S. (Eds.). (1992). *Portfolio portraits.* Portsmouth, NH: Heinemann.

Paulson, F. L., Paulson, P. R., & Meyer, C. A. (1991). What makes a portfolio a portfolio? *Educational Leadership, 48,* 60–63.

Swicegood, P. (1994). Portfolio-based assessment practices: The uses of portfolio assessment for students with behavioral disorders or learning disabilities. *Intervention in School and Clinic, 30*(1), 6–15.

Tierney, R. J., Carter, M. A., & Desai, L. E. (1991). *Portfolio assessment in the reading-writing classroom.* Norwood, CA: Christopher-Gordon.

Valencia, S. (1990). A portfolio approach to classroom reading assessment: The whys, whats, and hows. *The Reading Teacher, 43,* 338–340.

Using Computers to Observe and Record Behaviors

The computer revolution has affected nearly every aspect of education, and data-collection

Table 3.4 Possible Information to Include in Student Portfolios

Measures of Behavior and Adaptive Functioning
Anecdotal records or critical incident logs
Observations of behavior across settings and conditions
Behavior checklists
Interviews about interests, motivation, and attributions
Videotapes of student behaviors
Social skills ratings and checklists
Peer ratings and sociometric measures

Measures of Academic and Literacy Growth
Criterion-referenced tests
Curriculum-based assessments
Teacher-made tests in selected literacy or content-area domains
Analysis of oral reading such as informal reading inventories
Writing samples collected over time
Photographs of student projects
Running records in reading, writing, or math, such as "stories read and completed"
Classroom tests in spelling, math, etc.

Measures of Strategic Learning and Self-Regulation
Ratings and checklists of skills or strategies a student is using
Student self-evaluations of task performance
Miscue analysis procedure in oral reading
Interviews and questions about how a student performs in literacy and classroom tasks
Student thinks aloud: Verbal descriptions of strategies and operations used in different academic situations
Excerpts from teacher-student dialogue journals
Observations and ratings of study skills

Measures of Language and Cultural Aspects
Cultural interviews with students and parents
Primary language sample
Observations of student responses to changing social and classroom situations
Simulations and role-plays

Source: Swicegood, P. (1994). Portfolio-based assessment practices: The uses of portfolio assessment for students with behavioral disorders or learning disabilities. *Intervention in School and Clinic, 30,* (1), 9. Copyright 1994 PRO-ED. Used with permission.

technology is no exception. A variety of computer software and hardware is available for observing behavior and for recording and plotting data from direct observations. Laptop computers are capable of recording and storing data on a number of coded behaviors, or the data can be fed simultaneously into a monitor that displays a graphic record of the data as they are recorded. For example, the UPWARD system developed by Reith, Haus, and Bahr (1989) consists of 11 categories that include 97 specific teacher, student, and class behaviors. The observer codes data on a Zenith A-181 laptop computer. The system automatically formats and stores the data for direct use with most statistical analysis programs. Denny

and Fox (1989) developed a portable microcomputer and software system for observational data collection in school settings.

A disadvantage of many computer-based observational systems is that the observer must enter data at the computer keyboard. Even laptop computers can be cumbersome and obtrusive at times. Johnson et al. (1995) designed a system that allows for unobtrusive data collection in natural settings through a remote recording device that allows the observer to enter event, interval, duration, or latency data in settings other than those in which the computer is located. The case study at the end of this chapter describes this system.

Sophisticated computer technology is not out of the reach of classroom observers. Many schools now have microcomputers in some or all classrooms. Programs are available that will turn a classroom computer into a data-collection and plotting instrument (e.g., Zuckerman, 1987). Investigate these labor-saving data-collection and analysis systems with your school's technology specialist.

Assessing Reliability

If all human behavior could be observed and recorded automatically by machines (as the disk pecks or lever presses of laboratory animals are recorded), reliability of measurement would be a minor concern. However, we must rely upon our own powers of observation, and this raises the question of the accuracy of the observer's estimates. In the classroom, if the target behaviors result in a permanent product (math worksheet, spelling test, carburetor assembled), reliability of measurement is relatively certain. But most social behaviors are ephemeral; they leave no trace. Unless you are able to obtain an audio or video recording of the student's performance, your accuracy in observing and recording behavioral occurrences is a major concern. Human observers are biased rather easily, and their measures may be influenced by many subjective factors. Also, changes in observed behaviors may be due to errors of measurement rather than to actual changes in behavior resulting from intervention procedures.

For observational measures to be reliable, the behaviors to be observed must be specifically and objectively defined (Cooper, 1981), meaning observations must be confined to what the student actually does rather than reflecting a generalization or impression. Consider the difficulty you might have in measuring "hostile" remarks or "pesky" noises. Human behaviors are objectively defined if two or more persons agree on whether they occurred. It is unlikely that high interobserver agreement could be obtained for either of the behaviors we just mentioned. What is "hostile" or "pesky" to one person may not be to another. To make these behavioral definitions specific and objective, we would ask: What does the

pupil do that makes you interpret her remarks as hostile or her noises as pesky? To answer this question we might prepare a list of specific behaviors, the occurrence or nonoccurrence of which two independent persons could agree upon. She says to others, "Go to hell," "I don't like you," "Your momma," and so forth; she taps her pencil against her desk; she squeaks her chair; she belches.

It is not sufficient to develop definitions of target behavior about which two observers *could* agree, however. The primary criterion for evaluating the adequacy of a behavioral definition is the extent to which independent observers *do* agree that they have observed the same levels of behavior during the same observational period (Hall, 1973). Only then can we feel relatively confident that the data reflect what the pupil is actually doing and not measurement error. Several methods are used to assess agreement between observers. The simplest is **total reliability** (Kelly, 1977), determined by dividing the smaller obtained frequency by the larger and multiplying by 100. This method is appropriate for comparing total numerical counts of behaviors or products (Koorland & Westling, 1981). For example, if two observers counted seven and eight episodes of self-stimulation in a thirty-minute period, their reliability would be 7/8 x 100 = 88 percent. **Point-by-point reliability** is used when discrete units of observation, such as time intervals or trials, are being compared (Koorland & Westling, 1981). For each time interval or opportunity to observe the behavior, two observers may agree or disagree as to its occurrence (i.e., they both may "see" the behavior as defined, or they both may not see it, or one may see it although the other does not). Thus reliability is calculated by:

$$\frac{\text{Number of agreements}}{\text{Agreements} + \text{Disagreements}} \times 100 = \text{Percent of agreement}$$

If, for instance, off-task behavior is being observed in ten-second blocks for 30 minutes, there would be six observations per minute, or 180 observations for the thirty-minute period. If two observers agreed (that off-task behavior occurred or did not occur) on 150 of these observations and disagreed on 30, their reliability would be

$$\frac{150}{150 + 30} \times 100 = 83 \text{ percent}$$

To assess the reliability of occurrences and non-occurrences separately, use the point-by-point method. Insert the number of intervals in which one or both observers scored an occurrence (or nonoccurrence) as the denominator (e.g., agreement and disagreements regarding occurrences).

Tawney and Gast (1984) recommend that inter-observer agreement regarding *occurrences* be computed when the target behavior is reported to have occurred in less than 75 percent of the intervals observed. Only the intervals in which at least one observer recorded an occurrence are compared. On the other hand, agreement regarding *nonoccurrences* should be computed when the target behavior is observed in more than 75 percent of the intervals. This comparison involves only those intervals in which at least one observer recorded a nonoccurrence. Computing occurrence and nonoccurrence reliabilities separately provides a more rigorous and conservative estimate of interobserver agreement.

Reliability actually is a statistical concept. The above formulas yield **percentage of interobserver agreement** rather than true reliability. Statistical reliability of observational measures typically is computed by using Pearson's *r* or a comparable procedure. It is used when comparing data obtained from numerous recordings of behavior (Koorland & Westling, 1981). You are not likely to encounter occasions when it is important to determine statistical reliability; therefore, use one of the percentage agreement methods instead.

There are no hard-and-fast rules for determining how much agreement is enough. When observing low levels of behavior, a single disagreement may make a difference of several percentage points when the total reliability method is used. Generally, 80 percent agreement is considered satisfactory but 90 percent or better is preferred (Gast & Gast, 1981; Koorland & Westling

1981). Use periodic reliability checks to rule out gradual changes in the observers' interpretation regarding the occurrence or nonoccurrence of a behavior. Conduct reliability checks at least once during each program phase, and otherwise once a week, unless you are measuring permanent products. If interobserver agreement is below 80 percent, check with your reliability observer regarding scorable instances and noninstances of the behaviors observed before resuming formal data collection. If agreement is below 90 percent, follow the same procedure without interrupting formal data collection. However, in both cases conduct additional reliability checks to ensure that disagreements have been resolved.

The procedure you select to assess reliability will depend upon your measurement strategy. Total reliability is better suited to event, frequency, or rate data, or for determining scoring agreement on permanent products. The point-by-point approach is more useful when several behaviors are being observed and recorded simultaneously, when interval data are recorded, or when pupil responses to discrete learning trials are being measured. If you are unsure of the approach to use, consult someone more experienced in behavioral measurement.

Summarizing Data

Obviously, if your observations are recorded with a wrist counter, on scraps of paper, or on an interval data sheet, you will want to transfer the data to a central form, both for convenience and safekeeping. Such forms need not be elaborate, but they should contain all relevant information: dates, sessions, observation time, data taken, and program phase. Figure 3.7 is a data summary sheet for rate data measured in terms of responses per minute. Such forms centralize your data for easy reference and for transfer to a chart or graph.

Data summaries can be organized to eliminate the necessity of graphing or charting. For example, Nelson et al. (1979) developed an IEP performance chart to monitor progress on task

Figure 3.7 Rate Data Summary Sheet

Adviser **Magee   Jerry**
          (last)   (first)

Manager **Swenson Margaret**
          (last)   (first)

Protege **Issacs   Jean**
          (last)   (first)

Target **Offers to share with peers**

Phase	Session	Number of responses	Time (minutes)	Rate (number of responses per minute)	Consequence
baseline	1	0	30	0	
	2	0	30	0	
	3	10	30	.33	
	4	0	30	0	
	5	0	30	0	
Intervention 1	6	9	30	.30	1 min. free
	7	11	30	.35	time if .33
	8	5	30	.18	per min.
	9	9	30	.30	
	10	13	30	.42	
	11	8	30	.27	
	12	5	30	.18	
Intervention 2	13	16	30	.52	Sit by
	14	13	30	.42	preferred
	15	18	30	.58	peer if
	16	11	30	.35	.42 per min.
	17	16	30	.52	
	18	20	30	.62	
	19	17	30	.55	
	20	20	30	.64	
	21	17	30	.55	Lunch with
	22	20	30	.64	preferred
	23	20	30	.64	peer if
	24	18	30	.58	.52 per min.
	25	20	30	.64	
	26	20	30	.64	
	27	20	30	.64	
	28				
	29				
	30				

steps or short-term objectives. Figure 3.8 shows how the system can be used to summarize performance regarding several targeted social behaviors. In this figure an X indicates that a criterion was met for a particular behavior, a / (slash) indicates that a criterion was not met, and the daily total indicates whether the short-term objective was met for that day.

Another procedure was developed by Fabry and Cone (1980) for trial-by-trial recording (for recording student responses to individual prompts given by the teacher over a set of discrete trials). In this procedure, an X indicates a correct response and an O designates an error response. Figure 3.9 illustrates three uses of this procedure. The left-hand portion displays a summary of

Figure 3.8 IEP Performance Chart

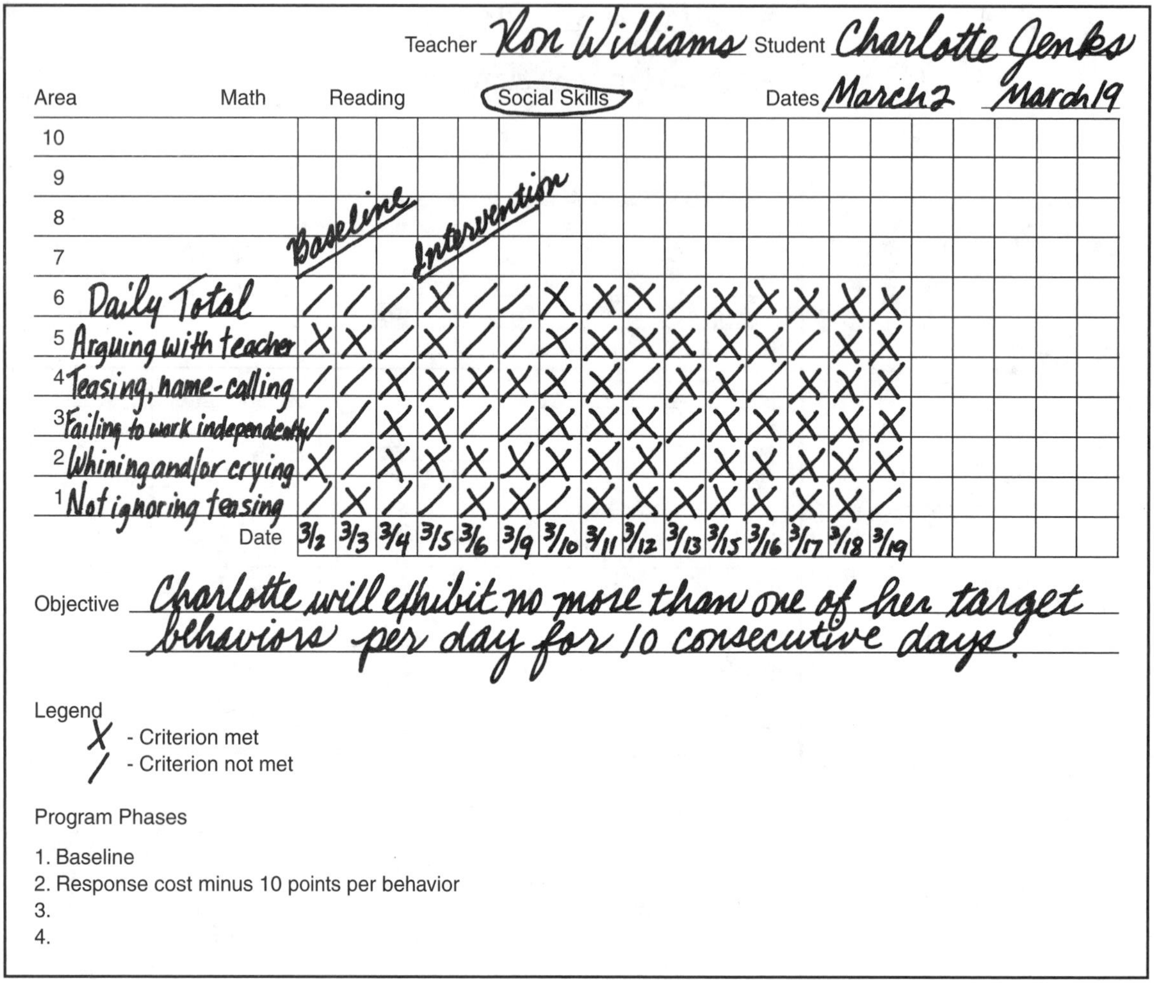

Teacher _Ron Williams_ Student _Charlotte Jenks_

| Area | Math | Reading | (Social Skills) | Dates _March 2_ _March 19_ |

Baseline Intervention

	3/2	3/3	3/4	3/5	3/6	3/9	3/10	3/11	3/12	3/13	3/15	3/16	3/17	3/18	3/19
6 Daily Total	/	/	X	/	/	X	X	X	/	X	X	X	X	X	
5 Arguing with teacher	X	X	/	X	/	/	X	X	X	X	X	X	/	X	X
4 Teasing, name-calling	/	/	X	X	X	X	X	/	X	X	X	/	X	X	X
3 Failing to work independently	/	/	X	X	/	/	X	X	X	X	/	X	X	X	X
2 Whining and/or crying	X	/	/	X	X	X	X	X	/	X	X	X	X	X	X
1 Not ignoring teasing	/	X	/	/	X	/	X	X	X	X	X	X	X	/	/

Objective _Charlotte will exhibit no more than one of her target behaviors per day for 10 consecutive days._

Legend

X - Criterion met

/ - Criterion not met

Program Phases

1. Baseline
2. Response cost minus 10 points per behavior
3.
4.

---

pupil responses to each trial across sessions. The middle portion shows these same data, but the teacher has charted correct responses cumulatively from the bottom of the chart and entered errors from the top down. A graph of these data may be produced by connecting the Xs representing the cumulative total of correct responses for each session. The right-hand portion summarizes the same students' performance, but the teacher also entered the number of each trial according to whether the response was correct or incorrect. Thus, trials 3, 4, 6, and 9 in session 1 were correct. These data also have been

transformed into a graph by connecting the cells representing the last correct trial per session. The advantage of this procedure is that the teacher can collect, summarize, and graph student performance while administering instructional trials.

A final variation of Fabry and Cone's (1980) system is to substitute time intervals for trials. Interval lengths are set according to a predetermined variable interval schedule (see the left side of Figure 3.9). The teacher sets a timer for the designated interval lengths and when it rings, enters the appropriate symbol for the pupil's response, as in Kubany and Slogett's (1973)

Figure 3.9 Auto-Graphing Data Forms

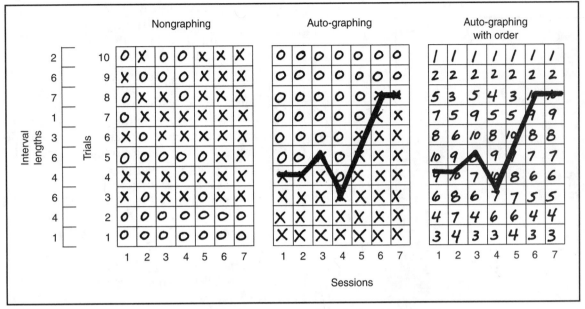

Source: Fabry, B. D. &. Cone, J. D. (1980). Auto-graphing: A one-step approach to collecting and graphing data.
Education and Treatment of Children, 3, 361–368. Used with permission.

procedure. These data may be arranged to create a graph, just as when trial-by-trial data are recorded.

Graphing and Charting

If you employ either of the charting systems just presented, you already may have a useful visual display. However, there are other meaningful ways to present visually. Remember that most teachers can get many kinds of data pertaining to student performance. Much of it is work samples, weekly test scores, or results of standardized achievement tests. Such data are used infrequently for program decision making because these samples are not organized to be useful for this purpose: they do not show trends in student performance or compare performance to predetermined criteria. Nongraphic data summary forms such as that depicted in Figure 3.7 do organize the data, but they fail to display trends or communicate clearly to anyone who is not intimately familiar with the program or student they represent. On the other hand, graphs and charts meet these goals. A **graph** typically uses only one

or two symbols to represent data (e.g., a dot or a triangle). A **chart,** however, displays from several to many symbols to represent the data. All types of graphs and charts serve three important purposes: they summarize data in a manner convenient for precise, daily decision making; they communicate program effects; and they provide reinforcement and feedback to those persons involved with the program.

There are as many types of charts and graphs as there are behaviors to monitor. However, these can be grouped into a few categories. The selection of any particular type depends on the considerations listed in Table 3.3, as well as on the type of data to be presented. A **bar graph** may be used to show progress toward a specific goal or objective. For example, Figure 3.10 shows a student's progress toward earning a class party through appropriate classroom behavior. This type of graph is useful for presenting data to be used by students because it is easily interpreted and may be reinforcing. Pupils may also be reinforced by filling in the graph each day.

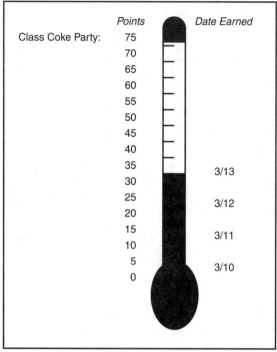

Figure 3.10 Susan's Progress Toward a Class Party

Another type of bar graph, shown in Figure 3.11, provides a better display of daily fluctuations in student performance. Bar graphs may be used to plot any kind of data and they are easily understood by pupils, parents, and other lay persons. An even simpler presentation is a star chart, shown in Figure 3.12. Charts such as these can be sent home to parents as daily or weekly reports. Charts that report the results of behavior (points earned, stars) instead of the behavior itself are reinforcing and do communicate readily, but they do not provide the kind of data useful to teachers for decision-making purposes.

The graph pictured in Figure 3.10 is **cumulative;** each day's total is added to the previous day's earnings. Line graphs may also be cumulative, as shown in Figure 3.13. Although you may plot cumulative time, percentages, frequencies, or rates of either appropriate or inappropriate behavior, if the graph is to be used by the student plot desired behavior (e.g., time in-seat instead of time out-of-seat) so that increases in level will be associated with gains, not losses.

Figure 3.11 Arnold's Percent of Assignments Completed

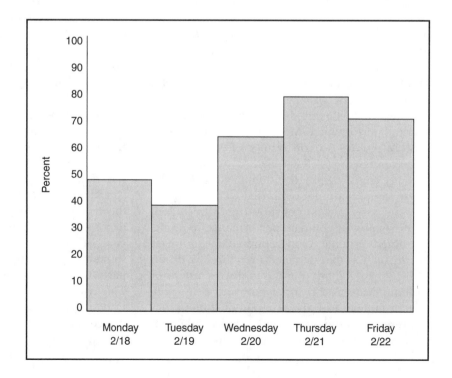

Figure 3.12 Mary's Good
Behavior Chart

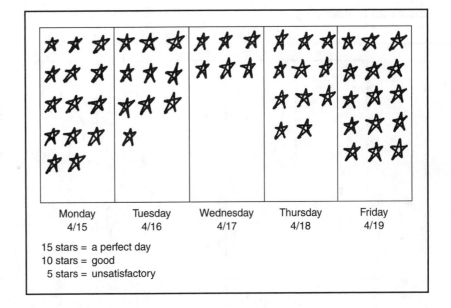

A noncumulative frequency graph, or **frequency polygon,** is the most common type used in behavioral research, and is the type most useful in data-based decision making. It may be used to report frequency, rate, or percent data. Frequency polygons are illustrated in Figures 3.14 and 3.15. Numerical frequency is plotted in Figure 3.14 and rate movements per minute is graphed in Figure 3.15.

Figure 3.13 David: Math
Facts Learned

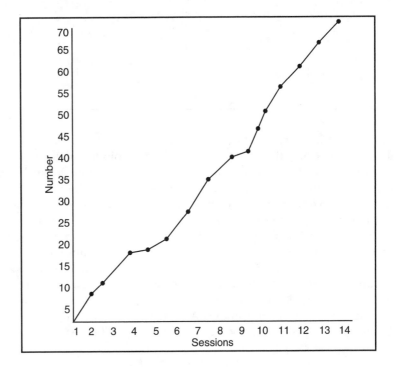

Figure 3.14   Kay: Talk Outs

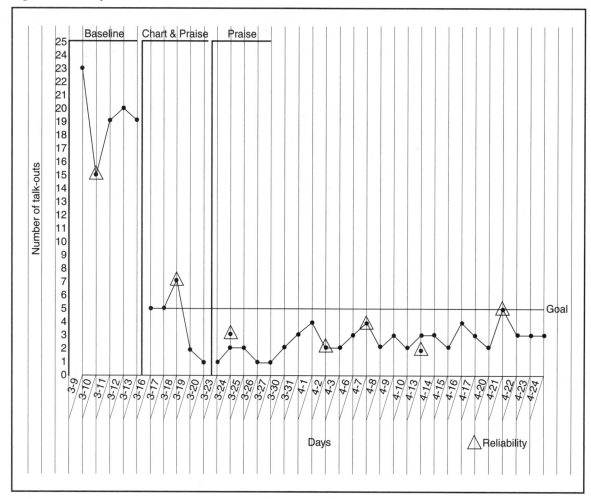

Figure 3.14 illustrates plotting on **equal interval** graph paper (i.e., the difference between a frequency of 15 and 16 is equal to the difference between that of 19 and 20). Figure 3.15 shows data plotted on **equal ratio** or semilogarithmic graph paper, on which equal changes in rate show up as identical changes in the slope of the data path regardless of their absolute rate. For example, a change in rate from .1 to .2 movements per minute or from 5 to 10 movements per minute, or an acceleration in rate of times 2, show up as identical slopes on the graph. Although equal ratio graph paper may be confusing to

those who are not accustomed to it, the rules for plotting data are learned quickly. Also, this standard semilogarithmic charting paper offers several advantages: it saves time in drawing and scaling graphs; it allows behaviors occurring anywhere between 1 time in 24 hours and 1,000 times per minute to be plotted on the same graph; it permits comparison across different times and activities when the amount of time or number of opportunities to respond varies; and once persons become familiar with the ratio scale, time is saved in reading and interpreting the plotted data (White, 1986). The major disadvantage of equal

Figure 3.15 Doug: Rate of Assignment Completion

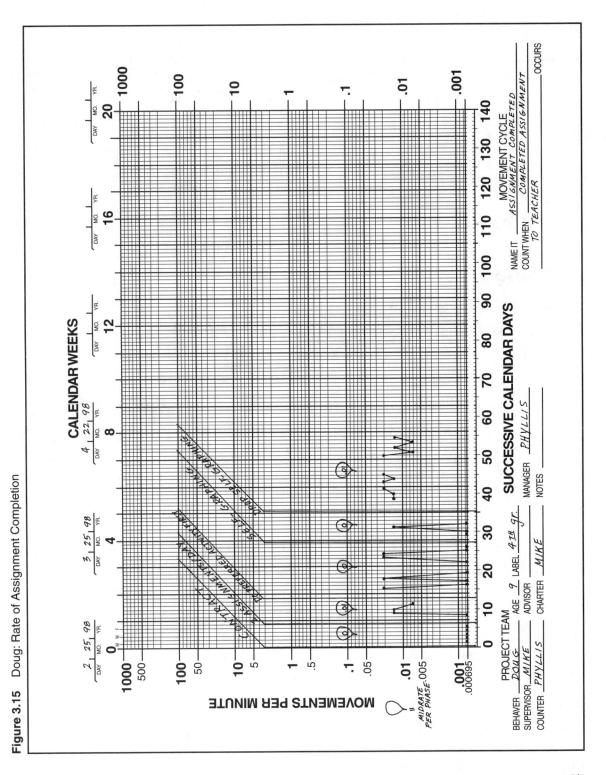

97

Figure 3.16   Progress Chart: Dolch Words

IEP Performance Chart	Teacher _Williams_									Student _Donnie_									
Area Math (Reading) Social Skills (circle one) Dates _Oct. 1_ to _Oct. 26_																			
10																			
9																			
8																			
7																			
6 6th 10 words										T/7	T/9	T/X	T/X	T/X	X				
5 5th 10 words								T/X	T/6	T/6	T/8	T/X	T/X	T/X	T/X	T/X			X
4 4th 10 words							T/X	T/X	T/X	T/X	T/X	-/9	T/X	T/X					-/8
3 3rd 10 words					T/9	T/X	T/X	T/X	T/X	T/X			-/8	T/X	T/X				X
2 2nd 10 words			T/7	T/9	T/X	T/X	T/X	T/X	T/X	-/9	T/X	T/X	X						X
1 1st 10 words	T/6	T/7	T/X	T/X	T/X	T/X	T/X		X		X								X
Date	10/1	2	3	4	5	10/8	9	10	11	12	10/15	16	17	18	19	10/22	23	24	25	26

Objective   _Given 110 Dolch sight words, presented on flash cards, Donnie will call each word correctly the first time for 5 consecutive sessions._

Legend

T/#	Training/number correct		X	Assessment, criterion met
T/X	Training/criterion met (10/10 words)		/#	Assessment, criterion not met, # correct

Comments _____

_____

ratio graphing is that it is cumbersome to collect data on students' responses per minute when each response is controlled by the teacher's instruction (e.g., "Do this". . . "Now do this" . . .) because, in order to measure only the pupil's rate of response, the teacher would have to subtract the time required to give each instruction from the time period in which response rate was measured (Tawney & Gast, 1984). (Standard semilogarithmic graph paper, called the Standard 'Celeration Chart, may be purchased from Behavior Research Company, Box 251, Kansas City, KS 66103.)

Graphs and charts may be designed to display either student progress or performance. A **progress graph** or **chart** shows the time it takes a student to master a set of objectives (Deno & Mirkin, 1978). For example, Figure 3.16 is a chart of a student's progress toward mastery of 110 words in the Dolch list. A **performance chart**

Figure 3.17   Performance Graph: Dolch Words

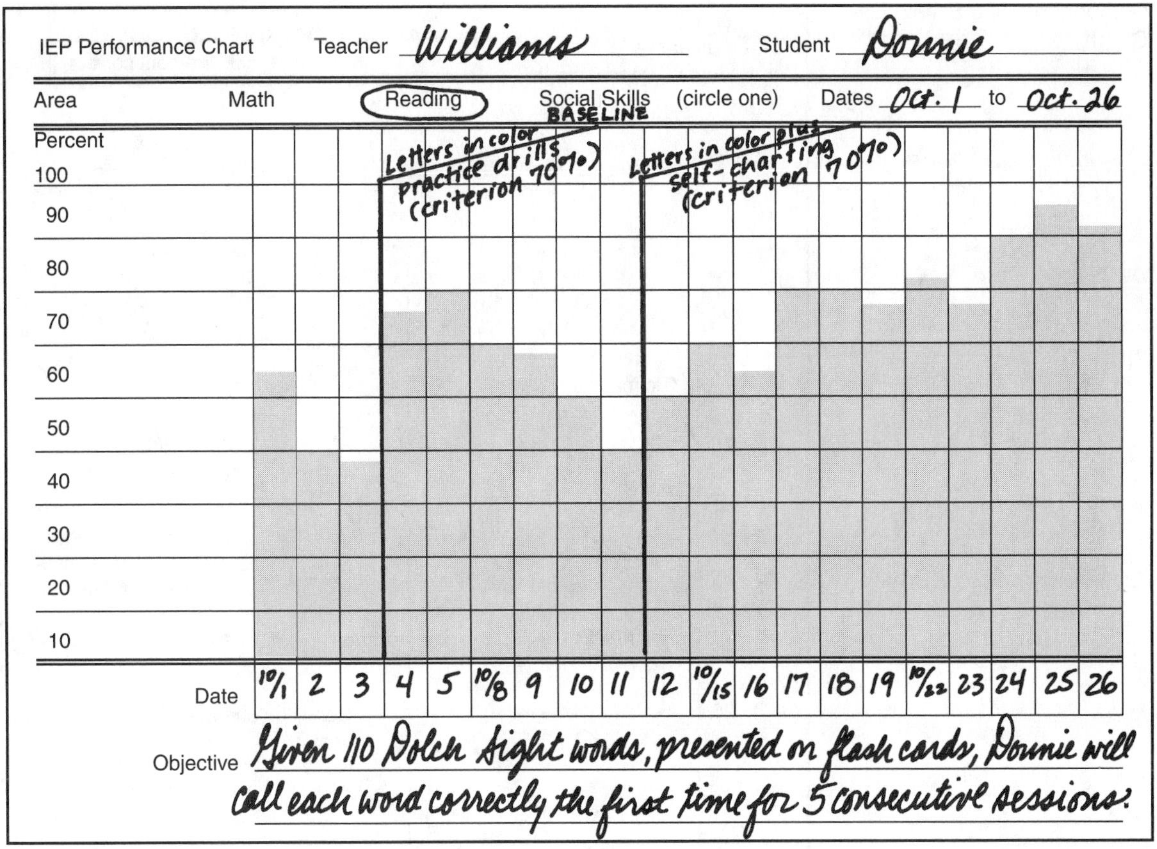

| IEP Performance Chart | Teacher *Williams* | Student *Donnie* |

Area   Math   (Reading)   Social Skills   (circle one)   Dates *Oct. 1* to *Oct. 26*

Objective: *Given 110 Dolch sight words, presented on flash cards, Donnie will call each word correctly the first time for 5 consecutive sessions.*

or **graph,** on the other hand, reports a change on a single task or behavior (Deno & Mirkin, 1978). The same type of data may be charted either way. For example, Figure 3.17 shows student daily performance on the same set of Dolch words. Whether you select progress or performance graphs depends on the kind of data you will be using to make decisions: daily performance or sequential progress (Deno & Mirkin, 1978). Your choice also will be influenced by your instructional strategy. If you have task-analyzed your terminal objective, for instance, progress charting will be more suitable. Performance graphs or charts are better suited for monitoring most social behaviors, unless you are using direct teaching procedures to shape a particular skill or behavior.

The communication function of charts and graphs is not fulfilled if they are cluttered or inconsistent or if the reader cannot follow what is being reported. Tawney and Gast (1984) indicate that graphic presentations of data should communicate to the reader: the sequence of baseline and intervention conditions, the time spent in each condition, the independent and dependent variables, the experimental design used, and the relationships among variables. Figure 3.18 identifies the major components of a frequency polygon or simple line graph. Because charts use a variety of symbols to represent the data, they require more elaborate legends, but the basic parts are the same. Condition lines are used to designate where changes in conditions are made. Generally, behavior graphs begin with a baseline condition, followed by intervention conditions that may include phase changes (adjustments in the intervention; e.g., a change in the

Figure 3.18 Basic Components of a Simple Line Graph

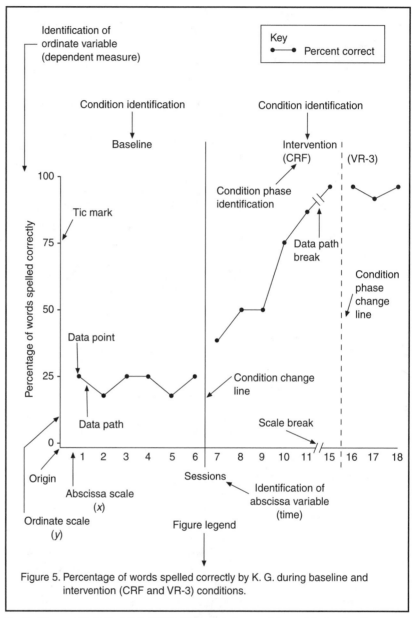

Figure 5. Percentage of words spelled correctly by K. G. during baseline and intervention (CRF and VR-3) conditions.

Source: Tawney, J. W., & Gast, D. L. (1984). *Single subject research in special education.* Upper Saddle River, NJ: Merrill/Prentice Hall. Used with permission.

schedule of reinforcement). Intervention conditions and phases should be labeled descriptively, but briefly, so the reader knows what conditions are in effect at any given time. The examples we have provided in this chapter illustrate the range of options possible without grossly violating these guidelines. With practice you will be able to construct useful graphs quickly and efficiently. Your pupils can learn to construct graphs and plot data too (self-graphing may be a reinforcer for students interested in their own progress). Readers interested in a more in-depth discussion of graph construction should consult Tawney and Gast (1984). A number of software programs are available for creating charts and graphs.

SUMMARY

This chapter has addressed the important area of monitoring student performance. The range of procedures for measuring human behavior is expanding rapidly. We have attempted to present important considerations regarding the collection and use of behavioral data in educational settings and to provide sample strategies which you may use in designing your own procedures for monitoring students' educational progress. Although there are no tangible incentives to encourage data-based instruction or intervention, research indicates that pupils whose teachers monitor their performance make greater progress than those who do not (Fuchs, 1986). Practice in data collection and graphing will increase your fluency and confidence.

 CASE STUDY

THE DIRECT OBSERVATION DATA SYSTEM (DODS)[1]

Happy Johnson, Department of Special Education, Trenton State College

Four students in Ms. Brady's regular fourth-grade class are classified as having EBD. One student in particular, Daryl, presents a unique challenge. Daryl is of average intelligence, but he has difficulty staying on task, rarely completes assignments, and as a result is not learning.

Ms. Brady contacted the Teacher Assistance Team in her school for some suggestions on how best to help Daryl. Ms Brady and the Teacher Assistance Team decided to focus on increasing Daryl's on-task behavior. It was decided that the team needed a clear picture of just how much time Daryl spent on and off task. Ms. Brady was asked to collect direct observational data on Daryl's off-task behavior for five consecutive days. She was to collect these data twice a day, once for 20 minutes during the morning session and once for 20 minutes during the afternoon session. At the end of each day the data were to be summarized and then graphed. It was agreed that the team would meet on the fifth day to review the results and plan an intervention to increase Daryl's on-task behavior. Although in agreement with the team's decision, Ms. Brady was concerned about how she would accomplish this additional task while carrying out her other duties (e.g., teaching, record keeping).

Mr. Blackhurst, a resource room teacher and a member of the Teacher Assistance Team, recommended that Ms. Brady use the *Direct Observation Data System (DODS)*. He explained that the *DODS* materials are a set of programs designed for use by regular and special education teachers, school psychologists, guidance counselors, classroom aides, parents, and anyone else who has a need to collect direct observational data (see Johnson, Brady & Larson, in press, for a complete explanation of the *DODS*). The purpose of the *DODS* materials is to facilitate the collection, summation, graphing, and reporting of assessment data.

Table 3.5   Direct Observation Data System (DODS)

Data selection advisor
Direct observation data systems
Occurrence/Event data collection program
Duration data collection program
Latency data collection program
Interval data collection program
Momentary time-sampling data collection program
Antecedent behavior consequence analysis program
Data analysis advisor
Direct observation data system utilities program

[1] Reprinted with author's permission

(continued)

Figure 3.19 Data Selection Adviser (DSA)

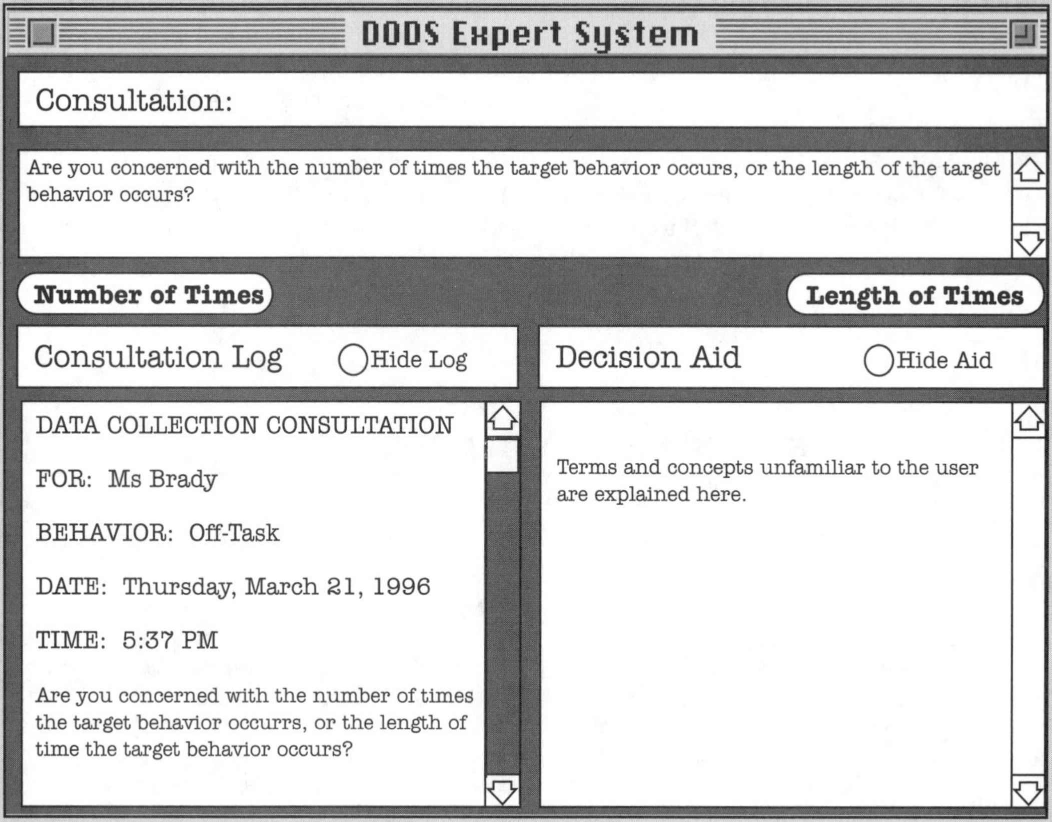

The *DODS* (Table 3.5) consists of four separate, yet interrelated computer programs: the Data Selection Advisor, the Direct Observation Data System programs, the Data Analysis Advisor, and the Direct Observation Data System Utilities Program.

Ms. Brady expressed reservations about being "computer illiterate." Mr. Blackhurst reassured her that the *DODS* was very user-friendly and since Ms. Brady had a computer and printer in her room, she could be trained in about half an hour. With tempered enthusiasm, Ms. Brady agreed.

Ms. Brady began by consulting the Data Selection Advisor (DSA) (Figure 3.19), an expert system designed to assist educators in the selection of an appropriate data-collection procedure. (See Barr & Feigenbaum, 1981, and Hofmeister & Ferrara, 1986, for an explanation of expert systems.) She partici-

pated in a dialogue with the DSA program by typing responses to system-generated questions designed to assess data-collection needs. This question-and-answer format is analogous to a consultation with an expert (e.g., behavioral consultant). The program maintained a consultation log of all system-generated questions and Ms. Brady's decisions. Also, a decision aid was available (see Figure 3.19) to explain unfamiliar terms and concepts. Based on the Ms. Brady's responses and the system's decision rules, the DSA recommended Ms. Brady use the Interval Data Collection Program contained in the DODS.

A unique feature of the DODS is that data may be collected using a remote recording device. (See Johnson, 1995, and Johnson et al., 1995, for a complete description of the remote recording device.) The remote recording device (Figure 3.20) consists of

(continued)

an adapted Macintosh mouse, a radio transmitter, and a radio receiver. Data are collected by depressing the button located on the radio transmitter each time a targeted behavior occurs. The device allows educators to record data when not near the computer. The computer can be located anywhere in the classroom (e.g., in a closet or drawer) or outside the classroom (e.g., in another room or in an office) and the radio transmitter can be held in the hand, clipped to a belt, or put in a pocket. Piloting of the remote recording device indicates that it has a range of 150–200 feet. A remote device has some particularly useful applications when working with special students in inclusive settings; data may be collected without awareness of others and also in nonclassroom settings (e.g., lunchroom, playground, community settings, field trips, at home).

Ms. Brady then turned her attention to the Interval Data Collection Program (Figure 3.21). This program allows the user to select the observation length and interval length and to record the targeted behavior if it occurs at any time during the interval (partial interval), or during the entire interval (whole interval). In order to mark the appropriate interval, the observer must be cued when each interval ends. In the past, observers set timers or used a stopwatch to signal the ending of an interval. The Interval Data Collection Program does away with this need. Whenever the targeted behavior occurs, the user clicks the mouse anywhere on the screen or, if using the remote

recording device, depresses the button located on the radio transmitter. The Interval Data Collection Program monitors the intervals and records the behavior in the appropriate interval.

The Interval Data Collection Program contains the following features: automated data collection (remote recording device) and summation; saving of student data to a cumulative record; graphing of data; and report writing. For each observation, the following data are summarized: total number of occurrences of the behavior, number of intervals when behavior occurred, and number of intervals when behavior did not occur.

Ms. Brady began to collect data on Daryl's off-task behavior. She placed the Interval Data Collection Program from the DODS on to the hard drive of her computer, connected the remote recording device, booted the program and was ready to collect data. While teaching math, Ms. Brady placed the radio transmitter of the remote recording device in her jacket pocket. Each time Daryl was off-task during the lesson, Ms. Brady depressed the button on the radio transmitter and the computer program marked the appropriate interval. If the interval had already been marked, the program ignored the signal from the radio transmitter. When the twenty-minute observation time ended, the program terminated the observation and summarized the data. When the math lesson was completed, Ms. Brady saved the data to a cumulative file and went to lunch, much relieved that her encounter with technology and data collection went so smoothly and successfully.

For the next five consecutive school days Ms. Brady used the Interval Data Collection Program of the DODS and the remote recording device to collect data on Daryl's off-task behavior. When it was time to meet with the Teacher Assistance Team and review the results, Ms. Brady booted up the Interval Data Collection Program, went to the cumulative file, and requested that Daryl's off-task data be graphed. The program immediately graphed the data and printed the graph.

Next, Ms. Brady used the Data Analysis Advisor portion of the *DODS* to analyze Daryl's performance over the last five days. The Data Analysis Advisor is an expert system designed to address this problem. Similar to the Data Selection Advisor mentioned above, the Data Analysis Advisor retrieves a student

(continued)

Figure 3.20 Remote recording device

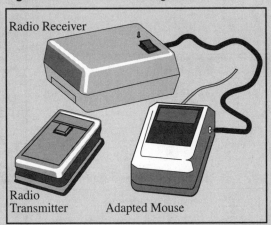

Radio Receiver

Radio Transmitter

Adapted Mouse

cumulative file, analyzes the data, reports the data analysis to the user, and on request, suggests instructional/behavioral refinements or intervention. The purposes of the Data Analysis Advisor are to assist educators in interpreting student progress data (e.g., progress toward instructional/behavioral objective), recommend refinements to existing educational/behavioral interventions (e.g., refine task analysis), or confirm the mastery of an educational/behavioral objective.

Finally, using the report printing function of the *DODS,* Ms. Brady printed a report summarizing Daryl's performance. With report, graphs, and recommendations in hand, Ms. Brady was off to meet with the Teacher Assistance Team.

The Teacher Assistance Team was very impressed with Ms. Brady's results. All team members agreed that Daryl was spending entirely too much time off-task and that this most likely was interfering with his learning. They set about creating a behavior change program to increase Daryl's on-task behavior and decided to use the *DODS* system to track Daryl's progress.

Development of the *DODS* was supported by research and development activities at Trenton State College and the University of Kentucky. Field tests of the occurrence/event, duration, and latency data-collection programs of the *DODS* indicate the following advantages: users can be easily and reliably trained, users report a substantial saving in time and paperwork, and users prefer using the *DODS* to traditional direct-observation data-collection methods (Johnson, 1995; Johnson et al., 1995). At this writing, further development plans include adapting the *DODS* for use on IBM and IBM-compatible platforms, developing a series of user manuals to accompany the *DODS* computer programs, and producing the *DODS* on CD-ROM disk.

Figure 3.21 Interval Data Collection Program

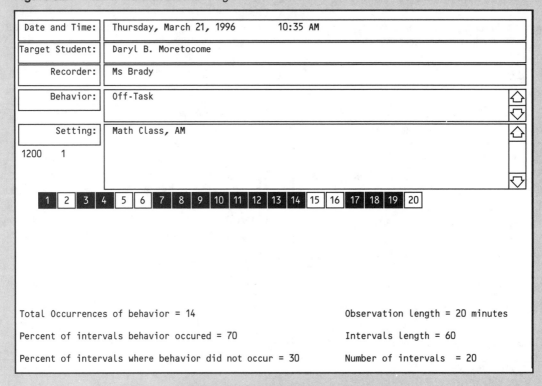

Date and Time:	Thursday, March 21, 1996 10:35 AM
Target Student:	Daryl B. Moretocome
Recorder:	Ms Brady
Behavior:	Off-Task
Setting:	Math Class, AM

1200   1

Total Occurrences of behavior = 14

Percent of intervals behavior occured = 70

Percent of intervals where behavior did not occur = 30

Observation length = 20 minutes

Intervals length = 60

Number of intervals = 20

DISCUSSION QUESTIONS

1. What are some of the factors that contribute to teachers' unwillingness to collect behavioral data? Suggest strategies for overcoming these resistances.

2. Suggest alternate recording strategies for the following behaviors and situations: a low-rate behavior that occurs on the playground; a high-rate behavior that occurs across a number of settings; a behavior that is characterized by its duration; a behavior that is continuous; several behaviors exhibited by more than one pupil.

3. Talk with a teacher who has used portfolios to document students' progress over time. What are some of the advantages and limitations of portfolio assessments compared with more traditional approaches?

4. If your school or program has access to a computer-based observational system, obtain a copy and experiment with different types of data collection. How does it compare with "hard copy" observational data-collection procedures?

5. Why is interobserver agreement an important consideration in measuring social behavior? How can it be influenced by such factors as low or high rates of targeted behaviors?

6. Describe the features of well-constructed graphs and charts and how these contribute to clear communication.

7. Differentiate between equal interval and equal ratio graphs and between performance or progress charts. What circumstances influence decisions about which to use?

REFERENCES

Barr, A., & Feigenbaum, E. A. (Eds.). (1981). *The handbook of artificial intelligence (Vol. 1).* Los Altos, CA: William Kaufman, Inc.

Belanoff, P., & Dickson, M. (Eds.). (1991). *Portfolios: Process and product.* Portsmouth, NH: Heinemann.

Cooke, N. L., Heward, W. L., Test, D. W., Spooner, F., & Courson, F. H. (1991). Student performance data in the classroom: Measurement and evaluation of student progress. *Teacher Education and Special Education, 14,* 155–161.

Cooper, J. O. (1981). *Measuring behavior* (2nd ed.). Columbus, OH: Merrill.

Denny, D., & Fox, J. (1989). Collecting and analyzing continuous behavioral data with the TRS model 100/102 portable laptop computer. *Journal of Special Education Technology, 9,* 181–189.

Deno, S. L., & Mirkin, P. K. (1978). *Data-based program modification: A manual.* Reston, VA: Council for Exceptional Children.

Fabry, B. D., & Cone, J. D. (1980). Auto-graphing: A one-step approach to collecting and graphing data. *Education and Treatment of Children, 3,* 361–368.

Fowler, S. A. (1986). Peer-monitoring and self-monitoring: Alternatives to traditional teacher management. *Exceptional Children, 52,* 573–581.

Fuchs, L. S. (1986). Monitoring progress among mildly handicapped pupils: Review of current practice and research. *Remedial and Special Education, 7* (5), 5–12.

Fuchs, L. S., & Fuchs, D. (1986). Effects of systematic formative evaluation: A meta-analysis. *Exceptional Children, 53,* 199–208.

Gast, D. L., & Gast, K. B. (1981). Educational program evaluation: An overview of databased instruction for classroom teachers. In *Toward a research base for the least restrictive environment: A collection of papers* (pp. 1–30). Lexington, KY: College of Education Dean's Grant Project.

Gelfand, D. M., & Hartmann, D. P. (1984). *Child behavior analysis and therapy* (2nd ed.). New York: Pergamon Press.

Graves, D. H., & Sunstein, B. S. (Eds.). (1992). *Portfolio portraits.* Portsmouth, NH: Heinemann.

Hall, R. V. (1973). *Managing behavior—behavior modification: The measurement of behavior (Part 1).* Lawrence, KS: H & H Enterprises.

Johnson, H. (1995). *Development and evaluation of an unobtrusive computer system for collecting direct observation data in the classroom.* Unpublished dissertation, University of Kentucky.

Johnson, H. J., Brady, S. J., & Larson, E. (in press). The use of microcomputer technology in inclusive childhood educational programs. *Journal of Computing in Childhood Education.*

Johnson, H., Blackhurst, A. E., Maley, K., Bomba, C., Cox-Cruey, T., & Dell, A. (1995). Development of a computer-based system for the unobtrusive collection of direct observational data. *Journal of Special Education Technology, 12*(4), 291–300.

Kauffman, J. M. (1993). *Characteristics of emotional and behavioral disorders of children and youth* (5th ed.). Upper Saddle River, NJ: Merrill/Prentice Hall.

Kelly, M. B. (1977). A review of the observational data-collection and reliability procedures reported in the *Journal of Applied Behavior Analysis. Journal of Applied Behavior Analysis, 10,* 97–101.

Koorland, M. A., & Westling, D. L. (1981). An applied behavior analysis research primer for behavioral change personnel. *Behavioral Disorders, 6,* 164–174.

Kubany, E. S., & Slogett, B. B. (1973). Coding procedure for teachers. *Journal of Applied Behavior Analysis, 6,* 339–344.

Lund, K., Schnaps, L., & Bijou, S. (1983). Let's take another look at record keeping. *Teaching Exceptional Children, 15,* 155–159.

Nelson, C. M., Gast, D. L., & Trout, D. D. (1979). A charting system for monitoring student progress in instructional programs. *Journal of Special Education Technology, 3,* 43–49.

Paulson, F. L., Paulson, P. R., & Meyer, C. A. (1991). What makes a portfolio a portfolio? *Educational Leadership, 48,* 60–63.

Reith, H., Haus, G. J., & Bahr, C. M. (1989). The use of portable microcomputers to collect student and teacher behavior data. *Journal of Special Education Technology, 9,* 190–199.

Scott, L. C., & Goetz, E. M. (1980). Issues in the collection of in-class data by teachers. *Education and Treatment of Children, 3,* 65–71.

Stokes, T. F., & Baer, D. M. (1977). An implicit technology of generalization. *Journal of Applied Behavior Analysis, 10,* 349–367.

Swicegood, P. (1994). Portfolio-based assessment practices: The uses of portfolio assessment for students with behavioral disorders or learning disabilities. *Intervention in School and Clinic, 30*(1), 6–15.

Tawney, J. W., & Gast, D. L. (1984). *Single subject research in special education.* Columbus, OH: Merrill.

Tierney, R. J., Carter, M. A., & Desai, L. E. (1991). *Portfolio assessment in the reading-writing classroom.* Norwood, CA: Christopher-Gordon.

Touchette, P. E., MacDonald, R. F., & Langer, S. N. (1985). A scatter plot for identifying stimulus control of problem behavior. *Journal of Applied Behavior Analysis, 18,* 343–351.

Valencia, S. (1990). A portfolio approach to classroom reading assessment: The whys, whats, and hows. *The Reading Teacher, 43,* 338–340.

Walton, T. W. (1985). Educators' responses to methods of collecting, storing, and analyzing behavioral data. *Journal of Special Education Technology, 7*(2), 50–55.

White, O. R. (1986). Precision teaching—precision learning. *Exceptional Children, 52,* 522–534.

White, O. R., & Haring, N. G. (1980). *Exceptional teaching* (2nd ed.). Columbus, OH: Merrill.

Zuckerman, R. A. (1987). *Data* [Computer program]. Kent, OH: Kent State University, Department of Special Education.

4

SELECTING AND EVALUATING INTERVENTIONS

OUTLINE

OBJECTIVES

After completing this chapter, you should be able to

◆ Describe six principles of applied behavior analysis and give examples from school situations.
◆ Describe professional, legal, and ethical guidelines affecting the use of behavioral interventions.
◆ Locate and use information systems and internet services that provide intervention planning resources.
◆ Identify appropriate and inappropriate intervention alternatives for given behaviors and circumstances, and provide a rationale for each decision.
◆ Visually analyze graphed data and write data decision rules.
◆ Identify the major types of single-subject research designs and give the uses and limitations of each.

In the preceding chapters, we described procedures for screening and identifying students who require intervention for their behavior problems, for assessing these students for the purpose of intervention planning, and for monitoring students' progress during intervention. Using these procedures, you decide with which students you will intervene and what behaviors will be the focus of your interventions. Further, you assess these behaviors and form some tentative hypotheses regarding why they are occurring. Finally, you design strategies to monitor behaviors in the settings in which they occur or where they are expected to occur. This chapter describes strategies for selecting and evaluating interventions based upon those assessments.

Behavioral interventions are derived from a set of principles that explain the relationship of human behavior to immediate environmental variables that exert powerful influences. We begin with a brief explanation of these principles, followed by a description of systematic procedures used by behavior analysts to influence behavior. Next, we present guidelines that affect the choice of procedure, followed by a discussion of intervention planning. We conclude with a description of specific procedures for evaluating interventions formatively, that is, for the purposes of determining their effectiveness and making adjustments to intervention strategies based on these evaluations.

PRINCIPLES OF APPLIED BEHAVIOR ANALYSIS

Applied behavior analysis implies that the practitioner is interested in more than the simple behavior management. It implies an interest in understanding behavior and its functional relationship to environmental events (Baer, Wolf, & Risley, 1968). The behavior analyst therefore studies behavior in the context of the immediate situation. Specifically, he examines stimuli that precede and follow the behavior. Diagrammatically, the model may be represented as A-B-C: A stands for antecedent stimuli, which precede behavior (B), and C designates those stimuli that occur predictably as consequences of the behavior (Worell & Nelson, 1974; see also Chapter 2).

The following principles describe how this model operates. A word of caution before proceeding: Under no circumstances should specific behavior analysis techniques be used by practitioners who do not thoroughly understand the principles upon which they are based. These techniques are a powerful set of tools but they are easily misapplied. Therefore, you should master them through reviewing such basic texts as Alberto and Troutman (1995), Cooper, Heron, and Heward (1987), Ferster and Culbertson (1982), or Wolery, Bailey, and Sugai (1988), as well as through competent supervised practice in the implementation and evaluation of behavior management procedures.

Principle I

Behavior is controlled by its **consequences.** This principle is the heart of behavior analysis, yet it is also the least understood. Most persons assume that behavior is controlled by preceding, or antecedent, stimuli. Consider the teacher who wants a pupil to sit down. She might say, "Sit down." This clearly is an antecedent (A) to the student sitting (B). If the child sits, it is obvious that the antecedent controlled his behavior. But what if the pupil does not sit down after receiving the instruction? The normal tendency is to repeat the command until it is followed, varying voice intensity and adding gestures or threats. Antecedent stimuli effectively control behavior when they enable the behaver to discriminate that certain consequent stimuli will follow certain behavior. Thus, the pupil is more likely to sit if he knows there is a predictable relationship between

sitting (or remaining standing) and consequent events. Repeated association with consequences enables the student to learn that sitting upon command will likely be followed with positive consequences, or that remaining standing is likely to result in aversive consequences. He has thus acquired a discrimination. If he consistently sits upon request, this behavior is under antecedent **stimulus control.** Unfortunately, many teachers fail to provide predictable consequences for students who do not follow their instructions, with the result that pupils learn to rely on other discriminative stimuli: how often the command has been repeated, how loudly, or how red the teacher's face is.

Consequences can affect behavior in three ways. Some consequences *strengthen* or *increase* the frequency of the behavior they follow; others *weaken* or *decrease* behavior; whereas other consequences *maintain* preceding behavior at a preestablished level. On the other hand, *neutral* consequences have no effect on the behavior they follow. Only consequences that strengthen, weaken, or maintain behavior have a functional relationship to that behavior. Moreover, consequences are always defined by their effects: strengthening consequences increase behavior, weakening consequences decrease it, and maintaining consequences keep behavior at the current level.

Principle II

Behavior is strengthened or maintained by **reinforcement.** Reinforcement functions in two ways. **Positive reinforcement** occurs when the presentation of a consequence maintains or strengthens behavior over time. Remember that procedures, as well as consequences, are defined by their effects. For example, Madsen, Becker, Thomas, Koser, and Plager (1968) found that when first-grade teachers told their pupils to sit down, higher rates of out-of-seat behavior occurred. Thus, the command to sit down, (or, more precisely, the teacher attention that accompanied it) given when students were out-of-seat, actually served as positive reinforcement for out-of-seat.

Behavior also may be strengthened or maintained if it avoids or terminates an aversive stimulus. This is called **negative reinforcement.**

Examples of behaviors controlled by negative reinforcement include slowing down upon seeing a radar trap, closing the window to stop a draft, adjusting the water temperature before stepping into the shower, or sitting upon command to avoid a reprimand from the teacher. Because it emphasizes aversive stimuli, negative reinforcement may promote escape and avoidance behaviors other than those the teacher intends to strengthen. For instance, a child may learn to avoid reprimands by not coming to school. Therefore, the major emphasis in behavior management is on positive reinforcement.

Principle III

Behavior is weakened by withholding the consequences that have maintained it. This process is called **extinction.** For example, if your attention has consistently followed a pupil's out-of-seat behavior, and you withhold attention each time the student is out-of-seat, such behavior will be weakened over time. However, for extinction to work you must know *which* consequences have been supporting the behavior, and these consequences must be under your control. Out-of-seat behavior, for instance, may be maintained by reinforcement from the student's peer group instead of (or in addition to) teacher attention. If so, ignoring out-of-seat behavior will have little effect. Such examples emphasize the analysis component of behavior analysis, for only through careful study of antecedents, behaviors, and consequences can you understand their interrelationships and apply appropriate procedures.

Attempting to weaken behavior through extinction takes time. At first, you will likely see an immediate, but temporary, increase in the undesired behavior. Hold your ground when this occurs and give the procedure time to work. If you do not achieve the desired effect after a fair trial (depending on the student's past history of reinforcement for the behavior), use another procedure.

Principle IV

Behavior also is weakened by **punishment.** There are two classes of punishment. The first involves presenting an aversive consequence immediately after a response has occurred (e.g., a verbal reprimand for being out-of-seat). The second involves removing a positive consequence following a response (e.g., taking away a minute of recess time or a token for being out-of-seat). This type differs from extinction because the consequence being removed is arbitrarily chosen rather than the consequence that maintains the undesired behavior. Also, something actually is taken away, rather than being withheld. Just as with reinforcement or extinction, punishment is defined by its effects (i.e., the behavior must decrease in frequency when the aversive consequence is applied). Therefore, you must analyze the procedure over a period of time. For example, if your verbal reprimands result in increased out-of-seat behavior, punishment has not been implemented. Thus, reinforcing or aversive consequences are not defined by the practitioner's judgment of their value to the student. For example, if standing in the corner for talking-out results in an increase in this behavior, the consequence functions as a reinforcer.

Principle V

Consequences must consistently and immediately follow the behaviors they are meant to control. A planned, systematic relationship between a behavior and a consequence is referred to as a **contingency.** Although some contingencies in the environment are naturally systematic and predictable (failing to adjust cold water to warm before stepping into the shower results in goose pimples), many are not. A teacher sometimes may allow pupils to leave their seats without permission and at other times reprimand them. To the extent that such practices diminish the predictability of a contingency, so too is the teacher's control over behavior weakened. Consistency is one of the most taxing requirements of effective behavior management, but in the long run, effort here will save a great deal of frustration and suffering.

Principle VI

Behavior also is strengthened, weakened, or maintained by **modeling** (Bandura, 1969). Modeling involves the alteration of one's behavior through imitating the performance of that behavior by a model. Models may be live or vicarious, adults or children, and the behavior imitated may be appropriate or inappropriate. Children more readily imitate the behavior of models who are similar to them in some way, who have high status, and who have been reinforced. If a model's behavior is punished, the same behavior is more likely to be suppressed by the imitator (Bandura, 1969). It is important to apply planned consequences consistently to all students who serve as models for others.

Although these principles have been described separately, they seldom operate in isolation. For example, teachers often apply positive reinforcement to desired behavior (e.g., in-seat) and extinction to incompatible undesired behavior (e.g., out-of-seat). In this and the following chapters we will present a number of strategies based on these principles. First, however, remember that the complexity of behavior analysis and of behavior management interventions requires that practitioners be well versed in these principles, as well as in data-collection and evaluation procedures. An alternative is to have access to a consultant with demonstrated competence in the principles and techniques of behavior analysis.

SYSTEMATIC PROCEDURES TO INFLUENCE BEHAVIOR

The above principles explain the effects of environmental events on behavior and how these effects may be enhanced or weakened. Using their knowledge of these principles, behavior analysts have designed procedures to strengthen or weaken behavior. These are summarized in Table 4.1. Note that we have arranged them in two groups according to their influence on behavior: those that maintain or increase behavior (enhancement procedures) and those that decrease behavior (reductive procedures). You also may have heard these sets of procedures referred to as those that *accelerate* or *decelerate* behavior. Within each category, we have listed procedures from those that are least intrusive or restrictive to those that are most intrusive or restrictive. **Intrusiveness** refers to the extent to which interventions impinge or encroach on students' bodies or personal rights (Wolery et al.,

1988) as well as the degree to which they interrupt regular educational activities. Thus, more intrusive interventions potentially involve the risk of interfering with students' rights (e.g., to freedom of movement, bodily integrity), of exposing them to physical risks (e.g., through restraint or aversive stimuli), or of interrupting their normal educational programs. (Those interventions that pull the teacher away from normal instructional routines also are intrusive because such an interruption affects the educational program for other students.) **Restrictiveness** involves the extent to which an intervention inhibits students' freedom to be treated like all other pupils (Barton, Brulle, & Repp, 1983). We describe each of the major enhancement and reductive procedures briefly here. More detailed descriptions appear in Chapters 6 through 10, along with examples of how these are applied singly and in combination with other methods. In reviewing these, it is important to keep in mind that this hierarchy is based on our own beliefs regarding which interventions are more or less intrusive or restrictive. Other authorities may place the same interventions in a different hierarchy, although there is growing consensus about the relative intrusiveness/restrictiveness of alternate reductive procedures in particular (e.g., see Nelson & Rutherford, 1988; Wolery et. al., 1988). Also note that although we describe these procedures separately, in practice they are usually combined as intervention packages that are applied together to increase their effects on behavior.

Table 4.1 Enhancement and Reductive Procedures

Enhancement Procedures	Reductive Procedures
Self-regulation	Differential reinforcement
Social reinforcement	Extinction
Modeling	Verbal aversives
Contracting	Response cost
Activity reinforcement	Time-out
Token reinforcement	Overcorrection
Tangible reinforcement	Physical aversives
Edible reinforcement	
Tactile and sensory reinforcement	

Behavioral Enhancement Procedures

Self-Regulation   **Self-regulation** actually includes three procedures: **self-monitoring, self-evaluation,** and **self-reinforcement.** We consider these the least intrusive and least restrictive of the enhancement procedures because after students have been trained in self-regulation they may apply these procedures across a wide range of situations without interrupting ongoing activities. Most students learn to monitor their own performance ("Am I doing this right?"), evaluate it ("Yes, that's right"), and administer reinforcement or corrective feedback ("I'm doing a good job so far") without systematic training. However, pupils exhibiting behavioral disorders often appear deficient in these skills (Polsgrove, 1979). Although self-regulation procedures have shown much promise in terms of changing behavior (Nelson & Polsgrove, 1984), because they are usually private events, it is difficult to objectively establish the degree to which students use them. However, changes in overt behaviors that result from self-regulation procedures (e.g., self-recording, verbal reports, target behaviors) may be monitored to evaluate the extent to which these strategies are used. One factor in its success appears to be training in self-regulation prior to allowing students to control reinforcing events (i.e., to decide when they have earned reinforcement) (Polsgrove, 1979). A number of self-regulation strategies are described in the self-mediated interventions sections of Chapters 6 through 10.

Social Reinforcement   Like self-regulation, social reinforcement consists of several operations: feedback, attention, and approval. However, social consequences are mediated by another person. Social reinforcement may be delivered easily and nonintrusively. Used by itself, contingent social feedback has been shown to have only weak effects, but attention and approval have been found to be powerful reinforcers for both typical learners and students with disabilities, particularly those who are developmentally younger (Nelson, 1981). Teacher attention, even when paired with frowns, warnings, and reprimands, may be a potent reinforcer, especially with students who tend to be ignored except when they misbehave (Walker, 1995). Furthermore, it has been shown that such students receive proportionately more teacher attention than pupils who are nondeviant (Walker, 1995; Walker, Hops, & Fiegenbaum, 1976), which may strengthen their undesired behaviors. Nevertheless, teacher attention and approval (e.g., praise), when contingent upon desired student behavior, are very effective in strengthening or maintaining these behaviors. Naturally, for attention and praise to control student behavior successfully, they must have been established as **conditioned reinforcers** through repeated pairings with previously established reinforcers. Their effectiveness also depends upon whether strong competing reinforcers exist for undesired behavior, and whether the teacher uses them contingently and delivers them immediately following desired behavior (Nelson, 1981; Shores, Gunter, Denny, & Jack, 1993). Praise is more effective when it is genuine, describes the desired behavior exhibited, and is applied consistently. However, it should not disrupt the behavior being emitted and should not involve the same phrase (e.g., "Good") time after time (Wolery et al., 1988). With older pupils or those with more severe disabilities, social consequences tend to work better in combination with other behavior enhancement procedures.

Modeling   Having another person demonstrate desired behavior has been used successfully to accelerate these behaviors in students of all ages and levels of disability (Stainback, Stainback, & Dedrick, 1979). Also, vicarious modeling through films or printed materials has been effective with students who do not have severe cognitive impairments. Modeling is useful especially for teaching complex behaviors such as social skills (Gelfand & Hartmann, 1984). Modeling is most effective if the model is highly regarded by the student (e.g., a school athlete), the model is like the student in some way (e.g., age or sex), the student observes the model receive reinforcement for the desired behavior, the modeled behavior is in the target student's repertoire, and the target student is reinforced on other occasions when he displays the desired behavior (Bandura, 1969). Undesired behaviors also may be reduced if students observe a model who receives aversive consequences as a result of the target behavior. As with social reinforcement, modeling is likely to be used in conjunction with other procedures and is a component of behavioral rehearsal and role-playing, both of which are used in several social skills training packages.

Contracting A behavioral **contract** is a formal, written agreement negotiated between the student and other persons. A contract usually specifies the behavior(s) to be increased (or decreased), the consequences to be delivered contingent upon satisfaction of the contract's terms, and the criterion for determining whether the terms of the contract have been fulfilled (Rutherford & Polsgrove, 1981). Although contracts are more intrusive in terms of the time required to negotiate, write, monitor, and fulfill, they do not restrict the student's freedom to participate in normal educational activities.

Activity Reinforcement Providing opportunity to engage in preferred or **high-probability behaviors** contingent upon completion of less preferred or **low-probability behaviors** (Premack, 1959) is an effective reinforcement procedure with both typical students and those with disabilities. It is a relatively intrusive procedure because the reinforcing activity must be identified and access to it made contingent upon the occurrence of desired target behaviors. However, high-probability behaviors do not necessarily have to be such major events as a class party or an extra recess; the opportunity to engage in a preferred academic task (e.g., reading, tutoring a peer) can be used as a reinforcer for a less-desired academic activity (e.g., working on a composition). Activity reinforcers often are used as **back-up reinforcers** in token systems or behavioral contracts.

Token Reinforcement A **token economy** is a behavior management system involving nonsocial conditioned reinforcers (e.g., points, chips, paper clips, etc.) earned for exhibiting desired academic or social behaviors that may be exchanged for back-up reinforcers of predetermined token

value. Although tokens may be delivered quickly and easily, the time required to develop a token system makes this a more intrusive intervention. Token economies may be used with students individually, but they more often are applied with groups (see Chapters 5 and 6). They have been used with an extraordinarily wide range of populations and age groups and in numerous educational and treatment settings (Kazdin, 1983). A major problem with token systems is teachers' failure to phase out tokens in preparation for moving pupils to less restrictive environments.

Tangible Reinforcement Nonedible items (e.g., stickers) that are reinforcing for particular students are **tangible reinforcers.** Often they are used as back-up reinforcers in token economies, but they may also be used as reinforcers for desired student behavior. Many types of tangible reinforcers are inexpensive, but because the same item may not be reinforcing to every student, delivering the correct reinforcer to each student immediately contingent upon desired behavior makes this an intrusive procedure.

Edible Reinforcement Suffering the same drawbacks as tangibles, **edible reinforcers** also involve several other disadvantages. First, the student must be in a state of relative deprivation for the edible item. Thus, pretzels, popcorn, or even M & Ms® may be ineffective immediately after breakfast or lunch. Second, students have varying food preferences, which again makes delivering the right reinforcer to every student immediately contingent upon desired behavior rather difficult. Third, because these are consumable items, health factors such as food allergies, and parental preferences must be taken into account. Finally, many public schools have policies restricting the use of edible items in classrooms (Stainback et al., 1979). Edibles have been widely effective, especially with developmentally younger pupils. Fortunately, behavior analysis technology has advanced to the point where teachers seldom must rely exclusively on edible reinforcement.

Tactile and Sensory Reinforcement The application of tactile or sensory consequences that are reinforcing has been used almost exclusively with students exhibiting severe and profound disabilities, especially in attempts to control **self-stimulatory behaviors** (SSB) (Stainback et al., 1979). The teacher must first identify sensory consequences that appear to be reinforcing (e.g., vibration, movement, touch) and then arrange for these consequences to follow desired behavior. For example, if the student self-stimulates by rubbing her palm, the teacher can rub the pupil's palm immediately contingent upon a desired behavior. Alternately, the teacher can allow the student to rub her own palm when the desired behavior occurs. Among the risks of such a procedure is that of strengthening SSB even further. Before considering tactile or sensory reinforcement, evaluate such possibilities and consider parental wishes and whether the SSB interferes with the acquisition of more adaptive behaviors, or select toys or other devices for the student to use that provide sensory stimulation or feedback like that received through SSB (Wolery et al., 1988).

Behavioral Reduction Procedures

Procedures for reducing undesired student behavior have received an enormous amount of attention from professionals who deal with children and adults exhibiting behavioral disorders. Consequently, the professional literature on the topic of reductive strategies and techniques is extensive. It is matched by the tradition in our schools of attempting to control unwanted pupil behavior through reactive management strategies involving the administration of aversive consequences. Fortunately, this thinking is giving way to more proactive procedures, such as a recognition of the influence of a sound and relevant curriculum, interesting instructional activities, appropriate stimulus control, and positive classroom structure on increasing desired student behaviors (Rutherford & Nelson, 1995). These antecedent events clearly are prerequisite to the effective management of maladaptive behavior and are discussed at greater length in Chapter 5. In addition, as pointed out in the previous chapter, more attention is being given to analyzing the contributions of events that are antecedents to undesired pupil behavior (e.g., Conroy & Fox, 1994; Wehby, 1994), to the communicative function of aberrant behavior (e.g., Carr & Durand, 1985; Dunlap et al., 1993) as well as to identifying and strengthening desired replacement behaviors through differential reinforcement (LaVigna & Donnellan, 1986). However, behavioral enhancement procedures alone are not sufficient to decelerate undesired behavior in pupils who exhibit moderate to severe behavioral disorders (Axelrod, 1987; Gast & Wolery, 1987; Walker, 1995). The following continuum of reductive procedures is arranged from least to most intrusive and restrictive. It is likely that the more intrusive and restrictive procedures we describe will be aversive to both students and teachers.

Differential Reinforcement   Four strategies are involved in **differential reinforcement**. **Differential reinforcement of low rates of behavior** (DRL) is applied by providing reinforcement when the targeted behavior occurs no more than a specified amount in a given period of time (e.g., if fewer than three talk-outs are observed in a one-hour period, the student earns five bonus points). **Differential reinforcement of other behaviors** (DRO, which Dietz and Repp, 1983, renamed differential reinforcement of the *omission of behavior*) requires that the target behavior be suppressed either for an entire interval (whole interval DRO), or only at the end of an interval (momentary DRO). **Differential reinforcement of incompatible behaviors** (DRI) and **differential reinforcement of alternate behaviors** (DRA) involve reinforcing behaviors that are functionally incompatible with (i.e., cannot occur at the same time) or that are simply alternatives to the target behavior (Dietz & Repp, 1983). DRL is appropriate for relatively minor behavior problems that can be tolerated at low rates, whereas DRO, DRI, and DRA may be used with severe behavioral disorders. However, because direct consequences (i.e., loss of reinforcement) are not provided for target behaviors under DRI and DRA, they may take longer to work than DRL or DRO, and they may be ineffective if the target behavior has a long history of reinforcement or has been maintained by other sources of reinforcement (Polsgrove & Reith, 1983).

Extinction Withholding reinforcers (e.g., attention) will reduce undesired behavior if the reinforcer being withheld is the one that maintained the target behavior and is consistently and contingently withheld. However, this is a relatively weak procedure for controlling severe maladaptive behavior (Stainback et al., 1979) and is inappropriate for behaviors reinforced by consequences that are not controlled by the teacher (e.g., talking-out, aggression, SSB) or that cannot be tolerated during the time required for extinction to work, such as **self-injurious behavior** (SIB). Nevertheless, many pupil behaviors are maintained because they result in peer or teacher attention, and therefore extinction can be effective, particularly when combined with reinforcement procedures (i.e., differential reinforcement). **Sensory extinction** (Rincover, 1981) is an intrusive procedure in which the sensory consequences of SSB or SIB are masked so that reinforcement is effectively withheld (e.g., covering a table top with felt to eliminate the auditory feedback produced by spinning objects). The need to monitor student behavior carefully and to use special equipment limit the usefulness of sensory extinction beyond very specific circumstances (see Chapter 9).

Verbal Aversives Verbal reprimands have been used effectively with many mild and moderate behavior problems (Rutherford, 1983), but by themselves are less successful with severe behavior disorders. Van Houten, Nau, MacKenzie-Keating, Sameoto, and Colavecchia (1982) demonstrated that reprimands are more effective when accompanied by eye contact and when delivered in close proximity to the target pupil. They also demonstrated that reprimanding one student for behavior exhibited by another student reduced both students' behavior. When reprimands are associated with other aversive back-up consequences (e.g., response cost, timeout), they acquire conditioned aversive properties and subsequently are more effective when used alone (Gelfand & Hartmann, 1984).

Response Cost The removal of reinforcers contingent upon the occurrence of undesired target behaviors, or **response cost,** differs from extinction in that the reinforcer is taken away rather than withheld and is not the reinforcer that has maintained the target behavior. This procedure is used most often in token systems, in which tokens may be lost for displaying undesired behaviors. Variables that influence the success of response cost include the type of behavior on which it is used, the ratio of fines to reinforcers, and the amount of cost imposed (Polsgrove & Reith, 1983). Strategies involving response cost are described in Chapters 5 and 6.

Timeout Like differential reinforcement, **timeout** from positive reinforcement involves several possible strategies, ranging from planned ignoring to putting the student in a secluded place for a period of time (Nelson & Rutherford, 1983). Its effectiveness varies with the level of timeout used and its duration, with whether a warning signal precedes placement in timeout, with how it is applied, with the schedule under which it is administered, and with procedures for removing pupils from timeout (Gast & Nelson, 1977; Polsgrove & Reith, 1983; Rutherford & Nelson, 1982; Twyman, Johnson, Buie, & Nelson, 1993). Perhaps the most important variable affecting the success of timeout is whether the time-in setting is more reinforcing. When students may escape or avoid unpleasant demands or persons, or when they may engage in more reinforcing behavior (e.g., SSB) while in timeout, this clearly is not a good intervention to choose. It is also an inappropriate option when the student is likely to harm himself while in timeout. Timeout has been effective in reducing severe maladaptive behaviors when combined with procedures to enhance desired behavior (Nelson & Rutherford, 1988).

Overcorrection There are two types of overcorrection procedures. **Positive practice overcorrection** involves having the student repeat an arbitrarily selected behavior (e.g., arm movements) contingent upon the occurrence of an undesired target behavior (e.g., stereotypic hand wringing). **Restitutional overcorrection** requires the student to overcorrect the effects of her behavior on the environment (e.g., returning stolen items and giving one of her possessions to the victim). In general, both types of overcorrection have been effective, but the procedures are time consuming and often aversive to both students and staff.

Physical Aversives   Substances having aversive tastes and odors, electric shock, slaps, pinches, and spankings illustrate the range of physically aversive stimuli that have been used. Such procedures have been shown to be an efficient and effective means of reducing severe maladaptive behaviors (Rutherford, 1983; Stainback et. al., 1979). However, the frequency with which the use of such aversives are abused; the occurrence of undesired side effects; and the objections by parents, educators, and community groups have limited the application of these most intrusive and restrictive procedures. The Council for Exceptional Children (1993) adopted a policy statement regulating the use of physical interventions (see Table 4.2). Behavior management procedures that are not consistent with this policy are indefensible.

Even less defensibly, many school districts sanction the use of corporal punishment with students in spite of the absence of empirical studies demonstrating its effectiveness (Rose, 1983), and policy statements of professional organizations that specifically prohibit its use. The general trend has been away from using aversives and toward greater use of procedures to decrease undesired behaviors by increasing functional and desired replacement behaviors through behavior enhancement strategies.

Other Procedures   Other reductive procedures, such as in-school suspension and temporary exclusion from school, also are available. These procedures are quite disruptive to students' educational programs, and their use with pupils who have been certified as having disabilities is carefully regulated (Warboys, 1987). The development of an expanded range of reductive procedures fortunately has opened up numerous options to educators concerned with reducing maladaptive student behaviors. However, the increase of intervention alternatives has placed greater demands on practitioners to make appropriate choices. Behavior analysts have made this decision-making process easier by developing guidelines and decision models.

GUIDELINES FOR SELECTING AND DEVELOPING INTERVENTIONS

Walker, Colvin, and Ramsey (1995) identified two broad categories of interventions. **Universal interventions** are designed to affect all students in the same way under the same conditions. For example, a school-wide discipline plan, classroom token economy, or posted classroom rules are universal interventions. In contrast, **selected interventions** are designed for a specific pupil and are developed to meet the specific needs of that student and the adults who deal with her. Examples include a specific differential reinforcement program, behavioral contract, or a timeout contingency. Whereas universal interventions are appropriate for preventing behavior problems and generally less demanding to implement, selected interventions are used for individual behaviors that have proven resistant to efforts to change. Also, universal interventions are less powerful, but have their best impact on students whose behavior is marginally out of compliance with usual classroom expectations and standards. On the other hand, selected interventions are designed to exert powerful influence on the behaviors of students for whom universal interventions have had less impact than desired (Walker et al., 1995). Universal interventions, then, are appropriate for establishing the structure and expectations of a classroom or other setting. When such interventions are in place and used effectively, the need for selected interventions with more than a small number of students is reduced. The guidelines that follow are provided to assist in developing appropriate selected interventions; universal interventions will be discussed in Chapter 5.

Effective Behavior Support

As mentioned in Chapter 2, the emerging technology of effective behavior support is designed to address the communicative function of targeted problem behaviors and to teach and strengthen desired replacement behaviors that serve the same function. As described by Sugai (1995), effective behavior support (EBS) is based on four assumptions: a school-wide plan of

Table 4.2 CEC Policy on Physical Intervention

The Council recognizes the right to the most effective educational strategies to be the basic educational right of each special education child. Furthermore, the Council believes that the least restrictive positive educational strategies should be used, as it relates to physical intervention, to respect the children's dignity and personal privacy. Additionally, the Council believes that such interventions shall assure the child's physical freedom, social interaction, and individual choice. The intervention must not include procedures which cause pain or trauma. Lastly, behavior intervention plans must be specifically described in the child's written educational plan with agreement from the education staff, the parents, and, when appropriate, the child.

The Council recommends that physical intervention be used only if all the following requirements are met:
- The child's behavior is dangerous to herself/himself or others, or the behavior is extremely detrimental to or interferes with the education or development of the child.
- Various positive reinforcement techniques have been implemented appropriately and the child has repeatedly failed to respond as documented in the child's records.
- It is evident that withholding physical intervention would significantly impede the child's educational progress as explicitly defined in his/her written educational plan.
- The physical intervention plan specifically will describe the intervention to be implemented, the staff to be responsible for the implementation, the process for documentation, the required training of staff, and supervision of staff as it relates to the intervention and when the intervention will be replaced.
- The physical intervention plan will become part of the written educational plan.
- The physical intervention plan shall encompass the following provisions:
    - A comprehensive analysis of the child's environment including variables contributing to the inappropriate behavior;
    - The plan to be developed by a team including professional and parents/guardians, as designated by state/provincial and federal law;
    - The personnel implementing the plan shall receive specific training congruent with the contents of the plan and receive ongoing supervision from individuals who are trained and skilled in the techniques identified in the plan;
    - The techniques identified in the physical intervention plan are approved by a physician to not be medically contraindicated for the child (a statement from the physician is necessary); and
    - The impact of the plan on the child's behavior must be consistently evaluated, the results documented, and the plan modified when indicated.

The Council supports the following prohibitions:
- Any intervention that is designed to, or likely to, cause physical pain;
- Releasing noxious, toxic or otherwise unpleasant sprays, mists, or substances in proximity to the child's face;
- Any intervention which denies adequate sleep, food, water, shelter, bedding, physical comfort, or access to bathroom facilities;
- Any intervention which is designed to subject, used to subject, or likely to subject the individual to verbal abuse, ridicule, or humiliation, or which can be expected to cause excessive emotional trauma;
- Restrictive interventions which employ a device or material or objects that simultaneously immobilize all four extremities, including the procedure known as prone containment, except that prone containment may be used by trained personnel as a limited emergency intervention;
- Locked seclusion, unless under constant surveillance and observation;
- Any intervention that precludes adequate supervision of the child; and
- Any intervention which deprives the individual of one or more of his or her senses.

The Council recognizes that emergency physical intervention may be implemented if the child's behavior poses an imminent and significant threat to his/her physical well-being or to the safety of others. The intervention must be documented and parents/guardians must be notified of the incident.
- However, emergency physical intervention shall not be used as a substitute for systematic behavioral intervention plans that are designed to change, replace, modify, or eliminate a targeted behavior.
- Furthermore, the council expects the school districts and other educational agencies to establish policies and comply with state/provincial and federal law and regulations to ensure the protection of the rights of the child, the parent/guardian, the education staff, and the school and local educational agency when physical intervention is applied.

Source: Council for Exceptional Children. (1993). *CEC Policy on Physical Intervention.* Adopted by the Delegate Assembly, San Antonio, TX. Used with permission.

supporting desired student behavior is in place; the problem behavior produces consequences that are reinforcing to the student (i.e., direct positive reinforcement or escape/avoidance of aversive stimuli); alternative desired behavior has been identified that produces similar consequences; and all intervention agents, such as school personnel, family members, must know exactly how to implement EBS (i.e., the plan should be scripted, rehearsed, and monitored).

The EBS procedure consists of three steps (Sugai, 1995). First, the problem behavior is defined operationally (see Chapter 2). Second, a functional analysis is performed to identify setting events and immediate antecedents to the target behavior, describe topographies of the target behavior, identify its consequences, and formulate hypotheses regarding the function of the behavior. The third step consists of developing an EBS plan, which should ensure that the problem behavior will be irrelevant, ineffective, and inefficient in obtaining previously produced consequences. The specific plan focuses on proactive strategies to teach desired and replacement behaviors, to respond to infrequent social behavior errors, to precorrect[1] for chronic errors, and to systematically reinforce expected behavior. The plan also includes reactive strategies for when the problem behavior does occur. Scripts are prepared to guide interventionists through the most common problem situation (e.g., dealing with episodes of aggression on the playground). Practitioners should ensure that the problem behavior does not result in reinforcing consequences and should apply the least intrusive intervention. An EBS support plan is provided in the case study at the end of this chapter. Additional resources for developing positive intervention strategies for problem behaviors include Carr et al. (1994); Horner, O'Neill, and Flannery (1994); and Reichle and Wacker (1993).

---

[1]**Precorrection,** an instructional approach for managing problem behaviors that occur predictably (e.g., during transitions) (Colvin, Sugai, & Patching, 1993), is described in Chapter 5.

Using Reductive Procedures

Traditionally, practitioners have relied heavily upon the application of aversive consequences to reduce undesired behaviors. While the intervention technology described above is beginning to provide viable alternatives to this practice, the best practices for children and youth who exhibit chronic and severe acting-out behavior typically include planned aversive consequences as well as EBS (Walker et al., 1995). Verbal reprimands, response cost, timeout, overcorrection, and any physical aversive are all considered punishment procedures if they result in the deceleration of behaviors upon which they are contingent. (Based upon observations of its side effects, extinction also is perceived as an aversive event by students.) As Nelson and Rutherford (1988) observe, "the excessive and inappropriate use of aversive procedures constitutes one of the more sensitive areas of special education practice" (p. 143). Concerns regarding the potential and real abuse of aversives have led some professional organizations to adopt policies severely limiting the use of reductive procedures that involve aversive stimuli. For example, the Association for Retarded Citizens' resolution "calls for a halt to those aversive practices that (1) deprive food, (2) inflict pain, and (3) use chemical restraint in lieu of programming. . . ." (*The Association for the Severely Handicapped Newsletter,* 1986). The Association for the Severely Handicapped (1981) resolution

> supports a cessation of the use of any treatment option which exhibits some or all of the following characteristics: (1) obvious signs of physical pain experienced by the individual; (2) potential or actual physical side effects, including tissue damage, physical illness, severe stress, and/or death, that would properly require the involvement of medical personnel; (3) de-humanization of the individual experiencing a severe handicap because the procedures are normally unacceptable for persons who are not handicapped in community environments; (4) extreme ambivalence and discomfort by family, staff, and/or caregivers regarding the necessity of such extreme strategies or their own involvement in such intervention; and (5) obvious repulsion and/or stress felt by peers who are not handicapped and by (community) members who cannot reconcile extreme procedures with acceptable standard practice. . . .

Other professional groups (e.g., the Council for Children with Behavioral Disorders, 1990) have prepared detailed position statements addressing the use of punishment procedures. In addition, the Council for Exceptional Children, the National Education Association, and the National Association of School Psychologists have adopted positions against the use of corporal punishment with all students. The Council for Exceptional Children (1994) has drafted specific professional policies for the use of school exemption, exclusion, suspension, or expulsion, as well as physical intervention for students with disabilities.

Legal and Ethical Guidelines The position statements cited above were adopted for the purpose of guiding professional practice. However, they clearly do not prohibit all use of aversive procedures, nor are practitioners, especially those not belonging to the respective professional organizations, legally bound to follow these policies. Educators legally are required to follow federal and state laws that regulate the use of disciplinary procedures. As Yell and Peterson (1995) pointed out, a dual standard exists for disciplining nondisabled students and those with disabilities. The latter group includes those protected under IDEA and Section 504 of the Rehabilitation Act of 1973. In addition, the U. S. Supreme Court's *Honig v. Doe* (1988) decision established that normal disciplinary procedures customarily used for dealing with school children (e.g., restriction of privileges, detention, and removal of students to study carrels) may be used with students exhibiting disabilities. However, disciplinary procedures that constitute a unilateral decision to change the placement of students with disabilities are severely limited (Yell & Peterson, 1995).

According to Yell and Peterson (1995), disciplinary procedures may be placed in one of three categories. *Permitted procedures* include those that are part of a school district's disciplinary plan and are used with all students (e.g., verbal reprimands, warnings, contingent observation timeout, response cost, and the temporary delay or withdrawal of goods, services, or activities). Physical restraint or immediate suspension are permissible in emergency situations. No legal restrictions exist regarding the involvement of the police if a law has been violated (Maloney, 1994). *Controlled procedures* include interventions the courts have held to be permissible if they are used appropriately, are not abused, and are not used in a discriminatory manner. These include exclusion timeout, seclusion/isolation timeout, in-school suspension, and out-of-school suspension. Suspensions up to ten days are permitted, but the Court was unclear regarding whether this meant ten days per disciplinary incident or cumulatively for the school year.[2] *Prohibited procedures* are those that involve unilateral decisions (i.e., decisions not made by the student's IEP committee or educational team) affecting educational placement and include expulsions and indefinite suspensions. This applies even if the student's behavior is dangerous to himself or to others. The only exception allowed is when it can be proven that the behavior resulting in suspension or expulsion is not related to the student's disability, and courts have tended not to agree with IEP committees who have ruled that such is the case, especially with regard to students with EBD (Yell & Peterson, 1995).

Educators also are obligated to follow local school district policies regulating the use of aversives, but many districts do not have such policies, so your best source of guidance is case law. Barton et al. (1983) reviewed judicial rulings concerning the use of aversive techniques and found that except for *Morales v. Turman* (1973), which allowed slaps in extreme circumstances, all decisions have expressly forbidden corporal punishment for persons with disabilities. In *Wyatt v. Stickney* (1972) the use of electric shock was upheld under carefully defined conditions. Physical restraint and seclusionary timeout can only be used under supervised conditions and only when the failure of less restrictive techniques has been documented. To our knowledge, other aversive procedures have not been litigated.

---

[2]The Office of Civil Rights has stated that cumulative suspensions totaling more than ten days constitute a pattern of exclusion, and therefore are not permissible.

The absence of legal precedent for many reductive procedures and the observation that corporal punishment is used in many schools despite rulings against it may cause you to wonder whether to be concerned with these issues. The precaution offered by Barton et al. (1983) should clear up this ambiguity: "Any person who provides aversive behavioral therapies for handicapped persons without knowledge of the current legislative and litigative mandates governing such provision and concern for the rights of the individual invites both professional and personal disaster" (p. 5). In fact, the U. S. Supreme Court has ruled that if punishment is found to be excessive, the teacher or school officials who are responsible may be held liable for damages to the student (Singer & Irvin, 1987). Thus, you may avoid using punishment procedures altogether or use them carefully and with proper attention to student and parental rights (Wood & Braaten, 1983). Although reductive procedures are necessary with highly disruptive and aggressive pupils, they should be used in combination with procedures for teaching desired replacement behaviors. Further, as Wood and Braaten (1983) stated, corporal punishment "has no place in special education programs" (p. 71).

The possibility of legal sanctions is a compelling reason for school districts to adopt policies regulating the use of reductive procedures. Singer and Irvin (1987) suggested that students' and teachers' rights concerning intrusive or restrictive procedures should be safeguarded through establishing school district procedures that include the following:

◆ Obtaining informed consent, including a detailed description of the problem behavior, previously attempted interventions, proposed intervention risks and expected outcomes, data-collection procedures, and alternative interventions; and a statement of consent from the parents, including the right to withdraw consent at any time.
◆ Review by a school district human rights committee. (Such review procedures are not found in most school districts, but they should be developed.)

◆ Due process procedures to regulate school district actions when intrusive behavior management techniques are used. (Again, few school districts have developed such procedures. However, "formal IEP processes must be used if disciplinary methods for any [student] are a regular part of a handicapped child's educational program" [p. 50]. Intrusive interventions require a level of review beyond regular IEP procedures [e.g., human rights committee review].)
◆ Use of the least restrictive alternative, which refers to interventions that restrict a student's freedom no more than is necessary to achieve the desired goals (Budd & Baer, 1976). (Restrictive interventions must be aimed at educational objectives and those proposing an intervention must prove that less intrusive methods are not the best approach and that the proposed intervention is the least restrictive alternative.).

Wood and Braaten (1983) suggested that school district policies regarding the use of punishment procedures include definitions and descriptions of procedures that are permitted and those that are not allowed; references to relevant laws, regulations, court decisions, and professional standards; and procedural guidelines that contain the following elements:

◆ Information concerning the use and abuse of punishment procedures.
◆ Staff training requirements for the proper use of approved procedures.
◆ Approved punishment procedures.
◆ Procedures for maintaining records of the use of punishment procedures.
◆ Complaint and appeal procedures.
◆ Punishment issues and cautions.
◆ Procedures for periodic review of procedures used with individual students.

Resources that can be used in drafting such policies include guidelines in the professional literature for specific interventions such as differential reinforcement (Dietz & Repp, 1983), response cost (Walker, 1983), timeout (Gast & Nelson, 1977; Nelson & Rutherford, 1983), and for aversive procedures in general (Polsgrove & Reith, 1983; Wood & Braaten, 1983). Some professional and parental organizations, such as the Association for Retarded Citizens, have adopted guidelines for behavioral interventions (Sajwaj, 1977), and others (e.g., Council for Children with Behavior Disorders, 1990) have developed these. The CCBD guidelines are particularly useful for practitioners.

This discussion has considered the impact on and acceptability by persons directly affected by behavioral interventions. The IEP committee format provides a means of *socially validating* the goals, the appropriateness, and the acceptability of intervention procedures, that is, the extent to which caregivers and significant others agree with the objectives and methods of intervention programs (Wolf, 1978). In planning interventions for typical students, take care to assure that intervention objectives and procedures are seen as appropriate and necessary by those persons who are involved and concerned with pupils' well-being and educational progress. School policies regulating the use of behavior reduction procedures should therefore apply to all students, not just to those with disabilities.

The acceptability of practitioners' interventions also is a relevant issue, especially because some procedures will be recommended to regular educators working with pupils having disabilities in mainstream settings. Research on this issue has revealed that, in general, more restrictive interventions (e.g., timeout and psychoactive medications) are viewed as less acceptable than such interventions as positive reinforcement of desired behavior, although more restrictive procedures are seen as more acceptable with students exhibiting highly deviant behavior (Kazdin, 1981; Witt, Elliott, & Martens, 1984). Student and teacher ethnicity have also been suggested as factors affecting treatment acceptability (Pearson & Argulewicz, 1987). Witt and Martens (1983) recommended that professionals ask five questions regarding the acceptability of an intervention (even one whose effectiveness has been documented in the literature) before implementing it:

1. Is it suitable for mainstream classrooms?
2. Does it present unnecessary risks to pupils?
3. Does it require too much teacher time?
4. Does it have negative side effects on other pupils?
5. Does the teacher have the skill to implement it?

Considerations in Selecting Reductive Procedures   Legal and ethical factors also place limits on what reductive procedures can be used with pupils. However, these do not provide specific guidelines concerning which procedures represent the appropriate alternative for specific problem behaviors. Although decisions regarding these choices should be made by students' IEP committees, it is important that this group have guidance from persons who are technically knowledgeable about intervention procedures and their effects, side effects, advantages, and drawbacks. Furthermore, committees should feel comfortable that the recommendation to intervene with a reductive procedure occurs in the context of an educational environment that is positive, structured, and productive. In this section we provide guidelines from the professional literature for making intervention suggestions.

Braaten (1987) suggested three principles that govern the appropriate use of reductive procedures:

1. The priority given the target behavior justifies the level of intervention.
2. interventions based on positive reinforcement of incompatible or alternative behaviors have been demonstrated to be ineffective.
3. Less restrictive or intrusive procedures are attempted first.

We elaborate on each of these principles in the following discussion.

Priority of the Target Behavior   In Chapter 2, we introduced the *fair pair rule* (White & Haring, 1980), which applies to the identification of desired replacement behaviors for each undesired behavior targeted for reduction. Further, we indicated that desired replacement behaviors could be selected by assessing the skills pupils need in their current or potential future environments.

But what criteria should be used in deciding which of the student's undesired behaviors to target first? Braaten (1987) suggested a hierarchy of such behaviors. *Low-priority* target behaviors are those that are annoying but not harmful to others (e.g., teasing, off-task). *Mild-priority* targets include behaviors that frequently interfere with the achievement of classroom or individual student goals (e.g., defiance, pushing, minor property damage). *Moderate-priority* targets are behaviors that repeatedly or significantly interfere with goal achievement or with other class members (e.g. fighting, avoiding school, abuse of staff). Behaviors that are *high-priority* targets involve persistent, generalized alienation or agitation that is excessively disruptive to self and others (e.g., physical assault, stereotypic behaviors, total noncompliance). Finally, *urgent-priority* targets involve extreme risk and require expert intervention (e.g., behaviors that are life-threatening or that risk serious injury to self or others). By reviewing the student's problem behaviors with regard to this hierarchy, you can determine which behaviors may be ignored or monitored to ensure that they are not increasing to obtrusive levels and target these for intervention after higher priority undesired behaviors have been reduced.

Documentation That Enhancement Interventions Have Not Been Effective Braaten, Simpson, Rosell, and Reilly (1988) recommended that schools should use disciplinary procedures in accordance with the *principle of hierarchical application,* which requires that more intrusive procedures be used only after less intrusive procedures have failed. We hope that you have seen ample need to attempt interventions that strengthen desired behaviors before considering reductive procedures. By differentially reinforcing behaviors that are incompatible with or alternative to undesired targets, you may be able to avoid using punishment procedures entirely. In targeting replacement behaviors remember also to consider the possible communicative function of the pupil's maladaptive behavior (Carr & Durand, 1985). If you can identify a replacement behavior that serves the same communicative function and you can

systematically reinforce it, the chances are doubly good that you will not have to use aversive consequences to reduce the undesired target behavior. However, for strategies based on enhancement procedures to be most effective, remember that you should identify reinforcers for both desired and undesired behaviors and be able to control the pupil's sources of positive reinforcement. Furthermore, in documenting that reinforcing interventions have been ineffective, we assume that you have implemented the intervention systematically, collected data on its effects over an adequate period of time, and evaluated its effects on the target behavior with respect to level, trend, and stability (see pp. 129–133 for guidelines on data-based evaluation of interventions).

Use Less Restrictive or Intrusive Procedures This principle suggests that once the decision to use reductive procedures has been made you should consider those that intrude the least upon the student's body, rights, or curriculum. Consider a wide range of alternatives that address both the antecedents to and consequences of the undesired target behavior. Wolery et al. (1988) describe four categories of setting events that may influence behavior. The *instructional dimensions of the environment* include the types of materials, activities, and instruction that are provided as well as the sequence of activities. For example, if the target behavior occurs mainly when certain activities are scheduled, perhaps these activities are too difficult or are boring to the student. The *physical dimensions of the environment* that may influence behavior include lighting, noise, heat, the physical arrangement of the environment, and the time of day. Variables related to the *social dimensions of the environment* include the number of other students, the number of adults, the behavior of others toward the student, and the pupil's physical proximity to others. Finally, *changes in the environment* that potentially affect student behavior include changes in schedule, the physical arrangement of the setting, and the home environment. By being a careful student of the pupil's behavior and staying informed of changes in his other ecological settings, you should be able to identify antecedent conditions or variables that affect him. If a functional relationship between the target behavior and any of these variables is discovered, attempt interventions that address these factors before considering reductive consequences.

If you cannot identify a relationship between antecedent variables and undesired behavior, and if you have tried nonpunishment reductive procedures (i.e., differential reinforcement, extinction) and found them ineffective, you are now faced with choices from among the punishment options listed in Table 4.1. Two principles will help you make a selection. The principle of the **least intrusive alternative** (Gast & Wolery, 1987) indicates that the simplest effective intervention should be chosen when data are available regarding the general effectiveness of a given procedure. This principle implies that intervention agents must keep up with current research literature on behavioral interventions, which is reported in a variety of professional journals. We encourage you to subscribe to some of these journals independently or through your professional organization (e.g., Council for Children with Behavior Disorders, Council for Exceptional Children), and to allow some time each week for professional reading.

Although behavioral interventions have been proven effective across numerous settings, intervention agents, and target individuals, outcomes vary with the unique characteristics of persons and settings so effectiveness always is relative. Thus, the question of what works must address with whom and under what circumstances (Nelson, 1987). Another principle, the **criterion of the least dangerous assumption,** is useful when conclusive data are not available regarding the effectiveness of a particular intervention and the circumstances surrounding it. As stated by Donnellan (1984), "in the absence of conclusive data, educational decisions should be based on assumptions that, if incorrect, will have the least dangerous effect on the student" (p. 142). For example, an intervention package involving DRI and response cost could be assumed to have less dangerous effects than one

that includes overcorrection. One cautionary note: In applying behavior reduction procedures, be sure to continuously evaluate their effectiveness. A less restrictive or intrusive intervention that is ineffective not only is a waste of your time, it also may contribute to the student's increasing adaptation to more aversive consequences (Azrin & Holz, 1966).

While this discussion has focused on reductive procedures, be aware that strategies based on positive reinforcement also can be misapplied and abused (P. S. Strain, personal communication, April 1986). For example, inappropriate contingencies of reinforcement may directly support undesired behavior, as when teachers attend to maladaptive student performances while ignoring adaptive behavior when it occurs. One reason that interventions involving aversive procedures are evaluated more critically is that their misuse usually involves greater risks to the student (although there are several exceptions, such as the teacher who attends to SIB).

Decision Models for Reducing Undesired Behaviors

The guidelines and considerations described here provide a basis for making tentative decisions about intervention alternatives. However, a more detailed analysis is necessary to match precisely the intervention strategy to the characteristics of the pupil, the setting, and the target behavior. Several decision models have been devised for this purpose (e.g., Evans & Meyer, 1985; Gaylord-Ross, 1980; Wolery et al., 1988). The common elements of these models are the formation of hypotheses regarding why problem behavior is occurring and systematic assessment of these hypotheses through manipulation of potential maintaining variables. For example, the model developed by Gaylord-Ross (1980) includes reinforcement, ecology, curriculum, and punishment components. In terms of *reinforcement,* if you hypothesize that a student's behavior is maintained by positive reinforcement and that the teacher controls the reinforcer, extinction would be a viable intervention. On the other hand, if the behavior is maintained by negative reinforcement (e.g., the student escapes or avoids tasks or settings by engaging in the target behavior), the task itself can be modified to make it less aversive or you can remove the opportunity to escape by putting the student through the task. Or if the behavior occurs due to an insufficient amount of positive reinforcement, increasing the density (i.e., amount and availability) of reinforcement through differential reinforcement might be the best choice.

Interventions based on *ecological* hypotheses stress determining whether problem behaviors occur because of crowding, the lack of engaging objects, or the presence of environmental pollutants (heat, noise, light). Changes in these variables constitute the appropriate intervention in such cases. (However, Conroy and Fox [1994] observed that more remote events occurring in other settings, such as the home, may need to be considered.) Hypotheses based on *curriculum* variables derive from the observation that problem behaviors vary according to particular tasks. Interventions addressing this component involve making appropriate adjustments in the curriculum (e.g., modifying overly difficult tasks, changing nonpreferred tasks).

Punishment is the last component in the Gaylord-Ross (1980) model, which indicates that the other hypotheses should be entertained first. We cannot overemphasize the importance of trying to "read" the pupil's behavior correctly; interventions chosen without regard for maintaining variables may be doomed to failure. For example, if a student's disruptive behavior is maintained by escape from undesired tasks, timeout would be ineffective in reducing this problem. The systematic, continuous assessment of pinpointed target behaviors in the settings in which they occur is crucial to identifying their relationships to variables that may influence them, to selecting appropriate intervention strategies, and to evaluating and adjusting these interventions.

Resources for Intervention Planning

Fortunately for the practitioner, tremendous growth has occurred in the amount of resource materials for developing interventions for social behaviors. Included in these are social skills curricula (see Chapter 10), which represent proactive strategies for teaching appropriate social skills and replacement behaviors. Other resources present strategies for the management of specific problem behaviors. For example, Algozzine (1993) developed a practical guide for dealing with a variety of instructional and behavior management problems. The practitioner can look up a particular behavior problem in this loose-leaf notebook (e.g., physical aggression toward peers, off-task behavior) and locate alternate strategies for dealing with it. The guide includes reference citations and additional readings for each strategy.

A number of such quick reference guides have been published by Sopris West. These include *The Tough Kid Book* (Rhode, Jenson, & Reavis, 1993) and the *Tough Kid Tool Box* (Jenson, Rhode, & Reavis, 1994), which present a number of suggestions and materials for assisting in the development of proactive behavior management strategies and ideas for dealing with students who are noncompliant, disruptive, and aggressive. Project RIDE (Responding to Individual Differences in Education) (Beck & Gabriel, 1990) and Project RIDE for Preschoolers (Utah State Office of Education, 1993) are building- and classroom-based support systems for teachers, including computer tactics banks and video libraries that present and illustrate a number of proven, cost-effective strategies. Table 4.3 lists these and other resource materials. Sopris West also provides training to school districts that adopt these materials. In using such resources, it is important to recognize the need for adequate training or access to skilled consultation to avoid the tendency to apply the tactics presented in "cookbook" fashion, without appropriate accommodation to individual circumstances.

The Council for Exceptional Children has published a mini-library on working with behavioral disorders. These short booklets contain useful information for practitioners about issues and strategies concerning working with students

Table 4.3 Resource Materials for Dealing with Problem Behaviors

Available from Sopris West, 1140 Boston Avenue, Longmont, CO 80501

Title, Author	Description
Administrative Intervention: A School Administrator's Guide to Working with Aggressive and Disruptive Students, Black & Downs	A step-by-step approach to dealing with out-of-control students from onset of behavior to student's reentry into the classroom
Bully-Proofing Your School: A Comprehensive Approach for Elementary Schools, Garrity, Jens, Porter, Sager, & Short-Camilli	A comprehensive process that assists elementary school staff in recognizing and intervening in bullying situations and that empowers other students to assist victims of bullying and to deny bullies the peer reinforcement that perpetuates their behavior
Interventions: Collaborative Planning for Students at Risk, Sprick, Sprick, & Garrison	Three effective processes for collaborative intervention planning and 16 proven interventions presented via a manual and audio cassettes
Managing Acting-Out Behavior: A Staff Development Program to Prevent and Manage Acting-Out Behavior, Colvin	Two videotapes and a manual that describe the various stages of acting-out behavior and provide nonconfrontational strategies for dealing with it
Project RIDE (elementary and secondary versions), Beck & Gabriel	A comprehensive resource for solving both academic and social student problems in the regular classroom, a process for accommodating those students who neither qualify for pull-out programs nor can function successfully in the regular classroom, and a prereferral procedure to special education services
Project RIDE for Preschoolers, Utah State Office of Education	Like Project RIDE, provides a comprehensive guide to dealing with difficult-to-teach children through a resource manual, computer-based tactics bank, and video demonstration tapes
The Teacher's Encyclopedia of Behavior Management: 100 Problems/500 Plans, Sprick & Howard	Designed for elementary and middle/junior high school teachers, includes 3 to 5 detailed, step-by-step plans to assist teachers in developing a plan that fits the origin, duration, and severity of the problem situation
The Tough Kid Book: Practical Classroom Management Strategies, Rhode, Jenson, & Reavis	A resource for both regular and special education teachers that presents straightforward alternate strategies for dealing with disruptive student behaviors
The Tough Kid Tool Box: A Collection of Classroom Tools, Jenson, Rhode, & Reavis	A compilation of ready-to-use materials for managing and motivating tough-to-teach students

Available from The Council for Exceptional Children, Dept. K30950, 1920 Association Drive, Reston VA 22091-1589
CEC Mini-Library, Working with Behavioral Disorders, Edited by L. M. Bullock and R. B. Rutherford, Jr.
Use this mini-library as a reference to help staff understand the problems of specific groups of youngsters with behavioral problems.
Teaching Students with Behavioral Disorders: Basic Questions and Answers, Lewis, Heflin, & DiGangi.
Conduct Disorders and Social Maladjustments: Policies, Politics, and Programming, Wood, Cheney, Cline, Smith, & Guetzloe.
Behaviorally Disordered? Assessment for Identification and Instruction, Algozzine, Ruhl, & Ramsey.
Preparing to Integrate Students with Behavioral Disorders, Gable, Laycock, Maroney, & Smith.
Teaching Young Children with Behavioral Disorders, Zabel.
Reducing Undesirable Behaviors, Polsgrove.
Social Skills for Students with Autism, Simpson, Myles, Sasso, & Kamps.
Special Education in Juvenile Corrections, Leone, Rutherford, & Nelson.
Moving On: Transitions for Youth with Behavioral Disorders, Bullis & Gaylord-Ross.

who exhibit problematic behaviors (see Table 4.3; the appendix to this text includes a bibliography of intervention resources).

The rapid development of computer-based information services also has produced numerous on-line resources for practitioners with access to computers with modems and Internet accounts.[3] The Internet offers practitioners access to a variety of electronic mail (e-mail) services, including "gopher" searches of library data bases and access to "listservs". A listserv is a public or private electronic mailing list that provides a way of sending one notice to many persons on many different computer systems. Listservs are one of the more popular ways to disseminate information, share opinions, and get advice through the Internet. When you subscribe to a listserv you get a copy— in your electronic "mailbox"—of every message sent to the list. You also have the ability to send your messages to all other subscribers by sending them to one central address for quick electronic distribution to everyone on the list. Thousands of lists are available on a wide range of topics (W. Ross, personal communication, May 1995). Table 4.4 presents some of the lists pertaining to those working with children with disabilities.

Developing an Intervention Plan

IEPs for pupils certified as having EBD should contain objectives and strategies for targeted social behaviors. (We often are surprised to read IEPs for such pupils that contain no plans for intervening with their social behavior problems.) However, these strategies lack the specificity needed to guide intervention efforts on a day-to-day basis. Moreover, students who are not certified as having disabilities will not have IEPs.[4] Wolery et al. (1988) indicated that a specific intervention plan should be developed for each social behavior that is targeted for reduction. The components of an intervention plan include: a *behavioral objective, what* will be done, *who* will do

it, *how* it will be done, *when* it will be done, *when* it will be reviewed, *who* will review it, and *what* will happen if the plan is ineffective or if undesired side effects occur. Given the many legal, ethical, and practical considerations that must be taken into account in using reductive procedures, such plans are best worked out by a team. Initial intervention plans can be developed by IEP committees, but for daily decision making and for those students who do not have IEPs, planning teams should include persons who are readily available to review data, discuss problems, and make decisions about plan revisions as required. Data-based evaluation strategies, which are valuable tools for intervention teams, are discussed in the following section.

EVALUATING BEHAVIORAL INTERVENTIONS

Powerful intervention strategies, especially those that are restrictive or intrusive, require precise and sensitive evaluation procedures to ensure that students do not spend unnecessary amounts of time in ineffective programs. Good evaluation procedures also protect those who carry out interventions, in that they provide feedback that may be used to adjust or change procedures that are inappropriate, incorrectly applied, or simply do not work as planned. Unlike assessment, which yields information regarding the current status of a student, evaluation involves assessing the impact of a program on a pupil's current status. Evaluation may be **summative,** occurring after teaching and learning have taken place, or **formative,** which means it occurs as skills are being formed (Howell, Kaplan, & O'Connell, 1979). Traditionally, most educational programs are evaluated summatively (e.g., once or twice a year), when it is too late to make any program changes based on the data obtained. Formative evaluation, however, is an integral part of the teaching process.

Two sets of behavioral procedures are used in conducting formative evaluations of student programs. The first, **data-based decision making,** involves comparing student performance or progress to a desired level and making adjustments based

---

[3]Many school districts and even some states are establishing linkages to such computer-based information linkages as SpecialNet. In addition, the development of the World-Wide Web is making available vast amounts of information to subscribers with modems and appropriate software. Some states (e.g., Iowa, Kentucky) are developing web pages containing resources for understanding and managing student behavior.

[4]Students with disabilities who are not identified by IDEA are protected under Section 504 of the Rehabilitation Act of 1973 and should have a written educational plan that includes disciplinary plans (Yell & Peterson, 1995).

Table 4.4   Internet On-Line Resources

List Name	Description	Server
ADA-LAW	Americans with Disabilities Act Law discussion	@ndsuvm1
ALTLEARN	Alternative approaches to learning	@sjuvm
AUTISM	SJU autism and developmental disabilities	@sjuvm
BEHAVIOR	Behavioral & emotional disorders in children	@asuacad
BGEDU-L	Educator's forum on reform	@ukcc.uky.edu
BLIND-L	Computer use by and for the blind	@uafsysb
BLINDNWS	*Blind News Digest*	@ndsuvm1
BULLY-L	Bullying and victimization in schools list	listserv@nic.surfnet.nl
CDMAJOR	Communication disorder discussion list	@kentvm
CHATBACK	Planning forum for CHATBACK UK & Int'l, educational net for disabled children	@sjuvm
COMMDIS	Speech disorders	@rpitsvm
DDFIND-L	Forum for networking on disabilities	@gitvm1
DISRES-L	Disability research list	@ryerson
DRUGABUS	Drug abuse education list	listserv@umab.bitnet
EFFSCHPRAC	Effective school practices list	mailserv@oregon.uoregon.edu
KIDINTRO	Penpal group for children	listserv@sjuvm.stjohns.edu
KIDSNET	Global K-12 network planning list	kidsnet-request@vms.cis.pitt.edu
MULTC-ED	Multicultural education discussion	listserv@umdd.umd.edu
L-HCAP	Handicapped people in education	@ndsuvm1
SCR-L	Study of cognitive rehabilitation	@mizzou1
TALKBACK	Kids forum for CHATBACK, disabled children	@sjuvm
TEACHEFT	Teaching effectiveness discussion	listserv@wcupa.edu
SPCEDS-L	Special education students list—Suny/Buffalo	@ubvm

Social Integration Handicap Issues in ICIDH
Address   DS-H-SI@NIHLIST.BITNET
Server   LISTSERV@HIHLIST.BITNET

Child Abuse
Address   ABUSE-L@UBVM.BITNET
Server   LISTSERV@UBVM.BITNET
Contact   Ann S. Botash <BOTASHA@VAX.CC.HSCSYR.EDU>
The ABUSE-L list was formed to serve as a forum for professionals to discuss topics related to child abuse.

Mental Health and the Legal System
Address   LEGALTEN@world.std.com
Server   majordomo@world.std.com
Contact   Jonathan Hurwitz <jsh@hsri.org>
The Evaluation Center @ HSRI has been working on plans to set up an internet listserv to facilitate assessment of the impacts of interventions in the broad area of interface between the mental health system, the criminal justice system, and the courts.

(continued on next page)

Table 4.4 (*continued*)

Discussion of Topics in Special Education

Address	spedtalk@virginia.edu
Server	MAJORDOMO@VIRGINIA.EDU
Contact	John Wills Lloyd <john1@virginia.edu>

Spedtalk is an open, unmoderated list hosted by the University of Virginia. It is a forum for people to discuss current issues about practices, policies, and research in special education. Although many of the long-standing participants in spedtalk are affiliated with institutions of higher education, either as students or professors, the list is open and includes people from other backgrounds as well, particularly teachers, researchers, and clinicians.

Department of Education/OERI Institutional Communications Network (INET)

Address	gopher gopher.ed.gov

National Institutes of Allergy and Infectious Disease (NIAID)

Address	gopher niaid.nih.gov

NIH Server includes reports from GAO, the president, Department of Labor, and the National Institute of Health. The NIH Server is also adding full text of government documents including the "National Performance Review."

Address	ftp cu.nih.gov	(128.231.64.7)

ADA BBS
202/514-6193
Daniel A. Searing
Department of Justice, Disability Civil Rights Div.
Washington, DC
2400

CARE NET BBS
219/233-1261
Marlin Sheffield
820 Whitehall
South Bend, IN 46615
1200
Weekdays; 10PM–5PM, weekends; 10PM–9PM

This FIDO BBS has one message conference dedicated to disabilities and special education. The system began early in 1985 and currently operates part-time.

Resource Access
504/897-9204
Richard Butler
New Orleans, LA
Maternal/children's health, disability, and disease information

Well-Net
415/968-1126 or 415/968-8798
Community Health Information Project
222-C View St.
Mt. View, CA 94141
A nationwide bulletin board for persons with disabilities.

on this comparison (Deno & Mirkin, 1978). The second procedure is to apply a **single-subject research design** to identify and isolate specific variables that have a direct cause-effect relationship to target behavior. We discuss these procedures separately, although both have much in common and may be used simultaneously.

Data-Based Decision Making

The professional who is directly responsible for managing the target student in settings where targeted behaviors occur must be able to evaluate interventions continuously and make or recommend adjustments in intervention procedures on the basis of these evaluations. Data-based decision making is a technology designed to assist practitioners in conducting ongoing formative evaluations of student performance as part of the teaching process. It uses data collected systematically to measure targeted academic and social behaviors.

One of the first skills required for data-based decision making is determining what the collected data are telling you. In other words, you must know how to analyze data. There are two approaches to behavioral data analysis: statistical and visual. The debate between proponents of both approaches has been long standing and lively. We advocate the visual method because visual analysis is more conservative (Parsonson & Baer, 1978). In addition, visual inspection is more realistic for practitioners.

Formative evaluation, then, is based upon ongoing data collection. These data are used to decide when to change an instructional or behavior management program as well as which components of a student's program to alter, remove, or replace. Obviously, this task cannot be accomplished without data that are sensitive to variations in students' daily performances and that are reliable measures of those performances. If your data are sensitive and reliable, you can make good program evaluation decisions from visual analysis.

Formative evaluation based on visual data analysis (data-based decision making) is a search for **functional relationships,** looking for environmental variables that affect the target behavior being measured. This is accomplished by systematically manipulating certain independent variables (curriculum, reinforcement, instructions, etc.) one at a time while keeping other variables as constant as possible.

Before implementing an academic or social intervention, assess the student's current performance. Instead of a static pretest approach, which may not represent the pupil's typical performance, measure target behavior across several sessions or days. Your intervention data then can be compared to this preintervention or **baseline data** to determine whether your program is effective. Thus, the purpose of collecting baseline data is to determine current levels and trends in behavior, as well as to see whether any environmental variables present during the baseline period are affecting it.

There are no hard and fast rules for determining the length of a baseline condition. Length depends on the level of the behavior, its variability, and whether it shows a **trend** in the direction of the criterion level, as well as such factors as the effects of the target student's behavior on others and the amount of time left in the school term (Gelfand & Hartmann, 1984). If baseline data are highly variable or show a trend in the direction of the desired criterion level, consider extending the baseline phase while looking for sources of variation or factors contributing to trends. A minimum of three baseline data points generally are recommended for academic target behaviors (e.g., White & Haring, 1980), although White (1971) demonstrated that a minimum of seven data points is needed to project a reliable performance trend. You should collect five to seven baseline data points on social behavior targets, unless circumstances prohibit it.

Baseline data provide a relative standard against which subsequent program changes may be evaluated, so it is essential to analyze these data as carefully as those gathered during intervention conditions. The visual display of data via graphs and charts provides a convenient summary across various baseline and intervention conditions. Within these conditions, the data may be characterized in terms of level, trend, and stability. Straightforward and useful procedures for analyzing data about these characteristics on simple line graphs have been developed.

Analyzing Level   *Level* refers to the magnitude of the data in terms of the scale value on the ordinate, or Y-axis, of the graph. Tawney and Gast (1984) describe two characteristics of level that are important in data analysis. Within a given condition, level may be analyzed with regard to stability and change. *Level stability* refers to the variability of the data points around their median.[5] Data that vary no more than 15 percent from the median value would be considered stable. Level stability reflects the degree to which behavior is affected by planned or unplanned variables. For example, unstable data following the introduction of an intervention suggest that the other variables may be influencing the behavior as much as the intervention procedures (Tawney & Gast, 1984).

Level change refers to the amount of relative change in the data within or between conditions. To compute *level change within a condition,* find the ordinate values of the first and last data points in the condition, subtract the smallest from the largest, and note whether the change is occurring in a therapeutic (improving) or contratherapeutic (decaying) direction, based on the intervention objective. Knowledge of the amount of level change within a condition is useful for deciding whether it is appropriate to change conditions. For example, if a level change is occurring in a therapeutic direction during baseline conditions, it may be unnecessary to begin an intervention. *Level change between adjacent conditions* (e.g., baseline and intervention) is computed by identifying the ordinate values of the last data point of the first condition and the value of the first data point of the second condition, subtracting the smaller from the larger, and noting whether the

change is in an improving or decaying direction. The amount of level change between baseline and intervention conditions is an indication of the immediate impact of the intervention on the target behavior (Tawney & Gast, 1984).

Another important characteristic to consider when evaluating changes in data between conditions is the amount of *overlapping data points.* This is calculated by noting the proportion of data points in adjacent conditions that fall within the same range. For example, if more than 50 percent of the data points during an intervention condition fall within the range of baseline data points, it may be concluded that the intervention has only weak effects (Parsonson & Baer, 1978). However, the trend of the intervention data must also be considered.

Analyzing Data Trends   Data paths seldom follow straight lines, nor do they increase or decrease in even increments. This can create difficulty in making reliable judgments about whether rates of behavior are accelerating, decelerating, or remaining relatively stable. A relatively simple way to analyze data trends is to draw **trend lines** (also called *lines of progress*) that depict the general path of the data within a condition. This can be done by the *freehand method,* which involves drawing a line of "best fit" that bisects the data points (Parsonson & Baer, 1978). This method takes very little time but the trend lines produced are likely to be inaccurate (Tawney & Gast, 1984). A more reliable procedure is the *split-middle method* (White & Haring, 1980) explained in Figure 4.1. This method may be used to analyze trends in data plotted either on equal interval or semilogarithmic graph paper, and with a little practice you can do it quickly.

Data trends often reveal important and useful information. For example, an increasing (accelerating) trend indicates that the target behavior probably is being reinforced. A level trend suggests that reinforcement is serving to maintain the behavior at its current rate. A decreasing (decelerating) trend indicates that extinction or punishment contingencies are in effect. Such trends may show that contingencies unknown to or unplanned by intervention agents are operating. For example, if a baseline trend is in the

---

[5]The median is determined by finding the middle data point on the ordinate. To do this, simply count up from the abcissa, or X-axis, until you reach the middle data point; for example, if there are seven data points in the condition, the median is the fourth data point. There are three data points above and three below it. If there is an even number of data points in a condition, the median will fall halfway between two data points.

Figure 4.1 Line of Progress

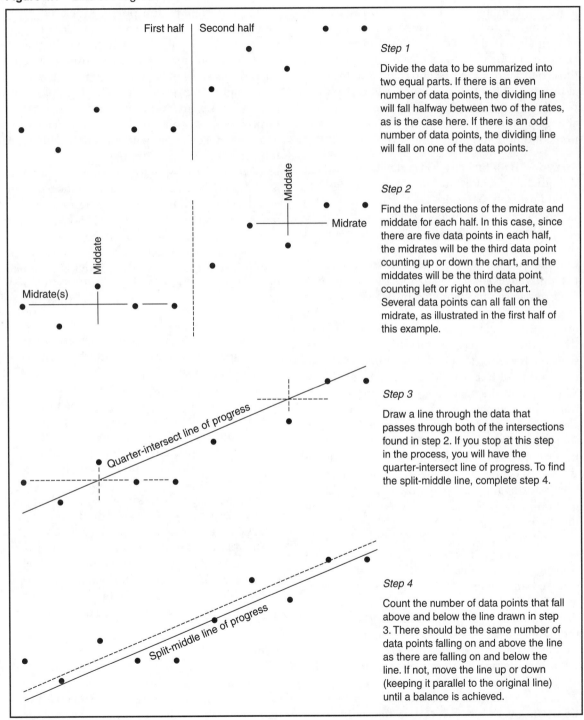

First half | Second half

Step 1

Divide the data to be summarized into two equal parts. If there is an even number of data points, the dividing line will fall halfway between two of the rates, as is the case here. If there is an odd number of data points, the dividing line will fall on one of the data points.

Middate

Middate

Midrate

Step 2

Find the intersections of the midrate and middate for each half. In this case, since there are five data points in each half, the midrates will be the third data point counting up or down the chart, and the middates will be the third data point counting left or right on the chart. Several data points can all fall on the midrate, as illustrated in the first half of this example.

Midrate(s)

Step 3

Quarter-intersect line of progress

Draw a line through the data that passes through both of the intersections found in step 2. If you stop at this step in the process, you will have the quarter-intersect line of progress. To find the split-middle line, complete step 4.

Step 4

Split-middle line of progress

Count the number of data points that fall above and below the line drawn in step 3. There should be the same number of data points falling on and above the line as there are falling on and below the line. If not, move the line up or down (keeping it parallel to the original line) until a balance is achieved.

Source: White, O. R., & Haring, N. G. (1980). *Exceptional teaching* (2nd ed.). Upper Saddle River, NJ: Merrill/Prentice Hall. Used with permission.

131

direction of your intervention criterion, and you implement an intervention, it would be difficult to attribute a continued change in a therapeutic direction (were this to occur) to the intervention because the behavior was changing anyway. On the other hand, if the baseline trend is stable or in a direction opposite to the intervention criterion, you could justifiably hypothesize that therapeutic changes following the initiation of an intervention condition were the result of your procedure.

Analyzing Data Stability   The stability of data is the variability of individual data points around the trend line. Gable, Hendrickson, Evans, and Evans (1988) suggest drawing a **window of variance** around the trend line to indicate the amount of desired stability around the trend. This is done by drawing parallel dotted lines representing a 15 percent range above and below the trend line. (This range can be computed by determining the medians for both halves of the data within a condition and calculating values within 15 percent of these, but it is simpler to estimate this variance visually.) Howell et al. (1993) recommended that the window of variance should encompass at least 80 percent of the data points. Any extreme variation or sudden change in your data that is not associated with a planned condition indicates that something unanticipated is affecting the target behavior, and you should attempt to find out what it is through conducting further functional analyses. This information may help you adjust the intervention or control extraneous variables affecting the student's performance.

Determining data trends during intervention also may help you assess functional relationships and troubleshoot your program. Parsonson and Baer (1978) provided several guidelines. For example, stable intervention data following a variable baseline indicates that recurring baseline variables perhaps are the treatment variables (e.g., differential teacher attention that was not controlled systematically during baseline). Weak program effects are suggested by variable intervention data or by considerable overlap between data points in baseline and intervention phases. This problem is

less critical if the overlap diminishes later during the intervention phase. A delayed therapeutic trend in the intervention data (i.e., no positive change followed by a change in the desired direction) may indicate the presence of initial training steps that are redundant or a waste of time. Figure 4.2 presents stylized graphs illustrating several intervention trends, and their interpretation. As you become more proficient in analyzing data visually, you also will be able to interpret trends more accurately.

Data trend analysis tells you whether a program is working and can prompt you to remove or revise an intervention, but waiting for a trend to emerge may take too long. Practitioners who must make day-to-day program decisions need rules to expedite their decision making. Fortunately, empirical data decision rules have been developed for academic targets (Deno & Mirkin, 1978; White & Haring, 1980). To implement these rules, follow these steps:

1. Determine a desired terminal criterion level. This may be established arbitrarily by the curriculum, by assessing peers, or from data obtained in previous programs with the student, or from normative data on the target behavior, if available. Plot this on the graph at a location corresponding to when you expect the criterion to be reached (see Step 2).
2. Set a date when you want to meet the criterion. Also plot this on the graph.
3. Obtain and plot baseline assessment data for three days (or sessions), if more than one instructional session takes place each day.
4. Draw a **line of desired progress** from the last day of baseline to the criterion level and date.
5. Change the program if the student's progress fails to meet or exceed the line of desired progress for three consecutive days or sessions (White & Haring, 1980).

Figure 4.3 illustrates a data decision graph for an academic target.

Data decision rules for social behaviors are not as clear-cut, because student performance, rather than sequential progress, generally is measured. Therefore, it is more difficult to establish a line

Figure 4.2 Interpretation of Data Trends

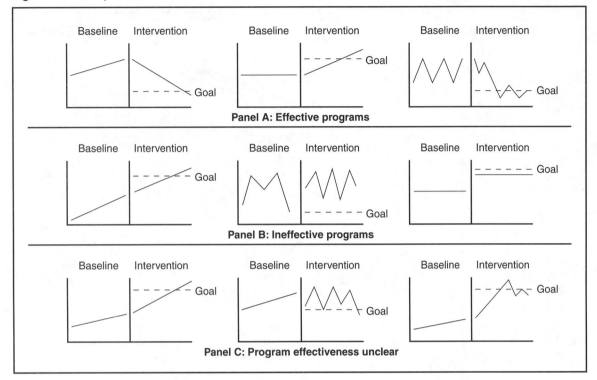

of desired progress. You may, however, set your criterion in terms of a *daily level of performance* and base your decisions on the following steps:

1. Set and graph terminal criterion level and date, just as for academic targets.
2. Obtain five to seven days (or sessions) of baseline data (more if the data are extremely variable or a therapeutic trend is apparent).
3. Write a data decision rule for the program (e.g., change the program if performance does not meet criterion in a particular phase for three consecutive sessions or days).
4. Collect intervention data and adjust the program according to your rule.

These are guidelines rather than rules; they are intended to be applied flexibly. Different behaviors and circumstances will require different data decision guidelines. Figure 4.4 shows data regarding a social behavior change program employing these data decision guidelines.

When setting criterion levels for targeted social behaviors, keep in mind an **ecological ceiling** (Howell et al., 1993). This means simply to acknowledge that it is unrealistic (and unfair) to expect target behaviors to increase or decrease to rates above or below those of peers in the same settings. Thus, a zero rate of talk-outs is an unreasonable criterion if the usual rate of peer talk-outs is five per hour. By assessing peers who are exhibiting acceptable rates of the target behavior, you can establish reasonable criterion levels (see Chapter 2). Lines of desired progress or performance should terminate at the appropriate ecological ceiling rather than at an arbitrarily chosen rate.

Single-Subject Research Designs

By using data decision rules and by learning to visually analyze data, you should become skilled at systematically evaluating interventions and making appropriate decisions. However, while data-based decision-making procedures are extremely useful

Figure 4.3   Data Decision Graph: Academic Program

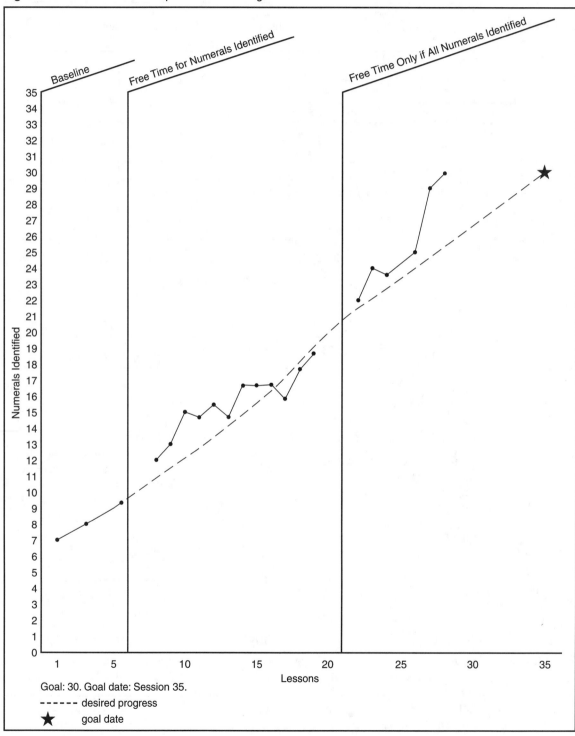

Goal: 30. Goal date: Session 35.

------ desired progress

★   goal date

134

in determining whether an intervention is working, they do not provide a convincing demonstration that the intervention is responsible for changes in target behaviors. Other uncontrolled factors may influence the behavior simultaneously with the intervention, and these offer **competing explanations** for observed changes (e.g., something else in the setting was altered, the student became more mature, gained insight). Single-subject research designs control for the effects of such extraneous variables through systematic manipulation of intervention variables over time while the target behavior is monitored.

At this point, many teachers say they do not care whether these variables are uncontrolled as long as something works to change behavior. The problem with this attitude is that it may lead to using nonfunctional procedures or complex

Figure 4.4 Data Decision Graph: Social Behavior Program

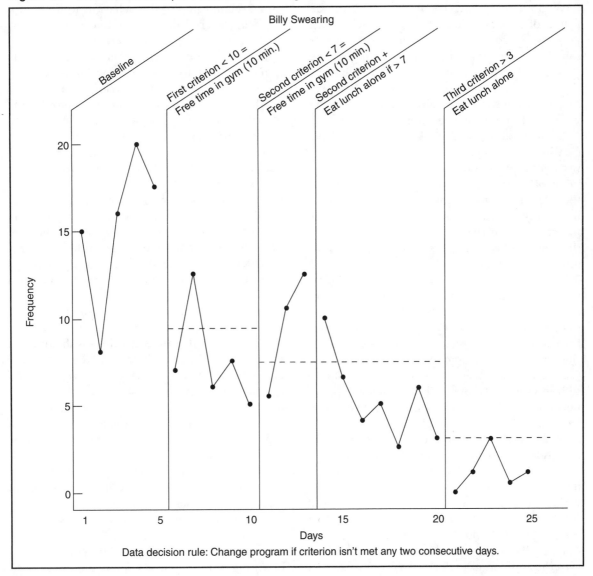

interventions that place extensive demands on the teacher. For instance, a teacher designed a group-oriented contingency (see Chapter 5) to control a group's disruptive behavior. The game involved points, back-up consequences, and much of the teacher's time. It was, however, very effective and the teacher used the game with subsequent groups for several years. Unfortunately, the effects weren't always as dramatic as the first time. Had the teacher been able to determine which components of the game were responsible for its effectiveness, the interventions could have been adjusted to the demands of each new situation. Further, some components could have been dropped, thereby simplifying the procedure and reducing the response cost to the teacher. The point is that you should use the simplest procedures that also are effective. If praise is an effective reinforcer, why develop an elaborate token economy?

Single-subject research designs are useful not only in controlling for the effects of unsystematic variables and for isolating the essential components of intervention "packages"; understanding them also will help you interpret studies reported in the research literature. The reference lists at the end of each chapter will give you an idea of the journals reporting research in areas of interest or concern to you.

Now, we briefly describe three single-subject research designs. For more comprehensive explanations, you may wish to consult a single-subject design book (e.g., Tawney & Gast, 1984). The information in our discussion of data-based decision making regarding the length of baseline phases and the determination of stability or trends in data through visual analysis applies here as well. You also may apply data-decision rules within phases of a single-subject design.

Withdrawal and reversal designs, also referred to as A-B-A-B designs, involve collecting preintervention (baseline) data (A), followed by an intervention condition (B), a withdrawal or reversal of intervention procedures (A), and finally reinstatement of the intevention (B). If the target behavior, continuously measured during all conditions, changes in accordance with the condition in effect, it may be concluded

that the intervention is effective. Although A-B-A-B designs are commonly referred to as **reversal designs,** Tawney and Gast (1984) indicate that a "true" reversal design involves a reversal of intervention contingencies in which the intervention is withdrawn from one behavior (e.g., in-seat) and simultaneously applied to an incompatible behavior (e.g., out-of-seat). The purpose of this manipulation is to demonstrate that the intervention procedure (e.g., teacher attention delivered contingent on the target behavior) has a functional relationship to the behaviors to which it is applied. Reversal designs are uncommon in the applied research literature because of the understandable reluctance of researchers and practitioners directly to reinforce undesired behavior once it has been reduced. **Withdrawal designs,** on the other hand, involve simply removing the intervention during the second A condition. In other words, baseline conditions are reinstated. Figure 4.5 shows a withdrawal design used to evaluate the effects of timeout contingent on a student's temper tantrums. It may be concluded that timeout was effective in this case because the pupil's rate of tantrums decreased when the intervention was applied. (The second replication of baseline and intervention conditions establishes timeout as the variable that probably was responsible for the observed effects. Without this replication we could not be sure that timeout was responsible for changes in the target behavior, because other uncontrolled events may have been introduced at the same time as the timeout contingency.) Changes in levels and trends of the target behavior in accordance with repeated introduction and withdrawal of the intervention demonstrates that manipulation of the timeout contingency controlled the student's tantrums, regardless of any uncontrolled events that may have taken place.

Multiple baseline designs provide a means of evaluating an intervention without a return to baseline conditions. The effectiveness of a program is demonstrated by applying it sequentially across different students, across different behaviors in the same student, or across different conditions or settings with the same student and behavior. If the measured behaviors change in the desired direction only when the intervention is applied, it may be concluded that the intervention is effective. Figure 4.6 illustrates a multiple baseline design across behaviors. The teacher's goal was to increase the pupil's oral responses to questions. Baseline data were collected on two classes of oral responses: simple yes-no answers and more elaborate verbal responses. Next, intervention was applied to yes-no responses only, while baseline data were collected on other verbal responses. After a stable trend in the former was apparent, intervention was applied to other verbal responses. The conclusion that the teacher's procedures were responsible for the changes in the pupil's oral responses is allowed because neither class of verbal behavior changed until the intervention was applied. The same sequence is followed in the other types of multiple baseline designs; that is, baseline data are collected across multiple students or settings and then the intervention is staggered across students or settings.

Multiple baseline designs are applicable to a variety of situations. However, they require two or more replications (two or more students, settings, or behaviors), prolonged baselines, and target behaviors that can be separately altered without changing the rate of the behavior still in baseline (Tawney & Gast, 1984).

A variation on the multiple baseline is the **multiple probe design.** It differs from the former in that data *probes,* or periodic assessments, rather than continuous data, are recorded for the settings, behaviors, or students to which the intervention has not yet been applied. This variation is useful particularly if you are unable to monitor all target behaviors each day (Tawney & Gast, 1984).

Figure 4.5 Tantrums

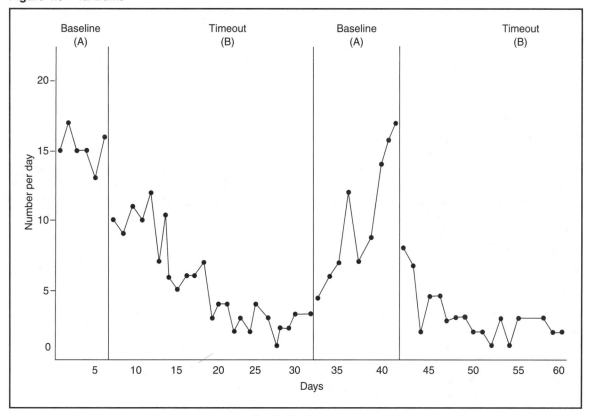

Figure 4.6 Percent of Verbal Responses per Opportunity

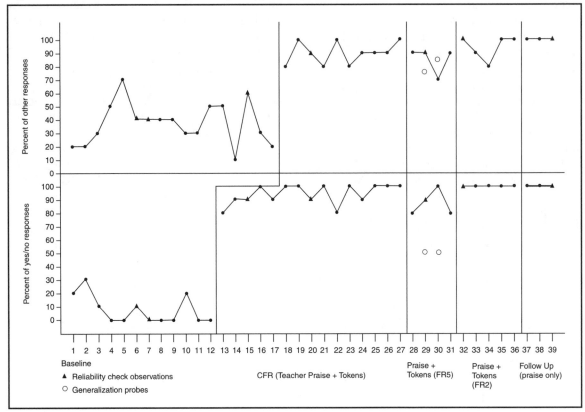

The **changing criterion design** (Hartmann & Hall, 1976) actually is a variation on the multiple baseline design, but it may be used with only one student, one behavior, or in only one setting. Following the baseline phase, an intervention program is applied through a series of increments in criterion levels. If the rate of the target behavior changes as the criterion is altered, it may be concluded that the intervention was responsible (Hartmann & Hall, 1976). For example, Figure 4.7 shows a changing criterion design used to evaluate a program to increase a student's time in his classroom. Each week, the criterion was increased in terms of time in the classroom. Chris's performance also increased in response to these criterion changes. This design especially is appropriate for evaluating programs in which a stepwise progression is desired (Tawney & Gast, 1984).

SUMMARY

Designing intervention strategies from among the variety of behavior change procedures currently available requires complex decisions that are best made by a team of professionals and advocates for the students involved. Professional guidelines and school district or agency policies should be considered in making such decisions. Ultimately, it is the responsibility of primary behavior change agents to make informed decisions regarding intervention strategies from among the range of available behavior enhancement and reductive procedures. These choices should be based on their knowledge of the current research literature, of ethical and legal constraints, and of the characteristics of the student and the settings in which interventions are to be applied. Frequently these procedures must be

Figure 4.7 Chris: Time
Spent in Classroom

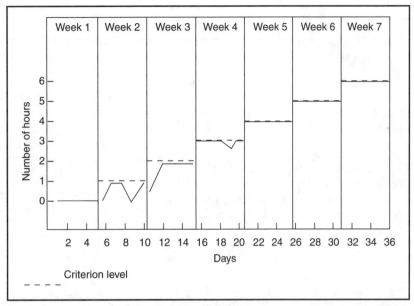

Source: Worell, J., & Nelson, C.M. (1974). *Managing instructional problems: A case study workbook.*
New York: McGraw-Hill, p. 216. Used with permission.

combined or used in novel ways to fit the circumstances in which they are to be used. Formative evaluation procedures based on continuous and precise measurement of target behaviors therefore are needed for studying and for adjusting interventions. Formative evaluation reduces the chances that students will be subjected to ineffective or unnecessarily aversive procedures. These skills are the basic tools of applied behavior analysis practitioners.

 CASE STUDY

THE DEVELOPMENT OF INDIVIDUALIZED BEHAVIOR SUPPORT PLANS[1]

George Sugai, Ph.D., Behavior Research and Teaching, College of Education, University of Oregon

[1]Reprinted with the author's permission. The author acknowledges Geoff Colvin, Betsy Fernandez, and Rob Horner for their assistance in the development of the Quickie Behavior Support Plan Sheet. Preparation of this manuscript was supported in part by the U. S. Department of Education, Office of Special Education and Rehabilitation, Grant HO29N30003. Opinions do not necessarily reflect the policy of the U.S. Department of Education and no official endorsement should be inferred.

Most students are successful in school because they possess learning histories that enable them to benefit from the universal strategies we use to teach academic content and to manage their social behaviors. These strategies include instruction in large groups, grade-level basal curricula, enforcement of school-wide and classroom-wide rules, use of standardized consequences for appropriate and inappropriate behaviors, and so on (Colvin, Kameenui, & Sugai, 1994; Kameenui & Darch, 1995). When these students make errors, we provide simple corrections that involve minimal amounts of assistance and effort (e.g., verbal corrections, simple demonstrations,

(continued)

and additional practice). For example, if Caesar blurts out an answer to a question instead of raising his hand, his teacher reminds him of the rule for raising hands and has him verbally repeat the rule and demonstrate what the rule-following behavior looks like. If Caesar is like most students, he will remember to raise his hand at the next opportunity. A few students may require two or three corrections before they become successful at meeting the rules and expectations of the classroom and school, but they usually are not identified as chronic offenders or difficult to teach.

Unfortunately, not all students are like Caesar, and many students come to our classrooms unprepared to benefit from the simple behavior management strategies that are used regularly by teachers to maintain a controlled learning environment. In fact, a significant but small proportion of our students do not respond to strategies that are effective with most students, and the challenges they present often consume more than 80 percent of teachers' instructional time (Sugai & Horner, 1994). These students experience academic and social failure because they lack the prerequisite skills and/or have learned responses that are incompatible with the expectations of the school and classroom environments. For example, little improvement is seen in Cleo's talking-out behaviors even when her teacher gives frequent verbal reminders and reprimands, takes away privileges, has her practice the desired responses, or sends her to the principal for a "firm" message about the importance of following teacher directions. In fact, when corrected or punished, Cleo's behaviors escalate; she uses profanity, intimidates peers and adults, and destroys classroom and school property.

Students like Cleo who display chronic problem behaviors require behavior support plans that are specialized, comprehensive, and individualized. Behavior support plans must be specialized because general classroom management strategies and school-wide discipline systems are ineffective in responding to the intense and chronic nature and history of the problem behavior. Behavior support plans must be comprehensive to accommodate those times and places when problem behaviors are likely; maximize opportunities for the student to be behaviorally successful across settings, people, and time;

and improve our capacity to respond when problem behaviors do occur. Finally, plans must be individualized because strategies that work with the larger student body do not align with and accommodate the student's unique learning history and persistent behavior patterns.

Fortunately, we know many features that make behavior support plans specialized, comprehensive, and individualized (Horner, O'Neill, & Flannery, 1993; Sugai & Tindal, 1994; Wolery et al. 1988):

1. Functional assessments are used to develop testable explanations or hypotheses about factors that maintain the occurrence of problem behavior and inhibit displays of more acceptable responses.
2. Instructional strategies are used to teach and/or enhance more acceptable replacement responses to the problem behavior (e.g., social skills instruction, self-management strategies).
3. Strategies are included to weaken and eliminate problem behavior.
4. Planned strategies for crisis prevention and intervention are used when problem behavior becomes too severe or escalates to the point where students might injure themselves or others.
5. Strategies for manipulating setting events and antecedent factors are used to occasion more appropriate responding.
6. Teaching scripts (i.e., lesson plans) are used to improve the fidelity with which plans are implemented by staff.
7. Strategies for measuring and evaluating the effects and outcomes of the plan are used on an ongoing basis so timely plan modifications can be made.

Unfortunately, many schools discover that their capacity to develop and implement plans that include these features is severely curtailed, if not halted altogether, because of common school barriers (e.g., lack of time, untrained staff members, insufficient resources, and poor organizational structures and procedures) (Colvin, Kameenui, & Sugai, 1994; Sugai & Horner, 1994). When these barriers exist, teachers become frustrated; for example, effective plans are not immediately available, not understood, or too complicated to be implemented accurately or at all,

(continued)

and the problem behavior worsens because of inconsistent or inaccurate implementation.

This paper describes a strategy for improving the efficiency with which behavior support plans can be developed and implemented. A Quickie Behavior Support Plan sheet is described in detail, and examples are provided. In addition, requisites for using this planning sheet are described.

REQUISITES

To develop and implement comprehensive behavior support plans for individual students with chronic problem behavior, program and building staff must be prepared to dedicate time and resources to establishing a system that sustains and reinforces behavior support planning. The following requisites should be considered (Sugai & Horner, 1994; Todd, Sugai, & Horner, in preparation):

1. Establish a building or school-wide team that has as its primary responsibility the management of behavior support systems for individual students with severe behavior challenges. Depending on the size of the school staff, this team could be directly responsible for developing and implementing individual behavior support plans, or it could oversee the activities of smaller behavior support teams that might do the actual intervention planning and implementation.
2. Establish the behavioral capacity within the school to provide specialized behavior support. This behavioral capacity could come from an individual staff member or from a small group of individuals who collectively have expertise in the following areas: functional assessment, social skills instruction, behavioral interventions, instructional and curricular adaptations, and data collection and evaluation.
3. Establish a system by which teachers can request assistance in a timely manner, that is, a simple, one-page request for assistance is used to initiate the process for receiving behavioral support; a functional assessment and a behavior support plan are completed within 10 working days; and a strategy for immediate assistance is provided within 24 hours.

FUNCTIONAL ASSESSMENT AND DEVELOPMENT OF A COMPETING BEHAVIOR PATHWAYS ANALYSIS

The development of behavior support plans must be based on information obtained through functional assessments (Carr et al., 1994; Horner, O'Neill, & Flannery, 1993; Sugai & Tindal, 1994). Regardless of the functional assessment method used (e.g., teacher/parent interviews, student interviews, direct observations, rating scales), the outcome must be statements that describe the relationship between the problem behavior and the environmental context in which the behavior is displayed (i.e., setting events, triggering antecedents, maintaining consequences) (Horner, 1994; Lewis & Sugai, 1994). In addition, the functional assessment must give information that enhances our ability to identify effective, efficient, and relevant replacement behaviors (i.e., functional equivalence) for the problem behavior (Horner & Day, 1991; Todd et al., in preparation).

After functional assessment information has been collected, the competing pathways form, shown in Figure 4.8, is completed (Horner, O'Neill, & Flannery, 1993; O'Neill et al., in press). This form serves as a simple, practical, and efficient means of summarizing and organizing functional assessment information and of developing effective, efficient, and relevant replacement behaviors for the problem behavior. To complete this form, the behavior support team fills in each of the shapes with corresponding functional assessment information. When completed, a relational representation of the problem behavior, desired alternative behavior, acceptable alternative behavior, and environmental influences (setting events, triggering antecedents, and maintaining consequences) is displayed.

Figure 4.8 illustrates Theora's problem behaviors, which consist of putting her head down on her desk, covering her head with her coat, and refusing to initiate tasks, are hypothesized as being maintained by task avoidance/escape (negative reinforcement). Although her teacher ultimately wants Theora to initiate and complete difficult tasks without assistance, he has selected an acceptable alternative response ("asking the teacher for assistance") that is maintained by the same consequence that sustains the problem behavior.

(continued)

Figure 4.8 Theora's competing Behavior Pathways Form

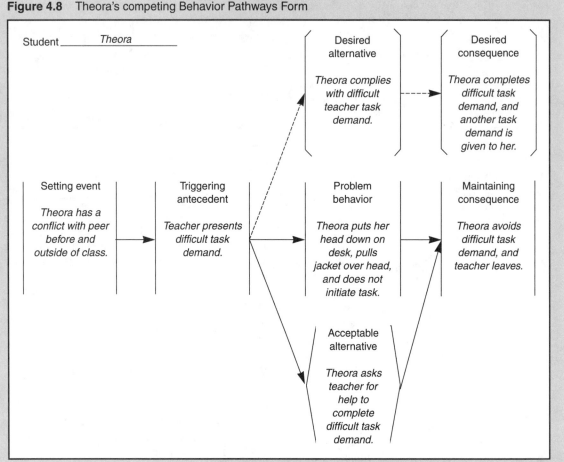

Figure 4.9 illustrates a second competing pathways summary. Information from a functional assessment suggests that Geoff's problem behaviors are maintained by adult and/or peer attention; setting events do not appear to be a factor; he is unlikely to display the desired behavior ("select alternative activities when done with work") because gaining adult and/or peer attention is more desirable and accessible (i.e., positively reinforcing) than working independently; and teaching him to solicit teacher attention when he is done with his work is more relevant than selecting alternative activities, but more tolerable to the classroom environment than making disruptive comments.

QUICKIE BEHAVIOR SUPPORT PLAN SHEET

After the competing pathways summary is completed, a behavior support plan is developed. To accommodate the barriers described previously (e.g., limited time, resources, and behavioral expertise), a Quickie Behavior Support Plan Sheet is recommended (see Figure 4.10) (Sugai, 1994). This single-page form is designed to be completed by a behavior support team within 30 minutes. Although a more comprehensive and detailed plan will be necessary for extremely challenging behavior problems, the Quickie Plan Sheet gives teachers a set of

(continued)

Figure 4.9　Geoff's competing Behavior Pathways Form

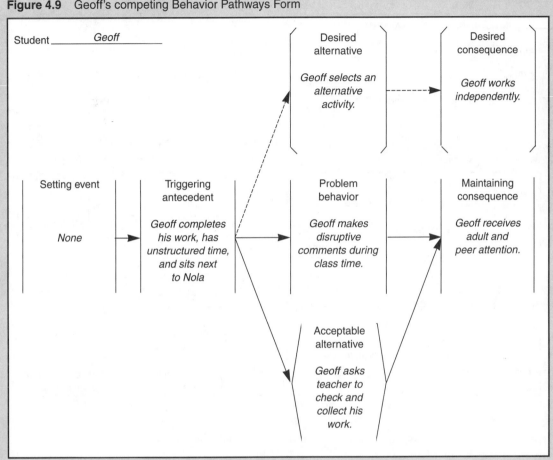

Student _____ *Geoff* _____

Desired
alternative

*Geoff selects an
alternative
activity.*

Desired
consequence

*Geoff works
independently.*

Setting event

None

Triggering
antecedent

*Geoff completes
his work, has
unstructured time,
and sits next
to Nola*

Problem
behavior

*Geoff makes
disruptive
comments during
class time.*

Maintaining
consequence

*Geoff receives
adult and
peer attention.*

Acceptable
alternative

*Geoff asks
teacher to
check and
collect his
work.*

intervention responses that can be implemented immediately. The Quickie Behavior Support Plan has a number of unique features that have been designed to increase development and implementation activities:

1. The initiation and completion of each step is prompted by a single question.
2. The answer for each question must fit within the space provided.
3. The sequence of steps needed to complete the plan sheet is prompted by arrows which are numbered (counterclockwise direction) from 1 to 9.

4. Assessment information is summarized on the left side of the sheet (Steps 1 through 4), and intervention information is summarized on the right hand side (Steps 5 through 8).
5. Each assessment pinpoint has a corresponding intervention strategy, that is, Steps 1 and 8, Steps 2 and 7, Steps 3 and 6, and Steps 4 and 5.
6. A simple data decision rule to initiate a timely review of performance progress is indicated in the box designated as Program Evaluation Criteria.

Procedurally, the goal of the behavior support team is to complete the Quickie Behavior Support Plan Sheet within 30 minutes. At the end of the

(continued)

Figure 4.10 Geoff's Quickie Behavior Support Plan

Student _____ Geoff _____ Teacher _____ Ms. Fernandez _____ Date _4/29/95_

School _____ Cheers M. S. _____ Prepared by _____ Ms. Fernandez _____

Program Evaluation Criteria: *If three consecutive problem days, call EBS meeting.*

Start here 1

What does problem behavior look like?	*Makes disruptive comments about peers.* *Touches property of others.*

2

Where and when does problem behavior occur?	*In P.E. (7th period).* *During health class (3rd period), especially, when with Nola.* *Unstructured activities.*

3

What are early signs of problem behavior?	*Begins looking around room.* *Begins asking for teacher help.* *When work/tasks are completed.*

4

What is expected behavior at this time and place?	*Ask teacher to check and collect work.* *Select alternative activity when done with tasks.* *Enter and maintain positive peer engagements.* *Ask before touching property of others.*

5

What positive feedback can be given when expected behavior occurs?	What	When	By Whom
	Praise when finished with work. *Play game with peers at end of class.* *Give access to games.*	☐ Immediately ☐ ___ Minutes ☐ Hourly ☐ Daily ☐ Weekly ☐ _____	*All teachers.*

6

What can be done when early sign is observed?	*Offer alternative activity.* *Stay close to G.* *Ask G. to assist teacher.*

7

What can be done to increase occurrence of expected behavior?	**Environmental manipulation** *Move Nola to another table.* *Give specific sequence of activities to be completed.*
	Reminder/Prompt *Ask: "What can you do when you're finished with work? How will you ask for help?"*

8

What can be done when problem behavior occurs?	What	When	By Whom
	1. *Ask to return to seat.* 2. *Ask to see A.P.* 3. *Give office referral.*	☐ Immediately ☐ ___ Minutes ☐ Hourly ☐ Daily ☐ Weekly ☐ _____	*All teachers.*

Do plan 9

(continued)

144

Figure 4.11 Measurement Tool Used to Monitor Geoff's Performance

Date Crit.	1	2	3	4	5	6	7	8	9	10	11	12	13	14	15	# opp	#/% p	#/% d	#/% a
	p d a	p d a	p d a	p d a	p d a	p d a	p d a	p d a	p d a	p d a	p d a	p d a	p d a	p d a	p d a		/	/	/
	p d a	p d a	p d a	p d a	p d a	p d a	p d a	p d a	p d a	p d a	p d a	p d a	p d a	p d a	p d a		/	/	/
	p d a	p d a	p d a	p d a	p d a	p d a	p d a	p d a	p d a	p d a	p d a	p d a	p d a	p d a	p d a		/	/	/
	p d a	p d a	p d a	p d a	p d a	p d a	p d a	p d a	p d a	p d a	p d a	p d a	p d a	p d a	p d a		/	/	/
	p d	p d	p d	p d	p d	p d	p d	p d	p d	p d	p d	p d	p d	p d	p d		/	/	/

At end of structured activity, did Geoff display problem, desired, or acceptable behavior? (circle)

meeting, each teacher is given a copy of the completed plan sheet so the plan can be implemented immediately. Finally, a measurement strategy is developed to monitor the effectiveness of the program. To be useful in applied settings, measurement strategies must be simple to implement, not interfere with teaching, assess outcomes that are related directly to problem and replacement behaviors, and facilitate decision making.

The Quickie Behavior Support Plan shown in Figure 4.10 is based on Geoff's functional assessment information and the resulting competing pathways analysis and focuses on teaching Geoff a more acceptable replacement response ("ask teacher to collect/check work") before beginning activities during unstructured time.

To measure the effectiveness of the plan summarized in the Quickie Behavior Support Plan and at the end of each structured activity, Geoff's teacher indicates whether he displays problem, desirable, or acceptable behavior, and a daily summary is generated. A simple recording tool (see Figure 4.11) is used to minimize the amount of interference that might be associated with data collection.

CONCLUDING COMMENT

This paper illustrates how behavior support planning can be made comprehensive, specialized, and individualized through the use of simple forms and formats. The Quickie Behavior Support Plan Sheet is only one example that was developed for a particular school to improve its behavior support system for students with severe problem behavior. The actual form is less important than the features that are represented, such as being immediately usable, based on functional assessment information, and teacher friendly. In addition, the form's structure makes the behavior support planning process accessible to all teachers, not just those with specialized behavioral skills.

The success of the form and format, however, are predicated on the presence of a team that oversees the provision of effective behavioral support, collectively possesses behavioral competence, and can develop and implement a system of support that can provide an immediate response to a request for assistance. When these requisites exist, students with severe problem behaviors are more likely to receive comprehensive, individualized, and specialized behavioral programming.

DISCUSSION QUESTIONS

1. Give an example showing how each of the following principles affects behavior in classroom situations: positive reinforcement, negative reinforcement, extinction, punishment, modeling.
2. Why is the concept of a contingency important in determining the effectiveness of behavioral change procedures? Give examples of both planned and unplanned contingencies.
3. What procedures and policies should be addressed in developing guidelines for behavioral interventions in schools? Develop a model set of guidelines.
4. A student engages in disruptive behavior almost every day in math class. This results in her being placed in timeout for the remainder of the math class. Comment on the effectiveness and appropriateness of this intervention.
5. Describe alternate intervention strategies for reducing the disruptive behavior of the student described in question 4.
6. How do data levels, trends, and stability affect decisions about changing intervention conditions?
7. What is a functional relationship? How is a functional relationship demonstrated between an intervention and a target behavior?
8. For what behaviors and circumstances are the following designs appropriate: withdrawal, reversal, multiple baseline, multiple probe, changing criterion?

REFERENCES

Alberto, P. A., & Troutman, A. C. (1995). *Applied behavior analysis for teachers.* Englewood Cliffs, NJ: Prentice-Hall.

Algozzine, R. (1993). *Problem behavior management: Educator's resource service.* Gaithersburg, MD: Aspen Publishers.

The Association for the Severely Handicapped Newsletter. (1986, February). Volume 12, No. 2.

Axelrod, S. (1987). Doing it without arrows: A review of Lavigna and Donnellan's Alternatives to punishment: Solving behavior problems with non-aversive strategies. *The Behavior Analyst, 10,* 243–251.

Azrin, N. H., & Holz, W. C. (1966). Punishment. In W. K. Honig (Ed.), *Operant behavior: Areas of research and application* (pp. 380–447). New York: Appleton Century-Crofts.

Baer, D. M., Wolf, M. M., & Risley, T. R. (1968). Some current dimensions of applied behavior analysis. *Journal of Applied Behavior Analysis, 1,* 91–97.

Bandura, A. (1969). *Principles of behavior modification.* New York: Holt, Rinehart, & Winston.

Barton, L. E., Brulle, A. R., & Repp, A. C. (1983). Aversive techniques and the doctrine of least restrictive alternative. *Exceptional Education Quarterly, 3,* 1–8.

Beck, R., & Gabriel, S. (1990). *Project RIDE: Responding to individual differences in education* (elementary and secondary version). Longmont, CO: Sopris West.

Braaten, S. (1987, November). Use of punishment with exceptional children: A dilemma for educators. Paper presented at the 11th annual Conference on Severe Behavior Disorders of Children and Youth, Tempe, AZ.

Braaten, S., Simpson, R., Rosell, J., & Reilly, T. (1988). Using punishment with exceptional children: A dilemma for educators. *Teaching Exceptional Children, 20,* 79–81.

Budd, K. S., & Baer, D. M. (1976). Behavior modification and the law: Implications of recent judicial decisions. *Journal of Psychiatry and the Law, 4,* 171–244.

Carr, E. G., & Durand, V. M. (1985). Reducing behavior problems through functional communication training. *Journal of Applied Behavior Analysis, 18,* 111–126.

Carr, E. G., Levin, L., McConnachie, G., Carlson, J. I., Kemp, D. C., & Smith, C. E. (1994). *Communication-based intervention for problem behavior: A user's guide for producing positive change.* Baltimore: Paul H. Brookes.

Colvin, G. (1992). *Managing acting-out behavior: A staff development program to prevent and manage acting-out behavior.* Longmont, CO: Sopris West.

Colvin, G., Kameenui, E., Sugai, G. (1994). Reconceptualizing behavior management and school-wide discipline in general education. *Education and Treatment of Children, 16*(4), 361–381.

Colvin, G., Sugai, G., & Kameenui, E. J. (1994). *Curriculum for establishing a proactive school-wide discipline plan (Project PREPARE).* Eugene, OR: University of Oregon.

Colvin, G., Sugai, G., & Patching, B. (1993). Precorrection: An instructional approach for managing predictable problem behaviors. *Intervention in School and Clinic, 28,* 143–150.

Conroy, M. A., & Fox, J. J. (1994). Setting events and challenging behaviors in the classroom: Incorporating contextual factors into effective intervention plans. *Preventing School Failure, 38*(3), 29–34.

Cooper, J. O., Heron, T. E., & Heward, W. L. (1987). *Applied behavior analysis.* Columbus, OH: Merrill.

Council for Children with Behavioral Disorders. (1990). Position paper on use of behavior reduction strategies with children with behavioral disorders. *Behavioral Disorders, 15,* 243–260.

Council for Exceptional Children. (1993). *CEC Policy on Physical Intervention.* Adopted by the CEC Delegate Assembly, San Antonio, TX.

Council for Exceptional Children. (1995). *What every special educator must know: The international standards for the preparation and certification of special education teachers.* Reston, VA: Author.

Deno, S. L., & Mirkin, P. K. (1978). *Data-based program modification: A manual.* Reston, VA: Council for Exceptional Children.

Dietz, D. E., & Repp, A. C. (1983). Reducing behavior through reinforcement. *Exceptional Education Quarterly, 3,* 34–46.

Donnellan, A. M. (1984). The criterion of the least dangerous assumption. *Behavioral Disorders, 9,* 141–150.

Dunlap, G., Kern, L., dePerczel, M., Clarke, S., Wilson, D., Childs, K. E., White, R., & Falk, G. D. (1993). Functional analysis of classroom variables for students with emotional and behavioral disorders. *Behavioral Disorders, 18,* 275–291.

Evans, l. M., & Meyer, L. H. (1985). *An educative approach to behavior problems: A practical decision model for interventions with severely handicapped learners.* Baltimore: Paul Brookes.

Ferster, C. B., & Culbertson, S. (1982). *Behavior principles* (3rd ed.). Englewood Cliffs, NJ: Prentice-Hall.

Gable, R. A., Hendrickson, J. M., Evans, S. S., & Evans, W. H. (1988). Data decisions for instructing behaviorally disordered students. In R. B. Rutherford, Jr., C. M. Nelson, & S. R. Forness (Eds.). *Bases of severe behavior disorders in children and youth* (pp. 75–89). San Diego, CA: College-Hill Press.

Garrity, C., Jens, K., Porter, W., Sager, N., & Short-Camilli, C. (1994). *Bully-proofing your school: A comprehensive approach for elementary schools.* Longmont, CO: Sopris West.

Gast, D. L., & Nelson, C. M. (1977). Legal and ethical considerations for the use of timeout in special education settings. *Journal of Special Education, 11,* 457–467.

Gast, D. L., & Wolery, M. (1987). Severe maladaptive behaviors. In M. E. Snell (Ed.), *Systematic instruction of the moderately and severely handicapped* (3rd ed.) (pp. 300–322). Upper Saddle River, NJ: Merrill/Prentice Hall.

Gaylord-Ross, R. (1980). A decision model for the treatment of aberrant behavior in applied settings. In W. Sailor, B. Wilcox, & L. Brown (Eds.), *Methods of instruction for severely handicapped students* (pp. 135–158). Baltimore: Paul Brookes.

Gelfand, D. M., & Hartmann, D. P. (1984). *Child behavior analysis and therapy* (2nd ed.). New York: Pergamon Press.

Hartmann, D. P., & Hall, R. V. (1976). The changing criterion design. *Journal of Applied Behavior Analysis, 9,* 527–532.

Honig v. Doe, 479 U.S. 1084. (1988).

Horner, R. H. (1994). Functional assessment: contributions and future directions. *Journal of Applied Behavior Analysis, 27,* 401–404.

Horner, R. H., & Day, H. M. (1991). The effects of response efficiency on functionally equivalent, competing behaviors. *Journal of Applied Behavior Analysis, 24,* 265–278.

Horner, R. H., O'Neill, R. E., & Flannery, K. B. (1993). Building effective behavioral support plans from functional assessment information. In M. Snell (Ed.), *Instruction of students with severe disabilities* (pp.187–214). Upper Saddle River, NJ: Merrill/Prentice Hall.

Horner, R. H., O'Neill, R. E., & Flannery, K. B. (1994). Effective behavior support plans. In M. E. Snell (Ed.). *Instruction of students with severe disabilities* (pp. 184–214). New York: Macmillan.

Howell, K. W., Fox, S. L., & Morehead, M. K. (1993). *Curriculum-based evaluation: Teaching and decision making* (2nd ed.). Pacific Grove, CA: Brooks/Cole.

Howell, K. W., Kaplan, J. S., & O'Connell, C. Y. (1979). *Evaluating exceptional children: A task analysis approach.* Upper Saddle River, NJ: Merrill/Prentice Hall.

Jenson, W. R., Rhode, G., & Reavis, H. K. (1994). *The tough kid tool box: A collection of classroom tools.* Longmont, CO: Sopris West.

Kameenui, E. J., & Darch, C. B. (1994). *Instructional classroom management.* White Plains, NY: Longman.

Kazdin, A. E. (1981). Acceptability of child treatment techniques: The influence of treatment efficacy and adverse side effects. *Behavior Therapy, 12,* 493–506.

Kazdin, A. E. (1983). Failure of persons to respond to the token economy. In E. B. Foa & P. M. G. Emmelkamp (Eds.), *Failures in behavior therapy* (pp. 335–354). New York: Wiley.

LaVigna, G. W., & Donnellan, A. M. (1986). *Alternatives to punishment: Solving behavior problems through non-aversive strategies.* New York: Irvington.

Lewis, T. J., & Sugai, G. (1994). Special issue: Social behavior assessment within schools. *Diagnostique, 19*(2–3), 1–4.

Madsen, C. H., Jr., Becker, W. C., Thomas, D. R., Koser, L., & Plager, E. (1968). An analysis of the reinforcing function of "sit down" commands. In R. K. Parker (Ed.), *Readings in educational psychology* (pp. 265–278). Boston: Allyn & Bacon.

Maloney, M. (1994). How to avoid the discipline trap. *The Special Educator,* Winter Index, 1–4.

Morales v. Turman, 364 F. Supp. 1078. (1973).

Nelson, C. M. (1981). Classroom management. In J. M. Kauffman & D. P. Hallahan (Eds.), *Handbook of special education* (pp. 663–687). Englewood Cliffs, NJ: Prentice-Hall.

Nelson, C. M. (1987). Behavioral interventions: What works and what doesn't. *The Pointer, 31*(3), 45–50.

Nelson, C. M., & Polsgrove, L. (1984). Behavior analysis in special education: White rabbit or white elephant? *Remedial and Special Education, 5,* 6–17.

Nelson, C. M., & Rutherford, R. B., Jr. (1983). Timeout revisited: Guidelines for its use in special education. *Exceptional Education Quarterly, 3,* 56–67.

Nelson, C. M., & Rutherford, R. B., Jr. (1988). Behavioral interventions with behaviorally disordered students. In M. C. Wang, M. C. Reynolds, & H. J. Walberg (Eds.), *The handbook of special education: Research and practice* (Vol. 2, pp. 125–153). Oxford, England: Pergamon Press.

O'Neill, R. E., Horner, R. H., Albin, R. W., Storey, K., & Sprague, J. R. (in press). *Functional analysis of problem behavior: A practical guide* (2nd ed.). Pacific Grove, CA: Brooks/Cole.

Parsonson, B. S., & Baer, D. M. (1978). The analysis and presentation of graphic data. In T. R. Kratochwill (Ed.), *Single subject research: Strategies for evaluating change* (pp. 101–165). New York: Academic Press.

Pearson, C. A., & Argulewicz, E. N. (1987). Ethnicity as a factor in teachers' acceptance of classroom interventions. *Psychology in the Schools, 24,* 385–389.

Polsgrove, L. (1979). Self-control: Methods for child training. *Behavioral Disorders, 4,* 116–130.

Polsgrove, L., & Reith, H. J. (1983). Procedures for reducing children's inappropriate behavior in special education settings. *Exceptional Education Quarterly, 3,* 20–33.

Premack, D. (1959). Toward empirical behavior laws: I. Positive reinforcement. *Psychological Review, 66,* 219–233.

Reichle, J., & Wacker, D. P. (1993). *Communicative alternatives to challenging behavior.* Baltimore: Paul H. Brookes.

Rincover, A. (1981). *How to use sensory extinction: A non-aversive treatment for self-stimulation and other behavior problems.* Lawrence, KS: H & H Enterprises.

Rhode, G., Jenson, W. R., & Reavis, H. K. (1993). *The tough kid book: Practical classroom management strategies.* Longmont, CO: Sopris West.

Rose, T. L. (1983). A survey of corporal punishment of mildly handicapped students. *Exceptional Education Quarterly, 3,* 9–19.

Rutherford, R. B., Jr. (1983). Theory and research on the use of aversive procedures in the education of moderately behaviorally disordered and emotionally disturbed children and youth. In F. H. Wood & K. C. Lakin (Eds.), *Punishment and aversive stimulation in special education* (pp. 41–64). Reston, VA: Council for Exceptional Children.

Rutherford, R. B., Jr., & Nelson, C. M. (1982). Analysis of the response-contingent timeout literature with behaviorally disordered students in classroom settings. In R. B. Rutherford, Jr., (Ed.), *Severe behavior disorders of children and youth* (Vol. 5, pp. 79–105). Reston, VA: Council for Children with Behavioral Disorders.

Rutherford, R. B., Jr., & Nelson, C. M. (1995). Management of aggressive and violent behavior in the schools. *Focus on Exceptional Children, 27*(6), 1–15.

Rutherford, R. B., Jr., & Polsgrove, L. (1981). Behavioral contracting with behaviorally disordered and delinquent children and youth: An analysis of the clinical and experimental literature. In R. B. Rutherford, Jr., A. G. Prieto, & J. E. McGlothlin (Eds.), *Severe behavior disorders of children and youth* (Vol. 4, pp. 49–69). Reston, VA: Council for Children with Behavioral Disorders.

Sajwaj, T. (1977). Issues and implications of establishing guidelines for the use of behavioral techniques. *Journal of Applied Behavior Analysis, 10,* 531–540.

Shores, R. E., Gunter, P. L., Denny, R. K., & Jack, S. L. (1993). Classroom influences on aggressive and disruptive behavior of students with emotional and behavioral disorders. *Focus on Exceptional Children, 26*(2), 1–10.

Singer, G. S., & Irvin, L. K. (1987). Human rights review of intrusive behavioral treatments for students with severe handicaps. *Exceptional Children, 54,* 46–52.

Sprick, R., Sprick, M., & Garrison, M. (1993). *Interventions: Collaborative planning for students at risk.* Longmont, CO: Sopris West.

Stainback, W., Stainback, S., & Dedrick, C. (1979). Controlling severe maladaptive behaviors. *Behavioral Disorders, 4,* 99–115.

Sugai, G. (1994). *Quickie behavior support plan.* Eugene, OR: University of Oregon, College of Education, Behavioral Research and Training.

Sugai, G. (1995, June). Pro-active classroom management. Workshop presented at the Springfield School Improvement Conference, Springfield, OR.

Sugai, G., & Horner, R. (1994). Including students with severe behavior problems in general education settings: Assumptions, challenges, and solutions. In J. Marr, G. Sugai, & G. Tindal (Eds.), *The Oregon conference monograph* (pp. 102–120). Eugene, OR: University of Oregon.

Sugai, G., & Tindal, G. (1993). *Effective school consultation: An interactive approach.* Pacific Grove, CA: Brooks/Cole.

Tawney, J. W., & Gast, D. L. (1984). *Single subject research in special education.* Upper Saddle River, NJ: Merrill/Prentice Hall.

Todd, A., Sugai, G., & Horner, R. H. (in preparation). *Effective behavior support implementation guide.* Eugene, OR: University of Oregon, College of Education, Effective Behavior Support Project.

Twyman, J. S., Johnson, H., Buie, J. D., & Nelson, C. M. (1993). The use of a warning procedure to signal a more intrusive timeout contingency. *Behavioral Disorders, 19,* 243–253.

Utah State Office of Education (1993). *Project RIDE for preschoolers.* Longmont, CO: Sopris West.

Van Houten, R., Nau, P. A., MacKenzie-Keating, S. E., Sameoto, D., & Colavecchia, B. (1982). An analysis of some variables influencing the effectiveness of reprimands. *Journal of Applied Behavior Analysis, 15,* 65–83.

Walker, H. M. (1983). Applications of response cost in school settings: Outcomes, issues, and recommendations. *Exceptional Education Quarterly, 3,* 47–55.

Walker, H. M. (1995). *The acting-out child: Coping with classroom disruption* (2nd ed.). Longmont, CO: Sopris West.

Walker, H. M., Colvin, G., & Ramsey, E. (1995). *Antisocial behavior in school: Strategies and best practices.* Pacific Grove, CA: Brooks/Cole.

Walker, H. M., Hops, H., & Fiegenbaum, E. (1976). Deviant classroom behavior as a function of combinations of social and token and cost contingency. *Behavior Therapy, 7,* 76–88.

Warboys, L. M. (1987, November). Special education and school discipline: Legal issues. Paper presented at the 11th annual Conference on Severe Behavior Disorders of Children and Youth, Tempe, AZ.

Wehby, J. H. (1994). Issues in the assessment of aggressive behavior. *Preventing School Failure, 38*(3), 24–28.

White, O. R. (1971). *A pragmatic approach to the description of progress in the single case.* Unpublished doctoral dissertation, University of Oregon, Eugene.

White, O. R., & Haring, N. G. (1980). *Exceptional teaching* (2nd ed.). Upper Saddle River, NJ: Merrill/Prentice Hall.

Witt, J. C., Elliott, S. N., & Martens, B. K. (1984). Acceptability of behavioral interventions used in classrooms: The influence of amount of teacher time, severity of behavior problem, and type of intervention. *Behavioral Disorders, 9,* 95–104.

Witt, W. C., & Martens, B. K. (1983). Assessing the acceptability of behavioral interventions used in classrooms. *Psychology in the Schools, 20,* 510–517.

Wolery, M., Bailey, D. B., & Sugai, G. M. (1988). *Effective teaching: Principles and procedures of applied behavior analysis with exceptional students.* Boston: Allyn & Bacon.

Wolf, M. M. (1978). Social validity: The case for subjective measurement or how applied behavior analysis is finding its heart. *Journal of Applied Behavior Analysis, 11,* 203–214.

Wood, F. H., & Braaten, S. (1983). Developing guidelines for the use of punishing interventions in the schools. *Exceptional Education Quarterly, 3,* 68–75.

Worell, J., & Nelson, C. M. (1974). *Managing instructional problems: A case study workbook.* New York: McGraw-Hill.

Wyatt v. Stickney, 344 F. Supp. 373. (1972).

Yell, M. L., & Peterson, R. L. (1995). Disciplining students with disabilities and those at risk for school failure: Legal issues. *Preventing School Failure, 39* (2), 39–44.

CLASSROOM BEHAVIOR
MANAGEMENT

OUTLINE

OBJECTIVES

After completing this chapter, you should be able to

◆ Explain what is meant by "bringing a student's behavior under stimulus control" and give examples of behaviors and of the antecedent stimuli that control them.
◆ Describe how a cycle of pupil misbehavior and teachers' use of aversive behavior management practices may lead to a crisis.
◆ Indicate which aspects of classroom setting events are likely to influence pupil behavior and how they may be altered to increase the probability of desired behavior.
◆ Describe the characteristic features of token systems and three types of group-oriented contingencies.
◆ Describe the advantages and disadvantages of level systems and their application in classroom management programs.
◆ Indicate how the characteristics of students with severe disabilities and of adolescents, as well as the settings in which they are educated, affect classroom behavior management.

The most complex and demanding task of educators who work with students exhibiting serious problem behaviors is the day-to-day classroom behavior management. Pupils who are chronically disruptive, defiant, withdrawn, or aggressive, or who engage in nonfunctional stereotypic behaviors and possess minimal social or functional communicative skills often are difficult to handle even in one-to-one situations. The teacher who works with such pupils must be able to manage them in group settings, which means establishing a productive and orderly classroom environment in which to implement IEPs and in which to work on specific target

behaviors. In other words, effective individual programming cannot occur if the classroom is chaotic or in a constant state of crisis. The purpose of this chapter is to help you develop the skills necessary to create productive learning environments.

As discussed here, *classroom behavior management* refers to the management of pupil behavior in group settings, which, in its broadest sense, is only part of classroom management. Organizing the curriculum, arranging and individualizing instruction, evaluating students' learning, and communicating the outcomes of instruction to others also are important components. However, managing behavior is a necessary, if not sufficient, condition for accomplishing your major goal—facilitating pupils' learning. The teacher who cannot maintain behavior within reasonable limits through positive management procedures will face constant frustration and personal dissatisfaction and is likely to find those same feelings expressed by students and their parents.

Therefore, this chapter focuses on management decisions and strategies aimed at the *prevention* of crisis situations (i.e., occasions in which one or more students exhibit behaviors that are dangerous or extremely disruptive and not under your stimulus control). We emphasize variables that have been shown to affect the classroom environment: paying attention and praising students; establishing stimulus control over pupil behavior; using rules and consequences; applying interventions appropriately; and using group behavior management strategies. These strategies represent *universal interventions* as defined by Walker, Colvin, & Ramsey (1995); they are applied to all students in a group, and address the "margins" in which the boundaries between acceptable and unacceptable student behavior typically are not clear. The objective of preventative classroom behavior management is to analyze and structure classroom social interactions in such a way as to minimize behaviors requiring crisis intervention. Management procedures and systems intended for specific behavior problems are emphasized in subsequent chapters. Many crisis situations can be prevented through careful assessment, effective educational programming and behavioral support, and appropriate group behavior management. Thus, classroom management should be viewed as a set of proactive strategies that reduce the need for selected interventions for specific pupils.

The most essential prerequisites to effective classroom management are an appropriate and functional academic curriculum and effective instructional practices (Shores, Gunter, Denny, & Jack, 1993; Sugai & Tindal, 1993). An appropriate and functional curriculum is one that meets each student's individual needs and that *he* perceives as important and meaningful. In the case of students with IEPs, this prerequisite often is assumed

to be a given; unfortunately, research does not bear out this assumption. The correspondence between student assessment data and instructional goals often is poor (Shores et al., 1993). A curriculum that is poorly matched to students' aptitudes and interests (e.g., too difficult, too easy or boring) is likely to be aversive, thus setting the stage for escape and avoidance behavior.

An extensive body of research describes effective teaching practices. It is beyond the scope of this text to describe these in detail; however, Sugai and Tindal (1993) devised an "effective teaching profile" of these skills, which provides a succinct summary of the outcomes of research on instruction as well as a self-assessment checklist (see Figure 5.1).

Conversely, Johns and Carr (1995) have identified a number of negative behavior management techniques that effective teachers seldom exhibit:

◆ Forcing a student to do something she doesn't want to do.
◆ Forcing students to admit to lies.
◆ Demanding confession from students.
◆ Using confrontational techniques.
◆ Asking students why they act out.
◆ Punishing students.
◆ Making disapproving comments.
◆ Comparing a student's behavior with other students' behavior.
◆ Yelling at students.
◆ Engaging in verbal battles.
◆ Making unrealistic threats.
◆ Ridiculing students.

Engaging in these practices greatly increases the chances that students with EBD, as well as those on the "margins" with respect to classroom behavior, will act out. They provide fertile soil for the cultivation of crisis situations (see pp. 155–157). To the extent that you can avoid these practices and practice the effective teaching skills listed in Figure 5.1, you and your students will experience a much more productive classroom climate.

Our focus on acting-out (externalizing) behavior problems may appear to overlook behavioral deficits, that is, the absence of socially desirable behaviors. However, many students whose

Figure 5.1   Teaching Behaviors of Effective Teachers

Effective Teaching Profile

Place an X on the scale to indicate the extent to which the teacher displayed the best teaching practices. Connect each X to display a teaching profile.

Yes_____No   1. Brisk pacing

Yes_____No   2. Specific explanations and instructions for new concepts

Yes_____No   3. Allocated time for guided practice

Yes_____No   4. Cumulative review of skills being taught

Yes_____No   5. Regular and varied assessments of learning of new concepts

Yes_____No   6. Regular and active interactions with individual students

Yes_____No   7. Frequent and detailed feedback

Yes_____No   8. Varied forms of positive reinforcement

Yes_____No   9. Positive, predictable, and orderly learning environment

Yes_____No   10. Maintenance of student attention within and across instructional activities and materials

Yes_____No   11. Reinforcement for task completion

Yes_____No   12. Appropriate selection of examples and nonexamples

Yes_____No   13. Consistent application of contingencies for rules and expectations

Yes_____No   14. Appropriate use of model/demonstrations

Yes_____No   15. Appropriate use of behavioral rehearsal (role-plays)

Yes_____No   16. Smooth transition within and between lessons

Yes_____No   17. High rates of correct student responding

Source: Sugai, G. M., & Tindal, G. A. (1993). *Effective school consultation: An interactive approach.* Pacific Grove, CA: Brooks/Cole. Used with permission.

behavioral excesses create classroom management problems also are deficient in academic skills and appropriate social behaviors. Classroom behavior management aimed at preventing or reducing the occurrence of behaviors that interfere with productivity and learning will be more effective if the curriculum simultaneously addresses pupils' social skill deficits. Students who consistently break rules of conduct, whose inappropriate behaviors repeatedly disrupt classroom order, or who fail to correct their undesired behavior when exposed to the teacher's available disciplinary measures should be assessed with respect to desired academic, social, and school survival skills, and their deficits in these areas should be remediated through appropriate curricular interventions (see Chapter 7).

This chapter begins with a discussion of the goals of classroom behavior management. Because students with behavior problems may react catastrophically to certain management practices, situations leading to behavioral crises are described next. We then discuss the kinds of assessment decisions teachers must make each day in order to remain in touch with students' behavior. This is followed by an overview of classroom behavior management interventions, including how to use them appropriately. Next is a discussion of special considerations for working with pupils exhibiting severe disabilities and with secondary age pupils. Finally, procedures for evaluating management strategies are described.

GOALS OF BEHAVIOR MANAGEMENT

The primary goal of behavior management, especially for students exhibiting problem behavior, is to bring their behavior under **stimulus control.** This means that pupils respond appropriately to antecedent stimuli (A) without always having to experience the consequences (C) of their behavior. For example, stimulus control over behavior has occurred when students respond to the request "Take out your science books" by getting out the appropriate text and *not* by leaving their seats, shouting, or daydreaming. The teacher who has stimulus control over pupil behavior experiences a minimum of crisis situations and both teacher and pupils work in an orderly and productive atmosphere.

The behavior of most children is at least partially under stimulus control by the time they begin public school. However, a significant number (both those with disabilities and nondisabled students) do not respond appropriately to antecedent stimuli. Limited stimulus control over pupils' behavior greatly increases the probability of a crisis situation. Therefore, your first management task is to prevent crises by bringing pupil behavior under the control of such antecedent stimuli as teacher directions and instructional materials. This is accomplished by systematically applying positive consequences to appropriate responses made in the presence of those stimuli. For instance, if you want pupils' desks to be the stimulus that controls in-seat behavior, apply positive consequences (attention, praise, tokens) for students who sit at their desks, and apply different consequences (ignoring, verbal reprimands, loss of tokens or privileges) for students who are not at their desks.

Developing stimulus control over the behavior of "problem" students requires many systematic applications of consequences. Begin by reinforcing approximations of the desired behavior (e.g., praising a student for only a few seconds of in-seat behavior). As Sugai (1995) emphasizes, teachers' behavioral expectations often are considerably above students' abilities to perform. Therefore, he advises that after you have identified the *behavior you expect,* decide what *behavior you can settle for* and build it through **shaping.** It is important to begin with the behavior the student gives you rather than the behavior you demand. If you expect too much initially, the student will fail, and you are more likely to engage in the unproductive reactions listed by Jones and Carr (1995; see p. 153). Through systematic differential reinforcement, bring the desired behavior under stimulus control (e.g., teach the student to exhibit "in-seat" when requested) and gradually increase the requirement for reinforcement (e.g., praising only when the pupil has been in-seat for a minute or longer) until the desired goal has been reached (e.g., the student remains in-seat as long as the others). The process of reinforcing closer and closer approximations to desired behavior must be carried out slowly and systematically, and the hierarchy of steps must be adjusted according to the behavior of individual students. This again emphasizes the importance of behavior analysis and underscores the need for a thorough understanding of behavior principles and their application.

The specific management goals expressed by teachers are likely to include increasing such desired student behaviors as attending to tasks, remaining in-seat, following teacher directions, using time productively, and giving correct academic responses (Gresham & Reschly, 1987). As we noted in Chapter 2, these behaviors correspond to a "model behavioral profile" (Hersh & Walker, 1983), but they have little to do with developing students' peer relationship skills (Gresham & Reschly, 1987). Teachers are also concerned about decelerating behaviors that are dangerous, disruptive, or incompatible with the completion of academic tasks. The majority of pupils likewise want to achieve these goals, so negotiate with students when setting expectations for classroom behavior. Your expectations will more likely be accepted if you consider those of your students.

SITUATIONS THAT CREATE MANAGEMENT CRISES

You may be tempted to blame behavior problems on underlying "pathology" supposedly inherent in students who have been certified as "behaviorally disordered" or "emotionally disturbed." This is inappropriate, and although not all classroom misbehavior is attributable to inappropriate classroom behavior management, pupils who have been reinforced for their tantrums, defying authority, aggressive acts against others, or being noncompliant will exhibit such behavior in situations when others will not. The key to effective control of these behaviors lies in the teacher's ability to analyze and adjust variables in the immediate environment; specifically, antecedents and consequences.

These same variables also happen to be responsible for most crisis situations. This observation has been documented in a number of studies. For example, White (1975) and Thomas, Presland, Grant, and Glynn (1978) studied rates of teacher approval and disapproval and found that most teachers gave disapprovals at higher rates than they gave approvals. Both sets of investigators suggested that teachers experience greater reinforcement for using disapprovals (i.e., the use of disapprovals is strengthened through negative reinforcement, in that disapprovals quickly, though temporarily, terminate undesired child behavior). Thomas et al. (1978) also conjectured that teachers feel appropriate behavior deserves little recognition.

Walker and Buckley (1973) and Walker, Hops, and Fiegenbaum (1976) investigated the rates of teacher praise and disapproval toward children who are behaviorally deviant and nondeviant and also studied the behaviors upon which these responses were contingent. They found that teachers interacted significantly more with children who are deviant and that the majority of these interactions consisted of attending to inappropriate behavior. Walker (1995) observed that negative teacher attention increases inappropriate child behavior. Recall that Madsen, Becker, Thomas, Koser, and Plager (1968) also found that teacher attention to inappropriate behavior (out-of-seat) in children who are behaviorally "normal" increased the rate of this behavior. Thus, teacher attention to undesired behavior, though negative, may function as positive reinforcement. This has been documented by Buehler, Patterson, and Furniss (1966) and Solomon and Wahler (1973).

Furthermore, both of these studies demonstrated that peer attention to inappropriate responses exerted more powerful control over child behavior than did the adult reactions.

Shores et al. (1993) conducted numerous studies of the interactions between regular and special education teachers and students with EBD. They found that rates of positive reinforcement ranged from once every 2 hours to once every 15 minutes. For example, teachers responded less than half the time to students raising hands and requesting assistance with tasks. The net effect of such teacher neutrality may be to create an extremely lean schedule of positive reinforcement, which could encourage pupil escape and avoidance behaviors. At the same time students with histories of aggressive behavior received 6 to 20 times more negative consequences from their teachers than students with EBD who were considered nonaggressive and those not identified as EBD (Shores et al., 1993). Finally, Carr, Taylor, and Robinson (1991) found that teachers tended to assign students with problem behaviors easier tasks than students who were compliant.

As Walker (1995) found, the cumulative effect of disproportionate teacher attention (in addition to peer support and attention) to acting-out children's misbehavior is to strengthen undesired behavior patterns. The unfortunate result of this combination of events is a classroom situation in which the teacher relies on progressively more aversive management practices (public scoldings, sending children to the principal's office, spankings, etc.). These measures may have temporary suppressive effects for some students, but they have no effect or a strengthening effect on undesired behaviors of other pupils. These tactics are not likely to succeed over time, particularly if the peer group reinforces deviant behavior. Moreover, continued use of aversive consequences that are ineffective in reducing undesired behavior may result in increased tolerance for such consequences (Azrin & Holz, 1966). The persistence of undesired behavior under such circumstances may encourage teachers to use aversive consequences to control the behavior. Patterns of unintentional teacher reinforcement of problem behaviors lead to cycles characterized by high levels of student misbehavior and aversive teacher countercontrol (Shores et al., 1993).

A common side effect of aversive teacher control is power struggles between the teacher and some, or all, pupils. Like adults, children react negatively to aversive management. If they sense that the teacher is reacting from frustration or feels out of control of the situation, they may respond with even more intensive misbehavior. Thus, avoid behavior management practices that are not carefully and thoughtfully chosen, that involve little or no pupil input, and that consist largely of reacting negatively to inappropriate student behavior.

Two other mistakes are made even by experienced teachers of pupils with EBD. The first is to assume that students know what is expected of them. An indication of this problem is the absence of clear rules for classroom behavior. Either rules are nonexistent or they are worded too generally (e.g., "show respect for other persons, use good manners"). Vague rules may be operationalized so that pupils understand them (e.g., showing respect means keep hands and feet to yourself, do not interrupt when others are talking, take turns, etc.), but often they are not. The second mistake is to punish students for their failure to exhibit a behavior that they do not know how to perform (e.g., following directions, remaining in-seat). This problem relates to the failure to correctly discriminate the difference between a skill deficit and a performance deficit, which was discussed in Chapter 2. It is most often a response to students' noncompliance. Although noncompliance may reflect a pupil's *decision* not to follow a rule or direction, it may also indicate that the student *does not know* what behavior is expected, that there are *obstacles* to the student performing as desired, or that the student *lacks the skills* to exhibit the desired behavior. Therefore, before punishing their nonperformance, be sure that your students can line up properly, bring required materials to class, take time-outs appropriately, or tie their shoelaces. Also remember to attempt to correct the problem first through interventions based on positive reinforcement.

As suggested earlier, another potential cause of crisis situations involves setting goals or selecting curricula that are inappropriate for students. Appropriate goals and curricula are fair, functional, and meaningful to students. Undesired behavior may be one way (perhaps the only way) the student has of saying "This is too hard," "I don't like this," or "This is baby stuff." Inappropriate expectations or curricula generate frustration, dissatisfaction, and rebellion, thus setting the stage for behavior problems. If the teacher reacts punitively, he may initiate a self-perpetuating cycle of crises. By functionally analyzing problem behaviors in relationship to variables inherent in specific curricula and settings, you can identify potential causes and address them without resorting to procedures that involve aversive consequences. If your goals and curricula are fair and important to students, you can also prevent many problems from occurring in the first place.

The following questions make up an informal checklist that you can use to assess the potential sources of problem behaviors:

◆ Is what I am teaching useful or important to the students?
◆ Do the pupils know what I expect them to do?
◆ Are there any obstacles to the students performing as desired?
◆ Do students have the ability to perform as expected?
◆ What are the consequences of desired performance?
◆ What are the consequences of nonperformance?
◆ When does the problem behavior occur?
◆ What is different about students who are not displaying the problem behavior?
◆ How can I change my instruction to help pupils develop the skill I am trying to teach?

EFFECTIVE CLASSROOM BEHAVIOR MANAGEMENT

We have indicated that the goals of classroom behavior management are to develop stimulus control over pupil behavior and to prevent crisis situations from occurring. These must be accomplished in group settings where the teacher is responsible for delivering instruction. Consequently, appropriate classroom management interventions are those that are less intrusive and restrictive; they may be accomplished without significant interruption of ongoing activities and without removing students or instructional staff from the teaching setting.

The least intrusive and most natural behavior management strategies are, of course, good teaching practices. The literature on effective teaching indicates that such behaviors as using brisk instructional pacing, reviewing students' work frequently, giving systematic and constructive corrective feedback, minimizing pupil errors, providing guided practice, modeling new behaviors, providing transitions between lessons or concepts, and monitoring student performance are strongly related to pupil achievement and attitudes toward learning. These instructional behaviors are beyond the scope of this text but are clearly important elements of effective classroom management. Consult Bickel and Bickel (1986), Brophy and Good (1986), Kameenui and Darch (1995), and Rosenshine and Stevens (1986) for reviews of the research and information on effective teaching. Because of their impact on students' classroom behaviors, you should strive to develop these vital teaching skills.

The classroom behavior management procedures considered here are designed to specifically influence the behaviors that teachers desire in their pupils: compliance with teacher requests and instructions, on-task behaviors, cooperative interactions with others, and low rates of noise and disruptions. Most practitioners prefer the least intrusive management strategies that produce these results. Indeed, the most appropriate group behavior management procedures are those that are more natural and easier to implement. For example, praise and attention are more natural and easier to administer than tokens, and tokens are easier to deliver than edible reinforcers. Similarly, extinction and response cost are less intrusive behavior reduction procedures than timeout or overcorrection. Each teacher must decide what range of interventions is best

for his particular classroom. In practice, the procedures that you choose will be based on your own experience and feelings of competence with them. Effective classroom behavior managers use a range of enhancement and reductive interventions, and they develop the ability to "read" situations and behaviors on the spot and apply interventions appropriately and in a timely fashion. Develop proficiency with a range of interventions so that you too can use them effectively.

A wide variety of universal interventions are described in literature dealing with both students exhibiting disabilities and nondisabled students. We present those found useful for organizing social interactions with your pupils and in preventing most extreme behavior problems—or, if they do occur, for helping you decide what to do. The appropriate context for a classroom behavior management program is a school-wide disciplinary plan (Colvin, Kameenui, & Sugai, 1993; Walker et al., 1995) that connects the teacher's strategy with expectations and consequences that exist throughout the school building. School-wide disciplinary plans are described in Chapter 6.

Thus, a management system is a flexible, operating framework, not a rigid, intolerant set of rules and consequences. As a matter of principle, use the system most natural (i.e., most like management practices used in regular classrooms) and easy to operate. Artificial systems usually must be diminished for pupil behavior to generalize to classroom environments in which naturalistic management practices prevail. In accordance with this principle, we present management procedures in an ascending order of complexity, along with factors that influence the effectiveness of the procedures used.

Factors Affecting Classroom Management

In addition to positive and aversive consequences, five environmental variables are known to affect behavior. These are the antecedent stimuli; the contingencies of reinforcement or punishment; the contiguity, or timing, of reinforcement or punishment; the schedule of reinforcement in effect; and the persons who control the available consequences. These are the variables you must consider, and can adjust, in developing or altering a management system. For example, what rules and instructions will you provide students? How will you relate specified desired and undesired behaviors to planned consequences? Can you deliver these consequences immediately following behavior so as to maximize their effectiveness? If not, what alternatives can you use? Which schedule of reinforcement is best under various circumstances? Do you control the consequences of pupil behavior? If not, who does, and how can you enlist the aid of these agents to help you establish desired behavior patterns?

Thinking about how you will answer these questions before entering the classroom can help you avoid serious problems later. However, do not expect to prevent all problems at this stage, and do not walk into the classroom with a fully developed management system. Each system must be individually tailored and should be developed in cooperation with students, not imposed upon them. In the following discussion, we describe five approaches to group classroom management.

Manipulating Antecedent Stimuli

As we indicated earlier, antecedent stimuli include a range of things and events that may influence student behavior, some of which (e.g., students' sleep schedules, nutrition, events occurring at home) are beyond your control. However, if you can identify patterns in your students' behavior that apparently are not related to school or classroom factors, you may be able to establish links with parents or other professionals who can give you information to functionally analyze the relationship of these setting events to student behaviors. Perhaps you can then have input on collaborative interventions to alter their influence on behavior. Within the classroom, such *setting events* as the physical arrangement, schedule of events, instructional materials, and teacher proximity have been shown to affect student behavior. These variables can be managed through structuring. Additional strategies based on the manipulation of antecedent variables include modeling, behavioral momentum, and pre-correction.

As defined by Haring and Phillips (1962), **structuring** refers to clarifying the relationship between behavior and its consequences. For many children and youth exhibiting behavioral disorders, this relationship has been anything but clear, either because of an absence of rules, inconsistent application of consequences for behavior, or ability to out-manipulate the adults who control these consequences. Such pupils enter education programs with the expectation that their wishes will prevail or that the social world is a chaotic place where nothing can be predicted. Haring and Phillips designed the structured approach to make these youngsters' environment more predictable as well as to provide a basis for behavior change.

Our use of the term *structuring* differs somewhat from that of Haring and Phillips. For our purposes *structuring* refers to a range of antecedent variables that the teacher may use to influence pupil behavior: the planning of physical space, daily schedule, rules, teacher movement patterns, and stimulus change.

Physical Space Imagine you have just walked into the room where you are going to spend the next nine months with students who have behavioral problems. Perhaps the room is arranged as the previous teacher left it, or maybe you find yourself staring at nothing more than boxes and packing crates. Your first thought might be, "How can I arrange this to suit what I want to do here?" The answer to the first part of this question depends on how much thought you have given to the second part; that is, the arrangement of your classroom is determined by how you intend to use it.

Following are several considerations intended to help you plan for the full use of your classroom, not restrict it.

1. *How many students* will you have in the room at one time? Twenty students impose more restriction on room use than ten. However, you can plan to use different areas for more than one activity; a science area can also be used for art, provided equipment can be stored and retrieved easily.

2. *How close together* should your pupils sit? The answer to this depends on both the behavioral patterns of your students and their activities.

Extremely active or disruptive children should sit farther apart, and independent seatwork calls for less physical proximity than a group project. Even in regular classrooms, students need space between them to decrease the probability of off-task pupil interactions and increase the probability of on-task behavior during lessons in which peer interactions are not desired (Gunter, Shores, Jack, Rasmussen, & Flowers, 1995).

3. *What kinds of activities* will be taking place in your classroom? You will want to provide some physical activity, particularly if you have young children or if your curriculum includes activities requiring space for free movement. *Will two or more kinds of activities* be going on simultaneously? One student listening to rap music as earned reinforcement can be disruptive in the middle of your civics group. It is wise to set up separate areas if space permits. If not, adjust your schedule so that quiet activities go on at one time and noisy or physical activities at another.

4. Consider also whether any students *need to be isolated,* and if so, whether only for certain activities or for most of the day. By *isolation* we mean physical (usually visual) separation from classmates, not timeout (although this too is a consideration in planning the physical layout of your classroom). **Study carrels** or **cubicles** are a popular method of isolating easily distracted pupils, but they are expensive. Perhaps students in a workshop program can construct one or two for you or you can make one yourself out of an old refrigerator crate. If none of these options is possible, a desk in the corner gives at least some limiting spatial structure. Using a cubicle or separate desk space need not be punishing. If you explain it as a way to get work done on time, a student may appreciate the opportunity. When cubicles are called "offices" and students understand they are used to facilitate studying, competition frequently develops over access to them. One word of caution, however: Under no circumstances should a study carrel be used as a means of permanently separating a disruptive or slow student, or as a timeout area. All children deserve as much educational and personal assistance as you can provide. "Out of sight, out of mind" is not an acceptable strategy.

5. Finally, you should consider *how movement in the classroom* is to be regulated. When pupils need help, will they come to you or will you go to them? Will student movement be restricted ("Raise your hand to get permission") or free? Will you require them to line up before leaving the room or not? How will you regulate movement to and from learning centers or the free-time area? How will students be monitored in these areas? Regardless of whether you want an open, free classroom or a highly structured one, you will need to make decisions such as these and design your classroom accordingly. (See Figure 5.2.)

Obviously, there are other factors to consider when planning your classroom. Much of what you do will be dictated by elements you will not discover until you see your room—the amount of storage space or the location of windows, lights, blackboards, sink, and counters. Look at your potential classroom when you interview for a job. Otherwise, you might end up in a storage closet or a converted locker room!

Daily Schedule   This part of structure has to do with your *general daily routine*—how you sequence your classes and activities. A dependable classroom routine is good for both you and your pupils; students generally like the security of a routine, and if you nearly suffer a breakown trying to get through the math period, there is some comfort in knowing that in thirty minutes you can get to that biology project both you and the pupils like.

The job of setting up a daily schedule often is half done for you. Recesses, lunch, and planning periods usually are determined by school administrators, and like it or not, you will have to organize your day around these set activities. Such scheduled events can be used to good advantage simply by applying *Grandma's Law*[1]:"First eat your vegetables, then you may have your dessert" (Homme, 1970). Applying the law to a schedule

---

[1]Grandma's Law actually is an euphemism for the Premack Principle (Premack, 1959).

Figure 5.2   Floorplan of an Engineered Classroom

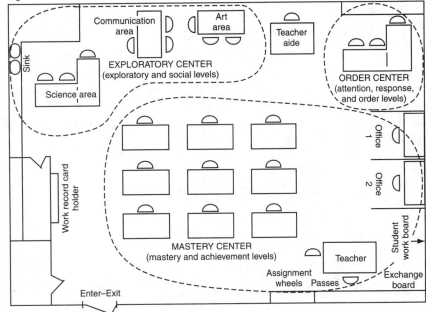

Source: Hewett, F. M. (1968). *The emotionally disturbed child in the classroom.* Boston: Allyn & Bacon. p. 243. Used with permission.

means teaching handwriting just before recess and requiring work to be done before recess.

You might also consider Grandma's Law when trying to decide what should come first in the school day. It is useful to schedule the least enjoyable tasks first (math, reading, spelling, or whatever for a given student or class). Thus, you not only reward task completion with a higher probability behavior, you also get pupils over a big hurdle early in the day. On the other hand, Hewett (1968) suggested beginning with a warm-up activity, usually a simple direction-following task, to get the children settled and ready for work. Another strategy is to alternate lessons that are easy and more difficult, more active and less active. Table 5.1 shows a sample class schedule for primary-age students with behavioral and learning problems.

Consider several other variables when setting up a daily schedule. Obviously, routine should be balanced by a *reasonable variety* of activity, lest school become boring or aversive. But variety does not mean keeping your pupils guessing what is going to happen from one day to the next. You

can plan both variety and routine if you vary specific tasks frequently but depart from the routine schedule less often.

Table 5.1   Daily Program for a Primary Self-Contained Classroom

Time	Task
8:50	Enter room, take seats, get ready to work
9:00	Math
9:45	Juice and cookie break
10:00	Social skills (group)
10:30	Recess
10:45	Reading, language arts (group)
11:30	Reading, language arts, other (individual)
12:00	Lunch
12:30	Recess
12:45	English, social studies, science (group)
1:30	Finish individual work (PE Tues/Thurs)
2:00	Music, library, or arts and crafts (outside room)
2:30	Finish group work
2:45	Listen to story
2:55	Clean up, ready for dismissal
3:00	Dismissal

Another consideration is the *physical activity* of your pupils during the day. Children need to have some times in the day set aside for physical games and activities. Even though you can work for long periods in one place, do not assume that nine-year-olds can do the same. Plan for some physical activity at least every hour, even if it is only to stand and stretch or to get a drink of water.

Make sure your *pupils understand the schedule*. Telling them is not enough. Use direct instruction to teach the schedule and take students through it several times before assuming they know the routine. However, do not be afraid to change the schedule if it is not working satisfactorily. This is good advice for secondary school teachers. Junior and senior high school schedules can be complicated, and pupils without the skills to get around properly may get into trouble.

Rules Rules are verbal statements regulating behavior. Not only do they tell pupils which behaviors will be tolerated and which will not, they also serve as cues to the teacher as to which behaviors should be followed with which consequences. Worell and Nelson (1974) provide some guidelines for establishing rules:

1. Select the fewest possible number of rules. Too many rules are difficult to remember, and frequently are so specific that pupils easily can find exceptions to them. For example, one teacher, who was concerned about fighting in the classroom, developed long list of rules: "No hitting," "No shoving," "No biting," "No name-calling," and so forth. She later substituted just one rule, "Remain in your seat during our quiet seatwork," because in-seat behavior was incompatible with behaviors leading to and involved in fighting.

2. Use different rules for different situations. Obviously, rules for classroom activities should be different from playground, lunch line, or bus-waiting-area rules. Some pupils need to be taught that different situations call for different behavior. Clearly stated rules can help them make this discrimination.

3. Rules should be stated behaviorally and they should be enforceable. Thus, the rule "show respect toward others" invites differing interpretations of

what constitutes respect or disrespect and is not easily enforceable. The rule "No talking when my back is turned" is behaviorally stated but would be difficult to enforce. Rules that are not enforceable invite tattling as well as testing, both of which can lead to disruptions.

4. Rules should be stated positively; that is, they should describe appropriate and desired student behaviors rather than those to avoid. This focuses attention on positive replacement behaviors rather than on inappropriate pupil activity. For example, the rule "Wait to be called upon before speaking" is preferable to "No talking."

5. Rules should be reasonable. The most common response to an unreasonable rule is to challenge it, which may lead to a serious power struggle. Another option is to give up rather than try to meet the expectation. Thus, the rule "All homework must be in before first period" is reasonable only if all students are capable of meeting it; that is, no one has a night job and the homework is within all pupils' ability to complete. The best way to ensure that rules are reasonable is to develop them with students.

6. There must be consistent consequences for rule fulfillment or infraction. This does not mean the use of threats or lectures. Rule consequences should be posted with the rules themselves or taught until all pupils know them thoroughly. Posted rules and consequences, incidentally, are a tremendous help to substitute teachers or new classroom paraprofessionals. Without consequences, rules have little effect on behavior (Madsen, Becker, & Thomas, 1968; O'Leary, Becker, Evans, & Sudargas, 1969; Walker, 1995). Therefore, consistent teacher follow-through is critical, including praise or points for following rules and systematic withdrawal of attention or other reinforcers (or presentation of aversive consequences) for their infraction. Avoid bending the rules for specific pupils or situations unless you have planned it with students in advance.

Teacher Movement Patterns Teachers who spend more time among their students exert greater stimulus control over their behavior than teachers who remain at their desks. Gunter et al.

(1995) observed that increasing the amount of time teachers spent away from their desks during independent activities increases student academic engagement. Fifer (1986) found that increased teacher movement decreased undesired student behavior and increased positive interactions between pupils and teacher. Teacher movement also increases proximity to students, and closer proximity is associated with the increased power of both social reinforcement and punishment (Shores et al., 1993).

The effective instruction literature includes research demonstrating that teachers who develop skill in being constantly aware of what their students are doing have a valuable behavior management strategy (Brophy & Good, 1986). Therefore, circulate among your students, looking around the room and delivering feedback, praise, and attention.

Stimulus Change A **stimulus change** means altering the discriminative stimuli for a particular response. For example, students who talk excessively or fight may be discriminative stimuli for these behaviors. By separating them the teacher is using stimulus change. The effects of stimulus change on behavior usually are temporary unless acompanied by differential application of consequences (Nelson, 1981; Sulzer-Azaroff & Mayer, 1977). Transfer to a special class is a type of stimulus change, and Walker et al. (1976) observed a 13 percent increase in appropriate behavior when children who acted out were placed in an experimental classroom. By itself, this technique does not have the power to alter more disruptive behavior (Walker, 1995).

Modeling Broden, Bruce, Mitchell, Carter, and Hall (1970) and Strain, Shores, and Kerr (1976) observed positive behavior changes in some nontarget children when positive consequences were applied to a target pupil's behavior. Kazdin (1973) suggested that reinforcement becomes a discriminative stimulus for nonreinforced peers because it signals the probability that similar behavior on their part will be reinforced. If students have a history of positive reinforcement for appropriate behavior, a statement such as "I like the way Tommy is waiting his turn" increases the probability that other pupils will imitate this behavior. However, to be effective with more disruptive children, modeling should be accompanied by the consistent application of consequences.

Behavioral Momentum Behavioral momentum is based on the observation that the performance of a behavior may act as a discriminative stimulus for the continuation of that behavior (Carr, Newsome, & Binkoff, 1976). Reactive behavior management strategies, in which the teacher waits for behavior to occur before applying punishing consequences, may strengthen behavior that is reinforcing in itself (Davis & Brady, 1993). Behavioral momentum actually is a proactive, nonaversive strategy for developing behavioral compliance. The teacher issues a set of simple requests that are discriminative stimuli for compliance responses (i.e., high-probability requests) immediately prior to giving a request identified as the discriminative stimulus for problem behavior (i.e., low-probability request). The "momentum" developed by responding appropriately to high-probability requests increases the probability of compliance with the low-probability request. For example, the teacher may deliver several requests that have been discriminative of compliance ("Show me your finger," "Point to your nose," "Tell me your name") and intersperse in the chain a low-probability request ("Point to the blue triangle"). For behavioral momentum to be effective, the student must have a history of responding appropriately to other examples of compliance requests in the same response class (Davis & Brady, 1993). Successful compliance always should be followed with reinforcement. This strategy has been effective with developmentally young children.

The strategy of permitting students to make *choices* among tasks and curricula has shown promise with students exhibiting behavior problems. Although an extensive body of research literature is developing on allowing students with cognitive disabilities to make choices, this research is only beginning to be applied to students with behavioral problems. Dunlap et al. (1994) demonstrated that allowing an elementary-aged student with EBD to choose tasks and instructional materials resulted in increased academic engagement and reduced disruptive behavior.

Pre-correction   Pre-correction is a strategy originally used to make adjustments in academic instruction before a student had an opportunity to make errors (Colvin, Sugai, & Patching, 1993; Kameenui & Simmons, 1990). Pre-correction is applied in instructional areas in which the teacher anticipates the student will make errors. Walker et al. (1995) described the application of pre-correction to social behavior in seven steps:

1. Identify the context and the likely problem behavior.

2. Specify the expected behaviors.
3. Systematically modify the context.
4. Conduct behavioral rehearsals.
5. Provide strong reinforcement for expected behaviors.
6. Prompt expected behaviors.
7. Monitor the plan (Walker et al., pp. 176, 178).

Figure 5.3 is a pre-correction checklist and plan for a student who has experienced difficulty entering the classroom following recess.

Informal or Naturalistic Techniques

Earlier we cited evidence that the typical behavior management practices of teachers who work with

Figure 5.3   Example of a Completed Pre-Correction Checklist and Plan for Dominic

Pre-Correction Checklist and Plan	Teacher _____ Sarah Enlow _____ Student _____ Dominic Smith _____ Date ___ 11 ___ / ___ 15 ___ / ___ 91 ___
☐ 1. Context	*Students entering classroom immediately after recess.*
Predictable behavior	*Students shouting, laughing, and pushing before complying with teacher direction.*
☐ 2. Expected behavior	*Enter the room quietly, go to desks, begin task, keep hands to self.*
☐ 3. Context modification	*Teacher meets students at door, has them wait and then go to desk to begin entry tasks.*
☐ 4. Behavior rehearsal	*Teacher reminds students just before recess of expected behaviors. Asks Dominic to tell what are expected behaviors.*
☐ 5. Strong reinforcement	*Students are told that if they cooperate with teacher requests, they will have additional breaks and 5 extra minutes for recess.*
☐ 6. Prompts	*Teacher gives signals at the door to be quiet and points to activity on chalkboard. Teacher says "hush" to noisy students and praises students who are beginning work.*
☐ 7. Monitoring plan	*Teachers uses a watch to measure how long it takes for all students to get on task and counts how many students begin their tasks immediately (within 10 seconds).*

students exhibiting problematic behaviors are not conducive to pupil achievement or desired social behavior. It appears that teachers lack training in effective behavior management practices. Shores (1993) interviewed 20 teachers regarding their use of behavior management strategies with students with EBD. Practically all of the teachers he interviewed reported that they learned about the classroom management strategies they were using from other teachers or from their own experience; only one teacher reported learning about the system she used from a teacher preparation program. The following sections present strategies that have been proven effective when teachers are taught to use them competently.

As we indicated in Chapter 4, teacher-administered social reinforcement includes three kinds of teacher behavior: feedback, attention, and approval. *Feedback* typically occurs as a consequence of particular behaviors (finishing a task, breaking a rule). However, by itself, the effects of feedback are weak (Madsen, Becker, & Thomas, 1968; O'Leary et al., 1969). On the other hand, *contingent teacher attention* has been shown to influence behavior strongly. Attention differs from approval in two ways: it need not involve any verbal behavior and it is not necessarily positive.

Using teacher attention involves applying differential reinforcement. When appropriate behavior occurs, the teacher attends, stands near, touches, looks at, or interacts with the student. Inappropriate behavior is placed on extinction by looking away, moving to another part of the room, or calling attention to another child. Providing differential attention has been successful in eliminating regressive crawling (Harris, Johnston, Kelly, & Wolf, 1964), reducing aggression (Brown & Elliot, 1965), increasing following instructions (Schutte & Hopkins, 1970), and accelerating correct academic performance (Zimmerman & Zimmerman, 1962).

However, in order for teacher attention to function effectively, it must become a **conditioned reinforcer** (a consequence that has acquired reinforcing properties through association with previously established reinforcers). To establish attention as a conditioned reinforcer, it should be repeatedly paired with the presentation of a consequence that already has been demonstrated to be reinforcing, such as praise, points, or tangibles (e.g., food). The latter consequences gradually and systematically are faded until attention alone produces the desired effect. This process may take time for many pupils with severe problem behaviors. Other students may reveal an extensive repertoire of inappropriate attention-getting behaviors (e.g., raising a hand and saying, "Hey teacher!"; getting up to ask a question). Clearly stated rules governing how teacher attention may be solicited are helpful, but they serve little purpose if you even occasionally respond to the inappropriate activity. Managing such pupils' behavior requires a high degree of self-monitoring and self-control.

Teacher approval or *praise* involves the same contingencies as attention and may be verbal or nonverbal. However, in using approval the teacher usually specifies the desired behavior verbally, such as "I like the way you are working" or "You really did a good job on your algebra assignment." Nonverbal approval (smiles, pats on the back) also may be effective (Kazdin & Klock, 1973). The contingent use of approval is more critical than the amount of approval, per se (Becker, Thomas, & Carnine, 1971; Kazdin & Klock, 1973), but use contingent praise four times as often as verbal aversives (Alberto & Troutman, 1995).

A major problem with attention and approval is getting teachers to use the technique. Breyer and Allen (1975) were unsuccessful in their attempts to train a teacher with 23 years of teaching experience to praise appropriate behavior and ignore inappropriate behavior. However, they did persuade the teacher to implement a token system, which resulted in positive changes in rates of teacher approval and disapproval. Some teachers feel the number of available ways to praise student performance is limited. Table 5.2 illustrates that this is not the case. We hope you will make liberal use of these and other statements in your daily interactions with students.

Also remember that reductive procedures are more effective when they occur in a reinforcing social climate. Therefore, we urge you to administer positive reinforcers (e.g., attention, praise,

Table 5.2 Sample Praise Statements

1. You're doing a good job!	41. Keep working on it, you're getting better.
2. You did a lot of work today!	42. You're doing beautifully.
3. Now you've figured it out.	43. You're really working hard today.
4. That's RIGHT!!!	44. That's the way to do it!
5. Now you've got the hang of it.	45. Keep on trying!
6. That's the way!	46. THAT'S it!
7. You're really going to town.	47. You've got it made.
8. You're doing fine!	48. You're very good at that.
9. Now you have it!	49. You're learning fast.
10. Nice going.	50. I'm very proud of you.
11. That's great!	51. You certainly did well today.
12. You did it that time!	52. That's good.
13. GREAT!	53. I'm happy to see you working like that.
14. FANTASTIC!	54. I'm proud of the way you worked today.
15. TERRIFIC!	55. That's the right way to do it.
16. Good for you!	56. You're really learning a lot.
17. GOOD WORK!	57. That's better than ever.
18. That's better.	58. That's quite an improvement.
19. EXCELLENT!	59. That kind of work makes me very happy.
20. Good job, (name of student).	60. Now you've figured it out.
21. You outdid yourself today!	61. PERFECT!
22. That's the best you've ever done.	62. FINE!
23. Good going!	63. That's IT!
24. Keep it up!	64. You figured that out fast.
25. That's really nice.	65. You remembered!
26. WOW!	66. You're really improving.
27. Keep up the good work.	67. I think you've got it now.
28. Much better!	68. Well, look at you go!
29. Good for you!	69. TREMENDOUS!
30. That's very much better.	70. OUTSTANDING!
31. Good thinking!	71. Now that's what I call a fine job.
32. Exactly right!	72. You did that very well.
33. SUPER!	73. That was first-class work.
34. Nice going.	74. Right on!
35. You make it look easy.	75. SENSATIONAL!
36. Way to go!	76. That's the best ever.
37. Superb!	77. Good remembering!
38. You're getting better every day.	78. You haven't missed a thing.
39. WONDERFUL!	79. You really make my job fun.
40. I knew you could do it.	80. You must have been practicing.

Source: Walker, H. M., Golden, N., Holmes, D., McConnell, J. Y., Cohen, G., Anderson, J. , Connery, A., & Gannon, P. (1981). *The SBS social skills curriculum: Teaching interactive competence and classroom survival skills to handicapped children.* Eugene, OR: University of Oregon. Reprinted with permission.

points) four times more than reductive procedures. When students are used to receiving positive reinforcement and know which behaviors are likely to earn reductive consequences, withholding of reinforcement is more effective in reducing undesired behavior, thereby lowering the necessity for more intrusive and aversive procedures (Ferster & Culbertson, 1982).

Finally, be aware that verbal praise and approval may be ineffective if misapplied. As Brophy (1981) has pointed out, much teacher praise "is not systematically contingent on desirable behavior, lacks specification of the behavioral elements to be reinforced, and/or lacks credibility" (p. 15). To be effective, praise should be genuine, warm, and spontaneous; specifically describe the desirable student behavior; be used with all pupils, even those with large repertoires of undesirable behaviors (i.e., find some behaviors to praise in every student each day); avoid disrupting ongoing appropriate pupil behavior; and be varied in delivery and not overused so that it becomes meaningless (Wolery et al., 1988).

Rationale for Group Management Systems

Whereas modeling and teacher reinforcement are more or less informal and naturalistic management techniques, token systems and group-planned contingencies are universal interventions that require proportionately more strategic planning and effort during implementation. However, in programs for students with EBD (as well as those in a significant minority of regular classrooms) the number of pupils who require some type of behavior management is sufficient to require a group plan. Behavior analysis techniques could be applied to individuals but this tactic would present several problems. First, it would be necessary to identify and deliver individual consequences to each pupil. Although tokens, for example, can be delivered easily to many students, and later exchanged for individual back-up reinforcers, delivering different consequences immediately contingent upon the behavior of individual pupils can be complicated and exhausting. (One reason the number of pupils in classes for students with EBD is restricted by state laws is because so much individual programming is required.)

Delivering reinforcers immediately is virtually impossible unless you can establish a conditioned reinforcer for all students. As we have seen, praise can become a conditioned reinforcer by pairing its delivery with an existing reinforcer. Use both points and praise statements as conditioned reinforcers. Points offer the advantage of being concrete and additive; once a student reaches a specified total, he may exchange points for back-up reinforcers.

Group management systems also are flexible: They may be applied to an entire group of students, to individuals within the group, or to any

combination. Thus, two pupils may receive the same number of tokens for performing different tasks or for reaching different criterion levels. Within such a system, individualization is accomplished by adjusting reinforcement contingencies. The same conditioned reinforcer is given to all pupils, but for different behaviors or on different reinforcement schedules.

Token Systems The token economy is a widely used classroom management system. Token systems have been used in regular and special classrooms, with children exhibiting mild to severe disabilities, with preschoolers and adults, and with social and academic behaviors (Kazdin & Bootzin, 1972). They also may be adapted to fit any situation, or they may be combined with a variety of other management strategies (see Walker, 1995). The essential ingredients of a token system include tokens, *back-up reinforcers* (tangibles or activities) for which tokens may be exchanged, *contingencies* specifying the conditions under which tokens may be obtained or lost, and the *exchange rate* of tokens for back-up reinforcers.

A variety of back-up reinforcers is possible: classroom or school privileges, activities, trinkets, clothes, costume jewelry, toys, or even such large items as bicycles. Some community agencies (e.g., the Chamber of Commerce, Volunteers of America, church groups, labor unions) may be willing to conduct drives or donate items. Cast-off items from your basement or attic may prove valuable in a token system. However, remember that preferred activities also are effective reinforcers, and they are much less expensive and present no storage problems. Therefore, consider using such activities as listening to music, talking with a peer, or playing a game as back-up reinforcers.

Because tokens are conditioned reinforcers, their value derives from association with previously established consequences. Teach students to value tokens by pairing their presentation with an existing social or tangible reinforcer or by **reinforcer sampling,** that is, giving pupils a number of tokens and letting them purchase back-ups immediately (Ayllon & Azrin, 1968). Over a period of days, fade out the paired reinforcer or delay token exchange and make receipt of tokens contingent upon desired behaviors. As your system evolves, increase the length of intervals between token exchanges. This teaches pupils to delay gratification and encourages saving for larger items, which, incidentally, are desirable behaviors in our economic system.

Token systems offer a number of advantages. Because each student can select from a variety of back-up reinforcers, pupil satiation and loss of reinforcer power are not likely problems. Also, tokens can be delivered more easily than individualized tangibles, and simply by announcing that a student has earned a token, your praise and approval develops as a conditioned reinforcer. If tokens are awarded contingent upon academic performance, incompatible social behaviors are reduced in most cases (Ayllon & Roberts, 1974; Hundert & Bucher, 1976; Marholin & Steinman, 1977; Robinson, Newby, & Ganzell, 1981). Also, with such contingencies, little time is lost from teaching as a result of behavior management. In addition, the requirement that tokens be awarded influences the teacher to interact frequently with pupils. With activities as back-ups, the cost of the system is minimal. Specific guidelines for setting up a classroom token system are presented in Chapter 6.

Group-oriented Contingencies   Token systems are powerful behavior management systems, but they do not necessarily take into account the dynamics of children in group settings. Also, because reinforcement is based on individual performance, the teacher must deal with record keeping. Individual differences in the amount of reinforcement may create jealousy, competition, and theft of tokens (Hayes, 1976).

On the other hand, contingencies related to group characteristics take advantage of social reinforcers controlled by the peer group and are adaptable to a variety of situations. **Group-oriented contingencies** also reduce the number of individual consequences the teacher must deliver, which saves time from behavior management duties.

The basic characteristic of group-oriented contingencies is group reinforcement. Whether the

target is an individual student or the entire class, the group shares in the consequences of the behavior. In many cases, group-oriented contingencies are devised to deal with specific problem behaviors. Nevertheless, they can be used to establish appropriate behaviors and to prevent problems. Litow and Pumroy (1975) described three categories of group-oriented contingencies: dependent, independent, and interdependent.

With **dependent group-oriented contingencies,** the performance of certain group members determines the consequences received by the entire group. For example, Carlson, Arnold, Becker, and Madsen (1968) eliminated a second grader's tantrums when a class ice cream party was made contingent on the child going without a tantrum for two days. Coleman (1970) improved appropriate behaviors and decreased out-of-seat and talking-out in four elementary pupils in separate classrooms by awarding them candy to share with peers.

Dependent group-oriented contingencies are most effective when group members are less disruptive than the target child or children (Hayes, 1976). Therefore, these contingencies may not be suitable with groups of students whose behavior is not under appropriate stimulus control. The teacher must be careful that peer influence does not become peer pressure (Hayes, 1976). This is not likely if the contingency involves group reinforcement rather than cost, if the desired behavior is in the pupil's repertoire, and if the initial contingency is not set too high.

The identifying characteristic of **independent group-oriented contingencies** is that the same consequence (e.g., free time) is applied to individual group members (Litow & Pumroy, 1975).[2] One of the best-known variations of independent group-oriented contingencies is **contingency contracting**

---

[2]Token systems actually fall within this definition as well, in that individual pupils receive the same consequence (tokens) and the amount of reinforcement is independent of what others earn. Token systems were treated separately mainly for convenience. However, independent group-oriented contingencies more frequently are directed at a common target behavior, whereas token systems may be used with individual target behaviors.

(Homme, 1970), in which access to a high-probability behavior (one that has a high probability of occurrence) is made contingent upon a low-probability behavior. Contracts are negotiated individually, but access to high-probability behaviors may be arranged on a group basis by setting aside a special area for such activities, called a reinforcing event (RE) area. Pupils also may select a variety of reinforcing events from an **RE menu** (Homme, 1970). Even undesired behavior may be used as a reinforcer for low-probability desired behavior (Homme, 1971). Contracting is low cost and effective (Cantrell, Cantrell, Huddleston, & Woolridge, 1969; White-Blackburn, Semb, & Semb, 1977), but the process takes time. Chapter 6 contains suggestions for contracting with pupils and sample contingency contracts.

Individual pupils' contingent access to a common reinforcer also is a successful variation of independent group-oriented contingencies. Osborne (1969) made free time contingent upon the in-seat behavior of six preadolescent girls with hearing impairments. Schulman, Bailey, and Huntsinger (1976) used masking tape to mark one-square-yard "territories" around fourth graders' desks. Violation of classroom rules caused an immediate twenty-minute loss of territory. This contingency effectively controlled out-of-seat and inappropriate verbal behavior. Wolf, Hanley, King, Lachowicz, and Giles (1970) devised a timer game to control the out-of-seat behavior of 16 students in an after-school remedial class. A kitchen timer was set for intervals varying around an average of twenty minutes. When the timer went off, all pupils in their seats earned tokens exchangeable for a variety of activities and tangibles. The timer game is useful not only for shaping pupil behavior, but also in training teachers to use tokens and praise. However, it is important to fade out the timer gradually, so that appropriate pupil behavior, rather than the timer bell, becomes the discriminative stimulus for reinforcement.

Unfavorable peer pressure is less probable with independent group-oriented contingencies because each student earns consequences independent of the group. However, this procedure also fails to take advantage of the peer group's potent social reinforcement and thus may have less impact on children who seek peer attention through deviant behavior. Speltz, Shimamura, and McReynolds (1982) found that dependent group-oriented contingencies were better than independent contingencies in producing higher rates of academic productivity and improved group interactions with most of the children with learning disabilities they studied.

In **interdependent group-oriented contingencies,** consequences are applied to the group contingent upon each member reaching a specified level of performance (Litow & Pumroy, 1975). Such contingencies may be positive or negative. The "Good Behavior Game" (Barrish, Saunders, & Wolf, 1969) is an interdependent group-oriented contingency that is easy to operate. A class is divided into two or more teams and each team accumulates marks. These are written on the blackboard, indicating that someone on the team has exhibited a target behavior (desired or undesired, depending on the contingency). At the end of the day, the team with the most (or fewest) marks gains a privilege. This game has been successful in reducing disruptive behavior (Barrish et al., 1969; Harris & Sheman, 1973; Medland & Stachnik, 1972), and to increase group on-task behavior (Darch & Thorpe, 1977).

Sulzbacker and Houser (1968) conducted a classic study involving interdependent group-oriented contingencies. Fourteen special class students displayed high rates of using the "naughty finger" (third finger, extended) or referring to it. It was arranged for students to receive a special ten-minute recess at the end of the day. The teacher mounted ten cards, each one corresponding to a minute of recess time, in the front of the room. If she saw the naughty finger, or heard anyone refer to it, she turned over one card, indicating that a minute of recess had been lost. The contingency quickly reduced the target behaviors.

Switzer, Deal, and Bailey (1977) effectively reduced stealing in a second-grade class by using contingent recess time. Interdependent contingencies are particularly well suited to problems such as stealing because of the difficulty in identifying the guilty parties. However, monitor peer interactions carefully. Axelrod (1973), for example, found both group and individual contingencies equally effective in two special classes, but the interdependent group contingency resulted in more verbal threats to peers whose behavior resulted in point losses.

With some special equipment and a little ingenuity, you can manage even difficult problems with interdependent contingencies. For instance, Schmidt and Ulrich (1969) used a decibel meter to monitor the noise level of a fourth-grade class. After determining the baseline level, a criterion of 42 decibels was used as a basis for awarding additional gym and break time. If the noise level remained under 42 decibels for ten consecutive minutes, a two-minute addition to gym or break time was awarded. Wilson and Hopkins (1973) linked a voice-operated relay to a decibel meter and a radio. Classroom noise above a set criterion level automatically turned off a radio that was tuned to a popular music station. This strategy was effective in reducing the noise level in four junior high school home economics classes.

Comparisons of individual and group-oriented contingencies show that the latter are at least as effective as individual contingencies and are easier for teachers to manage (Axelrod, 1973; Darch & Thorpe, 1977; Drabman, Spitalnik, & Spitalnik, 1974; Kazdin & Geesey, 1977; Rosenbaum, O'Leary, & Jacob, 1975). The social status of some children may be improved by group-oriented contingencies and cooperative peer interactions may be fostered (McCarty, Griffin, Apolloni, & Shores, 1977). However, pupils with high peer social status may become more disruptive under group contingencies, and one pupil may be reinforced at the cost of others (Hayes, 1976; O'Leary & Drabman, 1971). Individual child characteristics, peer interaction patterns, and situational influences should be considered in setting up group contingencies (Hayes, 1976). A combination of contingencies may be more effective than group or individual contingencies alone (Hayes, 1976; O'Leary & Drabman, 1971).

Levels Systems   A **levels system** is a comprehensive behavior management strategy that establishes a hierarchy of increasing expectations for behavioral improvement with increasing student reinforcement and decreasing behavioral structure. Levels systems are used to help students progress from the academic and social skills they exhibit upon entry into the system to levels at which they may be expected to make successful transitions to less restrictive settings. Typically, students advance through a sequence of four or five levels, each associated with higher expectations for academic performance and social behavior, as well as with greater student autonomy and access to more naturalistic reinforcers. For example, at level one, a student may be expected to follow basic classroom rules, attempt all academic assignments, and work in a 1:1 relationship with the classroom teacher or paraprofessional. At more advanced levels, expectations may include fulfilling the terms of individual contingency contracts, completing assignments with a high degree of accuracy, and working independently in group settings, which may include participation in mainstream classes. Advancement through the levels is based upon periodic assessments of student progress against specific criteria for academic and social behaviors. Considerations in the development of a levels system include the following (Reisberg, Brodigan, & Williams, 1991):

1. Clearly define the levels or steps in the system.
2. Clearly define the desired behaviors students must exhibit to progress through the system.
3. Clearly define inappropriate behaviors (and their consequences) that prohibit student advancement or will cause students to regress at each level.
4. Clearly define the reinforcers students may earn at each level.
5. Clearly define the criteria for placement and movement within the system.
6. Develop procedures for continuous evaluation and measurement of student performance.
7. Develop procedures to facilitate frequent communication between all parties.

For a complete description of levels systems as a strategy for helping students transition to less restrictive settings, see Chapter 11.

Although levels systems enjoy widespread popularity in more restrictive educational programs for students with behavioral problems, their efficacy in promoting successful transitions to less restrictive environments has not been demonstrated (Smith & Farrell, 1993; Scheuermann, Webber, Partin, & Knies, 1994). Scheuermann et al. (1994) suggested that levels systems may, in fact, violate some legal requirements associated with the due process and the least restrictive environment regulations of IDEA. Specifically, the right to an education in the least restrictive environment may be abridged, in that access to general education classrooms is treated as a privilege and is not based on whether the student can benefit from such participation. In addition, to the extent that criteria for placement in levels systems and movement among levels are the same for all students, levels systems are not consistent with the individualized program requirement of the law. Even the placement of students in mainstream school settings based on their status in the levels system (e.g., lunch in the cafeteria) violates their right to have decisions regarding their participation in such settings made by their IEP teams. Scheuermann et al. proposed a model for designing individualized levels systems based on the curriculum for a given student.

Using Reductive Procedures in Classroom Behavior Management

Although behavior enhancement procedures should dominate classroom management, many students are adept at manipulating situations so that their inappropriate behavior results in positive reinforcement. Also remember that teacher attention, even when accompanied by reprimands or other negative reactions, may be positively reinforcing to some pupils. Students who constantly are punished may develop a tolerance for aversive consequences and the accompanying attention may be a powerful reinforcer, especially if the pupils' appropriate behaviors largely are ignored. Used by itself, positive reinforcement of appropriate behavior generally is thought to be effective in maintaining low rates of undesired behavior of pupils with relatively mild behavior problems, but even with these students it should not be assumed that positive reinforcement alone will be effective. For example, Pfiffner and O'Leary (1987) found that increasing the density of positive reinforcement alone was ineffective in maintaining acceptable levels of on-task behavior and academic accuracy in first-through third-grade students with academic or behavioral problems, unless they had previously experienced negative consequences. Research with individuals exhibiting more severe behavior disorders consistently indicates that a combination of positive reinforcement and punishment procedures is superior to either reinforcement or punishment alone (Shores, Gunter, & Jack, 1993; Walker & Hops, 1993).

Chapter 4 included guidelines and policies regarding the use of aversive consequences. Subsequent chapters present intervention procedures for dealing with inappropriate behavior and problem or crisis situations. This discussion of reductive procedures should help you establish a repertoire of interventions to apply to behavior before it gets out of control. For example, what should you do if a pupil breaks a rule, ignores a direct request, or persistently engages in off-task or disruptive behavior? Having command of a range of reductive interventions can help you quickly resolve such problems before they become crisis situations.

Remember that the range of reductive procedures used in classroom management is limited by the need for strategies that are less intrusive and restrictive. Nevertheless, several procedures can be applied with minimal interruption of instructional interactions: extinction, verbal reprimands, response cost, and timeout. In the following discussions, keep in mind that we, like Polsgrove (1991), advocate the use of such techniques only in the context of systematic positive reinforcement of desired behaviors through strategies involving differential reinforcement.

Extinction You will recall from the previous chapter that extinction involves withholding reinforcement that is thought to be maintaining maladaptive behavior. Therefore, extinction is likely to be ineffective in reducing behaviors for which you cannot identify or control the reinforcer (e.g., social interactions between pupils, bullying, or self-stimulatory behavior) or in reducing a behavior that has been maintained by intermittent positive reinforcement (Gelfand & Hartmann, 1984). It has been used with success in reducing mild behavior problems (e.g., disruptive classroom behavior, off-task, and tantrums) and, in combination with differential reinforcement of appropriate behavior, in reducing more serious problems such as aggression (Alberto & Troutman, 1995). If your attention has maintained the target behavior and you initiate an extinction procedure, be prepared for a temporary increase in rate and intensity. Thus, the student who repeatedly calls out to get your attention may increase his calling out and perhaps add standing up, yelling, or coming to you for several days after you first apply extinction. Alberto and Troutman (1995) suggest some strategies to help you control your attention under such circumstances: become involved with another student, read or write something, recite something to yourself, carry a worry rock or beads, or leave the room (if possible). Again, if you cannot tolerate a temporary increase in the behavior, extinction is not a good choice. Also consider alternatives if you cannot control other sources of reinforcement (e.g., peer reactions) for the target behavior, if the target behavior is likely to be imitated by other pupils, if you are not able to withhold your attention consistently, or if alternative behaviors that can be reinforced have not been identified (Alberto & Troutman, 1995).

Verbal Reprimands Of the range of verbal aversives used by adults to influence children's behavior (i.e., warnings, threats, sarcasm, ridicule, etc.), reprimands are the most effective and ethical. Other types usually are not applied immediately or consistently following undesired behavior; they imply consequences that may not be carried out (e.g., "If you do that one more time, I'll kick you out of class for a week!"), or they involve evaluations that are personally demeaning to students (e.g., "You're the worst student I've ever had."). Reprimands provide immediate feedback

to students that their behavior is inappropriate and they serve as discriminative stimuli that punishment contingencies are in effect. Their effectiveness in controlling mild and moderate behavior problems has been demonstrated amply (Rutherford, 1983). However, they should be used with caution because one provides attention when delivering a reprimand and this can be a potent reinforcer. Therefore, reprimands should be brief and to the point (e.g., "No hitting") rather than accompanied by lectures or explanations. Obviously, the student should know in advance which behaviors are not allowed so that a reprimand is not an occasion for a discussion (e.g., the pupil says "What did I do?"). O'Leary, Kaufman, Kass, and Drabman (1970) found that soft, private reprimands were more effective than those given loudly and in public. When reprimanding, get close to the student, make eye contact, give the reprimand, and move on (Van Houten et al., 1982). If the student fails to correct his behavior, provide a more intrusive back-up consequence (e.g., response cost) instead of another reprimand or a threat. Note: Never ask a pupil whether he "wants" to go to timeout, the principal's office, and so forth. Such verbalizations merely invite the student to challenge your statement (e.g., "No, you can't make me!").

Response Cost This punishment technique involves the loss of a reinforcer, contingent upon an undesired behavior (Kazdin, 1972; Polsgrove, 1991). The consequence lost may be an activity, such as a privilege or a portion of recess time, or a token (Rutherford, 1983). Response cost has been used successfully with various children in different settings without the undesirable side effects (escape, avoidance, aggression) sometimes observed with other forms of punishment (Kazdin, 1972). It is easily used in conjunction with a token system (Walker, 1983, 1995), and compares favorably with positive reinforcement in controlling behavior (Hundert, 1976; Iwata & Bailey, 1974). On the other hand, McLaughlin and Malaby (1972) found positive reinforcement to be more effective, presumably because the teacher had to attend to disruptive students when taking away points.

Response cost contingencies can be arranged so as to limit this kind of attention. For example, you can post the number of points or minutes of an activity that can be lost for given rule violations and simply give the pupil a nonverbal signal (raising a finger, pointing) indicating what has been lost. (Examples of cost penalties are given in the next chapter.) It is important to maintain a balance between cost penalties and reinforcers earned, so that a pupil does not get "in the hole" with no chance of obtaining any positive reinforcers. Once all opportunity to earn reinforcers has been lost, you hold no contingencies over undesired behavior; that is, there's no reason for the student to behave appropriately. As with any aversive system, you should negotiate systematic response cost penalties with your pupils before they are used.

Timeout Exclusionary levels of timeout (i.e., when the pupil is removed from the immediate instructional setting) are intrusive and restrictive. Therefore, they should only be used as back-up consequences when less intrusive interventions have not been effective. However, these forms of timeout (exclusion and seclusion) are only two of six timeout levels that have been used (Nelson & Rutherford, 1983; Rutherford & Nelson, 1982).

Three levels of timeout may be used in the instructional setting. *Planned ignoring* involves the systematic withdrawal of social attention for the length of the timeout period. Like extinction, it will be effective if teacher attention during time-in is associated with positive reinforcement, and other sources of reinforcement can be controlled during timeout. *Reduction of response "maintenance" stimuli* is based upon systematically enriching the time-in setting through the addition of positive reinforcers for behaviors incompatible with or alternative to the undesired behavior (i.e., using differential reinforcement). When timeout is imposed, these reinforcers are withheld. For example, Foxx and Shapiro (1978) gave disruptive students a "timeout ribbon" to wear while they were exhibiting appropriate behavior. The ribbons were discriminative stimuli for staff to deliver high levels of reinforcement. When a student misbehaved, her ribbon was removed and

reinforcement was withheld for three minutes. Salend and Gordon (1987) used a group contingency timeout ribbon procedure to reduce inappropriate verbalizations in students with mild disabilities. **Contingent observation** requires the student to remain in a position to observe the group without participating or receiving reinforcement for a specified period. As we have emphasized before, timeout is not a good choice if time-in activities are not reinforcing to the student or if timeout provides him the opportunity to engage in behavior that is more reinforcing. Having the pupil take timeout without leaving the setting offers the advantage of being able to observe his behavior during the timeout condition. We do not recommend using another level of timeout (*timeout with restraint*) because of the possibility that physical contact may be highly reinforcing to the student. However, Rolider and Van Houten (1985) successfully applied a movement suppression timeout procedure, in which the pupil was positioned in a corner with her chin against the corner, hands behind her back, and both feet touching the wall for two to three minutes. Plan in advance the levels of timeout and procedures to follow when using this intervention. Also, timeout periods should be brief (one to five minutes) and students should be taught how to take timeout appropriately before it is used.

No matter how mild, use procedures that involve aversive stimuli systematically in conjunction with positive reinforcement, and monitor their effects carefully. Master a hierarchy of such consequences and plan specific techniques for each level in the hierarchy so you will have alternate intervention strategies for any given behavior or situation. Then when you apply a selected consequence, use it at maximum intensity (e.g., a firm "No" instead of a plaintive "It hurts my feelings when you do that"). Give students choices when applying consequences (e.g., "You may go back to work or you may take a timeout"). This indicates to pupils that they have control over the consequences they receive. If the student returns to work, give positive reinforcement (e.g., praise, a point). If undesired behavior persists, apply the stated consequence. Reinforce student decisions to take point or timeout penalties by praise and attention after the penalty has been paid (e.g., "I appreciate the way you took your timeout"). Note, however, that reinforcement for accepting consequences appropriately should not be equal to or greater than the reinforcement the student would receive for appropriate behavior in the first place. If pupils can obtain strong reinforcers by engaging in undesired behaviors then taking a mild penalty, they will learn to exhibit such behaviors to initiate the chain of events leading to reinforcement. Reserve more restrictive procedures (e.g., overcorrection or suspension) for situations in which it is documented that the above procedures have been ineffective, and pay careful attention to due process and to other procedural considerations discussed in Chapter 4.

CONSIDERATIONS FOR SEVERE BEHAVIOR DISORDERS

The classroom behaviors of children and youth with developmental disabilities that include severe behavior disorders[3] present somewhat different management problems than their less involved peers. Basically, their teachers can expect to see a more limited repertoire of behavior, including more limited social, academic, and self-help skills as well as more stereotypic behavior patterns that interfere with learning (Kauffman, 1993; Gast & Wolery, 1987; Spradlin & Spradlin,

---

[3]Although the term "severe behavior disorders" traditionally is used to refer to individuals displaying autistic or psychotic behavior patterns, it has not been demonstrated that differentially certifying such pupils has any educational utility (Kauffman, 1993). The topography of the behaviors exhibited by children with autism may vary from that of children exhibiting severe developmental or cognitive disabilities, but these differences have not proven sufficiently reliable to warrant differential diagnosis. Furthermore, the function of the various topographies of severe behavior problems is the same: whether a child is self-abusive or has tantrums, the teacher should perform an A-B-C analysis and systematically apply appropriate consequences. Finally, the behavioral repertoires of children with severe disabilities and the educational goals and intervention strategies developed for them as a group are similar. Therefore, in this text, we do not attempt to differentiate a set of methods unique to persons with severe behavior disorders from those used with severe disorders in general.

1976). Here we identify some of these differences and the management procedures that have proven to be effective with this population.

Spradlin and Spradlin (1976) found that the selection of appropriate target behaviors for change and of appropriate strategies for continuously measuring them was critical to success in managing the behavior of pupils with severe disabilities. They recommend concentrating on the following initial targets:

1. Limiting behaviors. This category includes behaviors that limit the student's access to public education programs. Often these are the behaviors that cause management problems. To be a pupil in most public schools the individual must be able to function in a group setting (i.e., for the most part, behavior must be under stimulus control by the teacher or by the setting). Many of the behaviors that limit pupils' access to public schools also interfere with learning: stereotypic behaviors (rocking, handflapping, fingerplays, etc.); tantrums; seriously disruptive behaviors; and behaviors that are dangerous to the pupil or to others, such as headbanging, throwing objects, or aggression.

2. Self-help skills. These include toileting, dressing, feeding, and getting around in the environment. Deficits in these areas impose practical limitations on the student's ability to function in a public school.

3. Social skills. To be successful in a group setting, pupils need to exhibit appropriate social interactions, to attend to teacher instructions and educational materials, to follow verbal instructions, and to have a repertoire of imitative behaviors.

These behaviors constitute the initial teaching targets for students with severe disabilities. Classroom management of such individuals will be easier if you assess your pupils in these areas and design individualized education programs to fit each student's needs.

Behaviors in these three categories operate along the same principles as outlined at the beginning of Chapter 4, and they respond to systematic alteration of consequences. However, the learning needs and behavioral characteristics of these pupils are sufficiently different to require specialized procedures. The first of these is a greater emphasis on 1:1 instruction, dictating a smaller pupil-teacher ratio. Generalized stimulus control is more difficult to establish, and therefore, the teacher and classroom aides must work more intensively with each child. Precise command of such techniques as differential reinforcement, stimulus fading, prompting, time delay, and other procedures for developing appropriate stimulus control are invaluable skills (Gast & Wolery, 1987; Spradlin & Spradlin, 1976; Wolery, Ault, & Doyle, 1992).

Identifying effective reinforcers also can be more difficult with learners who have severe disabilities. Although most of these pupils respond to contingent social behavior (attention and praise), primary reinforcers (food, water) must be used in some cases. Public school policy often forbids the contingent feeding of meals (Spradlin & Spradlin, 1976). Teachers who work with low-functioning students with severe behavioral disorders must make do with less potent reinforcers, attempt to alter school policies, or identify alternate consequences.

In using reinforcement with pupils with severe disabilities, you should reinforce desired behavior immediately, meaning you must have a reinforcer that you can deliver promptly in small units. Pieces of crackers, pretzels, potato chips, raisins, bites of cereal, or sips of milk are good alternatives to candy, cookies, and ice cream. By pairing these items with praise, you can develop the latter as an effective conditioned reinforcer, even for low-functioning pupils. If a pupil's responsiveness to social praise and attention is not established after a fair trial, consider using such stimuli as lights, buzzers, bells, or tactile stimulation. These have been used as conditioned reinforcers by some researchers (Wolery et al., 1988).

It also is crucial to design an appropriate curriculum for each student. Individual programs must be broken down into small, sequential steps presented repeatedly and systematically until the pupil reaches a specified behavioral criterion.

By now you should have the impression that a major key to effective behavior management of persons with severe disabilities is sound educational programming. This is the essence of good behavior management with any group or population. If your curriculum is not based on functional skills that pupils need to learn in order to be more effective both in and out of school, education will not be reinforcing. In too many programs for students with severe disabilities, the curriculum consisted largely of cutting and pasting, coloring and painting, playing with blocks or other toys, or making potholders. Such activities take up time; if students find them more reinforcing than inappropriate behavior (which often is not the case), behavior problems are under control. However, few functional (i.e., useful and generalized) skills are developed.

Finally, as a teacher of students with severe disabilities, you must consider how to control behaviors that interfere with learning. Some of these behaviors (e.g., self-stimulation through rocking, twirling objects, engaging in fingerplays) are more reinforcing than the behaviors you want. Also, some pupils may have developed extensive repertoires of disruptive or dangerous behavior that, through intermittent reinforcement, has become highly resistant to extinction. Before you can teach more functional and appropriate skills, therefore, you often must employ procedures for reducing these behaviors. The contingent presentation of aversive consequences has demonstrated the best results, but punishment is also the most controversial approach (Stainback, Stainback, & Dedrick, 1979). Alternatives include extinction, overcorrection, response cost, and timeout. However, all of these techniques are difficult to implement if the pupil's behavior is not under stimulus control. Consequently, you must shape appropriate responses to these interventions through differential reinforcement, prompting, and stimulus fading.

CONSIDERATIONS FOR SECONDARY SCHOOL STUDENTS

The difficulties in working with adolescents with behavior disorders are so imposing that until recently few special programs existed. Less than 20 years ago school exclusion was not uncommon as an intervention with adolescents who had behavior problems[4] (Nelson, 1977). Programs for these youths, whether in regular classrooms or special alternative settings, must provide two essential ingredients: structure and consistency. These are not easy to accomplish in traditional secondary schools where students change classes and are managed by five or six teachers.

With adolescents, particularly those having EBD, there is a greater probability of power struggles and defiance toward authority figures. A structured curriculum, in which both teacher and pupils know the expectations, consequences, and routine, will be invaluable. Establish rules and consequences well in advance of potential crisis situations and develop them in conjunction with pupils. Remember to have in mind a continuum of interventions for undesired behavior, which permits you to more fairly match consequences to offenses and reduces the likelihood that a given intervention will lose its effectiveness through overuse. The same is true of reinforcers. Deliver praise and attention liberally and have a variety of reinforcers available in the classroom. These should also be available in the school, the home, and the community. Teacher verbalizations accompanying the use of aversive procedures should be reduced and simplified. This technique will help avoid unproductive confrontations and arguments.

As with any group of students, it is extremely important to analyze continuously and to adjust the curriculum for adolescents. Both subject matter and learning activities must be relevant to pupils' immediate lives; otherwise, students either will not attend classes or will engage in more reinforcing behaviors, which may be highly undesirable. Therefore, the curriculum must be individualized and adjustments must be made in students' programs on the basis of continuous evaluation of their performances. Important components of curricula for this age group are social skills and school survival skills that students will find useful in their current and future settings (see Kerr,

Nelson, & Lambert, 1987; Walker et al., 1995; also Chapter 7).

Encourage pupils to participate in all aspects of the curriculum. This includes permitting them to make choices among tasks, curriculum, materials, and instructional sequences. In addition, they should be involved in selecting and prioritizing their own social goals, in making decisions about the classroom structure, and in setting consequences and contingencies. Contingency contracting is a productive technique for involving adolescents in decisions about their educational programs (see Rutherford & Polsgrove, 1981). Bear in mind that pupil participation does not mean pupil control. Adolescents with EBD are not likely to possess well-developed decision-making skills (Rutherford, 1975), yet they can be adept at manipulating social situations, especially if the teacher lacks confidence. The teacher remains the final authority, but as students develop greater competency in making decisions, their participation can be increased systematically. The ultimate goal of pupil participation in decision-making is self-regulation. Students must be taught to set goals for themselves, to monitor and evaluate their behavior accurately, and to self-administer reinforcement (Mace, Brown, & West, 1987; Polsgrove, 1979).

Several adaptations are useful for the application of consequences with adolescents. First, whenever possible, teachers should emphasize consequences that are the logical outcomes of behavior. For example, the logical consequence of stealing is arrest, not sympathetic counseling or exoneration. In school, the logical consequence of being tardy may be detention.[5] Although it is difficult to identify many truly "natural" consequences to human social behaviors that can be applied systematically, even those that must be contrived can be presented as logical and consistent outcomes of behavior. Thus, if a rule is broken, the stated consequence is applied. This reduces

---

[4]Recall from Chapter 1 that students with EBD have the lowest rate of school completion of any category of students with disabilities.

[5]In contrast to the policy of some school districts, suspension is *not* a logical consequence of truancy. On the contrary, such practices may directly reinforce truancy.

power struggles because pupils learn to see the teacher as someone who follows the rules, not as one who capriciously or maliciously applies punishment. Consistency in applying such consequences also teaches self-control; pupils learn to anticipate predictable consequences for behavior, and therefore can choose to engage in or suppress their behavior based on this knowledge.

Second, in designing behavior management systems, the teacher of adolescents must consider the reinforcers controlled by the peer group. Peer reinforcement can be much more powerful than adult reinforcement for almost any age group, but this is especialy true for adolescents. The behavior reinforced by peers may be contrary to the goals of the program (Buehler et al., 1966). Therefore, it is prudent to design systems that increase the probability that peer influence will be exerted in accordance with your objectives. Group-oriented contingencies are ideally suited for this purpose.

Third, conditioned reinforcers can be easily administered or withheld. Further, it should be possible to conduct transactions involving these reinforcers with a minimum of teacher verbalization. Many special education programs for adolescents use point systems. Points meet the requirements just mentioned and are especially useful when response cost contingencies are employed.

Fourth, back-up reinforcers for adolescents should be considered carefully. The range of activities and tangibles that serve as reinforcers for secondary-age pupils is wide, and the same reinforcer is not likely to work with all students. The potent influence of peers can be harnessed by including peer interactions as back-up reinforcers. Also, because many adolescent reinforcers lie outside the school, it is wise to arrange contingencies in the home and local community. This involves enlisting the aid of parents, social agency personnel, employers, and girlfriends and boyfriends as agents of reinforcement. For example, MacDonald, Gallimore, and MacDonald (1970) trained volunteer mothers to serve as attendance counselors for adolescents. These counselors made "deals" with their clients and other persons who controlled the students' reinforcers. One such contingency required that a

boy fulfill the terms of his contract before being allowed into a local pool hall. Another boy's girlfriend saw him only if he had met his contingency. Parents can control access to cars, peers, television, and special events such as concerts. By negotiating for such back-up reinforcers to be delivered or withheld at home, the teacher can increase effective control of behavior in school.

Finally, teachers should give thought to the selection and application of techniques for managing undesired behaviors. The physical size of adolescents renders some interventions impractical (e.g., physical punishment). Other techniques should be avoided becuse they increase the probability of further conflict (e.g., public reprimands). Teachers should incorporate response cost contingencies into a group management system as a first step intervention. Such contingencies help develop control over inappropriate pupil reactions when other aversives must be employed. For example, students will learn to take self-imposed timeouts if there are meaningful cost penalties for failure to do so and if points and social reinforcers are used to shape appropriate responses to timeout contingencies. However, response cost contingencies should be developed thoughtfully and evaluated continuously. Under some conditions, the removal of reinforcers has increased rates of undesired pupil behaviors (Santogrossi, O'Leary, Romanczyk, & Kaufman, 1973).

In every secondary program we have observed, the bottom line of the reductive continuum has been temporary exclusion from school. However, if the pupil for whom this intervention is considered has been certified as having a disability, legal restrictions on the use of both suspension and expulsion must be considered. The prevailing view of the courts is that a student cannot be expelled from school if the behavior triggering such an intervention is related to her disability (*Honig v. Doe*, 1988). Furthermore, in such cases the school has the burden of proving that the disabling condition and the behavior problem are not related. If the disability and behavior are related, the school may take emergency measures, but courts disagree on these measures. The Office of Civil Rights has offered the opinion that suspensions totaling less than ten days of the school year are not in violation of a pupil's right to a free and appropriate education (Warboys, 1987). However, some school districts interpret the Supreme Court's *Honig v. Doe* decision to mean ten-day suspensions for each incident. Any school district that finds it necessary to use more than one suspension should carefully examine its policy and instructional program. Suspension should never be substituted for adequate instructional programming and disciplinary measures that permit students to remain in school. Temporary suspension must be negotiated with school officials and parents, who should work out procedures for communicating with the home when this consequence is applied. Ideally, parents should be instructed in how to manage their child during exclusion (what privileges should be withheld, what activities should be permitted, etc.), and home visits should be conducted to ensure that the procedures agreed upon are being implemented effectively. Homework should be assigned and enforced during the exclusion period. The period itself should be brief (one to three days), and alternative procedures should be developed for students who approach the ten-day limit. This intervention specifically is *not* recommended if a responsible adult will not be home to supervise the pupil, if the adult has no control over the student's behavior, or if that individual is unlikely to implement the strategy as designed. If school exclusion is contemplated as an intervention, school personnel should carefully evaluate the potential for competing reinforcers (e.g., access to drugs, peers, delinquent activities, avoidance of school demands) to strengthen patterns of behavior that result in school exclusion. Therefore, it is important that this intervention be closely monitored.

In-school suspension is a less restrictive alternative to sending students home, and it permits better supervision of pupils while they are in suspension. It is somewhat like a detention hall where students work and receive a minimum of privileges. The need for adequate space and personnel to manage the suspension room limits this intervention. It also can be completely ineffective if avoiding scheduled classes is more reinforcing than participation, or if supervisory staff are not qualified to work with students who have

disabilities. Therefore, the effects of in-school suspension should be monitored continuously for all students. For pupils with disabilities, this restrictive intervention should be subjected to a human rights review, it should be written into students' IEPs, and its effects should be carefully evaluated. If it can be argued that suspension has denied a pupil his civil rights, you may be subject to litigation. This is another reason for giving careful thought to using this intervention. (In-school suspension is discussed in Chapter 6.)

EVALUATING CLASSROOM MANAGEMENT PROGRAMS

The basic question teachers ask about a classroom management program is, Has it been effective? Generally, this refers to whether the teacher's goals have been met. Yet this is only one part of evaluation. Other important questions are: Did pupil behavior change as a result of the program or because of uncontrolled variables? What components of the program were responsible for these changes? The answers to these questions require systematic data collection and experimental manipulation, which are imposing tasks for the classroom teacher. However, you should be sufficiently competent in using single-subject research designs to identify the mechanisms of your management system responsible for its success or for any problems. (These designs are described in Chapter 4.)

Published research on classroom management systems has yielded the following general results:

1. Total management packages appear more effective than separate components or combinations of components (Greenwood, Hops, Delquadri, & Guild, 1974; Herman & Tramontana, 1971; MacPherson, Candee, & Hohman, 1974; Walker, Hops, & Fiegenbaum, 1976; Walker & Hops, 1993).
2. The most important component of management systems is the application of contingent extrinsic consequences (Ayllon, Garber, & Pisor, 1975; Becker, Madsen, Arnold, & Thomas, 1967; Hayes, 1976; Porterfield, Herbert-Jackson, & Risley, 1976).

3. Reinforcement and response cost seem to work equally well (Hundert, 1976; Iwata & Bailey, 1974; Kazdin, 1972), although this may not be the case if teacher attention accompanies the removal of reinforcers (McLaughlin & Malaby, 1972).

4. Group-oriented contingencies seem as effective as individual contingencies and are more efficient to administer (Drabman et al., 1974; Kazdin & Geesey, 1977; Rosenbaum et al., 1975); however, negative peer interactions with group contingencies are possible (e.g., Axelrod, 1973).

5. The optimum management package, particularly for highly disruptive students, appears to be a combination of group and individual contingencies (O'Leary & Drabman, 1971; Polsgrove & Nelson, 1982; Walker, 1995; Walker et al., 1995).

Summary

Planning and operating a positive and productive classroom environment are important elements of success in teaching any group of students at any level. Without effective behavior management, teachers and pupils both are likely to be dissatisfied with the time they spend in school. This chapter has provided information about classroom management strategies that will help you establish stimulus control over student social behaviors in group settings. When the group norm is appropriate and desirable behavior, individual behavior problems are less likely to occur, and if they do, you can manage them without having to worry simultaneously that other students are going to be out of control. The following points summarize the procedures that are critical to your success in managing classroom social behavior.

1. Collect data on target behaviors. This is the most critical feature of effective classroom management, but it is also the one most often left out. Without objective, reliable measures of the behaviors targeted for change, you will have no basis on which to judge the effectiveness of your management program or for making decisions regarding program adjustments. Data collection should occur on a daily basis, and if you relate it to the academic program (such as when the system is based on academic performance rates or accuracy), this process need not be a significant additional burden. Remember too that students can be taught to monitor and record their own academic and social behavior.

2. Set goals that are specific, clear, and fair. The most effective classroom management goals are stated behaviorally and include clear criterion statements. This enables you, your pupils, and others to evaluate progress clearly. Your management goals should be based upon baseline data and communicated to everyone having an interest in the management program.

3. Set contingencies that are clear and fair. Contingencies are the "rules" of the system; they specify which consequences will follow which behaviors. The best contingencies are few in number, are positively stated, and are easily understood. The ideal contingency is one in which the response automatically produces the consequence, but in education, the natural consequences of behavior often are ong term and tend to be ineffective in the short run (e.g., failure to turn in assignments results in a failing semester grade). Therefore, devise contingencies that relate behavior to immediate consequences, even if these contingencies must be arbitrary and artificial.

4. Negotiate the system with pupils. If you open yourself to pupil input, you will likely find that your students also are distressed by a chaotic and confusing classroom environment or by being unable to meet teacher or parental expectations for academic performance. Students can participate in identifying target behaviors and setting goals for classroom management. In addition, they can help you operate the program: monitoring behavior, giving tokens, tutoring classmates, keeping records of points saved and spent, or operating a token store. If you develop a management system with students, it will be more to their liking than if you impose it on them.

5. Make systematic program adjustments based upon observable changes in target behaviors. Conscientious data collection, if not accompanied by responding to the data with improvements and adjustments, is a pointless activity. Depending on the kind of data you collect and the trends and patterns you observe, you may find it necessary to add or delete components, revise them, or create program modifications for individual pupils.

6. Base the selection and application of any management system on a careful study of each individual situation. Classroom management programs are not fixed entities applied to all groups of children. Rather, they are infinitely flexible and varied and may be designed to suit any set of

circumstances. The variables you should take into account in setting up a program include the target behaviors; the sociometric status, age, and other characteristics of your group; the enthusiasm and effort you are willing to put into the program; your ability and willingness to adjust the program; and the long-range effects of the system on students and on you. This may seem like an overwhelming array of variables, but it is actually no more than you should consider when implementing any intervention, whether it be a new reading curriculum or a recess period.

 CASE STUDY

USING THE TIMER GAME TO REDUCE DISRUPTIVE CLASSROOM BEHAVIOR[1]

Karen Hensley

In my first year as a special education teacher, I was assigned to a primary-level (ages six through eight) self-contained class for children with EBD. Not being trained in this area, I was pretty nervous and insecure from the beginning. The first few weeks of school reinforced my apprehension.

I had established a token system, using points for completing academic assignments and for following classroom rules. Points were exchanged each day for free time to engage in such quiet play activities as puzzles, games, assembling models, and coloring. However, the system didn't prevent off-task behavior and inappropriate social interactions, which frequently disrupted the classroom routine and atmosphere. My pupils (four boys and one girl) would attempt to gain attention or distract others through talking, name-calling, arguing, and occasional open warfare.

STRATEGY

I had enrolled in a graduate-level behavior management class during my first semester of teaching; now I elected to do my class project on disruptive classroom

behaviors. I realized that if the students followed my classroom rules requiring teacher permission to talk or to leave one's seat, disruptive behavior would occur less often. Therefore, I selected talking-out and out-of-seat as target behaviors. I also identified nonverbal noises as a target, because my students often used this tactic to distract other pupils or to get my attention. For recording purposes, I defined these as follows:

1. Talking out—pupil speaks or makes verbal noises without turning over his "Help" sign and waiting for teacher attention.
2. Out-of-seat—pupil's bottom is no longer touching the chair but pupil doesn't have teacher permission to be up.
3. Nonverbal noises—repeated kicking, tapping, or other motions that result in an audible sound that is noticeable to me.

My aide and I collected baseline data on these behaviors for six days; I observed three ten-minute time samples each day, scattered across several independent work periods. For recording purposes, I divided each ten-minute period into 40 fifteen-second intervals. If any of the target behaviors occurred in an interval, I entered a code in the box corresponding to that interval (T = talking-out,

(continued)

[1] Used with the author's permission.

O = out-of-seat, N = noises). We entered only one symbol per behavior in each interval, no matter how many times it occurred or how many students were doing it. I found that I could measure these behaviors reliably while performing other teaching duties. I attached recording sheets to the clipboard I normally carry with me during independent work.

The intervention strategy consisted of a timer game. I set a kitchen timer for an average of ten minutes. When the timer rang, my aide or I gave all students who were showing appropriate behavior

a point along with verbal praise. At the end of the period, these points could be exchanged for "special" free time, provided the student had earned 80 percent of the possible points. Students who failed to meet this criterion had to remain in their seats during free time.

During baseline, I observed that talking-out occurred more frequently than out-of-seat or nonverbal noises (see Figure 5.4). Since it was also the problem of greatest concern to me, I began the timer game with this behavior alone (a multiple baseline design

Figure 5.4   Reduction of Disruptive Behavior

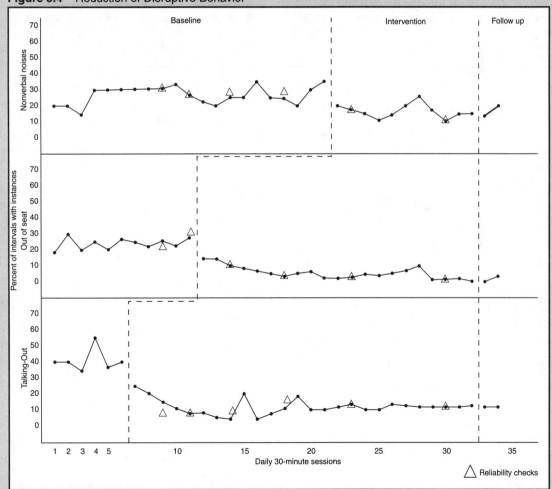

(continued)

was used in my study). After six days, I added out-of-seat behavior to the contingency and added nonverbal noises on day 22. Reliability observations were made by my aide at regular intervals. Our independent records showed that we were consistently in agreement.

On the 33rd day I began phasing out the timer. Gradually, I lengthened the interval between timer rings from an average of 10 minutes to an average of 20 minutes. I did this so that students' good behavior would become a discriminative stimulus for awarding points rather than the sound of the timer. Also, I conducted two follow-up checks to assess generalization and maintenance. The first was conducted in the school library during independent work supervised by the librarian. The second was done during another period in my class.

OUTCOME

Figure 5.4 shows the percentages of disruptive behavior for all students. All three behaviors steadily decreased. This decrease was least dramatic for nonverbal noises, probably because these were most difficult to detect. By the end of my intervention, all three behaviors were occurring during less than 10 percent of the work period. These changes were maintained during my follow-up observations.

At this writing, I am still fading out the timer game. Soon I will drop the timer altogether and just catch my pupils "being good" as a basis for awarding points. I also plan to drop the special free time. My original goal, which was to reduce the occurrence of these three behaviors to less than 20 percent, has been met, and my classroom is a much quieter and more productive place in which to work.

DISCUSSION QUESTIONS

1. When Ms. Peters says to her students, "Please line up quietly to go to the lunch room," her first-grade pupils immediately line up in single file with no disruptive behavior. When Ms. Thomas issues the same request to her class, there is a great deal of running, shouting, and fighting among her first-grade students to be first in line. Explain the difference between the behavior of these two groups in terms of stimulus control and suggest how Ms. Peters may have established stimulus control over the behavior of lining up.
2. Ms. Thomas often uses a loud voice, threats, and spankings to attempt to control her class, but her pupils are among the most unruly in the building. Use your knowledge of behavior analysis to explain why this happened.
3. If you were to set up a resource room for elementary-age pupils with EBD, how would you structure it? How would you structure a resource room differently for junior high school students?
4. Design group behavior management systems based on each of the following: dependent group-oriented contingency; independent group-oriented contingency; interdependent group-oriented contingency.
5. How would you plan a behavior management strategy for a school day for adolescents with severe disabilities? How would your strategy differ for adolescents with mild disabilities?

REFERENCES

Alberto, P. A., & Troutman, A. C. (1995). *Applied behavior analysis for teachers* (4th ed.). Columbus, OH: Merrill.

Axelrod, S. (1973). Comparison of individual and group contingencies in two special classes. *Behavior Therapy, 4,* 83–90.

Axelrod, S. (1987). Doing it without arrows: A review of Lavigna and Donnellan's alternatives to punishment: Solving behavior problems with non-aversive strategies. *The Behavior Analyst, 10,* 243–251.

Ayllon, T., & Azrin, N. H. (1968). *The token economy: A motivational system for therapy and rehabilitation.* New York: Appleton-Century-Crofts.

Ayllon, T., Garber, S., & Pisor, K. (1975). The elimination of discipline problems through a combined school-home motivational system. *Behavior Therapy, 6,* 616–626.

Ayllon, T., & Roberts, M. (1974). Eliminating discipline problems by strengthening academic performance. *Journal of Applied Behavior Analysis, 7,* 71–76.

Azrin, N. H., & Holz, W. C. (1966). Punishment. In W. K. Honig (Ed.), *Operant behavior: Areas of research and application* (pp. 380–447). New York: Appleton-Century-Crofts.

Barrish, H. H., Saunders, M., & Wolf, M. M. (1969). Good behavior game: Effects of individual contingencies for group consequences on disruptive behavior in a classroom. *Journal of Applied Behavior Analysis, 2,* 119–124.

Becker, W. C., Madsen, C. H., Arnold, C. R., & Thomas, B. A. (1967). The contingent use of teacher attention and praise in reducing classroom behavior problems. *Journal of Special Education, 1,* 287–307.

Becker, W. C., Thomas, D. R., & Carnine, D. (1971). Reducing behavior problems: An operant conditioning guide for teachers. In W. C. Becker (Ed.), *An empirical basis for change in education* (pp. 129–165). Chicago: Science Research Associates.

Bickel, W. E., & Bickel, D. D. (1986). Effective schools, classrooms, and instruction: Implications for special education. *Exceptional Children, 52,* 489–500.

Breyer, N. L., & Allen, G. J. (1975). Effects of implementing a token economy on teacher attending behavior. *Journal of Applied Behavior Analysis, 8,* 373–380.

Broden, M., Bruce, C., Mitchell, M. A., Carter, V., & Hall, R. V. (1970). Effects of teacher attention on attending behavior of two boys at adjacent desks. *Journal of Applied Behavior Analysis, 3,* 205–211.

Brophy, J. (1981). Teacher praise: A functional analysis. *Review of Educational Research,* 51, 5–32.

Brophy, J., & Good, T. L. (1986). Teacher behavior and student achievement. In M. C. Wittrock (Ed.), *Handbook of Research on Teaching* (3rd ed.). (pp. 328–375). New York: MacMillan.

Brown, P., & Elliott, R. (1965). Control of aggression in a nursery school class. *Journal of Experimental Child Psychology, 2,* 103–107.

Buehler, D., Jr., Patterson, G. R., & Furniss, J. M. (1966). The reinforcement of behavior in institutional settings. *Behavior Research and Therapy, 4,* 157–167.

Cantrell, R. P., Cantrell, M. L., Huddleston, C. M., & Woolridge, R. L. (1969). Contingency contracting with school problems. *Journal of Applied Behavior Analysis, 2,* 215–220.

Carlson, C. S., Arnold, R. R., Becker, W. C., & Madsen, C. H. (1968). The elimination of tantrum behavior of a child in an elementary classroom. *Behavior Research and Therapy, 6,* 117–119.

Carr, E. G., Newsome, C. D., & Binkoff, J. A. (1976). Stimulus control of self-destructive behavior in a psychotic child. *Journal of Abnormal Child Psychology, 4,* 139–153.

Carr, E. G., Taylor, J. C., & Robinson, S. (1991). The effects of severe behavior problems in children on the teaching behavior of adults. *Journal of Applied Behavior Analysis, 24,* 523–535.

Coleman, R. (1970). A conditioning technique applicable to elementary school classrooms. *Journal of Applied Behavior Analysis, 3,* 293–297.

Colvin, G., Kameenui, R. J., & Sugai, G. (1993). Reconceptualizing behavior management and school-wide discipline in general education. *Education and Treatment of Children, 16,* 361–381.

Colvin, G., Sugai, G., & Patching, B. (1993). Pre-correction: An instructional approach for managing predictable problem behaviors. *Intervention in School and Clinic, 28,* 143–150.

Darch, C. B., & Thorpe, H. W. (1977). The principal game: A group consequence procedure to increase classroom on-task behavior. *Psychology in the Schools, 14,* 341–347.

Davis, C. A., & Brady, M. P. (1993). Expanding the utility of behavioral momentum with young children: Where we've been, where we need to go. *Journal of Early Intervention, 17,* 211–223.

Drabman, R., Spitalnik, R., & Spitalnik, K. (1974). Sociometric and disruptive behavior as a function of four types of reinforcement programs. *Journal of Applied Behavior Analysis, 7,* 93–101.

Dunlap, G., dePerczel, M., Clarke, S., Wilson, D., Wright, S., White, R., & Gomez, A. (1994). Choice making to promote adaptive behavior for students with emotional and behavioral challenges. *Journal of Applied Behavior Analysis, 27,* 505–518.

Fifer, F. L. (1986). Effective classroom management. *Academic Therapy, 21,* 401–410.

Ferster, C. B., & Culbertson, S. (1982). *Behavioral Principles* (3rd ed.). Englewood Cliffs, NJ: Prentice-Hall.

Foxx, R. M., & Shapiro, S. T. (1978). The timeout ribbon: A non-exclusionary timeout procedure. *Journal of Applied Behavior Analysis, 11,* 125–143.

Gast, D. L., & Wolery, M. (1987). Severe maladaptive behaviors. In M. E. Snell (Ed.), *Systematic instruction of the moderately and severely handicapped* (3rd ed.). (pp. 300–322). Columbus, OH: Merrill.

Gelfand, D. M., & Hartmann, D. P. (1984). *Child behavior analysis and therapy* (2nd ed.). New York: Plenum.

Greenwood, C. R., Hops, H., Delquadri, J., & Guild, J. (1974). Group contingencies for group consequences in classroom management: A further analysis. *Journal of Applied Behavior Analysis, 7,* 413–425.

Gresham, F. M., & Reschly, D. J. (1987). Issues in the conceptualization, classification, and assessment of social skills in the mildly handicapped. In T. R. Kratochwill (Ed.), *Advances in school psychology.* Hillsdale, NJ: Lawrence Erlbaum Associates.

Gunter, P. L., Shores, R. E., Jack, S. L., Rasmussen, S., & Flowers, J. (1995). Teacher/student proximity: A strategy for classroom control through teacher movement. *Teaching Exceptional Children, 28* (1), 12–14.

Haring, N. G., & Phillips, E. L. (1962). *Educating emotionally disturbed children.* New York: McGraw-Hill.

Harris, F. R., Johnston, M. K., Kelly, C. S., & Wolf, M. M. (1964). Effects of positive social reinforcement on regressed crawling of a nursery school child. *Journal of Educational Psychology, 55,* 35–41.

Harris, V. W., & Sherman, J. A. (1973). Use and analysis of the "good behavior game" to reduce disruptive classroom behavior. *Journal of Applied Behavior Analysis, 6,* 405–417.

Hayes, L. A. (1976). The use of group contingencies for behavioral control: A review. *Psychological Bulletin, 83,* 628–648.

Herman, S. H., & Tramontana, J. (1971). Instructions and group versus individual reinforcement in modifying disruptive group behavior. *Journal of Applied Behavior Analysis, 4,* 113–119.

Hersh, R. H., & Walker, H. M. (1983). Great expectations: Making schools effective for all students. *Policy Studies Review, 2,* 147–188.

Hewett, F. M. (1968). *The emotionally disturbed child in the classroom.* Boston: Allyn & Bacon.

Hewett, F. M., & Taylor, F. D. (1980). *The emotionally disturbed child in the classroom: The orchestration of success* (2nd ed.). Boston: Allyn & Bacon.

Homme, L. E. (1970). *How to use contingency contracting in the classroom.* Champaign, IL: Research Press.

Homme, L. E. (1971). Human motivation and environment. In W. C. Becker (Ed.), *An empirical basis for change in education.* Chicago: Science Research Associates.

Honig v. Doe (1988). 108 S. ct. 592.

Hundert, J. (1976). The effectiveness of reinforcement, response cost, and mixed programs on classroom behaviors. *Journal of Applied Behavior Analysis, 9,* 197.

Hundert, J., & Bucher, B. (1976). Increasing appropriate classroom behavior and academic performance by reinforcing correct work alone. *Psychology in the Schools, 13,* 195–200.

Iwata, B. A., & Bailey, J. S. (1974). Reward versus cost token systems: An analysis of the effects on students and teacher. *Journal of Applied Behavior Analysis, 7,* 567–576.

Johns, B. H., & Carr, V. G. (1995). *Techniques for managing verbally and physically aggressive students.* Denver, CO: Love.

Kameenui, E. J., & Darch, C. B. (1995). *Instructional classroom management: A proactive approach to behavior management.* Reston, VA: Council for Exceptional Children.

Kameenui, E. J., & Simmons, D. C. (1990). *Designing instructional strategies: The prevention of academic learning problems.* Columbus, OH: Merrill.

Kauffman, J. M. (1993). *Children's behavior disorders* (5th ed.). Columbus, OH: Merrill.

Kazdin, A. E. (1972). Response cost: The removal of conditioned reinforcers for therapeutic change. *Behavior Therapy, 3,* 533–546.

Kazdin, A. E. (1973). The effects of vicarious reinforcement on attentive behavior in the classroom. *Journal of Applied Behavior Analysis, 6,* 71–78.

Kazdin, A. E., & Bootzin, R. R. (1972). The token economy: An evaluative review. *Journal of Applied Behavior Analysis, 5,* 343–372.

Kazdin, A. E., & Geesey, S. (1977). Simultaneous-treatment design comparisons of the effects of earning reinforcers for one's peers versus for oneself. *Behavior Therapy, 8,* 682–693.

Kazdin, A. E., & Klock, J. (1973). The effects of nonverbal teacher approval on student attentive data. *Journal of Applied Behavior Analysis, 6,* 643–654.

Kerr, M. M., Nelson, C. M., & Lambert, D. L. (1987). *Helping adolescents with learning and behavior problems.* Columbus, OH: Merrill.

Litow, L, & Pumroy, D. K. (1975). A brief review of classroom group-oriented contingencies. *Journal of Applied Behavior Analysis, 8,* 341–347.

MacDonald, W. S., Gallimore, R., & MacDonald, G. (1970). Contingency counseling by school personnel: An economical model of intervention. *Journal of Applied Behavior Analysis, 3,* 175–182.

Mace, F. C., Brown, D. K., & West, B. J. (1987). Behavioral self-management in education. In C. A. Maher & J. E. Zins (Eds.), *Psychoeducational interventions in the schools: Methods and procedures for enhancing student competence* (pp. 160–176). New York: Pergamon Press.

MacPherson, E. M., Candee, B. L., & Hohman, R. J. (1974). A comparison of three methods for eliminating disruptive lunchroom behavior. *Journal of Applied Behavior Analysis, 7,* 287–298.

Madsen, C. H., Jr., Becker, W. C., & Thomas, D. R. (1968). Rules, praise, and ignoring: Elements of elementary classroom control. *Journal of Applied Behavior Analysis, 1,* 139–150.

Madsen, C. H., Jr., Becker, W. C., Thomas, D. R., Koser, L., & Plager, E. (1968). An analysis of the reinforcing function of "sit down" commands. In K. R. Parker (Ed.), *Readings in educational psychology* (pp. 265–278). Boston: Allyn & Bacon.

Marholin, D., & Steinman, W. (1977). Stimulus control in the classroom as a function of the behavior reinforced. *Journal of Applied Behavior Analysis, 10,* 465–478.

McCarty, T., Griffin, S., Apolloni, T., Shores, R. E. (1977). Increased peer teaching with group-oriented contingencies for arithmetic performance in behavior disordered adolescents. *Journal of Applied Behavior Analysis, 10,* 313.

McLaughlin, T. F., & Malaby, J. (1972). Intrinsic reinforcers in a classroom token economy. *Journal of Applied Behavior Analysis, 5,* 263–270.

Medland, M. B., & Stachnik, T. J. (1972). Good behavior game: A replication and systematic analysis. *Journal of Applied Behavior Analysis, 5,* 45–51.

Nelson, C. M. (1977). Alternative education for the mildly and moderately handicapped. In R. D. Kneedler & S. G. Tarver (Eds.), *Changing perspectives in special education* (pp. 185–207). Columbus, OH: Merrill.

Nelson, C. M. (1981). Classroom management. In J. M. Kauffman & D. P. Hallahan (Eds.), *Handbook of special education* (pp. 663–687). Englewood Cliffs, NJ: Prentice-Hall.

Nelson, C. M., & Rutherford, R. B., Jr. (1983). Timeout revisited: Guidelines for its use in special education. *Exceptional Education Quarterly, 3,* 56–67.

O'Leary, K. D., Becker, W. C., Evans, M. B., & Sudargas, R. A. (1969). A token reinforcement program in a public school: A replication and systematic analysis. *Journal of Applied Behavior Analysis, 2,* 3–13.

O'Leary, K. D., & Drabman, R. (1971). Token reinforcement programs in the classroom. *Psychological Bulletin, 75,* 379–398.

O'Leary, K. D., Kaufman, K. F., Kass, R. E., & Drabman, R. S. (1970). The effects of loud and soft reprimands on the behavior of disruptive students. *Exceptional Children, 37,* 145–155.

Osborne, J. G. (1969). Free-time as a reinforcer in the management of classroom behavior. *Journal of Applied Behavior Analysis, 2,* 113–118.

Pfiffner, L. J., & O'Leary, K. D. (1987). The efficacy of all-positive management as a function of the prior use of negative consequences. *Journal of Applied Behavior Analysis, 20,* 265–271.

Polsgrove, L. (1979). Self-control: Methods for child training. *Behavioral Disorders, 4,* 116–130.

Polsgrove, L. (Ed.). (1991). *Reducing undesirable behaviors* (CEC Mini-Library: Working with behavioral disorders). Reston, VA: Council for Exceptional Children.

Polsgrove, L., & Nelson, C. M. (1982). Curriculum interventions according to the behavioral model. In R. L. McDowell, F. H. Wood, & G. Adamson (Eds.), *Teaching emotionally disturbed children* (pp. 169–205). Boston: Little, Brown.

Porterfield, J. K., Herbert-Jackson, E., & Risley, T. R. (1976). Contingent observation: An effective and acceptable procedure for reducing disruptive behavior of young children in a group setting. *Journal of Applied Behavior Analysis, 9,* 55–64.

Premack, D. (1959). Toward empirical behavior laws: I. Positive reinforcement. *Psychological Review, 66,* 219–233.

Reisberg, L., Brodigan, D., & Williams, G. (1991). Classroom management: Implementing a system for students with BD. *Intervention in School and Clinic, 27,* 31–38.

Robinson, P. W., Newby, T. J., & Ganzell, S. L. (1981). A token system for a class of underachieving hyperactive children. *Journal of Applied Behavior Analysis, 14,* 307–315.

Rolider, A., & Van Houten, R. (1985). Movement suppression timeout for undesirable behavior in psychotic and severely developmentally delayed children. *Journal of Applied Behavior Analysis, 18,* 275–288.

Rosenbaum, A., O'Leary, K. D., & Jacob, R. G. (1975). Behavioral intervention with hyperactive children: Group consequences as a supplement to individual contingencies. *Behavior Therapy, 6,* 315–323.

Rosenshine, B., & Stevens, R. (1986). Teaching functions. In M. C. Wittrock (Ed.), *Handbook of research on teaching* (3rd ed.). (pp. 376–431). New York: Macmillan.

Rutherford, R. B., Jr. (1975). Behavioral decision model for delinquent and predelinquent adolescents. *Adolescence, 11,* 97–106.

Rutherford, R. B., Jr. (1983). Theory and research on the use of aversive procedures in the education of moderately behaviorally disordered and emotionally disturbed children and youth. In F. H. Wood & K. C. Lakin (Eds.), *Punishment and aversive stimulation in special education* (pp. 41–64). Reston, VA: Council for Exceptional Children.

Rutherford, R. B., Jr., & Nelson, C. M. (1982). Analysis of the response-contingent timeout literature with behavioraliy disordered students in classroom settings. In R. B. Rutherford, Jr. (Ed.), *Severe behavior disorders of children and youth* (Vol. 5). (pp 79–105). Reston, VA: Council for Children with Behavioral Disorders.

Rutherford, R. B., Jr., & Polsgrove, L. (1981). Behavioral contracting with behaviorally disordered and delinquent children and youth: An analysis of the clinical and experimental literature. In R. B. Rutherford, Jr., & A. G. Prieto (Eds.), *Severe behavior disorders of children and youth* (Vol. 4). (pp. 49–69). Reston, VA: Council for Children with Behavioral Disorders.

Salend, S. J., & Gordon, B. D. (1987). A group-oriented timeout ribbon procedure. *Behavioral Disorders, 12,* 131–137.

Santogrossi, D. A., O'Leary, K. D., Romanczyk, R. G., & Kaufmann, K. R. (1973). Self-evaluation by adolescents in a psychiatric hospital school token program. *Journal of Applied Behavior Analysis, 6,* 277–287.

Scheuermann, B., Webber, J., Partin, M., & Knies, W. C. (1994). Level systems and the law: Are they compatible? *Behavioral Disorders, 19,* 205–220.

Schmidt, G. W., & Ulrich, R. E. (1969). Effects of group contingent events on classroom noise. *Journal of Applied Behavior Analysis, 2,* 171–179.

Schulman, J. A., Bailey, K. G., & Huntsinger, G. M. (1976). Territory and classroom management: An exploratory case study. *Behavior Therapy, 7,* 240–246.

Schutte, R. C., & Hopkins, B. L. (1970). The effects of teacher attention on following instructions in a kindergarten class. *Journal of Applied Behavior Analysis, 3,* 117–122.

Shores, R. E. (1993, April). General classroom management strategies: Are they effective with violent and aggressive students? Paper presented at the Council for Exceptional Children Annual Convention, San Antonio, TX.

Shores, R. E., Gunter, P. L., Denny, R. K., & Jack, S. L. (1993). Classroom influences on aggressive and disruptive behaviors of students with emotional and behavioral disorders. *Focus on Exceptional Children 26*(2), 1–10.

Shores, R. E., Gunter, P. L., & Jack, S. L. (1993). Classroom management strategies: Are they setting events for coercion? *Behavioral Disorders, 18,* 92–102.

Smith, S. W., & Farrell, D. T. (1993). Level system use in special education: Classroom intervention with prima facie appeal. *Behavioral Disorders, 18,* 251–264.

Solomon, R. W., & Wahler, R. G. (1973). Peer reinforcement control of classroom behavior. *Journal of Applied Behavior Analysis, 6,* 49–56.

Speltz, M. L., Shimamura, J. W., & McReynolds, W. T. (1982). Procedural variations in group contingencies: Effects on children's academic and social behaviors. *Journal of Applied Behavior Analysis , 15,* 533–544.

Spradlin, J., & Spradlin, R. (1976). Developing the necessary skills for entry into classroom teaching arrangements. In N. G. Haring & R. Schiefelbusch (Eds.), *Teaching special children* (pp. 232–267). New York: McGraw-Hill.

Stainback, W., Stainback, S., & Dedrick, C. (1979). Controlling severe maladaptive behaviors. *Behavioral Disorders, 4,* 99–115.

Strain, P. S., Shores, R. E., & Kerr, M. M. (1976). An experimental analysis of "spillover" effects on the social interaction of behaviorally handicapped preschool children. *Journal of Applied Behavior Analysis, 9,* 31–40.

Sugai, G. (1995, June). Pro-active classroom management. Workshop presented at the Springfield School Improvement Conference, Springfield, OR.

Sugai, G. M., & Tindal, G. A. (1993). *Effective school consultation: An interactive approach.* Pacific Grove, CA: Brooks/Cole.

Sulzbacker, S. I., & Houser, J. E. (1968). A tactic to eliminate disruptive behaviors in the classroom: Group contingent consequences. *American Journal of Mental Deficiency, 73,* 88–90.

Sulzer-Azaroff, B., & Mayer, G. R. (1977). *Applied behavior analysis procedures with children.* New York: Holt, Rinehart, & Winston.

Switzer, E. B., Deal, T. E., & Bailey, J. S. (1977). The reduction of stealing in second graders using a group contingency. *Journal of Applied Behavior Analysis, 10,* 267–272.

Thomas, J. D., Presland, I. E., Grant, M. D., & Glynn, T. L. (1978). Natural rates of teacher approval and disapproval in grade-7 classrooms. *Journal of Applied Behavior Analysis, 11,* 91–94.

Van Houten, R., Nau, P. A., MacKenzie-Keating, S. E., Sameoto, D., & Colavecchia, B. (1982). An analysis of some variables influencing the effectiveness of reprimands. *Journal of Applied Behavior Analysis, 15,* 65–83.

Walker, H. M. (1983). Applications of response cost in school settings: Outcomes, issues, and recommendations. *Exceptional Education Quarterly, 3,* 47–55.

Walker, H. M. (1995). *The acting-out child: Coping with classroom disruption* (2nd ed.). Boston: Allyn & Bacon.

Walker, H. M., & Buckley, N. K. (1973). Teacher attention to appropriate and inappropriate classroom behavior: An individual case study. *Focus on Exceptional Children, 5,* 5–11.

Walker, H. M., Colvin, G., & Ramsey, E. (1995). *Antisocial behavior in school: Strategies and best practices.* Pacific Grove, CA: Brooks/Cole.

Walker, H. M., Golden, N., Holmes, D., McConnell, J. Y., Cohen, G., Anderson, J., Connery, A., & Gannon, P. (1981). *The SBS social skills curriculum: Teaching interactive competence and classroom survival skills to handicapped children.* Eugene, OR: University of Oregon.

Walker, H. M., & Hops, H. (1993). *The RECESS program for aggressive children.* Seattle, WA: Educational Achievement Systems.

Walker, H. M., Hops, H., & Fiegenbaum, E. (1976). Deviant classroom behavior as a function of combinations of social and token reinforcement and cost contingency. *Behavior Therapy, 7,* 76–88.

Warboys, L. M. (1987, November). Special education and school discipline: Legal issues. Paper presented at the 11th annual Conference on Severe Behavior Disorders of Children and Youth, Tempe, AZ.

White, M. A. (1975). Natural rates of teacher approval and disapproval in the classroom. *Journal of Applied Behavior Analysis, 8,* 367–372.

White-Blackburn, G., Semb, S., & Semb, G. (1977). The effects of a good-behavior contract on the classroom behaviors of sixth-grade students. *Journal of Applied Behavior Analysis, 10,* 312.

Wilson, C. W., & Hopkins, B. L. (1973). The effects of contingent music on the intensity of noise in junior high home economics classes. *Journal of Applied Behavior Analysis, 6,* 269–275.

Wolery, M., Ault, M. J., & Doyle, P. M. (1992). *Teaching students with moderate to severe disabilities.* New York: Longman.

Wolery, M., Bailey, D. B., Jr., & Sugai, G. M. (1988). *Effective teaching principles and procedures of applied behavior analysis with exceptional students.* Boston: Allyn & Bacon.

Wolf, M. M., Hanley, F. L., King, L. A., Lachowicz, J., & Giles, D. K. (1970). The timer game: A variable interval contingency for the management of out-of-seat behavior. *Exceptional Children, 37,* 113–117.

Worell, J., & Nelson, C. M. (1974). *Managing instructional problems: A case study workbook.* New York: McGraw-Hill.

Zimmerman, E. H., & Zimmerman, J. (1962). The alteration of behavior in a special classroom situation. *Journal of the Experimental Analysis of Behavior, 5,* 59–60.

STRATEGIES FOR SPECIFIC PROBLEM BEHAVIORS

6

DISRUPTIVE BEHAVIOR

OUTLINE

OBJECTIVES

After completing this chapter, you should be able to

◆ Explain the five types of behavior management interventions and give examples of each.
◆ List ten reinforcers appropriate for an elementary or secondary classroom.
◆ Design a token economy.
◆ Select and carry out a group contingency.
◆ Design and carry out a self-monitoring procedure.
◆ Select the best intervention for a student's disruptive behavior.

This chapter focuses on behaviors that disrupt the ongoing learning process in a classroom. Behaviors that we call *disruptive* are a serious problem for regular classroom and special education teachers. There is no single precise description of disruptive behavior because youngsters can misbehave in a variety of ways. Students can climb on furniture, grab other classmates' materials, make obscene noises or gestures, throw spitballs, verbally or physically defy the teacher, touch their classmates, or run through the hallways. We are concerned about these behaviors not only because they disrupt the ongoing educational activities of the classroom but because they demand much teacher time and attention. The teacher's feelings of pressure and emotional tension that result may affect classroom management practices. Teachers want calm and productive classrooms; students, too, find disruptive behaviors disturbing (see Mullen, 1986).

How do you decide whether to intervene to correct a problem behavior? Consider first whether the behaviors "interfere with the freedom or personal comforts of another individual" (Worell & Nelson, 1974, p. 50). Many behaviors will annoy and irritate you. However, as a veteran middle school teacher once advised, "In this classroom, you must pick your battles carefully—you can't take on everything!" Next, consider the *function*, or *meaning*, of the behavior. Here are some possible reasons why students disrupt classroom activities:

◆ To gain your attention (positive or negative).
◆ To get the attention or approval of classmates.
◆ To avoid doing work.
◆ To gather information; for example, to "test" the limits of your authority or to find out whether the rules will be enforced.
◆ To make the classroom a more interesting place!

Table 6.1 illustrates disruptive behaviors. You might include these target behaviors as you plan **interventions,** conduct **direct observations,** or write **Individualized Education Programs** (IEPs). It's important to have teaching team agreement on **target behaviors, rules,** and sanctions. After all, the behaviors that "bug" you may not even faze your colleagues.

Now let us turn to the intervention strategies available to you. We present five categories of interventions: **school-wide, environmentally mediated, teacher-mediated, peer-mediated,** and **self-mediated.** In each section we define the approach and provide multiple examples of strategies to use in your classroom or school.

SCHOOL-WIDE INTERVENTIONS

Behavior management approaches taken by districts or schools are the focus of this section. It is important that you know the disciplinary policies of your district, especially if you are a new teacher.

Policy is generally decided by the board of school directors and is available from the district's law office or from your teachers' union. Understanding these policies is crucial, as it not only explains students' rights and responsibilities but also explains your rights and responsibilities as a classroom teacher or support professional. The district's discipline code may include dress code, rights of protected students (e.g., those with disabilities), sanctions that the board may take against students, due process safeguards (e.g., disciplinary hearings that you may be asked to attend), safety and security measures (e.g., weapons policies, procedures for students who use alcohol and other drugs), and truancy and attendance guidelines.

Federal and state governments distribute additional policies and regulations. If you work in a public school, request your state's guidelines for the education of protected students and the general education guidelines for discipline. Federal guidelines also affect your discipline policies. For a copy of the Individuals with Disabilities Education

Table 6.1 Sample Definitions of Disruptive Behaviors

1. *Talking out.* The student speaks without permission or interrupts the teacher and another student who are talking to each other.

2. *Out of chair.* The student moves from his chair when not permitted. Such movement may include leaving the chair to open the window, remove items or threaten to remove items from the teacher's or other students' desks, name-calling, and moving around the room.

3. *Modified out of chair.* The student moves from his chair with some part of the body still touching the chair (excluding sitting on feet).

4. *Noise.* The student creates any audible noise other than vocalization.

5. *Rocking.* The student lifts one or more of his chair legs from the floor while he is seated in his chair.

6. *Noncompliance.* The student fails to initiate the appropriate response as requested by the teacher.

7. *Other.* The student clearly violates school or classroom rules or engages in behavior that prevents him from engaging in learning tasks and that are not otherwise specifically defined. Such behavior must be determined by the rules in operation in students' classrooms. Examples of such behavior may include engaging singly in activities or tasks not approved by the teacher or related to the assigned academic tasks (i.e., combing hair, writing on desk, looking at or handling objects within the immediate area surrounding his desk or work area, acting inappropriately to the academic task at hand).

Source: The information in this table was reprinted with permission from Rhode, G., Morgan, D. P., & Young, K. R. (1983). Generalization and maintenance of treatment gains of behaviorally handicapped students from resource rooms to regular classrooms using self-evaluation procedures. *Journal of Applied Behavior Analysis, 16,* 171–188.

Act (IDEA) and the Americans with Disabilities Act, contact your school district's law department, compliance officer, or special education department. In the continental United States, you may also call the National Information Center for Children and Youth with Disabilities at 1-800-695-0285.

Detention

Detention takes place either before or after school or during lunch time, for a thirty- to sixty-minute period. At the beginning of the year, plan a school-wide or an individual detention program using the following steps:

1. Find out students' transportation options. Contact parents to explain detention and to work out transportation. If before and after school times are not practical, consider a lunch-hour detention that requires students to eat in a designated classroom.
2. Establish certain days and times for detentions. Limit detention to a few days a week so that you can supervise the detention students without being distracted by other activities. Daily detention may be too ambitious and can create faculty "burn-out!"
3. Choose assignments students will complete. It may not be feasible for students to complete work they did not finish in class if they require your help or special materials (e.g., film, lab equipment).

Once you have planned detention, consider the following application guidelines:

◆ Assign detention through printed forms that explain the rule violation and the date of the assigned detention. These detention slips should be convenient to use, even when a teacher stops a student in the hall between classes. That is, the slips should be small and handy for teachers in the halls. Because others will need notification, either carbon-set slips or slips with a perforated "receipt" work best.
◆ Notify parents in writing *before* the child serves the detention. This allows parents to arrange for transportation. The parental detention notice should describe the rule violation and the

date and time of the detention. Include the telephone number of a school staff person who can answer parental questions. Figure 6.1 shows a detention slip with these features. Notice its clarity; it is designed for student readers, too.

◆ Plan detention for a time when it will be enforceable. For example, an early-morning detention may have to be rearranged for an afternoon time.
◆ Have adequate work on hand for students. If students fail to bring their own work, then apply a consequence. For example, you might impose another detention. Do not excuse students from detention because they do not bring work—they will learn to beat the system.
◆ Post and review firm rules for behavior during detention. Detention should not be fun.
◆ Establish rules for "excused" absences from detention. For example, require that parents contact you directly in the case of dental visits that conflict with the detention schedule.
◆ Consider asking someone to act as a coordinator who is responsible for detention schedules and parental contacts; this may make the system more efficient. Perhaps a dean or a vice-principal can handle the parental phone calls, and a secretary can schedule detentions, in-school suspensions, and makeups.
◆ Reinforce colleagues who conduct the detention periods, whether the duty is assigned or voluntary. Managing a disgruntled group after school is no picnic.
◆ Be sure that detention is assigned for less serious infractions and that in-school suspension is assigned for more serious ones. This supports the notion of progressive discipline along a continuum of sanctions.
◆ You may wish to run your own detentions for infractions of classroom rules. Here, "central detention" may address violations of school-wide rules, or it may also be used for violations of your classroom detentions.
◆ As with all disciplinary programs, build into the detention system a regular review. Some discipline committees meet on a regularly scheduled basis for this purpose.

◆ At the end of each month (at least), review the list of students assigned to detentions. See how many are repeat offenders. Consider an alternate punishment for these students or revamp detention. Students should hesitate before committing a rule violation that incurs detention. Remember that rules must be reasonable in the first place if the system is to work properly.

In-School Suspension

In-school suspension (ISS) varies widely in its applications. The crucial elements include:

◆ A reinforcing setting from which the student is removed.
◆ A non-reinforcing environment to which the student is sent.
◆ Carefully articulated contingencies that govern the student's passage from one environment to the other.

The in-school suspension room serves as the non-reinforcing environment, so the regular (or special education) class should be the more reinforcing environment. The rules governing ISS should outline how a student enters and exits from ISS. Specific guidelines for in-school suspension appear in Table 6.2.

Because in-school suspension is misused so often, we offer some troubleshooting ideas:

◆ Check the legal implications of your in-school suspension program for students who are protected under the Individuals with Disabilities Education Act (IDEA), the Americans with Disabilities Act (ADA), state standards and regulations, and local policies and procedures. Be sure that all staff members, students, and parents are informed about the rules for ISS. Additional tips include:
◆ Inform students' parents about each instance of ISS.
◆ Staff the ISS room with paraprofessionals and/or professionals who have good behavior management skills.
◆ Avoid letting ISS become just another study hall or tutorial program.
◆ Prohibit students from socializing in ISS.
◆ Monitor referrals to the ISS room. Check referring teachers and those students repeatedly referred.

Figure 6.1   Detention Slip

Dear Parent/Guardian,
   Your child, _____, broke a rule at school today. This is what he or she did: _____

_____

   The school has a rule that your child must now go to a detention. In other words, your child will have to come to school at 3:00 P.M. on *January 16* to do school assignments. Your child will be able to go home at 4:00 P.M. To get home from school, your child can take the school activities bus for $0.50. Or you may make other travel plans for your child.

   Please know that detention is serious. If your child does not come on time, with schoolwork, to the detention period, then we will have to keep your child in the In-School Suspension Room for one school day. This means that your child will have no regular classes for one entire day.

   We have told your child about the detention. If you have any questions, you may call Dean Whittaker at 556-9087 between 9:00 A.M. and 3:00 P.M. tomorrow. If you do not call us, we will look for your child at the detention.

Mrs. Marsh, Teacher

January 15

Source: Reprinted with permission from Kerr, M. M., Nelson, C. M., & Lambert, D. L. (1987). *Helping adolescents with learning and behavior problems.* Upper Saddle River, NJ: Merrill/Prentice Hall.

Table 6.2 Guidelines for In-School Suspension

1. Be sure that the individual in charge of ISS can manage misbehavior. Preferably, teachers should be handpicked for this assignment. If one individual is not in charge all day, then rotate teachers through the ISS duty, with perhaps a permanent para-professional on duty.

2. Do not allow students to enter ISS at any time except the beginning of the school day. Midday entries are disruptive and create additional problems (e.g., parents who are not notified in advance, failure to get enough appropriate assignments from regular teachers, ect.).

3. When students check into school on the day of their ISS, have them meet in a central location. In one successful program, students meet in the dean's office, where they receive a brief orientation to the ISS policies and a reminder of the infraction that earned them ISS. Students then go to ISS in a group, accompanied by the dean.

4. Have students' work already organized when they arrive to serve their ISS day. Do not allow students to circulate throughout the building collecting assignments; this may turn into a reinforcer!

5. When students go to the restroom, do not let them go in groups. One or two students per trip should be the rule.

6. ISS students probably should have lunch in the ISS room. The alternative, allowing then to eat with the other students, may earn them vocal recognition from their peers and create cafeteria disruption.

7. Students who misbehave in ISS should be required to return for an additional day.

8. Time spent in ISS should be work time—no talking to one another or to the adults unless the talk relates to assignments. You may choose to set up carrels to facilitate this atmosphere.

9. At the end of the student's ISS time, an adult should review with the student alternatives to the behavior that warranted ISS placement. Somehow, the ISS teacher should communicate to the regular staff the student's compliance with the punishment.

Source: Reprinted with permission from Kerr, M. M., Nelson, C. M., & Lambert, D. L. (1987). *Helping adolescents with learning and behavior problems.* Upper Saddle River, NJ: Merrill/Prentice Hall.

◆ Check to see if ISS is reducing behavior problems. If not, review the guidelines and adjust the ISS program accordingly. Remember, by definition a disciplinary consequence is not punishing unless it reduces the behavior you designate.

◆ Involve all staff in developing the ISS program guidelines.

Exclusion from School

Suspensions that exclude a student from school are commonly used to correct misbehavior. There may be a good justification for excluding a student from school (e.g., protecting the safety and welfare of other students), but **expulsions** are ineffective when used as a routine practice. Moreover, legal problems may arise when a student with disabilities is excluded from instruction. Some districts have faced serious legal challenges due to the overrepresentation of certain ethnic, racial, or gender groups in their group of suspended students (Uchitelle, Bartz, & Hillman, 1989; also see this source for a discussion of alternatives to suspension.)

Other School-Wide Disciplinary Programs and Practices

Detention, rules, and in-school suspension are only three examples of a school-wide discipline plan. Research has shown that *school-wide discipline planning works* (Colvin, Kameenui, & Sugai, 1993; Nelson, Colvin, Petty, & Smith, 1995). Here are the guidelines offered by the University of Oregon's Project PREPARE (Colvin et al., 1993):

1. Take a consistent approach to discipline problems; it is important to send clear and consistent messages to students.
2. Approach discipline as an instructional opportunity, preparing students before expecting them to act in a certain way, offering them practice, review, and feedback. Consider the steps outlined by Colvin et al., 1993, for teaching students how to behave during transition times:

   Identify the transition behaviors and the times when these behaviors are needed.
   Identify times when you can explain the transition rules and behaviors.
   Identify ways to practice and times to practice.
   Identify reminder times and strategies.
   List reinforcers.
   Name correction procedures.

   Does this format remind you of a lesson plan? That is the idea. Additional detailed lesson plans for teaching appropriate behaviors during elementary school transition times are available by writing to J. Ron Nelson, Ph.D., Eastern Washington University, Department of Applied Psychology, Cheny, WA 99004.
3. Think of discipline as a tool to improve school success, not as an "end unto itself" (p. 369).
4. Use preventive and proactive approaches more than reactive responses.
5. Ensure that administrative and teaching leaders are fully involved in the planning process.
6. Agree among yourselves to change and participate as you develop your school's discipline approaches.
7. Take time to learn new approaches. After all, one study showed a 50 percent decrease in office referrals for schools that set up this approach. (Colvin et al., 1993, pp. 369–370)

In summary, school-wide discipline planning based on sound policies will prevent many behavioral crises. Inclusionary practices, which are more effective than exclusionary practices, greatly enhance a school's functioning and safety. Let's turn now to classroom-level strategies.

ENVIRONMENTALLY MEDIATED INTERVENTIONS

By *environmentally mediated strategy,* we mean that some aspect of the environment is altered to prevent or to manage behavioral problems. For example, you might modify your rules, curricula, schedules, seating, and the general physical plan of your room. Two important ideas may help you when considering environmental strategies. First, altering the environment is not itself a powerful intervention strategy. Second, all other strategies depend on a sound environment that discourages disruptive behavior and that supports the other, more powerful interventions. In other words, environmental modifications are *necessary* if other strategies are to be successful, but not *sufficient* to change misbehavior.

Begin by analyzing your classroom from a student's point of view. Chapter 5 has helpful suggestions.

Preschool and Primary School Environments

Two simple modifications can help students stay in their assigned areas. The first strategy is to mark the floor around each child's desk with masking tape, designating his "yard" or assigned area. Reinforce pupils who remain in their yards and do not reinforce students who are out of their yards. The second intervention is a signaling device (see Figure 6.2) that the student can use to show whether teacher assistance is needed. This procedure reduces the need for students to be out-of-seat to get teacher attention.

Elementary and Middle School Environments

One handy and proven environmental intervention is a clock light, described by Greenwood, Hops, Delquadri, and Walker (1977) as a wireless, remote-control clock used by the teacher to signal **on-task** and **off-task behavior** to students. A green light attached to the clock shows students that they are on-task; a red light reminds students that they are not attending to their work. During a lesson,

Figure 6.2   Signaling Device for a Child's Desk

the teacher can operate the clock light from a remote-control switch at her desk. Immediate feedback to students is one feature of this successful intervention. By designating a length of time that students must be on-task (the clock measures the time cumulatively), teachers can assign reinforcing activities tied to the on-task contingency. Adams (1984) described an inexpensive design for assembling a clock light.

Many of the suggestions offered for young children are applicable to older students as well. Students in the older group, however, are more likely to travel from classroom to classroom and may therefore require assistance in transitions from one location to another. Hall passes are recommended for this age level and may be made of inexpensive materials. In addition, you may wish to mark the traffic pathways with colored tape or decorative footprints.

Secondary School Environments

Large-scale environmental changes are not practical at the secondary level. Instead, it is important to emphasize to students the specific behavioral requirements for each classroom. For example, students should have a clear notion of the criteria for arriving at class on time. Does a student need to be in a seat, in the classroom, or at the door when the bell rings? Areas of the school building that are off-limits to students should be clearly marked, and traffic patterns, especially in crowded areas such as stairwells, should be clear. Adult visibility is important. A survey in urban middle schools (Kerr, 1986) indicated that disruptions in the hall were less common when deans and faculty members remained visible during the changing of classes. This all-out effort lets students know that staff members support each other in a consistent program of discipline.

Special Education Environments

It is crucial that your special education environment prepare students for the regular education placements to which they will be mainstreamed. Be sure that you have ample spaces and opportunities for students to practice group participation skills that will help them succeed in the regular education setting. As much as possible, model your classroom after the mainstream classrooms to which your students will be going.

Many special education settings use cubicles. Like many aspects of environmental planning in the classroom, the effectiveness of cubicles has not been thoroughly examined. However, two research studies provide information on the effectiveness of this environmental manipulation. Shores and Haubrich (1969) found that attending behavior was increased by the use of cubicles but that children's performance on math and reading activities was not affected. In a follow-up study, these authors found that a reinforcement intervention was necessary to improve academic performance, despite improvements in attention obtained through the use of cubicles (Haubrich & Shores, 1976). Each classroom should provide quiet spaces in which students may work individually. Cubicles may serve this function adequately, but they will not replace appropriate academic programming. Overreliance on segregated, individual seating arrangements such as cubicles will defeat the purpose of teaching children to interact appropriately in a group.

TEACHER-MEDIATED INTERVENTIONS

The classroom teacher, through direct interaction with students, plays a primary role in modifying their behavior. This section tells how to increase your effectiveness as a behavioral change agent.

Reviewing Rules

The first intervention (Runyon, Donohue, & Pishevar, 1995) includes a review of classroom rules to encourage primary-school-aged children to monitor their own classroom behavior.

1. Introduction of Rules After selecting target behaviors, the teacher develops a poster or bulletin board to display on-task behavior and rules. He reviews desired classroom behaviors with the class (e.g., listen and sit quietly, assignment completion, no hitting). Adults model appropriate and inappropriate behavior. For example, the teacher may say, "I'm going to sit quietly and listen to Bob while he is talking." As Bob speaks, the teacher sits quietly and makes eye contact. Next, the adults model in appropriate behavior (e.g., talking simultaneously), ask what was undesirable about the interaction, and ask how they could do better in the modeled situation. After this identification of on-task behavior and classroom rules, the teacher gives an explanation of the contingency management program.

2. Review Activity Children hear the following explanation and and see a star chart. (Refer to Figure 6.3.)

"Every 15 minutes or four times during the first class, we will have a 'star check.' I will ask you to come to the 'star chart' one at a time. You will review the rules and wonderful behaviors we just discussed. If you tried to complete your work, raised your hand to talk, and listened, then you earn a sticker next to your name. After class, you may pick a prize from the 'mystery bag' because you earned two out of four stickers and you are a 'Classroom Star.' Later, those of you who earn the most stickers get a chance to be a 'star checker' and monitor the 'star chart.'"

Children then approach the board ("star chart") one at a time. This allows the instructor to continue teaching and peers to proceed with classwork. A "star check" is conducted every 15 minutes.

During a "star check," the teacher's aide (and/or "star checker") reviews classroom participation with each child. For example, the aide might say "Bob, did you raise your hand to speak out in class?" The child picks a sticker for the chart if both the child and "star checker" agree. The aide provides descriptive praise for appropriate classroom behavior (e.g., "That's right, you raised your hand and waited to be called on. You were a model student today."). When the child denies inappropriate behavior, the teacher's aide (and/or "star checker") points out the violation (e.g., "Do you remember when you jumped out of your seat and ran across the room while the teacher was talking? I wish I could give you a sticker but I can't because you did not remain seated or wait to be called on. Next time I'm sure you'll get one.").

3. Reinforcement At the end of class, children with two stars get to choose a prize from the "mystery bag." Class members with the most stickers get to be peer monitor ("star checker"). To ensure that peer monitors are providing classmates with descriptive praise, adults should coach the child during the "star check."

As behavior improves, contingencies may gradually become more stringent. For example, children must earn stickers for three time periods to receive a prize from the "mystery bag." The time intervals may also be increased (i.e., a "star check" is performed during twenty- or thirty-minute intervals instead of every 15 minutes).

Public Posting

Public posting is a successful, relatively simple strategy that combines an environmental intervention with a teacher-directed approach. In public posting, students receive visual feedback about their performance (e.g., a poster telling them how well they have performed a given behavior). Two recent studies illustrate the versatility of this intervention. Both were conducted with secondary school students, but there is no reason why the public posting strategy would not be effective with

Figure 6.3 Class Rules and Star Chart

CLASS RULES
1. No hitting
2. Raise your hand to ask permission to talk
3. Listen and remain seated
4. Complete assigned class work
5. No name-calling

Star Check Interval	1	2	3	4
Name				
John	★			★
Laura		★	★	
Bob				
Larry	★	★	★	★
Tom	★	★		★
Sue	★	★	★	
Pete	★	★	★	
Joe	★	★	★	★
John			★	
Sara	★	★	★	★

Source: Runyon, M. K. , Donohue, B., & Pishevar, R.(1995). *Positive reinforcement and peer monitoring: A method for managing disruptive classroom behavior in elementary school-aged children.* Texts and figures have been adapted and reprinted with permission from the authors.

younger students as long as they understand the contents of the poster.

Jones and Van Houten (1985) used public posting to change seventh graders' disruptive behavior (i.e., noises, pushing, teasing, "showing off," leaving seats) during science and English classes. Before trying the posting, the authors instituted pop quizzes to see whether these would remediate the misbehavior, but they were not entirely successful, so the authors turned to the public posting of each student's daily quiz score. The public posting resulted in decreased disruptive behaviors as well as in similar or improved quiz scores for the seventh graders. Here is a description of the poster that Jones and Van Houten used:

Three 70 cm x 56 cm white bristol board sheets covered with clear plastic laminate were used as feedback posters. Each poster contained the names of the students in whose classroom it was used. In addition, the poster provided space to record five consecutive daily academic quiz scores, the highest daily quiz score and the highest weekly score by each student's name. Further, the daily scores, the highest daily score, and the highest weekly score of the class as a whole were recorded on the poster. Red and black grease crayons were used to record the quantitative data noted above on each poster. Black 3" and 1" lettering was used for all printed material on the chart. Letters were formed with the use of letter stencils and filled in with felt-tipped black markers (p. 94).

In a second study of public posting, Staub (1987) sought to improve the rambunctious hall behavior of middle school students during change of classes. Large posters at each end of a very busy corridor gave students the following information: the percentage change in the daily occurrence of disruptive behavior (as compared with the day before) and the "best record to date" of decreasing disruptive behaviors. To enhance the public posting strategy, the dean gave verbal feedback and praise matching the posters to each classroom during the first minute of classes. This simple and inexpensive intervention proved successful in reducing the disruptive behaviors of the middle school students.

Monitoring Teacher Verbal and Nonverbal Behavior

What you say or do not say may be your most powerful strategy for remedying disruptive behavior. We all know teachers who are "naturals" at disciplining students. These individuals have distinctive speaking voices that command students' attention without screaming. You, too, can have an authoritative but courteous voice. First, ask a colleague to role-play some situations with you. Pretend that you are stopping a rambunctious student in the corridor. Ask your colleague to tell you honestly how you sound. Do you sound angry and out of control? Do you convey authority without losing your "cool"? Are you meek or apologetic? Now practice again. This activity might seem silly at first, but it makes you more aware of your verbal reactions, especially in stressful situations.

Next, concentrate on your facial expressions, gestures, and posture. Ask a colleague for feedback on how you look. Research has shown that 80 percent of the message received by a person in a stressful situation is *nonverbal*. **Self-monitoring** is a great (and even fun) way to gain control of your verbal and nonverbal messages. Here is a simple activity to help you monitor your verbalizations (e.g., praise, reprimands, nags, repeated requests) and body language (e.g., hands on hips, tightened fists, clenched jaw, pointing a finger, standing too close, arms folded across chest):

1. Obtain at least 50 pennies or paper clips.
2. Place the pennies or paper clips in one pocket.
3. Each time you find yourself giving a designated verbal statement or using a gesture you'd like to avoid (e.g., pointing at students), move a penny or a paper clip to the other pocket.
4. At the end of the day, count the items in each pocket and record your score.
5. Tally the number of times you used the verbal statement or gesture and record this on an individual chart. Try to improve your record the next day.

Reprimands

Admonishing students who misbehave is a teaching tradition. Studies have shown that you can **reprimand** more effectively by using the following guidelines:

- *Make your reprimand privately, not publicly* (O'Leary, Kaufman, Kass, & Drabman, 1970). Humiliating or embarrassing a student is likely to increase that student's resentment and may create an unsafe situation (The Gun Institute, 1993). Raising your voice repeatedly merely desensitizes students to your reprimands. Students may be more inclined to listen to what you are saying when you use a normal speaking voice.
- *Look at the student while you are speaking* (Van Houten, Nau, MacKenzie-Keating, Sameoto, & Colavecchia, 1982). Do not insist that the student give you eye contact, however, as this may violate a student's cultural traditions or humiliate him.
- *Stand near the student while you are talking to her* (Van Houten et al., 1982). However, a good idea with anyone is to remain at least one leg length away from the individual, to honor that individual's personal space needs (National Crisis Prevention Institute, 1987).
- *Do not point your finger at the student.* This habit, shared by many educators, can be very difficult to break. Try self-monitoring your gestures, or ask students to help you.
- *Do not insist on having the last word*, especially with teenagers.

The Praise-and-Ignore Approach

Sometimes we ignore problem behaviors, only to be disappointed in the results. Our failure to control behavior may be due to a misunderstanding of the basic principles that underlie this intervention. Here are four guidelines for an effective praise-and-ignore approach:

1. Remember that ignoring will not work unless the reason for the student's behavior is to gain your attention. Use an A-B-C analysis to determine this.
2. Remember that when an ignoring intervention is successful, disruptive behavior will increase before decreasing. Do not give up when students test to see if you will give in and pay attention to their antics.
3. Develop ways in which other adults can distract you from the student who is being disruptive so that you do not find yourself giving the student attention. Let others present know to ignore the student's disruptive behavior.
4. Be sure to **praise** the student for appropriate behaviors. Ignoring without praise will not work—it's merely "going cold turkey."
5. Consider the "peak" of the extinction curve before you begin this strategy. *If you will not be able to tolerate (ignore) the behavior as it accelerates, select a different strategy.* Remember that *the problem behavior almost always worsens (e.g., swearing may escalate to hitting) before it gets better as the ignored child tries to get your attention.*

Differential Reinforcement of Other Behaviors

Differential Reinforcement of Other Behaviors, or **DRO,** is a strategy whereby you reinforce the nondisruptive behaviors when they occur during a specified time interval. One simple way to use the DRO approach is through a timer game (an approach illustrated in the Chapter 5 case study).

Differential Reinforcement of Low Rates of Behavior

Differential Reinforcement of Low Rates of Behavior has been applied to swearing (Epstein, Repp, & Cullinan, 1978), talking out (Dietz &

Repp, 1973), inappropriate questioning, and negative verbal statements. Teasing and name calling were targeted by Zwald and Gresham (1982). Here are the steps they took:

1. The teacher posted and discussed class rules, telling the group the maximum number of teasing/name-calling occurrences allowed to still obtain reinforcement for that day.
2. The teacher made a mark on the blackboard for every teasing/name-calling verbalization. These verbalizations were not discussed or reprimanded.
3. Each boy selected **positive reinforcement** from a reinforcement menu mutually decided upon by the teacher and class members. The reinforcement menu for each day consisted of a hot drink (hot chocolate, tea, or coffee), free reading, or listening to radio.
4. To prevent the number of teasing remarks from getting out of hand if the students went beyond the limit set for the day (thereby losing that day's reinforcement), the teacher gave a larger reward at the end of the week if the group had five or fewer "extra" recorded teasing remarks for the week. The large reinforcer was 20 minutes of free time on Friday.
5. A line graph was posted so that class members could graphically see their progress. The extra teasing remarks (the number of remarks that exceeded the imposed limit) were recorded on a bar graph so the students could observe whether they would obtain free time at the end of the week (p. 430).

Trice and Parker (1983) reduced obscene words in a resource room by using DRL and a **response cost.** Specific words were targeted, and each time a student said one of the six targeted words, he got a colored marker. At the end of the period, the markers were tallied and the students' behavior was posted on a graph. A five-minute detention (the response cost) was required for each marker. Under the DRL condition, students received praise each time the tally fell below the mean tally for the day before; students whose tallies were higher received no comment. The authors cited the response cost procedure as more immediately effective than the DRL procedure.

Physical Interactions with Students

Most of your interactions with student problems will be, and certainly should be, verbal, not physical. We advise that you do not engage in any physical interactions that you would deem inappropriate with an unfamiliar adult. Whereas a handshake may be appropriate and courteous, touching a student in any other way may lead to problems, especially with students who have a history of acting-out behaviors or have been victims of abuse. Naturally, there will be good exceptions to this rule, but a conservative stance is usually best. Adolescents who are developing their own sexual identities are often confused about physical affection. Hypersensitive to your initiations, they may misunderstand your intentions. This likelihood increases when teenagers are under stress, angered, or embarrassed.

Physical interventions for aggressive students create their own problems. Avoid physical confrontations whenever possible, taking precautions to protect yourself and others. Maintaining the recommended leg-length distance is one way to develop the habit of honoring students' personal space needs.

Contingency Contracting

We call a written explanation of contingencies a **contingency contract.** This is a useful procedure, even for young children (Allen, Howard, Sweeney, & McLaughlin, 1993). General guidelines for implementing a contingency contract would include the following:

- Explain to the student what a contract is. Your explanation will depend upon the conversational level of the child, but it may be helpful to use examples of contracts that the student will encounter.
- Share examples of contracts with the student.
- Ask the student to suggest tasks that might be included in a contract between student and teacher. Write these down.

- Suggest tasks that you would like to see the student accomplish, and write these down.
- Decide on mutually agreeable tasks. If a third party is to be involved in the contract, be sure that the party also agrees on the tasks that you have selected.
- Discuss with the student possible activities, items, or privileges that the student would like to earn. Write these down.
- Negotiate how the student will earn the reinforcers by accomplishing portions or all of the tasks.
- Identify the criteria for mastery of each task (time allotted, achievement level, how the task is to be evaluated).
- Determine when the student will receive the reinforcers for completing tasks.
- Determine when the contract will be reviewed to make necessary revisions or to note progress.
- Make an extra copy of the contract. Give this copy to the student and any third party involved. **Home-based contracts,** as they are called, have proven quite successful (Canter & Canter, 1991; Crary, 1990; Kelley & McCain, 1995; Smith, 1994). Smith (1994) offered parents of K–7 students a workshop and workbook, invited them to identify school behaviors of concern to them, and then set up weekly parent-teacher evaluation charts. Once a week students received a simple "yes" or "no" from their teacher, telling whether or not they had met the behavioral goal. Parents issued rewards and certificates when children met their weekly goals. These *parent-initiated contracts* improved the children's behavior and were appreciated by the parents.
- Sign the contract; get the student to sign the contract; and if there is a third party involved, ask the third party to sign the contract.

Figure 6.4 provides an example of a contract for a disruptive child. Notice that it is a home-based contract, in which the parents have agreed to participate. Involving parents (or other persons important to the child) is an excellent way to strengthen a contingency contract. At the bottom of the home-based contract is an important feature: the review date. This frequent review allows everyone involved to offer suggestions for how the procedure can be improved before major problems arise. Did you also note that the reinforcers within the contract tend to be educational activities? By selecting special privileges that enhance your academic program, you move away from the tendency to "bribe" students into improved performance.

We will address contracting again when we come to self-monitoring. First, let's turn to another powerful contingency management tool, the **token economy.**

Token Economy Programs

Token economies have been successful in decreasing such disruptive behavior as jumping out-of-seat, and they have been successful in increasing attention and academic performance (see Chapter 5). Following are the resources you will need for initiating a token economy program:

◆ Back-up reinforcers appropriate for your classroom group.
◆ Tokens appropriate for your group.
◆ A kitchen timer, if you plan to reinforce behaviors by measuring their duration.

Figure 6.4 Home-Based Report

I, ___Randy___ (student), agree to do the following at school:
1. ___Try not to interrupt the teacher___
on this schedule: ___during social studies class___
2. ___Try to work without disturbing other kids___
on this schedule: ___during math___
I, ___Mr. Jameson___ (teacher), agree to provide assistance as follows:
___Arrange for Randy to take part in the social studies discussion, by calling on him daily.___
___Move Randy away from the gerbils.___
We, ___the Bergers___ (parents), agree to provide privileges as follows:
___provide Randy with ✓ marks on the chart posted in the kitchen. When Randy earns 50 ✓s, he can buy a gerbil. We will also try to have conversations about the news at home.___
We have read and discussed this contract in an after-school meeting on ___2/16___. and we hereby sign as a way of making our commitment to this arrangement.
We will all meet on ___2/28___, to reevaluate the contract.
Signed ___Randy Berger___ (student)
___JJ Jameson___ (teacher)
___Anita Berger___ (parent)
___George Berger___ (parent)
Date ___2/16___

◆ A monitoring sheet on which to record the tokens or points earned.
◆ Token dispensers, containers, or devices to denote the gain or loss of tokens.

You will need a couple of hours to get materials together and to get the monitoring sheets duplicated. Then plan to spend about 30 minutes a day for the first week of the program introducing the tokens and orienting students to the program. After the first week, the program should require no more than 20 minutes a day in addition to the time spent delivering tokens. (Note: Programs may differ in the amount of time required.)

To begin the program, select target behaviors for your class. Some of the behaviors you list should be ones you presently take for granted. Select easy behaviors to ensure all students can earn a few tokens from the beginning of the program. Select target behaviors that are compatible with your classroom rules. Include behavioral targets from your students' IEPs. Sample target behaviors developed for a primary classroom token economy could include the following:

◆ Say hello to teachers when you arrive at school.
◆ Hang up your coat when you come to school.
◆ Put your lunch away when you arrive at school.
◆ Pick up your work for the day and take your seat.
◆ Eat lunch within the allotted time.
◆ Line up for activities outside the room.

To ensure that the selected target behaviors are appropriate, ask yourself the following questions:

1. How can I describe this behavior in words the student(s) can understand?
2. How can I measure this behavior when it occurs? If the behavior is measured in terms of time (on-task for ten minutes, no outburst during a fifteen-minute period, solving a certain number of math problems within a specified amount of time), assign the tokens or points on the basis of a token-to-time ratio. If the behavior is measured in terms of **frequency** (percent correct on a worksheet, number of positive verbal comments to a peer, number of independent steps in a self-care task), award tokens or points on the basis of a token-to-frequency ratio.
3. How will I know when this behavior is exhibited?
4. How important is this behavior? You will not be able to initiate the program with all of the behaviors you identify, so you may have to rank them. Start with some behaviors that you can modify successfully.
5. Is the behavior one that you wish to reduce or eliminate? You can handle this behavior in two ways. The first approach is to reward a behavior that is incompatible with the problem behavior. For example, reward in-seat behavior to reduce classroom wandering. The second approach is to fine the student. We call this a **response cost.** If the student wanders around the room, he loses a privilege.
6. Does this behavior occur in other settings? If so, you may want to extend the token economy program to include other classes or the home. You will need to monitor the behavior in those settings, so include space on your monitoring form or develop a different form for those settings.

As you present these target behaviors or rules to your students, remember that research has shown that a daily review of the rules strengthens the effectiveness of the token economy (Rosenberg, 1986). Use this supplemental activity by calling on students and asking them to state the rules and the tokens or points that the behaviors can earn. Rosenberg (1986) found that a mere two-minute review each day improved students' responses to the token economy intervention.

Selecting reinforcers and fines is the next step. If your students can help, let them develop a list of reinforcers. Think of items or events that will be enjoyable and that can be obtained within the school. Some ideas for involving students in identifying their own reinforcers might include the following:

◆ Ask students to draw, write, or select from a set of pictures those items or events that appeal to them.

◆ Allow students some free time, and observe what they choose to do.
◆ Allow students to "sample" reinforcers by placing them in an accessible place and recording which items the students select frequently.

Selecting tokens is the next step. These may take the form of checkmarks, stamps, or other marks on a form. However, you may want to use tangible items, especially with young children. In considering the types of tokens to use, you must consider the following variables:

◆ The age of the students.
◆ The skill level of the students.
◆ The likelihood that students will destroy, eat, or cheat with respect to the tokens.
◆ The expense of the tokens.
◆ The durability of the tokens.
◆ The convenience of using the tokens.
◆ Tokens that are being used in other programs within the same setting. (Do not use these!)

Once you have chosen tokens for your program, select an appropriate container or form for them. Counterfeiting may be prevented by using a special color marking pen, by awarding tokens at specified times, or by awarding bonus points for honesty and deducting points for cheating.

You may have seen token economy programs that were included in a **levels system.** A levels system lists and organizes behavioral targets and their consequences in a kind of hierarchy or set of levels (Schuermann, Webber, Partin, & Knies, 1994). Our example in this section includes four levels. There are advantages (such as efficiency) to having levels for your token economy, but the levels system must carefully consider the legal rights of protected students. To review Chapter 5 guidelines, here are some possible legal concerns (as cited by Schuermann et al., 1994):

1. *Ignoring the IEP process.* Examples include requiring all students to enter at the first level, requiring class consensus before allowing a student to move to a level, establishing target behaviors based on group instead of individual needs, advancing or moving down based on group performance, or

any other action that is not part of an individualized consideration of the student's needs.

2. *Overlooking the concept of Least Restrictive Environment (LRE).* Examples include denying students' access to the general education setting through a requirement that students must earn the right to attain regular education placement. Other examples include restricted access to peers during class or lunch. The checklist in Figure 6.5 will help you evaluate your levels system.

As students learn to manage their behavior, their reinforcers should reflect their increasing ability to handle classroom freedom. Moreover, their reinforcers should provide them with a smooth transition to the less restrictive mainstream environment where frequent and tangible reinforcers are not common. After all, we cannot expect any child to leave a special education classroom willingly if that classroom resembles a toy department.

Another component of your token economy will facilitate the development of new—and unexpected—skills. Issue "bonus points" for spontaneous behaviors that you would like to recognize but did not include in your monitoring forms.

Finally, be sure that you review your token economy program with your students at least once a month. Remember that you will have students at different levels at the same time, so you will need to examine how each student is functioning. If you find that a student is not moving from one level to another, make the higher level a bit easier to reach, or reexamine your lower level to see why the student is not succeeding. This review is similar to the strategy teachers use in assessing students' progress in academic curricula or materials. Through careful initial planning and regular monitoring of students' progress, your token economy will be a success. Here are some tips for making your token economy successful (Bicanich, 1986):

Do
◆ Include your students, whenever possible, in planning your token program.
◆ Deliver the reinforcement only as a consequence of the desired behavior.
◆ Let the student know why a reinforcer is being given.

Figure 6.5   Level System Checklist

Answer each of the following questions regarding your level system.

I. Access to LRE

A. Are mainstreaming decisions made by each student's IEP committee, regardless of the student's status within the level system?

    If no, check below: **Yes   No**

    ___ 1. Students are required to attain a predetermined level before they can attend a mainstream class.

    ___ 2. Mainstream classes are predetermined (e.g., P.E. for students on Level 2, P.E. and music for students on Level 3, etc.)

II. Placement in the level system

A. Are students initially placed in the level system at the level that is commensurate with their needs and strengths?   **Yes   No**

B. Is initial placement in the level system based on current, valid assessment?   **Yes   No**

III. Curriculum

A. Does each student have individual target behaviors designated in addition to those designated for the whole group?   **Yes   No**

B. Are group expectations considered by each student's IEP committee to determine whether those expectations are appropriate for each individual student?   **Yes   No**

C. Are criteria for mastery of target behaviors determined individually?   **Yes   No**

D. Is the sequence of target behaviors developed individually for each student, based on that student's needs and areas of strength?   **Yes   No**

E. Are target behaviors differentiated as skill deficits or performance deficits?   **Yes   No**

F. Are reinforcers individualized?   **Yes   No**

G. Do you avoid using access to less restrictive environments/activities and nondisabled peers as reinforcers?   **Yes   No**

IV. Procedures

A. Are advancement criteria (criteria for movement from one level to the next) individualized for each student?   **Yes   No**

B. Are advancement criteria based on recent, relevant assessment data as well as expectations for age peers in general education environments?   **Yes   No**

C. Does each student's IEP committee determine whether advancement criteria are developmentally appropriate for a particular student?   **Yes   No**

D. Are behavior reductive strategies used separately from the level system (i.e., downward movement is not used as a consequence for inappropriate behavior or for failure to meet minimum criteria for a given level)?

    If no, check below:

    ___ 1. Downward movement is used as a consequence for inappropriate behavior.

    ___ 2. Downward movement is used as a consequence for failure to earn minimum points for a certain number of days.

V. Efficacy

A. Is each student's progress through the level system monitored?   **Yes   No**

B. Is there a problem-solving procedure if data indicate a lack of progress through the level system?   **Yes   No**

C. Do students consistently "graduate" from the level system?   **Yes   No**

D. Do behaviors that are addressed in the level system maintain over time and generalize across environments?   **Yes   No**

E. Do students who complete the level system maintain successfully in less restrictive environments?   **Yes   No**

F. Are self-management skills incorporated into the level system?   **Yes   No**

Each "No" response indicates a potential problem with your level system. For information on how to remediate the problem, refer to the corresponding section in the text.

Source: Scheurmann, B., & Webber, J. (1996). Level systems: Problems and solutions. *Beyond Behavior, 7,* 13. Reprinted with permission.

- ◆ Give some free tokens at the beginning of your program.
- ◆ Reduce tokens gradually so that more work is done for each reinforcer.
- ◆ Review all rules frequently.
- ◆ Exchange tokens formally.
- ◆ Consider reinforcers that are controlled by the peer group.
- ◆ Change reinforcers whenever boredom sets in. (If you become bored, your students have probably been bored for some time!)
- ◆ Make the number of tokens needed consistent with the difficulty or effort required to perform the behavior.
- ◆ Keep reinforcers appropriate to your system's levels.
- ◆ Keep a record of tokens earned for everyone to see.
- ◆ Include behavior/reinforcers and response cost/fines on the same classroom poster but in separate columns.
- ◆ Combine praise with tokens so that social reinforcement can eventually be used alone.
- ◆ Withdraw material reinforcers gradually and let social reinforcement maintain the behaviors.
- ◆ Encourage students to compete with themselves to earn tokens as they improve their own behavior.

Do Not

- ◆ Use tokens that students can obtain outside your system.
- ◆ Give away the best reinforcers at the beginning; high-level reinforcers (the best ones) should cost more and be more appealing.
- ◆ Spend tokens for your students; let them choose for themselves.
- ◆ Let students stockpile tokens.
- ◆ Let students "go in the hole."

The two case studies at the end of this chapter illustrate token economy programs for young children and teenagers, respectively.

Timeout From Reinforcement

Timeout from reinforcement was introduced in Chapter 5. As you recall, this potentially powerful procedure takes away or reduces the reinforcers students might otherwise enjoy (Alberto & Troutman, 1995). Detention and in-school suspension are school-wide interventions that build upon the concept of timeout from reinforcement.

PEER-MEDIATED INTERVENTIONS

What? Turn over behavior management to the very class giving you such a hard time? It may sound completely out of the question. Yet many studies have proven that peers can be trained effectively to change their classmates' behaviors. Here are some reasons to adopt peer-mediated strategies:

1. Peers make good behavioral managers. The research has proven this repeatedly (Lloyd, Crowley, Kohler, & Strain, 1988). In fact, several studies have shown that peers teach skills as well as or better than adults do (Kohler & Strain, 1990).
2. Nondisabled students from toddlers to high schoolers can model and teach their peers, making it a highly versatile tool.
3. Both those teaching and those taught have benefited in the many studies of peer tutoring, whether the targets were social or academic behaviors (Lloyd et al., 1988; Sugai & Chanter, 1989).
4. Carefully implemented peer-mediated interventions provide invaluable opportunities for appropriate social interaction among children with disabilities or within an integrated setting.
5. Through teaching others, children learn to discriminate between appropriate and inappropriate social responses (Sugai & Chanter, 1989).

Peer-mediated interventions take advantage of a student's peer group to alter problem behaviors or to teach new ones. These interventions are especially appealing to adolescents, who prefer their contemporaries. The entire class can be involved in changing an individual's disruptive behavior or the disruptive behavior of the whole class.

Group Goal-Setting and Feedback

This intervention is based on a group discussion in which peers "vote" on a fellow student's behavior. Each student receives a behavioral goal. Either daily or twice a week, students meet in a highly structured, twenty-minute group discussion to vote and give feedback under adult direction. Here are some target goals for your consideration:

◆ Rob will help another student during recess.
◆ Mario will go from class to the library without getting a detention slip.
◆ Cristina will not swear during her morning classes.
◆ Alexa will stay awake in classes after lunch.
◆ Bonifacio will attend his last class.

The goals are very specific. You may wonder why they are not more ambitious; after all, wouldn't we want Alexa awake all the time? Should Bonifacio attend all classes? Two rationales support these goals. First, the behavior may be specific to a particular class. Second, the goal should shape successive approximations. We will succeed in changing behavior if we break the goal into small, attainable target behaviors and reinforce students for mastering them.

Steps for directing **group goal-setting** and feedback are outlined in Table 6.3.

Peer Monitoring

To give you an idea of the versatility of peer-mediated interventions—even with younger children—take a look at a **peer-monitoring** procedure.

Table 6.3 Strategy for Conducting Group Goal Setting and Feedback

1. For each student in the group, develop a social behavior objective written in language the student can understand. Typical goals might be to speak up in the class discussion times, to share materials with others on the playground, to play baseball without teasing my classmates, or to play with at least one other child at recess.

2. Write each student's name, goal, and the date on which the goal was announced on a separate sheet in the group notebook. Record the feedback of the student's peers each day during the group session.

3. Schedule a 15- to 20-minute daily session for the group goal-setting and feedback sessions.

4. Ask everyone to sit in a circle for the group session. Instruct students that this is a time when everyone will speak and that no one is to speak out of turn. Explain further that each student has some behavior that warrants improvement and that the time will be spent talking about our behavior goals.

5. Explain to each student on the first day of the group goal-setting session what her goal is for the next week or two. It is recommended that individual goals be maintained for at least 10 school days.

6. On subsequent days of the group goal-setting session, turn to the first student sitting next to you in the group, announce that student's goal, and state either "I think you made your goal today" or "I don't think you made your goal today." Then provide limited feedback in the form of a statement to support your evaluation. A typical evaluation statement might be, "I like the way you cooperated with Charlie on the playground" or "I don't like the way you took the baseball away from Jane."

7. Request that the student sitting next to the target individual now evaluate that individual's progress toward the goal. Reinforce eye contact with the target student and other constructive feedback. Be certain that each student in the group provides both an evaluation and a feedback statement. Repeat this process until each student in the group has provided the target individual with an opinion and a feedback statement.

8. Tally the votes of making or not making the goal and announce the result. If the student has made the goal, invite others in the group to give her a handclap or other reinforcement you have chosen. If the student has not made the goal, the group makes no response.

9. Repeat this process until all members of the group have received feedback on their goals.

10. If the group has developed a consistently productive performance, you may decide to allow one of the students to be the group leader. This student then reads each student's goals and requests feedback from members of the group. These goals could still be teacher assigned, or in the case of an advanced group, the goals could be self- or peer assigned.

Source: From Kerr, M. M., & Ragland, E. U. (1979). PowWow: A group procedure for reducing classroom behavior problems. *The Pointer, 24,* 92–96. Reprinted with permission of the Helen Dwight Reid Educational Foundation. Published by Heldref Publications, 4000 Albemarle St., N. W., Washington, D. C. 20016. Copyright 1986.

Carden-Smith and Fowler (1984) taught kindergarten children to issue and withdraw points from their classmates. To introduce the strategy, they initiated a teacher-directed points program. The eight children received or lost a point for obeying or disobeying each of these "rules": cleaning up after play, waiting appropriately, and going to and from the bathroom appropriately. After a few training sessions, the class was divided into two teams that changed membership each day. Each child on each team then earned (or lost) teacher-distributed points for the designated behaviors. In this system, the token exchange was simple: children with three points each day could vote on and participate in play activities; children with two points could participate but not vote; children with one point were required to remain inside and complete clean-up chores.

The peer-mediated feature of the program built upon the introductory teacher-directed program. During the peer-mediated intervention, the teacher appointed a team captain who issued and withdrew points from classmates. (The privilege of team captain was awarded students who had earned three points the previous day.) The program showed that even young children with learning and behavior problems could manage a basic token economy. Remember to get approval through the IEP process before using this procedure.

Peer Management

Students can learn to reinforce and ignore their classmates misbehavior, through a strategy called **peer management,** or *peer confrontation.* Peer confrontation is a combined teacher-directed and peer-mediated intervention in which elementary school students modify one anothers' problem behaviors (Salend, Jantzen, & Giek, 1992; Sandler, Arnold, Gable, & Strain, 1987). The peer confrontation works this way: The teacher calls on the group with questions such as, "Who can tell Jake what problem he is having with his behavior?" or "Who can help Sarina figure out a different way to be acting right now?" The teacher then selects a volunteer, who explains the problem behavior and offers an alternative. Students learn this strategy through teacher-led, practice, and role-playing. Here are some guidelines for using peer confrontation effectively:

1. To minimize embarrassment, consider calling upon the entire group for a quick assessment of the class members' behavior: "How are we doing? Does anyone notice a problem we need to correct?"
2. Watch for signs that students are avoiding the activity or the approach or are trying to "gang up on one another." These effects of punishment were observed only initially in two studies (Salend et al., 1992; Sandler et al., 1987) but you may find that your group responds differently.
3. Emphasize positive responses when you teach the system to your students. Role-play correct responses.
4. Don't use this approach unless you have a good relationship with your students, as they may feel that you are singling out their behavior publicly. Encourage students to offer behavioral alternatives and to de-emphasize comments regarding the problem behaviors. One of the advantages of peer interventions such as this one is that it gives students an opportunity to solve behavioral problems and to express alternatives in words that make sense to their peers.
5. Be sure children's participation is cleared through their IEP teams, if applicable.

Peer Extinction and Reinforcement

Recall what you read earlier in this chapter about the importance of reviewing classroom and school rules with students. Could you use peer managers to review and provide feedback on rule following and rule violations?

Group-Oriented Contingencies

The basic ingredient of a **group contingency** is group reinforcement. Litow and Pomroy (1975) described three types of group contingencies: **dependent, independent,** and **interdependent.** In a **dependent group contingency** the peer performance of certain group members determines the consequence received by the entire group (Williamson, Williamson, Watkins, & Hughes, 1992).

This arrangement works best when the behavior of the large group is better than that of the target student or students (Hayes, 1976). This may not be the best plan for a group whose behavior is generally disruptive. The primary characteristic of **independent group contingencies** is that the same consequence is applied to individual group members (Litow & Pomroy, 1975). Contingency contracting is an independent group contingency. In an **interdependent group contingency,** each student must reach a prescribed level of behavior before the entire group receives a consequence. To be sure that a group-oriented contingency does not create negative peer pressure, observe these guidelines:

◆ Use a group reinforcement rather than a response cost.
◆ Be sure that the behavior target and criteria are within the students' reach.
◆ Include "language loopholes" that make the contingency easier to master and harder to sabotage. Here are some examples:

as soon as . . . whenever . . . if . . .
◆ "Easy in . . . easy out": Use the principle of successive approximations.
◆ Avoid language that implies an ultimatum, such as: "If you don't do . . ., then I will do . . . ." "Unless you do . . ., we will not do . . . ."
◆ Get a colleague to help you as you write your contingencies. Consider together the "worst case" scenario for your proposed group-oriented contingency and modify your contingency accordingly.

Table 6.4 illustrates the three types of group contingencies. Pay special attention to each example. Can you identify the "loophole" in each one? How was an ultimatum avoided?

One nice variation of a group contingency is the "Hero Procedure," in which one student earns reinforcers for the rest of the group. As one teacher described this intervention (Briand, personal communication, 1986), "Not only does this procedure help to improve the target student's

Table 6.4 Group Contingency Arrangements

Type of Group Contingency	Examples
Interdependent	If each student comes to class on time, the whole class will earn 5 points extra on his next science test.
	When each student finishes the worksheet of a day, each student will put one bean in a bean container. When the container weighs a pound, the whole class can have a free time for 15 minutes before leaving school.
	If everyone remembers to bring his math books to class for four consecutive days, they will not be assigned homework for the fifth day of class.
Independent	Each student who finishes his research project on time will receive a food coupon for a fast-food restaurant.
	Each student who does not exceed one unexcused tardy for an entire week will receive a homework pass.
	Each student who gets through music class without a teacher reprimand will receive a certificate to take home.
Dependent	If a student who returns to the regular classroom from the in-school suspension room has a good day (i.e., no warnings and classwork completed), all students will get to drop their lowest daily classwork grade. (This recognizes the supportive role of classmates.)
	Three students in this class got detention last week for pushing in the class. If these three students do not get detention for two weeks, the entire class will get to play pogs for indoor recess.

behavior, but it also stops other class members from reinforcing that behavior that you have deemed inappropriate—they want to get the reinforcers!" Here is an example of a group-oriented procedure that incorporates a hero procedure:

> This will be a three-week mathematics estimation contest. If anyone in your class guesses the correct number of cubes in the container, everyone in the class will receive a prize. If more than one person (within or across classes) guesses the correct number, more than one class will receive prizes. If no one guesses the correct answer, then the person guessing closest to the correct number during week 3 will be the winner and his/her class will receive prizes. Each week you will receive written information about whether you guessed correctly or were too high or too low in your estimation (Williamson et al., 1992, p. 418).

Good Behavior Game

The Good Behavior Game (Barrish, Saunders, & Wolf, 1969) is yet another variation on a group contingency. This intervention involves teams of students competing on the basis of their behavior in the classroom (Saigh & Umar, 1983; Salend, Reynolds, & Coyle, 1989). Salend et al. (1989) used the Good Behavior Game in an individualized format to improve the behaviors of high school students in a special education classroom. Students joined a team according to their target behaviors (e.g., inappropriate verbalizations, cursing, drumming/tapping). Each team, therefore, had a common goal. Salend et al. (1989) reported that the teams created positive peer pressure and that students enjoyed being rewarded for their behavioral improvements. This individualized approach (basing the team target behaviors on identified needs of students) is a good way to comply with the requirements of your students' IEPs.

Figure 6.6 is a consultant's description of the Good Behavior Game for a group of "rowdy" sixth graders. Finally, we turn to interventions implemented by students themselves.

SELF-MEDIATED INTERVENTIONS

One of our goals with students who are disruptive is to promote self-control of their problem behaviors.

In recent years we have learned more about such valuable tools as self-instruction and self-evaluation (Hallahan, Lloyd, & Stoller, 1982; Lam, Cole, Shapiro, & Bambara, 1994; Rueda, Rutherford, & Howell, 1980). (For a review of self-management research with students who have behavioral disorders, see Nelson, Smith, Young, & Dodd, 1991.) In this section we focus on three procedures: **self-monitoring, self-evaluation,** and **self-instruction.**

Self-Monitoring

Self-monitoring or **self-recording** allows the student to record his own behaviors. Perhaps you have tried self-monitoring for dieting, smoking cessation, or tracking your physical fitness goals. Another way to think of self-management is the correspondence between what we say we are doing (or will do) and what we do (Miller, Strain, Boyd, Jarzynka, & McFetridge, 1993). Some authors call this a "say-do-reinforcement" or "do-say reinforcement" model (Paniagua, 1990). Before you begin a self-monitoring program, consider the suggestions in Table 6.5.

One of your decisions in designing this intervention is to select a practical monitoring form. Figure 6.7 shows the monitoring form used by Keith.

Space is provided for tallies each day and period, although you might find that your student will at first need to monitor in only one or two periods a day. Printing the target behavior definition at the bottom of the form is a good idea; it helps the child remember what she is monitoring. The form could be modified for an older or more sophisticated student.

Once you have trained a student to self-record, you can move to a behavior management program. During the first few days of the program (at least three days), ask the student to self-record disruptive behaviors without additional intervention. The data from these sessions will provide you with a baseline assessment of the student's performance. The next step in this program is to establish contingencies under which the student receives a reinforcer for reducing the number of disruptions per session. A student

Table 6.5   Guidelines for Self–Management Strategies

1. Consult the section on token economy programs for ideas about selecting appropriate target behaviors.
2. Decide how this behavior might be measured most easily by the student.
3. Some studies have shown that students perform better when they record an academic behavior rather than merely recording whether they are on-task (Lam et al., 1994). Students may use a self-correction aid to see if they have completed a math problem right, for example. Even though this procedure takes a bit of time, the results indicate that it is a preferable approach.
4. Be sure your students can correctly identify the target behaviors, through explanation, discussion, and practice.
5. Consider using a question format. For example, the student's form might read: "Did I get this problem right?"   YES __   NO __
6. Reinforce students not only for improvements in their performance but also for not cheating! Unannounced teacher-monitoring of the student's target behaviors will allow you to see if the student is recording his behavior honestly.
7. If a student is oppositional to the procedure, supplement it with a positive contingency for cooperation or with another strategy (Lam et al., 1994).
8. Try to make the self-monitoring as minimally intrusive as possible (Reid & Harris, 1993).
9. Choose a behavior that is relevant to the student (Reid & Harris, 1993).
10. Work with the student to develop a procedure that is enjoyable, not a chore (Reid & Harris, 1993).

might use a contract form to record the reinforcement to be earned by controlling problem behaviors. In still another approach the student might self-reinforce without using tokens or contracts. For some students, self-recording alone may reduce disruptions.

Whether you use self-monitoring alone or as part of a larger behavior management system, encourage students to reduce disruptions and increase appropriate behavior relative to their own baseline performance. For example, a student whose baseline assessment indicates that he is off-task 80 percent of the period could be encouraged to improve his performance little by little until he reaches a mutually agreed-upon goal (e.g., on-task 80 percent of the period). By setting small but reasonable goals for students and gradually increasing expectations for their behavior, you help ensure that the self-monitoring program will be successful. This strategy is referred to as **shaping of successive approximations** (see Chapter 5).

Self-Evaluation

Self-evaluation requires a student to assess the quality of her behavior, while in self-monitoring the student simply counts her behavior. Even very young children can learn to self-evaluate their behaviors. Miller et al. (1993) taught four preschoolers with disabilities to self-evaluate their

behaviors with a "thumbs up" or "thumbs down" signal as the teacher pointed to visual depictions of appropriate behaviors on a poster. Behaviors included cleaning up the play area, following teacher instructions, and interacting with peers appropriately.

Self-Instruction

In a self-instruction program, the student is trained to whisper statements that will help accomplish the task. Table 6.6 provides guidelines for using a self–instruction procedure. Be sure to analyze the self-instructional task before attempting to use this procedure with a student.

SUMMARY

This chapter offers you many suggestions for managing or preventing disruptive behavior. School-wide strategies include detention and in-school suspension. In these, as in all approaches, we urge close communication among staff and with families. Our teacher-mediated strategies include the ever-popular token economy—an outstanding way to set up classroom-wide contingencies. To enhance your overall contingency management, plan group contingencies. Finally, the self-management strategies promote generalization of new behaviors to other settings.

Figure 6.6 A Consultant's Description

Dear Mrs. Schaeffer,

I'm aware from our conversation that you are having a difficult time with your sixth graders. You told me that they can't seem to get to class on time and that it takes them at least 10 minutes to settle down.

I talked with you briefly about the possibility of trying out a game that requires team members to work toward a goal to win a reward. Here are some specifics about setting up this game:

1. It's been called the "Good Behavior Game," but your class can choose any name for it (e.g., "Party!, Party Possibilities").
2. If you have not yet established and posted conduct rules for your room, do so before you start the game.
3. To set up rules, talk with the students and allow them input. Suggest your own ideas and consider theirs. Agree upon a limited number of reasonable rules, and write them behaviorally in language the students understand. Examples:

   • Do not kick, hit, shove, or push other students.
   • Keep your hands and feet to yourself.
   • Raise your hand when you want to say something.
   • Talk when it's your turn.

   Set up contingencies (the relationships between behaviors and their consequences), and maintain consistent consequences when rules are broken.
4. Find out what might be powerful reinforcers for the students. Poll them, or offer them the possibility of free time for the last half of a Friday class each week. (I will use this as a sample reinforcer for the remainder of this program description.)
5. Divide the class into two teams.
6. Review rules and contingencies with the students.
7. State that 80% of each team's members will be required to reach or exceed this goal: to have at least one marker left out of three next to their names at the end of class each day. If 80% of a team reaches this goal, team members will be rewarded with free time on Friday. The 80% criterion (as opposed to a higher percentage) is set to prevent the same one or two disruptive students from ruining a team's chances of winning free time. Unreasonably high criterion levels might lead to low morale and lack of motivation among team members. For students who have serious behavior problems, repeated failures to achieve the goal in a game where "all must achieve to receive" could lead to their being ridiculed, ostracized, or scapegoated. Prevent this by specifying a reasonable criterion and by setting up individual problems and/or contingencies for the extremely disruptive students.
8. Explain to the students that the goal must be reached in one specified class period during the first week. During the second week, it must be achieved in two specified classes. Continue adding a period per week until you're at the point where the goal must be achieved during all periods the students are with you for instruction.
9. Hang a poster or use bulletin boards for each team, listing the members. At the beginning of each class, every student should have three markers next to his or her name. (For markers, use rock concert ticket stubs, small, laminated mock "record albums," or some other easily made or acquired items.)
10. Remove one marker from beside a student's name each time he or she breaks a rule (e.g., punches somebody, arrives late).

Figure 6.6
continued

11. At the end of the period, determine if 80% of each team's members have at least one marker next to their names. If 80% or more of one team achieved criterion, they win the privilege of receiving 20 minutes of free time during the last half of a Friday class. At this time, they will be free to go to the cafeteria for a "party." Enlist the aid of another staff member who can supervise the students as they talk, listen to radios or tape players, and drink cans of pop that they've brought or bought. The other team will be required to complete work in the classroom during the same period on Friday. If 80% of both teams achieve the goal, then all students will be awarded free "party" time.

12. Run the game for entire class periods. Even though most of this group's problems occur during the first 10 minutes, you don't want to operate it for 10 minutes and then leave 30 minutes open to possible disruptions. Set the rules and contingencies for the full 40 minutes. Self-control will probably be hardest to demonstrate during the initial 10 minutes, but it may get easier once they get over that "hump" each day. And we hope that it will increase throughout the course of the game.

13. Remember to provide lots of positive verbal reinforcement for both group and individual team improvements.

14. Again, severely disruptive students may be good candidates for individualized behavior management programs. You may want to consider what you'll do, though, when students occasionally lose all three markers in the same class. To prevent their getting completely out of control once they've broken three rules and lost all markers, perhaps you could arrange the following: If a student breaks four rules in once class period, he or she receives one day of detention. If he or she breaks five rules, he or she is assigned to two days of detention, and so on.

Good luck with this game!

Mrs. Prisby

Source: Prisby, personal communication, 1987

Figure 6.7 Self-Monitoring Form

	Reading	Math	Language Arts	Science	Social Studies	Total
Monday	//		/	//	/	⑥
Tuesday	/	/	/		/	④
Wednesday	//		//		///	⑦
Thursday		/	///	/	//	⑦
Friday	/	/	///			⑤

I will put a tally mark in the box each time I get out of my seat without asking permission during class. I know I am out of my seat when my backside is not touching my chair and I have not asked permission to leave my seat.

Name **KEITH**   Date Begun **2-22**   Teacher **COVALASKI**

Table 6.6 Guidelines for Training Students to Use Self-Instruction

1. Analyze the task for the student, listing necessary steps. For example, the task might involve specific steps such as reading the problem, writing out the necessary information, and performing the operations. Or the task might be more generic, requiring steps such as getting out pencil and paper, opening the text to the correct page, not talking to others, signaling when help is needed.

   Consider including specific questions about task demands, planning statements, self-guiding instructions, coping statements for errors, and self-praise statements.

2. With help from the student, rewrite the steps in the student's conversational style. For example, one primary school student developed these self-instructions:

   "Okay, to be a good student, I need to stay in my seat, not bother others, and complete my assignment. I have to take my time and do the work the way Mrs. Smith showed me. Good, I did it. Right on!"

3. Practice the self-instruction procedure with the student. Begin by saying the words together aloud. Then whisper as the student self-instructs aloud. Finally, have the student whisper alone.

4. Enable the student to use the self-instructions in the classroom. If possible, allow the student to whisper quietly; this may be more effective (and easier to monitor!) than covert, or silent, rehearsal.

Note: The material for this table was taken from Albion, F. *Development and implementation of self-monitoring/self-instruction procedures in the classroom.* Paper presented at CEC's 58th Annual International Convention, Philadelphia, 1980.

 CASE STUDY

TOKEN ECONOMY[1]

Wyllie Keefer

My classroom is a part-time resource room with the students coming on various schedules. My 13 students are in sixth, seventh, and eighth grades, with the majority of students in eighth. The age group is between eleven and fourteen years old. There is such a diversity of abilities among the students that grade-level curriculum is difficult to assess on a general basis. Some students are nonreaders, some do not know their multiplication tables, while others are on grade level but behavior problems have deterred them from academic success.

When needed, the students who are the readers or mathematicians are the classroom peer tutors. Their special abilities come in handy when other students are having difficulties in their mainstream classes or particular assignments in the resource room. Two of my students are extremely talented in

art and are always excited and interested in any lesson or project dealing with art.

Our school day begins at 7:40 A.M. and ends at 2:33 P.M. There are eight periods a day; each period is 42 minutes long. Most of my students spend first period in my room (directly after first period is homeroom). First period usually goes very well, with a calm environment.

I bring my students to my room from study halls, for extra monitoring time, if I sense there may be trouble brewing or a potential crisis. Many days my students are sent to my room to have tests read to them, to get help with classwork/assignments, or if their behavior is disrupting a mainstream class. I have a full-time aide so there are always two adults in our room for the kids to model. Together with our students' current IEP teams, we designed a four-level behavior chart listing "Earners" and "Losers." To be sure that our students really understood the four levels, we made four posters. Each poster showed the "Earners" and "Losers" for

(continued)

---

[1] Reprinted with the author's permission.

Figure 6.8 Levels System Poster

Earners

Level I		Level II		Level III		Level IV	
Behaviors	**Cost**	**Behaviors**	**Cost**	**Behaviors**	**Cost**	**Behaviors**	**Cost**
Try to follow classroom rules	$2	Respect others	$3	Ignore other student's inappropriate behavior	$4	Follow classroom rules all day	$5
Be in seat when bell rings	$2	Bring book, pen/pencil & worksheet to class	$3	Participate in class	$4	Complete all assignments and turned in	$5
Stay in your seat	$2	Bring homework & worksheets to class	$3	Hand in completed assignments 80% of the time	$4	Use appropriate behavior 90% of the time	$5
Raise your hand	$2	Neat papers	$3	Work without disturbing others	$4	Be self-monitored 90% of the time	$5
Use kind & courteous language	$2	Appropriate behavior on bus, in hallways or in cafeteria	$3	Keep checkbook current and correct	$4	Have no discipline offenses all week	$5
Write down assignments	$2	Remain on task 70% of the time	$3	Organize school work	$4		
Have all teachers fill out deposit slip	$2	Start and try to complete assignments 70% of the time	$3				
Greet adults and classmates	$2	All teachers filled out deposit slip	$3				

Losers

Level I		Level II		Level III		Level IV	
Break a classroom rule	$1	Have physical or verbal outbursts	$10	Fail to turn in assignments	$3	Receive anecdotals, DT, ISS, or OSS	$20
Use vulgarities, swearing, or inappropriate gestures	$5	Argue	$2	Disrupt class	$15	Miss assignments	$4
Be out of seat	$1	Not be prepared	$2	Cheat on checkbook	$3	Break a classroom rule	$4
Be tardy	$1	Be off-task	$2	Receive anecdotals, DT, ISS, or OSS	$3		
Receive anecdotals, DT, ISS, or OSS	$5	Receive anecdotals, DT, ISS, or OSS	$10				
Have physical or verbal outbursts	$5	Fail to keep checkbook up-to-date	$2				
Fail to keep checkbook up-to-date	$1						

Monitoring

To be monitored at the end of each period (5 min.) Also on Fridays (1/2 hour)	To be monitored at the end of each period (5 min.) Also on Fridays (1/2 hour)	To be monitored at the end of each day Also on Fridays (1/2 hour)	To be monitored at the end of each week on Fridays (1/2 hour)

that level. We placed the posters next to each other on our classroom wall. We included the values assigned to these behaviors so there was no question as to how much a behavior earns or loses (see Figure 6.8).

The selection of behaviors to be targeted is a group activity. The students are asked to contribute their ideas of expected or appropriate behaviors in school to include, along with my expectations.

(continued)

I divided the chalkboard into four sections and labeled them Level I to Level IV. The students then participated and decided which behaviors would be listed at which level.

◆ Level I—Behaviors everyone can do, easy to achieve.
◆ Level II—Slightly more demanding than Level I.
◆ Level III—Bigger effort, trying to make a change.
◆ Level IV—Major effort, highest level.

BONUSES

Students can earn extra points (money) when they go "beyond the call of duty" and do something out of the ordinary. For example, a student of mine recently found a wallet filled with money, credit cards, and a driver's license. Other students were arguing over how they would split the cash. My student grabbed the wallet from them and turned it into the office. As it turned out, the wallet belonged to the art teacher. She was not only relieved but impressed that one of the "special" students had fought to do the right thing. This deed of honor earned a lot of bonus bucks! Bonuses will always be positive and awarded as surprises. Other examples would be when one student compliments another, lends a pencil, or helps another student or teacher. In my particular environment, there are many opportunities to reward behavior, however small!

The design of our checkbook money system is twofold. Each student receives his own personal checkbook. With help from the art teacher, the class creates their own checkbook covers made from heavy cardboard and wallpaper samples. I have designed checks and withdrawal slips.

For *earners,* the student receives *deposits;* for *losers, withdrawals.* Behaviors are assigned a dollar amount. Each period the student self-monitors the behaviors that were exhibited, negative or positive. At the end of the period, we schedule five minutes to go over their checklist and we agree on deposits or withdrawals earned. Mainstream teachers also have checklists and are familiar with our system. They have a supply of previously made deposit slips with money amounts and behaviors on them. They check each behavior earned or lost during that particular period. Each student brings back the deposit slip to enter the earned or lost amounts into their accounts.

The second advantage of using a fictitious banking system is to teach the students, for their employable future, that if they do a good job, they will get a paycheck, or perhaps a bonus/raise. If they do a bad job, argue, or forget their responsibilities, they can be fired, lose pay, and so on. They learn how to keep and balance a checking account, along with practicing basic, consumer math.

The banking system is not only a self-monitoring system but is also an interdependent contingency. Every student is responsible for her behaviors, and the class can benefit or lose out, together. My former classroom was an "every person for himself" classroom. I changed it because I believe a group plan helps students learn that together everyone achieves more. The more "money" each student "earns," the more reinforcers the group has to choose from.

The students know how often their behavior will be monitored by referring to the timeframe listed at the bottom, at each level, of the chart posted in the classroom. They are reminded when we go over the plan together before implementation.

The reinforcers and response costs are posted in the classroom. Students know that anecdotals (office referrals), DT (detention), ISS (in-school suspension), and OSS (out-of-school suspension) are included as "losers," based on our school-wide plan.

When I initially introduced the idea of a banking system for behavior, I was delighted that my students thought it would be a lot of fun and a challenge. (They did suggest that the plan include *real* money!) They helped me make a list of reinforcers that they would like to be able to earn with their "bank accounts" (see Table 6.7).

Here are my troubleshooting guidelines:

◆ *If a student loses the checkbook:* Student's behavior for that period goes to zero.
◆ *If students cannot decide on the same reinforcer for the week:* The class must resolve this problem among themselves. They may discuss the situation, vote majority rules, secret ballot or other ways the students come up with to solve the problem, or they may vote to have alternate choices.

(continued)

Table 6.7   Reinforcers to Accompany Banking System

Reinforcers			
Level I—Minimum Balance $12	Level II—Minimum Balance $24	Level III—Minimum Balance $36	Level IV—Minimum Balance $48
10 minutes of free time at the end of each period	Mrs. Keefer to buy new game for the room	Get a pet (hamster, rabbit, gerbil) for the classroom	Walk to bowling alley (bowl for two periods)
Skip a homework assignment	Make a treat in the home-ec room	Help work in the school store	Paint wall mural in classroom
Movie day	Go to library for an extra period	Eat lunch at the high school	Use weight room at high school
Popcorn party	Have a free day	Walk to Taco Bell or Dairy Queen	Go to Heights Elem., read to a class
Can of pop	Have a pizza party	Use gym for free time	Hold a car wash for the faculty
Candy store coupon	Skip a test	Do a special tech-ed project	Walk to Heights Plaza
Computer time	Listen to music in room	Do a special art project	Take a field trip

◆ *If a student does not move up to the next level:* An individual contract will be made between the teacher and student. The student will choose a particular reinforcer they would like to earn.

◆ *If a mainstream teacher will not cooperate:* For example, a student chooses to "buy" a test or homework assignment and the teacher does not agree. The mainstream teacher must then decide to offer other reinforcers that are acceptable and achievable in their room.

INCLUDING NEW STUDENTS

Before a new student arrives in class, we review the program within their IEP team. We figure an average balance for her initial deposit into the checking account. Depending on which level the class is on, the new student will be observed for two weeks and an individual adjustment will have to be made as to her needs and level.

MODIFICATIONS TO THE SYSTEM

Controlled/creative tinkering is an important factor to consider when designing and making successful any behavioral management plan. Problems may arise at any point of my banking/checkbook plan. I discuss problems with the students as a group. They have helpful suggestions, ideas, and negative comments. This plan is for them and I take their concerns or the question/problem at hand and deal with it on an individual basis. Sample modifications are to "up the ante"; to increase the dollar amounts for deposits; to provide earners or losers; or, to re-arrange the levels or change the reinforcers.

SUMMARY OF THE STEPS FOR THE BANKING SYSTEM

1. Discuss behavior management plan with students. Introduce the Bank checking account system.
2. Help each student make a checkbook out of heavy cardboard and wallpaper samples.
3. Complete each checkbook with a check register, checks, and a supply of deposit slips. (The teacher designs and copies behavior deposit slips.)
4. IEP teams, students, and teachers will decide upon behavior earners and losers (to be sorted into in Levels I–IV) and the reinforcers the students want to earn.
5. Draw charts for earners, losers, and reinforcers. Post it in the classroom.

(continued)

6. Each Monday, the class decides on which reinforcers the whole class will be working toward for the week.

7. Each Monday, deposit the following dollar amounts into their accounts:

Level I	$10.00
Level II	$20.00
Level III	$30.00
Level IV	$40.00

8. Each period, check off behaviors on preprinted deposit slips.

9. Instruct each student to keep their checkbooks current.

10. Students *add* earners, *subtract* losers, and enter total deposits or withdrawals on their check register.

11. Monitor students according to the level timetables.

12. Supplementary procedures: If a student does not cooperate, consider the following consequences:

> Written assignment as to why they are having problems
> Extra assignments to earn a (+) higher balance
> Detention

13. Bonus points/additional money earned entitles a student to:

> Choose an additional *reinforcer*
> Become Bank President, monitoring some part of the system
> Offer suggestions from the students

14. If the students have saved enough money, at any time, they may write a check to "buy" the following:

Study Hall pass	$3.00
A homework pass	$10.00
A detention pass	$15.00
A day of In-School Suspension pass	$20.00

(I have discussed this with the administration, and they have given me their approval.)

 CASE STUDY

A COMBINATION PROGRAM CREATED FOR AN INCLUSIVE PRESCHOOL CLASSROOM: TOKEN ECONOMY AND SELF-MONITORING[1]

MeShelda Jackson

The following program describes a token economy in combination with a self-monitoring system for a preschool classroom of typically developing children, children with behavioral disorders, a teacher, a teacher's aide, and a part-time speech-language pathologist. The childrens' ages range from three to five years. Some of the behaviors identified by their IEP teams include temper tantrums, kicking, pushing, and hitting. Self-management is incorporated through the children's use of a self-monitoring sheet.

**COMPONENT ONE:
CLASSROOM RULES POSTERS**

First, the IEP teams select appropriate behaviors for the classroom and its learning centers. Next, we classroom teachers take pictures of each child displaying the appropriate behavior in the classroom and at their centers. The general classroom rules are posted in the front of the room. Next the children and the adults discuss and show pictures of inappropriate and appropriate behaviors in the classroom and at each learning center. Then my aide and I post pictures of the children exhibiting appropriate behaviors on the rules chart, one for each center area and one general chart for the classroom. The pictures allow

(continued)

---

[1] Reprinted with the author's permission.

CASE STUDY

the children to identify themselves exhibiting appropriate behavior. Before the children go to their centers each day, we review the rules (see Figure 6.9).

COMPONENT TWO: TOKEN ECONOMY

The tokens for the token economy system are kept in each adult's apron pocket. Circles are used as tokens for the charts. The yellow circles means the child gets the number of circles by that specific rule.

The white circles mean that the child loses the number of circles by that rule. Each child starts the day earning tokens for exhibiting any of the appropriate behaviors previously discussed. A child can earn up to four circles in one center. Each time they exhibit the positive behavior, they get a yellow circle to place on their self-monitoring sheet. If they do not exhibit the appropriate behavior, they lose one or more white circles. If they have earned all four circles

Figure 6.9 Examples of Charts for Classroom Rules

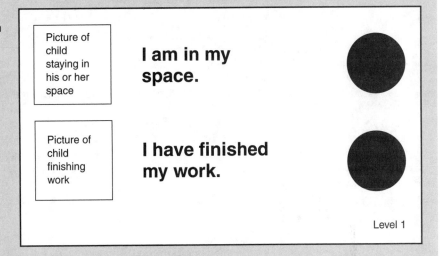

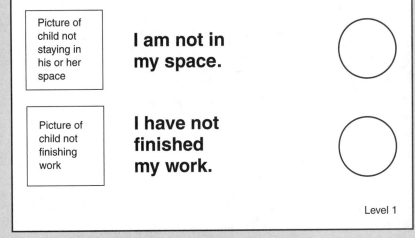

(continued)

when time is up at the learning center, they can se-lect from reinforcers previously decided upon before they go to their next activity. Here is a list of sample reinforcers chosen by the adults and children:

    stickers
    hugs
    having a book read to you
    emptying the wastebasket
    holding the flag for the morning
    pledge
    erasing the board
    feeding the fish
    leader of the line (recess, lunch, or
    other field trips)
    being in charge of a game or activity
    watering the plants
    free time in the center of your choice
    choosing a friend with whom to play
    sitting with the teacher at lunch

COMPONENT THREE: PEER MANAGEMENT

At the end of each center activity, the children decide if anyone did not exhibit the appropriate behavior. We all discuss how to improve the behavior for the next center activity.

The teachers' job is to praise the specific posi-tive behaviors whenever we see it. Any one of us in the room can distribute tokens. When the appro-priate behavior is exhibited, we provide the circle as soon as possible. We keep a separate card on each child that explains his behavior/s to be decreased.

We then record on the card the frequency and the area where the behavior occurred. The teacher should record positive and disruptive behaviors that occur. A check is added every time the child exhibits the target behavior or positive behavior. For each level, the behaviors are checked all during the day after each center activity.

If the child continues to perform inappropriate be-havior (hurting, throwing, hitting, or kicking, etc.) after the loss of circles, then the first step is to re-mind the child about the appropriate behavior and review the rule with her. The next consequence is to remove the child from the activity and ask her to sit in a chair for two minutes, away from the activity. She has to state the rule before returning to play. If the child continues to demonstrate inappropriate be-havior, the positive reinforcer previously earned for that level is taken away (response cost).

Figure 6.10 Behavior Checklist for Teachers

Student's Name _____

Behavior _____

Center	Mon	Tue	Wed	Thu	Fri	Total
Reading						
Math						
Science						
Art						
Play						
Music						
Teacher						
Classroom						
Total						

DISCUSSION QUESTIONS

1. Which strategies are preferable for younger students? Older students?
2. When are peer-mediated strategies preferable to teacher-mediated approaches?
3. How can several strategies be combined to reduce disruptive behaviors?
4. What are some possible mistakes one might make in implementing a token economy?
5. For what disruptive behaviors is self-monitoring a good choice?
6. What is the importance of levels within a token economy?
7. Describe the hierarchy of timeout from reinforcement strategies.
8. How can parents be involved in interventions for disruptive behavior?
9. What can a teacher do to *prevent* disruptive behavior?
10. Give three examples of ways we measure disruptive behaviors.

REFERENCES

Adams, G. L. (1984). An inexpensive wireless, remote-controlled clock light. *Education and Treatment of Children, 7*(1), 75–79.

Alberto, P. A., & Troutman, A. C. (1995). *Applied behavior analysis for teachers: Influencing student performance* (4th ed.). Upper Saddle River, NJ: Merrill/Prentice Hall.

Allen, L. D., Gottselig, M., & Boylan, S. (1982). A practical mechanism for using free time as a reinforcer in classrooms. *Education and Treatment of Children, 5*(4), 347–353.

Allen, L. J., Howard, V. F., Sweeney, W. J., & McLaughlin, T. F. (1993). Use of contingency contracting to increase on-task behavior with primary students. *Psychological Reports, 73*, 905–906.

Barrish, H. H., Saunders, M., & Wolf, M. M. (1969). Good behavior game: Effects of individual contingencies for group consequences on disruptive behavior in a classroom are reviewed with the class. *Journal of Applied Behavior Analysis, 2*, 119–124.

Bicanich, P. (1986). *So you want to try a token economy.* Unpublished manuscript, University of Pittsburgh.

Carden-Smith, L. K., & Fowler, S. A. (1984). Positive peer pressure: The effects of peer monitoring on children's disruptive behavior. *Journal of Applied Behavior Analysis, 17*(2), 213–227.

Canter, L., & Canter, M. (1992). *Parents on your side.* Santa Monica, CA: Lee Canter and Associates.

Colvin G., Kameenui, E. J., Sugai, G. (1993). Reconceptualizing behavior management and schoolwide discipline in general education. *Education and Treatment of Children, 16*(4), 361–381.

Dietz, S. M., & Repp, A. C. (1973). Decreasing classroom misbehavior through the use of DRL schedules of reinforcement. *Journal of Applied Behavior Analysis, 6*, 457–464.

Epstein, M. H., Repp, A. C., & Cullinan, D. (1978). Decreasing obscene language of behaviorally disordered children through the use of a DRL schedule. *Psychology in the Schools, 15*, 419–423.

Greenwood, C. R., Hops, H., Delquadri, J., & Walker, H. M. (1977). *Program for academic survival skills (PASS): Manual for consultants.* Eugene, OR: University of Oregon, Center at Oregon for Research in the Behavioral Education of the Handicapped.

Gun Safety Institute (1993). Personal Communication. Cleveland, OH.

Hallahan, D. P., Lloyd, J. W., & Stoller, L. (1982). *Improving attention with self-monitoring: A manual for teachers.* Charlottesville, VA: University of Virginia Learning Disabilities Research Institute.

Haubrich, P. A., & Shores, R. E. (1976). Attending behavior and academic performance of emotionally disturbed children. *Exceptional Children, 42*, 337–338.

Hayes, L. A. (1976). The use of group contingencies for behavioral control: A review. *Psychological Bulletin, 83*, 628–648.

Jones, D. B., & Van Houten, R. (1985). The use of daily quizzes and public posting to decrease the disruptive behavior of secondary school students. *Education and Treatment of Children, 8*(2), 91–106.

Kelley, M. L., & McCain, A.P. (1995). Promoting academic performance in inattentive children: The relative efficacy of school-home notes with and without response cost. *Behavior Modification, 19*(3), 357–375.

Kerr, M. M. (1986). *Report on adult interviews: Arsenal Middle School.* Unpublished manuscript, University of Pittsburgh.

Kerr, M. M., Nelson, C. M., & Lambert, D. L. (1987). *Helping adolescents with learning and behavior problems.* Upper Saddle River, NJ: Merrill/Prentice Hall.

Kerr, M. M., & Ragland, E. U. (1979). PowWow: A group procedure for reducing classroom behavior problems. *The Pointer, 24,* 92–96.

Kohler, F. W., & Strain, P. S. (1990). Peer-assisted interventions: Early promises, notable achievements, and future aspirations. *Clinical Psychology Review, 10*(4), 441–452.

Lam, A. L., Cole, C. L., Shapiro, E. S., & Bambara L. M. (1994). Relative effects of self-monitoring on-task behavior, academic accuracy and disruptive behavior in students with behavior disorders. *School Psychology Review, 23*(1), 44–58.

Litow, L., & Pomroy, D. K. (1975). A brief review of classroom group-oriented contingencies. *Journal of Applied Behavior Analysis, 8,* 341–347.

Lloyd, J. W., Crowley, E. P., Kohler, F. W., & Strain, P. S. (1988). Redefining the applied research agenda: Cooperative learning, pre-referral, teacher consultation, and peer-medicated interventions. *Journal of Learning Disabilities, 21*(1), 43–58.

Miller, L. J., Strain, P. S., Boyd, K., Jarzynka, J., & McFetridge, M. (1993). The effects of classwide self-assessment on preschool children's engagement in transition, free play, and small group instruction. *Early Education and Development, 4*(3), 162–181.

Mullen, J. A. (1986). Teacher and student ratings of the disturbingness of common problem behaviors. *Behavioral Disorders, 11*(3), 168–176.

National Crisis Prevention Institute, Inc. (1987). *Nonviolent crisis intervention: Participant workbook.* Brookfield, WI: National Crisis Prevention Institute, Inc.

Nelson, J. R., Colvin, G., Petty, D., & Smith D. J. (1995). *The effects of a school-wide instructional discipline program on students' social behavior in common areas of the school.* Unpublished manuscript, Eastern Washington University.

Nelson, J. R., Smith, D. J., Young, R. K., & Dodd, J. M. (1991). A review of self-management outcome research conducted with students who exhibit behavioral disorders. *Behavioral Disorders, 16*(3), 169–179.

O'Leary, K. D., Kaufman, K. F., Kass, R. E., & Drabman, R. S. (1970). The effects of loud and soft reprimands on the behavior of disruptive students. *Exceptional Children, 37,* 145–155.

Paniagua, F. A. (1990). A procedural analysis of correspondence training techniques. *The Behavior Analyst, 13,* 107–119.

Rhode, G., Morgan, D. P., & Young, K. R. (1983). Generalization and maintenance of treatment gains of behaviorally handicapped students from resource rooms to regular classrooms using self-evaluation procedures. *Journal of Applied Behavior Analysis, 16*(2), 171–188.

Rosenberg, M. S. (1986). Maximizing the effectiveness of structured classroom management programs: Implementing rule-review procedures with disruptive and distractible students. *Behavioral Disorders, 11*(4), 239–247.

Rueda, R., Rutherford, R. B., & Howell, K. W. (1980). Review of self-control research with behaviorally disordered and mentally retarded children. In R. B. Rutherford, A. G. Prieto, & J. E. McGothlin (Eds.), *Severe behavior disorders of children and youth* (Vol. 3, pp. 188–197). Reston, VA: Council for Exceptional Children.

Saigh, P. A., & Umar, A. M. (1983). The effects of a good behavior game on the disruptive behavior of Sudanese elementary school students. *Journal of Applied Behavior Analysis, 16*(3), 339–344.

Runyon, M. K., Donohue, B., & Pishevar, B. (1995). *Positive reinforcement and peer monitoring: A method for managing disruptive classroom behavior in elementary school aged children.* Unpublished manuscript.

Salend, J. S., Jantzen, N. R., & Giek, K. (1992). Using a peer confrontation system in a group setting. *Behavioral Disorders, 17*(3), 211–128.

Salend S. J., Reynolds, C. J., Coyle, E. M. (1989). Individualizing the Good Behavior Game across type and frequency of behavior with emotionally disturbed adolescents. *Behavior Modification, 13*(1), 108–126.

Sandler, A. G., Arnold, L. B., Gable, R. A., & Strain, P. S. (1987). Effects of peer pressure on disruptive behavior of behaviorally disordered classmates. *Behavioral Disorders, 12*(2), 104–110.

Scheuermann, B., Webber, J., Partin, M., & Knies, W. C. (1994). Level systems and the law: Are they compatible? *Behavioral Disorders, 19*(3), 205–220.

Shores, R. E., & Haubrich, P. A. (1969). Effects of cubicles in educating emotionally disturbed children. *Exceptional Children, 36,* 21–24.

Smith, S. E. (1994). Parent-initiated contracts: An intervention for school-related behaviors. *Elementary School Guidance & Counseling, 28,* 182–187.

Smith, D. J., Young, R., West, R. P., Morgan, D. P., & Rhode, G. (1988). Reducing the disruptive behavior of junior high school students: A classroom self-management procedure. *Behavioral Disorders, 13*(4), 231–239.

Staub, R. W. (1987). *The effects of publicly posted feedback on middle school students' disruptive hallway behavior.*

Unpublished doctoral dissertation, University of Pittsburgh.

Sugai, G., & Chanter, C. (1989). The effects of training students with learning and behavior disorders to modify the behavior disorders of their peers. *Education & Treatment of Children, 12*(2), 134–151.

Trice, A. D., & Parker, F. C. (1983). Decreasing adolescent swearing in an instructional setting. *Education and Treatment of Children, 6,* 29–35.

Uchitelle, S., Bartz, D., & Hillman, L. (1989). Strategies for reducing suspensions. *Urban Education, 24*(2), 163–176.

Van Houten, R., Nau, P. A., MacKenzie-Keating, S. E., Sameoto, D., & Colavecchia, B. (1982). An analysis of some variables influencing the effectiveness of reprimands. *Behavior Journal of Applied Analysis, 15,* 65–83.

Williamson, D. A., Williamson, S. H., Watkins, P. C., & Hughes, H. H. (1992). Increasing cooperation among children using dependent group-oriented reinforcement contingencies. *Behavior Modification, 16*(3), 414–425.

Worell, J., & Nelson, C. M. (1974). *Managing instructional problems: A case study workbook.* New York: McGraw-Hill.

Zwald, L., & Gresham, F. (1982). Behavioral consultation in a secondary class: Using DRL to decrease negative verbal interactions. *The School Psychology Review, 11*(4), 428–432.

IMPROVING SCHOOL
SURVIVAL SKILLS AND
SOCIAL SKILLS

OUTLINE

OBJECTIVES

After completing this chapter, you should be able to

- Describe three assessment approaches for problems in social skills and school survival skills.
- Describe three environmental modifications to improve social skills and school survival skills.
- Plan a teacher-mediated intervention for a student with poor social skills.
- Plan a comprehensive sequence of peer-mediated interventions for a socially withdrawn child.
- Select a social skills curriculum for a particular class group.
- Use a group contingency procedure to modify off-task behaviors.
- Develop a self-monitoring procedure to improve students' academic productivity.

SCHOOL SURVIVAL SKILLS: AN INTRODUCTION

The first part of this chapter addresses limitations in school survival skills, those behaviors that enable a student to get the most from instructional interactions. Research has shown that many students simply do not learn to adjust to the demands of the school setting (Kerr & Zigmond, 1984). Consider these vignettes:

- Andy was never really a troublemaker, but he just didn't seem to "get his act together" at school. His projects were always incomplete and he often showed up late for classes, resulting in repeated detentions. Sometimes he forgot he had detention and wound up having to go to the in-school suspension room for a day or two. We never seemed to find the right intervention for Andy, and he developed a reputation as a "loser."

◆ Yvonne just didn't seem to fit into any classroom. She wasn't exactly a behavior problem, but she was no angel either. For example, she would never answer the questions I asked, and I found myself repeating questions to her just because she was daydreaming during our discussions. Sometimes I actually wondered if she had a neurological problem, but her pediatrician said she was fine. Let's face it: Yvonne was a "space cadet."

◆ How could I ever forget Corrado? I never could put my finger on his problem. He was a nice enough kid but he was totally disorganized. His assignments always looked like they had been run over, and his test papers were decorated with doodles. No amount of lecturing could ever change that kid. I wonder what ever happened to him?

◆ I guess you call five-year-old Lila unmotivated or lazy. She really got under my skin because she never did what I asked the first time. Every request turned into a battle. She was fine as long as you didn't ask her to do anything.

These recollections may sound familiar to you. Some researchers might call these children *attention deficit disordered* (Kauffman, 1989). Regardless of the term you use, the behaviors will be your real concern. Table 7.1 lists definitions for some of the behaviors we discuss in this section of the chapter.

ASSESSING LIMITATIONS IN SCHOOL SURVIVAL SKILLS

Many of the problems in Table 7.1 will be obvious to you and to the other teachers. In a large secondary school, however, you may not have a chance to compare notes with a student's other teachers. Consider using a pencil-and-paper checklist for assessing a student's specific skill limitations. Figure 7.1 displays the School Survival Skills Scale, which is appropriate for middle and high school students.

As you read through the items of the School Survival Skills Scale, consider the skills and problems thought to be most important for high

school students (Kerr, Zigmond, Schaeffer, & Brown, 1986).

Important Skills

1. Meets due dates.
2. Arrives at school on time.
3. Attends class every day.
4. Exhibits interest in academic work.
5. Accepts consequences of behavior.

Problem Behaviors

1. Seldom completes assignments.
2. Cannot follow written directions.
3. Gives "back talk" to teacher.
4. Falls asleep in class.
5. Is quick to give up.

Focus your intervention efforts on these skills and problems first. By the way, similar lists have resulted from work with elementary school children (Kerr & Zigmond, 1984; McConnell et al., 1984; Walker & Rankin, 1983). Notice the emphasis on compliance and academic productivity; as you prepare children for mainstreaming at any grade level, be sure to give these skills special attention.

Another increasingly important skill for students included in mainstream classes is homework completion (Roderique, Polloway, Cumblad, Epstein, & Bursuck, 1994). A useful assessment is the *Homework Problem Checklist* (Anesko, Schoiock, Ramirez, & Levine, 1987); see Figure 7.2. (You may obtain a copy of this checklist by contacting the authors at the State University of New York at Stony Brook.)

As you analyze a student's classroom performance, consider the research on children's perceived control and autonomy in the classroom. Children hold **strategy beliefs** (about what it takes to perform well) and **capacity beliefs** (whether the child has "what it takes"). In the academic domain, a clear picture emerges (Skinner et al., 1990). The children most actively engaged in the classroom are those who believe effort is an important cause of school success and failure, and they themselves can exert effort (high-effort strategy and capacity beliefs); that although ability is not necessary for success, they

Figure 7.1   School Survival Skills Scale

Date _____

Student's Name _____
                          (please print)

Teacher's Name _____
                                          (please print)

Circle the appropriate response.

Student's Grade   9   10   11   12

This student is in your class for:

Student's Sex   M   F

Homeroom   Social Studies

Student's Special Ed Classification

English   Science

SED   LD   EMR   VH   HI   PH

Math   Other _____

Directions: *Please read each statement and circle the corresponding letter that best describes this student's typical behavior. Be sure that you mark every item.*

This student	Never	Sometimes	Usually	Always	Not Observed
1. ...stays awake in class.	N	S	U	A	X
2. ...gets to class on time.	N	S	U	A	X
3. ...complies with requests of adults in authority.	N	S	U	A	X
4. ...stays calm and in control of emotions.	N	S	U	A	X
5. ...brings necessary materials to class.	N	S	U	A	X
6. ...is persistent even when faced with a difficult task.	N	S	U	A	X
7. ...asks for help with school when necessary.	N	S	U	A	X
8. ...responds to others when they speak.	N	S	U	A	X
9. ...arrives at school on time.	N	S	U	A	X
10. ...completes assigned work.	N	S	U	A	X
11. ...behaves appropriately in a variety of settings.	N	S	U	A	X
12. ...manages conflict through nonaggressive means	N	S	U	A	X
13. ...organizes study time efficiently.	N	S	U	A	X
14. ...can concentrate on work without being distracted by peers.	N	S	U	A	X
15. ...works well independently.	N	S	U	A	X
16. ...accepts the punishment if caught doing something wrong	N	S	U	A	X
17. ...turns in assignments when they are due.	N	S	U	A	X
18. ...speaks appropriately to teachers.	N	S	U	A	X
19. ...follows written directions.	N	S	U	A	X
20. ...talks calmly to an adult when perceived to be unjustly accused.	N	S	U	A	X
21. ...uses time productively while waiting for teacher.	N	S	U	A	X
22. ...attends class.	N	S	U	A	X
23. ...exhibits interest in improving academic performance.	N	S	U	A	X
24. ...is good at taking tests.	N	S	U	A	X
25. ...appropriately handles corrections on classwork.	N	S	U	A	X
26. ...identifies the central theme of a lecture (demonstrates by stating or writing the main ideas and supporting facts).	N	S	U	A	X

Please Check to Make Sure All Items Are Marked

Source: From *The School Survival Skills Curriculum* by Zigmond, N., Kerr, M. M., Schaeffer, A., Brown, G., & Farra, H. (1986). Pittsburgh: University of Pittsburgh. Reprinted with permission.

Table 7.1 Definitions of School Survival Skills and Deficits

Skill or Deficit	Definition	Author
On task	…any time a student [has] his or her eyes focused on a book, paper, or self-monitoring question card, [has] eyes closed or word covered and lips moving, [is] writing words, or [is] checking words.	Harris (1986)
Preparation	The student is preparing to work or completing an activity or participating in the routine procedures of the class. The following are considered preparation. 1. Getting books or paper 2. Looking for materials 3. Sharpening a pencil 4. Flipping through pages of a book to find the correct page 5. Moving into a structured group 6. Putting materials away 7. Passing in homework or classwork 8. Waiting for teacher direction 9. Waiting for teacher's help	Kerr & Zigmond (1984)
Off-task	The student is off-task if she is not paying attention to or participating in a class activity or if she is not working on a class assignment or project. Examples of off-task behaviors are the following: 1. Student looks at fingernails. 2. Student reads a note from a friend. 3. Student puts head down on desk during math. 4. Student folds her paper into a small triangle. 5. Student stares at teacher during individual reading time. 6. Student stares at blank chalkboard. 7. Student draws faces on paper during math class. 8. Student reads a comic book during language arts. 9. Student wanders around room. 10. Student writes a letter (Note: you must be able to see this to know that it is off-task).	Kerr et al. (1987)
On-task	The student is on-task if she is working. Students engaged in one of the following are considered on-task or attending: 1. Looking at teacher in absence of inappropriate behavior 2. Looking or working at the chalkboard 3. Writing or taking notes 4. Reading book or assignment 5. Raising hand to ask or answer questions about classwork 6. Asking questions related to classwork 7. Questions or statements to the teacher regarding one's grades or performance on a test or paper 8. Talking to teacher if teacher initiates conversation 9. Peer-tutoring/working	Kerr et al. (1987)

Table 7.1   (*continued*)

Skill or Deficit	Definition	Author
Using others' name	Addressing others by name to get attention, or to initiate or maintain a conversation.	Mathur & Rutherford (1994)
Using manners	Using social manners while conversing with people 1. Saying please, thank you, excuse me	Mathur & Rutherford (1994)
Positive statements about self	Making statements that demonstrate positive self-concept, interests, and hobbies. 1. I am proud of myself. 2. I am responsible. 3. I am good at music.	Mathur & Rutherford (1994)
Positive statements about others	Making statements that include compliments and praise for others to peers sitting nearby, parents, family, teachers, staff, friend, or anyone special. 1. I am proud of you. 2. You look nice. 3. She is very kind.	Mathur & Rutherford (1994)
Positive statements about present and future	Making positive statements about the subject's present and future events and activities. 1. We are having so much fun today. 2. This food tastes good. 3. When I get out of here, I will go to school, get a job, do something nice.	Mathur & Rutherford (1994)

themselves are smart (low-ability strategy beliefs and high-ability capacity beliefs); and that they have access to powerful others and are lucky (high-powerful others and luck capacity beliefs). In contrast, children who are most disaffected from school activities believe they are incapable of exerting effort and are not smart (low effort and ability capacity beliefs); that powerful others and luck are needed to succeed, but they themselves cannot influence others and are unlucky (high strategy and low capacity for powerful others and luck); and that they don't know the causes of success and failure in school (high unknown strategy beliefs). Pairs of strategy and capacity beliefs for each of the five causes examined in the academic domain (effort, ability, powerful others, luck, and unknown) are strong predictors of children's behavior and emotion in the classroom (Patrick, Skinner, & Connell, 1993).

Students' beliefs are not the only ones that influence academic performance. Your own perceptions, beliefs, standards, and expectations play a significant role in your students' study habits. Studies of effective schools have demonstrated that teachers with higher classroom expectations take more responsibility for seeing that their students learn. Moreover, these effective teachers believe in their ability to help students (Fuchs, Fuchs, & Phillips, 1994). As you develop your own standards and expectations, ask yourself these questions:

◆ Is there a clear expectation for an alternative, appropriate behavior in this setting? Be sure your students have clear, appropriate expectations for performance. Are the rules posted or orally reviewed for the student?

◆ Is the behavioral expectation developmentally appropriate for this student? Perhaps the environment or the social situation is too demanding (or too boring) for a student at this developmental level.

Figure 7.2 Homework Problem Checklist

Child's Sex _____
Child's Grade _____
Child's Age _____

Child performs (−1) below grade level in most subjects
(0) on grade level in most subjects
(+1) above grade level in most subjects

For each statement check one:	Never (0)	At Times (1)	Often (2)	Very Often (3)
Fails to bring home assignments and necessary materials (textbook, dittos, etc.)				
Doesn't know exactly what homework has been assigned.				
Denies having homework assignment.				
Refuses to do homework assignment.				
Whines or complains about homework.				
Must be reminded to sit down and start homework.				
Procrastinates, puts off doing homework.				
Doesn't do homework satisfactorily unless someone is in the room.				
Doesn't do homework satisfactorily unless someone does it with him/her.				
Daydreams or plays with objects during homework session.				
Easily distracted by noises or activities of others.				
Easily frustrated by homework assignment.				
Fails to complete homework.				
Takes unusually long time to do homework.				
Responds poorly when told by parent to correct homework.				
Produces messy or sloppy homework.				
Hurries through homework and makes careless mistakes.				
Shows dissatisfaction with work, even when he/she does a good job.				
Forgets to bring assignment back to class.				
Deliberately fails to bring assignment back to class.				

Source: Reprinted with permission from Anesko, K. M., Schoiock, G., Ramirez, R., and Levine, F. M. (1987). The homework problem checklist: Assessing children's homework difficulties, *Behavioral Assessment, 9,* 179.

233

◆ Has the student received training in alternative appropriate behaviors? If you're unsure about a student's skills, review these skills as a teaching assessment. Remember that some students require regular review and practice in order to maintain their self-help and social skills.

◆ Has the student suddenly lost the skills? If so, then contact as many other persons involved with the student as possible. See if there is a health or family change that may be responsible for the sudden behavioral change. Remember, many problem behaviors may be the result of anxiety or depression and this may reflect a serious but treatable problem.

◆ Has the problem occurred before? Can you identify any similarities between the episodes? Consider using an A-B-C analysis to determine what causes or maintains the behavior. Perhaps the behavior is being reinforced.

◆ Are other students engaging in the same behavior? There's a possibility that the student is imitating others. Reevaluate the contingencies for the other students. Are they being reinforced? How can you alter the contingencies for the target student and peers?

Once you have answered these questions, you will want to ensure that your school and classroom environment support your efforts to improve your students' on-task behavior. The following guidelines for curricular modifications include ways to prevent a child from experiencing the repeated failure or the unwarranted success that can be demoralizing to a child's sense of self-worth and achievement. The goal is to make the classroom environment demanding but predictable, allowing students a sense of control and accomplishment.

◆ Schedule ample time for a student working at a typical pace to complete the assignment, but, if you have planned a task carefully, do not give in to a student's complaints that it is too long.

◆ Place work materials in a designated storage area, off your desk, so that the student must take responsibility for picking up and returning work.

◆ Plan tasks that will challenge students but will occasionally allow them to experience some failure so that they will learn how to handle frustration. On the other hand, let students know when an assignment is difficult or encompasses new knowledge or skills.

◆ Let students know how they are performing. Help students develop a sense of competence by sharing your evaluations with them. Encourage self-evaluation by asking questions ("How do you think you worked in algebra today?" "Did you organize your study time well for this exam?").

◆ Do not assist students every time they request help. Establish guidelines for requesting help (perhaps a signaling device on the student's desk) and follow these guidelines. Encourage students to help themselves by using the dictionary, reference books, or answer keys. Promote peer assistance and **peer tutoring** (discussed later in this section).

With these general guidelines in mind, let's turn now to interventions that you can use to improve your students' work habits.

INTERVENTION STRATEGIES TO IMPROVE SCHOOL SURVIVAL SKILLS

Managing Transitions

Hall monitors can check non-classroom areas for unauthorized student "trespassers." Security guards serve this purpose in some schools; in others, parent volunteers monitor the halls. Help these personnel individualize (when appropriate) their strategies for dealing with students with disabilities. In turn, these youth should receive (and review as often as necessary) a clear explication of class attendance and of hall-monitoring policies. In this explanation, you and other teachers should make the real-world link to individuals with whom students may have similar interactions (e.g., ticket takers at athletic events, concerts, and movies; department store security agents and dressing-room monitors). Talk about managing interactions (especially confrontations) with persons in these hall monitor-positions. Of course, it is important to discuss school hall monitoring before the student develops problems (or a poor reputation) with security staff.

If they are to be effective, hall passes must be produced in a way that prevents counterfeiting. Like tokens in a token economy program, hall passes should be durable (if they are to be reused), unique (to avoid counterfeit), convenient to produce, and age-appropriate.

Random attendance checks may control absenteeism and tardiness. Each day (or check), a teacher chooses a class period to monitor but does not announce it in advance. After taking attendance, he reads the names of the late or absent students for penalties. Alternatively, he should recognize or reinforce students who were on time.

Van Houten's (1981) research on public posting offers principles that warrant consideration: his work involves publicly listing the names of persons who have (or have not) engaged in a target behavior.

To follow this procedure, post a schedule of daily activities (for younger students) or classroom periods (for older students) that accounts for time within thirty-minute intervals (younger students) or for class periods. The schedule should be specific about what the activity requires of the students, especially if a change of classes is required. Many teachers have found it helpful to post a shorter schedule adjacent to the overall one for changeable aspects of the school day. For example, this "little" schedule might include weekly sessions with a speech therapist, special school-wide events, or vacation days.

For junior high or high school students, provide an 8½-by-11-inch printed schedule for their notebooks. If you work with a student who has tantrums or seems easily upset when the school schedule changes arrange a time to review the schedule with the student and suggest that she use a highlighter pen to mark special or important dates (the date a term paper is due, the date and time for auditions for the school chorus, or the deadline for ordering class rings).

Your classroom should include a large wall clock to help students who want to remain on schedule. It may also be useful in giving students some idea about how much time has elapsed during a work period and how much time remains for them to complete work. To assist elementary school students in becoming independent in time management, announce that it is time to check the clock and ask one student to tell the group how much time remains in the period. Repeat this process until each student is able to use the clock independently. "Beat the buzzer," a strategy wherein students are asked to complete their clean-up or move to their new activity before the buzzer sounds, facilitates the transition of young and developmentally delayed children (Wurtele & Drabman, 1984). Sainato, Strain, Lefebvre, & Rapp (1987) successfully modified this teacher-directed intervention by having children move to their next activity and ring a bell themselves when they arrived. Fowler (1986) described a peer-mediated transition strategy for kindergartners elected as team captains:

> They assigned points for appropriate behavior to team members and to themselves on report cards depicting a picture of each transition activity. Depending on their performance, children earned various levels of participation in the day's daily outdoor activity. Following the peer-monitoring procedure, a self-monitoring procedure, in which children assigned themselves checks on their report cards, was implemented (reported in Sainato, 1990, p. 293).

Managing Homework

Studies have shown that if planned correctly, homework enhances academic performance (Epstein, Polloway, Foley, & Patton, 1993). In an attempt to raise academic standards, many schools are placing special emphasis on homework completion, especially for students in integrated regular education classes. Nevertheless, students with classroom behavioral and learning problems may experience similar difficulties with homework completion (Epstein et al., 1993). Consider these suggestions as you develop your own homework policy:

◆ Assess your students' homework difficulties, including the perceptions of their parents and other teachers. The *Homework Problem Checklist* (Epstein et al., 1993) is a useful interviewing tool.

◆ Present very clear and specific directions with all assignments.

◆ Teach students time-management skills (presented later in this section).

◆ Make it relevant! Help the student understand the connection with his mainstream classwork. Share sample assignments from regular education or less restrictive settings (Epstein et al., 1993).

◆ Assign homework that emphasizes proficiency, maintenance of skills *already learned,* or generalization of those skills and knowledge to another situation or example. Be sure that the homework is neither too novel nor too complex (Cooper, 1989). A good rule of thumb is to assign homework on which an unsupervised student would achieve 70 percent to 80 percent accuracy (Epstein et al., 1993).

◆ To ensure that you can provide adequate and timely feedback on homework, be as efficient as you can. Consider self-correcting assignments, peer-monitored homework, or other assistance.

◆ Keep in mind that elementary-level students primarily learn good study habits and independent review strategies from their homework assignments (Cooper, 1989; Rosenberg, 1989). Short, successful assignments work best.

◆ Establish the routine early in the school year. Begin with written explanations to parents and students about homework schedule and subjects. Collect homework after each assignment. Provide homework folders for students to take back and forth from school to home; these may help those who are likely to misplace their papers.

◆ Don't assume that a student will understand spoken homework assignments. Encourage the use of written assignments. (You may write them for younger students; older students may use an assignment book.)

◆ Involve parents. Have parents sign completed homework but do not expect parents to teach their students material that has not been learned in school. (Parent-developed ideas

for helping students with disabilities organize their schoolwork and schedules are available in *Education Advocacy: Steps for parents.* To receive a copy, contact United Mental Health, Inc., at (412) 391–3820, or write to UMH at 1945 Fifth Avenue, Pittsburgh, PA 15219.)

Modifying the Curriculum

Many students require modifications of the regular curriculum. Here is an example of a "Curriculum Modification Ladder":

1. Can the student do the same as peers?
(e.g., paragraph writing)
If not, can . . .

2. the student do the same activity but with adapted expectations?
(e.g., write five sentences about a topic)
If not, can . . .

3. the student do the same activity but with adapted expectations and materials?
(e.g., write five sentences about a picture)
If not, can . . .

4. the student do a similar activity but with adapted expectations?
(e.g., select and rearrange words to make a sentence)
If not, can . . .

5. the student do a similar activity but with adapted materials?
(e.g., arrange words on a card to make a sentence about a picture)
If not, can . . .

6. the student do a different, parallel activity?
(e.g., use a computer typing program or put pictures in a computer)
If not, can . . .

7. the student do a different activity in a different section of the room?
(e.g., do a computer game matching pictures to words)
If not, can . . .

8. the student do a functional activity in a different section of the school?

Figure 7.3 Primary School Planning Form

Today my homework is:

Reading: next story ☐

long   medium   (short)   none

Science: bring in leaves ☐

long   (medium)   short   none

Writing: copy lesson over ☐

(long)   medium   short   none

Bring in: money for lunch ☐

Name: Jon   All Done! ☐

Today: October 20

[Circle how long you think you need to do the lesson.]

(e.g., matching pictures to words with younger students, peer helper or instructional aide[1])

TEACHING SCHOOL SURVIVAL SKILLS

One of your best approaches to improving your students' time on task is to teach them the important skills they lack. Two publishers, Research Press and Sopris West, offer study skills curricula for this purpose.

A handy tool for improving time-management skills is an assignment sheet or notebook (Zigmond et al., 1986). Even young children can begin thinking about the length of assignments and how to accomplish them. Figure 7.3 shows a planning form for a primary school child; Figure 7.4 is a form for high school students.

Combining Contingency Management With Other Strategies

When you develop contingency contracts, token economies, group-oriented contingencies, or other reinforcement and response-costs systems, remember to include school survival skills. By emphasizing these skills you communicate the importance of good student work habits. Highly valued by regular classroom teachers, these skills are essential for students who are working in mainstream classrooms.

---

[1]DeBoer, A. L., & Fister, S. (1995). *Strategies & Tools for Collaborative Teaching.* Longmont, CO: Sopris West.

Figure 7.4 High School Student's Grade and Progress Monitoring Form

As of Friday, <u>Sept. 11</u>

<u>Course</u>   <u>Grade</u>

French level three .... `70`

     comments   <u>I was well prepared for the two small quizzes we had,</u>

<u>one on grammar and the other on vocabulary</u>

American Literature Advanced .... `—`

     comments   <u>no grades thus far: working on a short paper due</u>

<u>Monday — will be our first grade</u>

History .... `85`

     comments   <u>This is the same as last week. I expect a test next</u>

<u>week.</u>

Elementary Physics .... `41`

     comments   <u>I was barely able to grasp a simple principle and did</u>

<u>poorly on a quiz. Afterwards I went in for HELP. I understand it</u>

<u>now.</u>

Algebra and Trigonometry Advanced........................... `90`

     comments   <u>I am keeping up so it is not so bad as I might have</u>

<u>expected.</u>

Smith, Schumaker, Schaefer, and Sherman (1982) conducted a study in which students were trained to improve classroom participation, bringing about positive changes in a classroom previously troubled by disruptive behavior and poor group discussion. The key variables included teacher-posted rules for discussions, praise for student contributions, teacher restatement of the contribution, teacher-outlined discussion questions, graded student contributions, and public posting. An expanded version of the steps used to promote classroom discussion is displayed in Table 7.2 .

This study illustrates an excellent "combination intervention." Students were given clear direction, feedback, reinforcement, praise, and public recognition. The teacher also assisted students with note-taking methods by giving them outlines or lists of questions before each discussion. Students took notes, previewed the material, and then prepared for relevant classroom discussion. We can assume that grades served as strong and effective reinforcers because classroom discussion and participation improved. A response cost also was included in a clear hierarchy of expectations.

Another illustration of a combination strategy was offered by Kastelen, Nickel, and McLaughlin (1984), who used rapid teacher feedback, public posting, and teacher praise to improve the on-task and academic performance of an eighth-grade English class. Students received points for several school survival skills: bringing materials to class, starting to work promptly, reading as directed, and completing assignments correctly. Students' points were posted on a large display chart and were accompanied by teacher praise when a day's performance exceeded the previous one. The students' academic productivity dramatically improved.

In a study by Bahr, Fuchs, Fuchs, Fernstrom, & Stecker (1993), combining contingency contracts with self-monitoring proved to be an effective way to reduce the problem behaviors intervention of middle school students. Students learned to monitor their work completion as well as their off-task behaviors. The contingency contract specified the type of monitoring (inspection of the work or checking a self-monitoring form), a reward, and a schedule for rewards. Group contingencies are powerful peer-mediated strategies that can be especially useful for older students whose poor academic skills are the result of having too much fun in the classroom. (Refer to Chapters 5 and 6 for guidelines.)

Table 7.2 Ten Steps to Promote Classroom Discussion

Step 1. Hand out this list of rules pertaining to the discussion proceedures. The rule for the students are as follows:

1. Raise your hand when you have something to say.
2. Speak only when you are called on.
3. If classmate is called on, put your hand down and listen quietly.
4. If you have something to add after your classmate is finished, raise your hand again.

Step 2. Explain to the class why you think classroom discussion is important.

Step 3. Designate a "recorder" to mark a point for student contributions that appear relevant. Contributions can be in the form of a question, answer, or comment.

Step 4. Give examples of relevant statements.

Step 5. Give examples of irrelevant statements.

Step 6. Explain to the class and the classroom recorder that one point will be subtracted for irrelevant statements and disruptions (e.g., out of seat, talking out, or hand-waving).

Step 7. Discuss your discipline hierarchy. If anyone loses three points during one discussion period, he will be sent to the office and will have to attend an afternoon detention.

Step 8. Let the students know that their total number of points earned or lost will determine their daily grade. Explain the point system as follows (the difference between the number of points earned and the number of points lost):

Six or more = A
Five = A–
Four = B+
Three = B
Two = B–
One = C+
No points = C
Minus One = C–
Minus Two = D
Minus Three = F

Step 9. Post the weekly average of the discussion grades.

Step 10. At the end of the semester, average the weekly grades and convert them into 25% of their final grade.

Source: Reprinted with permission from Kerr, M. M., Nelson, C. M., and Lambert, D. L. (1987). *Helping adolescents with learning and behavior problems.* Upper Saddle River, NJ: Merrill/Prentice Hall, p. 130.

Compliance Training

Students with severe disabilities or young students who ignore classroom rules and refuse to comply with teachers' requests may benefit from a procedure called compliance training (Schoen, 1986). The purpose of **compliance training** is to modify oppositional behavior and to train students to respond quickly to adult directions. In other words, compliance training is used when a student's behavior indicates he is not under the verbal stimulus control of an adult. The following steps are guidelines for planning and implementing a compliance training program:

1. Write down at least ten behaviors of which the student is capable.
2. Select simple behaviors that can be done typically within fifteen seconds of your request.
3. Do not command the student to talk or to say something, as you cannot enforce this request.
4. Think of behaviors that the student perhaps will not do now but can do.
5. Following are examples of behaviors to use in compliance training: Come here; Sit down; Pick up_____; Give me _____; Shake hands; Stand up.
6. Once you have developed a list of behaviors, write them on a compliance training chart.
7. Plan a time during the day (usually about ten minutes) when you can work with the student.
8. Make the first request. If the student responds within fifteen seconds, give the student praise or the previously designated reinforcer.
9. If the student does not respond in fifteen seconds, physically prompt the response.
10. Praise the physically prompted response but do not provide an additional reinforcer.
11. Do not use the verbal request at times during the day when you are physically unable to prompt the student's response.
12. Do not make repeated requests of the student for any response. One request is enough.
13. If necessary, schedule more than one session per day per student.

Once a student has mastered the requests in the initial compliance training program, add additional commands to the list. Gradually you should notice that the student complies promptly to most adult directions.

PEER-MEDIATED APPROACHES

Peer tutoring, a successful way of structuring academic activities to involve peers, relies upon the principles of **peer modeling** and peer teaching. The peer tutor must be a student who wants to do the tutoring, who may or may not have the content area skills but who can follow teacher directions and learn from a model. Use your judgment when pairing students for tutoring. Do not select a tutor who may embarrass or criticize the target student. When using a cross-age peer tutor (someone from another class), plan a schedule that is mutually convenient and decide how to evaluate the student tutor's involvement. Studies have shown that peer tutoring for students with disabilities in general education settings is more effective if those students are tutors for at least part of the time. However, students with disabilities do not require pairing with nondisabled students for this intervention to work (Mathes & Fuchs, 1994).

The selection of the task for peer tutoring is an important step. Give first priority to the subject area in which the target student has difficulty. Choose academic tasks that are best taught through a "model or prompt + feedback or praise" format. Good choices include spelling, vocabulary, sight words, and foreign language vocabulary; math facts; scientific formulas; and dates and names in social studies. Select academic tasks that require discrete responses and simple evaluation procedures (e.g., keeping a written tally of number correct and errors; sorting flashcards into mastered and nonmastered piles). Plan tasks that require relatively brief fifteen- to twenty-minute sessions. Trained tutors are more successful than those who are inexperienced (Fuchs, Fuchs, Bentz, Phillips, & Hamlett, 1994). While tutor preparation should be specific to the content of the lessons, general guidelines for tutor training would include the following:

1. Pinpoint the task and analyze it before you begin.
2. Collect all needed materials.
3. Explain the goal of tutoring to the tutor.
4. Explain the task to the tutor, as much as you think is needed.
5. Instruct the tutor in the use of the materials.
6. Explain how the data are to be collected.
7. Role-play the actual tutoring procedures with the tutor.
   a. Model the teaching and the feedback/praise with the tutor and the target student.
   b. Ask the tutor to try being the student for a couple of steps.
   c. Provide feedback to the tutor.
   d. Role-play some problems the tutor may encounter.
   e. If needed, train the tutor to use particular phrases to reinforce the student.
   f. Provide the tutor with sample data and have her record them.
   g. Meet with the tutor before the first session to review the procedures.
   h. Meet daily after the tutoring session to answer questions.
   i. Reinforce the tutor for her efforts.

For a detailed explanation of tutor training in elementary mathematics, see Fuchs et al. (1994). Preparation of preschool tutors is described in Tabacek, McLaughlin, & Howard (1994). Procedures for implementing a classroom-wide peer tutoring program is described in Greenwood, Delquadri, & Carta (1988).

In the future, computers may facilitate classroom peer-tutoring programs. The *Classroom-wide Peer Tutoring Guru* software assists teachers in planning, implementing, monitoring, and trouble-shooting (Greenwood, Delquadri, & Bulgren, 1993).

SELF-MANAGEMENT STRATEGIES

In this section we describe programs in which the student serves as the primary agent of change. These strategies, which were introduced in Chapter 6, are strongly recommended for dependent students or students who are manipulative or oppositional when confronted with adult demands. Moreover, "such procedures are considered particularly appropriate for facilitating the educational success of students with disabilities in mainstream environments, where resources for external management programs may be limited" (Sabatos, 1986, p. 23).

Recording one's own behavior is an effective way to increase academic productivity and on-task behavior (Glomb & West, 1990). A question may arise in planning this intervention: What *should* the student monitor? The WATCH Program teaches adolescents to follow these steps:

(a) Write down an assignment when it is given and write a due date; (b) Ask for clarification or help on the assignment if needed; (c) Task-analyze the assignment and schedule the task over the days available to complete the assignment; and (d) Check all work for completeness, accuracy, and neatness (Glomb & West, 1990, p. 235).

Figure 7.5 displays the assignment planner. (You can obtain a copy of the WATCH lessons and WATCH assignment planner by contacting Nancy Glomb at the Department of Special Education, Utah State University, Logan, UT 84322-6500.)

Compare the student's self-monitoring data with your reliability checks on performance. Hertz and McLaughlin (1990) awarded tickets to middle school students when their self-monitoring scores closely matched those of their teachers. Students then exchanged tickets for reinforcers.

A critical aspect of a successful self-management program is the reduction or fading out of teacher participation in the program. Once a student has shown consistent ability to self-monitor or self-instruct behavior, reduce your involvement in the program. Consider the steps outlined in Table 7.3 for elementary school children, but this "game" might not be appropriate for adolescents. Rather, meet with the student to discuss termination of the self-evaluation activities and to recognize achievement of the student's goal. Self-management strategies may be used in combination. For example, a student

Figure 7.5 Academic Self-Management

Week of _____ to _____ **WATCH** Name _____

Assignment Planner and Point Card

Assignment_____

Special Requirements

a. Due Date _____

b. _____

c. _____

d. _____

e. _____

Do I understand the assignment? ◯

Do I need to ask for help? ◯

		Citizenship/ Points	Watch/ Points	Total
Monday _____	I C/A/N	◻___	◻___	◻___
Tuesday _____	I C/A/N	◻___	◻___	◻___
Wednesday _____	I C/A/N	◻___	◻___	◻___
Thursday _____	I C/A/N	◻___	◻___	◻___
Friday _____	I C/A/N	◻___	◻___	◻___

Assignment_____

Special Requirements

a. Due Date _____

b. _____

c. _____

d. _____

e. _____

Do I understand the assignment? ◯

Do I need to ask for help? ◯

		Citizenship/ Points	Watch/ Points	Total
Monday _____	I C/A/N	◻___	◻___	◻___
Tuesday _____	I C/A/N	◻___	◻___	◻___
Wednesday _____	I C/A/N	◻___	◻___	◻___
Thursday _____	I C/A/N	◻___	◻___	◻___
Friday _____	I C/A/N	◻___	◻___	◻___

Table 7.3 Guidelines for Reducing Teacher Input in Self-Management Programs

1. For self-management programs that involve a group of students, divide the group into two teams. List students' names, according to teams, on the chalkboard.

2. Announce that only one group will be lucky and have its self-management records checked each day. The same group will be eligible for bonus points.

3. Flip a coin each afternoon, designating one group heads and one tails. The winning team has self-monitoring cards checked for reliability with teacher records. If each member of the team has a reliable score, team members then win bonus points or reinforcers.

4. Remember, promote the idea that being checked is a privilege.

5. Continue this procedure for at least seven school days.

6. During the next stage of the fading program, announce that a new game is beginning.

7. Place all students' names, written on paper strips, into a jar. Draw two names each day. These two lucky students receive the opportunity to earn bonus points or reinforcers.

8. After a period of at least seven school days, adjust the program so that you draw only one name. Maintain this stage of the program for at least one school week.

9. At the completion of the final phase, discontinue checking.

Note: Material presented in this table was taken from Alford, F. (1980). *Self-management for teachers.* Nashville, TN: George Peabody College for Teachers.

might monitor his behavior, record it, and then graph his results. DiGangi, Maag, & Rutherford (1991) combined self-monitoring with self-graphing for two older elementary school students and found that academic performance and on-task performance improved even more when the students graphed the results of their self-monitoring.

RECOGNIZING AND ASSESSING SOCIAL WITHDRAWAL

The final part of the chapter will help you work with students who do not get along well with others. Many children and adolescents with behavior disorders have very poor social skills. Their inability to respond in social situations and make friends can lead to the disruptive, aggressive, or offensive behaviors you read about in other chapters. This chapter addresses social skill deficits that lead to **social withdrawal.** Chapter 8 describes additional social skills instruction for **aggressive** students.

Social withdrawal, a very serious problem, refers to a cluster of behaviors that result in an individual escaping or avoiding social contact. This may be intentional, as in extreme cases of elective mutism

(an uncommon syndrome involving a refusal to speak by someone who can talk), or it may reflect a broader lack of social competence, as often found in children or adults with retardation, psychotic behaviors, or autism. Social withdrawal may result from a lack of specific social skills or it may have its origins in a history of rejection and punishment associated with social interaction. In many cases, social withdrawal may be maintained by **negative reinforcement:** the child continues the specific form of withdrawn behavior because she escapes or avoids social contact, which apparently constitutes an aversive stimulus for her. In other cases, behaviors incompatible with social interaction, such as self-stimulation, may be maintained by self-produced reinforcement. Thus, social withdrawal covers a broad and complex range of problem behaviors.

For a long time, social withdrawal was not considered a serious problem in the field of special education or in related disciplines. Even today an extremely quiet child, seldom enjoying the benefits of positive relationships with others but creating no observable problems for his teachers, may drift unnoticed from one school year to the next. Yet, the consequences of untreated social withdrawal can be extremely serious. Unless a child can learn to interact with others at a reasonably competent level, access to less restrictive settings and subsequent learning opportunities may be seriously curtailed.

As stated in earlier chapters, rating scales and checklists are useful assessment and monitoring techniques for an initial look at a student's problem behaviors. For example, you might use a problem behavior checklist or the evaluation checklists taken from a social skills curriculum to get a general picture of the social skill problems experienced by one of your students. To make this **assessment** especially helpful, solicit the ratings from as many significant others as possible, including the parents, teachers, and other professionals who know the child. Do not overlook the student's previous teacher, who might be a valuable source of information.

The information you gather from checklists and ratings can give you a starting place for further, more finely grained assessments, including behavioral interviews and direct observations. Moreover, a curriculum-based checklist can clue you in on where to begin in the sequence of skills taught in that particular instructional program. Finally, a checklist or rating scale allows you to compare quickly the views of several individuals about the student's behavior.

Interviews are especially important in the assessment of social skills because others in the child's life are apt to have strong convictions about the student's social relationships and functioning. Some questions you might ask in a social assessment interview include the following:

◆ Who are this student's friends?
◆ What social situations are difficult for this student?
◆ What "social mistakes" does this student make?
◆ Does this student initiate social interactions?
◆ What social skills does this student have?
◆ What do others say about this student's social behavior?
◆ What skills does this student need to be more socially successful?
◆ Can this student maintain a social interaction?

◆ In what situations is this student socially successful?
◆ What behavior does this student exhibit in these situations?

Analogue measures refer to a role-play or behavioral rehearsal in which an individual demonstrates how he would respond in a given social interaction (Cartledge & Milburn, 1983). You have probably used analogue measures and not realized it. For example, you may have asked a student to describe how he would respond to a certain social situation. Analogue procedures may help you understand a student's social perception and the skills he needs to learn in order to respond successfully to a given social situation.

Direct observations allow you to look at social skills and related problem behaviors. These skills and problems will be the focus of your planning and teaching activities. Table 7.4 offers examples taken from research studies. Use the observational strategies discussed in earlier chapters to monitor social interactions. Review the section on interval recording for specific guidelines.

REMEDIATING SOCIAL WITHDRAWAL
General Considerations

There are some strategies that you should always avoid when dealing with social withdrawal. One of these is coercion, or punishment, designed to "make the child come out of herself." Unfortunately, classmates often ridicule and tease their withdrawn peers, making initiating simple interactions even more difficult for the student. Try to help classmates recognize that social withdrawal is a problem for that student, and consider using one of the peer-mediated interventions to assist her.

Another strategy to avoid is leaving the isolate individual alone. Isolate children who are left alone for long periods may develop additional serious problems, rather than learning skills that improve their social interactions. Timeout procedures are thus inappropriate interventions for the socially withdrawn.

Table 7.4 Sample Definitions of Social Behaviors

Behavior Category	Definitions	Authors
Motor-gestural	This included all positive physical contacts such as brushing another person's arm while reaching for something; cooperative use of an object such as looking at a book with another person, exchanging pens, taking turns placing puzzle pieces; touching and/or manipulating the same object or parts of the same object; all other gestural movement directed to another person such as handling an object, pointing, motioning to "Come" or "Go away," shaking head to indicate "Yes" or "No," and waving.	Dy, Strain, Fullerton, & Stowitschek (1981)
Vocal-verbal	This included all positive vocal expressions or verbalizations which by virtue of content, e.g., "Hey you," "Uh-huh" (while nodding), clearly indicated that the person was directing the utterance to another individual.	
Approach gestures	…consisted of any deliberate behavior of the child which involves the hand(s), arm(s), or other body parts in a motion directed to another child, e.g., an inward circular hand and arm motion, repeated bending and straightening of forefinger while arm extended towards a peer.	Gable, Hendrickson, & Strain (1978)
Play organizer	Verbalizations or responses to verbalizations wherein a child specifies an activity, suggests an idea for play, or directs a child to engage in a play behavior.	Odom, Hoyson, Jamieson, & Strain (1985)
Share	Offers or gives an object to another child or accepts an object from another child by taking the object in hand or using it in play.	
Share request	Asks a child to give an object to the speaker.	
Assistance	Helps another child complete a task or desired action which he or she could not complete or do alone.	
Complimentary statement	Verbal statement indicating affection, attraction, or praise.	
Affection	Patting, hugging, kissing, or holding hands with another child.	Odom, Hoyson, Jamieson, & Strain (1985)
Negative motor-gestural	Hitting, pushing, sticking out tongue, taking unoffered objects, or destroying others' constructions.	
Negative vocal-verbal	Crying, shouting, calling another child an ugly name, and refusal to engage in a requested behavior or corrections.	

A third approach to socially withdrawn students—one that has not proven effective—is to accept their social isolation as a developmental phase and simply to await their decision to approach their classmates. Unfortunately, many withdrawn children have not learned the social skills required to develop social relationships with their classmates and cannot learn them without help. Maturation as a singular intervention on social withdrawal is not effective; children do not simply outgrow this problem because the more they avoid people, the less opportunity they have to develop personally reinforcing situations.

Organizing the Environment to Promote Social Interaction

You can alter the environment of the classroom, playground, or free-play room to facilitate cooperative interactions. Given the seriousness of social skills problems, early interventions have dominated the research on children's social skills (Peterson & McConnell, 1993). (Additional information for teachers who want to facilitate social interaction among young children is available by writing to Carla A. Peterson, 101 Child Development, Iowa State University, Ames, IA 50011.)

Table 7.5 Facilitative and Nonfacilitative Activities across Settings with Mean Frequencies of Positive Social Behavior Per Five-Minute Session (in Parentheses)

	Facilitative Activities	*Nonfacilitative Activities*
Structured play	Going to a grocery store (25.3)	Road and car (9.96)
	Having a picnic (16.1)	Building with blocks (9.4)
	Playing doctor (13.6)	Kitchen (7.54)
	Washing babies (10.27)	Garage (7.2)
	Gluing (17.0)	Stencils (5.43)
	Doing puzzles (13.2)	Drawing (4.86)
	Parquetry (12.5)	Bristle Blocks (4.83)
	Stamping (10.0)	Playing with playdough (4.1)
Learning center	Working jobs (12.4)	Manipulatives (3.89)
	Doing puzzles (12.4)	Using rice table (3.3)
	Pasting (8.9)	Using water table (1.2)
	Parquetry (8.7)	Showing and Telling (8.3)

Source: Reprinted with permission from Odom, S., & Strain, P. (1984). Classroom-based social skills instruction for severely handicapped preschool children. *Topics in early childhood special education.*

Odom & Strain (1984) named activities that facilitated or inhibited social interactions in early childhood classrooms. These are shown in Table 7.5.

One study examined the effects of proximity on the social interactions of students with severe and profound multiple disabilities (Speigel-McGill, Bambara, Shores, & Fox, 1984). This investigation suggested that placing the students close to one another in pairs improved their social interactions, which consisted of head orientation, vocalizations, and gestures. These researchers observed more social interchanges at one foot than at five or ten feet.

TEACHER PROMPTING AND REINFORCEMENT

One intervention procedure is prompting and reinforcement. As the name suggests, this procedure requires you to prompt and reinforce an isolated pupil's peer interactions. Even though this procedure is fairly simple, research studies conducted over a number of years have indicated that it is successful, particularly with young children (Bryant & Budd, 1984; Odom & Strain, 1993). The following suggestions outline a teacher prompting and reinforcement procedure:

1. Arrange the free-play area as directed in the section on environmental modification. Invite the target individual and the nontarget students to play in the free-play area for a period of at least fifteen minutes.

2. **Prompt** a nondisabled student to initiate play with the target individual by using a phrase such as, "Why don't you ask Kylea if she would like to play with the blocks?" This type of prompt is a play organizer.

3. Use a prompt such as, "Hand Tommy the truck," to share a material.

4. Use a prompt when asking the child to assist another student. You may do this by using a phrase such as, "Help Kathy roll the truck into the blocks."

5. Reinforce any interactions between the students, but try not to interrupt their play by focusing on the behaviors of one child. Make your reinforcement as brief as possible; research has shown that teacher reinforcement tends to interrupt the ongoing social interaction of two children.

6. Once the students have established a fairly steady rate of interacting with one another during free-play times, reduce the number of prompts and reinforcement instances that you provide. For example, if you have been prompting the students on an average of once every thirty seconds or once every minute, reduce the number of prompts to one every three to five minutes.

7. Remember that a peer trainer can be used to provide prompting and reinforcement. If you feel that you have gotten the intervention off to a good start, consider using a peer to maintain it.

Social Skills Instruction

Several social skills teaching packages have appeared recently in the commercial marketplace. (For a review of social skills curricula and supplementary materials, see *The Social Skills Planning Guide* by Alberg, Petry, and Eller, published in 1994 by Sopris West.) Let's look at the key features of social skills curricula:

◆ *Modeling.* The first step in most social skills teaching programs is to introduce students to examples of the social skill through live, audio, or video modeling. Usually, one skill, broken down as much as possible, is the focus of each vignette or lesson. To incorporate peers, call on various students in your class to demonstrate social skills during a lesson.

◆ *Role-Playing.* After an initial demonstration, the social skills program may call for a role-play of the targeted skill. To facilitate this component, encourage students first to discuss the demonstration and to think of real-life situations in which they might use the skill. Following this discussion, arrange student-designed role-playing or follow a scripted role-play from the curricular materials. (Before teaching a lesson, be sure that you would feel comfortable role-playing the social skill yourself.)

◆ *Performance Feedback.* Letting students know how they performed the skill during the role-play is crucial. Some of the most helpful (and candid) feedback (e.g., approval, praise, constructive criticism) will come from the other group members. A good rule of thumb is to encourage positive, supportive feedback while indicating aspects of the behavior that the student could improve. Adult supervision is very important during this phase. A helpful strategy is to have the student immediately replay the scene so that the group can give feedback on the improved performance.

◆ *Generalization and Maintenance.* By now these terms are familiar. The chance to "overlearn" and repeatedly practice the social skills in other settings is vital to a youngster's social development, as demonstrated by Schumaker and Ellis (1982). Self-monitoring can be an

essential feature of this transfer-of-learning phase (Kelly et al., 1983). Many social skills programs include "behavioral homework" and notes sent home to reinforce the skills outside of the classroom. One way to increase the generalization of social skills out of school is first to ask parents which social skills are important to them. Also, try to incorporate different "trainers." In one consultation experience a teacher of junior high school students with moderate disabiilities "primed" various faculty colleagues to enter her classroom and initiate certain social interactions, including gentle teasing for a student having trouble with this kind of interaction. She simply posted her "social skills needs list" in the teachers' lounge each Monday.

In reviewing social skills programs, be sure that the essential components are included. Once you have chosen a curriculum, remember that your social skills instruction, like academics, must be individualized. Most curricula have "placement tests" to help you tailor your instruction to a student's needs.

Many teachers prefer to develop their own social skills lessons. Our case study by Li-Lin Chen at the end of this chapter describes her social skills program.

Token Reinforcement

Chapter 6 described token reinforcement in detail. Here, we call your attention to a study of token reinforcement to improve the social interactions of preschool children. Wolfe, Boyd, and Wolfe (1983) devised a system whereby targeted socially withdrawn children wore bright yellow "happy face" charts with boxes marked to indicate the intervals during which they played cooperatively. Happy face stickers placed on (or removed from) the charts constituted the tokens. Following is a description of the intervention (Wolfe et al., 1983):

> Training the target children to play in a cooperative, nonaggressive manner consisted of the following procedures. All children in the classroom were told that sharing time was about to begin, and

the target children were given their happy face charts to wear. All of the children in the class were then encouraged to find a play activity and a friend with whom to share the activity. Once the target children had found an activity and friend, a bell signaled that the play program had begun. During the next minute, general praise was given to the group of children for cooperative play (e.g., "I like the way everyone is playing") and specific praise was administered to the target children contingent upon appropriate play (e.g., "I like the way Jimmy is playing with Billy"). At the end of 1 minute, the bell rang and the teacher placed happy face stickers on the charts of target children who had engaged in cooperative play for the entire minute. Target children who had not earned a happy face were prompted to engage in cooperative play by the teacher and were reminded of the backup reinforcers they could earn (i.e., outside play time). In the event a target child did not engage in play following this prompt, a gentle physical prompt was used to lead the child to a play activity. This prompt was repeated every 3 to 5 minutes for any target child who did not engage in cooperative play. The cycle of 1-minute play periods, signaled by the bell, was repeated 15 times during each session.

At the end of the session the teacher counted the happy faces on each child's card and praised the child for his/her efforts to share with others. Initially, the backup reinforcer (10 minutes of outside play) was administered for earning eight or more stickers. This criterion was gradually increased over several sessions to 12 stickers. Children who did not earn enough tokens to go outside were allowed to look at books and play with toys inside the classroom while the other children went outside. Subsequently, they were reminded of this missed opportunity the following day before the training session was begun. The token reinforcement program continued in the morning for 20 sessions, and then was extended to include the afternoon sessions as well. Once a target child displayed an 80% rate of cooperative play on three consecutive sessions in either the morning or afternoon setting, a fading procedure was implemented that involved a gradual lengthening (over several sessions) of the required interval of cooperative play from 1 minute to 5 minutes. When the child was able to play for a 5-minute duration before reinforcement with an overall rate of cooperative play exceeding 80%, the happy face chart was discontinued.

Intermittent verbal praise was used in the classroom, and outside play was continued as a reward at the end of each session contingent upon an 80% rate of cooperative play (pp. 4–5).

You will notice that this intervention actually combined several of the teacher-mediated strategies we have recommended: prompting, praise, and feedback. This approach also incorporated peers as interventionists, which is discussed in the following section.

PEER-MEDIATED STRATEGIES

In a peer-mediated intervention a member of the individual's peer group, rather than an adult, is the primary agent of change in behavior. Why should you consider peer involvement in social skills training? Consider the response offered by Hollinger (1987):

> To date, social skills training interventions consistently focus exclusively on the children who are identified as those with the behavior problems or low social status. Yet social behavior and status are defined in part by other persons in the target child's life. Consequently, it may be important to consider peers' perceptions in social skills training, thus focusing on interactive exchanges rather than discrete behaviors (Strain et al., 1984). It seems especially important to address negative social perception biases among peers in their interactions with behaviorally disordered children (p. 22).

By including peers in the intervention, you increase the likelihood that they will alter their attitudes towards the socially handicapped child.

Few aspects of behavioral change have experienced such growth as the peer-mediated interventions for socially challenged children and adolescents. Entire volumes now offer suggestions for incorporating peers in social skills training (e.g., Strain et al., 1984). Naturally, we can highlight only the more basic, classroom-tested approaches here. We begin with peer-mediated strategies for young children or those who are more severely disturbed: peer imitation training, peer social initiation, and peer prompting and reinforcement.

Table 7.6 Peer Imitation Training: Selection of Peer Behavior Model

1. Select a student who attends school regularly to promote continuity of the intervention.
2. Select a student who frequently exhibits appropriate social skills with other students.
3. Select a student who can follow a teacher's verbal instructions reliably and can imitate a teacher model.
4. Select a student who can concentrate on the training task for at least 10 minutes per target individual.

Note: Material was taken with permission from Kerr, M. M. and Strain, P. S. (1979). The use of peer social initiation strategies to improve the social skills of withdrawn children. In A. H. Fink (Ed.), *International perspectives on future special education.* Reston, VA: Council for Exceptional Children.

PEER IMITATION TRAINING

Peer imitation training requires a classmate of the isolate child to model appropriate social behaviors for the student to learn. Peer imitation training is particularly well suited for students with severe behavioral disorders who do not exhibit appropriate social behaviors. This training is the most intensive peer-mediated intervention we describe, for it involves not only the peer model but an adult who prompts and reinforces the isolated student. Table 7.6 gives you ideas for selecting a good peer behavior model.

Once you have selected a peer model, begin the program. Table 7.7 provides general guidelines for conducting a peer imitation session. You may want to modify them according to the chronological and intellectual level of the peer model selected.

In Table 7.7 the peer model is cued to demonstrate target behaviors. The peer model should demonstrate social behaviors from a predesignated list, repeating them until the withdrawn student consistently imitates them. One source for generating a list of target behaviors is the IEP for the isolate student. For example, you may want the student to learn how to ask other children to play.

Table 7.7 Steps in Conducting a Peer Imitation Training Session

1. Seat the children about two feet apart and facing one another.
2. Station a trainer behind each child in a "shadowing" style.
3. The trainer behind the peer model whispers in the child's ear to cue the target behavior (e.g., "Kevin, drink from your cup.").
4. The model child drinks from his cup.
5. The trainer behind the target child says, "See what Kevin's doing? You do it too!"
6. If the target imitates the modeled behavior, the trainer offers verbal praises and affectionate pats.
7. If the target does not imitate the modeled behavior, the trainer behind the target physically guides (handshapes) the desired behavior (e.g., guides the hand-held cup to the child's mouth).
8. The trainer gradually fades physical guidance and continues to reinforce successive approximations.
9. When the target can successfully imitate the peer model while seated across from each other, move the training to a less structured setting (e.g., a free-play situation).
10. When the peer model exhibits an appropriate behavior, approach the target and say, "See what Kevin's doing? You do it too!"
11. Provide physical guidance if the target fails to imitate.
12. Fade physical guidance and reinforce successive approximations.

Note: This table was contributed by Thomas P. Cooke.

In this case, you might have the peer model say a standard phrase such as, "I want to play with you. Here is a toy." This is a verbal target behavior. You might also want the student to learn motor skills such as how to hand a toy to another child without throwing it. You would then direct the model to offer a toy gently so that the isolate child could observe this and learn to do it. Other examples of suitable target behaviors are smiling, pushing a toy, adding a block to a tower, throwing a ball, offering a verbal compliment, sharing, hugging, and patting. Remember that target behaviors are not always selected from play activities but might be behaviors from a self-help or prevocational activity, as illustrated in Table 7.7.

It is important that you think about where you would like the peer imitation to take place. Cooke, Cooke, and Apolloni (1978) suggested that peer imitation training take place in the most natural setting possible. In research conducted on young children, they found that pupils performed better when training was conducted in their classroom instead of an individual session room. If your peer imitation intervention relates to play behaviors, plan training in a free-play area of the classroom or during an outside recess period. If you are attempting to use peer imitation training for, say, self-help or pre-academic skills, then shift the intervention session to a setting that has the materials for these activities. You may find it helpful in the initial sessions to conduct the training when other students are not present. This enables the student who is challenged to pay close attention to the peer model. The private peer training also allows you to give more attention to the intervention sessions.

Peer Social Initiation

In **peer social initiation,** the peer trainer is required to make social bids to a withdrawn child or children. These bids may be vocal-verbal or motor-gestural (asking the isolate child to play, giving the isolate child a toy, or helping the child to use a particular material). This procedure has been used successfully with both children who are severely behaviorally disordered and those with normal to mild disabilities (James & Egel, 1986; Ragland, Kerr, & Strain, 1978; Strain, Shores, & Timm, 1977).

In addition to using the general resources listed for peer interventions, you may want to make a set of cue cards to assist the peer trainer in carrying out his role. Each cue card should display a picture of a toy or play activity that the isolated child enjoys. Peer trainers need a little reminder to move from one play material to another during the training session, which the cue cards accomplish when displayed in the play area.

Select a peer trainer for this intervention according to the criteria listed in Table 7.7. Research studies reveal the ability of even very young children (three years old) or children who are developmentally delayed (moderately retarded) to carry out this simple intervention (Young & Kerr, 1979). Table 7.8 outlines the basic steps of preparing a peer trainer for intervention sessions. If you are working with a peer trainer who is developmentally delayed, this training may take longer than the four twenty-minute sessions suggested. In addition, you may find it helpful to provide frequent, tangible reinforcers to a trainer who is developmentally delayed.

When you are ready to schedule intervention sessions on a daily basis, allow enough time to enable the peer trainer to work with one isolate student at a time for a ten-minute interval. Do not plan to ask the trainer to work with several students at one time because it becomes too difficult a role for the peer trainer and is not sufficiently intensive an intervention for the withdrawn pupils. Rather, "taking turns" is preferred. You may notice, however, that while the peer trainer is working with one student, others in the group play more cooperatively and frequently with each other.

The first few days of a peer social initiation intervention may leave you with the discouraging feeling that this intervention will not work at all. This is because when first approached by the peer trainer, isolate children have a natural tendency to ward off these approaches through temper tantrums and other oppositional behaviors. You and the peer trainer must not give up at this point. Rather, the peer trainer should continue to make initiations toward the children, and you should reinforce these efforts. You may find that in the initial session, you will also need

Table 7.8 Peer-Mediated Social Initiation Procedure: Preparing the Peer Trainer

1. Explain to the peer trainer what is expected during the training sessions. Modify the explanation to suit the conversational level of the individual. Examples of this brief explanation are, "Try your best to get other children to play with you," "To get others to play with you, give them a toy."

2. Train the peer trainer to expect rejection. This is accomplished by the adult's taking the role of an isolated individual. In every other instance of the peer trainer making a social initiation toward the adult, ignore the initiation. Pause for ten seconds or more, then explain to the child that your ignoring the initiation is a behavior the trainer is likely to encounter with the isolate student. Explain this in a manner that encourages the trainer to continue trying. For example, you can say something like, "Children will not always want to play, but you need to keep trying very hard."

3. Repeat the role play, first training the peer to hand you a toy or to otherwise make a motor-gestural initiation. Then train the student to make vocal-verbal initiations.

4. Carry out the role play using each of the toys or play materials that are in the free-play setting. Cue the peer trainer about any toys that have a particular appeal to the isolate individual. Introduce cue cards depicting each toy at this time, if necessary.

5. Continue practicing the role plays during daily twenty-minute practice sessions until the peer trainer can reliably make repeated social initiations towards you. Keep in mind that peer training in the research reported has typically required at least four sessions, with additional sessions needed for a severely handicapped peer trainer.

6. Be sure to reinforce the peer trainer's participation during each training session.

Note: Material was taken with permission from Kerr, M. M. and Strain, P. S. (1979). The use of peer social initiation strategies to improve the social skills of withdrawn children. In A. H. Fink (Ed.), *International perspectives on future special education.* Reston, VA: Council for Exceptional Children.

to prompt, either physically or verbally, the isolate student's responding to the peer trainer. This initial difficult period generally lasts no more than four or five sessions, after which pupils cooperate and begin to enjoy their interactions. Table 7.9 displays the basic steps in conducting the intervention sessions.

Peer Prompting and Reinforcement

Peer prompting and reinforcement, like teacher prompting and reinforcement, refers to the use of a trainer to assist withdrawn children in playing with each other. Again, verbal and physical prompts and frequent reinforcers are used. Research on this procedure has not been extensive,

Table 7.9 Peer-Mediated Social Initiation Procedure: Conducting the Intervention Sessions

1. Set aside at least six minutes for each target individual during the play session.

2. Try to use the same free-play area with the play materials suggested each day.

3. Before each intervention session, review with the peer trainer the activities that are most likely to succeed.

4. Remind the peer trainer before each session that the pupils may not respond at first but to keep trying.

5. Remind the peer trainer to play with only one target individual at a time. It helps if the adult in the session reminds the peer trainer when to change toys and when to begin play with another student.

6. Reinforce the peer trainer for attempting to play with the withdrawn individuals. If the session is going slowly, you may wish to reinforce the peer trainer during the session. Otherwise, provide the peer trainer with some form of reinforcement at the end of the session.

Table 7.10 Peer-Mediated
Prompting and Reinforcement
Strategy

1. Select a peer as suggested in the previous intervention strategies.

2. Plan at least four 20-minute training sessions to prepare the individual for her role as peer trainer.

3. Explain to the peer trainer that you want assistance in helping other children to learn to play. Explain further that the role of peer trainer is helping children play with each other and letting them know they are doing a good job.

4. Train the peer trainer by inviting two children into the play session, and practice with the trainer prompting and reinforcing them for playing together. Unlike other peer-mediated procedures, training for peer prompting and reinforcement should take place "on the job," using the isolate students from the beginning.

5. By modeling the strategies with the isolate children present, assist the peer trainer to think of ways to prompt and reinforce the isolate children.

6. Remind the peer trainer before each intervention session to try to get the two children to play with each other rather than directly with the peer trainer.

7. Set aside the time and materials and location described in previous peer training intervention for the actual training sessions.

8. Remember to reinforce the peer trainer for efforts after each session.

but the initial work has shown that a peer trainer could successfully use the procedure to increase the cooperative play behavior of two children who are severely behaviorally disordered (Strain, Kerr, & Ragland, 1979). Consider the peer prompting and reinforcement strategy as a followup to peer social initiations. Once an isolate student begins to respond reliably to the peer trainer, a different playmate can be introduced by using the peer prompting and reinforcement strategies described in Table 7.10. Do not train a peer to carry out both interventions (peer social initiations; prompting/reinforcement) at once; this would be too complex a task.

Peer Management Strategy

Young students who are socially withdrawn may benefit from playing "class manager," a role studied by Sainato, Maheady, and Shook (1986). In their study the withdrawn kindergartners took turns directing pleasurable classroom activities: feeding the class pet, ringing the "clean-up bell," collecting milk money, and opening two play areas. This effort succeeded in improving social interactions and sociometric ratings.

Peer Coaching

Peer coaching, like peer imitation, involves students and adults who provide instruction. The purpose of this intervention is to teach withdrawn pupils social skills to gain them peer acceptance. Children who are socially withdrawn realize more opportunity to engage in social learning if they are trained to increase their acceptance by peers. In a study by Oden and Asher (1977), third- and fourth-grade children who were socially isolated were coached in skills for making friends. The coaching procedure was designed to be used in schools. This intervention requires the adult to train children verbally in social skills, give them the opportunity to practice their social skills by playing with a peer, and finally, review the training procedure with their teacher/coach (see Oden, 1980, for a detailed description of the coaching procedure).

Peer Tutoring

Research by Franca, 1983, and Maher, 1982, demonstrated that academic peer tutoring can have a positive influence on peer social interactions, although researchers cannot always document how and why (Cook, Scruggs, Mastropieri, & Casto, in press; Scruggs, Mastropleri, Veit, & Osguthorpe, 1986). Franca (1983) found that adolescents with behavior disorders who tutored one another in fractions played more cooperatively in a physical education class. In this study students were assigned to pairs and given specific tutoring scripts.

Peer-tutoring guidelines, as presented earlier, may help your students expand their opportunities to practice both social and academic skills. Consider peer tutoring as a supplementary social skills training activity, relying on more direct interventions to teach new social skills (see Scruggs et al., 1986; Scruggs, Mastropieri, & Richter, 1985).

Another goal for peer tutoring may be a shift in attitudes toward children who are behaviorally challenged. Shisler, Osguthorpe, and Eiserman (1987) found that nondisabled sixth-graders rated their tutors with behavior disorders more positively after their tutoring experience. According to Johnson and Johnson (1984), the tutoring may allow nondisabled students to view their peers with disabilities in a different, less stereotyped role (Shisler et al., 1987).

This section closes with a look at the benefits of peer-mediated interventions for *all* students. Rob, a child with no disabilities, has learned helpful ways to accommodate his classmates with special needs. His ideas are listed in Figure 7.6.

SELF-MEDIATED STRATEGIES

Self-management strategies for the remediation of social withdrawal have not been explored extensively in research literature. However, newly emerging self-management strategies offer promise for an isolate student who is aware of her difficulty and wishes to have a role in remedying it. For example, this intervention might be very useful in a regular classroom for adolescents or in a classroom of youngsters with behavior disorders who are returning to a regular classroom. The self-management strategies discussed here are similar to those discussed in other chapters; the primary difference is in the target behavior selected. In choosing target behaviors for self-management procedures, it is a good idea to have the student participate.

The primary resource for helping students carry out a self-managed intervention for social withdrawal is a self-recording data sheet. Students should record their own performances to show visibly their progress towards meeting the goal of increased social interactions. (Chapter 6 contained information on developing a self-recording sheet.)

The purpose of self-recording is to make the student aware of positive interactions with others and how to increase them. Thus the intervention is twofold. First, the teacher or counselor describes to students examples of social initiations and responses. Second, students collect data on their own interactions. A third component, self-reinforcement, may supplement the intervention, or the teacher or counselor may provide the reinforcement to the student. Here are examples of target behaviors for a student to record:

- Raising my hand in classroom discussions to say something.
- Asking a question during the class meeting.
- Helping another student in my class on an assignment.
- Answering a question when another student asks me something.
- Saying "hello" to one of my classmates.
- Asking my classmate to eat lunch next to me.
- Asking someone in my class to play with me at recess.
- At recess, telling others they are doing a good job.
- Lending someone a pencil or paper during class.
- Sitting next to one of my friends during lunch.
- Bringing a toy for someone else to play with in school.
- Telling someone what I did after school yesterday.
- Signing up to tutor another person in my class.
- Asking someone else to help me with my self-recording project.

Self-monitoring is a good way to extend your social skills training program, as suggested by Kelly et al. (1983), who found that self-monitoring improved the social interactions between adolescents who had behavior disorders and their vocational supervisors. In this case, self-monitoring was combined with role-playing and didactic training. Students rated themselves and

Figure 7.6 Helping a Child with Disabilities

Helping a Child with Disabilities
by Rob Perrone, age eight

1. Call the child by his or her name, not "the handicapped kid."
2. Be kind to the child, and remember: this involves patience.
3. When you start out, ask the teacher, "May I help this child?"
4. Wait until the teacher says you can do it.
5. After the teacher says "Yes," then you go over to the child.
6. Ask the child what they're doing, or what they're writing, or what they're interested in.
7. Then probably ask them, [not in a mean way, but nicely], "You know, I've heard that you kind of have some trouble in doing..."
8. The child will say, "Yeah, but... I still have some friends."
9. Then you say, "I'm here to help you out with your disability and help you do things like your classmates."
10. Then, say it's time to line up for gym and the child is in a wheelchair, you would say, "I'm going to help you in gym, also. I'll come and help you along with your teacher to play the sport."

YO! THIS IS A NEW PART OF THE PRESENTATION!!

11. If the child has trouble in behavior... approach them not like you're a really sweet person. But more like, "Hey, yo, Dude, What 'ya doin?" so they feel comfortable. Then, if they start acting up, just say, "Calm down, [whatever their name is. Not like "Bad kid," or "Sick Kid,"]
12. Do not say this even with a kind voice—no matter what—to this child: "I know that you're not very good at behavior and you're not well-liked."
13. SURE, SURE. I KNOW YOU WANT TO KNOW WHY? WELL:

First of all, it would seem mean to them. Second of all, it would be like telling them that just because they have a simple disability that they can't be liked. Third of all, it would just probably make them do the same thing.

Figure 7.6 Helping a Child with Disabilities (continued)

14. For a kid who just plays a little too rough, first of all, don't say, "Do you want to play this sport that he DOES like." [Now I know it sounds kinda mean, but the sport he likes he probably plays too rough.] Your first move when you come into the room is to definitely ask the teacher. See if the teacher will give you some information on how to work well with this child. Say, "When you have gym class, I'll probably come and help you out a little bit in case you start getting a little rough. Because the school doesn't want anyone to get hurt." Whatever you do, don't start screaming at the kid. This probably isn't my best advice for the rough-housing kid, Ask the teacher if you want really good information, because mine's probably not right. My advice might not be the best.

15. And if the child is shy, invite him to take a walk with you with his mom or something or a friend. This only works in a city. When you see a pigeon, say, "I'm gonna get that bird." And then run after it. That works because it's funny and it will get the child to laugh. Believe me, I did it to my best friend, and it worked.

16. If the child does not have trouble in behavior but--say--listening, then you would use this approach. Probably try to make the activity a little more fun or humorous. Or a little more exciting, so he or she would want to look at it. Make sure that you get the message but make sure that it is still a little humorous or fun.

Approach #2: You might just tell another student to tell them, "Can you say to this kid, "Hey Buddy! You know how I get all my good grades?" I try to listen my best, so I hear everything the teacher is saying so I get the maximum amount you are supposed to learn."

Whatever you do, don't tell them that just because you can't listen well means that you won't get good grades. Because they might get good grades in one thing but not in another thing.

then discussed their ratings with their teacher. When students monitored their interactions, their social skills showed greater generalization to a setting for which they were not trained. A second study (Kiburz, Miller, & Morrow, 1984) achieved similar results with an eighteen-year-old learning to greet others and initiate conversations in a residential setting.

SUMMARY

This chapter began with remedies for students who lack school survival skills—those behaviors necessary to meet one's academic potential. School survival skills are crucial for students mainstreamed to least restrictive classrooms, and several strategies have proven effective in preparing students for this transition to regular education. Try one of these interventions—after you have determined through careful assessment what skills a student lacks.

This chapter concluded with a focus on the social skill problems of your students. Beginning with checklists to gather global opinions about students' functioning, we moved to the more precise assessments, sociometric measures and direct observations. In addition to measuring a student's one-to-one interactions, consider how well a student functions within a group context. Moreover, you must adapt group activities within the classroom to the individual strengths and weaknesses of the students while challenging them to improve their ability to work with others. The capacity to function within small and large groups is crucial to mainstreaming. Many strategies were highlighted in this chapter, from environmental modifications for young children to social skills curricula for adolescents. In general, the more didactic, curriculum-based approaches are well-suited to students whose limitations are mild to moderate or who have the skills but lack consistency and judgment about when and how to use them. The prompting and reinforcement strategies, conducted by the teacher or by a trained peer, meet the needs of young students or those with more severe disabilities whose social interactions may still be rudimentary.

 CASE STUDY

TEACHING SOCIAL SKILLS[1]

Li-Lin Chen

This week the goals of my social skills program are that students will initiate a conversation, make eye contact, and smile with adults (teachers). In addition, students must get at least five marks on the group contingency according to the agreement between their self-recording charts and the teachers' recording sheet. On Monday students will practice initiating a conversation with an adult or a teacher. On Tuesday they must make eye contact as well as starting a conversation with adults (teachers). On Wednesday they will initiate a conversation with eye contact as well as smile at the adults (teachers). (Naturally, our program continues throughout the year.)

_____
[1]Reprinted with author's permission.

Monday
Homeroom (15 minutes)

00:00–00:05 (Teacher's greeting)

The teacher says, "Good morning everyone! How are you today?"

She lets students feel free and comfortable to talk.

00:06–00:15 (Introduction of today's topic)

The teacher talks about today's topic, starting a conversation with the following questions:

How do you start a conversation?
What do you do when you meet someone?

(continued)

What are some other ways you can start a conversation?

Why is conversation important?

(Students can respond or ask questions if they do not understand. The teacher lists what they say on the blackboard and keeps a list on paper so that she and the students can discuss it next time.)

The teacher talks about the self-recording procedures to the entire class—including when and how to record. The teacher then asks students to start a conversation with any adult (teacher) in math, art, music, English and social skills classes, not including the homeroom period. She hands out paper to every student and explains how to use the self-recording chart by drawing a chart on the board. Then they copy the chart onto their paper. They can place a "Y" mark on their chart if they initiate a conversation with adults (teachers) before, within, or at the end of the classes. The maximum total marks that can be earned for the week is 21. Each needs to write his name, the date, and the topic of the day on his recording chart so that he can learn to be responsible for it and also to remember what he should do for the day. The chart will be like the one in Figure 7.7.

The teacher must tell students the reason why other teachers are joining them to record their behavior by starting a conversation with teachers, in class or out of class, every day. Then they will talk about the group contingency: where it will be placed (public posting in this classroom), how the group contingency will apply in starting a conversation with adults (teachers), and how the entire class or each individual will earn rewards—the teacher lets them recommend rewards and vote for the most popular for the entire class (assuming that they like free time, reading storybooks, and computer games).

THE GROUP CONTINGENCY

When each student has earned five "Y" marks in a week on their self-recording chart (this must agree with the records kept by their teachers), the whole class will have a ten-minute free conversation time in the social skills class the following week. (Where there is disagreement, the teacher clarifies by talking to the student and those teachers.)

A point will be earned for each additional "Y" mark over five "Y" marks.

Each student who accumulates nine points by Friday can choose a favorite storybook to read with a friend during free time or recess time next week.

Each student who accumulates more than ten points by Friday can play a fifteen-minute computer game with a friend during recess or free time next week.

3rd Period (60 minutes)

00:00–00:10 (Review)

The teacher asks how they initiated a conversation with their math teacher. She lets the students respond freely. She asks how they started the conversation. How did they record for themselves? What did they say?

00:11–00:25 (Introduction to starting a conversation with adults)

The teacher mentions the morning's response list and then discusses it in depth. She explains to students what it means to start a conversation and how

Figure 7.7　Self-Recording Chart

Name				
Date				
Purpose				
Math	Social Skills	Music	English	Art

(continued)

they can start a conversation with adults (teachers). Give good examples from the math class. (Remember to make sure that each student understands how to initiate a conversation.)

00:26–00:40 (Demonstration of the skill)

The teacher will ask a student to volunteer to role-play initiating a conversation. For example, the volunteer will act as a bookstore owner and the teacher as a customer. The teacher might say, "Good morning! I am looking for a cookbook. Can you help me?" The teacher will then give each student in the room the opportunity to initiate a conversation.

00:41–00:55 (Role-play of the skill)

The teacher pairs off students and gives them some situations to let them practice with their partners such as in a restaurant, a clothing store, a bookstore, an ice cream store, or a flower shop. After they practice one situation, the teacher asks them how they did and asks one of the pairs to come forward to demonstrate. The teacher then begins a discussion with the class about how their example can be improved. During this discussion the pair can incorporate the improvements into their situation. So as not to embarrass the pair, the discussion should accentuate the postitives as well as pointing out the areas that need improvement. If time allows, each pair should be given the opportunity to demonstrate their role-play situation in front of the class.

00:56–00:60 (Reinforcement)

Ask the students what they remember.
Review the procedures of self-recording.
Remind students of the rewards for the whole class or each individual.

The End of the Day (15 minutes)

00:00–00:15 (homework)

The teacher begins by collecting all of the self-recording charts. (The teacher should also collect the other teachers' charts and make sure that they agree with the students'.) Next, the teacher passes out the homework sheet to each student and explains what they need to do at home (see Figure 7.8). The sheet should be signed by their parent and returned during homeroom period the following morning.

Tuesday
Homeroom (15 minutes)

00:00–00:05 (collecting parents' slips)

The teacher collects the parents' slips from all students, and asks how they did with their assignments and if there are any questions. (Remember to call student's parent if they do not turn in the slip and write down specific student's response.)

00:06–00:15 (Review of self-recording charts)

Under each student's name on the group contingency poster, the teacher writes each student's total marks. The poster should be placed on the wall where everyone can obviously see it. If there is a disagreement about the marks, the teacher arranges time to meet with the student and teachers, encouraging those students who have only a few marks, and praising those who gained many marks. Then the teacher will hand out paper and ask the students to draw their self-recording chart. It should include each student's name, date, and the topic of the day, as defined by the teacher. The teacher announces that they can mark a "Y" when they initiate a conversation with adults (teachers) in math and social skills classes. After the social skills class, they will record a different social behavior according to today's criterion.

3rd Period (60 minutes)

00:00–00:15 (Recording marks in your social skills class and introducing the new social skill)

The teacher marks a "Y" on the recording chart when any student starts a conversation with her. She praises those students who initiate a conversation, especially those ten students with behavioral problems.

Next, the teacher introduces today's behavioral skill—initiating a conversation and also making "eye contact" with adults (teachers) by asking questions or showing examples:

(continued)

Figure 7.8   Homework Sheet

Dear Parents,

Good evening! Thank you for taking the time to read this letter. The purpose of this letter is to ask for your help with your child's homework. The focus of this week at school is emphasis on initiating a conversation while making eye contact, and smiling with adults (teachers). This process has been divided into three steps. The first step is to initiate a conversation with adults (teachers). The second step is not only initiating a conversation but also making eye contact with adults. The third step is initiating a conversation, making eye contact and smiling while talking with adults (teachers). Today please pay attention to and encourage your child to start a converstaion with you when your child wants to watch TV, to have a drink, to ask you to sign this sheet, to ask permission to play with neighbors, etc. On Tuesday, it would be helpful if you could take your child to the library or a bookstore where he or she could practice initiating a conversation while making eye contact with adults. On Wednesday, possibly you could take him or her to a friend's home where your child is able to practice initiating a conversation, making eye contact, and smiling while talking to adults. Please do not hesitate to call me if you have any questions. I will be very glad to hear from you. Have a nice evening! Please remember to detach the answer slip from this homework sheet, sign it, and remind your child to return it to me. Thank you again.

Sincerely,

Carol

08/02/95

- -

I agree to guide my child to finish his or her homework.

Signature _____

Date _____

What do you do when you meet someone? (For example, when you saw your friend in the mall, what did you do? Did you wave your hand or call his or her name?)
What else did you do besides talking?

(continued)

Did you look at your friend or did you
avoid looking at him/her?

After students respond to these questions, the
teacher asks them why they reacted the way they
did and explains why we need eye contact when
talking to people. She also discusses some exceptional situations such as when speaking to people
with different cultural backgrounds.

00:16–00:30 (Demonstration of the
skill)

The teacher tells them about her own story:

I am shy; therefore, I try not to talk to people. One
time, Lillian, one of my best friends, saw me and
called my name, so I had to talk to her. She
made direct eye contact while speaking to me,
which made me very uncomfortable and I felt like
going away. However, I respected her and didn't
want to embarrass her, and because she was so
nice, I was encouraged to look at her while
talking to her. That experience helped me to
make the effort to look at people when I am
talking to them.

The teacher asks for a discussion about her incident with Lillian, asking what they would have
done. The teacher then speaks directly to each
student, making sure to make eye contact. The
class should then discuss each student's reaction
to this and ask the students to describe how it
made each feel.

00:31–00:45 (Role-play)

The teacher should ask for four volunteers or pick
four students for a role-play situation. One will be a
waiter. Three of them will be friends going to have
dinner at the Pizza Hut. The waiter gives them
menus. They need more time to think, so they ask
him to come back later. After he comes back,
everyone takes a turn to order his or her own pizza.
The teacher will then initiate a discussion of the role-
play and ask for feedback from the class.

The teacher asks another four students to come
forward, with one student acting as a children's
bookstore manager and the others as customers.
Each customer will request a book that they want
and buy it. They need to initiate conversations and

make eye contact. Once again, the teacher asks for
a discussion of this role-play situation and asks for
feedback from the class.

The teacher should pair off the students and have
them take turns practicing being a taxi driver or passenger. The taxi driver needs to know where to go,
so his passenger needs to give him the directions.
Both of them should make eye contact during their
conversations. The teacher should try to monitor
each pair and offer help where needed. The pair that
demonstrates the best activity should replay their situation for the whole class. Their peers can give them
feedback and opinions.

00:46–00:60 (Review)

The teacher should ask students to sit in a circle
(the teacher sits with them). Discuss what they
learned in the last 45 minutes. How did they feel
when the teacher asked them to come forward to
role-play? During this time they can ask questions
and express their opinions. The teacher reminds
them that they mark a "Y" only when they initiate a
conversation and make eye contact with the adults
(teachers).

The End of the Day (15 minutes)

00:00–00:15 (Homework)

The teacher collects and checks students' self-
recording charts to see how they are doing in
math, music, English, and art classes (the teacher
should also collect the teachers' recording sheet).
If some students do not earn any mark today, the
teacher encourages them to try again tomorrow.
Explain the next homework assignment. Their
mother or father should take them to a library or
bookstore. Their job is to initiate a conversation
with some of the people who are there, remem-
bering to make eye contact.

Wednesday
Homeroom (15 minutes)

00:00–00:10 (Talking about the homework)

The teacher will begin by asking where students' parents took them and how they initiated a
conversation: "Did you make eye contact? Was it

(continued)

very difficult? Why or why not?" The teacher writes their responses and feelings on the board to keep as a record.

00:11–00:15 (Review of self-recording charts)

The teacher records each students total marks on the group contingency poster under their names, discussing the marks each student earned on Monday and Tuesday. She reminds the students about the class reward and the individual student rewards and the conditions on which they are based. This can encourage those students who have not reached five marks to do better. Next, the teacher hands out paper and asks them to draw their self-recording chart, including name, date, and today's topic (the teacher will announce this to the class). Once again the teacher reminds them to mark a "Y" on their self-recording charts for their math and social skills classes according to yesterday's criterion (starting a conversation and making eye contact with adults (teachers). After the social skills class, the self-recording chart will be based on today's criterion.

3rd Period (60 minutes)

00:00–00:15 (Recording marks in your class and introducing the new social skill)

The teacher will mark a "Y" on her recording sheet when any student starts a conversation as well as makes eye contact. She praises those students verbally. Then, the teacher introduces today's social behavior: initiating a conversation, making eye contact, and adding a "smile." She gets them started by beginning the discussion as follows:

Do you remember the role-play situation yesterday which included three friends and a waiter at the Pizza Hut? (If they do not remember, ask one volunteer student to describe it.) *If the waiter had said "Good evening" without smiling, how would that make you feel?* (Let students discuss this question.) *Then, if one of the three friends ordered pizza without a smile, how would the waiter respond? Would he smile in return? Why or why not?*

These discussions among the students help them to discover how important it is to smile and make eye contact when talking to someone.

00:16–00:30 (Demonstration of the skill)

The teacher walks around the classroom and chooses students randomly, asking "How are you?", making sure to smile and make eye contact. Then the teacher asks how this made them feel and begins a discussion with the students.

00:31–00:45 (Role-play)

The teacher groups students in pairs and gives them some situations from which to choose to practice with their partners (a shoe store, a candy store, a movie theater, etc.). The teacher asks them to pay much attention to their smile when their partners start a conversation and to be sure to make eye contact with each other. If their peers do not smile while practicing, their partners should correct them right away and practice it again. (During their role-play, the teacher needs to observe their role-play and choose one of the pairs to demonstrate for the entire class.) If time permits, the teacher can invite other pairs to come forward.

00:46–00:60 (Review)

The teacher begins a discussion by asking: "Do you like it when someone talks to you with a smile on their face? Why or why not? Can anybody tell me what social skills we learned this week?" (The teacher may need to give them some hints.) Next, the teacher looks at the group contingency and encourages their efforts, reminding them of the class reward and individual rewards to provoke them to practice the social skills they have learned.

The End of the Day (15 minutes)

00:00–00:15 (Homework)

The teacher collects and checks students' self-recording charts to see how they are doing in other classes. If any students did not receive marks since Tuesday, she arranges a time to meet with those students privately. She discusses their previous homework assignments and encourages them to practice their skills initiating conversations, making eye contact, and smiling while making conversation.

DISCUSSION QUESTIONS

1. What are the most important school survival skills for mainstreamed students?
2. How can you assess school survival skills?
3. What are five ways you can increase the opportunities for your students' skills to generalize to other, less restrictive settings?
4. What environmental modifications can assist a student who is overly dependent on the teacher?
5. What is the most effective way of using self-instruction as an intervention for on-task behavior?
6. What are the dos and don'ts of social skills interventions? Discuss them.
7. Why is there such emphasis on peer-mediated interventions?
8. What does research suggest about environmental modifications for improving social skills?
9. Will peer tutoring lead to improved social skills? Why or why not?
10. What are the essential components of a social skills intervention? Illustrate them.

REFERENCES

Anesko, K. M., Schoiock, G., Ramirez, R., & Levine, F. M. (1987). The Homework Problem Checklist: Assessing children's homework difficulties. *Behavioral Assessment, 9,* 179–185.

Bahr, M. W., Fuchs, D., Fuchs, L. S., Fernstrom, P., Stecker, P. M. (1993). Effectiveness of student versus teacher monitoring during prereferral intervention. *Exceptionality, 4*(1), 17–30.

Bryant, L. E., & Budd, K. S. (1984). Teaching behaviorally handicapped preschool children to share. *Journal of Applied Behavior Analysis, 17*(1), 45–56.

Cartledge, G., & Milburn, J. (1983). Social skills assessment and teaching in the schools. In T. R. Kratochwill (Ed.), *Advances in School Psychology* (Vol. 3, pp. 175–236). Hillsdale, NJ: Lawrence Erlbaum Associates.

Cook, S., Scruggs, T. E., Mastropieri, M. A., & Casto, G. W. (in press). Handicapped students as tutors. *Journal of Special Education.*

Cooke, S. A., Cooke, T. P., & Apolloni, T. (1978). Developing nonretarded toddlers as verbal models for retarded classmates. *Child Study Journal, 8,* 1–8.

Cooper, H. M. (1989). *Homework.* White Plains, NY: Longman.

DeBoer, A. L., & Fister, S. (1995).Strategies & Tools for Collaborative Teaching. Longmont, CO: Sopris West.

DiGangi, S. A., Maag, J. W., & Rutherford, R. B. (1991). Self-graphing of on-task behavior: Enhancing the reactive effects of self-monitoring on on-task behavior and academic performance. *Learning Disability Quarterly, 14*(3), 221–230.

Epstein, M. H., Polloway, E. A., Foley, R. M., & Patton, J. R. (1993). Homework: A comparison of teachers' and parents' perceptions of the problems experienced by students identified as having behavioral disorders, learning disabilities, or no disabilities. *Remedial & Special Education, 14*(5), 40–50.

Fowler, S. A. (1986). Peer-monitoring and self-monitoring: Alternatives to traditional teacher management. *Journal for Exceptional Children, 52*(6), 573–581.

Franca, V. M. (1983). *Peer tutoring among behaviorally disordered students: Academic and social benefits to tutor and tutee.* Unpublished doctoral dissertation, George Peabody College of Vanderbilt University.

Fuchs, D., Fuchs, L. S., Reeder, P., Bahr, M. W., & Moore, P. (1989). *Mainstream assistance teams: A handbook on prereferral intervention.* Nashville, TN: Vanderbilt University.

Fuchs, L. S., Fuchs, D., Bentz, J., Phillips, N. B., & Hamlett, C. L. (1994). The nature of student interactions during peer tutoring with and without prior training and experience. *American Educational Research Journal, 31*(1), 75–103.

Fuchs, L. S., Fuchs, D., & Phillips, N. (1994). The relation between teacher's beliefs about the importance of good student work habits, teacher planning, and student achievement. *Elementary School Journal, 94*(3), 331–345.

Glomb, N., & West, R. P. (1990). Teaching behaviorally disordered adolescents to use self-management skills for improving the completeness, accuracy, and neatness or creative writing homework assignments. *Behavioral Disorders, 15*(4), 233–242.

Greenwood, C. R., Delquadri, J., & Bulgren, J. (1993). Current challenges to behavioral technology in the reform of schooling: Large-scale, high-quality implementation and sustained use of effective educational practices. *Education & Treatment of Children, 16*(4), 401–440.

Greenwood, C. R., Delquadri, J., & Carta, J. J. (1988). *Class wide peer tutoring.* Delray Beach, FL: Educational Achievement Systems.

Gresham, F. M., & Cavell, T. A. (1986). Assessing adolescent social skills. In R. G. Harrington (Ed.), *Testing adolescents* (pp. 93–123). Kansas City, MO: Test Corporation of America.

Hertz, V., McLaughlin, T. F. (1990). Self-recording effects for on-task behavior of mildly handicapped adolescents. *Child & Family Behavior Therapy, 12*(3), 1–11.

Hollinger, J. D. (1987). Social skills for behaviorally disordered children as preparation for mainstreaming: Theory, practice, and new directions. *Recent Advances in Special Education, 8*(4), 17–27.

Jackson, N. F., Jackson, D. A., & Monroe, C. (1983). *Getting along with others: Teaching social effectiveness to children.* Champaign, IL: Research Press.

James, S. D., & Egel, A. L. (1986). A direct prompting strategy for increasing reciprocal interactions between handicapped and nonhandicapped siblings. *Journal of Applied Behavior Analysis, 19*(2), 173–186.

Johnson, D. W., & Johnson, R. T. (1984). Classroom learning structure and attitudes toward handicapped students in mainstream settings: A theoretical model and research evidence. In R. L. Jones (Ed.), *Attitudes and attitude change in special education: Theory and practice* (pp. 118–142). Reston, VA: Council for Exceptional Children.

Kastelen, L., Nickel, M., & McLaughlin, T. F. (1984). A performance feedback system: Generalization of effects across tasks and time with eighth-grade English students. *Education and Treatment of Children, 1,* 141–155.

Kauffman, J. M. (1989). *Characteristics of children's behavior disorders* (3rd ed.). Upper Saddle River, NJ: Merrill/Prentice Hall.

Kelly, W. J., Salzberg, C. L., Levy, S. M., Warrenfeltz, R. B., Adams, T. W., Crouse, T. R., & Beegle, G. P. (1983). The effects of role-playing and self-monitoring on the generalization of vocational social skills by behaviorally disordered adolescents. *Behavioral Disorders, 9*(1), 27–35.

Kerr, M. M., & Zigmond, N. (1984). *School survival skills: Grant report for year three.* Unpublished document, University of Pittsburgh.

Kerr, M. M., Zigmond, N., Schaeffer, A. L., & Brown, G. (1986). An observational followup study of successful and unsuccessful high school students. *High School Journal, 71,* 20–32.

Kiburz, C. S., Miller, S. R., & Morrow, L. W. (1984). Structured learning using self-monitoring to promote maintenance and generalization of social skills across settings for a behaviorally disordered adolescent. *Behavioral Disorders, 10*(1), 47–55.

Maher, C. A. (1982). Behavioral effects of using conduct problem adolescents as crossage tutors. *Psychology in the Schools, 19,* 360–364.

Mathes, P. G., & Fuchs, L. S. (1994). The efficacy of peer tutoring in reading for students with mild disabilities: A best-evidence synthesis. *School Psychology Review, 23*(1), 59–80.

Mathur, S. R., & Rutherford, R. B. (1994). Teaching conversational social skills to delinquent youth. *Behavioral Disorders, 19*(4), 294–305.

McConnell, S. R., Strain, P. S., Kerr, M. M., Stagg, V., Lenkner, D. A., & Lambert, D. L. (1984). An empirical definition of school adjustment: Selection of target behaviors for a comprehensive treatment program. *Behavior Modification, 8,* 451–473.

Oden, S. (1980). A child's social isolation: Origins, prevention, intervention. In G. Cartledge & J. F. Milburn (Eds.), *Teaching social skills to children: Innovative approaches* (179–202). New York: Pergamon Press.

Oden, S., & Asher, S. R. (1977). Coaching children in social skills for friendship making. *Child Development, 48,* 495–506.

Odom, S. L., & Phillip S. (1984). Classroom-based social skills instruction for severely handicapped preschool children. *Topics in Early Childhood Education, 4*(3), 97–116.

Patrick, B. C., Skinner, E. A., & Connell, J. P. (1993). What motivates children's behavior and emotion? Joint effects of perceived control and autonomy in the academic domain. *Journal of Personality and Social Psychology, 65*(4), 781–791.

Peterson, C. A., & McConnell, S. R. (1993). Factors affecting the impact of social interaction skills interventions in early childhood special education. *Topics in Early Childhood Special Education, 13,* 38–56.

Ragland, E. U., Kerr, M. M., & Strain, P. S. (1978). Effects of social initiations on the behavior of withdrawn autistic children. *Topics in Early Childhood Special Education, 13,* 565–578.

Rosenberg, M. S. (1989). The effects of daily homework assignments on the acquisition of basic skills by students with learning disabilities. *Journal of Learning Disabilities, 22,* 314–323.

Roderique, T. W., Polloway, E. A., Cumblad, C., Epstein, M. H., & Bursuck, W. D. (1994). Homework: A survey of policies in the United States. *Journal of Learning Disabilities, 27*(8), 481–487.

Sabatos, M.A. (1986). *Private cues in self-monitoring: Effects on learning-disabled students' on-task performance and reading productivity during sustained silent reading.* Unpublished doctoral dissertation, University of Pittsburgh.

Sainato, D. M. (1990). Classroom transitions: Organizing environments to promote independent performance in preschool children with disabilities. *Education & Treatment of Children 13*(4), 288–297.

Sainato, D. M., Maheady, L., & Shook, G. L. (1986). The effects of a classroom manager role on the social interaction patterns and social status of withdrawn kindergarten students. *Journal of Applied Behavior Analysis, 19*(2), 187–195.

Sainato, D. M., Strain, P. S., Lefebvre, D., Rapp, N. (1987). Facilitating transition times with handicapped preschool children: A comparison between peer-mediated and antecedent prompt procedures. *Journal of Applied Behavior Analysis, 20* (3), 285–291.

Schoen, S. F. (1986). Decreasing noncompliance in the severely multihandicapped child. *Psychology in the Schools, 23*(1), 88–94.

Schumaker, J. B., & Ellis, E. (1982). Social skills training of LD adolescents: A generalization study. *Learning Disability Quarterly, 5,* 409–414.

Scruggs, T. E., Mastropieri, M. A., & Richter, L. (1985). Peer tutoring with behaviorally disordered students social and academic benefits. *Behavioral Disorders, 11*(1), 283–294.

Scruggs, T. E., Mastropieri, M., Veit, D T., & Osguthorpe, R. T. (1986). Behaviorally disordered students as tutors: Effects on social behavior. *Behavioral Disorders, 12*(1), 36–44.

Shisler, L., Osguthorpe, R. T., & Eiserman, W. (1987). The effects of reverse-role tutoring on the social acceptance of students with behavioral disorders. *Behavioral Disorders, 13*(1), 35–44.

Skinner, E. A., Wellborn, J. G., & Connell, J. P. (1990). What it takes to do well in school and whether I've got it: A process model of perceived control and children's engagement in school. *Journal of Educational Psychology, 82*(1), 22–32.

Smith, B. M., Schumaker, J. B., Schaefer, J., & Sherman, J. A. (1982). Increasing participation and improving the quality of discussions in seventh-grade social studies class. *Journal of Applied Behavior Analysis, 15,* 97–110.

Speigel-McGill, P., Bambara, L. M., Shores, R. E., & Fox, J. J. (1984). The effects of proximity on socially oriented behaviors of severely multiply-handicapped children. *Education and Treatment of Children, 7*(4), 365–378.

Strain, P. S. (1981). *The utilization of classroom peers as behavior change agents.* New York: Plenum Press.

Strain, P. S., Kerr, M. M., & Ragland, E. U. (1979). Effects of peer mediated social initiations and prompting/reinforcement procedures on the social behavior of autistic children. *Journal of Autism and Developmental Disabilities, 9,* 41–54.

Strain, P. S., Odom, S. L., & McConnell, S. (1984). Promoting social reciprocity of exceptional children: Identification, target behavior selection, and intervention. *Remedial and Special Education, 5,* 21–28.

Strain, P. S., Shores, R. E., & Timm, M. A. (1977). Effects of peer initiations on the social behavior of withdrawn preschool children. *Journal of Applied Behavior Analysis, 10,* 289–298.

Tabacek, D. A., McLaughlin, T. F., & Howard, V. F. (1994). *Teaching preschool children with disabilities tutoring skills: Effects on preacademic behaviors. Child & Family Behavior Therapy, 16*(2), 43–63.

Walker, H. M., & Rankin, R. (1983). Assessing the behavioral expectations and demands of less restrictive settings. *School Psychology Review, 12,* 274–284.

Wolfe, V. V., Boyd, L. A., & Wolfe, D. A. (1983). Teaching cooperative play to behavior-problem preschool children. *Education and Treatment of Children, 6*(1), 1–9.

Wurtele, S. K., & Drabman, R. S. (1984). "Beat the Buzzer" for classroom dawdling: A one-year trial. *Behavior Therapy, 15,* 403–409.

Young, C. C., & Kerr, M. M. (1979). The effects of a retarded child's social initiations on the behavior of severely retarded school-aged peers. *Education and Training of the Mentally Retarded, 14,* 185–190.

Zigmond, N., Kerr, M. M., Schaeffer, A. L., Brown, G. M., & Farra, H. E. (1986). *School survival skills curriculum* (limited published circulation). Available from Department of Special Education, 5M30 Forbes Quadrangle, 230 Bouquet Street, University of Pittsburgh, Pittsburgh, PA 15260.

AGGRESSIVE BEHAVIORS

OUTLINE

OBJECTIVES

After completing this chapter, you should be able to

◆ Offer four reasons students engage in antisocial behavior.
◆ Conduct a functional analysis of aggressive behavior.
◆ Name four ways to create a safe school environment.
◆ Identify alternatives to verbal confrontations with students.
◆ Implement three interventions for teaching prosocial behavior.

As you begin this chapter, consider these sobering facts from the Children's Defense Fund (1995):

◆ Every two days, guns kill the equivalent of a classroom full of American children.
◆ The average child witnesses 8,000 simulated murders and 100,000 other acts of violence on television before reaching the seventh grade.
◆ Homicide is now the third leading cause of death of children ages 5 to 14. Every five minutes a child is arrested for a violent crime.

School violence hurts students as well as their teachers. This chapter will offer suggestions on how you can help students whose primary behavioral problem is aggression, one form of **antisocial behavior** (Walker, Colvin, & Ramsey, 1995).

The interventions here may prevent these students from becoming antisocial adults, but only if you identify them and intervene early. Consider these facts:

◆ Antisocial behavior early in a child's school career is the single best predictor of delinquency in adolescence.
◆ Antisocial behavior that is not changed by the end of third grade should be treated as a chronic condition. . . . That is, it cannot be cured but can be managed with the appropriate supports and continuing interventions.
◆ Early intervention in home, school, and community is the single best hope we have of diverting children from this path. (Walker et al., 1995, p. 6)

DEFINING AND IDENTIFYING ANTISOCIAL BEHAVIOR

Students with antisocial behaviors often come to the attention of their teachers without formal assessments. Their behaviors are illustrated in Table 8.1.

To identify students at risk for developing antisocial behaviors, however, you may use a screening instrument. The Systematic Screening for Behavior Disorders (SSBD) (Walker & Severson, 1990) is a multistep approach, beginning with teacher nomination. If students are identified through the nomination process, their teacher then completes two brief rating scales. Observations supply additional information on those students whose scores suggest that they need intervention.

Documenting Aggressive Behavior

Some of the direct observational and interview strategies you learned in earlier chapters will help you document aggressive behavior. One tool you can use is Antecedent-Response-Consequence (ARC) Analysis. We begin with this assessment and continue with functional explanations for aggression, which the ARC may uncover. Because many aggressive acts take

Table 8.1   Illustrations of Antisocial Behavior

Pushing Shoving Spitting	Kicking Hitting	Defacing property Stealing	Performing physical, demeaning and humiliating acts that are not bodily harmful (e.g., de-panting) Locking in a closet or confined space	Using physical violence against family or friends	Threatening with a weapon Inflicting bodily harm
Gossiping Embarrassing someone	Setting up to look foolish Spreading rumors	Making ethnic slurs Setting up to take the blame	Publicly humiliating (i.e., revealing personal information) Excluding from group Rejecting socially	Maliciously excluding Manipulating social order to achieve rejection Participating in malicious rumor-mongering	Threatening with total isolation by peer group
Mocking Name-Calling Making dirty looks Taunting	Teasing about clothing or possessions	Teasing about appearance	Intimidating phone calls	Verbally threatening aggression against property or possessions	Using verbal threats of violence or of inflicting bodily harm
Threatening to reveal personal information Drawing graffiti Making public challenge to do something	Defacing property or clothing Playing a dirty trick	Taking possessions (lunch, clothing, toys)	Using extortion	Threatening to use coercion against family or friends	Using coercion Threatening with a weapon

Source: Reprinted with permission from Garrity, C., Jens, K., Porter, W., Sager, N., & Short-Camilli, C. (1996). Bully-proofing your school: A comprehensive approach. *Reclaiming Children & Youth: Journal of Emotional and Behavioral Problems, 5*, 35–39.

place suddenly and without warning, you can't really plan to observe and record systematically as you do with other behaviors. To circumvent this problem, we have an "after the fact" ARC checklist for recalling aggressive incidents. To begin, describe the aggressive or destructive behavior in the far left column, using as many specific terms as possible. Second, write the date and time period of the aggressive incident, if known. Next, identify the location and all other participants or observers. State whether the aggressive behavior was directed toward property and/or persons and identify any personal injury or property damage. Then describe as accurately as possible what happened before and after the aggressive behavior. Note whether you directly observed the behavior or received the report of it. Finally, add any comments helpful in predicting future aggression. Those involved should complete this form independently; they may have a tendency to "color" each other's account of what actually took place. Remember, you need an objective retelling of the situation. Try to capture each person's recollection soon after each incident. By comparing facts and independent impressions, you may form useful hypotheses about the antecedents ("triggers") to a student's aggressive behavior. For example, you may notice that a student is aggressive only toward younger students or only during unsupervised transition activities. The form may also reveal that aggressive behaviors are inadvertently reinforced by others. For example, a student cursed aloud to his easily embarrassed teacher because it resulted in expulsion from History, his most difficult subject. Can you detect any clues in Figure 8.1 that might explain Helen's actions?

Use the after-the-fact Antecedent Response Consequence Form to detect patterns in the aggression so that you and others can "see it coming" in the future. To predict aggression, it helps to have a good grasp of why aggression happens. What causes a student to act out? How do you make sense of the documentation on aggressive behaviors?

What We Know About Antisocial Behavior

Let us begin with a brief overview of research on antisocial behaviors.

Community conditions contributing to violence are those in which the social organizations (family and community standards) disintegrate and youth are not bonded to conventional norms. Although these tend to be low income areas, it is the lack of social organization and not poverty per se that contribute to violence. Low-income neighborhoods with strong social structures do not have the same level of crime. Socially isolated families with few resources and alternative activities for children are prone to produce violent youth.

Problem behaviors tend to cluster and it is uncommon for a child to engage in only one type of antisocial behavior. Violence is often associated with drug use, drug dealing, gang involvement, or absenteeism. The most powerful way of dealing with risk groups is to assess the combination of risk factors. No single factor is individually an overwhelming influence on violence.

Normal transitions (home to kindergarten or elementary school to middle school) are points when children are at greater risk of disruptive behavior and make excellent points for intervention.

Aggressive behavior in elementary school and lack of parental supervision in early adolescence are powerful predictors of subsequent criminal behavior. Youth who are involved in violence are likely to have witnessed it early in their lives.

Aggressive youths often misjudge or misinterpret others' behaviors as threatening and are prone to strike back. Feeling threatened also leads to the possession of weapons for self-protection. The use of weaponry increases the incidence of violence for youth who are not generally antisocial by nature.

Exposure to violence, in their homes and neighborhoods, can lead to symptoms similar to post-traumatic stress syndrome, like those seen in children raised in war zones.

Figure 8.1 Checklist for Assessing Aggressive Behaviors

Directions: Complete this checklist for each aggressive behavior the student has exhibited.

Person Completing Form _Mrs. Blouze_   Student _Helen A._   Date _Nov. 6_

Describe the behavior	When did this behavior most recently occur?	Where did this behavior take place?	Who else was in the setting?	Was the aggression directed towards anyone or towards property? Whom? What?	What was going on immediately (15 min.) before the aggressive behavior?	What happened immediately (15 min.) after the aggressive behavior?	Did you directly observe the behavior?	Comments: (Describe anything that was unusual about the schedule, setting, or student when the event took place, or anything you think would be helpful to consider.)
Came into room, threw book on desk, refused to open it. Threw book on floor. "Sassed" me. Refused to leave. Resisted, was verbally abusive, then hit me.	Yesterday	Regular Reading Class	Other Students (entire class)	More towards teacher	Was in art and came down the hall to reading class.	I told her again to open that book. Told her to pick it up. Told her to leave room. Took her hand to lead her. Buzzed the principal's office.	Yes	She seems to come to class already mad or upset.

Violence is not only a problem behavior of children and adults but an adaption to a violent environment. Understanding the way in which young people view this world and learn to relate to one another has a powerful effect on developing strategies to reduce violence. (Mulvey, 1993, pp. 8–9)

Now let us turn to explanations for an individual's antisocial behavior. First, the aggressive behavior may be under inappropriate stimulus control. A preschooler who has just discovered the joy of rough-and-tumble play may play roughly with all playmates, willing or not. A seventh grader taught to defend himself on the street deals the same way with his teachers.

A related problem has been described as attributional bias (Mulvey, 1993). A teenager may misinterpret or misread events involving the behaviors of others and react defensively, assuming that they are out to get her. Another explanation that follows a **social learning theory** approach is that the student's behavior has been, and continues to be, reinforced. Reinforcement may take many forms. For example, students may act tough because they are reinforced by the way other people react to them. By creating a crisis, these students stop all routines, gain abundant attention from peers, and scare, embarrass, or immobilize adults in authority. For example, throwing work materials or swearing at the teacher may give a student a way out of a difficult lesson; avoidance of the unpleasant work is the student's reinforcer.

Another explanation is that aggression communicates a student's wishes (Donnellan, Mirenda, Mesaros, and Fassbender, 1984). For example, students may use aggression to request attention, interaction, or an item; protest, refuse, or stop an activity; or express themselves.

To consider another explanation, aggressive behavior may be learned behavior, particularly if a student lives in a violent family, community, or culture. Studies have reported that over three-fourths of children surveyed had seen at least one act of violence (Mulvey, Arthur, & Reppucci, 1993). Much of this violence occurred at home and was witnessed by children in the primary grades. Teens involved in violence are more likely to have witnessed and experienced violence than their nonviolent peers. Sadly, many children rely on antisocial behaviors to survive victimization by others.

Explained yet another way, antisocial behavior may be caused by a social skills deficit. Many student simply lack the skills to manage difficult interpersonal situations. For example, a student may not know how to express a complaint without resorting to anger and profanity. A student who has never seen adults disagree peaceably cannot be expected to resolve conflicts effectively.

Finally, a teacher may inadvertently provoke a student to react aggressively. (For an interesting discussion of how teachers can address their own reactions to aggression, see pages 333–334 of *Conflict in the Classroom* by N. J. Long and W. C. Morse PRO-ED, 1996.) You will learn how to prevent volatile situations in the next section.

PREVENTION STRATEGIES

The best time to deal with aggressive behaviors is *before*, not after, the aggression takes place. Restraining a student who has already attacked a teacher is a last resort and does nothing to teach alternative behaviors or prevent future violence. How can you avoid unnecessary confrontations with your students? Here are a few ideas.

1. *"Misbehavior or Mother Nature?"*   The misbehavior may be part of a normal developmental phase. All adolescents sometimes feel the need to prove their increasing autonomy and individuality. Some of these ways are not much fun for adults! For example, teenagers often engage in verbal confrontations to prove that they can "win" with an adult. Adults may be caught off-guard and participate in these confrontations, making matters worse for everyone. As teenagers struggle to develop their own identities, they often reject adults' characteristics. This rejection may take the form of teasing adults. For example, we have had students say to us, "Did you really want your hair to look like that?" or "Haven't you gained an awful lot of weight since last semester?" Here is one of our favorites: "Is your mother still picking out your clothes for you, teacher?" Although you may not condone all expressions of a teenager's autonomy, you may feel better if you keep this behavior in its developmental context. One way to respond to teasing is to poke fun at yourself whenever possible. This lessens the tension and models a healthy sense of humor.

2. *"Pick your battles."*   An experienced middle school teacher once advised us, "You've already been a teenager. It's their turn!" Many confrontations are not worth the effort of winning; calmly turn down the invitation to do battle. When you let students win on inconsequential issues, you avoid major power struggles.

3. *"Later!"*   Suggest a later, private conference to the student who tries to create a public scene. Often the passage of time will reduce the student's vehemence. An absent-minded teenager may forget what was bothering him in the first place!

4. *"The last word can be lethal."*   Avoid needing the last word. As one principal said, "Teenagers need the last word a lot more than I do!" Many teacher assaults are the result of an adult's insistence on

getting the last word, rather than letting the student leave the interaction mumbling something under her breath. Statements such as, "I heard what you said! Now come back here and apologize!", can worsen an already tense situation. If a student is still really angry, you cannot have a rational conversation. Take time to talk about the issues later.

5. "Is anybody listening to me?" Listen! Students often tell us that this is really what they want. By listening to the student's complaint (just as a well-trained customer service representative would listen to your problems with a service or product), you may reduce the student's hostility and negotiate a good conclusion. Listening usually reduces the tension and lowers the emotional "thermostat."

6. "Sarcasm isn't funny." Sarcasm escalates tension. Adolescents are very sensitive to the subtleties of communications, and your well-intended wit may escalate a tense situation if misunderstood.

7. "Save face." Saving face is important to all of us. Embarrassing or humiliating a student never helps and could get you hurt. In fact, research by the Gun Safety Institute has shown that youth who are prone to carry guns believe that shame can only be undone through aggression (Clough, personal communication, February 25, 1993). For example, youth more likely to carry guns endorsed these beliefs: "If someone insults me or my family, it really bothers me, but if I beat them up, that makes me feel better." "If someone disrespects me, I have to fight them to get my pride back." "A kid who doesn't get even with someone who makes fun of him is a sucker." (Meador, 1992, p. 31)

8. "Don't sweat the small stuff." Ignore minor rule infractions when you think you can:

"Juan, sit down and open your book, please."
[No response.]
"Sarah, you're ready; why don't you get us started?"

9. "Set limits, but avoid ultimatums." Offer the student a choice, or an out whenever possible. The following conversations illustrate this idea. *Ultimatum:* "Janice, you either get to civics class right now or go to the office. This is no time for a

personal conversation!" *Setting limits, with two options:* "Janice, it's time for sixth period. If you can't stop your conversation with your friend now and move on to class, you will need to spend some of the afternoon break making up your work. The choice is up to you."

10. "Take charge of yourself." Stay in control of your own emotions. Irritable, overreactive teachers will experience repeated, unsuccessful confrontations. Students can always tell which teachers they can "set off." If you are angry, then take some time, cool off, and collect your thoughts. Not all challenges need an immediate response.

Studies have shown that teachers under stress become irritable, tired, bored, and even depressed. Here are some guidelines for managing the stress of teaching:

1. Maintain a balanced life-style, with plenty of fun activities and interests.
2. Set goals and manage your time so that you meet them.
3. Develop a social support network of positive individuals, some of whom are outside of your workplace.
4. Attitude is everything. . . . Pick a good one! Your attitude is under your control, even when everything else seems unpredictable.
5. Continue to learn and develop professionally. (Luckner, 1996)

Joining your colleagues in a team effort to make your school safe is also helpful in reducing your personal stress and vulnerability. In the next section we address strategies that involve the entire school.

SCHOOL-WIDE STRATEGIES

To convey a clear set of norms, we must ensure that all acts of aggression are treated similarly. Use the school-wide disciplinary practices described in the previous chapter to establish uniform and consistent policies for serious behaviors. Also, keep in mind these principles for maintaining a safe school:

◆ *Supervision and surveillance.* All adults in the school setting must take part in supervising the campus. Being alert and aware of your surroundings is a basic principle for personal safety. This includes greeting those whom you pass in the corridors; taking your part in supervising change of classes, outdoor play, and dismissals; reporting strangers promptly to the office; calling students by name when you see them; and frequently checking restrooms and out-of-the-way areas of the school. Some districts use video cameras on school buses to monitor behavior or video cameras at school entrances to verify the identify of visitors.

◆ *Intelligence and information.* A safe school is one in which students trust their faculty and staff and provide them with information or intelligence. As a leading school security expert says, "Information is the key to control." (Blauvelt, 1981) Students will generally report their suspicions of impending problems, if they have a sense of ownership in their school and "connectedness" to the adults working with them. This climate cannot exist when adults are unwilling to share authority with or listen to students. To increase your personal safety, avoid sarcasm, humiliation, and embarrassment tactics. (For additional information on school security, read *Effective Strategies for School Security* [Blauvelt, 1981] available from the National Association of Secondary School Principals.)

Architectural Design

Altering physical aspects of the school or classroom might not eliminate antisocial behavior but it may prevent some problems. Crime Prevention Through Environmental Design (CPTED) may interest those of you in districts considering new construction or remodeling older sites. Examples of how the architectural design may affect school crime are shown in Figures 8.2 and 8.3.

Metal Detectors and Searches

Metal detectors serve as a deterrent to those who would otherwise bring weapons to school or to school events. They are most effective when used on a random, unannounced basis or during specific high-tension situations. Prior to using metal detectors or conducting searches, check with your school district's legal department for the relevant laws and regulations in your area. Locker searches are one way to reduce the number of lethal weapons brought onto school campuses. Be sure that your school has issued prior, legally correct notices to students and their parents that their lockers may be searched and under what conditions the searches will take place. (Some districts have removed their lockers altogether or set up check rooms for coats.) Unintrusive spot checks are easier when districts require "see through" bookbags, now available in many retail stores.

Uniforms and Dress Codes

Many schools now encourage or require students to wear uniforms to eliminate the opportunity for gang members to show their gang colors or insignia, and to lessen competition over popular-label clothes and shoes. There is some evidence that dress codes are effective, especially when students participate in developing the guidelines (Mulvey et al., 1993). Dress codes differ from uniform requirements in that they spell out guidelines for the types of clothing and accessories allowed without prescribing specific garments. Some schools adopt both a dress code and an optional uniform policy so that students may choose whether to wear uniforms or not.

Silent Complaint Procedures

Silent complaint procedures allow students, staff, and families an anonymous way to report their concerns to school and law enforcement officials. Find out if your local law enforcement officials use a silent complaint form that you can adapt for school use. Distribute the form periodically to staff, students, and parents. You may want to use an open-ended format that asks such questions as, "Where in school do you not feel safe or comfortable?" Some districts have adopted an anonymous, toll-free, weapons report hotline (National School Safety Center, 1993). Check to see if your community has a hotline. (For additional ideas about how to assess the safety of your school campus see the *School Safety Checkbook* (1993) published by the National School Safety Center.

Controlling Environmental Factors That Contribute to Vandalism

In an attempt to understand some of the factors leading to school vandalism, Mayer, Nafpaktitis,

Butterworth, and Hollingsworth (1987) collected data in 28 schools. They found that a punitive school environment was a major factor in promoting vandalism. This finding confirmed earlier research showing that poor scholastic achievement was related to acts of vandalism (Gold & Mann, 1982). Mayer and his colleagues made three suggestions for altering the school environment, thereby reducing vandalism: make the school environment

Figure 8.2   Example of Architectural Design

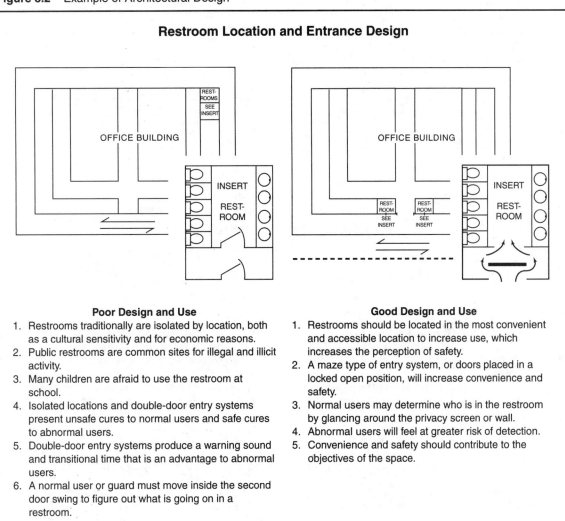

Restroom Location and Entrance Design

Poor Design and Use

1. Restrooms traditionally are isolated by location, both as a cultural sensitivity and for economic reasons.
2. Public restrooms are common sites for illegal and illicit activity.
3. Many children are afraid to use the restroom at school.
4. Isolated locations and double-door entry systems present unsafe cures to normal users and safe cures to abnormal users.
5. Double-door entry systems produce a warning sound and transitional time that is an advantage to abnormal users.
6. A normal user or guard must move inside the second door swing to figure out what is going on in a restroom.

Good Design and Use

1. Restrooms should be located in the most convenient and accessible location to increase use, which increases the perception of safety.
2. A maze type of entry system, or doors placed in a locked open position, will increase convenience and safety.
3. Normal users may determine who is in the restroom by glancing around the privacy screen or wall.
4. Abnormal users will feel at greater risk of detection.
5. Convenience and safety should contribute to the objectives of the space.

Source: Reprinted with permission from Crowe, T. D. (1990). Designing safer schools. *School Safety, Fall,* 9–13.

reinforcing and individualized for students, reduce the misuse of behavioral interventions, and substitute positive behavioral management approaches for the more punishing interventions.

Graffiti serves as a communication display for youth, especially for gangs, so its prompt removal is vital to school safety. First, photograph the graffiti to share with law enforcement officials, then paint it over immediately with graffiti-resistant paint. (For information about what graffiti means and how to remove it, contact The Graffiti

Information Network, P.O. Box 400, Hurricane, UT 84737, 801-635-0646.)

ENVIRONMENTALLY MEDIATED STRATEGIES

Stimulus Control

Rosen and Rosen (1983) designed a clever environmental modification for a first grader who stole from other students. To modify the behavior, the teachers marked all of the target child's possessions

Figure 8.3 Example of Architectural Design

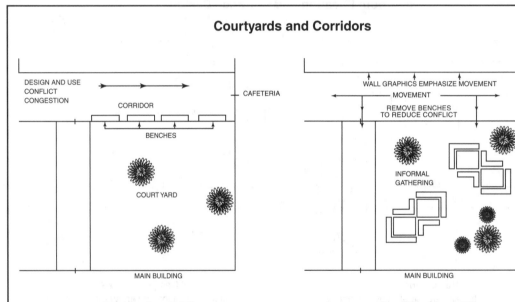

Courtyards and Corridors

Poor Design and Use

1. Many site planners or users of space fail to adequately define the intended purpose and uses of courtyards.
2. Corridor and courtyard confusion is exacerbated by placing benches and other furnishings along corridors.
3. Corridor and courtyard conflict often leads to congestion, noise, and personal conflict.
4. Groups of students or others often will colonize, or preempt, spaces, which creates further conflict and fear.
5. Normal users will avoid these areas. Abnormal users feel safer and at low risk of detection of intervention.

Good Design and Use

1. The intended purpose and use of courtyards and adjoining corridors are clearly defined in policy and in physical design.
2. Furnishings for courtyards that are intended for gathering behavior may be designed to break up group size or to provide only minimal comfort to shorten the staying time.
3. Portable rather than permanent amenities may be more effective, depending on intended use patterns. Accordingly, physical support is provided only when the specific behavior is desired.
4. Normal users will feel safer moving through these areas, while abnormal users will find it difficult to preempt these spaces.

Source: Reprinted with permission from Crowe, T. D. (1990). Designing safer schools. *School Safety, Fall,* 9–13.

with green circles. Every fifteen minutes the child's desk, person, and supply box were checked, and he was reprimanded and fined five points (under the token economy system) for every possession that did not have a green circle. If no stolen items were found, he received praise and points. Gradually, the teachers checked only once every two hours in order to reduce the level of intervention. During a later followup, the staff kept a list of the child's possessions and checked it whenever anyone reported a missing item. This simple procedure was very successful in eliminating the stealing, both in the classroom and in other settings.

Altering Classroom Density

Several researchers have examined classroom crowding as a factor in aggressive behavior (Hood-Smith, & Leffingwell, 1984; McAfee, 1987). McAfee studied students with behavioral disorders and mental retardation (the ages ranged from seven to sixteen) and noted that the amount of floor space available to students had an impact on their disruptive and aggressive actions. Densities of .90 square meters and .86 square meters significantly increased aggressive behaviors. To calculate how much space your students have, use McAfee's formula:

1. Measure the perimeter of the classroom and calculate the total area.
2. Subtract from this total the floor space that is not available to students "by virtue of its being occupied by objects such as cabinets, files, stacks of boxes, or any other objects that would preclude student work in that space" (p. 138). Include in available work space the students' desks and other furniture designed for their use.

TEACHER-MEDIATED STRATEGIES

Selecting Target Behaviors

Focus your attention on (1) identifying and modifying behaviors that immediately precede acts of aggression, destruction, or theft; and (2) identifying and modifying the not-so-immediate setting events that precede aggression, such as situations at home that "spill over" to school (Conroy & Fox, 1994). Look again at Figure 8.1 and note that one column is devoted entirely to immediate antecedent events. Antecedents are good target behaviors on which to intervene (e.g., teasing remarks, initial physical contact with another student, subvocal utterances, facial flush, movement of an arm to a fighting position). For example, intervene with a student fighter not after the fight has begun but when that student first teases or picks the fight; or stop and let a student "vent" verbally when you first notice that he has had a rough morning on the bus.

General Considerations

Two primary types of intervention enable teachers to address aggressive actions: the rearrangement of reinforcement contingencies for aggression, and the teaching of appropriate, prosocial skills that are incompatible with acts of aggression. These two approaches are based on a social learning theory model that presumes that aggressive acts are learned and that incompatible, prosocial skills can likewise be taught (Bandura, 1971). Contingency management for an aggressive individual requires that you pinpoint problem behaviors and provide negative consequences for them while providing positive consequences for actions incompatible with aggression. Contingency management has been discussed throughout this text in procedures such as token economies, contingency contracts, and timeout from reinforcement. This section explains how to manage the contingencies that influence aggressive behavior in your classroom.

With an aggressive student, it is important that all adults advocate the same position: aggressive behavior will not be tolerated. Otherwise aggression may be intermittently reinforced and thereby strengthened. This concept applies to bullying. Bullies intimidate their victims so that they will not report to authorities; knowing that they won't be punished is reinforcing to bullies. For bullying to cease, adults must know about it and do something to change the contingencies that maintain it. (For comprehensive coverage of bullying, see *Bully-proofing Your School* by Garrity, Jens, Porter, Sager, & Short-Camili, published in 1994 by Sopris West.)

Token Reinforcement and Response Cost

When using a token economy to reduce aggression, apply a response cost or fine to aggressive acts as well as to behaviors that predict aggression or destruction of property. The following lists display part of a teacher's classroom token economy for aggressive students:

Points may be earned for:

◆ Walking away from a fight.
◆ Ignoring someone who teases.
◆ Accepting teacher feedback.
◆ Keeping hands off others.
◆ Using an acceptable word instead of a swear word when angry.

Points will be lost for:

◆ Fighting or hitting.
◆ "Mouthing off" at a school visitor.
◆ Teasing a classmate.
◆ Threatening a classmate.
◆ Blocking a classmate's free movement in class or in the halls.

Note that students earn points for actions that inhibit aggression. Recall our discussion of the role that stimulus control plays in maintaining or reducing aggression. By identifying behaviors that inhibit aggression as well as those that provoke hurtful behavior, this teacher controlled the stimuli preceding aggression through token reinforcement and response cost.

Here are guidelines for implementing a response cost (RC) contingency:

◆ The RC system should be carefully explained before applying it.
◆ RC should always be tied to a reinforcement system, preferably involving points.
◆ An appropriate delivery system should be developed.
◆ RC should be implemented immediately after the target behavior or response occurs.

◆ RC should be applied each time an instance of a target behavior occurs.
◆ The student should never be allowed to accumulate negative points (that is, go in the hole with point totals).
◆ The ratio of points earned to those lost should be controlled.
◆ The social agent using response cost should never be intimidated from using RC by the target student.
◆ Subtraction of points should never be punitive or personalized.
◆ The student's positive, appropriate behavior should be praised as frequently as opportunities permit. (Walker et al., 1995, pp. 66-67).

Contracting

Contingency contracts have effectively reduced destructive actions, including fighting, property damage, fire-setting, and verbal aggression (Walker et al., 1995). In Figure 8.4 is a contingency contract with home-based reinforcement, developed for Helen, the sixth grader mentioned earlier. Notice that the conditions of the contract apply across classrooms as well as transition activities.

Timeout from Reinforcement

Many aggressive students, like classroom disruptors, fail to complete academic tasks because they are expelled from the instructional setting at each outburst. As a result aggressive students may develop a "double disability" requiring remediation in both academic and social skills. When using timeout with an aggressive student, remember that it is best (and easiest) to apply it *before* the child loses control or becomes assaultive. For this reason, behaviors pinpointed for timeout should be antecedents to aggression (teasing, threats, lifting an arm to "deck" someone). Also provide reinforcement for incompatible, acceptable actions once the student returns to the ongoing classroom activities. Occasionally a destructive student will attempt to destroy the timeout area. If possible, require the student to restore the area to its original condition before being allowed to leave it (i.e., use restitutional overcorrection). If the student is extremely destructive,

Figure 8.4   Contract for an Aggressive Student

I, __Helen Alison__ , understand that I have a problem with these behaviors:

1. __Talking back to my teachers when they tell me to do something.__

2. __Refusing to do or finish my schoolwork.__

3. __Getting into fights with other kids at lunch and at recess.__

This week I am going to work on these behaviors

1. __Talking back to my teachers.__

2. __Finishing my homework in the resource reading room.__

I know that if I do either one of these behaviors I will lose __my shopping trip Saturday to the mall with my friends__

to remind me that what I did was not right.

But, if I control these behaviors and have a week without them, I will get to

__Go to a movie with Jeanie, or get an extra 50¢ allowance__

as a reward.

Signed: __Helen Alison__   Date: __11/20__
              (Student)

__Mrs. Blouze__   Date: __11/20__
          (Teacher)

__Mr. Sider__   Date: __11/20__
     (Resource Teacher)

__Mrs. P. Alison__   Date: __11/20__
          (Parent)

We have read and discussed this contract in an after-school meeting on __11/20__
And we hereby sign as a way of making our commitment to this arrangement.

We will all meet on __11/28_____ to reevaluate the contract.

within-school interventions may have to be supplemented with external penalties. Examples are a legally imposed fine for destruction of public property, the requirement that a student pay for damage while parents withhold his allowance for other spending purposes, the assignment of a student to a custodial job for a designated period, or "grounding" an institutionalized student to a more restrictive physical environment until she demonstrates better care of property. In the case of timeout or punishment strategies, consult with your supervisor about school policies. Another form of timeout from reinforcement is the in-school suspension procedure you read about in Chapter 6. If this program is implemented properly and if the student is motivated by being with his friends in the regular school program, then the removal of friends through the in-school suspension assignment may reduce aggression. Unfortunately, very little research has been conducted on these school-wide interventions, so we cannot predict how effective they will be in deterring aggression. It is best that you monitor these interventions (especially home suspension) to see whether you are remediating or worsening the problem.

Overcorrection

One way to teach skills incompatible with problem behaviors is through positive practice **overcorrection,** a procedure in which the student is required to engage in a period of exaggerated alternative behaviors (e.g., exercises after an episode of an unwanted behavior). This procedure was applied to stealing, according to a report by Azrin and Wesolowski (1974). In this investigation, students with mental retardation who grabbed food from others' plates were reprimanded and prompted to return the stolen food. The thief was then told to obtain an identical item from a display area and to give it to the victim. This overcorrection procedure quickly eliminated all thefts. The authors cited four possible reasons for this procedure's success: in returning the stolen item, the thief no longer enjoyed its reinforcing qualities; securing another similar item was an unpleasant experience; the time spent in overcorrection lessened the amount of reinforcement available to the thief; and by returning items, the thief learned a new and incompatible behavior (Azrin & Wesolowski, 1974). Luce, Delquadri, and Hall (1980) used contingent exercise (functional movement training) for two elementary school students who were severely disturbed and were engaging in hitting and aggressive verbalizations. Whenever a student hit or threatened, he or she was prompted to do ten exercise sets. This procedure is detailed in Chapter 9. You might consider overcorrection to reduce aggressive or stealing behavior if you are working with students with serious disabilities or with young students. This strategy, when it involves contingent functional movement training, is not practical for an adolescent who is likely to be physically resistant.

Teaching Alternative Behaviors

Perhaps your most important task with aggressive students is to teach them alternatives to their angry behavior. After all, the contingency management procedures we have reviewed will help address the outbursts of an aggressive student but may fall short of offering the student new and better ways to solve problems with others. When faced with the task of teaching alternative behaviors, educators often ask: "Where should I begin?" We think you might find Table 8.2 helpful for targeting behaviors. The left-hand column contains behaviors that would lead to positive responses on the part of others, whereas the right-hand column outlines angry or hostile behaviors. This table might be a good discussion handout for your older students.

One of the most popular approaches to teaching alternative, prosocial behaviors to aggressive students is structured learning (Goldstein, 1987). Through this approach, students experience four training components: modeling, role-playing, performance feedback, and transfer of learning (Goldstein, 1987). Goldstein described the structured learning groups as consisting of from 6 to 12 participants who are assessed as having similar skill deficits. (See Goldstein, 1987, for a listing of assessment procedures.) Problem situations are task-analyzed and modeled for the students by their teacher or through audiovisual aids. Table 8.3 lists of these psychological skill areas.

After students have witnessed good ways to manage difficult situations, they role-play these skills themselves. Goldstein (1987) described the role-play as follows:

A brief, spontaneous discussion almost invariably follows the presentation of a modeling display. Trainees comment on the steps, the actors, and often the occurrence of the situation or skill problem in their own lives. Because our primary

Table 8.2 Appropriate versus Inappropriate Expressions of Anger and Their Effects

Expression	Appropriate		Inappropriate	
	Action	*Effect*	*Action*	*Effect*
1. Eye contact	Direct	People look back	Glaring	People look away
2. Tone of voice	Calm, polite, pleasant	People more likely to listen calmly, pleasantly	Loud, screaming, cursing	People less likely to listen, may yell back
3. Facial expression	Positive, relaxed, pleasant	People more likely to respond positively, look pleasant	Frowning, scowling, snarling	People more likely to walk away or look unpleasant
4. Body movement	Open position, relaxed stance, gestures not threatening	Feelings more likely to be recognized, problems more likely to be resolved, people more open to suggestion	Throwing, hitting, threatening, fist shaking	Person may respond physically and someone may get hurt, could result in legal action, property damage

Source: Larkin, D. (1986). Personal communication.

goal in role-playing is to encourage realistic behavior rehearsal, a trainee's statements about individual difficulties using the skill can often develop into material for the first role-play. To enhance the realism of the portrayal, the main actor is asked to choose a second trainee (coactor) to play the role of the significant other person in his or her life who is relevant to the skill problem. It is important that the main actor seeks to enact the steps just modeled. The main actor is asked to briefly describe the real problem situation and the real person(s) involved in it. The coactor is called by the name of the main actor's significant other person during the role-play. The trainer then instructs the role-players to begin. It is the trainer's main responsibility, at this point, to be sure that the main actor keeps role-playing and attempts to follow the behavioral steps in so doing. The role-playing is continued until all trainees in the group have had an opportunity to participate even if all the same steps must be carried over to a second or third session. However, even though the framework (behavioral steps) of each role-play in the series remains the same, the actual content can and should change from role-play to role-play; the skill

deficiency problem as it actually occurs in each trainee's real-life environment should be the content of each role-play. When the role-plays are completed, each trainee should be better armed to act appropriately in real situations. (p. 220)

The next stage of training is performance feedback, in which the actors in the role-plays receive comments on how they enacted the skills. Goldstein stressed the importance of specific encouraging comments here. Finally, students experience the transfer of training, a phase in which overlearning is emphasized. Students reexperience the modeling, role-plays, and performance feedback many times in order to ensure that they have really captured the important skills they lack. For more information, you might want to review Goldstein's *The Prepare Curriculum: Teaching Prosocial Competencies,* published in 1988 by Research Press.

To enhance a **social skills** curriculum, give students "behavioral homework assignments," writing assignments for their notebooks, "cue cards," and other learning aids. Moreover, try to

Table 8.3 Psychological Skill Areas for Aggressive Students

Asking for help
1. Decide what the problem is.
2. Decide whether you want help with the problem.
3. Identify the people who might help you.
4. Choose a helper.
5. Tell the helper about your problem.

Giving instructions
1. Define what needs to be done and who should do it.
2. Tell the other person what you want him to do and why.
3. Tell the other person exactly how to do what you want done.
4. Ask for the other person's reaction.
5. Consider that reaction and change your direction if appropriate.

Expressing affection
1. Decide whether you have warm, caring feelings about another person.
2. Decide whether the other person would like to know about your feelings.
3. Decide how you might best express your feelings.
4. Choose the right time and place to express your feelings.
5. Express affection in a warm and caring manner.

Expressing a complaint
1. Define what the problem is and who is responsible.
2. Decide how the problem might be solved.
3. Tell that person what the problem is and how it might be solved.
4. Ask for a response.
5. Decide whether you want to try again.
6. If it is appropriate, try again, using your revised approach.

Responding to contradictory messages
1. Pay attention to those body signals that help you know you are feeling trapped or confused.
2. Consider the other person's words and actions that may have caused you to have these feelings.
3. Decide whether that person's words and actions are contradictory.
4. Decide whether it would be useful to point out any contradiction.
5. If appropriate, ask the other person to explain any contradiction.

Responding to anger
1. Listen openly to the other person's angry statement(s).
2. Show that you understand what the other person is feeling.
3. Ask the other person to explain anything you don't understand about what was said.
4. Show that you understand why the other person feels angry.
5. If it is appropriate, express your thoughts and feelings about the situation.

Preparing for a stressful conversation
1. Imagine yourself in the stressful situation.
2. Think about how you will feel and why you will feel that way.
3. Imagine the other person(s) in that stressful situation. Think about how that person(s) will feel and why he (they) will feel that way.
4. Imagine yourself telling the other person(s) what you want to say.
5. Imagine the response that your statement will elicit.
6. Repeat the above steps, using as many approaches as you can think of.
7. Choose the best approach.

Determining responsibility
1. Decide what the problem is.
2. Consider possible causes of the problem.
3. Determine the most likely causes of the problem.
4. Take actions to test which are the actual causes of the problem.

Table 8.3 (*continued*)

Setting problem priorities
1. List all the problems currently pressuring you.
2. Arrange this list in order, from most to least urgent.
3. Take steps (delegate, postpone, avoid) to temporarily decrease the urgency of all but the most pressing problem.
4. Concentrate on solving the most pressing problem.

Dealing with being left out
1. Decide whether you're being left out (ignored, rejected).
2. Think about why the other people might be leaving you out of something.
3. Consider how you might deal with the problem (wait, leave, tell the other people how their behavior affects you, talk with a friend about the problem).
4. Choose the best way and do it.
5. Show that you understand the other person's feelings.
6. Come to agreement on the steps each of you will take.

Persuading others
1. Decide on your position and predict what the other person's is likely to be.
2. State your position clearly, completely, and in a way that is acceptable to the other person.
3. State what you think the other person's position is.
4. Restate your position, emphasizing why it is the better of the two.
5. Suggest that the other person consider your position for a while before making a decision.

Following instructions
1. Listen carefully while the instructions are being given.
2. Give your reactions to the instructor.
3. Repeat the instructions to yourself.
4. Imagine yourself following the instructions and then do it.

Responding to the feelings of others (empathy)
1. Observe another person's words and actions.
2. Consider what the other person might be feeling and how strong the feelings are.
3. Decide whether it would be helpful to let the other person know that you understand his feelings.
4. If appropriate, tell the other person in a warm and sincere manner how you think he is feeling.

Responding to a complaint
1. Listen openly to the complaint.
2. Ask the person to explain anything you don't understand.
3. Show that you understand the other person's thoughts and feelings.
4. Tell the other person your thoughts and feelings, accepting responsibility if appropriate.
5. Summarize the steps each of you will take.

Responding to persuasion
1. Listen openly to another person's position.
2. Consider the possible reasons for the other person's position.
3. Ask the other person to explain anything you don't understand about what was said.
4. Compare the other person's position with your own, identifying the pros and cons of each.
5. Decide what position to support, based on what will have the greatest long-term benefit.

Responding to failure
1. Decide whether you have failed.
2. Think about both the personal reasons and the circumstances that have caused you to fail.
3. Decide how you might do things differently if you tried again.

Table 8.3 *(continued)*

Dealing with an accusation

1. Think about what the other person has accused you of (whether it is accurate, inaccurate, said in a mean way or in a constructive way).
2. Think about why the person might have accused you (have you infringed on that person's rights or property?).
3. Think about ways to answer the person's accusations (deny, explain your behavior, correct the other person's perceptions, assert, apologize, offer to make up for what has happened).
4. Choose the best way and do it.

Dealing with group pressure

1. Think about what the other people want you to do and why (listen to the other people, decide what their real intent is, try to understand what is being said).
2. Decide what you want to do (yield, resist, delay, negotiate).
3. Consider how to tell the other people what you want to do (give reasons, talk to one person only, delay, assert).
4. If appropriate, tell the group or other person what you have decided.

Source: Reprinted with permission from Goldstein, A. P. (1987). Teaching prosocial skills to antisocial adolescents. In C. M. Nelson, R. B. Rutherford, & B. I. Wolford (Eds.), *Special education in the criminal justice system.* Upper Saddle River, NJ: Merrill/Prentice Hall, pp. 223–226.

link the skills with real-life situations by offering relevant teaching examples, role-plays, and discussion topics.

An outstanding program that incorporates social skills training and structured contingencies is the RECESS program developed by Walker, Hops, & Greenwood (1993). This program, designed for early intervention, has proven highly effective in reducing aggressive behavior in grades K–3. RECESS includes four components: social skills training similar to that outlined above, a response cost system, praise for cooperative behaviors, and individual and group reinforcement contingencies.

Hammond and Young (1992) developed excellent curricula for helping youth to manage their anger. In *Dealing with Anger,* students learn a three-step approach: "Givin' it; Takin' it; Workin' it out." Once again, the training offers modeling (through a series of videotaped examples), role-plays, visual clues (e.g., flashcards), and homework assignments. Students also learn to recognize and analyze components of angry interactions. *Dealing with Anger* and *PACT,* two curricula by Hammond et al., are available from Research Press (P.O. Box 9177, Champaign, IL 61826). Other social skills curricula and guidelines for teaching social skills are detailed in *A*

Resource Guide for Social Skills Instruction by Alberg, Petry, and Eller, published in 1994 by Sopris West. This excellent handbook, developed with the assistance of a U.S. Department of Education grant, provides information on social skills instruction at all grade levels and highlights exemplary curricula.

Remember, students with antisocial behaviors need contingency management as well as direct skills training. To maintain intervention gains and increase generalization or transfer of these skills across settings and persons, involve as many other persons as possible in the intervention planning and implementation. This chapter's case study demonstrates how skills training and contingency management work together to improve students' self-control.

CRISIS INTERVENTION WITH PHYSICAL AGGRESSION

In spite of your best efforts to prevent behaviors that threaten the physical safety of an aggressive student or of others in the classroom, a situation may erupt into violence before you can intervene. We hope that these instances will be rare if you employ the strategies described in this chapter. However, when violent behavior does occur, you should know what to do. If you work with potentially aggressive students, take an annual refresher class on nonviolent crisis intervention. These classes are often offered by local police departments or mental health programs. Be sure that your class is offered by a certified professional who has time to provide concrete examples.

It helps to have a well-rehearsed crisis response plan. The guidelines in Table 8.4 will help you prepare for this situation and prevent harm. This "drill" also alleviates the anxiety of adults in the building. Just compare this drill with others we use to prepare ourselves for potentially serious (yet less frequent) events such as a fire or tornado.

Occasionally you may work with a student whose aggression is a result of irrational thinking, hallucinations, or another psychiatric problem, or, you may want to help a student trying to cope with a violent family member. Consider these guidelines offered by an advocacy organization for families affected by mental illness:

Don't Threaten. This may be interpreted as a power play and increase fear or prompt assaultive behavior by the individual.

Don't Shout. If the person with a mental illness seems not to be listening, it is not because he or she is hard of hearing. Other "Voices" are probably interfering.

Don't Criticize. It will only make matters worse. It cannot possibly make things better.

Don't Squabble with other family members over "best strategies" or allocations of blame. This is no time to prove a point.

Don't Bait the individual into acting out wild threats. The consequences could be tragic.

Don't Stand over the individual if he or she is seated. Instead, seat yourself.

Avoid direct, continuous eye contact or touching the individual.

Comply with requests that are neither endangering nor beyond reason. This provides the individual patient with an opportunity to feel somewhat "in control."

Don't Block the Doorway. However, do keep yourself between the individual and an exit. (Adapted from the Alliance for the Mentally Ill of Southwestern PA, 1996)

PEER-MEDIATED STRATEGIES

A student's peer group can play a major role in intervention programs to reduce aggressive and destructive behaviors. For example, the peers may take part in a group contingency or learn to ignore

---

Table 8.4 Readiness Drill for Aggressive Events

1. With your principal and at least one other teacher whose room is nearby, develop a plan for getting help when the aggressive child loses control. This plan should include:
   a. transmitting a signal to the nearby adult or an alternate if that person is not available.
   b. the type of assistance you will need. For example, you might want the adult to come to your class and escort your other students out of the room so that they do not reinforce or taunt the target student.
   c. how you will notify the principal. You may want a second colleague to do this for you.
   d. how you will handle the aggressive student(s). This plan will depend in part on your school's policies. Interventions presented later in this chapter will help you.

2. Develop a "signal" that you can give to a dependable child in your classroom. This signal should be different from anything else the children may have encountered. For example, you might paint a wooden block a particular color. (If you also wish to notify the principal, you might want two such signals given to two students or their alternates.)

3. Select an alternate in the event that the designated child is absent the day you need to use your procedure.

4. Tell the students that you have an important drill for them to practice, like the fire and other drills to which they are accustomed. You do not need to declare the circumstances under which you would activate your readiness plan. If the students can read, give them a handout outlining the steps they are to take. If they are not capable readers, you might want to show an abbreviated set of steps on a poster.

5. Practice the drill, including the activities of the other adults. Begin with a weekly practice until the students and adults can complete the activities smoothly. Then have a monthly "surprise drill."

6. If at any time the drill does not proceed as you planned, revise the steps and inform everyone of the revision.

or respond in a new way to teasing or threats by the target student. Some of these peer-mediated procedures have been described in detail in previous chapters, so we will only mention them here.

Peer Confrontation

In this strategy, peers confront the inappropriate behavior of a classmate, identify the effects of the behavior, and engage in joint problem-solving (Arllen, Gable, and Hendrickson, 1996). Based on a model entitled "Positive Peer Culture" (Vorath and Brendtro,

1974), peer confrontation takes place both within a meeting format and during other times of the school day. The studies to date have taken place in small, elementary school, self-contained settings. In these respects the strategy is similar to Group Goal Setting and Feedback, (see Chapter 6).

Table 8.5 describes the steps to carry out peer confrontation.

Group Goal Setting and Feedback

Group goal setting and feedback, a strategy explained in Chapter 6, has been applied to

Table 8.5 Guidelines for Implementation.

The peer confrontation strategy is composed of five major parts. During each stage, the teacher should praise the target student(s) and peers for engaging in appropriate responses.

1. Identify the problem.
   - Identify the specific behavior(s).
   - Operationally define the target behavior(s) (e.g., verbal or gestural threats such as shaking a fist at another student; raising the middle finger; stating "I'll shoot you.").
   - Teach all students to identify positive and neutral behaviors of peers.
   - Teach all students to identify negative behaviors of peers (e.g., hitting, name calling).
   - Teach all students to discriminate between acceptable and negative behaviors.
   - Teach all students to identify target behavior(s) as they are exhibited naturally.
2. Determine the effects of the problem behavior on others.
   - Teach students to recognize various types of effects. Categories might include tangible effects (e.g., "all our equipment will be broken"), intangible effects (e.g., "we'll be late for class" or "he'll lose face"), short-term effects (e.g., "we'll get detentions"), or long-term effects (e.g., "we may not get to go on the field trip at the end of the project").
   - Teach students to predict possible effects resulting from a specific behavior.
3. Conduct problem solving.
   - Teach students to precisely describe the problem behavior (e.g., "Mike's hand is in the air; he's getting ready to hit").
   - Discuss the consequences of the behavior.
   - Brainstorm alternative target student responses. Prompt students to offer a number of positive behavioral options to the target student.
4. Deliver mild punishment—as appropriate.
   - This might take the form of a verbal reprimand, presented in close proximity to the target student.
5. Provide "booster training" (e.g., periodic retaining) to ensure appropriate performance.
6. Monitor the long-term effect of behavior changes on the target student(s).

Source: Reprinted with permission from Arllen, N. L., Gable, R. A., & Henderickson, J. M. (1996). Using peer confrontation to reduce inappropriate student behavior. *Beyond Behavior, 7*(1), 22–23.

aggressive behaviors on the playground (Kerr, Strain, & Ragland, 1982). In this study preadolescent students participated in daily group goal-setting and feedback sessions to improve their recess activities, originally described by their teacher as follows:

> The kids go outside for a thirty-minute recess and start right off arguing about what game to play. Once that's settled, they bicker about who will pick teams. After teams are finally chosen, a fight breaks out over unfair membership on the two teams. About ten minutes before the bell rings, they get down to playing baseball or something. By the time recess is over they've almost killed each other fighting about the rules. . . . (Ragland, personal communication, 1981)

Peer Reporting

Young students may improve their social interactions and reduce aggression through an activity designed by Kauffman, Grieger, and Grieger (1976):

1. Set aside approximately ten minutes per day for this activity. You will also need "happy face" badges (or a similar item) for each student. These should fit onto a hook or flannelboard and should also be attached to a child's clothing or desk.
2. At the designated time, assemble the group and ask that students take turns nominating someone who had been friendly and stating what the friendly act was.
3. A nominated child is eligible to receive a "friendly badge." Be sure the badge is received from a peer, not the teacher.
4. Discourage students from describing themselves.
5. Don't praise or otherwise recognize students who are not nominated. (This is a modification of the original method.)
6. If students cannot nominate a peer, encourage them to do so the next day (pp. 308–313).

Self-Mediated Strategies

Because aggression is an interpersonal behavior, self-management strategies alone will not remediate the problem. However, self-monitoring in combination with contingency management and the learning of alternative behaviors may succeed.

At least two reports suggest combining self-management with other activities for aggressive students. Kendall and Finch (1976) successfully used self-instructions with a token response cost for aggressive outbursts. Self-recording (described in Chapter 6) with points for accurate assessment of aggressive behaviors has been used with contingency contracting to reduce problem behaviors of early adolescent boys in a residential setting (Bardill, 1977). Figure 8.5 illustrates a self-recording form in combination with a contingency contract and "hero" procedure (group contingency). We believe that you will find self-control strategies especially helpful in supplementing the direct instruction, **modeling,** and role-play strategies included in your skills teaching programs.

Summary

We hope you understand the importance of a thorough analysis of aggression attained through careful documentation early in a student's school career. As part of a larger team making your school safe, you can develop policies and school-wide strategies that discourage acts of aggression. Several environmental changes are available to solve specific problems. Most strategies, however, are teacher-mediated, requiring a high degree of control of your emotions and reactions. Solid management of contingencies and direct skills instruction are two of your best tools. Few studies have reported self-mediated strategies, but self-monitoring can contribute to a more comprehensive approach. Our chapter concludes with a case study depicting a multifaceted approach with sixth graders. Following the case study is a list of violence prevention resources. The list includes a brief description and ordering information for curricula, school safety projects, community programs, and other resources.

Figure 8.5

Date _____   Today Sam earned _____

Class _____

	Yes	No
Did I stay in my seat?		
Did I raise my hand quietly and wait until the teacher called on me?		
or		
Did I do my work quietly?		

When I hear the timer, I will ask myself these questions. I will put a check in the Yes or No column.

Contract

I, Sam Mc Donald, agree to follow class rules. I will pay special attention to

1. _____

   _____

2. _____

   _____

In art and library classes. When I beat my last score in the Yes column for both questions, I will be able to pick an activity from the list. When I beat my score five times, the class will be allowed to pick an activity.

We have read and agreed to the things written here on _____ (date). We will meet in one month to talk about the things written here.

_____
(student)

_____
(parent)

_____
(teacher)

Source: Booth, L. (1995). Personal communication. Reprinted with permission of the author.

 CASE STUDY

ANGER MANAGEMENT SKILLS LESSONS[1]

Dawn E. Cois

BACKGROUND INFORMATION

A class of sixth-grade students exhibiting behavioral problems is in need of social skills training. In

[1] Reprinted with permission of the author.

particular, these ten students need to increase their social skills in interacting with adults. The faculty at this school is extremely cooperative and resourceful and will assist in the behavioral program for these students. Students are in my classroom for homeroom (15 minutes), third period (60 min-

(continued)

utes) and at the end of the day (15 minutes), five days a week.

BEHAVIORAL OBJECTIVE

When given a task request or directions from an adult, students will respond without talking back angrily or using inappropriate language (profanity).

LESSON PLAN

Introduction

Students will be given an introduction on the target behavior (i.e., responding appropriately to adult requests or directions), its value to them and the consequences for noncompliance. Open discussion will follow with students' volunteering examples of good encounters and bad encounters with adults.

Teacher: I need the class's help on a problem I have. Today Mrs. Lewis asked me to stay after school to help her finish the school newsletter. Well, I've stayed after school three times this week already to help with planning for the new weather station and the Tropicana Speech Contest, and tonight I have company coming over. Besides, I was in a hurry to get to the office to run off some copies and only had a few minutes before I had to be back in the classroom, so I really didn't have time to talk. You know what that's like, don't you? When you're in a hurry and people are bugging you for time that you don't have? Well, I paused for a second and simply told her "No way! I'm not staying after school another day. I have a life too. Find someone else or do it yourself. Why is it that I have to do everything around here anyway?" Well, she looked kind of angry and replied, "Sorry I asked you! It won't happen again."

Well, I really like Mrs. Lewis and I felt sort of bad that I responded that way, but I didn't have time to apologize or explain myself so I just kept going. Anyway, remember how we talked about having an egg-drop contest next month? Well, Mrs. Lewis was going to help me with it since she's done this activity before. I really don't know much about it. Now she's mad at me and I don't know how to ask her for her assistance. What do you think she'll say if I ask her stay after school next week to help me with this project?

What can I do to make things better so that our friendship isn't ruined?
How can I get her to still help me on this project?
Could I have avoided this problem if I had handled her request to stay after school differently?
What could I have said that would have sounded better and not made her angry?

We all do this sometimes, just blow up on people instead of talking politely and calmly when people ask us to do things, especially when they are things we don't really want to do. But in the end we just make people mad at us and then they don't want to help us when we need them. The funny thing about this is that if we would only take a moment to think the situation through, we could make our own lives a lot easier and know that the people around us will support us.

First, we need to think about what it is that the other person is asking of us. Is it a reasonable request? Is it something we can do? If not, what do we need that will better enable us to do it? Is it a fair request?
Second, we need to think about the consequences. What will happen if we do what is being asked of us? What will happen if we do not? Is there a good reason why we can't or shouldn't do this?
Third, we need to control our impulses to say things angrily. If we can do what is being asked of us, we should. If we can't, we need to calmly explain why we can't. Staying calm means that we don't say things that are offensive or use profanity. There's always a nice way to respond if we take the time to think about it.
Last, we need to reward ourselves for taking the time to think the situation through and responding appropriately.

This is especially important when any of you are dealing with adults. Adults make a lot of requests on kids, especially teachers. But their job is to help you get a good education and prepare you to undertake whatever careers you may choose when you leave school. When you are all adults, you'll find you'll have a lot of responsibilities and you'll need to rely on many of the skills you've acquired in school. Parents

(continued)

also ask a lot of you. But they too usually have your best interests in mind.

Would anyone like to share a situation they may have encountered with a teacher in the past? What was asked of you and how did you handle it? Good and bad situations are encouraged to be shared. Bad situations are discussed with suggestions on ways that it could have been handled better.

Modeling

Teacher: Let's first review the four steps we just talked about to help us better deal with adults when they ask us to do something. (Students volunteer the four steps while the teacher writes them down.)

1. Is it a reasonable and fair request?
2. What will be the consequences of my actions?
3. I need to respond politely and calmly.
4. Reward myself for handling the situation well.

(Students are given index cards with these four steps written on them.)

Now Mrs. B. and I will demonstrate how to use these four steps in a situation that is a little worse than the one I had with Mrs. Lewis. In this situation, I'm going to play the role of a sixth grader who is being told by a teacher to take work detention for not completing an assignment that she knows she did. In this role-play I'm going to think aloud so that you can hear how I work through the four steps on your cards.

Mrs. B: Kathy, I'm really disappointed in you this week. You didn't hand in your book report even though I gave the class extra time on Monday to finish it. Here's your detention slip. You won't be allowed free time today with the rest of the class. Instead you need to report to the detention room to finish your work. I want this detention slip signed by one of your parents and returned to me on Monday along with your completed book report.

Teacher (sixth grader): (1) Is this fair and reasonable? No! I did the assignment and I know I handed it in. (2) What will be the consequences if I do it? Well, I'll miss free time, my parents

will be angry with me, and I'll have to do the assignment all over again. What will happen if I get angry and refuse to do it? Well, I'll be sent to the principal's office and my parents will be called. That will make them even angrier at me. I'll still have to go to work detention or possibly have to sit in the office during free time, the principal will be angry with me, and I'll still have to redo the assignment. Is there another alternative? Yes, I can explain to Mrs. B. that I did the assignment and already turned it in. If I'm nice, maybe she'll listen to me. (3) Be calm and polite. Mrs. B., I worked hard on that book report and finished it on Monday when you gave us that extra time in class to work on it. I'm sure I turned it in. I remember putting it in the homework box. Maybe you misplaced it?

Mrs. B.: No, if it was in the homework box with the rest of the book reports I would have gotten it. I don't lose papers. But. . . . if you say you did it, maybe you thought you turned it in and didn't. Perhaps you should check your desk and see if you still have it.

Teacher (sixth grader): I don't think so, but I'll check anyway. Look, Mrs. B., you were right. It's here in my desk.

Mrs. B.: Well, it's late, but at least I know you did it and that it was an accident that it wasn't turned in, so I won't deduct any points. I'm glad we resolved this and that you don't have to take detention. Perhaps you should keep a record of your assignments and cross them off after you've turned them in rather than when you've completed them so that this won't happen again. I'll help you organize an assignment sheet if you'd like.

Teacher (sixth grader): OK. Thanks, Mrs. B. (4) Reward myself. Wow, I handled that great and got her to listen me. It got me out of detention and hot water with my parents.

Let's talk about that situation. (Students talk about how the four steps were used to help resolve the problem. Teacher also leads the class to discuss how that situation could have turned bad.)

(continued)

Practice/Role-Play

Teacher: Now we're all going to have a chance to practice using these four steps with some practice situations that I've made up. First, we'll practice these skills as a class and then we'll pair up with partners to practice. I'll play the teacher role and let each of you respond to a situation using one of the four steps. Remember to think the steps aloud so that the rest of us know how you're working this out. When I walk next to you, it's your turn to respond, OK? If you get nervous and can't come up with something, then the person beside you can offer you some suggestions to help you out. Does anyone have any questions or comments before we begin?

Situation One   Tommy is talking to Randy beside him about the football game last night while the teacher is giving instructions.

Teacher: Tommy, the rules of this classroom are that you shouldn't be talking when the teacher is talking. I want you to move you desk next to mine and stay in for 15 minutes of your recess.

(Students are each given a chance to respond to one of the four steps in responding appropriately in this situation)

Situation Two   Sam is being accused of writing on his desk when he knows he did not do it.

Teacher: Sam, why is there writing all over your desk? That's school property and you have no right to destroy or vandalize it! I want you to stay in at recess and wash not only you desk, but everyone's desk in this classroom!

Situation Three   Rita is having problems understanding division problems. She put her best effort into her assignment but still did poorly.

Teacher: Rita, you missed thirteen out of the fifteen math problems on you homework assignment. I want you to redo this assignment for homework tonight and I want every problem done correctly. Do you understand?

Now I'd like you all to divide into pairs with the person sitting next to you. Mrs. B. and I will give you each a card with a situation. Each person will take a turn being the teacher for his or her own situation while the other person role plays a student. Remember to talk aloud through the four steps. The person playing the teacher will be the recorder. As the recorder, you will check off each step as the student does it. At the end of each role-play, the recorder will then compliment his or her partner on one thing he or she did well and then offer one suggestion on how else the situation could have been handled.

Practice Situations

1. You stayed after class to ask your teacher a question about the assignment. Now you're late getting to your next class and running down the hall.

   Teacher: No running in the halls! Come here. I want you to go back to the end of the hall and walk this time.

2. You are Ralph. You and your grandparents flew in from California yesterday, and the family all went to a relative's for a family get-together. Your family didn't get home till after 11:00 P.M. so you didn't have time to get your spelling assignment completed.

   Teacher: Ralph, I don't have your spelling assignment. The test is tomorrow and it's important that you practice these words. I want you to stay in from recess and complete this assignment. I also want you to write each word five times tonight for homework and hand it in tomorrow.

3. Your name is Tommy, and you are anxious to get to gym class because they are playing basketball, a sport that you are real good at. Mrs. K. stops you in the hall and asks if you wouldn't mind helping her carry some boxes of books to the library. She promises you that she will write a note to your next teacher explaining why you are late.

4. You are Karen and your mother went into labor in the middle of the night. You were told this morning that she delivered a baby girl. You have not yet gone to the hospital to see your mother or your new baby sister. You're quite excited and haven't been able to pay attention in class.

   Teacher: Karen, this is the third time that I've had to ask you to look up here and pay attention. Do I need to move you up to the front of the room to keep your attention?

(continued)

5. You are running to catch a football on the playground when you accidently collide with another student. The other student jumps up angrily and begins screaming accusations that you knocked him over on purpose. A teacher arrives promptly on the scene and hears the other student's accusations.

6. Your name is Dave and you're having a really bad day. You and your best friend are fighting, you got in trouble at home last night and are grounded for the weekend, and another student has just yelled at you for missing the ball in a volleyball game during gymclass. You yell back at the student and push him.

   Teacher: Dave, report to the office. No fighting is allowed in this school. I'll be up after class to give you a detention slip. (After class:) Dave, this kind of conduct is serious. Why did you push John?

7. Larry has found that he is missing his lunch money and accuses you (Tim) of stealing it. You brought your lunch but have extra money in your pocket that you brought to buy extra cookies with. You know that you did not take Larry's lunch money.

   Teacher: Tim, Larry says that he saw you go into his desk when he went up to sharpen his pencil. He claims you have his lunch money in your pocket. Didn't you pack a lunch today? Stealing someone else's money is a crime and will have to be reported to your parents.

8. Yesterday's math assignment was really tough for you (Bob). You attempted the problems but just couldn't get it. Your mom's visiting the hospital a lot lately to see your grandma, so she wasn't around to help you, and your dad was too busy with your younger brothers. Now the teacher has asked you to put one of the problems on the board and explain it to the class.

   Teacher: Bob, I asked you to come up and put problem 4 on the board and explain to the class how you got your answer. I want you to do it now!

9. While cleaning up at the end of art class, Andy accidently bumped into you (Roy) and made you spill your paint dish all over the floor and the walls.

   Teacher: Roy, look at this mess! I want you to stay and wash the entire floor and walls until all this paint is cleaned up.

10. During reading class, Frank throws a spitball at Julie, which hits her directly in the head. The teacher has seen the direction that the spitball came from, but mistakenly thinks you (Danny) threw it.

    Teacher: Danny, that was totally uncalled for. I want you to stay in the first 15 minutes of recess and sweep the entire floor. Also, I'd like you to apologize to Julie right now!

Generalization/Transfer Activities

To ensure generalization of the new skills taught (i.e., four self-management steps) and to better enable students to respond to requests or directions from adults in an appropriate way, it is important that these skills be practiced across settings, situations, and people. Thus, the other teachers in the building have agreed to "create" situations in which the student will be required to use these skills. Students will not be forewarned about these situations, but they will be told that they are expected to self-monitor their use of these skills in their other classrooms. Additionally, they will be told that their other teachers have been informed about this self-management program and have agreed to reward each student that successfully demonstrates the use of these skills in a situation with them, if one should occur. Students will be given a self-monitoring checklist which will be explained, modeled by the teacher, and then practiced by the students.

Practice Session Using the Self-Monitoring Checklist

Teacher: I was told by a student from one of my other classes that someone in this classroom was given the answers to the math test yesterday. Since I don't know who it was, you will all have to retake a different math test that will be twice as hard. I'm very disappointed that someone from this class would cheat. Does anyone have any comments before we begin the test?

(continued)

First Student: I don't think it's fair that we should all be punished for something that one person did. Besides, you don't know for sure whether the kid who told you that was telling the truth. How did he know?

(Students are prompted to check off the first step under third period if they have not already.)

Second Student: If we refuse to take the second test, we could get a failing grade. If we take the test, we could do poorly since it's twice as hard. If we get angry and yell, we might get in trouble plus a failing grade. But if we talk to the teacher nicely and convince her that it is wrong to punish us all, we might get out of it.

(Students are prompted to check off the second step under third period if they have not already.)

Third Student: Mrs. Cois, if someone from an earlier period gave someone in our class the answers to the test, wouldn't that be just as wrong as the person taking the answers? So why isn't that class being punished, too, since you don't know who gave the answers?

Teacher: I hadn't thought of that. You are quite right, Andy. Giving the answers is just as wrong as getting them.

Fourth Student: Couldn't you look at the tests with the same scores and see if there are any that have all the same right and wrong answers? Maybe you could talk to those kids and see if any of them did it.

Teacher: That's a good idea, too. Maybe I'd find some clues by looking at the tests.

Fifth Student: Instead of punishing all of us, why don't you just give different tests to each class from now on so that people can't cheat?

(Students are prompted to check off the third step under third period if they have not already.)

Teacher: That would certainly help to keep this from happening again. It may have happened before and I just didn't know about it. Well, you've all been pretty helpful with ways to identify the cheaters and keep this from happening again. And you're right that the other class shouldn't get off the hook if you're being

Figure 8.6

Self-Monitoring Checklist									
Name _____				Date _____					
Class _____				Teacher _____					
	Home room	1st period	2nd period	3rd period	lunch	4th period	5th period	6th period	Home room
1. Is it a reasonable and fair request?									
2. What will be the consequences of my actions?									
3. I need to respond politely and calmly.									
4. I need to reward myself for a good job.									
Total points (1 pt/situation)									

(continued)

punished. I guess it isn't fair to punish nine innocent people because of one student, so you won't have to take this other test. But be warned that future tests will be different for all classes.

Sixth Student: We did a great job. No one lost their cool or yelled swear words or anything nasty. We just stayed calm and came up with some good reasons why it wasn't fair and how she could find the cheaters.

(Students are prompted to check the fourth step under third period if they have not already.)

After students have been instructed on how to use the self-monitoring checklist, they will be instructed to record only situations where the teacher's request or direction makes them feel angry or upset. Students will be shown a video on "anger" so that they are more aware of the signs for anger. Discussion will follow with students talking about

their own warning signals of anger. Lastly, students will be instructed to use the self-monitoring checklist during all periods.

Each of the five collaborating teachers will be instructed to set up situations with two different students a day to ensure that each student is receiving at least one practice session a day. Additionally, parents will be notified prior to implementing this behavior design and asked to sign an agreement to participate in assignments at home. The program, expectations, and monitoring system will have been explained to parents so that they can provide situations where their child(ren) can extend their practice to the home environments. Parents will be asked to monitor their child's performance utilizing these four steps and compare their evaluation with that of their child. Parent signatures will be required on the parent's evaluation which will be returned to the school for bonus points.

Figure 8.7 Letter to Parents

Dear Parents,

As previously discussed, you have agreed to assist _____ in practicing a new four-step strategy to assist him or her in dealing appropriately with adult requests or directions. This means that _____ will not talk back angrily, use offensive language, or refuse to do what is asked of him or her. The attached monitoring checklist is for you to complete. Please read the directions carefully. Additionally, you should have your child go over it with you since he or she has practiced completing it in school. Your child will also be completing his or her own monitor sheet.

When finished with this homework assignment, you may compare your evaluation scores with his or her scores and talk about any discrepancies. If your child has the same score you have, you may give him or her an extra five points by writing your initials on the line marked "5 bonus points."

Thank you for participating with this program. Your support is essential to the success of any program. We hope this program will provide the participating students with better skills to deal with adults appropriately by encouraging them to think about their actions.

Good luck and feel free to call me if you have any issues or concerns that you would like to discuss.

Sincerely,

Ms. D. Cois

(continued)

Figure 8.8

Directions: Please complete the information at the top of the checklist. You have agreed to make **two requests** of your child and monitor his or her response. You may choose one or both of the requests already provided or fill in requests of your choice in the other boxes. These requests need to be *direct* and *specific* as to what you want and when you want it completed. An example might be, "Sam, I want you to set the table right now since dinner will be ready in five minutes. Please don't forget the napkins."

If your child responds as requested in a calm and polite manner, you may assume that she or he thought through the four steps before responding. You may then check each box under the appropriate request column. Four checks in a column for one situation earns two points. If your child fails to respond appropriately, remind him or her to follow the four steps. If he or she still does not comply with your request, place zeros in each of the boxes under that situation and fill out the comment section as to what your child's response was.

After two requests have been made and recorded on the checklist, you can compare your checklist with that of your child. If your child has the same scores you have, you may give him or her an extra five points by writing your initials on the line marked "5 bonus points."

Monitoring Checklist

Name _____ Date _____

Parent's Signature _____ 5 Bonus Points _____

Request/Direction

Four Steps	Assist with preparing dinner	Complete homework without TV on	Other	Other
1. Is it a reasonable and fair request?				
2. What will be the consequences of my actions?				
3. I need to respond politely and calmly.				
4. I need to reward myself for a good job				
Total Points (1 pt/situation)				

Comments _____

_____

_____

(continued)

Group Contingency

Students will self-monitor their responses in all classes to adult requests and directions. Appropriate responses using the four-step strategy will earn one point for each situation. Inappropriate responses (talking back angrily or using inappropriate language) will earn a zero for each situation. For every point, students will earn a penny that will be put in the coin roller. If there are no inappropriate responses (zeros) from anyone during that week, an extra 5 pennies will be earned. When the class has earned 50 pennies, the class will be allowed to play a math game of their choice during third-period math class the following day and given a free homework ticket to be used at their discretion.

Self-monitoring checklists will be randomly monitored. Any checklist found to be inaccurate will cost the individual a day without being able to earn any points.

DISCUSSION QUESTIONS

1. Why is it important to understand the underlying reasons for aggressive behavior?
2. When would you use an "After-the-fact" A-B-C analysis?
3. Why is social skills instruction important for most students who have antisocial behaviors?
4. List five actions to avoid when dealing with students who may have aggressive behaviors.
5. What can you do about bullying?
6. When should you use crisis intervention strategies?
7. Name four strategies for avoiding confrontations.
8. Describe the components of a good social skills training program.
9. Why is role-playing important in social skills instruction?

REFERENCES

Alberg, J., Petry, C., & Eller, A. (1994). *A resource guide for social skills instruction.* Longmont, CO: Sopris West.

Alliance for the Mentally Ill. (1996). The Crisis. *Voice, 3,* 3, 6.

Arllen, N. L., Gable, R. A., & Hendrickson, J. M. (1996). Using peer confrontation to reduce inappropriate student behavior. *Beyond Behavior, 7*(1), 22–23.

Azrin, N.H., & Wesolowski, M.D. (1974). Theft reversal: An overcorrection procedure for eliminating stealing by retarded persons. *Journal of Applied Behavior Therapy, 7,* 578–581.

Bandura, A. (1971). *Social learning theory.* New York: General Learning Press.

Bardill, D. R. (1977). A behavior contracting program of group treatment for early adolescents in a residential treatment setting. *International Journal of Group Psychotherapy, 27,* 389–400.

Blauvelt, P. (1981). Effective strategies for school security. Richmond, VA: National Association of Secondary School Principals.

Children's Defense Fund. (1995). *State of America's Children.* Washington, D.C.: Children's Defense Fund.

Conroy, M. A., & Fox, J. J. (1994). Setting events and challenging behaviors in the classroom: Incorporating contextual factors into effective intervention plans for children with aggressive behaviors. *Preventing School Failure, 38,* 29–34.

Crowe, T. D. (1990). Designing safer schools. *School Safety* (Fall), 9–13.

Donnellan, A. M., Mirenda, P. L., Mesaros, R. A., & Fassbender, L. L. (1984). Analyzing the communicative function of aberrant behavior. *Journal of the Association of the Severely Handicapped, 9,* 201–212.

Garrity, C., Jens, K., Porter, W., Sager, N., & Short-Camilli, C. (1994). *Bully-proofing your school.* Longmont, CO: Sopris West.

Garrity, C., Jens, K., Porter, W., Sager, N., & Short-Camilli, C. (1996). Bully-proofing your school: A comprehensive approach. *Reclaiming Children & Youth, 5,* 36.

Gold, M., & Mann, D. W. (1982). Alternative schools for troublesome secondary students. *The Urban Review, 14,* 305–316.

Goldstein, A. P. (1987). Teaching prosocial skills to aggressive adolescents. In C.M. Nelson, R.B. Rutherford, Jr., & B.I. Wolford (Eds.), *Special education in the criminal justice system* (pp. 215–250). Upper Saddle River, NJ: Merrill/Prentice Hall.

Goldstein, A. P. (1988). *The prepared curriculum: Teaching prosocial competencies.* Champaign, IL: Research Press.

Hammond R., & Young, B. (1991). Dealing with Anger [video]. Champaign, IL: Research Press.

Hood-Smith, N. E., & Leffingwell, R. J. (1984). The impact of physical space alteration in disruptive classroom behavior: A case study. *Education, 104,* 224–230.

Kaufmann, J. M., Grieger, T., & Grieger, R. M. (1976). Effects of peer reporting on cooperative play and aggression of kindergarten students. *Journal of School Psychology, 14,* 308–313.

Kendall, P. C., & Finch, A. J. (1976). A cognitive-behavioral treatment for impulse control: A case study. *Journal of Consulting and Clinical Psychology, 44,* 852–857.

Kerr, M. M., Strain, P. S., & Ragland, E. U. (1982). Component analysis of a teacher-mediated peer-feedback treatment package: Effects on positive and negative interactions of behaviorally handicapped students. *Behavior Modification, 2,* 278–280

Long, N. J., & Morse, W. C. (1996). Conflict in the classroom. Austin, TX: PRO-ED.

Luce, S. C., Delquadri, J., & Hall R. V. (1980). Contingent exercise: A mild but powerful procedure for suppressing inappropriate verbal and aggressive behavior. *Journal of Applied Behavior Analysis, 13,* 583–594.

Luckner, J. (1996). Juggling roles and making changes: Suggestions for meeting the challenges of being a special educator. *Teaching Exceptional Children, 28,* 24–28.

Mayer, G. R., Nafpaktitis, M., Butterworth, T., & Hollingsworth, P. (1987). A search for the elusive setting events of school vandalism: A correlational study. *Education and Treatment of Students, 10,* 259–270.

McAfee, J. K., (1987). Classroom density and the aggressive behavior of handicapped students. *Education and Treatment of Students, 10,* 134–145.

Meador, S.A. (1992). Changing youth's attitudes about guns. *School Safety* (Fall), 31.

Mulvey, E. (1993). *Safe Schools Report.* Unpublished manuscript. University of Pittsburgh, Pittsburgh, PA.

Mulvey, E., Arthur, M., & Reppucci, N. (1993). The prevention and treatment of juvenile delinquency: A review of the research. *Clinical Psychology Review, 13,* 133–167.

National School Safety Center, (1990). *School safety checkbook.* Westlake Village, CA: Author.

Ramsey, E. (1995). *Antisocial behavior in school: Strategies and best practices.* Pacific Grove, CA: Brooks/Cole.

Vorath, H., & Brendtro, L. (1974). *Positive peer culture.* Chicago: Aldine Press.

Rosen, H. S., & Rosen, L. A. (1983). Eliminating stealing: Use of stimulus control with an elementary student. *Behavior Modification, 7,* 56–63.

Walker, H. M., Colvin, G., & Ramsey, E. (1995). *Antisocial behavior in school: Strategies and best practices.* New York: Brooks/Cole.

Walker, H. M., Hops, H., & Greenwood, C. (1993). *RECESS: A program for reducing negative-aggressive behavior.* Seattle, WA: Educational Achievement Systems.

Walker, H. M., & Severson, H. (1990). *Systematic screening for behavior disorders.* Longmont, CO: Sopris West.

9

STEREOTYPIC BEHAVIORS

OUTLINE

OBJECTIVES

After completing this chapter, you should be able to

◆ Define the various types of self-injurious and self-stimulatory behaviors.
◆ Conduct a functional analysis of a stereotypic behavior.
◆ Discuss the theoretical concepts underlying self-stimulatory behavior.
◆ Choose an effective intervention for self-injurious behavior.
◆ Discuss the ethical issues in carrying out aversive and restrictive interventions.
◆ Assist in conducting a sensory extinction intervention.

The behaviors described in this chapter may be the most complex that you will ever confront in teaching. Sadly, they are also serious—if not life-threatening—to the students who exhibit them. Let's look first at what is meant by **self-injurious behavior** and **self-stimulatory behavior** and the terms associated with them.

SELF-INJURIOUS BEHAVIORS

The terms *self-injurious,* **self-mutilating,** and *self-destructive* describe behaviors that hurt the person exhibiting them. These terms are commonly used for chronic, repetitive acts of individuals with severe disabilities (Favell, 1982). In this chapter we use *self-injurious behavior,* or SIB, because it is the term

you are most likely to hear and use. Note that although this term conceivably consists of all acts of self-injury, including suicide and substance abuse (Schroeder, Schroeder, Rojahn, & Mulick, 1981), we do not refer to these behaviors in this chapter.

Favell (1982) summarized into five categories the various kinds of SIB reported in research literature:

1. Striking oneself (e.g., face slapping, head banging against objects).
2. Biting or sucking various body parts (e.g., "mouthing").
3. Pinching, scratching, poking, or pulling various body parts (e.g., eye-poking, hair-pulling).

4. Repeatedly vomiting, or vomiting and reingesting food (i.e., "rumination").
5. Consuming nonedible substances (e.g., eating objects, cigarettes: **pica;** eating feces: **coprophagia**). (p. 1)

These generic categories are reflected in the research definitions of SIB in Table 9.1. These descriptions not only illustrate problem behaviors but give you and your multidisciplinary IEP team ideas for writing target behavior descriptions. Also, note the measurement approaches used by the various authors. These may help you decide how to measure the SIB of your students.

The studies cited are attempts to resolve the serious problems of SIB individuals. This is a new area for researchers and classroom teachers, and you may find that your previous experience and training in the management of SIB are limited. Still, you must try to understand these often frightening behaviors because they can result in serious injury to a student, such as retinal detachment (Favell, 1982), loss of an appendage or of the use of a sensory modality, or a skull fracture. It is imperative that you recognize the significance of SIB and respect the highly systematic interventions designed to treat it.

Let's review some explanations for why these bizarre behaviors occur. Understanding the motivational conditions of SIB is a rapidly developing area for research, often called **functional analysis** (Carr & Durand, 1985; Durand & Carr, 1985).

Durand and Carr (1985) cited four motivational conditions for self-injury. The first, social attention, refers to the maintenance of the behaviors through the verbal or nonverbal feedback of others (Carr & McDowell, 1980). Second, self-injury may be maintained through tangible consequences (e.g., access to play activities). Third, the student may exhibit self-injury to avoid a situation he dislikes (e.g., a difficult self-help lesson). Finally, the sensory feedback a student receives from injuring himself may be reinforcing to him.

Durand and Crimmins (1987) developed an assessment for determining the functional significance of self-injury, the Motivation Assessment Scale (MAS). You and your supervisor might use this instrument (available from V. Mark Durand, State University of New York at Albany) to gain a better understanding of a student's stereotypic behaviors.

A functional analysis of self-injury suggests the purpose for the behavior, and once we understand why a student injures herself, we can move to teaching her alternative behaviors for achieving the same goals. Carr and Durand (1985) illustrated this approach in a communication training program for children with developmental disabilities. Very carefully selected and trained phrases enabled the children to satisfy their needs without resorting to self-injury. Carr & Durand (1985) wrote of another illustration:

> As we have seen, it is essential to match the consequences involved in alternative behaviors to the assessed motivating conditions. Problems may arise if such a match is not made. For example, if a teacher chose to stand up and walk away from a boy who hit himself for attention, then his self-injurious behavior may very well decrease in frequency over time. However, if his self-injurious behavior were escape motivated, having the teacher walk away might produce an increase in self-injurious behavior since the teacher's leaving would be associated with removal of task demands. That is, the teacher would be providing the child with what he wanted, namely, a cessation of the task. This contingency would strengthen self-injurious behavior. The case just discussed illustrates the extreme importance of designing treatment intervention based on the specific motivation of the self-injurious behavior. (p. 175)

SELF-STIMULATORY BEHAVIORS

These actions, like SIB, are repetitive and frequent but do not cause physical injury. **Ritualistic** and **stereotypic** are global terms also used to describe self-stimulatory behaviors. For purposes of this chapter, however, we adopt **self-stimulatory behavior** (SSB), the term most commonly used, to describe "behaviors that are stereotyped and performed repetitiously, and that fail to produce any apparent positive environmental consequences or physical injury" (O'Brien, 1981, p. 117). Examples of self-stimulatory behaviors appear in Table 9.2.

Table 9.1 Definitions of Self-Injurious Behaviors

Behavior	Definition	Measurement Procedure	Authors
Ear pulling and gouging	Closure of fingers, fingernails, or hand on ear with a pulling or digging motion	Occurrence or nonoccurrence of self-injurious behavior during continuous, 10-sec. intervals	Iwata, Dorsey, Slifer, Bauman, & Richman (1994)
Eye gouging	Any contact of any part of hand within the ocular area.		
Face slapping	Forceful contact of the open hand with the face.		
Hair pulling	Closure of the fingers and thumb on hair with a pulling motion away from the head.		
Handmouthing	Insertion of one or more fingers into the mouth.		
Head banging	Forceful contact of the head with a stationary environmental object.		
Head hitting	Forceful contact of the hand with any part of the head.		
Neck choking	Forceful closure of both hands around the neck.		
Self-biting	Closure of the upper and lower teeth on the flesh of any portion of the body.		
Pica	Ingestion of or attempt to ingest nonnutritive items	10-second continuous interval record	Rojahn, McGonigle, Curcio, & Dixon (1987)
Self-injurious behavior (SIB)	Behavior directed against own body, which causes physical damage or presents a health hazard. These SIB types are likely to occur: head hitting (hit her head with her extremities), pinching, thigh slapping, hand pounding on hard surfaces, eye gouging with fingers		
Hand or arm biting	Insertion of the hand or arm into the mouth beyond the lips	Frequency, duration measures	Jenson, Rovner, Cameron, Peterson, & Kesler (1985)
Hand biting	Placing hands into mouth and biting down upon the skin with teeth	Frequency count	Luiselli (1984b)
Self-injurious behavior (SIB)	A tantrum that involves hitting head against the wall or floor, scratching at face, or hitting in the head or upper chest with clenched fists	Frequency count	Rolider & Van Houten (1985)
Mouthing objects	Placing any inappropriate objects such as rocks, napkins, cloth, part of toys, and dirt into his mouth		
Self-injurious behavior (SIB)	Striking face, head, neck, throat, torso, or extremities with closed hand (fist), open hand (palm), or extended fingers	Frequency count	Luiselli (1986)
	Striking face, head, neck, throat, torso, or extremities with any object held in the hand(s)		
	Striking the head against any fixed surface such as a wall, floor, tabletop, or partition		

Table 9.1   *(continued)*

Behavior	Definition	Measurement Procedure	Authors
Self-biting	Self-biting behavior was defined both in terms of frequency of daily occurrence and intensity of each occurrence and was scored when any part of the participant's body was pressed between her upper and lower teeth. The intensity of each occurrence was gauged according to the following five-point scale:	Frequency and intensity	Neufeld & Fantuzzo (1984)
	1. No teeth marks or lesions 2. Teeth marks not breaking skin 3. Scraping skin but no bleeding 4. Breaking skin and bleeding 5. Breaking skin, bleeding, and biting others attempting to restrain her		

Controversy surrounds (and may eventually alter the usage of) the term *self-stimulation* because it implies a questionable motivation for the behavior (Baumeister, 1978). Even today, some authors prefer the term *stereotyped movements* because it is "without inference and purely descriptive" (O'Brien, 1981, p. 118).

Like SIB, self-stimulatory behaviors are seen most often in those with severe behavioral disabilities. Research on the nature of SSB has revealed that this serious behavior problem may be maintained by the perceptual reinforcement that it provides to the self-stimulating individual (Lovaas, Newsom, & Hickman, 1987). Some of the important concepts put forth by these authors will help you understand why SSB is so difficult to eliminate in most individuals:

1. Many self-stimulatory behaviors are "so elaborate and idiosyncratic" (p. 46) that children must have learned them somehow. It is simply inconceivable that a child could be born with such complex behavioral preferences.

2. Children with SSB show a wide range of different kinds of SSB. These self-stimulatory behaviors are nearly identical, regardless of the culture in which the children were reared.

3. Withdrawal of social reinforcers and attention has not reduced these behaviors, which leads us to believe that these self-stimulatory behaviors are not the result of a "common social reinforcement history" (p. 46).

4. While engaged in SSB, children seem to be totally absorbed in their behaviors and become very difficult to interact with socially or instructionally.

5. When children do receive behavioral treatment, they often respond by developing new versions of SSB in place of the targeted behaviors.

6. "The most reliable and inevitable consequences of self-stimulatory behaviors are the perceptual or sensory stimuli that these behaviors produce" (p. 46).

7. SSB is a high-probability behavior, so SSB itself can be seen as a reinforcing event. (Review Chapter 5 on the concept of reinforcement.)

To better understand the particular role of perceptual reinforcement in SSB, consider these points made by Lovaas et al. (1987):

1. The child controls the perceptual reinforcers; these reinforcers are not controlled by others or the environment.

2. Perceptual reinforcers are primary reinforcers. Also, they are quite durable and not as vulnerable to satiation as other reinforcers.

When does a child begin to exhibit self-stimulatory behaviors? Research has shown that these behaviors begin in infancy in some individuals with developmental delays and, in most cases, before

Table 9.2 Definitions of Self-Stimulatory Behaviors

Behavior	Definition	Measurement Procedure	Authors
Scream	Vocalization above normal conversational level that contains no words.	Response rate per minute, using a stopwatch during a 10-minute session.	Bittle & Hake (1977)
Running and hopping	Normal running mixed with hops without any apparent attempt to move to a particular place	Response rate per minute, using a stopwatch during a 10-minute session.	
Arm waving	Extending arms at a 90° angle from one's side, moving them in a circular motion.	Response rate per minute, using a stopwatch during a 10-minute session.	
Finger wiggling	Putting hands in front of face spreading fingers apart, and then slowly flexing and extending them one at a time in sequence.	Response rate per minute, using a stopwatch during a 10-minute session.	
Looking out the corner of eyes	Turning head in one direction while moving eyes in the opposite direction without any apparent attempt to focus on an object.	Response rate per minute, using a stopwatch during a 10-minute session.	
Mouthing	Placing one or both hands, any fingers, or a toy in or on the mouth	Scoring each 10-second interval in a 10-minute session as to whether self-stimulation or appropriate play occurred. (If both occurred, then only self-stimulation was scored.)	Coleman, Whitman, & Johnson (1979)
Head back	Tilting the head back at an angle of 45° to the normal upright position.		
Body motion	Any back and forth movement of the head and shoulders and the torso with the back moving away from and toward the chair back at least twice in a row.		
Bouncing	Bouncing up and down in the seat with up and down leg motion or kicking.		
Public masturbation	Putting either hand inside pants and directed toward penis. Hand was defined as in pants whenever one fingernail disappeared from view. Response ended when hand or fingers were removed from pants. Public masturbation meant that the behavior occurred anywhere outside the child's bedroom or bathroom.	Rate of masturbation responses per day, measured during six 5-minute time samples.	Cook, Altman, Shaw, & Blaylock (1978)
Rubbing saliva	Placing fingers into mouth for 1–2 seconds, wetting them with saliva, and then rubbing the fingers together as student removed them from mouth.	Frequency count	Luiselli (1984a)

Table 9.2 (*continued*)

Behavior	Definition	Measurement Procedure	Authors
Tongue protrusion	Thrusting tongue out of mouth and exposing it for several seconds.		
Stereotypy	Excessive manipulation of the environment (turning the water taps on and off, opening and closing doors, etc.), pacing back and forth or in circles, rocking back and forth or from side to side, finger pilling (a continuous motion of rubbing thumb and fingertips together or on her clothing), and continuous nonsense vocalizations (repeated out of context phrases at a rapid pace).	Occurrence or nonoccurrence of the behavior. If the behavior occurred at all during the minute, the interval was scored for the presence of stereotypy.	Rolider, Williams Cummings, & Van Houten (1991).

the age of two years in most cases (Berkson, McQuiston, Jacobson, Eyman, & Borthwick, 1985).

How does a child "learn" to engage in SSB? Consider this illustration (Lovaas et al., 1987):

An autistic child initially twirls a string in a variety of different ways. Sooner or later (through trial and error) a pattern of string movements is discovered that is particularly attractive to look at (i.e., that strongly reinforces twirling the string). With practice, he or she learns to perform exactly the right manipulation of the string to achieve the preferred pattern and tends to perform only that topography and closely related topographies most of the time. Consider another example: A child will retrieve and then skillfully manipulate a variety of objects (dishes, sinkstoppers, balls, etc.) to make them rotate or spin. Once the object comes to a resting position he or she will resume the behavioral sequence. In such an example, the child's spinning of various objects may be an acquired response, an operant, whose visual consequence (the spinning object) is the perceptual reinforcer that shapes and maintains the response. In the example of the child who repeatedly arranges (lines) objects such as toys, books, or shoes in neat rows across the living room floor, "objects in a line" may constitute a positively reinforcing perceptual consequence, shaping and maintaining the lining behavior. (p. 49)

How does SSB persist? SSB is highly reinforcing, and individuals engaged in SSB simply may not have other, alternative behaviors in which to engage.

As you study intervention possibilities later in this chapter, you will notice an emphasis on controlling the perceptual experiences of self-stimulating individuals. Also, you will learn how very carefully all assessments and interventions must be implemented if a program is to have any success with this difficult and durable set of behaviors. If you work with students with severe disabilities, the behaviors listed in Table 9.2 are probably familiar. Research has uncovered 50 types of SSB (LaGrow & Repp, 1984), only a few of which are included.

Self-stimulatory behaviors are not harmful in themselves but may, in time, change to self-injurious behaviors through a slight shift in topography (O'Brien, 1981). Furthermore, several researchers have reported that SSB dramatically limits an individual's attention to learning activities, thus reducing the potential skills repertoire of an already deficient learner (Foxx & Azrin, 1973). It would seem then that considerable effort should be expended toward the reduction of these troublesome behaviors. Indeed, this is now the generally accepted course of treatment.

A Note About SIB and SSB Assessment and Interventions

The format of other chapters has been modified to accommodate the unusual issues surrounding the management of SIB and SSB problems. The major difference between this chapter and others is that fewer procedures are outlined in step-by-step fashion. We describe a few assessment and intervention procedures that you can implement with little supervision or outside help. Our exclusion of certain procedures will not be popular with many educators, who argue that "we already have these students in our classrooms—why not go ahead and tell us how to use all of the interventions available?" We can only reiterate our concern that you may inadvertently misuse a procedure because of problems with time, support personnel, supervision, effectiveness data, and approvals. As Judith Favell (1982) stated in her monograph on self-injurious behavior for the American Association of Behavior Therapy:

> The apparent simplicity of these techniques may be misleading. They are complex procedures which require a high degree of competence to design and conduct. The improper use of any procedure may place a self-injurious client at severe risk. (p. 20)

Despite their documented effectiveness, many interventions are prohibited in school settings because they create discomfort for the target student. Aversive procedures (always a last resort) have been replaced with more positive interventions in recent years (Van Houten, 1993; Iwata et al., 1994). Therefore, a second consideration is the use of alternative, nonaversive procedures that might be suggested through a good functional analysis. For example, you might discover that SIB occurs primarily when instructional demands are placed on the child—a finding described by Carr, Newsom, and Binkoff (1976). By changing the instructional schedule or the environmental demands, you may affect SIB. Iwata et al. (1994) studied individuals with visual impairments and reported that those who engaged in eye-poking may have increased their visual stimulation. Bright flashing lights or massages of the eye area contingent upon no self-injurious behaviors might work as interventions, if implemented properly.

Lovaas and Favell (1987) stated that

> If a program cannot conduct alternative interventions in a high-quality fashion, then it should not employ aversive procedures. (p. 320)
>
> . . . the use of aversive and restrictive interventions should only be considered in the context of several

issues surrounding their use. Such techniques are justified only when their effects are rigorously evaluated, caregivers are fully trained and adequately supervised in all dimensions of habilitative services, when a meaningful functional analysis of the child's problem has been conducted, alternative and benign treatments have been considered and are in place, parents and others are fully informed, and there is general agreement that the means justify the ends. (p. 324)

Furthermore, as Lovaas and Favell pointed out in their 1987 essay:

> These complexities illustrate the need for a "functional analysis" of what is reinforcing a particular client's problem behavior in order to prescribe an adequate treatment, whether that treatment contains aversive consequences or not. This requirement raises again the question of whether a facility or agency has adequately trained staff to conduct such a functional analysis before any kind of treatment is employed. It is a serious concern that because some programs do not have the expertise and resources to functionally analyze problem behavior, they employ aversive procedures in an attempt to override the reinforcers maintaining them. Quite the opposite should be true. Only programs that are capable of conducting an adequate analysis of problem behavior should be allowed to employ aversive and restrictive treatments. (p. 318)

Now let's turn to the assessment procedures for SIB, followed by a discussion of interventions (environmental and teacher-mediated).

ASSESSMENT OF SIB

The data you collect in performing multilevel assessments of SIB will help you

◆ Recognize physiological and/or biological factors in SIB.
◆ Analyze the interaction between SIB and environment variables.
◆ Summarize information so that you can get assistance from a behavioral consultant.
◆ Learn procedures that will prove useful in monitoring progress of subsequent interventions.

The last is especially critical because, as Favell (1982) stated, "it is not possible to predict in advance if a given procedure or set of procedures will be effective in an individual case" (p. 21). Favell went on to recommend that thorough analysis of the behaviors precede any pinpointing of behaviors for intervention:

> A prior analysis of biological and environmental conditions and consequences which may be maintaining the client's self-injury, and the explicit inclusion of that information in the design of [the intervention should be conducted]. . . . Such an analysis must be done situation by situation, since different situations control different rates and intensities of self-injury, and because even in situations in which self-injury does occur, the behavior may serve very different functions. For example, at times the behavior may serve to escape demands, at others it may function to obtain attention. (p. 18)

You may want assistance in conducting a comprehensive behavioral analysis; certain health-related information could be provided by the school nurse or physician with help from the student's parents. Complete this step before proceeding with any intervention, because this medical history is critical to determining whether the student has recently had or now needs a comprehensive physical and neuropsychiatric examination, as well as comprehensive testing for syndromes thought to cause SIB (Lesch-Nyan Syndrome, Cornelia de Lange's Syndrome). It is helpful to keep a daily log of bruises, cuts, and other injuries that may appear, as well as of SIB such as pica, vomiting, and rumination. Be sure to record any oral or topical medications (e.g., lotion for chapped or scratched skin) administered.

An environmental analysis calls for several items of information gathered in various settings and demand-situations. Figure 9.1 outlines components of an ecological approach. (See Iwata, Dorsey, Slifer, Bauman, & Richman, 1994, for a more detailed discussion of variables that contribute to SIB.) Because SIB varies within and across individuals, it is critical that you carry out a comprehensive individualized functional analysis (Iwata et al., 1994).

Naturally, the first item on the form requests a specific definition of the problem behavior or behaviors. Since SIB is rarely confined to one

environment, say, school, we have included items that reflect different settings and different times of day. These variables are combined in question 4, which asks for information regarding possible alternative behaviors. Research on SIB individuals suggests that injurious behavior may be decreased by reinforcing alternative, noninjurious behaviors (Mulick, Hoyt, Rojahn, & Schroeder, 1978). Therefore, it is important for you to consider alternative behaviors to substitute for SIB.

Question 5 asks for demands on the individual. Again, studies have indicated that levels of SIB may be altered by the presence of demands (Iwata et al., 1994), or by activities the student finds particularly stressful. Questions regarding consequation for SIB (7 and 8) reflect the need for a thorough understanding of what has maintained, reduced, or increased SIB in the past. Before designing and initiating a new intervention, your consultant and multidisciplinary team should examine closely the data on prior attempts at intervention (see question 9).

A completed environmental analysis should provide your intervention team with specific settings, time, and adult actions for further examination. For a more complete review of SIB research on environmental variables, see Schroeder et al. (1981).

INTERVENTION STRATEGIES FOR SIB

Following are strategies to decrease self-injurious behaviors. Some you will be able to implement by yourself, while other programs require outside help.

Environmental Changes

As mentioned earlier, your multidisciplinary team, treatment team, or behavioral consultant may want to alter one or more of the following antecedent circumstances in order to determine their effects on SIB:

◆ The demands placed on an individual during a specific part of the daily routine (or the reinforcement the student receives for compliance with that demand).

Figure 9.1 Environmental Analysis Forms for SIB

Student _____ Age _____

Date _____ Teacher _____

1. What is (are) this student's self-injurious behavior(s)? Describe specifically.
   _____
   _____

2. List all the settings in which this behavior is exhibited.
   _____
   _____

3. At what times of day does the student engage in the SIB?
   _____
   _____

4. What activities could the student engage in, throughout the day, if he were not injuring himself?

Time	Alternative Activity
7–8 am	
8–9	
9–10	
10–11	
11–12	
12–1 pm	
1–2	
2–3	
3–4	
4–5	
5–6	
6–7	
7–8	
8–9	
9–10	
10–11 pm	

5. What demands are made of the student immediately prior to episodes of SIB? (Use an A-B-C analysis to determine this.)

Demand	Setting	SIB

6. Are there particular antecedent events that you associate with this student's SIB?
   _____
   _____

7. When the student engages in SIB, what happens?

Setting	Consequence

8. List all interventions you presently use to control the SIB (e.g., verbal statements, restraints, punishment, DRO).
   _____
   _____
   _____
   _____

9. Do you have data on these interventions? _____ Please provide, if yes.
   _____
   _____
   _____

◆ The available, reinforceable alternative activities that the student can engage in.

◆ The physical restraints used with a client and the schedule for applying and removing them (see Favell, McGimsey, & Jones, 1978).

◆ The student's daily routine, with the possibility of rearranging stressful events.

It is imperative to remember that any such alteration depends on a thorough analysis of each individual's behavior.

Environmental Safety Considerations

To prevent a self-injurious student from further harm, take safety precautions in your classroom. Remove any chemicals that may be toxic (e.g., typewriter correction fluid; cleaning supplies; medications; and paint). Take the position that a self-injurious child or adolescent does not possess the judgment necessary to determine what might be dangerous. Remove sharp objects such as scissors, pens, needles, paper clips, and thumbtacks. It may be necessary to cushion hard surfaces if the student pounds them with head or body.

Restraint Devices

SIB is sometimes treated through the application of various kinds of restraints (Dorsey, Iwata, Reid, & Davis, 1982; Neufeld & Fantuzzo, 1984; Rincover & Devany, 1982). This intervention does not prevent self-injurious behaviors themselves, but it attempts to limit the harm of the stereotypic behavior. The disadvantages associated with restraints are (1) they do not teach new behaviors or eliminate the targeted ones, (2) they interfere with learning alternative behaviors (and may interfere with hearing and other senses), and (3) the appearance of a restraint may cause others to ostracize the child (Baumeister & Rollings, 1976). If your staff is considering a restraint procedure, consult Neufeld and Fantuzzo (1984) for the technical design of a "Bubble" restraint that does not interfere with other behaviors and that was successful in treating hand-biting. This chapter's case study illustrates a safe alternative to restraints, which effectively reduced face slapping in one individual.

Differential Reinforcement of Other Behaviors (DRO) Program

Differential reinforcement of other behaviors (DRO) is a term frequently cited in descriptions of programs for SIB (or SSB) individuals. DRO procedures often accompany other interventions. Research has not proven DRO as successful as the "suppression interventions" in eliminating SIB (Dorsey, Iwata, Ong, & McSween, 1980; Iwata et al., 1994), but we often rely on DRO to teach the student vitally needed alternative behaviors (Jenson, Rovner, Cameron, Peterson, & Kesler, 1985). The basic notion of a DRO program is the reinforcement of intervals at a time during which the SIB (or other undesirable behavior) does not occur. For example, students might be reinforced initially each time they engage in ten seconds, then fifteen, then twenty seconds of non-SIB behavior.

In some programs based on the DRO procedure, reinforcement is administered for intervals of time during which certain behaviors incompatible with SIB are exhibited (e.g., putting together a puzzle without biting one's hand). These programs are then termed DRI, or differential reinforcement of incompatible behaviors. Table 9.3 provides a step-by-step procedure for conducting a DRO or DRI program.

Overcorrection

Overcorrection procedures have been used with conflicting results to modify self-injurious behaviors (Bierly & Billingsley, 1983; Carey & Bucher, 1986; Gibbs & Luyben, 1985; Iwata et al., 1994; Luiselli, 1984a, 1984b). During an overcorrection procedure, the student engages in practice of nonstereotyped behaviors while at the same time undergoing the removal of positive reinforcement for these behaviors. The goals of overcorrection programs, both restitutional and positive practice, have been described by their developers, Foxx and Azrin (1973).

In restitutional overcorrection, the self-injury is interrupted and the student is required to restore her immediate environment to an improved condition by practicing appropriate behaviors. To conduct a restitutional overcorrection

Table 9.3 Guidelines for Using a DRO or DRI Procedure

1. Set aside a block of time (e.g., 15 minutes daily or several such times per day) to conduct the training.

2. Arrange for a staff member to spend time with (or near, in later stages) the student during these sessions.

3. Record rate-per-minute baseline data on the problem behaviors, and chart them. Continue recording data throughout the program.

4. Select an appropriate behavior to reinforce (preferably one that is incompatible with the problem behavior). Be sure to choose a behavior that you can count easily by the frequency or interval method. If you cannot count it, you will have difficulty knowing when to reinforce it!

5. Select a powerful reinforcer for the student. Be sure you can remove the reinforcer from the student if response cost is to be incorporated into the procedure.

6. Gather the reinforcers, a container for them (e.g., clear plastic cup), and a data record sheet, and ask the student to sit across the table from you.

7. Say, "It's time to work (play)," and give the student the necessary items to engage in the appropriate (other) behavior (e.g., ballpoint pens to assemble and place in a tray, a toy car to roll toward you, a favorite stuffed animal to cuddle without self-stimulating).

8. Beginning with a "rich" schedule of reinforcement, provide the student with the reinforcer for each appropriate "other" behavior (each pen assembled) or for a brief interval of appropriate behavior (e.g., 5 to 10 seconds of play with the teacher using a toy). If you use response cost, keep the reinforcers in the container until the end of the session.

9. If you desire, you can implement a response cost procedure at the same time. For this procedure, take away one (or two) of the reinforcers at each instance of the problem behavior after saying, "NO (*problem behavior*)!"

10. As the data indicate progress (e.g., a reduction in the response per minute of problem behaviors), you can "thin" the reinforcement schedule: you reinforce less frequently and require longer and longer intervals of time spent in the appropriate "other" behavior.

11. Be sure to praise the student at each time of reinforcement and to change the reinforcer if it seems no longer effective.

12. Do not use the verbal reprimand, "NO (*problem behavior*)" at times when you cannot remove the reinforcer until you see definite, stable behavior improvement.

---

procedure properly, you must first define the problem behaviors. Table 9.1 provides well-specified target behavior statements. **Restitutional overcorrection** is used for self-injurious and oppositional behaviors but not for self-stimulatory behaviors, which do not upset the environment. For example, restitutional overcorrection might be recommended for a child who smears feces, injures the inside of his mouth, or in some other way harms himself or damages his environment. Table 9.4 displays examples of overcorrection activities.

Correctly implementing overcorrection requires considerable staff time, so you will need help conducting this program. Review the guidelines, and once again, do not undertake this or any other SIB intervention without supervision from someone who has been trained to use overcorrection. Also, remember that overcorrection programs may require approval from the review committee and the student's parents. Check with your supervisor about this. Table 9.5 provides guidelines for implementing restitutional overcorrection.

Positive practice overcorrection is similar to restitutional overcorrection (see Table 9.6). Unlike restitutional overcorrection, it does not require the learner to restore the environment.

Table 9.4 Suggested Restitutional and Positive Practice Activities for Self-Stimulatory and Self-Injurious Behaviors

Problem Behavior	Suggested Overcorrection Activity
Mouthing objects, injuring inside of mouth	Brush teeth with an oral antiseptic (mouthwash) and wipe lips with washcloth soaked in mouthwash. Periodically encourage student to spit out the rinse.[a]
Head weaving	Functional Movement Training for 5–7 minutes: Guide student to hold his head in each of three positions, up, down, and straight, for 15 seconds. (Give instructions in a random order.)[a]
Clapping	Guide student through a series of hand positions, or Functional Movement Training. For example, have the student hold hands out, above her head, together, and behind back, holding each position for 15 seconds.[a]
Hand flapping "airplaneing"	Hold each of these positions for 15 seconds, repeating the entire series 15 times: hands on head, hands straight up, hands on shoulders, hands on hips.

[a] *Source:* These activities were taken from Foxx, R. M., & Azrin, N. H. (1973). The elimination of autistic self-stimulatory behavior by overcorrection. *Journal of Applied Behavior Analysis, 6,* 1–14.

Table 9.5 Guidelines for Using Restitutional Overcorrection

1. Define the problem behavior or behaviors specifically.

2. Record baseline data on the rate or frequency of the problem behavior for at least three days. (Continue data collection during the program.)

3. Select a verbal cue to use when the student engages in the problem behavior. For example, "no throwing" or "no smearing."

4. Select a restitutional activity that is relevant to the problem behavior (see Table 9.4 for ideas). Be sure this activity sequence is long and extensive enough to have an impact on the student.

5. Decide when the program will be in effect each day, and then arrange an adequate amount of time and staff assistance to implement the program. An adult must be available for at least 45 minutes per problem behavior instance in the initial days of the program.

6. When the student engages in the problem behavior, give the verbal cue and proceed with the restitutional activity. Be prepared to prompt the student physically to complete the activities.

7. Avoid eye contact, unnecessary physical contact, and unnecessary conversation during restitutional overcorrection.

8. If the student reengages in one of the designated problem behaviors during the overcorrection procedure, start the activities again.

9. *Never* use the verbal cue without the restitutional overcorrection activities until the problem behaviors are reduced to a low and stable rate.

10. Be sure to provide ample opportunity during the rest of the day for the student to receive attention for appropriate behaviors.

11. *Remember:* This program may require parental/guardian permission and should be implemented under the supervision of a professional competent in this aspect of behavior modification. Medical approval of this program should be obtained prior to the student's participation in it.

Source: The material in this table was taken from Foxx, R. M., & Azrin, N. H. (1973). The elimination of autistic self-stimulatory behavior by overcorrection. *Journal of Applied Behavior Analysis, 6,* 1–14.

Positive practice overcorrection is used for behaviors that do not upset the environment or for behaviors for which no restitutional activity can be reasonably developed. Refer again to Table 9.4 for suggested positive practice activities. Positive practice overcorrection procedures are frequently described as successfully reducing the level of self-stimulatory or self-injurious behaviors. However, there is evidence to suggest that new forms of injurious behaviors may appear if they are not also included in the overcorrection procedure (Epstein, Doke, Sajwaj, Sorrell, & Rimmer, 1974). To avoid this negative side effect, be sure that your overcorrection procedure is closely monitored by a trained behavioral program specialist and that more acceptable replacement behaviors are reinforced.

Gibbs and Luyben (1985) showed that timeout from reinforcement (i.e., preventing the individual from engaging in the preferred stereotypic behavior) was a critical feature of successful overcorrection. Accordingly, we classify *positive* practice overcorrection as a restrictive procedure. This is in keeping with the advice of Foxx and Bechtel (1982) who suggested that the phrase *positive practice* be dropped from the term. (We have maintained the traditional title to assist readers who are acquainted with the two subtypes of overcorrection and who know of other, more purely educative uses of positive practice overcorrection.) However, one study suggested that you can maintain the effectiveness of the overcorrection by reinforcing the students for correctly practicing the designated behavior (Carey & Bucher, 1986). Correct responses, performed without physical guidance from the adult, earned the child edibles and praise. The child received no feedback for approximate responses.

Table 9.6 Guidelines for Using Positive Practice Overcorrection

1. Define the problem behavior or behaviors specifically.

2. Record baseline data on the rate or percent of intervals of occurrence of each behavior. Continue collecting data throughout the overcorrection program.

3. Select a verbal cue to use when the student engages in the problem behavior.

4. Select a positive practice overcorrection activity, such as Functional Movement Training (see Table 9.4). Be sure the activity is sufficiently lengthy and intensive to modify the student's behavior.

5. Decide when the program will be in effect each day, and then arrange an adequate amount of time and staff assistance to implement the program. An adult must be available for at least 45 minutes per problem behavior instance in the initial days of the program.

6. When the student engages in the problem behavior, give the verbal cue and proceed with the positive practice activity. Be prepared to physically prompt the student to complete the activities.

7. Avoid eye contact, unnecessary physical contact, and unnecessary conversation during positive practice overcorrection.

8. If the student reengages in one of the designated problem behaviors during the overcorrection procedure, start the activities again.

9. *Never* use the verbal cue without the overcorrection activities, until the problem behaviors are reduced to a low and stable rate.

10. Be sure to provide ample opportunity during the rest of the day for the student to receive attention for appropriate behaviors.

11. *Remember:* This program may require parental/guardian permission and should be implemented under the supervision of a professional competent in this aspect of behavior modification. Medical approval of this program should be obtained prior to the student's participation in it.

Source: The material in this table was taken from Foxx, R. M., & Azrin, N. H. (1973). The elimination of autistic self-stimulatory behavior by overcorrection. *Journal of Applied Behavior Analysis, 6,* 1–14.

Remember that positive practice overcorrection is considered a punishment procedure that must be applied contingently after an episode of the target behavior, so you cannot schedule the practice sessions but must interrupt your classroom activities to conduct the practice contingently (Gibbs & Luyben, 1985). Moreover, the timeout from the preferred stereotypic behavior is a valuable component of the intervention and strengthens the view that overcorrection is a restrictive intervention requiring special consent and approval.

Positive practice overcorrection can be applied if the student is physically smaller than the adult in charge. Some students, however, are too strong and resistant to complete a functional movement training series. In the initial days of an overcorrection program, a student may struggle with you to continue self-injurious behaviors instead of following the positive practice activities (Luiselli, 1984a, 1984b). When working with a student whose physical stature prevents you from conducting the typical overcorrection functional movement exercises, your consultant may suggest exercises that only partially involve the student's body. For example, DeCatanzaro and Baldwin (1978) used a forced arm exercise, relying only on the arm involved in self-injurious acts. The teacher gently pumped the student's arm up and down once per second, repeating this action 25 times. Foxx (1978) offered the following guideline for using overcorrection with a counteraggressive individual:

> if the overcorrection requires the involvement of two trainers instead of one, the danger of physical injury is greatly increased, and the procedure will not be implemented correctly. (Foxx, 1978, cited in Schroeder et al., 1981, p. 83)

Remember that the student must receive positive attention at times other than during the overcorrection activities. Conduct a daily DRO program to teach the student functional skills.

Movement Suppression Procedure

The **movement suppression procedure** is a variation of timeout from reinforcement in which the student is punished for any movement or verbalization while in timeout (Rolider & Van Houten, 1985; Rolider, Williams, Cummings, & Van Houten, 1991). In the Rolider and Van Houten study, DRO alone (praise and candy every fifteen minutes of no targeted behavior) was compared with movement suppression timeout plus DRO. The movement suppression intervention consisted of the parents or school staff placing the child in the corner, restraining his movements manually, and directing him not to move or talk. This lasted for three minutes. This procedure was replicated with slight modifications across cases of SIB in two other children; all reports were successful.

If you are on a team that is deciding which of several related interventions to try, review the Rolider et al. studies (1985; 1991); they provide comparative information on movement suppression plus DRO versus other treatments (e.g., contingent restraint, exclusionary timeout, corner timeout, and timeout in a wheelchair, respectively).

ASSESSMENT OF SSB

Perhaps the first decision to be made with regard to referring a problem with SSB is whether it warrants treatment. In the event that a stereotypic behavior has become self-injurious, the decision is a quick "yes!" As pointed out by O'Brien (1991), there are types of SSB that, if repeated over time, are self-injurious: "tapping knuckles on hard surfaces . . . flipping fingers in front of eyes focused on the sun, keeping hands in a tight fist around the collar of a shirt" (page 143).

An SSB individual may not gain access to less restrictive environments or to training programs within the present environment until the "annoying" SSB is reduced or eliminated (Baumeister, 1978; O'Brien, 1981). O'Brien illustrated this situation:

> Decreasing annoyance is a reason for treating self-stimulation. If parents, teachers, or peers reprimand, berate, or tease a client for self-stimulation, it should be treated. Similarly, treatment should be provided if clients are regularly required to accept less preferred sitting or sleeping arrangements because they self-stimulate. Requiring clients to sit in a

position farthest from the television set, sit at the least preferred table in the dining room, sleep in a less-preferred bed, or sit in a less-preferred seat on the bus are examples of this. When these types of annoyance can be reduced, it seems reasonable to treat self-stimulation. (p. 143)

In classroom situations you may choose to pursue the assessment of the problem because SSB interferes with a student's ability to attend to appropriate instructional or adaptive behavior tasks (Foxx & Azrin, 1973; Lovaas et al., 1987). To define an SSB problem, use the questions in Figure 9.2 to assemble information gathered from the student's teachers and the student's family. The information listed on this form will help you complete your functional analysis of the student's SSB.

As you read about interventions for SSB, you will understand why certain items of information are important to a thorough definition and analysis of SSB. For example, questions regarding the type of sensory stimulation a student appears to gain from SSB (questions 3 and 4) provide initial information for a sensory extinction program, whereas questions 7, 8, and 9 target information for a DRO or punishment program. You should also complete a health history form or ask the student's parents to do this.

You need to record specific samples of SSB in preparation for (or to monitor the effects of) an intervention program. Review Table 9.2; the third column describes measurement procedures used for SSB. Notice that interval-based measurements

Figure 9.2 Information-Gathering Form for SSB

Student _____ Date _____

1. What are the precise behaviors of concern?
2. Do these behaviors occur interchangeably, simultaneously, or separately?

3. Is any kind of sensory stimulation apparent (e.g., visual flickering, repetitive auditory signal)? In other words, what kind of *perceptual reinforcement* does the SSB provide the child?

4. Does the behavior appear only in selected settings (e.g., areas where there is a hard, smooth surface, well-lit areas)?

5. Do the behaviors prevent the student from engaging in an instructional activity? How?

6. Do the behaviors gain attention for the student from adults or peers? If so, what kind of attention? (Use an A-B-C analysis.)

7. Does the student cease self-stimulation when asked? For how long? When asked by whom? In what tone of voice?

8. Does the student stop these behaviors when alone? In the presence of whom?

9. Does the student stop the behaviors when engaged in certain activities? Specify these activities.

10. Could the self-stimulatory behaviors be considered developmentally age-appropriate for this student (e.g., masturbation)?

11. Is the student injuring himself?

12. Is the student presently involved in an intervention program? What is it? Where are the data on this program?

Name of person completing this form _____

Figure 9.3 Interval Record for Self-Stimulatory Behaviors

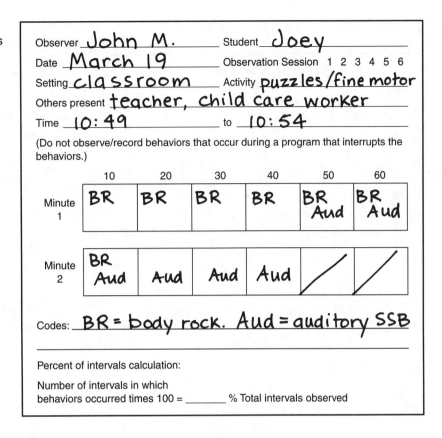

Observer __John M.__   Student __Joey__

Date __March 19__   Observation Session 1 2 3 4 5 6

Setting __classroom__   Activity __puzzles/fine motor__

Others present __teacher, child care worker__

Time __10:49__   to __10:54__

(Do not observe/record behaviors that occur during a program that interrupts the behaviors.)

	10	20	30	40	50	60
Minute 1	BR	BR	BR	BR	BR Aud	BR Aud
Minute 2	BR Aud	Aud	Aud	Aud	/	/

Codes: __BR = body rock. Aud = auditory SSB__

Percent of intervals calculation:

Number of intervals in which behaviors occurred times 100 = _____ % Total intervals observed

are often used. We suggest you record SSB using an interval record such as the one in Figure 9.3. (If you have questions about designing or using an interval record, reread Chapter 3.)

These assessment activities should provide information to facilitate the design of an appropriate intervention, although the task is still not simple. O'Brien (1981) offers these guidelines:

Should a decision be made to treat self-stimulation, a behavioral evaluation must be completed. The evaluation should determine the situations in which self-stimulation occurs, its topography, frequency, and duration, and its consequences. If during the evaluation it is found the self-stimulation occurred only under one condition (e.g., in front of a particular mirror, when wearing turtle-neck sweaters), and it was reasonable to restrict the client from this condition, that might be the preferred treatment. Should it seem unreasonable to restrict the client from a particular situation in

which self-stimulation occurred, it might be reasonable to apply sensory extinction (e.g., if self-stimulation occurs only at a wooden desk, the client should be seated in a soft-fabric chair). Should a behavioral evaluation determine that people regularly provide a consequence for the self-stimulation, that consequence should be reviewed as a possible reinforcer. Should the behavior evaluation determine that self-stimulation occurs in many different situations, that the sensory consequences would be difficult to modify, and that no other consequences are regularly provided, a program should be designed along the recommendations presented by Foxx and Azrin (1973), including teaching and reinforcing adaptive behaviors, interrupting self-stimulation, and scheduling an annoying consequence to follow such. When designing a treatment based on these recommendations, planners must address themselves to two treatment concerns: providing the least restrictive (less intrusive) plan and providing treatment that is effective. (pp. 144–145)

Intervention Strategies for SSB

Research in the area of self-stimulatory behavior has important implications for your work as a classroom teacher. Some of the following interventions are effective with self-stimulatory behaviors, while others are not.

Social Reinforcement Approaches

Evidence has shown that self-stimulatory behavior does not extinguish with the withdrawal of social reinforcement (Lovaas et al., 1987; Newsom, 1974). In other words, ignoring a self-stimulating child will not affect her problem behavior. The attention of others is simply not powerful enough to compete successfully with the perceptual reinforcement the child receives from SSB. While SSB may not respond favorably to extinction, a child's other behaviors may improve with this withdrawal of social reinforcement. You do not want to eliminate this strategy for a self-injurious child.

Sensory Preferences

Children engaged in SSB appear to have strong preferences for particular sensory experiences (e.g., either auditory or visual) (Lovaas et al., 1987). This finding underscores the importance of a painstaking analysis of the student's behaviors and the circumstances that maintain them.

Reinforcing Alternative Behaviors

The DRO approach described earlier might prove helpful in teaching the child alternative behaviors, but it does not seem fruitful as an intervention to eliminate SSB. This is a bit confusing for you because you may notice that the stereotypic behaviors do lessen when the DRO is implemented. This problem arises when—as has been observed—the self-stimulatory behaviors return once the DRO is terminated (Lovaas et al., 1987).

Enriching the Environment

No matter how interesting you make your classroom, environmental manipulation alone will not reduce self-stimulatory behaviors (Favell, McGimsey, & Schell, 1982; Murphy, Carr, & Callias, 1986). However, there is evidence that self-stimulating individuals prefer objects (e.g., toys) that give them their preferred mode of perceptual feedback (Favell et al., 1982), so you might want to consider this variable as you plan your classroom activities.

Perceptual Reinforcement

As you will recall, the key to understanding SSB is to view it as a form of perceptual reinforcement to the individual. Therefore, we believe that forthcoming research will prove sensory manipulation strategies to be the most effective. Some interventions for reducing SSB require outside behavior change agents, but in many you may play a major role. (Several procedures are described in "Intervention Strategies for SIB," so we will only mention them here.)

Environmental Safety Considerations

In the discussion of SIB we mentioned safety precautions to take in the classroom, unless an individual is to be restrained (a last resort). For ethical reasons restraints usually are not recommended for SSB students. It is difficult to justify the deliberate restraint of an individual whose behavior is hurting no one. Nevertheless, students who engage in self-stimulatory behaviors may incorporate some aspect of the environment as a part of their behavioral syndrome, thus creating a safety risk. Do not permit self-stimulatory students to use sharp objects, breakable items, or damaged toys as a part of a self-stimulatory sequence, for example. Toys that are safe for normal youngsters may present a hazard for a student who will use them inappropriately.

Sensory Extinction Procedure

A development in the alteration of self-stimulatory behaviors, sensory extinction, is based on the notion that certain individuals have a strong preference for one aspect of sensory input (e.g., tactile, proprioceptive, visual, or auditory) and engage in self-stimulatory behaviors to increase this sensory input (Aiken & Salzberg, 1984; Rincover & Devany, 1982; Rincover, Newsom, & Carr, 1979). For example, a child may spin objects for the auditory feedback (the sound of the plate spinning), may finger-flap (for the visual feedback of watching his finger movements), or tap his fingers (for the proprioceptive stimulation).

The first step in a sensory extinction program is to determine the sensory input the student receives while engaged in the behavior. He may exhibit a behavior that provides more than one type of sensory feedback; in that case, additional sensory analyses must be completed. One study described such an assessment procedure (Rincover, 1978):

> We observed each child throughout the day and consulted with the teachers in an attempt to identify possible sensory consequences of their self-stimulatory behavior. We found that Reggie would incessantly spin objects, particularly a plate, in a stereotyped, repetitive manner. However, when he twirled the plate, he would also cock his head to the side and lean toward it, seeming to listen to the plate as it was spinning. This suggested that the auditory feedback may have been an important consequence of Reggie's self-stimulation. Robert engaged in excessive finger-flapping, in which he had one or both hands in front of his face and vigorously moved the fingers (but not the arms) back and forth. In this case, two sensory consequences were identified for testing: the visual feedback from watching the finger movements, and the proprioceptive stimulation from the finger movement itself. Brenda's self-stimulatory behavior consisted of twirling objects such as a feather or string of beads in front of her eyes. For Brenda, as with Robert, both the visual and the proprioceptive components were targeted for testing.
>
> During sensory extinction sessions we attempted to eliminate a particular sensory consequence of a given self-stimulatory behavior. First, in order to eliminate the auditory feedback from Reggie's plate spinning, carpeting was installed atop the table in the classroom. The carpeting was .6 cm thick and completely covered the surface of the table. The surface of the carpet was hard and flat so as not to restrict the plate from spinning . . . no sound was audible from spinning the plate on the carpeted table. A second sensory extinction procedure was designed to mask the proprioceptive stimulation from finger-flapping (Robert) and object manipulation (Brenda). A small vibratory mechanism was taped to the back of each child's hand,

generating a repetitive low-intensity, high-frequency pulsation. Significantly, the vibrator did not physically restrict self-stimulatory behavior. The final sensory extinction procedure involved removing the visual consequences for each of the three children. For this purpose a blindfold was introduced consisting of a handkerchief, once folded, snugly placed over each child's eyes and tied behind the head. (pp. 302–303)

If you think an individual's self-stimulatory behavior reflects a strong preference for one aspect of sensory feedback, talk with a behavioral consultant who is trained in this procedure. In the study just cited (Rincover, 1978), daily twenty-minute sessions were conducted in which the child sat in a separate room with an adult. The child's preferred self-stimulation object was placed on a table before him or her. These sessions provided the children with experiences in which the preferred sensory feedback was eliminated. An additional benefit in using the sensory extinction procedure is that you may identify appropriate activities involving the preferred sensory input as potential reinforcers. For example, if a student prefers auditory input, you might try music or noisemaking toys to reinforce appropriate responses during teaching sessions.

Overcorrection

Overcorrection has been successful in some cases of SSB, as evidenced by a study by Luiselli (1984a), who targeted tongue thrusting and saliva rubbing (see Table 9.2). Positive practice was used, and the time period for each practice session was 30 to 40 seconds. If you decide to try overcorrection, refer to Table 9.5 and remember to monitor for the possibility that other SSB may emerge. (This was not the case in the Luiselli study.)

Facial Screening

This procedure has reduced stereotypic behaviors in a couple of studies (McGonigle, Duncan, Cordisco, & Barrett, 1982; Horton, 1987). To implement facial screening, briefly (e.g., one minute) cover the student's eyes with either your hand or a cloth bib (Van Hasselt, 1983) when the student engages in the target behavior, removing the screen when the student stops the stereotypic behavior. The positive features of this intervention, as cited by Van Hasselt (1983), are (1) it requires minimal training, (2) it appears to work effectively and rapidly, and (3) the improvements have been observed across settings and over time. Also, the procedure is only mildly aversive, but it may not be effective with physically strong and resistant children who struggle with the "screener."

The next four interventions are useful for teaching SSB individuals alternative behaviors, although they will probably not suppress the self-stimulatory behaviors.

Stimulus Variation

The purpose of stimulus variation is to increase the level of motivation and responsiveness exhibited by a student engaged in SSB. Although little research on this intervention has been conducted thus far, there is evidence to suggest that bored students may engage in SSB (Dunlap & Koegel, 1980). Review carefully the sequence and length of activities you present to students. Try to intersperse two or three target tasks among other tasks rather than focusing on 15 minutes of one task followed by 15 minutes of another.

Response-Reinforcer Procedure

In a response-reinforcer procedure, the immediate environment is manipulated so that the student, as a result of completing a task, has immediate access to a reinforcer physically imbedded within the task. The following description of a manual task is an example of a response-reinforcer (Bittle & Hake, 1977):

> The manual task involved removing eight wing nuts that secured the transparent side of each of six boxes mounted on a wall at the child's eye level. Each box contained a small piece of bologna sausage and a cup with .25 ounces of Coke®, known reinforcers for this child. Because the child averaged eleven seconds to remove a single wing nut, approximately ninety seconds was required to open one box and about nine minutes was required to open all boxes. The child was shown how to open the boxes prior to the study. (p. 909)

Why might a response-reinforcer procedure result in rapid learning acquisition? Perhaps it is because the reinforcer becomes immediately available as soon as the student engages in the correct response (completes the task). In other words, ". . . a functional response-reinforcer relationship may serve to highlight the contingency between the reinforcer and the intended target behavior" (Williams, Koegel, & Egel, 1981, p. 59).

Sensory Reinforcement

In contrast to the response-reinforcer intervention, a sensory reinforcement strategy provides the child with one or more sensory experiences that are deemed desirable to the child. Rincover and Newsom (1985) found that multiple sensory reinforcers were more effective than multiple edible reinforcers in increasing correct responses. When a single sensory reinforcer was compared with a single edible reinforcer, the results were about the same. The authors pointed out that "children may work longer and learn more when multiple-sensory events are used" (p. 245). Some of the sensory reinforcers they used include tickling, hand clapping, finger tapping or drumming with sticks by the adult on a surface near the child, singing (by the adult), playing music very briefly, and caressing. To create the multiple-sensory reinforcement arrangement, the adult varied the reinforcers given for correct trials.

DIFFERENTIAL REINFORCEMENT OF OTHER BEHAVIORS (DRO)

This procedure, described in an earlier section, is frequently applied to SSB as an accompaniment to behavior reduction procedures. Refer to Table 9.3 for steps in using DRO.

SUMMARY

Self-injurious and self-stimulatory behaviors are complex problems facing the teacher of students with developmental disabilities. Fortunately, new insights from research studies can provide new insights and relief to the classroom teacher seeking an end to stereotypic behavioral patterns. Consider the research-based interventions for self-injury and self-stimulation, fully respecting the complexity and intensity of some of these interventions and the assessments that must precede them. Our chapter closes with a case study about SIB.

 CASE STUDY

BEHAVIORAL AND NALTREXONE TREATMENT OF SELF-INJURIOUS BEHAVIOR[1]

Kristina Johnson, Cynthia R. Johnson, and Robert A. Sahl

The subject was a 7-year-old African-American boy with severe mental retardation and a long history of self-injurious behaviors. This was the first psychiatric hospitalization for this subject who had been diagnosed with autism at age 2. The subject's self-injurious, aggressive, and noncompliant behaviors began to worsen approximately 1 year prior to hospitalization, to the point where the subject sustained injury to his face (i.e., a large, swollen hematoma under his left eye due to repetitively striking this area with a closed fist). The parents, most recently, had been simply holding him on their laps to prevent self-injurious behaviors. The parents reported that he had become combative when they attempted to interrupt the self-injurious behaviors. The subject had lost interest or the ability to engage in the few self-help care skills that he had mastered, including eating skills.

The subject was initially evaluated at the ages of 2 and 3. These evaluation results included observations that the subject exhibited a wide scattering of abilities, many autistic-like behaviors, and a strength in gross motor areas. Another evaluation conducted at the age of five years confirmed the diagnosis of autistic disorder, and noted poor progress in the subject's development over the previous year. At that time, a trial of Haldol 0.5 mg was initiated to assist in improving the subject's activity level, tantrums, and to hopefully improve his social-relatedness. Apparently this was somewhat effective, and he was followed at the medical center on a regular basis for approximately one year. At this point, his aggression and head-slapping began to increase and his attention span decreased. Haldol was increased 1 mg b.i.d. and this was effective for approximately another year. When the aggression and head-slapping began, Haldol was once again increased to 1.5 mg/l mg b.i.d., following another increase to 1.5 mg b.i.d. However, due to the sedating effect, it was decreased back to 1.5 mg/lmg on a b.i.d. schedule. At this point, after the discontinuation of the Haldol, Tofranil was initiated at a dosage of 25 mg hs. This medication was then increased to 50 mg hs. and again increased to 75 mg hs., but it was apparently felt to be ineffective and was discontinued. At that time, the referral to Western Psychiatric Institute and Clinic had been made, and further treatment was deferred pending an inpatient evaluation. Upon admission, consent for treatment was obtained from the parents.

During inpatient hospitalization, psychoeducational evaluation utilizing the Bayley Infant Development Scale showed an age-equivalent of $5\frac{1}{6}$ months, indicative of severe to profound mental retardation. On the Vineland Adaptive Behavior Scale, the subject earned a behavior composite standard score of 23, with subtest scores as follows: Communication = 24; Daily Living Skills = less than 20; and Socialization = 24. A speech and language evaluation was also completed utilizing the Receptive Expressive Emergent Language Scale (REEL). His expressive score was 3 months and his receptive score was 4 months. The patient was able to vocalize approximately

[1]Reprinted with permission from Johnson, K., Johnson, C. R., & Sahl, R. A. (1994). Behavioral and naltrexone treatment of self-injurious behavior. *Journal of Developmental and Physical Disabilities, 6,* 2, 193–202.

(continued)

3 sounds, was unable to imitate, had object permanence for food, and overall low sensory skills.

Self-injurious behavior was defined as the forceful contact by the subject to the left side of his face, under his eye, with his fist. Ethical considerations precluded allowing unrestrained self-injurious behaviors to continue without intervention; therefore, physical and verbal interruption and redirection were implemented throughout all phases of the study. Due to the severity and frequency of the self-injurious behaviors, pediatric "no-no" arm splints were applied within 48 hours of the subject's admission to the hospital. Data were collected during structured periods by milieu-trained staff, with ongoing frequency counts of the subject's self-injurious behaviors across all settings, from wakeup to bedtime.

PROCEDURES

Baseline

Due to the intensity and frequency of the subject's self-injurious behaviors, baseline was necessarily brief. The frequency of the subject's self-injurious behaviors and attempts to self-injury were collected across a day.

Phase I Phase 1 involved a behavior treatment package of systematic splint fading, a faded differential schedule, and a 15-second hand restraint contingent on self-injury. Systematic splint fading began with the pediatric "no-no" splints being removed for 15 min twice per day, once in the morning during structured classroom time, and once in the afternoon during structured play activity. During this and all subsequent treatment phases 2 and 3, the subject was reinforced at the beginning of the session on a fixed interval schedule of 10 seconds, with verbal praise and edible reinforcers for the absence of self-injurious behaviors. Edible reinforcement (i.e., soda, cookies, candy, chips, crackers, and pretzels) was delivered and paired with the verbal statement, "Nice hands down." When the subject had achieved 10 consecutive intervals of 10 sec with no self-injurious behaviors, the fixed interval was faded to 30 sec. After 10 consecutive intervals of 30 sec with no self-injury, the fixed interval was faded to 60 sec. This continued again for 90 sec and 120 sec. Along with the faded differential reinforcement schedule, a brief hand restraint program was implemented.

Whenever the subject engaged in self-injurious behaviors when his splints were off, a brief hand restraint was implemented for 10 sec. This consisted of milieu staff citing, "No hitting," and holding the subject's hands on a flat surface without conversation for 15 sec when the behavior occurred.

Phase II During this phase, naltrexone 50 mg b.i.d. (3.8 mg/kg) was administered. The behavioral treatment package was continued as described above in Phase 1.

Phase III During this phase, placebo was administered as well as a continuation of splint fading, faded differential reinforcement schedule, and the brief hand restraint. This allowed for the removal of splints due to the reduction of the self-injurious behaviors. The subject had his splints off from 9 a.m. until 11 a.m., with a constant one-to-one supervision period. At 11:30 a.m., his right splint was replaced during lunchtime, leaving his left one off so that he could eat. Both splints were replaced at the end of lunch, from 12:15 p.m. to 1:00 p.m., and then from 1:00 p.m. until 3:30 p.m. both splints were removed. From 3:30 p.m. until bedtime both splints remained on, with the exception of being removed every hour for a total of 10 min for range of their motion exercises.

Phase IV In the final phase the naltrexone-placebo trial was discontinued, as well as the removal of splints, continuation of the brief hand restraint for 15 seconds was implemented whenever the self-injurious behavior occurred, the reinforcement being changed to a variable interval schedule of every 2 to 5 minutes.

Follow-up Follow-up data were recorded for 2 months after the subject's discharge to the school setting. The classroom aide collected frequency counts across each school day of self-injurious behaviors of the subjects. The contingent hand restraint for 15 sec was implemented whenever the self-injurious behavior occurred, with reinforcement being delivered every 3 to 5 minutes.

RESULTS

Mean total frequencies per day of self-injury across phases were recorded. At baseline, the subject engaged in self-injurious behaviors almost continuously during the initial two observation sessions,

(continued)

requiring splints to be applied within 48 hours of hospitalization. During unstructured settings, mean total frequency of self-injurious behaviors during baseline assessment was 544. In Phase 1, mean total frequency of self-injurious behavior was 197 (range = 1–1426). Hence a significant decrease in self-injurious behavior was observed to occur following implementation of splint fading, the brief restraint program, and a faded differential reinforcement schedule. The mean total frequency of self-injurious behavior in Phase 2 was 424 (range = 0–2051). In Phase 3, mean total frequency was 226 (range = 0–1488). In Phase 4, the behavioral treatment alone, mean total frequency was 34 (range = 0–377). During the last 12 days of hospitalization, the patient maintained zero rates of self-injurious behaviors across all settings. In follow-up, the subject's school personnel continued collecting total frequency counts of self-injurious behaviors on a daily basis. These data indicated that the mean total frequency for month one was 9.6, and the mean total frequency for month two was 5.1.

DISCUSSION

The combined use of splint fading, differential reinforcement, and a brief hand restraint successfully eliminated self-injurious behaviors in one child with severe profound mental retardation and autistic disorder. These results are similar to earlier reports of success with the combined use of DRO and restraint fading in the reduction of self-injurious behaviors (Cowdery et al., 1990; Parrish et al., 1985). This was in contrast to the lack of behavioral change noted during the naltrexone trial and is consistent with other reports (Szymanski et al., 1987; Davidson et al., 1983), but differed with the results supporting the efficacy of naltrexone (Barrett et al., 1989; Campbell et al., 1988; Herman et al., 1987).

One of the major challenges associated with the successful treatment of self-injurious behavior is to systematically program for maintenance and generalization of treatment in the home and school environment. In this study, attempts were made to promote generalization through (a) systematic fading of the use of restrictive physical restraints and simultaneous fading of reinforcement schedules to one that could be implemented in the child's natural environment,

(b) intense training with the parents and school personnel in the implementation of treatment procedures prior to the subject's discharge from the hospital, and (c) follow-up phone calls to the home and school setting in order to promote continuance of treatment and provide performance-based feedback and consultation.

Throughout the subject's hospitalization, the intensive training of parents and school personnel included the education of possible motivational factors for the subject's self-injurious behavior, a use of differential reinforcement, brief hand restraint, and strategies to promote maintenance of the program in their environments. The parents, as well as the school personnel, were quite active, motivated, and involved in this subject's hospitalization, although they lived some distance away. Phone contact with parents one day after discharge was made, reporting that they were consistently able to implement the behavior treatment package. School personnel collected total frequency counts across a day, and at the one- and two-month intervals, the generalization of treatment gains substantially continued in the school environment. Along with observed decreases in the frequency of SIB, anecdotal reports from school indicated decreased irritability and increased ability of this boy to sit in his seat for long periods of time. Significant gains in playing independently with toys for longer periods of time were also noted.

In the home environment, anecdotal reports from the subject's mother emphasized continued treatment gains at the 6-month period. Phone contact 1 year after discharge was made, with parental report that the subject's rate of SIB was minimal and the behavior treatment package that was recommended from his inpatient hospitalization was consistently being utilized. School personnel reported the subject was also doing well in their environment with minimal SIB rates. The schedule of reinforcement had been extended to every 8-10 minutes while the brief hand restraint was continued contingent on any SIB.

A number of limitations of this study should be noted. Optimally, reliability data should have been collected throughout all four treatment phases. In addition, as in many cases with self-injurious behavior, high variability makes any interpretation of treatment efficacy difficult. Admittedly, variations in

(continued)

the data collection may be accounted for by problems such as measurement error of observers. Another limitation of the study consisted of the medication only being administered at one dose over a short period of time. The dose was also higher than that used in some previous investigations (Barrett et al., 1989). Hence, the dose may have not been optimal and the medication trial might have continued longer with titrating dosages of medication.

DISCUSSION QUESTIONS

1. What are the major concepts of a perceptual reinforcement theory of self-stimulatory behavior? Discuss them.
2. What are the steps in conducting a functional analysis for self-injurious behavior and for self-stimulatory behavior? Describe each.
3. How would you use sensory extinction to reduce the auditory SSB of a child with developmental delays?
4. What is the importance of contingent practice and timeout in an overcorrection procedure for self-injurious behavior? Discuss it.
5. How is DRO best used for individuals with stereotypic behaviors? Will it suppress the stereotypic behaviors?
6. What criteria should you meet before trying an aversive or restrictive intervention?
7. What interventions have not proven effective in suppressing SSB? Why?
8. What are the advantages of facial screening?
9. What seems to be the most effective reinforcer for a child who engages in SSB?

REFERENCES

Aiken, J. M., & Salzberg, C. L. (1984). The effects of a sensory extinction procedure on stereotypic sounds of two autistic children. *Journal of Autism and Developmental Disorders, 14*(3), 291–299.

Barrett, R. P., Feinstein, C., & Hole, W. T. (1989). Effects of naloxone and naltrexone on self-injury: A double-blind, Placebo-controlled analysis. *American Journal of Mental Retardation, 93*, 644–651.

Baumeister, A. A. (1978). Origins and control of stereotyped movements. In C. E. Meyers (Ed.), *Quality of life in severely and profoundly mentally retarded people: Research foundations for improvement.* (AAMD Monograph, No. 3). Washington, DC: American Association on Mental Deficiency.

Baumeister, A. A., & Rollings, P. (1976). Self-injurious behavior. In N. R. Ellis (Ed.), *International review of research in mental retardation* (Vol. 9). New York: Academic Press.

Berkson, G., McQuiston, S., Jacobson, J. W., Eyman, R, & Borthwick, S. (1985). The relationship between age and stereotyped behaviors. *Mental Retardation, 23*, 31–33.

Bierly, C., & Billingsley, F. F. (1983). An investigation of the educative effects of overcorrection on the behavior of an autistic child. *Behavioral Disorders, 9*(1), 11–21.

Bittle, R., & Hake, D. F. (1977). A multielement design model for component analysis and cross-setting assessment of a treatment package. *Behavior Therapy, 8*, 906–914.

Campbell, M., Adams, P., Smolt, A., Tesch, L., & Curran, L. (1988). Naltrexone in infantile autism. *Psychopharmacology Bulletin, 24*, 35–139.

Carey, R. G., & Bucher, B. D. (1986). Positive practice overcorrection: Effects of reinforcing correct performance. *Behavior Modification, 10*(1), 73–92.

Carr, E. G., & Durand, V. M. (1985). Reducing behavior problems through functional communication training. *Journal of Applied Behavior Analysis, 18*(2), 111–126.

Carr, E. G., & McDowell, J. J. (1980). Social control of self-injurious behavior of organic etiology. *Behavior Therapy, 11*, 402–409.

Carr, E. G., Newsom, C. D., & Binkoff, J. A. (1976). Stimulus control of self-destructive behavior in a psychotic child. *Journal of Abnormal Child Psychology, 4*, 139–152.

Cowdery, G. E., Iwata, B. A., & Pace, G. M. (1990). Effects and side-effects of DRO as treatment for

SIB. *Journal of Applied Behavior Analysis, 23,* 497–506.

Davidson, P. W., Keene, B. M., Carroll, M., & Rockowitz, R. J. (1983). Effects of naloxone on self-injurious behavior: A case study. *Applied Research in Mental Retardation, 4,* 1–4.

DeCatanzaro, D. A., & Baldwin, G. (1978). Effective treatment of self-injurious behavior through a forced arm exercise. *American Journal of Mental Deficiency, 82,* 433–439.

Dorsey, M. F., Iwata, B. A., Ong, P., & McSween, T. E. (1980). Treatment of self-injurious behavior using a water mist: Initial response suppression and generalization. *Journal of Applied Behavior Analysis, 13,* 324–333.

Dorsey, M. F., Iwata, B. A., Reid, D. H., & Davis, P. A. (1982). Protective equipment: Continuous and contingent application in the treatment of self-injurious behavior. *Journal of Applied Behavior Analysis, 15,* 217–230.

Dunlap, G., & Koegel, R. L. (1980). Motivation of autistic children through stimulus variation. *Journal of Applied Behavior Analysis, 13,* 619–627.

Durand, V. M., & Carr, E. G. (1985). Self-injurious behavior: Motivating conditions and guidelines for treatment. *School Psychology Review, 14*(2), 171–176.

Durand, V. M., & Crimmins, D. B. (1987). Assessment and treatment of psychotic speech in an autistic child. *Journal of Autism and Developmental Disorders, 17*(1), 17–28.

Epstein, L. H., Doke, L. A., Sajwaj, T. E., Sorrell, S., & Rimmer, B. (1974). Generality and side effects of overcorrection. *Journal of Applied Behavior Analysis, 6,* 1–14.

Favell, J. (1982). *The treatment of self-injurious behavior.* New York: American Association for Behavior Therapy.

Favell, J. E., McGimsey, J. F., & Jones, M. L. (1978). The use of physical restraint in the treatment of self-injury and as positive reinforcement. *Journal of Applied Behavior Analysis, 11,* 225–241.

Favell, J. E., McGimsey, J. F., & Schell, R. M. (1982). Treatment of self-injury by providing alternate sensory activities. *Analysis and Intervention in Developmental Disabilities, 2,* 83–104.

Foxx, R. (1978). An overview of overcorrection. *Journal of Pediatric Psychology, 3,* 97–101.

Foxx, R. M., & Azrin, N. H. (1973). The elimination of autistic self-stimulatory behavior by overcorrection. *Journal of Applied Behavior Analysis, 6,* 1–14.

Foxx, R. M., & Bechtel, D. R. (1982). Overcorrection. In M. Hersen, R. M. Eisler, & P. M. Miller (Eds.), *Progress in behavior modification* (Vol. 13). New York: Academic Press.

Gibbs, J. W., & Luyben, P. D. (1985). Treatment of self-injurious behavior: Contingent versus noncontingent positive practice overcorrection. *Behavior Modification, 9*(1), 3–21.

Herman, B. H., Hammock, M. K., Aither-Smith, A., Egan, J., Chatoor, I., Werner, A., & Zelnik, N. (1987). Naltrexone decreases self-injurious behavior. *Annals of Neurology, 22,* 550–552.

Horton, S. V. (1987). Reduction of disruptive mealtime behavior by facial screening: A case study of a mentally retarded girl with long-term follow-up. *Behavior Modification, 11*(1), 53–64.

Iwata, B. A., Dorsey, M. F., Slifer, K. J., Bauman, K. E., & Richman, G. S. (1994). Toward a functional analysis of self-injury. *Journal of Applied Behavior Analysis, 27,* 197–209.

Iwata, B. A., Pace, G. M., Dorsey, M. F., Zarcone, J. R., Vollmer, T. R., Smith, R. G., Rodgers, T. A., Lerman, D. C., Shore, B. A., Mazaleski, J. L., Goh, H. L., Cowdery, G. E., Kalsher, M. J., McCosh, K. C., Willis, K. D. (1994). The functions of self-injurious behavior: An experimental-epidemiological analysis. *Journal of Applied Behavioral Analysis, 27,* 215–240.

Jenson, W. R., Rovner, L., Cameron, S., Peterson, B. P., & Kesler, J. (1985). Reduction of self-injurious behavior in an autistic girl using a multifaceted treatment program. *Journal of Behavior Therapy and Experimental Psychiatry, 16,* 77–80.

Johnson, K., Johnson, C. R., & Sahl, R. A. (1994). Behavioral and naltrexone treatment of self-injurious behavior. *Journal of Developmental and Physical Disabilities, 6*(2), 193–202.

LaGrow, S. J., & Repp, A. C. (1984). Stereotypic responding: A review of intervention research. *American Journal of Mental Deficiency, 88,* 595–609.

Lovaas, O. I., & Favell, J. E. (1987). Protection for clients undergoing aversive/restrictive interventions. *Education and Treatment of Children, 10*(4), 311–325.

Lovaas, O. I., Newsom, C., & Hickman, C. (1987). Self-stimulatory behavior and perceptual reinforcement. *Journal of Applied Behavior Analysis, 20*(1), 45–68.

Luiselli, J. K. (1984a). Therapeutic effects of brief contingent effort on severe behavior disorders in children with developmental disabilities. *Journal of Clinical Child Psychology, 13*(3), 257–262.

Luiselli, J. K. (1984b). Effects of brief overcorrection on stereotypic behavior of mentally retarded students. *Education and Treatment of Children, 7*(2), 125–138.

McGonigle, J. J., Duncan, D., Cordisco, L., & Barrett, R. P. (1982). Visual screening: An alternative method for reducing stereotypic behavior. *Journal of Applied Behavior Analysis, 3,* 461–467.

Mulick, J., Hoyt, R., Rojahn, J., & Schroeder, S. (1978). Reduction of a "nervous habit" in a profoundly retarded youth by increasing toy play: A case study. *Journal of Behavior Therapy and Experimental Psychiatry, 9,* 381–385.

Murphy, G., Carr, J., & Callias, M. (1986). Increasing simple toy play in profoundly mentally handicapped children: II. Designing special toys. *Journal of Autism and Developmental Disorders, 16,* 45–58.

Neufeld, A., & Fantuzzo, J. W. (1984). Contingent application of a protective device to treat the severe self-biting behavior of a disturbed autistic child. *Journal of Behavior Therapy and Experimental Psychiatry, 15*(1), 79–83.

Newsom, C. D. (1974). *The role of sensory reinforcement in self-stimulatory behavior.* Unpublished doctoral dissertation, University of California, Los Angeles.

O'Brien, F. (1981). Treating self-stimulatory behavior. In J. L. Matson & J. R. McCartney (Eds.), *Handbook of behavior modification with the mentally retarded.* (1st ed.). (pp. 117–150). New York: Plenum.

Parrish, J. M., Iwata, B. A., Dorsey, M. F., Bunick, T. J., & Slifer, K. J. (1985). Behavior analysis, program development, and transfer of control in the treatment of self-injury. *Journal of Behavior Therapy and Experimental Psychiatry, 16,* 159–168.

Rincover, A. (1978). Sensory extinction: A procedure for eliminating self-stimulatory behavior in developmentally disabled children. *Journal of Abnormal Child Psychology, 6,* 299–310.

Rincover, A., & Devany, J. (1982). The application of sensory extinction procedures to self-injury. *Analysis and Intervention in Developmental Disabilities, 2,* 67–81.

Rincover, A., & Newsom, C. D. (1985). The relative motivational properties of sensory and edible reinforcers in teaching autistic children. *Journal of Applied Behavior Analysis, 18*(3), 237–248.

Rincover, A., Newsom, C. D., & Carr, E. G. (1979). Using sensory extinction procedures in the treatment of compulsive-like behavior of developmentally disabled children. *Journal of Consulting and Clinical Psychology, 47,* 695–701.

Rolider, A., & Van Houten, R. (1985). Movement suppression time-out for undesirable behavior in psychotic and severely developmentally delayed children. *Journal of Applied Behavior Analysis, 18*(4), 275–288.

Rolider, A., Williams, L., Cummings, A., & Van Houten, R. (1991). The use of a brief movement restriction procedure to eliminate severe inappropriate behavior. *Journal of Behavior Therapy and Experimental Psychiatry, 22,* 23–30.

Schroeder, S. R., Schroeder, C. S., Rojahn, J., & Mulick, J. A. (1981). Self-injurious behavior: An analysis of behavior management techniques. In J. L. Matson & J. R. McCartney (Eds.), *Handbook of behavior modification with the mentally retarded.* (pp. 141–180). New York: Plenum.

Szymanski, L. J., Sulkes, S., Culter, A., & Stevens-Ous, P. (1987). Naltrexone in treatment of self-injurious behavior: A clinical study. *Research of Developmental Disorders, 8,* 179–190.

Van Hasselt, V. B. (1983). Facial screening. In A. S. Bellack & M. Hersen (Eds.), *Dictionary of behavior therapy techniques.* New York: Pergamon.

Van Houten, R. (1993). The use of wrist weights to reduce self-injury maintained by sensory reinforcement. *Journal of Applied Behavior Analysis, 26,* 197–203.

Williams, J. A., Koegel, R. L., & Egel, A. L. (1981). Response-reinforcer relationships and improved learning in autistic children. *Journal of Applied Behavior Analysis, 14,* 53–59.

10

PSYCHIATRIC PROBLEMS

OUTLINE

OBJECTIVES

After completing this chapter, you should be able to

- Describe the steps for interviewing a student who may have an emotional problem.
- Define each of the following terms: anorexia nervosa, bulimia nervosa, suicide, depression, drug and alcohol abuse, school and other phobias, anxiety disorder.
- Identify a student who is showing signs of a psychiatric problem.
- Make an informed referral for a student showing signs of a psychiatric problem.

This chapter deals with psychiatric or emotional problems that require treatment outside of school. Your role is one of collaborator, usually with in-school professionals and those from a mental health agency. Although we do not cover all of the possible psychiatric problems of children and adolescents, we hope to make you aware of those you are likely to identify in school-age children. The problems covered in this chapter include **depression, suicide, drug** and **alcohol abuse, eating disorders, anxiety disorders,** and **phobias** and extreme fears.

This chapter highlights some of the signs of psychiatric problems and offers you guidelines for recognizing and referring these disorders. Classroom teachers are good observers of children's normal and abnormal behaviors (Kerr & Schaeffer, 1987; Hoier & Kerr, 1987). After all, educators are the one professional group constantly in touch with normal child and adolescent behavior. You can decipher when a student's actions fall outside these norms.

Therefore, your primary role in helping children with serious emotional or psychiatric problems is to identify and refer them for more intensive services. Moreover, you may be called on to collaborate in the student's subsequent treatment, especially if you are a special educator, school counselor, psychologist, or social worker.

RECENT TRENDS IN SCHOOL PROGRAMMING

Student Assistance

A recent addition to many schools is the Student Assistance Program (SAP). SAPs are a response to the many and varied personal problems that students bring with them to school. The motivation behind the implementation of these programs is fundamentally educational. The sheer magnitude of many students' emotional predicaments makes working to their academic potential impossible. Initially, Student Assistance programs sprang up in response to the increasing concern of problems related to alcohol and other drug

---

This chapter was written by Deborah Lange Lambert.

use. Now the primary mission of Student Assistance is to identify troubled students and then connect them with a helping service in their school or community. When working in a school, ascertain whether or not an SAP or its equivalent exists.

IDENTIFYING PSYCHOLOGICAL PROBLEMS

Consider these general warning signs of a psychological problem:

1. A sudden change in behavior or mood.
2. A prolonged sad, unhappy mood.
3. Fatigue and lethargy, or excessive energy and euphoria.
4. A disinterest in activities that once were enjoyable.
5. A change in sleep (being sleepier or having difficulty sleeping).
6. A change in appetite or a remarkable weight loss.
7. Making statements about hurting oneself.
8. A sense of worthlessness or hopelessness.
9. A decline in grades.

We review these signs in our discussion of specific disorders, but first we offer some assessment strategies.

Interview Strategy

Interviewing is a good way to learn about a student's psychological problems. Have a conversation with the student. See the student privately and allow enough time (no less than thirty minutes). Let the student know that you are concerned and want to help.

1. If the student hesitates, gently offer an example of the worrisome behavior.

   "You seemed to have lost your interest in the track meet."

   "I've noticed that you seem more excited than usual. . . ."

   "You seem thin."

   "I notice you've been sleepy a lot lately."
2. Resist the urge to explain the symptom and/or offer advice. Refrain from comments like

"I guess your track team is not doing as well this year. No wonder you're less interested."

"Maybe you should eat more."

"Kids sometimes sleep too much when they're bored. Maybe you need to . . . ."

After all, you may guess incorrectly and throw the conversation off track.

3. Be a good listener so the student feels comfortable talking. Pay attention to how much you are actually listening versus counseling.
4. Do not badger! Here are some ways we badger.

   "I took time to talk with you, and this is all you have to say?"

   "Why don't you face facts; something is wrong with you!"

   "If you don't want help now, then don't come to me later."

   "Stop making excuses, and get your work done."
5. If the student does not want to talk, try another option.

   "Maybe this isn't a good time. We could meet after school."

   "I know you and Dr. Robb are rather close. Do you feel you might want to talk with him? I could check to see when he is available."

   "If you ever want to talk, just let me know."

   "Sometimes students are more comfortable expressing their problems in writing. Would that make things any easier for you?"
6. Be patient! Students with problems are not always articulate. It may take a little while for them to explain how they feel. Do not interrupt. Show the student that you are interested by looking at him and nodding your head.
7. Avoid judgments. This is no time to evaluate the student's perceptions.

   "Well, that is nothing to worry about."

   "How did you ever get into such a mess anyway?"

   "I hope you've learned your lesson."
8. Next, name some action that you can take with the student. If you cannot immediately think of a plan, at least show your acceptance and willingness to help.

"I am not sure how to tackle this problem, but we *can* think it through."

"Gee, this is a real problem. Let me give this some thought. We'll talk Wednesday, okay?"

"Now I see. How about if I share some of this with the counselor? I think she could help."

"I'd like to help you through this. How would *you* like to proceed?"

9. Close the conversation with reassurance (even if you cannot genuinely show acceptance of the student's views). Some students need information to help them view their situations more hopefully. If this is the case, offer it.

"I see why you were so worried about the quiz. You did not realize that everyone did poorly. I have decided to adjust everyone's grades."

"Suspension is serious, but no, it does not mean you fail the course."

"I know the seniors said they could vote you off the team, but that decision is made only by the coach."

10. Follow up on your commitment. Even if you have promised only to talk again, be sure you do. If you offered specific help, get it quickly.

11. Know how to help. Your work obligates you to know child and adolescent referral procedures, to understand the mental health services in your community, to know warning signs, and so forth.

12. Know how to handle confidentiality. Do not promise total confidentiality to a student; you may not be able to keep your word. Do not promise confidentiality, for example, in the case of suicidal or homicidal threats.

For very young children, you will need to interview the parents. Your school social worker or guidance counselor can assist you or you can informally ask questions based on your concerns. One helpful strategy is to share your concerns with the parent and ask if the same or other problems have been apparent at home. Sometimes this approach cues the parents to recall events that may not have seemed problematic to them at the time. Remember, follow the same guidelines in talking with a parent that you follow in talking with a student. Do not badger, explain the symptom, or pass judgment! Instead, listen with empathy. You will be in a better position to effect positive change if you focus on building a partnership with a parent without passing judgment.

Teacher Interview for Psychiatric Symptoms

One instrument for identifying psychiatric problems in children is the Teacher Interview for Psychiatric Symptoms (TIPS) developed by Kerr and Schaeffer (1987). Figure 10.1 displays some

Figure 10.1 Excerpts from the Teacher Interview for Psychiatric Symptoms

1. One of the feelings I'd like to know about is sadness. (This item refers to a mood of depression, sadness, "feeling bad.") Has (student's name) been feeling sad, unhappy, or miserable in school?

2. Does (student's name) appear to worry about things? Do you know of any current stressors that the student may be experiencing (at home or at school) that may be the reason for his or her worrying (e.g., parental divorce, boy/girlfriend problems, pending disciplinary action)?

3. Do you have a sense that (student's name) feels hopeless or pessimistic? Does she or he ever indicate that she or he has things to look forward to (e.g., movies, outings with family, basketball games, weekends)?

4. Does (student's name) have several friends with whom she or he plays or associates? If *no*, ask, does the student have a special friend with whom she or he plays or associates? When was the last time you noticed this student with a friend(s)?

5. When students are upset, sad, or angry, sometimes they think about hurting or killing themselves. Has (student's name) ever made a statement about wanting to hurt or kill herself or himself? Has she or he ever made a statement about not wanting to live?

questions from this interview, designed for counselors to ask teachers about worrisome students. The interview lasts approximately 45 minutes and can be conducted by telephone.

Teacher's Report Form of the Child Behavior Checklist

Developed by Achenbach and Edelbrock (1979), this checklist is commonly used around the world to screen children for psychiatric problems. The teacher completes the checklist in about 30 minutes, rating each problem statement as not true, somewhat or sometimes true, or very true or often true for the target student within the past two months. Here are some sample items:

◆ Clings to adults or too dependent.
◆ Is not liked by other pupils.
◆ Gets hurt a lot, accident-prone.
◆ Feels or complains that no one loves him/her.
◆ Is unhappy, sad, or depressed.
◆ Is afraid of making mistakes.
◆ Worries.

Frequently schools have their own assessment tools that require a minimal amount of time to complete while providing meaningful information. Figure 10.2 displays a student assistance form that goes to the student's teachers, administrator, counselor, and school nurse. Comparing a summary of this data to a student's perception of his performance can provide additional insight. With older students it is especially important to access the guidance counselor's transcript, where you can observe trends in grades, attendance, and tardiness. If you have referred students to a mental health clinic, you probably have completed one of these instruments.

The TIPS and the Child Behavior Checklist are only two of many available psychiatric screening instruments. Refer to Chapter 1 for a screening procedure (Walker, Severson, Haring, & Williams, 1986) for problem behaviors.

Direct Observations

For some psychiatric problems, you will be able to use a direct observation approach—or at least rely on your informal observations and impressions of a student.

DEPRESSION

Childhood **depression** is extremely difficult to diagnose, but it may be a warning of a serious psychiatric disorder. The diagnosis of depression begins with the criteria listed in the *Diagnostic and Statistical Manual of Mental Disorders* published by the American Psychiatric Association (*DSM IV*). Typical symptoms include dysphoria, irritability, changes in eating, sleeping, or energy, low self-esteem, and anhedonia. Depressed students do not always appear sad or unhappy; rather, pay attention to any sudden, unexplained change in behavior, even if it is acting-out or aggressive behavior. As an illustration of the complex and apparently paradoxical nature of childhood depression, here is an excerpt from a seven-year-old boy's hospital file.

> Eli returned to school after the death of his grandparents. His mother complained that in addition to becoming more withdrawn, he had been engaging in self-destructive and aggressive behavior. He had been running in front of automobiles and jumping down long flights of stairs in their apartment building. He had been increasingly aggressive toward his mother to the point that she had become quite fearful of him. She noted that for no reason he would come up to her and slap her. He would often call her a pig or a liar and have frequent tantrums. Other times, he would ignore his mother and refuse to eat.
>
> Eli's affect is depressed, and he has admitted to feeling sad. He spent his entire physical examination and first two therapy sessions sitting in a constricted manner, sobbing throughout. Eli related that sometimes in the (psychiatric) hospital he wakes up crying because he misses his mom so much (Mendelsohn, personal communication, 1981).

Depression in children and adolescents is marked by these warning signs: sadness (sometimes called *dysphoria*), low self-esteem, irritability, changes in appetite or sleep, impaired concentration, anhedonia (loss of pleasure in activities the child previously enjoyed), somatic complaints, and antisocial behaviors. If you observe any of the warning signs for two weeks or

Figure 10.2 Behavior Assessment Form

Teacher _____ Subject _____ Period _____

Student _____ Grade_____ Date _____

Check appropriate responses

A. ACADEMIC PERFORMANCE

___Present grade (this nine weeks)

___Declining grades, declining achievement

___Course grade to date

___Decrease in class participation

___Failure to complete assignments

___Disinterest in academic performance

___Short attention span, easily distracted

___Poor short-term memory (i.e., can't remember from one day to the next)

Specific Comments

_____

_____

_____

_____

B. SCHOOL ATTENDANCE

___Absenteeism (total absences)

___Number of absences in the last month

___Tardiness (please list dates)

___Absent from school; present at work

___Skipping class

___Frequent schedule changes

___Frequent visits to health office

___Frequent visits to counselor's office

Specific Comments

_____

_____

_____

_____

C. EXTRACURRICULAR ACTIVITIES

(Specify activity: _____)

___Attendance

___Withdrawal

___Performance level

Specific Comments

_____

_____

_____

_____

D. PHYSICAL SYMPTOMS

___Weight loss

___Reported insomnia

___Paleness, tiredness

___Alcohol or marijuana smell*

___Frequent complaints of nausea*

___Glassy, bloodshot eyes*

___Slurred speech*

___Inability to concentrate*

___Deteriorating personal appearance*

___Sleeping in class

___Physical injuries, bruises, cuts*

Specific Comments

_____

_____

_____

_____

E. ILLICIT ACTIVITIES*

___Possesses drug paraphernalia (roach clips, etc.)

___Carries a weapon

Specific Comments

_____

_____

_____

_____

F. DISRUPTIVE BEHAVIOR*

___Defiance of rules

___Alcohol- and/or drug-related clothing or jewelry

___Irresponsibility, blaming, denying

___Fighting

___Cheating

___Sudden outbursts of anger; verbally abusive to others

___Obscene language gestures

___Attention-getting behavior

___Extreme negativism

___Hyperactivity, nervousness

***Please provide comments when checking these behaviors.**

continued on next page

Figure 10.2 *(continued)*

Specific Comments

_____

_____

_____

_____

G. ATYPICAL BEHAVIOR*

___Model child, perfectionist

___Free talk about alcohol and other drug use

___Avoidance of contact with others

___Change in friends

___Erratic behavior/mood changes as viewed on day-to-day basis

___Abnormal interest in food/dieting

___Sudden popularity

___Constant adult contact

___Older or significantly younger social group

___Obsessive/compulsive behavior

___Extremely disoriented

___Unrealistic goals

___Inappropriate responses

___Depression

___Seeking adult advice without a specific problem

___Defensive attitude

___Social withdrawal, difficulty in relating to others

___Change in dress

Specific Comments

_____

_____

_____

_____

H. HOME PROBLEMS*

___Family

___Runaway

___Job

Specific Comments

_____

_____

_____

_____

ADDITIONAL COMMENTS

_____

_____

_____

_____

_____

_____

_____

_____

_____

_____

_____

_____

_____

_____

---

more, you should be concerned about the possibility of depression (American Psychiatric Association, 1980; Shaffer, 1985).

Eli's agitated depression—temper tantrums and acting-out behavior—rarely leads a lay person to think of depression. He probably has a bipolar disorder. According to Dr. Robert DeLong (1990), a renowned authority, the most prominent feature of a childhood bipolar illness is that emotions are extremely intense, especially irritability, anger, and rage. Fortunately, many of these children can be treated successfully with medication.

While childhood and adolescent depression has become an accepted clinical entity, one still finds professionals and others who argue its existence. Depression can be mistaken for other illnesses. When you learn about a child's lethargy, you often assume the child is merely bored in school or you look for medical reasons. You can overlook depression because some of the symptoms are considered "normal." For example, a parent may overlook his child's periodic school refusal or poor grades and chalk it up to a "bad phase." Generally, parents have extreme difficulty identifying a mood disorder such as depression. There continues to be a stigma associated with psychiatric illnesses. Hopefully, once medical reasons are ruled out, psychiatric possibilities are considered.

Age plays an important role in identifying childhood depression. As children get older, their chances of becoming depressed increases. Besides looking at characteristics that mark adult depression such as fatigue, suicidal ideation, and low self-esteem, you also need to look at failure to thrive, temper tantrums, school avoidance, withdrawal, daydreaming, and irritability. With younger students, you see less of the guilt, hopelessness, and despair that may accompany depression in adults. Appreciate the fact that depressive symptoms change with a child's developmental level.

How does a depressed student appear at school? What should you look for? Here are some examples of teacher-reported behaviors from a study by Kerr and Schaeffer (1987):

1. Dejected/Dysphoric Mood

   "Susan has been very depressed since she learned that her mother has cancer. She cries often and has difficulty completing schoolwork."

   "Bill has stated repeatedly that he is never happy but does not give a reason for his unhappiness. He lays his head down in class and does not complete his work."

2. Irritability/Temper

   "Cindy's defiant and irritable moods have become more severe as the year has progressed. She becomes angry at her classmates over the littlest thing. Although she does not harm other students, her behavior has warranted her removal from the classroom. This disciplinary action usually provokes more anger; she frequently slams her books down on a desk."

   "Michelle is easily irritated by many things and displays her temper by slamming a locker door or throwing books down on her desk."

3. Low Self-Esteem

   "After receiving a compliment about her appearance, Mary responded, 'I am not pretty at all.' She does not express pride in her academic accomplishments. Mary sees herself as unimportant and not worthy of attention."

4. Hopelessness

   "During a discussion of future plans, Ellen said, 'What is the future? Who knows if we have one?' She frequently comments, 'What does it matter?' or 'What's the use?'"

5. Anhedonia

   "Mark no longer seems to be interested in his favorite activities. He used to enjoy listening to music and being on the swim team but now avoids participating in those activities."

Schools are taking an active stand in identifying depression in youth. Depression in kids is *not* a passing phase; the average episode lasts seven months. Compare that to a student's calendar year of nine months. According to Maria Kovacs (1985), a chief researcher in this field, when childhood depression is *not* identified and treated early, the prognosis for recovery is less promising. Likewise, there is a high rate of recidivism among children with episodes of major depression. When mood disorders go untreated, they get worse. Depression interferes with everything in and out of school.

Because mood disorders affect intellectual functioning, depressed students often perform below their cognitive abilities. With depression, concentration is difficult and student motivation suffers. One may see a "Swiss cheese" learning pattern. Doing poorly scholastically can affect one's self-esteem dramatically. Parents often have a difficult time identifying depression in their child. More often, a school person notices academic or social problems that differ from the norm and makes a referral. When depression *is* treated, academic improvement occurs and self-esteem increases.

Another negative side effect of depression involves peer relations. Children and adolescents who are depressed tend to have fewer friends. Joaquim Puig-Antich (1985), the first psychiatric researcher to devote his career to childhood depression, remarked that while all psychiatric disorders affect children's social relationships, depression is by far the most impairing. Depression is damaging to school performance, friendships, and family relations. Even with therapy, social relationships do not improve as quickly as school performance. Typically treatment consists of therapy accompanied by medication.

Let us turn our attention from major depression to dysthymic depression. **Dysthymia** is a new classification of depression. Dysthymia generally lasts an average of three years and is accompanied by other psychiatric conditions. According to Dr. Kovacs (1985), dysthymia in children is "the most chronic and the most complicated" type of depression to diagnose and treat (p. 389). Symptoms are not always severe enough to warrant medical or psychiatric attention, so kids suffer in silence while adapting to their chronic pain. While the symptoms of a dysthymic disorder are less severe than with those of major depression, they are longer lasting. If you suspect a student suffers from dysthymia, identify the behaviors and seek outside help.

SUICIDE

The teenage suicide rate in the United States has increased by 226 percent since the 1960s (Brent, Perper, & Allman, 1987), making it the second leading cause of death in fifteen- to nineteen-year-olds (Pennsylvania Statistical Abstract, 1986). Moreover, research has shown that 1 in every 12 high school students has made a suicide attempt (Smith & Crawford, 1986). As you can see from these statistics, suicide is a problem you must be prepared to deal with if you work with adolescents.

What are the risk factors for suicide? A previous suicide attempt is a serious risk factor (Shaffer, 1986), as is threatening to take one's life. Seek professional help immediately for any student who talks about suicide or makes an attempt, regardless of how "serious" you think the student is. Drug and alcohol abuse are often implicated in a suicide (Brent et al., 1987). Under their influence, a vulnerable student may engage in risk-taking behaviors that she would otherwise avoid; these risks can include the fatal use of firearms (Brent et al., 1987). Access to firearms greatly increases the like-lihood of suicide in adolescents who are already vulnerable (Lester & Murrell, 1982). Exposure to a suicide or suicide attempt is another risk factor, sometimes referred to as *contagion* (Davidson & Gould, 1986). This contagion effect has prompted schools to adopt carefully planned postvention efforts when a suicide takes place among the student body. Postvention (as compared to prevention) refers to a set of actions that we take to prevent contagion *after* a suicide. Your school may have a postvention policy designed to lessen the risk of cluster suicides. Family variables in suicide include family conflict and a history of family psychiatric problems (including alcoholism). Indeed, a high percentage of suicide completers themselves had psychiatric problems, usually depression.

This finding underscores the importance of your early recognition of the signs of depression. First, increase your understanding of each risk factor. Try to learn about the families of your students. Second, know how to use your community mental health resources and drug rehabilitation agencies. Remember the warning signs for suicide:

- ◆ Hopelessness.
- ◆ Chemical abuse.
- ◆ Changes in eating or sleeping.
- ◆ Isolation from friends and family.
- ◆ A drop in academic achievement.
- ◆ Giving away valued possessions.
- ◆ Talking or writing about suicide or not wanting to live.
- ◆ A recent loss, such as divorce or death in the family, or a close friend moving away.

Reinforce the teenager's support network—family members, friends, and adults whom the student views as supportive: "Help in strengthening the [individual's] support system will be beneficial, as it is with all other psychiatric problems: with suicidal [individuals] it may be life-saving" (Strayhorn, 1982, p. 480).

Following are specific steps to take with a teenager who discusses or threatens suicide:

1. Listen!
2. Help the student reach a mental health service, even if you must accompany the student there.

3. Contact the student's family.
4. Do *not* leave the student alone.
5. Do *not* underestimate the student's situation or expressed intent to end her life or hurt herself.

DRUG AND ALCOHOL ABUSE

Educators and parents consistently identify drug use as a paramount problem confronting our schools. When thirteen- to eighteen-year-olds were asked to name the biggest problem facing them today, drug use was number one on their list. Educators and parents do not always agree on how schools should go about educating our students about alcohol and drugs, but both groups agree that open discussion in the classroom and at home is needed. Recognizing this widespread problem, most school districts have undertaken in-service training on drug and alcohol abuse prevention for their faculty and staff. School and community task forces have also joined hands to assess what works and what does not. Following are some important aspects of identifying and referring students at risk for drug and alcohol abuse. We begin with a review of the behaviors you might see in students who are engaged in substance abuse.

Alcohol and Other Depressants Remove from class any student who is intoxicated or in any identifiable stage of withdrawal. Do not confront the student with an accusation of drug use in front of peers. This may lead to opposition, resistance, or combativeness. When the student has been removed from the class, explain why and ask if you can be of help. School authorities and parents should be notified (and medical agencies if intoxication or withdrawal is severe). Refer the student to a counseling or rehabilitation program as soon as possible.

Marijuana It is the responsibility of frontline school personnel to provide adequate supervision to prevent marijuana use during school hours. Teachers, counselors, school psychologists—all of the individuals who have regular direct personal contact with the student—share this responsibility.

The most effective means of prevention of marijuana-related problems is the creation of a system of peer control based on educating students and families, the ability to convey an attitude of openness to communicate about drug and personal problems, and the appropriate structure in planning daily activities. It is important to demonstrate to the young person that you are concerned with his academic and social success and are not trying to control him unreasonably or remove his freedom in any other way. Pay attention to your students who are extremely interested in obtaining specific information about marijuana and other drugs. Information presented in textbooks or by the media may be inconsistent, fueling student debate and justification of usage. Also, students may seek knowledge to provide them with a means to "get high." In a nonjudgmental way, ask students about their curiosity.

To identify an acute marijuana episode, closely observe student behavior. A sudden uncharacteristic change in appearance, academic performance, or social functioning may be indicative. Apathy, drowsiness, and taking on drug culture mannerisms also alert you that marijuana use is being initiated or has become a significant problem.

Stimulants Intense agitation, unreasonable suspiciousness, and bizarre behavior may be indicators of stimulant use. Hostility and aggression may result. Extreme talkativeness and flushed skin that are uncharacteristic of a student may also indicate stimulant use. Avoid physical confrontation if possible.

Hallucinogens and Inhalants These chemicals usually severely disorganize behaviors so that medical or law enforcement intervention is necessary.

Narcotics Overt intoxication or narcotic withdrawal can be identified through close observation. Drowsiness and slurred speech may appear to be simple fatigue, except that the person cannot become fully alert when confronted and his pupils are constricted. Aggressiveness is unlikely to be a reaction of an individual under the influence of narcotics; however, agitation and impulsiveness are likely to accompany narcotic withdrawal. Significant withdrawal episodes require proper medical management. Do not rule out such intervention.

Do not attempt a power struggle with a student who appears to be under the influence of a drug. Certain drugs elicit combative behavior that can often be avoided if you do not respond impulsively to a physical threat.

Do not hesitate to seek emergency medical treatment for a student who appears to be experiencing a physical or emotional crisis. Sources of emergency care services, such as poison control, crisis intervention, and the police department, are often listed in the human services section of the telephone directory.

The classroom is not a place in which to attempt treatment of drug abuse. Prevention and identification are important activities for educators. It is appropriate to make individual referrals to proper agencies once drug use has been established, especially if it is the basis for disruptive behavior or poor academic performance. Table 10.1 summarizes the major drugs of abuse and their effects.

EATING DISORDERS

Professionals who work with adolescents need to know of the three major eating disorders: **anorexia nervosa, bulimia,** and **compulsive overeating.** With any eating disorder there is preoccupation with weight, size, and body image. Generally feelings of guilt and shame are associated with the behavior. The following vignette describes a teenager with anorexia nervosa:

> Katherine states that in February she went on a diet. At that time she was 127 pounds and five feet eight inches tall. She decided to cut down because she felt she didn't look good at that weight. She was surprised that she had so much willpower, and she was able to get down to 100 pounds. Katherine reports that around April her mother became uncomfortable with her dieting. By the end of April, her mother was really getting angry about her diet. She said that she exercised about half an hour each night and she would not eat sweets. She found herself being too occupied with counting calories. Katherine does not currently see herself as being too thin, so she does have a distorted body image. Katherine has always felt herself to be different from the other kids.

She has always been tall and was especially bothered by this in the seventh and eighth grades. When she was in ninth grade, her periods began. Her mother told her about periods and talked to her about sex. She also viewed some informational movies at school. Katherine was somewhat uncomfortable talking about this area. She reports that her periods stopped several months ago. Katherine reports a change in her personality since going on the diet. Before February she would become depressed only if her mother yelled at her, and her mother often became angry and upset. Now she becomes depressed over nothing, or so she feels, and just wants to be by herself, but she does no excessive crying. She does not feel that her current problems have had any effects on her friendships, though she has only one close friend, Natalie.

Russell (1985) cited criteria for anorexia nervosa.

1. Marked loss of weight that is self-induced, usually through a systematic avoidance of "fattening" foods (e.g., high-carbohydrate foods) and excessive exercise. Self-induced vomiting and purging are less frequent (cf. bulimia nervosa).
2. A specific psychopathology: an overvalued idea that fatness is a dreadful state to be avoided at all costs.
3. A specific endocrine disorder. In the female: amenorrhea is an early symptom. In the male: there is loss of sexual interest and potency. (pp. 629–30)

Bulimia, which often follows anorexia nervosa, is evidenced by these criteria (Russell, 1985):

1. Preoccupations with food associated with episodes of gross overeating.
2. Devices aimed at counteracting the "fattening" effects of the food ingested: especially self-induced vomiting or purging or alternation with periods of starvation.
3. The psychopathology of anorexia nervosa: fatness is so dreadful as to be avoided at all costs.
4. In "true" bulimia nervosa, there is a history of a previous episode of anorexia nervosa, possibly of minor severity. However, other forms of bulimic disorder may arise de novo. (p. 631)

Table 10.1 Common Drugs Abused by Youth

Tobacco: Nicotine, a stimulant, is the main ingredient in tobacco; it is more addictive than alcohol or marijuana. All tobacco products, even smokeless chewing tobacco and snuff, are addictive. Students are smoking in record numbers. Seventy percent of cigarette smokers who begin as teenagers will continue to smoke for forty years. Provocative advertisements appeal to young people and can influence their decision to start smoking. "Joe Camel" represents a controversial icon in the 90s.

Alcohol: Alcohol remains the number one drug of choice of teenagers. Teens receive very mixed messages about alcohol that creates a false sense of safety for some. The alcohol industry is targeting children and youth with media blitzes using talking frogs, party animals, and horses kicking footballs during major sporting events, and this recreational drug is filtering down to younger children. Newer products such as wine coolers and pre-mixed drinks make alcohol more palatable to the inexperienced user. The dangers of alcohol include dependency, automobile accidents involving people driving while under the influence, depression, accidental death, and suicide.

Marijuana: Marijuana is the first illicit drug that children and teens use. A generation ago, it was viewed as a "harmless" weed. With improved cultivation techniques, the most active chemical, delta-9-tetrahydrocannabinol (THC), has increased significantly. It would have taken twenty-five joints in the 1970s to equal the strength of one joint today. Hashish, a purified resin from the marijuana plant, has an even higher concentration of THC. Physical symptoms of users include reddening of the eyes, increased heart rate, relaxation, and increase in appetite. Dangers include loss of motivation, feelings of indifference, and developmental latency. Marijuana can be laced with PCP, cocaine, arsenic, or other chemicals.

Cocaine: Cocaine is a powerful central nervous system stimulant readily available to teenagers. The drug can be smoked or used intravenously. An added risk cocaine presents is its unpredictability in the effect on the user. Crack, which is smoked, is a less expensive, easy to procure, but more powerful form of the drug. The dangers of these drugs include dependency, weight loss, inability to concentrate, paranoia, cardiac arrest, and suicide.

LSD: Lysergic acid diethylamide (LSD), a popular hallucinogen, is practically considered a mainstream drug because of the high rates of experimentation. Typically, the drug is sold on small squares of paper saturated with the liquid. LSD is easy to hide and easy to use, while difficult to detect. The dangers related to its use include bizarre behavior, distorted thoughts, hallucinations, paranoia, "bad trips," feelings of invincibilty, and dependency.

Inhalants: Inhalant abuse is the deliberate misuse of chemicals to attain an intoxicated state, or "high"; it is becoming popular with young children. The "high" associated with certain chemicals, coupled with the lack of awareness of their harmful effects, is dangerous. Inhalants include a broad array of cheap and easily obtainable household products including aerosols, glue, paint thinner, gasoline, and nitrites (poppers). Problems may include irritability, headaches, drowsiness, confusion, memory loss, and unconsciousness. Using inhalants, even once, can be fatal.

Over-the-Counter/Look-Alike Substances: These drug-like substances are sold as diet aids, asthma/breathing medication, or "energy" supplements. Trade names include Minithins, Megatrim, Buzz, TurboTabs, and Heads Up. Each product stimulates the central nervous system. Dangers include overstimulation of the heart, stroke, mood swings, insomnia, dizziness, loss of appetite, and irritability.

Designer Drugs: There has been an upsurge in designer drugs, which can be produced in illegal labs. Typically, these drugs offer euphoric effects. Methamphetamine, known as crack, ice, or poor man's coke, is half the price of cocaine and easy to manufacture. Ecstasy or MDMA is a combination of a stimulant and a hallucinogen. The "party pill" or the Moroccan Quaalude is especially popular in the West. These street drugs are a special threat to our society. Users cannot be certain about what they are popping, snorting, or smoking. Because these chemical compounds are so varied, hospitals and treatment centers have difficulty detecting their presence with today's standard screening measures.

Other Drugs: Phencyclidine (PCP) or angel dust, mushrooms, anelobolic steroids, and heroine are dangerous. Anelobolic steroids are synthetic derivatives of testosterone that students use to enhance their physical performance in sports. Problems related to their use include aggressiveness, "roid rages," acne, high blood pressure, and damage to most body organs. Do not minimize the effects of these drugs.

Erin recalls her painful journey with bulimia:

Back in the seventies no one was talking about bulimia. In high school I was 5 feet 2 inches and weighed 96 lbs. As a teen I received a lot of positive attention because of my petite size. I attended a private all-girls school where eating was a popular social activity. I quickly learned how much I enjoyed binging. Soon my weight escalated, and one night after devouring 15 hot fudge sundaes I laid on the bathroom floor retching in pain. For relief, I made myself throw up. I discovered something magical. I could overindulge with my friends and then go off by myself to purge and prevent the weight gain.

Unfortunately I was not always able to purge after binging. For the next years I tried every crazy diet and my weight fluctuated between 94 and 130 lbs. One week I gained 17 lbs. after eating nothing but junk food—hot buttered donuts with bacon, chocolate milk, Oreos®, ice cream, Vanilla Wafers® with icing, and more. Little did I know that this activity would become chronic and progressive. Besides my weight fluctuating, my moods were all over the board. While I viewed myself as basically a happy person, I knew something was seriously wrong. This vicious preoccupation with food ended up dominating my life for the next 22 years until I sought help after feeling depressed, suicidal, and "out of control."

Compulsive overeating is generally recognized by these criteria (ICD, 1991):

1. Persistent thoughts about eating and feelings of being fat.
2. Buying clothes to hide the body.
3. Weight fluctuations of more than ten pounds due to dieting and overeating.
4. Secretive eating—in a car, bedroom, or bathroom.
5. Repeated and failed attempts to control weight.
6. Health complications such as high blood pressure and heart disease.

The following vignette describes an adolescent's problems with overeating and alcohol abuse.

A sixteen-year-old, found solace in comfort food (i.e., foods high in fat and sugar) and alcohol. He has clear memories of reaching for Coca Cola®, cookies, and his honey bear as a small child. As a teen he began to self-medicate with junk food *and* alcohol. Both of his parents were obese. When he was ten, he knew he was fat, but he did not want to diet even though the school nurse made the recommendation.

As an adolescent he recalls the euphoria he felt after drinking his first beer. He described the calmness as a feeling reminiscent of the feeling he had after binging on high-calorie food. He loved numbing himself and then drifting off to sleep.

At school, things seemed normal enough. He tried eating like everybody else but had trouble resisting pizza and cheeseburgers. Everyday he arrived home to an empty house. After walking through the door he went straight to the refrigerator and then to the pantry. He rarely brought his bookbag inside because he was too tired to bother. He began with milk and cereal and then moved on to cookies, cake, ice cream, leftovers, or anything available. Three hours later he would have a large meal with his family.

On Thursday and Friday his ritual changed as his parents worked later and there was no family dinner. On those nights he went to his parents' liquor cabinet and had a few drinks, climbed upstairs to his bedroom, and passed out. As the amounts of food and alcohol increased, his social life decreased. He began isolating himself from his friends. He felt more relaxed with food and alcohol than with people, even his friends. Once a counselor suggested he might be depressed. He did not understand what that meant. He did not care about much and wished people would leave him alone. He was not ready for help.

As Russell (1985) stated, "the very nature of the illness [is] that the [individual] tries to avoid measures that are aimed at reducing a gain in weight" (p. 632). Therefore, you will probably not succeed by encouraging or admonishing the student to eat better. Rather, your role is to inform parents and mental health professionals of your concerns. Above all, do not ignore the problem; the mortality rate for eating disorders can be as high as 25 percent (American Psychiatric Association, 1980). Often times students who are compulsive overeaters are seen by the school nurse. Generally the nurse will work with the family and the students. She will attempt to involve outside agencies who treat this disorder as an illness rather than as a lack of willpower.

ANXIETY DISORDERS

There are three types of anxiety disorders that children may experience: separation anxiety, avoidant disorder, and overanxious disorder (Hersov, 1985; American Psychiatric Association, 1980). **Separation anxiety** describes the problem of a child who has great difficulty when separated from significant others or familiar surroundings. **Avoidant disorder** is experienced by children who go to great lengths to avoid contact with any strangers. **Overanxious disorder** refers to children who are chronically fearful or worried about future events, demands made of them, their health, or their social and academic skills (Hersov, 1985).

Children may become anxious in response to a specific, stressful event (e.g., hospitalization, prolonged separation from parent, car accident). On the other hand, some children seem to have a general temperamental tendency to be worried and fearful (Thomas, Chess, & Birch, 1968). When a child's anxiety interferes with normal school and social functioning, consider a referral to a mental health professional.

Treatment for anxiety disorders can be multifaceted, including individual psychotherapy, behavioral relaxation, or desensitization techniques. Some children respond favorably to psychopharmacological interventions (Hersov, 1985).

In terms of classroom interventions, you may find the school survival skills described in Chapter 8 helpful in alleviating children's anxieties about school demands and deadlines. Time management can be especially helpful for an overanxious child. Other classroom suggestions will come from the child's therapist. Be sure to keep the person informed about the student's progress and problems.

PHOBIAS AND EXTREME FEARS

"Phobias are emotional disorders in which there is an abnormally intense dread of certain objects, or specific situations that normally do not have that effect" (Marks, 1969). Children's phobias may include fears of animals, death, insects, the dark, noise, and school (Rutter, Tizard, & Whitmore, 1970). Consider this illustration of a phobic child:

The presenting complaints at the time of the initial visit centered on Brenda's multiple fears. She is afraid of rain and lightning and is fearful of leaving the house without . . . one of her parents. While Brenda does attend school, she expresses discomfort at being there. Furthermore, her school performance is poor: Brenda has considerable difficulty with all school subjects.

Brenda acknowledged the first two fears—her being afraid of lightning and of leaving the house alone—but she would not expand on either. However . . . Brenda's fear of being alone became evident. So that she would not have to be without her parents in the waiting room, Brenda instructed her mother to request that the social worker finish talking with the mother prior to Brenda's completing her session with me.

With regard to school, Brenda did say that she disliked going to school. Brenda does not like her teacher, saying that her teacher is mean and always yells (Mendelsohn, personal communication, 1981).

Psychotherapeutic treatment of phobias may be categorized into four components described by Miller, Barrett, and Hampe (1974): development of a helping relationship with the therapist, clarifying what the feared object or situation is, helping the child become desensitized to the feared object or situation, and helping the child face the feared object or situation. Your role as an educator would be defined by the child's therapist.

In the case of school refusal, sometimes called **school phobia,** your role could be extensive. First, let's differentiate between school refusal and truancy. Truant students are not fearful of the school situation, whereas a school refuser may show fearfulness and anxiety such as somatic complaints, withdrawal from social interactions with other children, and a general inability to cope with demands to be independent of the family (Hersov, 1985). Consider this description by Hersov (1985):

Once back to school, on the first day contact must be maintained with child and parents by means of telephone calls to or from parents to gauge their own and the child's reactions to this first school attendance. Suggestions are made on how to deal with any new anxieties or attempts to manipulate parents to avoid school. If parents can manage unaided on successive mornings, they are praised and encouraged to take total responsibility for this, but support from clinic or school must be available if there are signs of faltering or loss of resolve in either child or parents. The child should be interviewed again after one week at school to sort out any existing or potential sources of stress and anxiety in the school or home situation which can then be discussed with teachers and parents. All concerned should be warned that the times of potential danger of breakdown of school attendance are after a weekend, after an illness requiring more than a day or two at home, the beginning of a new term, family illness or bereavement, and change to a new class or school. (p. 395)

SUMMARY

We hope that you have gathered information from the clinical vignettes and guidelines to help you identify and refer students at risk for psychiatric disorders. Do not hesitate to discuss a worrisome child with a colleague; you do not need to be absolutely sure about your concerns to make this inquiry. Be sure to document your concerns so that future professionals working with the child will have a better understanding of her history. Evaluation of results is discussed in Chapter 4; you might want to review this material before making notes in a child's record.

DISCUSSION QUESTIONS

1. How would you talk with a student who appears to be depressed?
2. Why is the identification of depression so important?
3. What are the warning signs for suicide?
4. What are the psychotherapeutic treatments for phobias?
5. How do truancy and school refusal differ?
6. What is an anxiety disorder?
7. What behavioral indicators might alert you to a student's use of alcohol, marijuana, cocaine, stimulants, narcotics, hallucinogens, or inhalants?
8. What are the warning signs for anorexia nervosa and bulimia nervosa?
9. What are the steps to take when an intoxicated student comes to your class?

REFERENCES

Achenbach, T. M., & Edelbrock, C. S. (1979). The child behavior profile: II. Boys aged 12–16 and girls aged 6–11 and 12–16. *Journal of Consulting and Clinical Psychology, 47*(1), 223–233.

American Psychiatric Association. (1980). *Diagnostic and statistical manual of mental disorders* (3rd ed.). Washington, DC: Author.

Brent, D. A., Perper, J. A., & Allman, C. J. (1987). Alcohol, firearms, and suicide among youth—Temporal trends in Allegheny County, Pennsylvania, 1960 to 1983. *Journal of the American Medical Association, 257*, 3369–3372.

Davidson, L., & Gould, M. S. (1986). *Contagion as a risk factor for youth suicide.* Unpublished manuscript.

Delong, R. (1990). Lithium treatment and bipolar disorders in childhood. *North Carolina Medical Journal, 5*, 152–154.

Hersov, L. (1985). School refusal. In M. Rutter & L. Hersov (Eds.), *Child and adolescent psychiatry: Modern approaches* (2nd ed.) (pp. 382–399). Oxford, England: Blackwell Scientific Publications.

Hoier, T., & Kerr, M. M. (1987). Extrafamilial information sources in the study of childhood depression. *Journal of the American Academy of Child Psychiatry, 27*, 21–33.

Kerr, M. M., & Schaeffer, A. L. (1987). *Teacher interview for psychiatric symptoms (TIPS).* (Available from Mary Margaret Kerr, Ed.D., or Alice L. Schaeffer, M.Ed., at Western Psychiatric Institute and Clinic, 121 University Place, University of Pittsburgh, 3811 O'Hara Street, Pittsburgh, PA 15213.)

Kovacs, M. (1985). *The natural history and cause of depressive disorders.* Washington, DC: American Psychiatric Association.

Lester, D., & Murrell, M. E. (1982). The preventive effect of strict gun control laws on suicide and homicide. *Suicide and Life-threatening Behavior, 12*, 131–139.

Marks, I. M. (1969). *Fears and phobias.* London: Heinemann.

Miller, L. C., Barrett, C. L., & Hampe, E. (1974). Phobias of childhood in a prescientific era. In A. Davids (Ed.), *Child personality and psychopathology: Current topics.* New York: Wiley.

The Pennsylvania Statistical Abstract. (1986). (28th ed.) Harrisburg, PA: Department of Commerce, Bureau of Statistics, Research and Planning.

Puig-Antich, J., Lukens, E., Davies, M., Goetz, D., Brennan-Quattrock, J., & Todak, G. (1985).

Psycho-social functioning in prepubertal major depressive disorders. *Archives of General Psychiatry 42,* 500–507.

Russell, G. F. M. (1985). Anorexia and bulimia. In M. Rutter & L. Hersov (Eds.), *Child and adolescent psychiatry: Modern approaches.* (2nd ed.) (pp. 625–637). Oxford, England: Blackwell Scientific Publications.

Rutter, M., Tizard, J., & Whitmore, K. (Eds.). (1970). *Education, health and behavior.* London: Longman. (Reprinted, 1981, Huntingdon, NY: Krieger.)

Shaffer, D. (1985). Depression, mania, and suicidal acts. In M. Rutter & L. Hersov (Eds.), *Child and adolescent psychiatry* (2nd ed.) (pp. 698–719). Oxford, England: Blackwell Scientific Publications.

Shaffer, D. (1986). Developmental factors in child and adolescent suicide. In M. Rutter, C. E. Izard, & P. B. Read (Eds.), *Depression in young people: Clinical and developmental perspectives* (pp. 383–396). New York: Guilford Press.

Smith, K., & Crawford, S. (1986). Suicidal behavior among "normal" high school students. *Suicide and Life-threatening Behavior, 16*(3), 313–325.

Strayhorn, J. M., Jr. (1982). *Foundations of clinical psychiatry.* Chicago: Year Book Medical Publishers.

Thomas, A., Chess, S., & Birch, H. G. (1968). *Temperament and behavior disorders in children.* New York: Universities Press.

U. S. Department of Health and Human Services. (1991). The international classification of diseases (4th ed.). Washington, DC: Author.

Walker, H. M., Severson, H., Haring, N., & Williams, G. (1986). Standardized screening and identification of behavior disordered pupils in the elementary age range: A multiple gating approach. *Direct Instruction News, 5*(3), 15–18.

PART

III

BEYOND THE CLASSROOM

11

EXTENDING
INTERVENTION EFFECTS

OUTLINE

OBJECTIVES

After completing this chapter, you should be able to

◆ Describe the relationship between the restrictiveness of treatment settings and the extent to which intervention effects generalize to other environments.
◆ Identify and describe obstacles to the maintenance and generalization of treatment effects.
◆ Describe strategies for achieving the maintenance and generalization of specific target behaviors.
◆ Describe procedures for assessing the expectations and tolerances of less restrictive settings for desired and maladaptive behaviors.
◆ Indicate factors to consider when planning for the transition of students to less restrictive school or post-school environments.
◆ Suggest strategies for accomplishing the successful transition of students to less restrictive environments.
◆ Explain the role of the special education teacher in working with parents and other professionals.

Up to now the major focus of this text has been on accomplishing changes in students' problem behaviors in settings where the primary intervention agent directly implements or supervises intervention procedures. In many cases, these **primary treatment settings** are individual classrooms that afford a high degree of stimulus control over pupils' behavior. Remember that there is a varied and powerful technology for accomplishing desired behavioral changes in settings in which intensive treatment may be applied. However, as we emphasized in Chapter 1, problem behaviors often occur in multiple settings. Furthermore, the effects of carefully designed and implemented interventions often do not generalize to other settings, nor do they tend to persist in primary treatment settings once intervention procedures are

withdrawn. The failure of intervention effects to maintain and generalize is a serious problem, especially for pupils whose behavior poses significant challenges to school personnel. This failure has been observed across many populations and age levels. For instance, Lane and Burchard (1983) conducted an extensive review of behavioral interventions with delinquent youth and observed an apparent relationship between recidivism and the restrictiveness of the treatment setting. Their conclusion is relevant to all professionals who attempt to serve children and youth in restrictive environments: "To the extent that delinquents and criminals are locked up in institutions, the rationale for doing so should be to punish, and/or to temporarily protect the community, not to rehabilitate. *Very restrictive environments make rehabilitation less likely to happen*" (p. 273, emphasis added). Although the task of educators is habilitative rather than rehabilitative, research concerning the maintenance and generalization of behavioral changes accomplished in single settings (e.g., special classrooms, residential treatment programs) indicates that the "albatross of generalization" (O'Leary & O'Leary, 1976) also plagues those who attempt to modify the behaviors of school-age children and youth in restrictive environments.

Thus, extending intervention effects beyond individual classrooms is a critical task. For students with EBD, this task is rendered more complex by the difficulties of including them in general education programs (Kauffman & Hallahan, 1995). Nevertheless, there are several practical reasons for attempting to generalize behavioral changes across settings and over time. First, as we have just suggested, many pupils with behavioral disorders have problems in other settings as well. They clearly need help in these environments too, and persons in these settings need assistance in dealing with them constructively. Second, the school environment actually is composed of many different settings, such as those just mentioned. This is obvious in secondary schools where pupils move from classroom to classroom and may participate in a variety of extracurricular activities. But even in elementary schools composed of self-contained classrooms, pupils function in a variety of settings. It is important both to assess these environments to determine what problems, if any, the target student is having in them and to generalize behavior changes accomplished in the primary treatment setting to these environments as well. Third, from an ecological view, a behavioral problem is not "owned" exclusively by the target pupil. Thus, it is inappropriate to expect all the change to occur in the student alone. Frequently, those who interact with students who exhibit behavior problems share ownership of the problem. In order for the pupil's behavior to change in the presence of these persons, their behavior must change as well. This is particularly important for generalizing behavioral changes to other settings. A fourth reason for extending treatment effects is to achieve social validation of important changes

that have occurred in other settings. For example, if you eliminate a pupil's stealing in your classroom but her parents still find her stealing at home, the problem has not been solved.

Finally, if you teach in a restrictive setting (such as a self-contained classroom or day treatment program in a regular school building, a special day school, residential program, or juvenile correctional facility), we hope that you plan to move your pupils into more natural environments. If you are working with secondary-level pupils, you must think about their successful transition to adult living and working environments. To accomplish these goals, you must involve a variety of other persons (e.g., other teachers, school administrators, bus drivers, parents, human services agency representatives, employers) in planning and implementing transition procedures.

This chapter describes strategies for extending the effects of interventions to other settings in which behavior changes also are needed. These interventions are discussed in three sections. The first describes maintenance and generalization procedures that have been developed through applied behavior analysts' research. The second section presents educational strategies for the successful transition of pupils to less restrictive school and adult environments. The last section describes strategies for working with parents and professionals outside of primary treatment settings. Obviously, these sets of procedures overlap considerably. Our discussion emphasizes issues that affect attempts to work across educational and noneducational settings.

MAINTENANCE AND GENERALIZATION PROCEDURES

The question of whether desired behavior changes extend across settings is one of generality. As Baer, Wolf, and Risley (1968) explain, "a behavior change may be said to have generality if it proves durable over time, if it appears in a wide variety of possible environments, or if it spreads to a wide variety of related behaviors" (p. 96). Generality therefore may be defined in terms of three effects. **Response maintenance** is the continuation or durability of behavior in treatment settings after the intervention has been withdrawn. Thus, if a pupil's targeted social skills in the special classroom continue to improve after social skills training procedures are discontinued, response maintenance has occurred. **Stimulus generalization** refers to the transfer of behaviors that have been trained in one setting, or in the presence of specific discriminative stimuli to settings or stimuli in the presence of which they have not been taught. An analogous term, **transfer of training,** more aptly describes the process of transferring behavior changes accomplished in training to new settings or in the presence of new discriminative stimuli (e.g., cues, persons, physical objects). For example, a student may use a social skill taught in the classroom with his peers in the cafeteria. **Response generalization** involves changes in untreated behaviors related to those behaviors targeted for intervention. For example, if a pupil is taught to suppress her physical attacks on other students, and her rate of verbal aggression also decreases (even though this behavior was not treated directly), response generalization has occurred. Such generalization across behaviors is more likely in responses that serve the same function (i.e., are followed by the same reinforcers) as the target behavior.

For educators, the critical questions regarding the maintenance and generalization of intervention effects include the following (Rutherford & Nelson, 1988):

1. Will desired behavior changes persist when students leave structured, highly controlled training settings?
2. Will pupils exhibit newly learned behaviors in nontraining settings, in the presence of other teachers or peers, and over time?
3. Will learning new skills facilitate the acquisition of similar behaviors that were not targeted for training in the original setting?

Next we examine the research concerning maintenance and generalization and describe specific procedures used to accomplish behavior changes across time, settings, and responses.

Maintenance and Generalization Research

Three decades ago, Baer, Wolf, and Risley (1968) described the parameters of applied behavior analysis. Their discussion of this new field clearly expressed a concern for the generality of the effects of behavioral interventions. Nearly ten years later Stokes and Baer (1977) reviewed 270 behavior analysis studies addressing generality. They found that in over half of these investigations, maintenance and generalization only were assessed, but not actually pursued or programmed. Rutherford and Nelson (1988) reviewed this literature a decade later and found that less than 2 percent of the approximately 5,300 applied research articles published between 1977 and 1986 addressed the maintenance and generalization of educational treatment effects, and less than 1 percent described studies in which maintenance and generalization were programmed systematically. Their analysis of this research was based on the nine procedures identified by Stokes and Baer (1977) as the major strategies for assessing or promoting generalization and maintenance of behavioral changes: Train and hope, sequential modification, introducing subjects to naturally maintaining contingencies, training sufficient exemplars, training loosely, programming indiscriminable contingencies, programming common stimuli, mediating generalization, and training to generalize. They concluded that although more researchers are addressing the generality of behavior changes, the "technology of generalization" called for by Stokes and Baer (1977) still was scattered and insufficient.

Rutherford and Nelson (1988) also noted that the complexity of intervention procedures, research designs, and methods of data collection required by such research contribute to the reluctance of investigators to study maintenance and generalization effects. For example, in designing procedures to manage inappropriate social behaviors, researchers usually impose a high level of stimulus control. They carefully define target behaviors; identify, control, and systematically manipulate specific environmental variables that affect these behaviors; and set reinforcement or punishment contingencies (often intrusive and artificial). On the other hand, programming for maintenance and generalization requires transferring stimulus control so that target behaviors come under the control of less precise and systematic variables. This "loosening" of stimulus control interferes with the demonstration of experimental control over treatment variables that affect target behavior. Therefore, maintenance and generalization research places unusual demands on researchers (e.g., for more time, more data collectors, more training for more persons, more extensive and elaborate data analysis), which increase the cost and effort of such research. These same obstacles also impede the ability of practitioners to conduct training for generality. Educators face additional barriers imposed by the educational system: most teachers are isolated from their colleagues when in direct contact with pupils, and they develop a sense of autonomy from others, even resenting intrusion into their classroom "domain."

Fortunately, maintenance and generalization training may be approached on two fronts: one focusing on procedures that influence the student's behavior during intervention so that it will maintain in other settings, and the other focusing on preparing other settings to support the pupil's new behaviors. If a teacher is unable to influence what goes on in other classrooms, for example, he still can select strategies that can be used in his own classroom. However, it is clear that maintenance and generalization programming is most effective when employed on both fronts, especially with students with more severe disabilities (Nelson & Rutherford, 1988). One such strategy is **transenvironmental programming** (Anderson-Inman, Walker, & Purcell, 1984), which consists of four components: assessing the behavioral expectations of specific generalization settings, teaching skills related to these expectations to students in the special education environment, selecting and using of techniques for promoting the transfer of skills across settings, and monitoring and evaluating student performance in generalization settings. Only the second component can be accomplished entirely in the primary treatment setting. Anderson-Inman et al. (1984) observed that monitoring and evaluating pupil behavior in targeted generalization settings is the most difficult aspect of transenvironmental programming because of the lack of training and support for regular education personnel. Consider these issues when reviewing the maintenance and generalization strategies presented later in this chapter.

Programming for Maintenance and Generalization

Stokes and Baer (1977) did not consider two of the nine strategies they described—namely, train and hope and sequential modification—to be techniques for programming generality of behavior across time, settings, or trainers. In *train and hope,* assessment probes are conducted in generalization settings but generalization is not specifically programmed. Yet, in their review, this category accounted for more than half of the studies addressing maintenance and generalization. Of the 103 studies specifically reviewed by Rutherford and Nelson (1988), train and hope accounted for 39 of them, or 38 percent of the total. *Sequential modification* was not considered a true generalization strategy because the procedure involves merely replicating the intervention procedures in other settings, without systematically programming for the durability of treatment effects once intervention is withdrawn. Procedures in this category accounted for nine (or 9 percent) of the studies reviewed by Rutherford and Nelson. Stokes and Osnes (1986) revised Stokes and Baer's (1977) remaining categories into 11 tactics grouped into three categories that emphasize the general principles underlying the classification:

1. Take advantage of natural communities of reinforcement.
   a. Teach relevant behaviors.
   b. Modify environments supporting maladaptive behaviors.
   c. Recruit natural communities of reinforcement.

2. Train diversely.
   a. Use sufficient stimulus exemplars.
   b. Use sufficient response exemplars.
   c. Train loosely.
   d. Use indiscriminable contingencies.
   e. Reinforce unprompted generalization.

3. Incorporate functional mediators.
   a. Use common physical stimuli.
   b. Use common social stimuli.
   c. Use self-mediated stimuli. (pp. 417–418)

Take Advantage of Natural Communities of Reinforcement The strategies incorporated in this principle emphasize using reinforcement normally available in the natural environment. For instance, appropriate social behaviors usually are followed by pleasant social responses from other persons, which is reinforcing to most individuals. Thus, the first strategy, *teach relevant behaviors,* involves adding to the pupil's social repertoire behaviors that are likely to set up reciprocal social interactions that strengthen further social initiations on the student's part, such as greetings and other positive social initiations, and effective language, communication, and interpersonal skills (Stokes & Osnes, 1986). Behaviors that are useful in generalization settings for gaining attention, inviting interactions, or generating praise effectively "trap" reinforcement; thus, the term **trapping effect** is used to describe the tactic of increasing behaviors that effectively capture naturally contingent reinforcement. When using this strategy, however, follow these suggestions.

First, assess generalization settings to determine what skills and behaviors are required or are likely to result in reinforcement. A skill that is taught in your classroom (e.g., greeting every pupil in the class with a handshake) may not be necessary or even desirable in another setting. Although this strategy is implemented in the primary treatment setting, the trainer obviously must assess the generalization setting to identify relevant behaviors. (A procedure that may be used for this purpose is described in the next section.)

Our second recommendation is to make sure that the student acquires sufficient proficiency in the skill. If the pupil does not use the skill fluently

(i.e., as well as other students in the generalization setting), she is less likely to be reinforced when she does use it. One way to increase the probability of reinforcement in generalization settings is to prompt it. In one study teachers had to prompt preschool children to interact with a withdrawn child in order to increase her social initiations enough to occasion their responses naturally (Baer & Wolf, 1970). Some pupils' social behaviors may not come under the control of peer responses without considerable training (e.g., see Gunter, Fox, Brady, Shores, & Cavanaugh, 1988), pointing out the need to carefully monitor settings in which generalization is desired. It also is important to go beyond providing training in only the primary treatment setting and simply hoping that the target behavior occurs in other environments. In fact, it is much more efficient and logical to train social skills in the settings where they are needed from the start (Nelson, 1988). Third, do not assume that the apparent existence of a natural community of reinforcement for one student's behavior assures that the same naturally occurring consequences will be reinforcing to another pupil (Stokes & Osnes, 1986).

As most teachers and parents know, peers sometimes provide consistent reinforcement of undesired student behaviors, and adults and peers in generalization settings may not adequately reinforce desired target behaviors. In such cases, it may be necessary to *modify environments supporting maladaptive behavior.* This tactic entails controlling the consequences that peers provide for undesired behavior. Managing peer reactions can be extremely difficult, given the number of students and settings that may be involved. Use peer-mediated procedures, such as dependent group-oriented contingencies and peer feedback, to shift reinforcement contingencies in order to support desired alternate behaviors. Under such contingency conditions, desired behavior becomes the discriminative stimulus for peer group reinforcement. However, you also may need to prevent reinforcement of undesired behavior by training peers, other staff, or parents to ignore maladaptive behavior and to attend systematically to desired replacement behavior

(Stokes & Osnes, 1986). Obviously, this strategy requires intervention in generalization settings.

Another strategy that can be used is to teach the target pupil to *recruit natural communities of reinforcement.* This consists of training the student not only to emit behaviors desired in the generalization setting but also to draw positive adult or peer attention to these behaviors. This strategy has been effective in recruiting adult attention (e.g., see Graubard, Rosenberg, & Miller, 1971; Hrydowy, Stokes, & Martin, 1984), but its success with peers has not been as well documented. However, Gaylord-Ross, Haring, Breen, and Pitts-Conway (1984) taught autistic adolescent boys to operate socially desirable objects (e.g., a video game and a tape player) and then to use them in social interactions with typical peers. The researchers observed generalized maintenance of those students' social interactions with typical pupils. Dependent group-oriented contingencies, in which the target pupil's desired behavior earns reinforcers desired by peers, also have been observed to increase peers' positive attention to the targeted student (Shores, Apolloni, & Norman, 1976). Initial training may be provided only in the primary treatment setting, but the trainer must be able to assess the pupil's skill in recruiting reinforcement in the generalization setting in order to adjust training procedures as needed.

Train Diversely The objective of this group of strategies is to arrange training conditions and response and reinforcement criteria to cover a range of possible circumstances that occur in generalization settings. As with other strategies, those in this category (except *reinforce unprompted generalization*) may be applied in the primary treatment setting, but they are much more effective when training occurs in generalization settings as well. The first strategy, *use sufficient stimulus exemplars,* tells you to arrange for more than one or a small set of discriminative stimuli to control the target behavior. Thus, conduct training in more than one setting or under more than one set of training circumstances (Stokes & Osnes, 1986). An application of this strategy that has been used successfully with pupils exhibiting autism involves

typical peers as discriminative stimuli for targeted social behaviors (Simpson, 1987); however, this tactic is much more effective with trained, as opposed to untrained, peer confederates (Hollinger, 1987; McEvoy & Odom, 1987). You also should augment peer-mediated strategies with direct instruction in generalization settings (Shores, 1987). Stokes and Osnes (1986) stress the importance of having a generalization plan to guide training across stimulus examples. Decide where and with whom generalization is desired and tailor your strategy according to the characteristics of these persons, stimuli, and settings.

The response analogue of the above strategy is to *use sufficient response exemplars,* which involves including more than one example of the target behavior(s) in the training. Using multiple-response examples is particularly important when attempting to generalize a complex behavior such as holding a conversation (Stokes & Osnes, 1986). In applying this strategy, the pupil is taught a range of correct responses that are appropriate in given situations and is reinforced for using them. Teaching several acceptable response variations also is useful for situations in which students may be required to exhibit different response topographies in different stimulus settings. For example, some greeting behaviors may be appropriate for a male coming up on a group of adolescent boys (e.g., "How's it going?" or "Hey, what's happening?") while other expressions are preferred for use in greeting members of the opposite sex (e.g., "Hi!" or "Hello, Sandy."). Getting a drink of water requires different response topographies when at a drinking fountain, a restaurant, or a sink.

Train loosely is closely related to the previous two strategies. Control over the training conditions and acceptable responses is loosened intentionally to permit greater flexibility in both the stimuli occasioning target behaviors and the reinforced behaviors. More tightly controlled initial training conditions will require proportionately greater attention to loosening stimulus control. Consequently, Stokes and Osnes (1986) recommended that the least tightly controlled yet effective initial training environment be used. Therefore, teachers who have students work in study carrels, who provide daily work in folders, who time seatwork assignments, and who have very specific response requirements for reinforcement may not be facilitating their pupils' success in less structured environments.

The objective of the strategy *use indiscriminable contingencies* is to loosen control over the consequences of behavior. The most common application is to use intermittent schedules of reinforcement to lessen the predictability of reinforcement while increasing the durability of target behaviors. Koegel and Rincover (1977) demonstrated that even noncontingent reinforcement maintained the imitation and direction-following behaviors of children with autism after systematic treatment contingencies were withdrawn. However, we do not recommend this approach unless pupils can be supervised continuously in generalization settings. Another application is to use vicarious reinforcement, for example, praising one student for appropriate behavior. Other pupils who observe this model are more likely to imitate the desired behavior (Kazdin, 1977; Strain, Shores, & Kerr, 1976). This has been referred to as a *ripple* or *spillover effect.* To make reinforcement less predictable, delay its delivery for some time after the target behavior has occurred or reinforce the behavior when it occurs simultaneously with other nontarget responses (Stokes & Osnes, 1986). One note of caution, however: you should be certain that desired responses are well established under systematic and plentiful schedules of reinforcement before making such reinforcement less discriminable. The last strategy in this category, *reinforce unprompted generalization,* involves monitoring in generalization settings and reinforcing spontaneous generalization of desired target behaviors when they occur or reinforcing the absence of maladaptive behaviors (Stokes & Osnes, 1986). Obviously, this strategy requires that persons in generalization settings be aware of target behaviors, monitor their occurrence, and apply the appropriate reinforcers contingently.

Incorporate Functional Mediators. The strategies included in this group attempt to take advantage of potential discriminative stimuli that are common to training and generalization settings. Again, assessment and training in generalization settings are critical to the success of these strategies. *Use common physical stimuli* means to ensure that physical discriminative stimuli are present in all settings in which target behavior is desired. Common work or play materials may be used to facilitate generalization. Marholin and Steinman (1977) found that by reinforcing the academic response rate and accuracy of special education pupils when the teacher was present, the academic materials became discriminative stimuli that occasioned working even when the teacher was not present. On the other hand, when the teacher merely reinforced on-task behavior, work productivity dropped when the teacher was out of the room, apparently because the teacher was the discriminative stimulus for academic responses in this condition. Peers are logical common stimuli in the next strategy, *use common social stimuli.* Significant peers and adults present in generalization settings may participate in training sessions in the primary treatment setting, either early in training or later, when transfer of training is contemplated (Stokes & Osnes, 1986). For example, Gunter et al. (1988) used typical peers who were present in generalization settings as discriminative stimuli in the training environment for the appropriate social initiations of students with disabilities. This tactic is an option when trainers cannot work in generalization settings, but assessment is necessary to ensure that interactions in these settings are consistent with the generalization plan.

A readily available source of common stimuli is the pupils themselves. Thus the final strategy, *use self-mediated stimuli,* involves having the student carry or deliver stimuli that are discriminative of appropriate responses. Instructions, prompts, reminders written on a card, or a string on a finger are tangible discriminative stimuli, whereas teaching the student to self-administer a verbal instruction or cue is intangible but more natural to generalization settings. Self-recording, self-assessment, and self-reinforcement are procedures that also employ self-mediated stimuli. This set of strategies potentially is one of the most useful and least intrusive for promoting transfer of training, but it is also difficult for researchers to evaluate the extent to which subjects use self-mediated procedures. Consequently, it is difficult to say that these procedures are responsible for some of the gains attributed to them. It also is important to realize that prior training in using self-mediated strategies is critical to ensuring their effectiveness in generalization environments (Polsgrove, 1979). Nevertheless, a number of studies have involved teaching students to self-monitor their performance. For example, Clees (1995) taught students with learning and behavioral disorders to self-record their daily schedules and observed significant and durable increases in the number of teacher-expected behaviors exhibited, even after withdrawing the self-recording intervention. Reid and Harris (1993) found that self-monitoring of performance and self-monitoring of attention had varied effects on students with learning disabilities. They concluded that a "best" strategy for teaching self-monitoring does not exist for all students and all tasks.

Cognitive behavior modification involves teaching students cognitive strategies to help them solve problems. These strategies incorporate an analysis of the tasks to be performed (or the social problems to be solved) and teaching the strategy through modeling, self-instruction, and self-evaluation (Meichenbaum, 1977). For example, if a student needed to learn how to control his temper, the teacher might teach him—through modeling, role-playing, and individual or group discussions—a set of steps to rehearse when he finds himself losing control (e.g., count to ten, leave the situation, repeat to himself that the other person is not trying to "get" him).

Such tactics frequently include an evaluation component. For example, Maag (1994) taught a girl to self-monitor situations that led to feelings of frustration. Her self-monitoring sheet included a description of the situation resulting in frustration, her expectations of that situation, her reactions, and whether the outcome was satisfactory to her.

The strategies that you design to extend treatment effects to other settings, persons, or specific discriminative stimuli, or over time will depend on your objectives for the student and situation. It is likely that a combination of strategies will be more appropriate to specific circumstances than a single procedure. Develop a generalization plan to guide your efforts and facilitate your evaluation of its effects. Figure 11.1 provides a format for this purpose. Use checklists like that illustrated in Figure 11.2 to identify resource persons to assist in generalization programming. Once you have gained fluency in writing intervention and generalization plans, you may find it more convenient to incorporate the latter into your intervention plan from the beginning.

In discussing maintenance and generalization training strategies, we have emphasized the importance of assessment and training in the environments where skills are expected or needed. Interventions that fail to address the demands and idiosyncrasies of generalization settings are not likely to produce effects that persist in these environments. Thus, severe limitations are imposed on intervention agents who are unable to gain access to these settings because their direct teaching responsibilities prohibit it, because other teachers will not tolerate observers in their classrooms, or because staff members will not cooperate with training procedures. The organization of most public school environments can be a significant obstacle to effective maintenance and generalization of treatment effects. Although you may have no authority to change factors such as teaching loads, you may be able to identify resources in the school in order to accomplish generalization objectives. Your own enthusiasm and dedication to helping your pupils will assist in recruiting reinforcement and support for your efforts. We have known educators who, through modeling, hard work, and determination, evoked similar efforts by their colleagues. As more school districts adopt teacher assistance teams or **interactive teaming models** (Thomas, Correa, & Morsink, 1995), better mobilization of the many resources available in schools (and communities) will follow.

Figure 11.1 Sample
Generalization Plan Format

Student _____ Target Behavior _____

Primary Treatment Setting _____

Intervention Plan (Include objective, procedures, data decision rules, review
       dates, etc.)

Outcome (Narrative description, dates plan reviewed/revised, data summaries or
       graphs, etc.)

Generalization Plan

    Objective

       Terminal Behavior

       Conditions (Settings, persons, reinforcers, schedule, etc.)

       Criteria

    Strategy (Procedures used, resources needed, etc.)

    Evaluation Plan (Data to be collected, when it will be collected, who will
            collect it, who will summarize/evaluate data, data decision
            rule, etc.)

    Outcome (Narrative description, dates plan reviewed/revised, data summaries
            or graphs, etc.)

PROGRAMMING FOR TRANSITION OF STUDENTS TO LESS RESTRICTIVE ENVIRONMENTS

This section describes strategies directed toward moving students to less restrictive educational settings,[1] to other programs or facilities where services are delivered, or to post-secondary school environments. Of course the maintenance and generalization procedures just presented may be applied to this goal. Our rationale for presenting transition strategies in a separate section is that movement of pupils to less restrictive environments is a common educational goal, and it involves transferring students and their entire repertoires of behavior to new settings. Thus it is a broader task than that of programming for the maintenance and generalization of specific target behaviors. In addition, the movement of students

---

[1]Recall that the concept of least restrictive environment is *not* synonymous with placement in a regular education classroom.

Figure 11.2 In-School Resource Checklist

Personnel Agencies	Willing to work with pupils?	Supportive of your program?	Cooperated with you previously?	Willing to collect data?	Supervision required?	Training required?	Willing to devote time above normal duties?	Reliably carried out procedures with pupils before?	Comments (Phone numbers, etc.)
Teachers									
Aides and volunteers									
Speech clinician									
Guidance counselor									
School psychologist									
Vice principal									
Principal									
Secretaries									
School nurse									
Custodian									
Bus driver									
Cafeteria workers									
Others									

among instructional settings is an activity peculiar to schools. Although it is desirable to generalize changes in those behaviors targeted in the primary treatment setting to these environments, each classroom teacher also has individual expectations for the behaviors required in his setting. Transition planning must take these expectations into account, and strategies for accomplishing the movement of pupils into less restrictive settings must involve a broad range of activities. Procedures have been developed for the specific purpose of facilitating this movement, especially in the case of students with disabilities. We describe strategies to facilitate transitions to less restrictive educational settings, other educational or treatment settings, and to adult environments separately, although many procedures, including those discussed in the previous section, are appropriate for any of these goals. We also consider follow-up assessment procedures because these are important for evaluating both pupils' status after leaving treatment settings and the effectiveness of the programs they received.

The key element in all transition activities is a **transition plan.** In effect, the eligibility assessment and multidisciplinary committee process conducted prior to students' entry into special education programs constitutes transition planning from regular to special education. All systematic transitions must include strategies for moving both the student and appropriate data from one location to another. Transition plans most often are associated with movement of students with disabilities from secondary school programs to post-secondary settings, but the components of all transition plans are the same: a statement of the goals and objectives to be achieved by the transition, and the procedures for their implementation, including the responsibilities of the sending and receiving program, the information to be transferred, and follow-up procedures (Edgar, Webb, & Maddox, 1987).

Transitions to Less Restrictive Educational Settings

Successfully reintegrating students into mainstream school life constitutes one of your most complex and difficult tasks. You must not only evaluate and develop appropriate pupil behaviors; you also must coordinate a number of environmental variables: schedules, curricula, materials, school staff, and other pupils, just to name a few. A technology for achieving this change on behalf of students with disabilities is developing; however, as Kauffman and Hallahan (1995) caution, the attitudes, strategies, and resources needed for achieving the successful full inclusion of students with significant behavioral challenges are not in place in the vast majority of school districts in the United States. Kauffman and Hallahan indicate that until such systems change, "full inclusion can provide only an illusion of support for all students, an illusion that may trick many into jumping on the bandwagon but is sure to produce disappointment, if not outrage, in its riders when the juggernaut crushes the students it was supposed to defend." (p. x).

A recommended strategy for accomplishing the reintegration of students into regular classrooms is *transenvironmental programming* (Anderson-Inman et al., 1984). As we mentioned earlier, transenvironmental programming consists of four steps. Following is a discussion of each step.

Assessing Mainstream Classrooms   The task of locating an appropriate mainstream class into which to reintegrate a student is greatly facilitated in schools with a climate that supports full inclusion. It is true that the mechanics and dynamics of such a climate are not in place on a large scale. Until they are, students who are hard to teach and to manage will not be welcome or successful in general education classes, regardless of lip service given to having "full inclusion school programs."

Fortunately, research is beginning to identify the factors that characterize such a climate. For example, Rock, Rosenberg, and Carran (1994) conducted a large-scale study in Maryland that identified variables that influence the reintegration[2] rate

---

[2]Students with EBD are the last of any group of students with disabilities to be identified—in terms of age and grade level—and placed in special education programs (U. S. Department of Education, 1994). Therefore, their entry into the educational mainstream is more accurately characterized as *reintegration*.

of students with EBD. They found three sets of variables that predicted higher rates of reintegration. Set 1 consisted of a "positive reintegration orientation," which included the following combination of program components:

1. Multiple options for reintegration, such as part-day, trial, and transitional reintegration.
2. Opportunity for special education teachers to learn reintegration class expectations.
3. Authority for the special teacher to participate in selecting the reintegration placement for a particular student.
4. Program-wide reintegration goals, including goal setting for students, when they are admitted to the program, and reintegration planning at the annual IEP review of each student.
5. Reintegration procedures that are written, documented, and easy-to-implement.
6. Training in reintegration that is provided to special teachers, including annual training in procedures and methods; regular, formal meetings to update reintegration information; and informal reintegration training sessions given by administrators to individuals or groups.

The best single predictor from this set was the ability of special education teachers to select the particular class into which the student would be reintegrated. In this regard, Wong, Kauffman, and Lloyd (1991) have developed procedures for selecting mainstream teachers to work with students certified as having EBD. On the basis of the effective teaching literature, they identified the following sets of characteristics of teachers who are likely to be successful with students with EBD:

♦ High expectations for students' academic performance and conduct.
♦ Selection of activities to maintain high rates of correct responding and low rates of off-task behavior.
♦ Frequent praise of desired student behavior.
♦ Infrequent use of criticism or punishment.
♦ Self-confidence in helping students learn and behave appropriately. (Wong et al., 1991, p. 111)

The second set of variables identified by Rock et al. (1994) consisted of the following combination of specific demographic characteristics:

1. The special education program was located in a wing of a comprehensive school building, as opposed to a separate building.
2. Program was within one mile of the most likely reintegration site.
3. Multiple reintegration sites were available, including less restrictive classes in the same building, in nearby public schools, in students' home school or previous school, or in another setting (such as a vocational center).
4. Program was public rather than private, and in a county that had a significantly higher rate of reintegration than others.
5. Program served students who were older rather than younger.
6. Program had smaller mainstream class sizes.
7. Classes were departmentalized or rotating, rather than self-contained.

Of this set, the best demographic predictors of reintegration rates were (1), (2), and (3) (Rock et al., 1994). Thus, the political climate regarding the reintegration of students with EBD as well as the social and physical demographics of the school are important factors in reintegration rate.

Set 3 consisted of a combination of teachers' characteristics and experiences:

1. Greater number of places a teacher had received reintegration training, including undergraduate school, graduate school, in-school training, inservice courses, access to professional literature, and other sites.
2. Higher number of students who have been reintegrated from a given teacher's class, and a higher number of students for whom the teacher had primary (case manager) or secondary (team member) reintegration planning responsibilties.
3. More years worked with children certified as EBD.
4. An "Advanced Professional" certificate from the Maryland State Department of Education (as compared to Standard, Temporary/Provisional, or none).

5. State certification in special education.

6. A higher level of overall teacher education (e.g., Master's as compared to Bachelor's degrees).

7. Teacher's educational specialization in special education.

The best single predictor in this set was the teacher's experience with reintegration. As the authors of this study pointed out, many other variables contribute to how much of this expertise a teacher has, including previous training, administrative and community support, and programmatic resources.

Another set of variables, consisting of special education teachers' opinions and attitudes, did not add significantly to the prediction of reintegration rate. However, as we have just mentioned, these variables were significantly related to other variables that already were predictive of reintegration rate (Rock et al., 1994).

Rock et al. (1994) also observed that a number of these variables are influenced by school administrators, who should ensure that (a) reintegration procedures are clearly defined and in writing, (b) schoolwide reintegration goals and expectations exist for all students, and (c) inservice teacher training is implemented as described in Set 1. However, as a classroom teacher, you may sit on a school council or site-based management team that makes decisions regarding such policies and staff training. As a special education teacher, you should be involved in the selection of classes into which your students are reintegrated and you should familarize yourself with reintegration expectations and procedures in your school (Rock et al., 1994).

A lively and sometimes contentious debate has developed regarding the participation of students with EBD in full inclusion programs (Kauffman & Hallahan, 1995). We believe that full inclusion is a desirable goal for these students but is not an appropriate strategy for all. Rather, as Edgar and Siegel (1995) observed, the needs of pupils with EBD (and their families) require a wide range of services that exceed those typically provided by the schools. Furthermore, without extended services, school programs are not likely to be successful. Edgar and Siegel (1995) also advised that teachers should argue "for programs that achieve desired outcomes regardless of the degree of inclusion, concede that no one program will ever meet the needs of all students, and advocate for the proactive testing of many program types rather than continued debates on what should be" (p. 252).

Preparing the Student   In describing strategies for developing students' competence with regard to the expectations and freedoms of the mainstream classroom, we begin with the assumption that you have improved the student's academic and social functioning to the point where he is able to profit from a less restrictive environment. If this assumption is met, the issue is one of generalization and maintenance of behavior change, which of necessity involves arrangements with other persons.

To help the student prepare for inclusion in a mainstream class, develop a hierarchy of student competencies and classroom structure that increasingly approximates the pupil behaviors and teacher expectations found in general education classrooms. One strategy to organize these variables is to establish a *level* or *phase system*. Ideally, a level system is coordinated with a continuum of placements in the school building. As Rock et al. (1994) suggested, the probability that critical behaviors will be maintained and generalized outside restrictive settings is enhanced by having a complete continuum of services available in the building. That is, rather than going directly from a self-contained, highly individualized program into a group-oriented regular classroom, students enter a class that more closely approximates the setting, demands, and expectation of the regular classroom (e.g., a resource room) and are phased into regular classrooms from there.

Entry and exit competencies for each level of program in this continuum can be specified. For example, Taylor and Soloway (1973) devised a service delivery system consisting of four levels. *Preacademic competencies* include such skills as paying attention, starting an assignment immediately, working continuously without interruption, following task directions, doing what one is told, taking part verbally in discussions, getting along with others, and demonstrating adequacy in perceptual-motor and language skills. *Academic competencies* include proficiency in all core subjects, as well as being accurate, being neat, efficient, and well organized. *Setting competencies* involve learning to profit from instruction provided in settings found in regular classrooms (independent work, large and small group work, etc.), and *reward competencies* range from responding to tangible reinforcers at the most basic level to being reinforced by social recognition and the acquisition of new knowledge and skills. Pupils are grouped according to their level of competence in these skill categories. They move up through the levels as they demonstrate more advanced competencies. The environments corresponding to each level consist of a self-contained setting, a resource room (with increasingly greater time spent in regular classrooms), and the regular classroom. Table 11.1 illustates Taylor and Soloway's (1973) level system of student competencies leading to functioning in a regular classroom.

Similar phase systems have been developed for secondary programs (e.g., Braaten, 1979; Vetter-Zemitszch et al., 1984) and for children and adolescents with severe behavior disorders in residential programs (e.g., Bauer & Shea, 1988; Hewett & Taylor, 1980; LaNunziata, Hunt, & Cooper, 1984). Within a given level, progress upward is maximized by a curricular emphasis on those competencies needed for the next higher level.

More than likely, you will not have the prerogative of developing a complete delivery system. However, most level systems are designed to operate in the context of an individual classroom. As the case study at the end of this chapter illustrates, you can arrange your own expectations for student behavior in terms of a hierarchy of competencies. If progress through the levels is associated with increasing independence and powerful (and naturalistic) reinforcers, student motivation to advance will pose few problems.[3] However, your system will work only if it is based on skills your pupils actually need for success in the less restrictive environments within your school or institution. Therefore, as suggested by the findings of Rock et al. (1994), you should begin by determining the minimum requirements of each environment. For example, what skills do pupils need to be manageable in regular classes in your building? Which behaviors are more likely to successfully trap reinforcement in the less-restrictive environment? In general, we believe these consist of appropriate social behavior, compliance with teacher requests and directions, and basic language proficiency.

These general skills, as well as the school survival skills described in Chapter 7, suggest some target behaviors for students you are considering moving to less restrictive settings. However, each classroom teacher's specific skill requirements vary, just as competence in and motivation to perform these skills vary from student to student; therefore, assess each environment separately. Thus, steps one and two of transenvironmental programming are ongoing and interactive.

In selecting target behaviors for intervention with the goal of the full inclusion of pupils with EBD in mind, assign appropriate social skills a high priority. The social skill deficits of students with disabilities, particularly EBD, are well documented. For example, Gresham, Elliott, and Black (1987) found that teacher ratings of social skills alone could be used to classify accurately 75 percent of a sample of mainstreamed pupils with mild disabilities. In other words, lack of social skills appears to be a factor that discriminates between children with disabilities and their peers who are not disabled. Use social skills rating scales such as those discussed in Chapter 2 to evaluate pupils' social skills relative to normative standards and to select target behaviors for training prior to mainstreaming placement.

---

[3]One cautionary note: level systems are patently *ineffective* if progress is less reinforcing to students than the peer and adult attention they receive for exhibiting problematic behaviors, if they do not receive meaningful reinforcement for advancement through the levels, including those levels that involve participation in mainstream classes or if they lack the skills needed for success at higher levels.

Table 11.1   A Level System of Student Competencies Leading to Regular Classroom Functioning

	Continuum of Settings and Competencies Required			
Levels	*Preacademic I Self-Contained Setting* ⟶	*Preacademic II Resource Setting* ⟶	*Academic I Resource Setting* ⟶	*Academic II Regular Class Setting*
Preacademic	*Major emphasis* Paying attention Beginning work immediately Working continuously Following directions Doing what one is told	*Minor emphasis* Behaviors stressed in preacademic *Major emphasis* Taking part in discussion Getting along with others	*Minor emphasis* Preacademic behaviors stated in preacademic I & II	Regular classroom
Academic	*Minor emphasis* Academic assignments Being accurate Being neat	*Major emphasis* Presenting basic school subjects Supplementing remediation with special materials and resources	*Major emphasis* School subjects Some remedial Some grade-level curriculum	Regular classroom
Setting	Student works independently at desk or booth 1:1 relationship with teacher	Student works in teacher/small group setting Student works independently in shared desk space Group interaction and cooperation emphasized	Regular classroom simulated Large group receives instruction from teacher Opportunities presented to function independently	Regular classroom
Reward	Checkmark system linked to tangible rewards for appropriate social and academic behaviors Any incentive considered that will motivate child	Checkmark system linked to free time Increased emphasis on social approval	Numerical grading system for effort, quality of work, and citizenship	Regular classroom

Source: This information is taken from Taylor, F. D., & Soloway, M. M. (1973). The Madison School Plan: A functional model for merging the regular and special classrooms. In E. N. Deno (Ed.). *Instructional alternatives for exceptional children.* Reston, VA: Council for Exceptional Children, pp. 147–149.

Of course, students also should be prepared to meet the academic expectations of less restrictive environments if they are to have successful experiences in these settings. The delineation of academic instructional strategies is beyond the scope of this book (see Kameinui & Darch, 1995; Mercer & Mercer, 1985). However, the general approach should be the same as for preparing students to meet the social demands of less restrictive settings: identify the academic expectations, assess the student with regard to these expectations, teach the pupil in the more

restrictive setting up to the criterion levels expected in the less restrictive environment, provide generalization training in the new setting, and follow up to determine whether the student is meeting expectations and to provide on-going support and technical assistance to the regular classroom teacher.

Several instruments have been developed to assess student behavior against the expectations of mainstream teachers. The *SBS Inventory of Teacher Social Behavior Standards and Expectations* (Walker & Rankin, 1980b) is a 107-item rating scale, divided into three sections, describing adaptive and maladaptive student classroom behavior. The first section consists of 56 items describing adaptive student behavior, which the mainstream teacher rates as critical, desirable, or unimportant to a successful adjustment in her classroom. The 51 items in Section II describe maladaptive behaviors that the teacher rates as unacceptable, tolerated, or acceptable. Section III asks the teacher to reevaluate the items she rated as critical and unacceptable in terms of (1) whether the behavior of a pupil rated as deviant on these items would have to occur at "normal" rates prior to the student being integrated into her classroom, or (2) whether she would require technical assistance for these behaviors following the student's placement. The *SBS Checklist of Correlates of Child Handicapping Conditions* (Walker & Rankin, 1980a) is a 24-item checklist describing conditions and characteristics commonly associated with disabilities that, if manifested by target pupils, often cause teachers to resist placement. The **Walker-Rankin Child Behavior Rating Scale** is a criterion-referenced scale on which the teacher in the sending setting assesses the target pupil's behavioral status on the items the potential receiving teacher designates as critical or unacceptable (Walker, 1986). These three instruments allow the sending teacher to directly compare the receiving teacher's expectations with the student's current behavior. Wong, Kauffman, and Lloyd (1991) developed a briefer system for matching students to prospective mainstream classrooms (see below).

Implementing Transition Strategies   In the process of assessing the mainstream classroom and establishing a match between the student's characteristics and the reintegration setting, you will develop relationships with the other building staff. Your relationship with the potential receiving teacher will be strengthened if you plan the student's academic program with him. In view of the likely possibility that the pupil may need special support and assistance not available to other students in the setting, you may need to help the teacher adapt instruction by providing special materials,

tutoring the pupil, or training the teacher in errorless or mastery learning procedures. If your school has formed teacher assistance teams, staff may be available to assist teachers in adapting instruction and management practices.

Use these teacher support services to facilitate the transition of your pupils to less restrictive settings. The more that dealing with students with behavior problems is seen as a responsibility shared by all professional educators and not just by those who are certified as "special," the more quickly professionals will learn the necessary skills and accept responsibility for guaranteeing these students their educational rights.

The settings in which social skills instruction takes place are important to consider. Whereas it is desirable to provide initial social skills training in settings that ensure a high level of stimulus control over instructional and response variables, the most effective maintenance and generalization strategies involve training in generalization settings. For instance, the use of multiple peer exemplars is a critical social skill generalization strategy, and research clearly supports using typical peers as confederates (Simpson, 1987). Further, although social skills are logical targets for trapping reinforcement, pupils with disabilities acquire these responses more efficiently when peer confederates are trained to interact with them rather than when students with disabilities simply are taught appropriate social responses and then placed in mainstream settings (Hollinger, 1987; McEvoy & Odom, 1987). In turn, more durable patterns of confederate interactions occur when students with disabilities are taught to make social initiations toward these peers (Gaylord-Ross & Haring, 1987). These strategies require that reciprocal social interactions between students be trained in generalization settings. This requirement is difficult for many school districts to implement because their other responsibilities restrict the staff members with expertise in social skills training (e.g., special education teachers) from working in settings with students who are not disabled. The most economical solution to this dilemma is to make social skills training the responsibility of regular education staff, but given the current pressures on general educators, this is not likely to happen (Braaten, Kauffman, Braaten, Polsgrove, & Nelson, 1988). The development of **collaborative consultation** models, in which regular and special education teachers work together in full inclusion classrooms, is a promising compromise (Hallahan & Kauffman, 1995; Idol, Paolucci-Whitcomb, & Nevin, 1986). Whether you seek employment as a regular or special education teacher, we strongly recommend that you investigate the amount of time and opportunity you will have to work with regular educators, as well as the school's strategies for promoting collaborative consultation.

Wong et al. (1991) developed procedures, based on the effective teaching literature, for establishing a match between the characteristics of teachers in mainstream classrooms and students who are being considered for inclusion. A *Mainstream Classroom Observation* form is completed by the special education teacher either during or immediately after directly observing a potential regular classroom (see Figure 11.3). Teachers who demonstrate recommended teaching behaviors then are interviewed to determine who would be a better match for a particular student. Following this interview, the special education teacher completes a *Student-Teacher Match* form (see Figure 11.4), which is based on the *SBS Inventory of Teacher Social Behavior Standards and Expectations,* (Walker & Rankin, 1980b) for selecting regular classroom teachers for mainstreamed students with EBD. This form also asks for information regarding the amount and kind of technical assistance the teacher would need for the student to be placed, as well as supportive plans for the student and teacher.

Monitoring and Follow-up Assessment The purposes of follow-up assessments are to monitor and evaluate the student's current status with regard to IEP or intervention objectives, to evaluate the effectiveness of the educational program or intervention for a pupil, or to evaluate the accuracy with which staff members implement intervention procedures. Follow-up data thus serve three functions: *to certify* that objectives have been reached; to provide *feedback* for use in revising programs for

future students; and to determine whether interventions are being *properly implemented.*

If the student has been certified previously as having a disability, follow-up data regarding IEP goals and objectives may be used as a basis for deciding that special education classification is no longer needed. In Chapter 1 we recommended that IEP committees specify criteria for decertification of pupils once conditions that caused them to be certified are remediated. IEPs should contain goals and objectives related to successful integration or reintegration into the educational mainstream; therefore, follow-up assessment in mainstream settings is needed for making decertification decisions. Follow-up evaluation of the maintenance and generalization of intervention effects is more specific and precise because the focus of assessment is on targeted behaviors. These assessments may or may not occur in settings outside the educational program.

The specific follow-up assessment procedures used depend upon the student's current educational placement. If the pupil is in your classroom, follow-up may involve conducting *measurement probes* of targeted behaviors after an educational program or intervention strategy has been terminated. If the student has been moved to a less restrictive setting, the same behaviors should be assessed, but the measurement strategy used will be influenced by the setting and the person conducting the assessment. For example, if you must rely on a regular classroom teacher to do the assessment, you probably will select a less technically demanding procedure than you would if you were conducting the assessment yourself. In such circumstances you may elect to have the teacher complete a behavior rating scale, evaluate the student against criteria for behaviors in her classroom (e.g., is the target pupil's frequency of disruptive behavior higher than, about the same as, or lower than that of the average student?). Frequency counts of discrete behaviors are preferable, and these data are even better when rates of similar behaviors collected on nontarget peers are available for comparison (see Chapter 2). However, such procedures require trained observers.

Figure 11.3 Mainstream Classroom Observation Form (MCO).

General Classroom Teacher ___K. C. Kray___ Date of Observation___3/18/98___

A. Use of Classroom Time

1. Percentage of time spent on academic learning — __90__ %
2. Percentage of time spent on group work — __75__ %
3. Percentage of time spent on independent work — __25__ %
4. Average amount of time spent in transition from one activity to the next — __2__ minute/sec
5. Average amount of time unassigned — __5__ minute/sec
6. Systematic way teacher deals with student wait-time — __X__ Yes _____ No

B. Instruction

1. Teacher gives clear and complete directions and instructions — __X__ Yes _____ No
2. Teacher's lessons are highly structured and clearly presented — __X__ Yes _____ No
3. Teacher's instruction is responsive to individual needs and the readiness levels of students — __X__ Yes _____ No

C. Questioning/Feedback/Student Involvement

1. Teacher encourages students to take an active role in learning — __X__ Yes _____ No
2. Teacher asks primarily low-order, content-related questions — _____ Yes __X__ No
3. Students are able to respond correctly to most of the teacher's questions — __X__ Yes _____ No
4. Teacher gives frequent positive feedback to correct student responses — __X__ Yes _____ No
5. Teacher gives sustaining feedback to incorrect student responses — _____ Yes __X__ No
6. Teacher seldom uses criticism in responding to student answers — __X__ Yes _____ No

D. Classroom Management

1. Teacher articulates positive expectations for students' academic success — _____ Yes __X__ No
2. Teacher monitors students' work during independent seatwork — __X__ Yes _____ No
3. Teacher communicates clear standards and expectations for behavior — __X__ Yes _____ No
4. Teacher consistently applies consequences for meeting standards and expectations — __X__ Yes _____ No
5. Teacher keeps students engaged in lessons — __X__ Yes _____ No
6. Teacher seldom has to intervene in behavioral problems — __X__ Yes _____ No
7. Teacher seldom uses punitive intervention — __X__ Yes _____ No
8. Teacher uses supportive interventions — __X__ Yes _____ No
9. Teacher's interventions appear to be effective — __X__ Yes _____ No

E. Classroom Climate

Teacher demonstrates the following characteristics (check if yes):

_____ Flexibility __X__ Consistency _____ Warmth __X__ Active Involvement with Students

__X__ Fairness __X__ Responsiveness _____ Humor

__X__ Firmness __X__ Patience

Source: Wong, K. L. H., Kauffman, J. M., & Lloyd, J. W. (1991). Choices for integration: Selecting teachers for mainstreaming students with emotional or behavioral disorders. *Intervention in School and Clinic, 27,* 108–115. Copyright PRO-ED. Used with permission.

Figure 11.4 Student/Teacher Match Form (STM).

General Classroom Teacher _____Mrs. K. C._____ Date _____3/19/98_____

Student To Be Mainstreamed _____Michael_____

	Teacher Willingness		Student Performances		
A. Types of Behavior Teacher Deems Critical for Success	Is Willing to Work on Behavior	Is not Willing To Work on Behavior	Exhibits Behavior Consistently	Exhibits Improving Behavior	Lacks Appropriate Behavior
1. Following directions	X	___	___	X	___
2. Completing assignments	X	___	___	___	X
3. Cooperating with peers	X	___	___	X	___
4.	___	___	___	___	___
5.	___	___	___	___	___

	Teacher Willingness		Student Performances		
A. Types of Behavior Teacher Deems Intolerable	Is Willing to Work on Behavior	Is not Willing To Work on Behavior	Does not Exhibit Behavior	Exhibits Behavior but Improving	Frequently Exhibits Behavior
1. Hitting and fighting	___	X	X	___	___
2. Disrupting others in class	X	___	___	X	___
3. Refusing to follow directions	X	___	___	X	___
4. Whining	X	___	X	___	___
5.	___	___	___	___	___

C. Kind and Amount of Technical Assistance Teacher Desires Help in designing a behavior management program for student: ongoing for student; ongoing support in helping student reduce intolerable behaviors; daily monitoring of student's performance in mainstream classroom.

Desired Technical Assistance Can Be Provided __X__ Yes _____ No

Comments Student's current behavior contract program can be modified for use in mainstream classroom.

D. Supportive Plans for Moving Student into Mainstream Classroom Special education teacher will meet general classroom teacher before placement date to discuss specific needs of student; student's behavior contract program will be reviewed. Special education teacher will introduce student to general classroom teacher and student will visit mainstream classroom before actual placement date. Special education teacher will monitor student's adjustment and progress on a daily basis (during resource period).

E. Contingency Plans in Case Student is Not Successful in Mainstream Classroom General classroom teacher and special education teacher will discuss presenting problems and try to address these without having to remove student from mainstream classroom. If difficulties persist, student will be taken out of mainstream classroom and returned to special class.

Source: Wong, K. L. H., Kauffman, J. M., & Lloyd, J. W. (1991). Choices for integration: Selecting teachers for mainstreaming students with emotional or behavioral disorders. *Intervention in School and Clinic, 27,* 108–115. Copyright PRO-ED. Used with permission.

Two of the instruments in the AIMS system (Walker, 1986) may be used to evaluate the adequacy of students' classroom and peer social adjustments in less restrictive settings. *The Classroom Adjustment Code (CAC)* is a five-second interval recording system that measures three categories of pupil and teacher behavior. The pupil behavior codes are *on-task, off-task,* and *unacceptable behaviors.* The teacher codes include *approval/feedback, providing instruction/command,* and *reprimand.* Thus, the *CAC* can be used to assess interactions occurring between teachers and target students. For example, *CAC* observations may reveal that a mainstream teacher consistently attends to undesired pupil behavior with punitive consequences, while at the same time ignoring desired behaviors. The second instrument, the *Social Interaction Code (SIC)* assesses three major classes of events associated with the pupil's social interactions with peers. These include the *structure or activity context* in which such interactions occur (five categories are used to assess whether the target student is alone or engaged in structured versus unstructured activities), the *type and quality of the pupil's interactive behavior* (assessed with five appropriate and five inappropriate behavior code categores), and *negative peer reactions* to the student's social behavior. The *CAC* and the *SIC* evaluate general interaction patterns rather than specific target behaviors, and observer training is required to use them properly. Of course, they could be used to measure adult-to-student or student-to-student interactions in other settings as well (e.g., work environments). The AIMS System is a useful package for planning and evaluating the transition of students to less restrictive educational environments.

Although data obtained from the above procedures cannot be compared to the graphs and charts used to analyze the student and his program while in your classroom, they can serve to *socially validate* that behavioral changes have taken place. Because others' perceptions of the student in his natural environment is the ultimate test of success in readjusting, these data should not be treated lightly. However, if you can obtain measures that are more comparable to the data you collected during intervention phases, a more specific analysis of the student's current status is possible. This can be important if target behaviors once again are problematic and you need to assess their occurrence in the new environment. If you are unable to collect these data, or if your presence in the environment influences the pupil's behavior, follow the guidelines presented in Chapter 3 for training other observers.

Finally, the length and schedule of follow-up assessments should be geared to the student, the behaviors, and the settings in which assessments are conducted. If you follow the suggestions in Chapter 3 (collect data that are sensitive to the changes you want to occur; measure only behaviors to which you will respond) follow-up data collection should not be unduly time consuming. You may want to monitor some behaviors closely (e.g., verbal threats having a history of leading to physical aggression); others may require less regular scrutiny because they are less important to the pupil's success in the new setting. Some data are easy to collect (e.g., number of assignments completed), whereas other data require more time and effort (e.g., time on-task). In general, use data that are readily available and that the classroom teacher, employer, or caregiver keeps and uses anyway.

Data pertaining to the student's adjustment to the expectations of the regular classroom environment thus can be as specific or general as necessary. The important point is to establish, and use, a feedback loop, in which you and your colleagues collect and respond to information about the student's performance. Figure 11.5 illustrates a simple daily evaluation form. The format may be adapted to suit the student's age, grade, or subject, or the student may evaluate himself and have the mainstream teacher sign it. Depending on circumstances, the student can bring the card to you or the classroom teacher may keep them for periodic review with you. You also may ask the classroom teacher to rate the frequency of behaviors he previously identified as critical or unacceptable on the SBS Inventory (Walker & Rankin, 1980b). For example, you can construct a three-point checklist of the behaviors that a teacher indicated as critical to success in

Figure 11.5 Sample Daily Teacher Report Card

Student's Name _____ Date_____ Class _____

Yes	No		Comments
_____	_____	Followed classroom rules	
_____	_____	Demonstrated appropriate social behavior	
_____	_____	Completed work on time	
_____	_____	Tried his/her best	

Teacher's Signature _____

her classroom: (1) indicates that the student is acceptably skilled, (2) indicates less than acceptable skill, and (3) indicates much less than acceptable skill. If you are monitoring specific target behaviors, however, you or the mainstream teacher should be able and willing to collect direct observation data. It is critical that you and the mainstream teacher meet regularly to review these data and design collaborative strategies to intervene when needed. As students demonstrate increasingly consistent adjustment, decrease the frequency of monitoring. Another strategy is to have the student rate or count her own behavior (see Chapter 3).

If the student has been transferred out of your building or even further away, follow-up will be sporadic, at best. Few agencies are interested in the status of clients once their direct service responsibilities have ended. Still, you may make telephone, e-mail, or conventional mail contacts to assess your former pupils' present status. No matter where former students are located, schedule follow-up contacts on your calendar so you will not forget. Initially, follow-up intervals should be brief (1 to 3 weeks). Thin the schedule as time passes (1, 6, and 18 months). At some point, you will be able to decide to discontinue evaluation. As with other phases of assessment, your data will suggest when you reach this point.

Another reason for conducting follow-up assessments is to evaluate the implementation of maintenance and generalization training procedures. These evaluations address the question of **procedural reliability** (Tawney & Gast, 1984), or the extent to which intervention procedures are being followed. The recommended format for such assessments is a behavioral checklist containing a list of intervention procedures that are checked (by an observer familiar with the intervention) according to whether they are implemented properly. Figure 11.6 illustrates a procedural reliability checklist for a DRO intervention. Intervention steps that are not being properly implemented indicate a need for feedback or retraining of the responsible persons. Assessment of procedural reliability is important, especially for identifying implementation failures when staff members report that a procedure "is not working."

Transitions to Other Settings

As a group, children and youth with significant behavior challenges are involved in numerous transitions. Although they are the last group of students with disabilities to be identified and placed in special education programs (U. S. Department of Education, 1994), they often have histories of multiple placements in the regular educational system prior to their referral to special education (Walker et al., 1987). The transitions they make include changes in school districts, classrooms, and programs (e.g., Chapter 1, remedial classes). Presumably, these alternate placements are attempts to meet students' needs, but it is likely that the motivation is to reduce disruptions to the settings from which the students are removed.

Figure 11.6 DRO Procedural Reliablity Checklist

```
Observer _____    Observation Dates _____
                                              Observations
                                          _____
                                          1       2       3

1. Length of DRO interval is set (interval
   length _____ secs/mins)             _____  _____  _____

2. Teacher accurately observes occurrence/
   nonoccurrence of target behavior
   during interval.                       _____  _____  _____

3. Behavior does not occur during interval. _____  _____  _____

   3.1. Teacher delivers reinforcer
        immediately upon end of interval.  _____  _____  _____

   3.2. Teacher resets interval timer.     _____  _____  _____

4. Behavior does occur during interval.   _____  _____  _____

   4.1. Teacher does not respond to behavior. _____  _____  _____

   4.2. Teacher resets interval timer.     _____  _____  _____
```

Students who have been identified as having EBD also are extremely mobile. Although in the previous section we discussed transitions to less restrictive educational settings, their transitions typically involve movement to more restrictive educational settings (Rock et al., 1994; Stephens & Lakin, 1995). Moreover, Stephens and Lakin (1995), in their study of students in separate facilities for children and youth with disabilities, found that facilities primarily serving students with EBD reported considerably greater turnover and shorter average lengths of stay than did facilities serving children with varying disabilities. Also, compared with day programs for students with varying disabilities, nearly twice as many students leaving day programs for students with EBD either had no next placement or the placement was unknown to the staff. Approximately 20 percent of those leaving day or residential programs for students with EBD were transferred to another separate facility.

As these findings suggest, the teacher of children and youth with EBD, whether in public school or separate day or residential programs, should expect the management of transitions to be a significant component of her job. Next, we describe transitions to more restrictive settings and to post-secondary school environments.

Transitions to More Restrictive Settings As we have just indicated, the typical movement of public school students with EBD is toward more restrictive environments. These include segregated special classes, special day programs in the public schools, day treatment programs, residential school programs, residential psychiatric facilities, and juvenile correctional programs. Unfortunately, such transitions often appear to be made for the convenience of the school and community rather than to meet the needs of the student.

Frequently, movement to more restrictive settings entails transitions between separate agencies (e.g., public schools and juvenile correctional or residential treatment programs). Edgar et al. (1987) identified three components to the transition process: (a) a *sending agency*, which has the student who is being transferred elsewhere, (b) a *receiving agency*, which gets the student, and (c) the *hand-off*, which is a process and a set of procedures for moving the student and his records from one agency to another. According to Edgar et al. (1987), six issues are involved between agencies when making transitions:

1. *Awareness.* Sending and receiving agencies need to learn about each other's programs and services. Unfortunately, most agencies operate without such information.

2. *Eligibility criteria.* The sending agency should have a working knowledge of the eligibility criteria of the agencies whose services may help their students or clients. Obviously, a lack of information about other agencies suggests that knowledge of eligibility criteria also is lacking.

3. *Exchange of information.* The receiving agency needs information before the client arrives. The transfer of student records is a universal problem. Often, records do not arrive in time to be used in placement or planning, and in many cases, the student has left the agency before her school records are obtained.

4. *Program planning before transition.* This should involve both sending and receiving agencies so that students are prepared for the programs they are about to enter and so their new programs will capitalize on the gains made in the old ones.

5. *Feedback after transition.* Feedback to the sending agency is essential for program evaluation and modification. Without it agencies are left to repeat the mistakes of the past, which often is the case.

6. *Written procedures.* Formal written procedures ensure that important hand-off activities take place. If only one staff person knows the procedures, there will be nothing in place should that person leave, unless procedures are formalized in writing.

If these issues are not addressed, students experience a lack of continuity in their educational programming, which may express itself in terms of repeating a curriculum they have completed already or being exposed to a curruculum that is inappropriate for their skills and needs. As a classroom teacher, you should be involved in transition activities at either the sending or receiving level to help ensure continuity of instructional and behavioral interventions. Your participation in site-based management teams will help you ensure that your agency's policies include important collaborative interagency linkages.

Transitions to Post-Secondary School Environments
PL 94–142 mandated that schools serve children and youth with disabilities through age 21, and subsequent amendments (PL 98–199, PL 99–457, and PL 101–436) have added specific emphasis to the provision of **transition services** to help these people adjust to adult living. Follow-up studies of the postschool status of youth with disabilities indicate that the special education enterprise has not been overwhelmingly successful in terms of preparing these young persons for successful post-school adjustment, particularly students with EBD (Chesapeake Institute, 1994; McLaughlin, Leone, Warren, & Schofield, 1994; U. S. Department of Education, 1994).

For two decades, the *criterion of ultimate functioning* (Brown, Nietupski, & Hamre-Nietupski, 1976) has influenced curriculum planning for pupils with moderate to severe disabilities. As explained in Chapter 2, this top-down approach to curriculum design begins with the assessment of the skill demands of the least restrictive adult environments in which the student is likely to function, and the curriculum is developed around pupils' skill deficiencies based on these expectations. However, determining which adult environments are least restrictive for students exhibiting widely varying levels of cognitive, academic, and social functioning is complex in itself and must be accomplished before the expectations of these settings can be assessed. Therefore, specific post-school objectives for students with less severe disabilities, based on assumptions about the limits of their future capabilities, are more difficult to develop while they are still in school. We are not suggesting that objectives relevant to post-school living cannot be developed for these students; appropriate social behaviors are useful in all adult settings and are needed by persons at all levels of cognitive functioning. Students who interview for jobs or admission to post-secondary schools, who go out on dates, or who visit their local hair salon need to employ these skills every day.

Unfortunately, it is apparent that the lack of such skills is a common denominator among individuals who display chronic maladjustments. For example, Walker and his colleagues (Shinn, Ramsey, Walker, Stieber, & O'Neill, 1987; Walker, Shinn, O'Neill, & Ramsey, 1987) identified behavioral differences between fifth-grade boys who were designated antisocial (on the basis of familial variables) and a control group of boys who were designated at risk for engaging in antisocial behavior. The behavior patterns that differentiated the antisocial group included less time engaged in academics, higher rates of negative interactions with peers, more school discipline contacts, and lower teacher ratings of social skills. The behavioral characteristics of older youth and adults who are at risk for criminal behavior or who are incarcerated reveal similar patterns (Nelson & Pearson, 1994; Nelson, Rutherford, & Wolford, 1987). Thus, early maladaptive social behavior patterns appear to be predictive of lifelong patterns of social failure (Robbins, 1966; Van Hasselt, Hersen, Whitehill, & Bellack, 1979). Early identification and remediation of social skills deficits in children who are at risk should be a major educational priority.

Planning for transitions to adulthood may not prevent the failure of all, or even many, students with behavior problems, but neither should it be assumed that the existence of problem behaviors condemns pupils to lives of crime or institutionalization. Transition programs for adolescents are useful for bridging the gap between school and productive adult experiences. If a transition plan is to be meaningfully linked to the student's post-school life, it should be initiated well before graduation. Transition plans must be developed with persons who have a stake in the pupil's post-school adjustment (e.g., parents, the student herself) and they should take into account planning for the wide range of options the student may consider as an adult. Clark, Unger, & Stewart (1993) describe four domains that should be considered in transition planning for students with EBD (see Table 11.2): alternatives such as college, military service, and independent living should be considered in addition to employment. Support services likely to be needed (e.g., mental health counseling, daily living support, vocational training) should be indicated, and representatives from agencies that provide services (e.g., community mental health, developmental disabilities council, vocational rehabilitation) should participate in drafting the transition

plan. Implementation of the plan should begin during the pupil's secondary school experience and should continue until the structure and support provided by the plan are no longer needed. If you are in a position to be involved in post-secondary school transition planning, consult Brolin (1995).

It would be naive to assume that school-based interventions alone are sufficient to enable adolescents with behavior problems to successfully enter adult living and working environments. Ideally, they also should have the benefit of **community-based training** during their public school years. Community-based instruction has played an important role in the curriculum of pupils with moderate and severe disabilities, and many good models are available (e.g., see Goetz, Guess, & Stremel-Campbell, 1987; Taylor, Bilken, & Knoll, 1987). Much less attention has been paid to teaching social skills to students with so-called "mild" disabilities in the community settings where these skills are critical to their successful adjustment. Given the recent data indicating that many adolecents with EBD fail to make adequate adjustments to adult life (Chesapeake Institute, 1994; Edgar, 1987; McLaughlin et al., 1994), appropriate changes in the secondary school curriculum for these students clearly are needed.

It is important to recognize that EBD is extremely durable and has deleterious long-term effects (Bullis & Paris, 1996). Therefore, one aspect of post-school transition is maintaining service coordination with agencies and the family to ensure that students continue to receive adequate support. As Walker and Bullis (1996) indicate, the goal for working with older adolescents and young adults with EBD probably should be accommodation; that is, to reduce the negative impact of their disability on successful adjustment. Alarm regarding the costs of a community-based support system to achieve the necessary level of accommodation should be balanced by the realization that these are no greater than the staggering costs of long-term institutionalization. Moreover, the client in a community-based service system is far more productive to society.

Table 11.2 Transition Domains

A. Employment
　　1. Competitive employment
　　2. Supported employment (individual and enclave)
　　3. Transitional employment opportunities
　　4. Work experience opportunities

B. Education opportunities
　　1. Workplace educational programs
　　2. High school completion or GED certificate
　　3. Vocational or technical certification
　　4. Associate's degree
　　5. Bachelor's degree or beyond

C. Independent living
　　1. Independent residence
　　2. Residence with natural, adoptive or foster family
　　3. Semi-independent living (e.g., nonlive-in case manager assists)
　　4. Supported living (e.g., supervised apartment)
　　5. Group home or boarding home

D. Community life: Skill development and activities related to domains A, B, and C
　　1. Leisure time activities and fun
　　2. Social interaction and problem-solving skills (e.g., self-advocacy)
　　3. Relationship development (e.g., friendships, intimate relationships)
　　4. Peer support groups
　　5. Emotional/behavioral management (e.g., anger control, relapse prevention, self-medication management)
　　6. Safety skills (e.g., prevent victimization, avoid dangerous situations)
　　7. Daily living skills (e.g., eating nutritious food, leasing an apartment)
　　8. Health care and fitness (e.g., stress management, physical activity)
　　9. Substance abuse prevention and maintenance
　　10. Sex education and birth control (e.g., prevention of sexually transmitted diseases and unwanted pregnancies)
　　11. Community resources (knowledge and utilization)
　　12. Transportation skills
　　13. Cultural/spiritual/religious resources

Source: Clark, H. B., Unger, K. V., and Stewart, E. S. (1993). Transition of youth and young adults with emotional/behavioral disorders into employment, education and independent living. *Community Alternatives: International Journal of Family Care,* 5(2), 19–46. Copyright Human Services Associates, Inc.

WORKING OUTSIDE THE CLASSROOM

Individual classrooms probably are the primary treatment setting for most students exhibiting problematic social behaviors. However, remember that undesired or maladaptive social behaviors may occur in many settings and that the successful management of a problem in one setting may not affect the same problem, or other problems, in other settings. Consequently, even if you serve students with behavior problems in a single classroom setting, your work will lead you into other settings, both within and outside the school. In this section we present a number of suggestions and strategies to increase your effectiveness with other professionals and lay persons in these settings.

Working with School Personnel

In a typical school building (or institution), there are a number of people you can use as resources for your students. The extent of their involvement may range from delivering social praise to taking pupils on after-school trips, from simply rating performance as acceptable or unacceptable to taking frequency data, and from following a plan worked out by you to collaborating in the development of a complete intervention strategy. Different persons may prove useful for different functions, and we hope the checklist in Figure 11.2 helps you develop a profile of your various personnel resources.

Before you approach anyone to assist you with a pupil or program, get your objective clearly in mind. Do you want to assess the generalization of change in a target behavior? Do you want to evaluate a trial mainstream placement? Do you want to establish other persons as social reinforcers? Do you want to maximize reinforcement by using stronger reinforcers outside your classroom? Do you need physical assistance handling an aggressive student in emergency situations? Each objective dictates a different tactic. When you enlist the cooperation of other people, explain clearly what you want them to do, as well as when and how they are to communicate to you regarding their work with the pupil or pupils.

Once again, a written plan is the best approach if the program is complex. Conflicts may arise between involved parties, such as teachers and school administrators; each party may want to impose its agenda on your program (the teacher wants the student to suit up for gym; the principal wants him to arrive at school on time). Remember, though, that the student is your client (the person who is to benefit from the program). This focus is somewhat different from the one you use when you are serving as a consultant, where your client is the person who comes to you with the problem. Many a good teacher has been rendered ineffective by trying to serve too many clients with conflicting demands. A written plan should specify objectives and roles at the outset, thereby preventing such episodes.

One such planning tool is a school-based **wraparound plan**[4] (Eber, 1995), a format for

planning the structure and support needed by a targeted student to function successfully across settings throughout a school day. This individualized plan is developed and implemented by a team of professionals and family members who know the student best. The wraparound plan must address the student's typical day and provide behavioral support where it is needed, as well as systematic reinforcement in settings in which the student typically behaves appropriately. It is driven by the needs of the student rather than the services traditionally available in the school. Thus, the resources, structure, and supports for each targeted student must be flexible and creative. For example, if managing unstructured times and settings (e.g., hallways, cafeteria, bus waiting areas) is a difficult task for the student, a wraparound plan might consist of enlisting the aid of a member of the school staff to escort him to his locker and then the classroom. Several peer "buddies" or mentors may be recruited to accompany him on the bus, in the halls and cafeteria, and to the restroom. Or teachers may stand outside their classroom doors during class breaks to monitor his behavior during transitions. As he makes progress, this structure may be loosened so that the pupil maintains a self-monitoring checklist, which is reviewed several times daily with his wraparound coordinator. Figure 11.7 (Eber, 1995) describes more of the features of a wraparound plan.

In working with school staff, remember that adults need support and reinforcement too; therefore, find out what teachers need, set up communication channels, and be sure to show your appreciation for someone's assistance. You can increase the likelihood of a wraparound plan being followed by meeting the teacher's need (e.g., arrange to help supervise difficult transition times) or providing needed materials (e.g., a checklist for regular classroom teachers to complete, a roll of smiley-face stickers for the cafeteria cashier or bus driver to put on the shirts of well-behaved students, a wrist counter for the librarian to use in counting talk-outs).

The school principal traditionally is regarded by pupils (and teachers) as the major disciplinarian

---

[4]As explained in Chapter 2, wraparound is an approach to planning and implementing services to students with needs in multiple life domains. It is not a set of services or an intervention strategy.

Figure 11.7 What Is Wraparound?

The wraparound process is based on individualized, needs-driven planning and services. **It is not a program or a type of service**. It is a value base and an unconditional commitment to create services on a "one student at a time" basis to support normalized and inclusive options for students with complex needs.

A child and family team, consisting of the people who know the student best, develop an **individualized plan**.

This plan is **needs driven** rather than service driven. Services are not based on a categorical model but on specific needs of the student, family, and teacher.

The plan is based on **needs identified by the family**.

The plan is based on **teacher expectations**.

The plan is **strengths based**. Human services traditionally have relied on the deficit model, focusing on pathology. Positive reframing to assets and skills is a key element in all individualized planning.

The plan focuses on **normalization**. Normalized needs are those basic human needs that all persons (of like age, sex, and culture) have.

The team makes a commitment to **unconditional care**. Services and interventions are changed to meet the needs of the student rather than referring her to another setting.

Academic and support services are created to meet the unique needs of the student. Though many plans rely on blending and reshaping categorical services, teams have the capacity to **create individualized supports and activities**.

Services are **based in natural school environments**. Restrictive settings are accessed only for brief periods of stabilization.

Services are **culturally competent**. The composition of the team ensures a fit to the person's culture and community.

Planning and services are **comprehensive**, addressing needs in three or more domain areas. These life domains are family, living situation, vocational/educational, social/recreational, psychological/emotional, medical, legal, and safety/crisis.

The plan is financially supported by **flexible** use of existing categorical resources or through a **flexible funding mechanism**.

Outcome measures are identified and measured often and are generated by parent and teacher expectations.

for a building. In view of this, having the principal deliver reinforcement can be a potent tactic, as several studies have demonstrated. Copeland, Brown, and Hall (1974) found in three separate studies that contingent principal recognition and praise increased attendance and academic performance. Brown, Copeland, and Hall (1972) involved a principal in administering tokens, playing basketball with pupils, and providing the opportunity to work on bicycles in the school basement, contingent upon appropriate school behaviors. The school counselor also can provide reinforcement or other services. Clore (1974) had a school-phobic child report to the counselor's office each morning, and

the counselor assisted in successfully phasing the student back into his classroom.

The school administrative staff may be helpful in other ways as well. For example, many reinforcing activities occur around the school office: pupils can deliver attendance slips or notes, answer the telephone, run the ditto machine, file, or perform other office tasks as reinforcement for desired behaviors. The main reason such opportunities are not taken is that teachers seldom think of them. Few persons will refuse to provide such experiences if you ask them (and remember to follow up with reinforcement).

Involving yourself has the further advantage of increasing your visibility to, and interaction with, school staff, which lessens the stigma attached both to teachers and students in segregated special classrooms. Volunteering to sponsor all-school activities such as clubs and social events will improve your standing with pupils outside your classroom. Also, do not shirk cafeteria or bus duty, and don't do all your work in the classroom where you are isolated from your colleagues. Instead, spend some of your time working in the teachers' lounge. In our experience, the more successful special education programs are run by teachers who are actively involved in the total school environment. When you are working with pupils with EBD, visibility and involvement are especially important because of the fear and misconceptions regarding persons with mental disabilities.

In developing intervention plans that wrap around a student and her school day, it is important to recognize that schools are rich in intervention resources. In addition to the school staff mentioned above, other students may be used as models, tutors, reinforcing agents, and monitors for wraparound plans. For students who need this level of structure, it is essential that functional analyses be performed to identify those settings and times of the day when wraparound support is needed. It also is important to schedule regular meetings with the wraparound team to ensure that the plan is being implemented properly and the student is making progress.

Working with Parents

The two general objectives of working with parents are (1) helping them meet their need to manage problem behavior in their home or neighborhood, and (2) assuring parents support of classroom objectives.[5] Each goal calls for a slightly different approach.

Parent Education If you and the parents agree on the need to apply behavior management strategies at home, you are putting yourself in a consultative relationship. Because parents have

learned to expect teachers to deal directly with their children and, consequently, may be less prone to let you help them, this relationship can be a difficult one. Also, parents of children with behavior problems (especially children who have been certified as having EBD) may be defensive about admitting their problems because, in the past, it was fairly common to attribute children's behavior disorders to faulty parenting. Fortunately, parents are becoming empowered to work actively on behalf of their children and are being included as equal partners with professionals in planning and implementing services (DeChillo, Koren, & Schultz, 1994; Friesen & Wahlers, 1993). Comprehensive *systems of care* have a distinctly family-centered focus, in which families are regarded as a source of support and strength, not of dysfunction and pathology (Duchnowski, Berg, & Kutash, 1995). Such national organizations as the Federation of Families for Children's Mental Health and the National Alliance for the Mentally Ill—Children and Adolescent Network have provided strong political advocacy where none has existed before.

Nevertheless, some professionals still hold the view that parents are the cause of their children's emotional and behavioral disorders and, because parents' interactions with school personnel tend to be negative, they may react to interactions with teachers as aversive stimuli. One way around this problem is to treat the task of helping parents more effectively manage their child as an educational issue, rather than as a problem requiring psychotherapy or analysis. We have found that presenting home management training as an educational program overcomes many resistances. Of course, this only works if the parents feel they need this type of assistance. Another suggestion is to maintain your focus on the child. Presenting ideas and techniques to help the parents solve or manage present problems is likely to meet with less resistance than giving them the impression that their parenting skills need a major overhaul.

When parents do recognize a problem and request your help, you have several options. One is to set up a specific program, following the consultation steps outlined in Table 11.3 for setting up a management program in the home. Note that these procedures are identical to those we recommend for use in the classroom for dealing with problem behavior. There is evidence that parents can successfully implement such procedures with professional guidance. For example, Christophersen, Arnold, Hill, and Quilitch (1972) taught two sets of parents who had five children between them to administer a token economy in their homes. The parents successfully altered 21 problem behaviors, including refusing to perform chores, bickering, teasing, whining, and refusing to go to bed. However, as the authors observed, these were not severe behavior disorders. Strain

Table 11.3   Specific Procedures for Establishing a Home Management Program

Objectives	Activities
1. Pinpoint and define behavior (operationally).	List and objectively define the family's major concerns about child's behavior.
	Rank those concerns from highest to lowest priority.
	List and objectively define the child's positive, adaptive, and desirable behaviors.
	Select one behavior of critical importance to the family. *Caution:* Probability of success is a prime factor in selecting a behavior to change.
2. Evaluate situations and environments in which the behavior occurs.	Evaluate the situations, environments, and circumstances under which the target behavior usually occurs.
3. Specify contingencies.	Evaluate the reactions of the parents and others after the problem behavior occurs.
4. Observe and record target behavior daily.	Develop a simple recording system and corresponding recording sheet.
	Observe and record target behavior using system and appropriate data sheet on a daily basis.
	Check on reliability between parents and parent counselor in defining target behavior.
	Make necessary adjustments in behavior definition or recording procedures.
5. Chart and inspect target behavior data.	Devise simple visual displays (charts) for target behavior.
	Record daily observations on charts.
	Inspect data for variability and trend before ending baseline period.
6. Devise intervention plans and establish performance expectations.	Develop appropriate reinforcing and punishing contingencies for specific target behavior.
	Ask parents what consequences have been effective or are likely to be effective with their child.
	Ask parents to describe techniques they have used before and to describe their effects.

	Interventions must be
	    Practical
	    Economical
	    Feasible
	    Realistic
	    Applicable
	    Effective

	Establish a desired rate (frequency/day) for target behavior.
	Establish a desired target date for the behavior and the respective desired rates.
	Establish sequentially placed interim rates and dates for the target behavior.

and Danko (1995) taught caregivers to implement a social skills training program and to encourage positive interactions between three three- to four-year-old children with autism and their siblings. The caregivers were quite succesful in applying the interventions and reported that they were simple to learn, easy to apply, and enjoyable.

Teaching parents the principles of applied behavior analysis constitutes one alternative to specific problem-solving consultation. A number of manuals are designed to teach these principles to parents (e.g., Becker, 1971; Patterson, 1975; Patterson & Gullion, 1971). Although these books have been given to parents to read on their own, we recommend that you provide specific instruction. A combination of training in behavioral principles and techniques and in specific problem-solving consultation has been found to be more effective than training in general principles and procedures alone (Glogowger & Sloop, 1976). The disadvantage of this approach is that it requires after-school time.

If you have several interested parents, a parent education group may be a useful strategy (Rinn, Vernon, & Wise, 1975). Several formats have been used. The format we prefer combines instruction in behavioral principles and procedures with specific problem-solving consultation. Parents show more interest in learning principles when they can immediately apply them to their children's behaviors. However, as Ferber, Keeley, and Shemberg (1974) found, a short-term parent course may be insufficient without long-term follow-up consultation for other problem behaviors. Also, aggressive children who display problems in the community may not be helped at all through parent education (Ferber et al., 1974). For these individuals, more extensive community-based intervention may be required. If you need to go this far, consider developing a comprehensive wraparound plan or referring the problem to another agency (see Chapter 12).

Parental Support of Classroom Goals   If parents are to support classroom goals, they should have input in identifying target behaviors and interventions. It also requires a school-home communication system, for parents can hardly be expected to support the objectives of a behavior change program if they do not understand them or have little access to information regarding their child's progress.[6] Traditional reporting systems (e.g., grade cards) are unsuitable for this type of communication because they are infrequent and they tend to communicate little useful information. Parental response to an unsatisfactory report card may be inappropriate, or parents may fail to respond at all to good reports. Therefore, we suggest a frequent (daily or weekly) reporting system that conveys meaningful information to parents and to which they may respond in a systematic manner. This implies that you have worked out a plan with the parents beforehand. Tell them what to expect (e.g., a daily or weekly report containing points their child has earned for academic work and for social behavior each day), when to expect it (e.g., every day after school), and how to respond to each report (e.g., praise when the point total is above 35, and for each subject or area for which 4 or more points are awarded).

In cases where you need more solid home support, work with parents to set up more explicit home contingencies based on their child's school performance. For example, they may provide extra privileges for good reports (specify the criteria for a "good" report) or lose privileges for a poor report. If required, you may even work out a menu of back-up home consequences similar to the classroom menu presented in Chapter 6. This provides for differential reinforcement and long-term savings for special privileges or treats (e.g., a movie, a fishing trip). It is preferable to work out the details of more elaborate systems with a simple contract among the pupil, parents, and you. All parties should sign and receive copies of the contract.

Figure 11.8 shows a variety of daily report cards (these also could be weekly). Panels A and B present forms useful for preschool and primary-age students. Panel C is a simple checklist for middle-grade students, and Panel D shows a

---

[6]IDEA requires that individual program objectives be developed in collaboration with parents and guarantees parents access to their child's school records.

Figure 11.8   Daily Report Cards

Date _____

Classroom Work

☐ Good 😊

☐ Bad ☹

_____
Teacher's Signature

A

Date _____

Classroom Behavior

☐ Good 😊

☐ Bad ☹

_____
Teacher's Signature

B

Date _____

Social Behavior
☐ Acceptable
☐ Unacceptable

Academic Work
☐ Completed on time
☐ Not completed
☐ Accuracy acceptance
☐ Accuracy unacceptable

_____
Teacher's Signature

C

Date _____

Reading   _____
Math   _____
Spelling   _____
Science   _____
P.E.   _____
Lunchroom   _____
Playground   _____
Social Behavior _____
Bonus Points   _____
Fines   _____   Total   _____
Total Points   _____   Possible _____

_____
Teacher's Signature

D

Subject _____   Date _____

_____ Is doing acceptable work and is keeping up with assignments
_____ Is not doing acceptable work
_____ Is behind on assignments
_____ Exhibits acceptable social behavior
_____ Exhibits unacceptable social behavior

Comments:

_____
Teacher's Signature

E

form for reporting daily points. Panel E is a checklist for mainstreamed, upper-level or secondary pupils. One problem with daily report cards is that students may lose them. If you advise parents to respond to a missing report as though it were poor or below criterion, this problem seldom persists. If you are concerned that parents fail to read the report, include in the contract an agreement that they are to sign reports and return them the next day. Graphs and charts such as those presented in Chapter 3 also may be sent home on a daily or weekly basis.

Home-school communication systems that use back-up home contingencies offer several advantages. First, they provide contingent consequences at home for performance in school. This can be a great help for students who do not respond well to school consequences (e.g., pupils who "do not care" if they miss recess or back-up reinforcers available at school). Second, they keep parents informed of their child's progress and get them involved in what is going on at school. Third, by emphasizing reinforcing consequences for good performance, they break down the common expectation among parents of children with behavioral problems that all school reports are bad reports. Furthermore, by teaching parents to reinforce their children, you may help break the criticism-punishment cycle that is prevalent in families with children who exhibit behavioral problems.

School-home communication systems need not be elaborate, and if properly used, they can be effective. Ayllon, Garber, and Pisor (1975), for instance, sent a good behavior letter home with students in a third-grade class for meeting criteria for good conduct. Receipt or nonreceipt of these letters resulted in differential consequences by the parents. Disruptive behavior, which averaged 90 percent during the baseline period and did not appreciably decrease in response to a school-based contingency system, dropped to 10 percent when the letter was instituted.

Your strategies for working with parents can be as varied as the students and parents themselves. Each situation calls for different measures, but you should be able to adopt a general strategy for all parents and children in your class. Several excellent texts on working with parents of exceptional children are available (e.g., Kroth, 1975; Kroth & Simpson, 1977; Kroth & Edge, 1997; Maag, 1996; Rutherford & Edgar, 1979; Wagonseller & McDowell, 1979), and we suggest you consult these sources for additional ideas and information.

Parents are essential partners for students who need the structure of wraparound service plans. As Eber (1995) emphasized, such plans should be based on needs identified by the family, as well as on teacher expectations. By including parents on the wraparound service team for their child, professionals not only gain important information about the child and her needs, but they also enlist an important ally in their efforts to help the student.

Working with Community Professionals and Agencies

Your work with children and youth exhibiting behavior problems will lead you into the domain of other professionals and agencies. Recent federal, state, and local efforts have been launched to reform the system of children's services toward greater coordination and integration (Nelson & Pearson, 1991). A system of care for children and youth with EBD and their families emphasizes more community services, less reliance on restrictive child placements, prevention of hospitalization and out-of-home placements, interagency collaboration, flexible and individualized services, and cost containment and efficiency (Stroul, Goldman, Lourie, Katz-Leavy, & Ziegler-Dendy, 1992).

The lack of interagency collaboration has been a major obstacle to achieving continuity of programming between public schools and other human service agencies. Remember that discontinuity in services contributes to the failure of treatment effects achieved in one setting to be generalized and maintained in other settings where these effects are expected and needed. As a professional attempting to extend the effects of interventions applied in educational settings or attempting to plan interventions across settings, you may work with a number of agencies such as the juvenile court, child welfare agencies, mental health centers, organizations serving children and youth with developmental disabilities, vocational rehabilitation agencies, medical clinics, and service organizations such as Big Brothers or Big Sisters, in addition to working with parents and parent groups. The professionals working in these agencies (or in private practice) include social workers, psychologists, psychiatrists, physicians, dentists, and lawyers. These individuals should be included on wraparound planning and implementation teams when students' needs extend beyond the school day. It is well beyond the scope of this book to acquaint you with the workings of these professions and agencies. However, we can provide a few guidelines for effective interaction and collaboration.

First, you should be aware of political realities. One of the foremost of these is that outside the school, special education is not viewed as the salvation of children with behavior problems. Do not expect other professionals to greet your suggestions and views with automatic respect and admiration. Your credibility with these people will come from your record with their clients. If you succeed in accomplishing goals with students and parents that are in accord with the agency's goals, or if you have solved problems addressed by the agency or professional, you are more likely to be viewed as effective. However, it is foolhardy to set up programs that oppose those established by another agency if you want to enjoy credibility with that agency. For example, if you develop a behavioral program with parents to deal with their child's enuresis while a psychiatrist is using psychoanalysis to treat the same problem, you are not likely to establish a good working relationship with that psychiatrist. A better tactic would involve demonstrating the effectiveness of your programs with other behaviors or students, and to offer suggestions as requested. Alternately, a strategy developed collaboratively by you and the psychiatrist could provide consistency throughout the child's day.

Second, learn to channel credit away from yourself toward the other professional whenever appropriate. However, do not suggest that the other professionals possess qualities or powers they do not have, and do not give credit where credit is not due. A good practice involves following the principle of contingently reinforcing practices with which you concur. For instance, if you approve of a psychologist's plan for dealing with school phobia, say, "I like this plan," not "You're a terrific psychologist" or "You have so much insight into this client." At times you need to overlook that it was you who suggested a particular plan in the first place.

Third, you should recognize that other professionals may not speak your language. You must be tolerant of the jargon of other professions while minimizing the use of your own. This is particularly important in the case of behavior analysis terminology. By selecting nontechnical but meaningful words (e.g., *reward* instead of *positive reinforcement*), you can avoid both semantic confusion and value clashes (Reppucci & Saunders, 1974).

Fourth, you should realize that most human service agencies often do not communicate well with one another. That is, juvenile court personnel may seldom contact the school and there may not be an automatic communication link between the school and the local mental health clinic. Communication among agencies requires someone who will initiate it and maintain it. Although interagency linkages are improving rapidly, frequently effective communication results from a dynamic individual rather than from agency policy. So, if you desire communication with other agencies, be prepared to take the initiative and follow through. Also, remember that communication will continue only as long as it is reinforced. Therefore, you need to acknowledge your appreciation of others' attempts to communicate and to make use of the communicated information. Further, be sure to communicate information that is useful to the treatment program being followed by the other agency. Irrelevant comments about a child's social history or the criminal record of his brother only serve to cloud issues and professional judgment.

Finally, whether you approach another agency or professional or they approach you, clarify the purposes of the involvement and your mutual responsibilities. Interagency **memoranda of agreement** formally commit agencies to working together, but these do not ensure effective collaboration among front-line staff and parents. A major advantage of a written **integrated** (or wraparound) **service plan** for a particular child and family is its clear delineation of roles and resonsibilities. If an agreement is plainly spelled out and understood by all (you are to count the frequency of Ronnie's pants-wetting during school hours, his parents are to record it at home, and both parties are to call in their data to the mental health service coordinator every Friday), there is a greater likelihood that interactions will be efficient, productive, and mutually reinforcing.

As you work with other professionals and human service agencies, you will learn which are most useful for specific purposes. You may find it helpful to maintain a checklist, using the format presented in Figure 11.9, to keep track of your contacts and the outcomes of your involvement. When working outside the school, keep in mind the limitations of your role. If you overextend yourself or intrude too far into another's territory, you may experience unpleasant consequences. At the least you are apt to find that your efforts do not produce the effects you desire. (Some limitations of the educator's role are discussed in Chapter 12.) The range of persons and professional or volunteer agencies in the local community that can assist your students is virtually endless. Each community has its own array of resources. These may be enlisted in the same manner as parents or in-school resources, and the guidelines we presented for working in those settings apply here as well. Particularly when working with professional agencies, make your requests consistent with the functions and philosophy of those within the agency (do not ask a psychoanalytically inclined social case worker to put a child in time-out) unless you are able to provide sufficient training and supervision to ensure reliable performance.

An early study by MacDonald, Gallimore, and MacDonald (1970) illustrated how a variety of persons may be used. They taught a parent and two school staff members (a counselor and a registrar) to contact persons in the communities of chronic school non-attenders These community contacts (mediators) established contingencies for the target pupils. The attendance counselors arranged contracts between pupils and the mediators, making reinforcement contingent upon school attendance. The mediators included relatives, a girlfriend, the guidance counselors themselves, and a pool hall proprietor. The reinforcers included privileges, money, and access to persons or places (time with a girlfriend, permission to enter a pool hall). This arrangement improved the school attendance of 26 nonattenders, whereas the attendance records of a control group of 15 pupils who received personal counseling by a trained school counselor did not improve.

Again, we must emphasize that the complex issues faced by students with EBD, their families, and the educators who serve them are such that schools are not, nor should they be, able to deal with them alone. As public schools become more active participants in developing integrated, comprehensive services for children and youth with EBD, new models of service delivery are emerging in the schools. These include intensive wraparound planning, collaborative day treatment programs, and family-linked services (see Illback & Nelson, 1996). These models compel educators to learn new skills and to assume increasingly more collaborative roles with parents and other professionals.

SUMMARY

Extending the effects of interventions that have been successfully applied in primary treatment settings is a complex task requiring intensive programming within these settings as well as assessment and intervention in those settings where these behavior changes also are needed and desired. We have described a variety of strategies addressing the goals of achieving the maintenance and generalization of treatment effects and the transition of students to less restrictive environments. Although the technology for achieving

Figure 11.9   Outside School Resource Checklist

Personnel Agencies	Willing to work with pupils?	Supportive of your program?	Cooperated with you previously?	Willing to collect data?	Supervision required?	Training required?	Willing to devote time above normal duties?	Reliably carried out procedures with pupils before?	Comments (Phone numbers, etc.)
Mental Health									
Child Welfare									
Juvenile Court									
Other Social Service Agencies									
Physicians									
Dentists									
Scout Club leaders									
Local Merchants									
Parents									
Volunteers									

these goals has advanced, helping students achieve desired behavior changes that endure over time and across settings continues to be difficult. A major factor seems to be the tendency to provide educational treatments, especially with pupils who are certified as having disabilities, in restrictive settings. Extending effects beyond the school environment is further complicated by problems of communication and the lack of collaborative relationships among educators, parents, and other professionals. However, research has demonstrated that generalization of desired intervention outcomes can occur when it is systematically planned and implemented. The challenge of the future is to alter the ways in which human service programs work to achieve better coordination and greater consistency on behalf of students and clients.

CASE STUDY

THE GARDEN SPRINGS PHASE SYSTEM[1]

Laura L. McCullough

The phase system I developed at my school is for a self-contained unit for students with EBD. Its objective is to provide a consistent guide for bridging the gap between the highly structured environment of a self-contained special education classroom and regular complex-style classrooms of an elementary (K–6) open school. The ultimate goal of my program is to provide the maximum mainstream experience appropriate for each student, and whenever possible, to return that student permanently to the regular public education system.

I believe that while a wide range of difference exists in the specific behavioral deficits for which children are certified as having EBD and are placed in special education classrooms, the most obvious common denominator for referral is an apparent lack of self-control. Therefore, if our task as special educators is to develop self-control abilities in children, what do we teach? Answers to this question have not come easily. However, I feel that we must do more than just make students quieter and smarter. My phase system is designed to teach a cognitive set of self-control principles while simultaneously providing a framework in which my students may learn to make choices based upon public consequences, privileges, and responsibilities. Since feedback is essential to the monitoring and maintenance of behavioral progress, my phase system continuum includes a set of criteria for evaluating specific behaviors at regular intervals.

The phase steps account for receiving a student who is exhibiting problematic behavior (entry level behavior); placing a student back in a regular program (exit level behavior); and a hierarchy of skills between. After determining the specific behavioral expectations important to survival in the environment to which my students are to return, I task-analyzed the behaviors into five component steps.

Phase I consists of the minimum acceptable student behaviors (what must the student do to maintain himself in a special class?). Phase V lists the desired outcome behaviors which appear necessary for inclusion in regular classrooms in my school. Phases II, III, and IV provide intermediate goals or benchmarks for measuring progress toward that inclusion. Tables 11.4 and 11.5 summarize student responsibilities and privileges, as well as some of the considerations used in making decisions about student progress through the phases. Students are provided a list (phase sheet) of specific behaviors for which they are responsible. At the end of the day, I review any behavioral observation data that I have collected. At this time, I also encourage the pupil to recall his day in reference to the phase requirements. I (and later the student) assign a + or − to each specific goal or behavior to indicate whether desired behaviors were demonstrated or lacking. Seven out of ten consecutive + days would, for example, constitute criterion (70 percent) for movement from Phase I to Phase II. Similarly, a Phase II student who receives only six out of ten consecutive + days has failed to maintain criterion at 70 percent and drops to Phase I the following day. I keep a public chart of students' location in the phase system, in addition to charting their daily point totals.

I maintain greater stimulus control at the lower phase levels to minimize undesired behaviors and noncontingent reinforcement. Students who do not advance through phase steps find themselves with little mobility, close supervision, and less choice. Once my authority has been established, I can begin to turn some of the control over to the student. As the requirements and expectations for desired behaviors expand at each level, the number of pupil choices is widened and flexibility increases. As students advance through the phases, they are permitted greater mobility in the classroom and school building, in addition to the opportunity for participation in regular classes. Consequently, students at

---

[1]Reprinted with permission from the author.

(continued)

Table 11.4 Garden Springs Phase System: Student Responsibilities

Phase I	Phase II	Phase III	Phase IV	Phase V Regular Class
		Academic		

State basic information
   Procedure
   Rules
   Points
   Names				

Start assignments	→ Start immediately	→ Start and finish work	→ Finish all work	→ Finish all work on time
Attempt all work	→ Stay on task	→ Complete work with 80% accuracy	→ Complete work with 90% accuracy	→ Complete work with 95% accuracy
Use help sign	→ Wait for help quietly	→ Do other work (waiting)	→ Work independently	→ Work in small group
Explain homework assignment	→ Take homework folder home	→ Homework folder is signed/returned	→ Complete all homework	→ Turn in all homework on time
Listen/repeat instructions	→ Remember instructions (restate later)	→ Follow short-range instructions	→ Follow long-range instruction	→

Attend class	→ Be punctual	→ Bring materials	→ Organize materials	→ Show responsibility for all
				   Materials
				   Assignments
				   Instructions

		Social		
State individual goal	→ State two goals	→ State three goals	→ State all individual goals	→ State all individual goals
	→ Begin daily evaluation of behavior with special education teacher	→	→ Regular teacher	→ Self-evaluate (weekly journal)
Try to follow class rules	→ State P.E./music/library rules	→ State regular class rules	→ Respond to regular class rules/consequences	→ Follow all regular class rules/consequences
Take time-out when told	→ Take time-out immediately when told (put head on desk)	→ Take time-out if necessary	→ Take time-out without putting head on desk	→ Take time-out internally (maintain cool)
Define self-control communication	→ Try to avoid fights, control verbal aggression	→ Talk calmly to staff and group session when angry/upset	→ Defer discussion until later time Ignore inappropriate behavior of others	→ Present problems at convenience of regular class teacher/schedule
		Daily Criterion		
Enter	70%	80% *Mainstreaming*	87%	93% *Exit*
No mainstream access	→ P.E./music/library access	→ Homeroom/lunch/recess access	→ Academic class access	→ All day! (as appropriate)

(continued)

Table 11.5 Garden Springs Phase System: Student Privileges

Example Items	Phase I	Phase II	Phase III	Phase IV	Phase V
Seat location	→ Assigned	→ Request considered	→ Variable	→ Any area by request	→ Regular class
Silent reading	→ In seat only	→ At group table	→ In reading pillow corner	→ Anywhere including floor (with pillows)	→ Regular class
Creative writing	→ Work in seat	→ Work at group table	→ With head-phone music	→ Music and snack	→ Regular class
Free time					
Materials	→ Art, games, Lagos	→ Plus records, tapes	→ Plus radio	→ Request by contract	→
Area time	→ In seat only	→ Free-time area	→ In room	→ Check out materials to regular class	→ Check out materials overnight take home
Cost	→ 25 points	→ 20 points	→ 10 points	→ Free	→
Class trips	→ Pay full cost	→ Pay self/ parent	→ Pay self/ guest	→ Pay self/ 2 guests	→ Free/contact agreement
Homework	→ Assigned	→ Request sequence	→ Request type task	→ Contract homework	→ Regular class
Mobility					
Restroom	→ Group supervision only	→ Paid escort for special trip	→ Alone with permission/ time limit	→ Inform teacher	→ Regular class
In building transit	→ No un-supervised mobility	→ Trial basis free to music/P.E.	→ Free to all scheduled classes (trial basis)	→ Free	→ Regular class
Classroom	→ In seat all times	→ Free access to trash, tissues, sharpener	→ Free access to materials, needs	→ Free	→ Regular class
Jobs	→ In class routine	→ Class/ building routine	→ Messages, flexible transit, class helper	→ Special jobs by contract Class leadership	→ Regular class Unlimited special contract
Feedback	→ Immediate	→ Frequent	→ Deferred by necessity	→ Intermittent	→ Regular class/weekly
Artificial reinforcers	→ Points: continuous	→ Points: end of each task	→ Points: twice daily	→ Points: once daily	→ Off points!
Intolerable behavior	← Place on homebound (start over)	← Homebound (two home-bounds = drop to Phase I)	← One home-bound = drop to Phase II	← One home-bound = drop to Phase III	← One home-bound = drop to Phase III or suspension

Note: Homebound consists of a one- to two-day school suspension. Student is sent home with specific academic assignments to complete, and parents are to supervise and restrict access to privileges (e. g., TV, playing outside).

(continued)

upper levels provide peer models to lower phase students who are more restricted.

The phase system also is a useful tool for communicating with school personnel and parents. Often alarmed by a student's certification, parents are more comfortable discussing the specific behaviors their children presently are exhibiting. The sequence of pupil responsibilities also is helpful for outlining a sequence of behaviors that are expected in the home or the educational mainstream. I urge parents to ask their children every day about their phase levels and to provide social reinforcement for advancement. Given consistent implementation over time, the regular classroom teachers seem to have more respect for and confidence in mainstreaming requests. In addition, regular classroom teachers find the phase system supportive. For example, they know they will not be stuck with a child whose behavior has seriously deteriorated because the system provides for dropping students back to lower levels if percentage criteria are not maintained.

Another advantage to phase mainstreaming is that generalization can be monitored and evaluated on the spot in the regular classroom. Students are exposed to a gradual transition from the rules and authority of a single special teacher to the rules and personal biases found in numerous settings. For instance, students reporting to regular physical education class are aware that the arrangement is made on a trial basis. Continued access is contingent upon conformity to the gym rules and appropriate response to the physical education teacher.

As students approach the upper phase steps (IV and V), artificial reinforcers (points) are withdrawn or transferred in favor of long-term natural reinforcement. Feedback is given less often and rewards are put on a more intermittent schedule. Token reinforcers (points) are faded and discontinued. If real academic or social progress has met with consistent systematic praise and peer encouragement, conversion to these natural reinforcers is accomplished smoothly. Regular staff personnel (principal, teachers, custodians, etc.) and parents who have learned to recognize and selectively attend to student improvements have tremendous positive influence on maintaining desired behavior at acceptable levels. They also may see an enormous sense of pride develop and spill over in a student who just couldn't make it before.

DISCUSSION QUESTIONS

1. Given that the generalization of treatment effects is much more difficult when interventions occur in restrictive settings, how could treatment procedures be designed to facilitate generalization within school environments? How might educational services be reorganized to make generalization of intervention outcomes more likely to occur?

2. Assume that you have reduced a student's aggressive behavior to an acceptable level in a special classroom environment, but she still exhibits verbal and physical aggression in other school settings. How would you assess these behaviors in other settings, and what strategies would you use to accomplish a generalized reduction in her aggression?

3. How would you prepare a student with EBD to be mainstreamed in a regular classroom?

Describe the procedures you would use in the special education setting and the strategies you would apply in the mainstream environment.

4. A parent of one of your students complains that his child is "unmanageable" at home (refuses to do chores, disobeys rules and direct requests, and fights with siblings). As a classroom teacher, what would you do?

REFERENCES

Anderson-Inman, L., Walker, H. M., & Purcell, J. (1984). Promoting the transfer of skills across settings: Transenvironmental programming for handicapped students in the mainstream. In W. R. Heward, T. E. Heron, D. S. Hill, & J. Trap-Porter (Eds.), *Focus on behavior analysis in education* (pp. 17–39). Upper Saddle River, NJ: Merrill/Prentice Hall.

Ayllon, T., Garber, S., & Pisor, K. (1975). The elimination of discipline problems through a combined school-home motivation system. *Behavior Therapy, 6,* 616–626.

Baer, D. M., & Wolf, M. M. (1970). The entry into natural communities of reinforcement. In R. Ulrich, T. Stachnik, & J. Mabry (Eds.), *Control of human behavior: Vol. II. From cure to prevention* (pp. 319–324). Glenview, IL: Scott, Foresman.

Baer, D. M., Wolf, M. M., & Risley, T. R. (1968). Some current dimensions of applied behavior analysis. *Journal of Applied Behavior Analysis, 1,* 91–97.

Bauer, A. M., & Shea, T. M. (1988). Structuring classrooms through level systems. *Focus on Exceptional Children, 21*(3), 1–12.

Becker, W. C. (1971). *Parents are teachers.* Champaign, IL: Research Press.

Braaten, S. (1979). The Madison School program: Programming for secondary level emotionally disturbed youth. *Behavioral Disorders, 4,* 153–162.

Braaten, S., Kauffman, J. M., Braaten, B., Polsgrove, L., & Nelson, C. M. (1988). The regular education initiative: Patent medicine for behavioral disorders? *Exceptional Children, 55,* 21–27.

Brolin, D. (1995). *Career education: A functional life skills approach* (3rd ed.). Upper Saddle River, NJ: Merrill/Prentice Hall.

Brown, L., Nietupski, J., & Hamre-Nietupski, S. (1976). The criterion of ultimate functioning and public school services for severely handicapped students. In A. Thomas (Ed.), *Hey, don't forget about me: New directions for serving the severely handicapped* (pp. 2–15). Reston, VA: Council for Exceptional Children.

Brown, R. E., Copeland, R. E., & Hall, R. V. (1972). The school principal as a behavior modifier. *Journal of Educational Research, 66,* 175–180.

Bullis, M., & Paris, K. (1996). Competitive employment and service management for adolescents and young adults with emotional and behavioral disorders. In R. J. Illback, & C. M. Nelson (Eds.), *Emerging school-based approaches for children and youth with emotional and behavioral disorders: Research on practice and service integration* (pp. 77–96). New York: Haworth Press.

Chesapeake Institute. (1994, September). *National agenda for achieving better results for children and youth with serious emotional disturbance.* Washington, DC: Department of Education, Office of Special Education and Rehabilitative Services, Office of Special Education Programs.

Christophersen, E. R., Arnold, C. M., Hill, D. W., & Quilitch, H. R. (1972). The home point system:

Token reinforcement procedures for application by parents of children with behavior problems. *Journal of Applied Behavior Analysis, 5,* 485–497.

Clark, H. B., Unger, K. V., & Stewart, E. S. (1993). Transition of youth and young adults with emotional/behavioral disorders into employment, education, and independent living. *Community Alternatives: International Journal of Family Care, 5*(2), 19–46.

Clees, T. J. (1995). Self-recording of students' daily schedules of teachers' expectancies: Perspectives on reactivity, stimulus control, and generalization. *Exceptionality, 5,* 113–129.

Clore, P. (1974). Chris: "School phobia." In J. Worell & C. M. Nelson. *Managing instructional problems: A case study workbook* (pp. 212–217). New York: McGraw-Hill.

Copeland, R. E., Brown, R. E., & Hall, R. V. (1974). The effects of principal-implemented techniques on the behavior of pupils. *Journal of Applied Behavior Analysis, 7,* 77–86.

DeChillo, N., Koren, P. E., & Schultz, K. H. (1994). From paternalism to partnership: Family/professional collaboration in children's mental health. *American Journal of Orthopsychiatry, 64,* 564–576.

Duchnowski, A., Berg, K., & Kutash, K. (1995). Parent participation in and perception of placement decisions. In J. M. Kauffman, J. W. Lloyd, D. P. Hallahan, & T. A. Astuto (Eds.), *Issues in educational placement: Students with emotional and behavioral disorders* (pp. 183–195). Hillsdale, NJ: Lawrence Erlbaum Associates.

Eber, L. (1995, April). *LASDE EBD network training developing school-based wraparound plan.* LaGrange, IL: LaGrange Area Department of Special Education.

Eber, L., Nelson, C. M., & Mills, P. (1997). School-based wraparound for students with emotional and behavioral challenges. *Exceptional Children, 63,* 539–555.

Edgar, E. (1987). Secondary programs in special education: Are many of them jusifiable? *Exceptional Children, 53,* 555–561.

Edgar, E., & Siegel, S. (1995). Postsecondary scenarios for troubled and troubling youth. In J. M. Kauffman & D. P. Hallahan (Eds.), *The illusion of full inclusion: A comprehensive critique of a current special education bandwagon* (pp. 251–283). Austin, TX: PRO-ED.

Edgar, E. B., Webb, S. L., & Maddox, M. (1987). Issues in transition: Transfer of youth from correctional facilties to public schools. In C. M. Melson, R. B. Rutherford, Jr., & B. I. Wolford (Eds.). *Special education in the criminal justice system.* Upper Saddle River, NJ: Merrill/Prentice Hall.

Ferber, H., Keeley, S. M., & Shemberg, K. M. (1974). Training parents in behavior modification: Outcomes of and problems encountered in a program after Patterson's work. *Behavior Therapy, 5,* 415–419.

Friesen, B. J., & Wahlers, D. (1993). Respect and real help: Family support and children's mental health. *Journal of Emotional and Behavioral Problems, 2*(4), 12–15.

Gaylord-Ross, R., & Haring, T. (1987). Social interaction research for adolescents with severe handicaps. *Behavioral Disorders, 12,* 264–275.

Gaylord-Ross, R. J., Haring, T. G., Breen, C., & Pitts-Conway, V. (1984). The training and generalization of social interaction skills with autistic youth. *Journal of Applied Behavior Analysis, 17,* 229–247.

Glogowger, F., & Sloop, E. W. (1976). Two strategies of group training of parents as effective behavior modifiers. *Behavior Therapy, 7,* 177–184.

Goetz, L., Guess, D., & Stremel-Campbell, K. (Eds.). (1987). *Innovative program design for individuals with dual sensory impairments.* Boston: Paul H. Brookes.

Graubard, P. S., Rosenberg H., & Miller, M. B. (1971). Student applications of behavior modification to teachers and environments or ecological approaches to social deviancy. In E. A. Ramp & B. L. Hopkins (Eds.), *A new direction for education: Behavior anlysis: 1971* (pp. 80–101). Lawrence, KS: University of Kansas Support and Development Center for Follow Through.

Gresham, F. M., Elliott, S. N., & Black, F. L. (1987). Teacher-rated social skills of mainstreamed mildly handicapped and nonhandicapped children. *School Psychology Review, 16,* 78–88.

Gunter, P., Fox, J. J., Brady, M. P., Shores, R. E., & Cavanaugh, K. (1988). Nonhandicapped peers as multiple exemplars: A generalization tactic for promoting autistic students' social skills. *Behavioral Disorders, 13,* 116–126.

Hallahan, D. P., & Kauffman, J. M. (1995). From mainstreaming to collaborative consultation. In J. M. Kauffman & D. P. Hallahan (Eds.), *The illusion of full inclusion: A comprehensive critique of a current special education bandwagon* (pp. 5–17). Austin, TX: PRO-ED.

Hewett, F. M., & Taylor, F. D. (1980). *The emotionally disturbed child in the classroom: The orchestration of success* (2nd ed.). Boston: Allyn & Bacon.

Hollinger, J. D. (1987). Social skills for behaviorally disordered children as preparation for mainstreaming: Theory, practice, and new directions. *Remedial and Special Education, 8*(4), 17–27.

Hrydowy, E. R., Stokes, T. F., & Martin, G. L. (1984). Training elementary students to prompt teacher praise. *Education and Treatment of Children, 7,* 99–108.

Idol, L., Paolucci-Whitcomb, P., & Nevin, A. (1986). *Collaborative consultation.* Rockville, MD: Aspen.

Illback, R. J., & Nelson, C. M. (Eds.). (1996). *Emerging school-based approaches for children and youth with emotional and behavioral disorders. Research or practice and service integration.* New York: Haworth Press.

Kauffman, J. M., & Hallahan, D. P. (Eds.). (1995). *The illusion of full inclusion: A comprehensive critique of a current special education bandwagon.* Austin, TX: PRO-ED.

Kazdin, A. E. (1977). Vicarious reinforcement and direction of behavior change in the classroom. *Behavior Therapy, 8,* 57–63.

Kerr, M. M., Nelson, C. M., & Lambert, D. L. (1987). *Helping adolescents with learning and behavior problems.* Upper Saddle River, NJ: Merrill/Prentice Hall.

Koegel, R. L., & Rincover, A. (1977). Research on the difference between generalization and maintenance in extra-therapy responding. *Journal of Applied Behavior Analysis, 10,* 1–12.

Kameinui, E. J., & Darch, C. B. (1995). *Instructional classroom-management: A proactive approach to behavior management.* Reston, VA: Council for Exceptional Children.

Kroth, R. L. (1975). *Communicating with parents of exceptional children: Improving parent-teacher relationships.* Denver, CO: Love.

Kroth, R. L., & Simpson, R. L. (1977). *Parent conferences as a teaching strategy.* Denver, CO: Love.

Kroth, R. L., & Edge, D. (1997). Strategies for communicating with parents and families of exceptional children (3rd ed.). Denver, CO: Love.

Lane, T. W., & Burchard, J. D. (1983). Failure to modify delinquent behavior: A constructive analysis. In E. B. Foa & P. M. G. Emmelkamp (Eds.), *Failures in behavior therapy* (pp. 355–377). New York: Wiley.

LaNunziata, L. J., Hunt, K. P., & Cooper, J. O. (1984). Suggestions for phasing out token economy systems in primary and intermediate grades. *Techniques: A Journal for Remedial Education and Counseling, 1,* 151–156.

Maag, J. W. (1996). *Parenting without punishment: Making problem behavior work for you.* Philadelphia: The Charles Press.

Maag, J. W. (1994, November). Teaching students self-control: From theory to practice. Workshop presented at the Seventeenth Annual Conference on

Severe Behavior Disorders of Children and Youth, Tempe, AZ.

MacDonald, W. S., Gallimore, R., & MacDonald, G. (1970). Contingency counseling by school personnel: An economical model of intervention. *Journal of Applied Behavior Analysis, 3,* 175–182.

Marholin, D., & Steinman, W. (1977). Stimulus control in the classroom as a function of the behavior reinforced. *Journal of Applied Behavior Analysis, 10,* 465–478.

McEvoy, M. A., & Odom, S. L. (1987). Social interaction training for preschool children with behavioral disorders. *Behavioral Disorders, 12,* 242–251.

McLaughlin, M. J., Leone, P. E., Warren, S. H., & Schofield, P. F. (1994). *Doing things differently: Issues and options for creating comprehensive school linked services for children and youth with emotional or behavioral disorders.* College Park, MD: University of Maryland and Westat, Inc.

Meichenbaum, D. (1977). *Cognitive-behavior modification: An integrative approach.* New York: Plenum.

Mercer, C. D., & Mercer, A. R. (1985). *Teaching students with learning problems* (2nd ed.). Upper Saddle River, NJ: Merrill/Prentice Hall.

Nelson, C. M. (1988). Social skills training for handicapped students. *Teaching Exceptional Children, 20*(4), 19–23.

Nelson, C. M., & Pearson, C. A. (1991). *Integrating services for children and youth with emotional and behavioral disorders.* Reston, VA: Council for Exceptional Children.

Nelson, C. M., & Pearson, C. A. (1994). Juvenile delinquency in the context of culture and community. In R. L. Peterson & S. Ishii-Jordan (Eds.), *Cultural and community contexts for emotional or behavioral disorders* (pp. 78–90), Boston: Brookline Press.

Nelson, C. M., & Rutherford, R. B., Jr. (1988). Behavioral interventions with behaviorally disordered students. In M. C. Wang, H. J. Walberg, & M. C. Reynolds (Eds.), *The handbook of special education: Research and practice* (Vol. 2) (pp. 125–153). Oxford, England: Pergamon.

Nelson, C. M., Rutherford, R. B., Jr., & Wolford, B. I. (Eds.). (1987). *Special education and the criminal justice system.* Upper Saddle River, NJ: Merrill/Prentice Hall.

O'Leary, S. G., & O'Leary, K. D. (1976). Behavior modification in the school. In H. Leitenberg (Ed.), *Handbook of behavior modification and behavior therapy* (pp. 475–515). Englewood Cliffs, NJ: Prentice-Hall.

Patterson, G. R. (1975). *Families: Applications of social learning to family life.* Champaign, IL: Research Press.

Patterson, G. R., & Gullion, M. E. (1971). Living with children. Champaign, IL: Research Press.

Polsgrove, L. (1979). Self-control: Methods for child training. *Behavioral Disorders, 4,* 116–130.

Reid, R., & Harris, K. R. (1993). Self-monitoring of attention versus self-monitoring of performance: Effects on attention and academic performance. *Exceptional Children, 60,* 29–40.

Reppucci, N. D., & Saunders, J. T. (1974). Social psychology of behavior modification: Problems of implementation in natural settings. *American Psychologist, 29,* 649–660.

Rinn, R. C., Vernon, J. C., & Wise, M. J. (1975). Training parents of behaviorally disordered children in groups: A three years program evaluation. *Behavior Therapy, 6,* 378–387.

Robbins, L. N. (1966). *Deviant children grown up: A sociological and psychiatric study of sociopathic personality.* Baltimore: Williams & Wilkins.

Rock, E. E., Rosenberg, M. S., & Carran, D. T. (1994). Variables affecting the reintegration rate of students with serious emotional disturbance. *Exceptional Children, 61,* 254–268.

Rutherford, R. B., Jr., & Edgar, E. (1979). *Teachers and parents: A guide to interaction and cooperation.* Boston: Allyn & Bacon.

Rutherford, R. B., Jr., & Nelson, C. M. (1988). Generalization and maintenance of treatment effects. In J. C. Witt, S. N. Elliott, & F. M. Gresham (Eds.), *Handbook of behavior therapy in education* (pp. 277–324). New York: Plenum.

Shinn, M. R., Ramsey, E., Walker, H. M., Stieber, S., & O'Neill, R. E. (1987). Antisocial behavior in school settings: Initial differences in an at risk and normal population. *Journal of Special Education, 21,* 69–84.,

Shores, R. E. (1987). Overview of research on social interaction: A historical and personal perspective. *Behavioral Disorders, 12,* 233–241.

Shores, R. E., Apolloni, T., & Norman, C. W. (1976). Changes in peer verbalizations accompanying individual and group contingencies. *Perceptual and Motor Skills, 43,* 1155–1162.

Simpson, R. L. (1987). Social interaction of behaviorally disordered children and youth: Where are we and where do we need to go? *Behavioral Disorders, 12,* 292–298.

Stephens, S. A., & Lakin, K. C. (1995). Where students with emotional or behavioral disorders go to school. In J. M. Kauffman, J. W. Lloyd, D. P. Hallahan, & T. A. Astuto (Eds.), *Issues in educational placement: Students with emotional and behavioral disorders* (pp. 47–74). Hillsdale, NJ: Lawrence Erlbaum Associates.

Stokes, T. F., & Baer, D. M. (1977). An implicit technology of generalization. *Journal of Applied Behavior Analysis, 10,* 349–367.

Stokes, T. F., & Osnes, P. G. (1986). Programming the generalization of children's social behavior. In P. S. Strain, M. J. Guralnick, & H. M. Walker (Eds.), *Children's social behavior: Development, assessment, and modification* (pp. 407–443). Orlando, FL: Academic Press.

Strain, P. S., & Danko, C. D. (1995). Caregivers' encouragement of positive interaction between preschoolers with autism and their siblings. *Journal of Emotional and Behavioral Disorders, 3,* 2–12.

Strain, P. S., Shores, R. E., & Kerr, M. M. (1976). An experimental analysis of "spillover" effects on the social interaction of behaviorally handicapped preschool children. *Journal of Applied Behavior Analysis, 9,* 31–40.

Stroul, B., Goldman, S., Lourie, I., Katz-Leavy, J., Zeigler-Dendy, C. (1992). *Profiles of local systems of care for children and adolescents with severe emotional disturbances.* Washington, DC: Georgetown University Child Development Center, CASSP Technical Assistance Center.

Tawney, J. W., & Gast, D. L. (1984). Single subject research in special education. Upper Saddle River, NJ: Merrill/Prentice Hall.

Taylor, F. D., & Soloway, M. M. (1973). The Madison School plan: A functional model for merging the regular and special classrooms. In E. Deno (Ed.), *Instructional alternatives for exceptional children* (pp. 145–155). Reston, VA: Council for Exceptional Children.

Taylor, S. J., Bilken, D., & Knoll, J. (1987). (Eds.). *Community integration for people with severe disabilities.* New York: Teachers College Press, Columbia University.

Thomas, C. C., Correa, V. I., & Morsink, C. V. (1995). *Interactive teaming: Consultation and collaboration in special programs* (2nd ed.). Upper Saddle River, NJ: Merrill/Prentice Hall.

U. S. Department of Education (1994). *Sixteenth annual report to Congress on the implementation of the Individuals with Disability Education Act.* Washington, DC: U.S. Department of Education, Office of Special Education and Rehabilitative Services.

Van Hasselt, B. B., Hersen, M., Whitehill, M. B., & Bellack, A. S. (1979). Social skills assessment and training for children: An evaluative review. *Behavior Research and Therapy, 17,* 413–437.

Vetter-Zemitzsch, A., Bernstein, R., Johnson, J., Larson, C., Simon, D., Smith, D., & Smith, A. (1984). The on campus program: A systematic/behavioral approach to behavior disorders in high school. *Focus on Exceptional Children, 16*(6), 1–8.

Wagonseller, B. R., & McDowell, R. L. (1979). *You and your child: A common sense approach to successful parenting.* Champaign, IL: Research Press.

Walker, H. M. (1986). The assessment for integration into mainstream settings (AIMS) assessment system: Rationale, instruments, procedures, and outcomes. *Journal of Clinical Child Psychology, 15,* 55–63.

Walker, H. M., & Bullis, M. (1996). A comprehensive services model for troubled youth. In C. M. Nelson, B. Wolford, & R. B. Rutherford (Eds.). *Developing comprehensive systems that work for troubled youth* (pp. 122–148). Richmond, KY: National Coalition for Juvenile Justice Services.

Walker, H. M., & Rankin, R. (1980a). The SBS Checklist of Correlates of child handicapping conditions. (Available from Hill Walker, Center on Human Development, Clinical Services Building, University of Oregon, Eugene, OR 97403).

Walker, H. M., & Rankin, R. (1980b). The SBS Inventory of teacher social behavior standards and expectations. (Available from Hill Walker, Center on Human Development, Clinical Services Building, University of Oregon, Eugene, OR 97403).

Walker, H. M., Shinn, M. R., O'Neill, R. E., & Ramsey, E. (1987). A longitudinal assessment of the development of antisocial behavior in boys: Rationale, methodology, and first year results. *Remedial and Special Education, 8*(4), 7–16; 27.

Wong, K. L. H., Kauffman, J. M., & Lloyd, J. W. (1991). Choices for integration: Selecting teachers for mainstreaming students with emotional or behavioral disorders. *Intervention in School and Clinic, 27,* 108–115.

THE CHALLENGES OF WORKING WITH STUDENTS WITH EBD

OUTLINE

OBJECTIVES

After completing this chapter, you should be able to

◆ Identify circumstances in which universal, targeted, and wraparound planning strategies are needed.
◆ Identify the major limitations that apply to educators working in school settings and describe the consequences of exceeding these limitations.
◆ Identify potential sources of conflict for educators working on behalf of students exhibiting behavioral disorders.
◆ Discuss strategies for working effectively within professional role boundaries.
◆ Identify signs of stress and burnout and suggest appropriate strategies for their reduction.
◆ Describe the advantages of participation on an interactive team.

Previous chapters have described a broad range of intervention strategies for dealing with an equally wide range of behavioral problems. Chapters 2 and 11 indicated that problem behaviors may be present in noneducational settings and discussed procedures for assessing and intervening in these settings. The present chapter considers the need to work collaboratively with other professionals and families to implement wraparound plans for students who often are affected by multiple service delivery systems. We begin with a brief discussion of universal, targeted, and wraparound approaches, which are used as a basis for making decisions regarding when to expand the scope of intervention planning through interactive teaming. Next is a description of some of the limits to the classroom teacher's role that indicate a need

for collaboration. The role of team member is an important extension of the functions traditionally served by educators; in view of the professional support and technical assistance needed by those who serve children and youth with EBD, a section has been added on this role. The relatively high attrition rate of teachers of students with EBD must be considered by any professional in this field. Therefore the final section presents information on teacher burnout.

SELECTING INTERVENTIONS REVISITED

In Chapter 4 we discussed two categories of intervention: *universal*, which are applied to all members or a group of population (e.g., a school-wide discipline plan, changes in scheduling and student monitoring procedures); and *targeted,* which are directed at specific pupils and behaviors that are not responsive to universal interventions. We cited research demonstrating that the need for multiple targeted interventions is reduced dramatically when effective universal interventions are in place. Universal interventions are presented in numerous methods texts, chapters, and articles on effective schools (Bickel & Bickel, 1986; Brophy & Good, 1986; Rosenshine & Stevens, 1986), school-wide discipline (Colvin, Kameenui, & Sugai, 1993), and classroom behavior management (Jones & Jones, 1995; Kauffman, Hallahan, Mostert, Trent, & Nuttycombe, 1993). Targeted interventions can be delivered, supervised directly, or orchestrated by school personnel with appropriate training in behavioral interventions. This text focuses on strategies involving targeted intervention methodology, based on the technology of applied behavior analysis and directed at influencing pupil social behavior.

As mentioned in Chapters 4 and 11, there exists a third level, or gate of intervention, through *wraparound planning,* in which teams of professionals and family members jointly create strategies that wrap around a given child and her needs in school, home, and community. Using the wraparound approach, a comprehensive interagency plan is developed that crosses multiple life domains. Wraparound planning involves identifying the student's strengths and other resources in the settings that make up the student's typical day. Both traditional and nontraditional intervention strategies are created and evaluated in terms of their impact on the progress and comfort of both the pupil and those who provide services to the pupil (Eber, 1996). The wraparound process developed from the system of care approach for children and youth who were involved with multiple service delivery systems (Stroul & Friedman, 1986). The goal of this approach has been to increase the intensity and effectiveness of services to children with EBD and their families in their home schools and communities, thereby reducing the need for out-of-community placement (Skiba & Polsgrove, 1996). The core values and guiding principles of a system of care are presented in Table 12.1. These values and

principals are reflected in the wraparound approach (see Table 1.8).

Recently, the wraparound process has been applied to planning and delivering more proactive services to children not at immediate risk for out-of-community placement. Many strategies presented in this text are appropriate for delivery through a wraparound approach; however, the policies, procedures, and technical assistance needed to ensure the effectiveness of this approach are beyond the scope of this text.[1] If school practices include effective universal and targeted interventions, the need for wraparound plans will be reduced significantly, *but they will not be eliminated.*[2] Therefore, it is necessary to have school-based staff who are capable of identifying when this level of intervention is needed, and who can initiate interactions with families, other school staff, and, when necessary, other agencies to develop comprehensive wraparound plans.

Essentially, this three-tiered conceptualization of intervention is a multiple-gated model, similar to the multiple-gated screening model presented in Chapter 1. Figure 12.1 illustrates this multiple-gated intervention model. Each intervention gate is entered by students for whom interventions have not been successful in previous gates. Therefore, progress toward more intensive intervention planning involves the compilation and analysis of data regarding what has worked and what has not in previous systematic attempts to affect problem behaviors. These outcome data will be invaluable to interactive teams who have the responsibility for wraparound planning and service coordination.

LIMITATIONS ON THE EDUCATIONAL ROLE

The consequences of overextending oneself or of overstepping one's professional boundaries can

---

[1] For information regarding wraparound planning and procedures, consult Eber, 1996; and Eber, Osuch, & Redditt, 1996.

[2] Gresham (1991) has conceptualized behavioral disorders in terms of resistance to intervention. He argures that the certification EBD should be applied only to students for whom appropriate universal and targeted interventions, provided in the context of a regular school program, have not been successful.

Table 12.1   Values and Principles for the System of Care

Core Values

1. The system of care should be child centered and family focused, with the needs of the child and family dictating the types and mix of services provided.

2. The system of care should be community based, with the focus of services as well as management and decision-making responsibility resting at the community level.

3. The system of care should be culturally competent, with agencies, programs, and services that are responsive to the cultural, racial, and ethnic differences of the populations they serve.

Guiding Principles

1. Children with emotional disturbances should have access to a comprehensive array of services that address each child's physical, emotional, social, and educational needs.

2. Children with emotional disturbances should receive individualized services in accordance with the unique needs and potentials of each child and guided by an individualized service plan.

3. Children with emotional disturbances should receive services within the least restrictive, most normative environment that is clinically appropriate.

4. The families and surrogate families of children with emotional disturbances should be full participants in all aspects of the planning and delivery of services.

5. Children with emotional disturbances should receive services that are integrated, with linkages between child-serving agencies and programs and mechanisms for planning, developing, and coordinating services.

6. Children with emotional disturbances should be provided with case management or similar mechanisms to ensure that multiple services are delivered in a coordinated and therapeutic manner and that they can move through the system of services in accordance with their changing needs.

7. Early identification and intervention for children with emotional disturbances should be promoted by the system of care in order to enhance the likelihood of positive outcomes.

8. Children with emotional disturbances should be ensured smooth transitions to the adult service system as they reach maturity.

9. The rights of children with emotional disturbances should be protected, and effective advocacy efforts for children and youth with emotional disturbances should be promoted.

10. Children with emotional disturbances should receive services without regard to race, religion, national origin, sex, physical disability, or other characteristics, and services should be sensitive and responsive to cultural differences and special needs.

Source: Stroul, B. A., & Friedman, R. M. (1986). *A system of care for children and youth with severe emotional disturbance.* Copyright CAASP Technical Assistance Center. Used with permission.

be unpleasant. Therefore, we provide guidelines derived from research, litigation, authoritative discourse, and experience. Recognizing the limits of the educational role not only helps you avoid aversive personal and professional consequences but also benefits you in two ways. First, you avoid overextending yourself in areas beyond your scope, which helps reduce your stress. Second, you function more effectively and more flexibly as a student advocate and as a member of an interactive team.

Our discussion of limitations is organized into three categories: ecological constraints, role constraints, and legal constraints. This division is arbitrary; in practical situations, the categories overlap considerably. Moreover, we believe the philosophy of services for persons with diverse needs in this country is shifting toward a more comprehensive and integrated focus, which demands that education become part of a system of care. The implication is that educators, especially those who work with children and youth who have experienced alienation and disempowerment because of their economic, cultural, and behavioral characteristics, no longer can function in isolation. The final section discusses teacher stress and burnout and the potential of wraparound planning to support the important work of the classroom teacher.

Figure 12.1 Multiple Gated Intervention Model

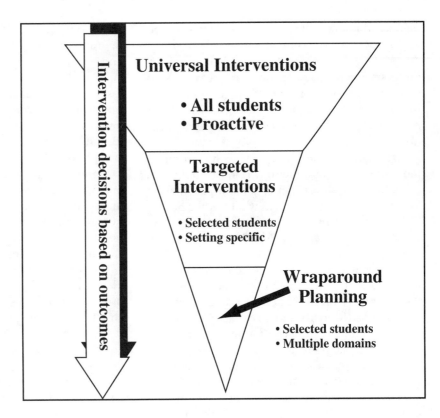

Ecological Constraints

Overextension and Intrusion Remember that problem behaviors do not occur only in educational settings. In particular, students with EBD display maladaptive behaviors or deficits in appropriate social skills across many settings. Caregivers and other persons who must deal with these individuals may lack the skills needed to design and implement sophisticated and effective intervention procedures. As a professional educator, you are constrained by the practical limits of your role. This means that you are sure to encounter circumstances in which you cannot manage all the student's environmental contingencies and reinforcers, nor can you train and supervise all those who do. It is important that you recognize these facts, even though you may have the expertise to deal with the student's problems. For example, there may be serious difficulties in the pupil's family interactions, or the student may be involved in a gang. If you know or think you know how to attack such problems, it may be tempting to try to

manage them yourself. However, this tactic presents several dangers. First, you may be overextending yourself; your official responsibility is to the student's educational program, unless you are acting in another professional role. If you are in a consulting role or have released time for parent training or community work, there is less conflict; nevertheless, one can easily become overextended when working with multiple-problem situations.

A related risk is that of intruding upon another professional's domain. If a family receives counseling from a mental health agency or if a probation officer is working on the pupil's delinquent behavior, do not initiate interventions without the prior consent of the other professional or agency. Then too you may risk providing ineffective treatment: You may find yourself working in areas or on problems for which you are not trained adequately. Paradoxically, the dangers of overextension are increased by your own effectiveness. That is, the better you are at your job, the more you may be called upon to help in other areas. It is very tempting to respond to the social reinforcement offered by your students, their families, and other professionals by increasing your participation in areas beyond your jurisdiction. However, this pattern may lead to undesired consequences for you and your pupils; thus, you should recognize this as a limitation on your role.

Extending yourself beyond your limitations is more likely if you are the only resource in the geographic area for a pupil or a family, as in rural locales. In more urban areas where other professionals are available, you may be the only one the student or family trusts. Providing assistance in these instances may represent a difficult decision.

Interagency and family collaborative service planning and delivery offer a viable solution to the problems of overextension and intrusion. School-based wraparound plans should include the use of family and community resources to support educational goals for individual students, as well as other life domains. At the same time, school services and resources should facilitate the achievement of family and community goals. Integrated service planning is, of course, a team effort. One way to identify the needs to be addressed in multiple life domain planning is to assess the pupil's ecology. An ecological asessment can be accomplished by interviewing the student or his caregivers. Wahler and Cormier (1970) developed three behavior checklists, reproduced here in Figures 12.2, 12.3, and 12.4, that can be used to map student ecological settings. Neither the problem behaviors nor the situations listed here are exhaustive, but the service coordination team can use these checklists as models to develop their own. Focus on specific behaviors and ask the interviewee in which of the settings they occur, or ask which behaviors present problems in each of the student's ecological settings. By entering checks in the appropriate rows and columns, you can develop a map of the student's problem behaviors in various settings and thereby gain a general understanding of the extent of such problems, as well as which behaviors the student displays in specific settings. Further questioning may reveal specific persons in

whose presence problems occur, typical reactions or approaches to handling problem behaviors, and so forth.

Note that these checklists depart from the philosophy of wraparound planning in that they do not probe for strengths and resources in the student or her ecology. Therefore, it is important to identify these and to incorporate them into service plans. A focus on building positive supports, as opposed to one that concentrates exclusively on reducing undesired behaviors, has been a major breakthrough in approaches to intervention and is much more likely to improve cooperation and collaboration with both families and community agencies.

If your school building or district has not implemented an integrated, team-based planning process for students with EBD, you may need to conduct the ecological assessment independently. If this is the case, after your interviews with caregivers and service providers you can make a decision whether to approach the problem situation yourself, to collaborate with other providers and family members, or to refer the student or caregiver elsewhere. The practice of referring students and families to other providers has been a common approach to dealing with children exhibiting significant emotional and behavioral problems. In many cases, this process has been a one-way ticket to "deep end" services (e.g., residential treatment) that remove the child from his community. The enormous costs and relative ineffectiveness of this strategy (Epstein, Nelson, Polsgrove, Coutinho, Cumblad, & Quinn, 1993) have driven the search for approaches to treatment that are not based on removal and containment. The system of care strategy for delivering intense treatment in natural settings has enabled many children to remain in their schools and communities (Rivera & Kutash, 1994; Stroul, 1993). The wraparound approach to service planning and delivery is a critical component of a system of care. Wraparound requires a team approach involving partnerships among parents and service providers. Therefore, participation in a service coordination team is an important addition to the role of special educators working with students with EBD.

Figure 12.2 Child Home Behavior Checklist

The following checklist allows you to describe your child's problems in various home situations. The situations are listed in the column at left and common problem behaviors are listed in the row at the top. Examine *each* situation in the column and decide whether one or more of the problem behaviors in the row fits your child. Check those that fit the best—if any.

	Always has to be told	Doesn't pay attention	Forgets	Dawdles	Refuses	Argues	Complains	Demands	Fights	Is selfish	Destroys toys or property	Steals	Lies	Cries	Whines	Hangs on or stays close to adult	Acts silly	Mopes around	Stays alone	Has to keep things in order	Engages in sexual play
Morning																					
Awakening																					
Dressing																					
Breakfast																					
Bathroom																					
Leaving for school																					
Play in house																					
Chores																					
Television																					
Afternoon																					
Lunch																					
Bathroom																					
Play in house																					
Chores and homework																					
Television																					
Company arrival																					
Evening																					
Father comes home																					
Dinner																					
Bathroom																					
Play in house																					
Chores and homework																					
Television																					
Company arrival																					
Bedtime																					

Source: R. G. Wahler & W. H. Cormier. The ecological interview: A first step in outpatient therapy. *Journal of Behavior Therapy and Experimental Psychiatry, 1,* 279–289. Copyright 1970. Pergamon Press, Ltd. Reprinted with permission of the *Journal of Behavior Therapy and Experimental Psychiatry.*

Figure 12.3 Child Community Behavior Checklist

The following checklist allows you to describe your child's problems in various situations outside the house. The situations are listed in the column at left and common problem behaviors are listed in the row at the top. Examine each situation in the column and decide if one or more of the problem behaviors in the row fits your child. Check those that fit the best—if any.

	Always has to be told	Doesn't pay attention	Forgets	Dawdles	Refuses	Argues	Complains	Demands	Fights	Is selfish	Destroys toys or property	Steals	Lies	Curses	Whines	Hangs on or stays close to adult	Acts silly	Mopes around	Stays alone	Has to keep things in order	Sexual play
In own yard																					
In neighbor's yard or home																					
In stores																					
Public Park																					
Downtown in general																					
Church or Sunday school																					
Community swimming pool																					
In family car																					

Source: R. G. Wahler & W. H. Cormier. The ecological interview: A first step in outpatient therapy. *Journal of Behavior Therapy and Experimental Psychiatry, 1,* 279–289. Copyright 1970. Pergamon Press, Ltd. Reprinted with permission

Thus, collaboration with other professionals is an important part of your role, and you should learn to function as a team member. Obviously, both you and your students will experience greater support if the professionals and agencies with whom you collaborate render high-quality service. Maintain a list of agencies and persons who have proven their worth to you and to your students. This list should include a variety of human service agencies to allow maximum flexibility in wraparound planning. For example, your local Agricultural Extension Office may employ a home economist or family nutritionist who can consult with families and help with such diverse problems as budgeting income or providing a diet that meets basic nutrutional requirements. In several instances we have collaborated with field nursing services on such problems as hygiene, diet, and general health care. Recreational therapists can help children gain access to camping programs and after-school and recreational activities.

Even sparsely populated areas may be served by a variety of such professionals, and you may begin to develop a community resource guide by contacting your county courthouse or your state's department of human services to find out what services are locally available.[3] As suggested in the previous chapter, whenever you work with other

---

[3] Trained volunteers are used extensively in the system of care developed in Alaska (the Alaska Youth Initiative). See Burchard, Burchard, Sewell, and VanDenBerg (1993).

Figure 12.4   Child School Behavior Checklist

The following checklist allows you to describe your student's problems in various situations. The situations are listed in the column at left and common problem behaviors are listed in the row at the top. Examine *each* situation in the column and decide if one or more of the problem behaviors in the row fits your student. Check those that fit the best—if any.

	Out of seat	Talks to others	Always has to be told	Doesn't pay attention	Forgets	Dawdles	Refuses	Argues	Complains	Demands	Fights	Is Selfish	Destroys toys or property	Steals	Lies	Cries	Whines	Hangs on or stays close to adult	Acts silly	Mopes around	Stays alone	Has to keep things in order	Sexual play
Morning: Teacher explains lesson																							
Teacher discusses with group																							
Silent work time																							
Cooperative work with other students																							
Oral reading or class presentation																							
Line up for lunch or recess																							
Hall																							
Playground																							
Lunch																							
Afternoon: Teacher explains lesson																							
Teacher discusses with group																							
Silent work time																							
Cooperative with other students																							
Oral reading or class presentation																							
Line up for recess or dismissal																							
Hall																							
Playground																							

Source: R. G. Wahler & W. H. Cormier. The ecological interview: A first step in outpatient therapy. *Journal of Behavior Therapy and Experimental Psychiatry, 1,* 279–289. Copyright 1970. Pergamon Press, Ltd. Reprinted with permission of the *Journal of Behavior Therapy and Experimental Psychiatry.*

professionals and parents, you should communicate your goals and objectives clearly.

Formal training and technical assistance in the wraparound process are beginning to emerge (Eber, 1994; Eber, Nelson, & Miles, 1997; Eber, Osuch, & Redditt, 1996), as is training in the development of systems of care (for information, contact the CASSP Technical Assistance Center, Georgetown University Child Development Center, 2233 Wisconsin Avenue, N. W., Suite 1204, Washington, DC 20007). Seek out such training and encourage others in the school community to do so as well. As the integration of services becomes more prevalent for children and youth with emotional and behavioral problems, educators will need to expand their information and skills in such areas as managed care (Malloy, 1995), child and family resources, and the effective use of human services in communities.

If you do not have the support of a building- or community-based interagency team and lack the opportunity to team informally with other providers, you may find yourself facing one of the most difficult solutions to the problem of being overwhelmed or overextended: saying no. If you or your school board have carefully defined and explained the limits of your services to your clientele initially, this should not alarm you. Nevertheless, there are tactful ways of saying no, and there are ways that reinforce people coming to you without building up false hopes that you will solve all their problems. Ideally, when you must say no, you will be able to refer the person or family to an appropriate service.

Advocacy   In your role as an advocate for students exhibiting problem behavior, you undoubtedly will find many shortcomings in the systems that serve them. These may include gaps in special educational provisions, or the lack of needed related services. When confronted by these problems, you have two choices: to campaign for the services your pupils require or to make do with what you have. The first option poses several questions: What educational or related services are most critical? Is the school or another agency responsible for providing these? What are the consequences to you of advocating for these services?

Figure 12.5 presents the service continuum originally described in Chapter 1, but here we have indicated for each level whether related services are likely to be needed, as well as which agency probably will have primary administrative responsibility for the educational program. These are important considerations because IDEA obligates the agency responsible for each pupil's educational program to provide a free and appropriate educational program in the least restrictive environment. In addition, the agency must obtain the necessary related services, which include "transportation and such developmental, corrective, and other supportive services as may be required to assist a handicapped child to benefit from special education" (*Federal Register,* 1977, p. 42479).

Guthrie (1993) offered guidelines for determining whether related services are needed to accomplish the goals and objectives specified on a student's IEP. These are reproduced in Figure 12.6. In determining the need for related services, be aware that additional educational and related services cost money, and traditionally IDEA's mandate has been interpreted as requiring the education agency (e.g., local school district) to be accountable for these services.[4] In the absence of specific interagency agreements, your school district may be responsible for providing or funding related services included on the IEP. If this is the case, we suggest that you advocate for an interagency planning group in your community to deal with the complex issues of multiagency services. (Alternately, you may contact the Federation of Families for Children's Mental Health, 1021 Prince St., Alexandria, VA 22314–2971, which may have an active chapter in your state, for suggestions regarding how parents can facilitate the development of appropriate related services.)

---

[4]The process of implementing a system of care typically involves planning how costs and resources are to be shared among agencies. Interagency memoranda of agreement are the vehicles used to establish fiscal and programmatic responsibility (see Skiba & Polsgrove, 1996).

Figure 12.5 Continuum of Services for Children and Youth with EBD

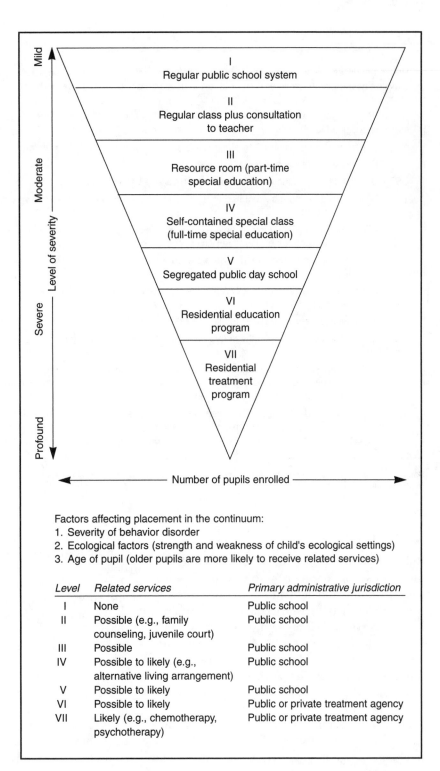

Level of severity

Mild
Moderate
Severe
Profound

I
Regular public school system

II
Regular class plus consultation
to teacher

III
Resource room (part-time
special education)

IV
Self-contained special class
(full-time special education)

V
Segregated public day school

VI
Residential education
program

VII
Residential
treatment
program

◄——————— Number of pupils enrolled ———————►

Factors affecting placement in the continuum:
1. Severity of behavior disorder
2. Ecological factors (strength and weakness of child's ecological settings)
3. Age of pupil (older pupils are more likely to receive related services)

Level	Related services	Primary administrative jurisdiction
I	None	Public school
II	Possible (e.g., family counseling, juvenile court)	Public school
III	Possible	Public school
IV	Possible to likely (e.g., alternative living arrangement)	Public school
V	Possible to likely	Public school
VI	Possible to likely	Public or private treatment agency
VII	Likely (e.g., chemotherapy, psychotherapy)	Public or private treatment agency

Figure 12.6   Child Study Team Determination of a Related Service

Related services are supplemental, corrective, developmental, or therapeutic resources other than basic educational services needed by the child or youth with an educational disability in order for the child to benefit from, participate in, or be provided specially designed instruction.

After IEP goals, objectives and implementers and services are identified, CST members discuss the objectives and services designed for the child or youth and decide whether:

a.   Specially designed instruction alone will facilitate mastery of the IEP goals and objectives

b.   Related services are needed.

CST members determine the need for any related service based on answers to the following questions:

1.   Will the child or youth be required to receive an education in a more restrictive environment if the related service is not provided?

2.   Will personnel assigned to any objective be unable to implement strategies and activities leading to mastery of the objective without the related service?

3.   Does the related service need to be provided within school facilities and during school hours in order for the child or youth to benefit from specially designed instruction?

4.   Does the related service directly affect the acquisition of skills or information identified as a goal or outcome of public education for all children?

5.   Is the related service required to allow the child or youth access to a public school program?

If the CST answers **yes** to **any** of these five questions, the need is a related service, and that service is included on the IEP.

If the CST answers **no** to **all** of these five questions or finds that the service requires provision by a licensed physician, the service being considered is determined to be solely for medical, health, or asthetic reasons. This service cannot be a related service and is not included on the IEP.

If a related service is identified, the CST members check the appropriate box on the IEP. Then the service is identified by type and nature (e.g., health services, catheterization; special transportation, bus with lift; physical therapy, strengthening exercise) and such a statement is written in the comments section on the Conference Summary Report.

Source: Adapted from P. Guthrie (1993). *ARC determination of a related services.* Bowling Green KY: Warren County Public Schools. Reprinted with permission of the author.

Role Constraints

Role constraints apply to those required interventions not suited for a person in your professional role, meaning the limitations in this category overlap considerably with ecological constraints. Related services such as psychotherapy or family counseling fit this category. Although you may feel qualified to provide informal counseling and the service you provide may be effective, you may not possess the professional authority (credentials or training) to render the service.

Another constraint exists if you are working in a day treatment or residential setting where the treatment program is prescribed and supervised by another professional. For example, a pupil may be institutionalized for treatment of a severe behavior disorder or delinquency. In such a case, the treatment program probably will be developed and supervised by a psychologist or correctional worker, and the education program will be part of the total treatment package. In these situations, you may not be free to make unilateral treatment decisions or to implement programs that affect the student outside the school program.

Failure to recognize role constraints can result in wasteful duplication of effort. This often happens with children and youth with EBD because they come to the attention of several agencies. Another undesirable consequence results in the provision of conflicting treatment programs. For example, a psychiatrist may give a pupil cathartic play therapy for aggressive behavior while you use contingency management for the same problem. If you assume too much of another professional's treatment responsibility, you may face professional sanction or at least suffer bad public relations in certain quarters. However, the most harmful consequence of overstepping role boundaries is that it erodes the effectiveness of all treatment or educational programs through professional conflict and disharmony. Students exhibiting severe behavior problems need consistency in their environment, and this is impossible when different agencies or professionals pull in different directions or haggle with each other over territorial issues.

Several of the responses to the ecological limitations we discussed in the previous section also will help you deal with role constraints. For example, you can clarify the goals and purposes of your program and concentrate on doing a credible job within your specific role. This point is well illustrated in the history of education programs for children and youth with EBD. Many early educational programs were established in residential treatment or psychiatric settings. Initially, these educational programs were regarded as little more than day care or as an adjunct to medically oriented treatment. However, such professional leaders as Bettelheim, Berkowitz, Rothman, Fenichel, Hobbs, Redl, Long, Morse, Haring, Phillips, Whelan, Wood, and Hewett have been instrumental in the development of a uniquely educational perspective and have helped establish credibility for the educator's role in treatment programs (see Kauffman, 1993; Kauffman & Lewis, 1974).

Hewett and Taylor's (1980) description of the opening of an educational program at the University of California at Los Angeles's Neuropsychiatric Institute (NPI) illustrates how educators have had to reconceptualize their role as distinct from that of other professionals. The school program originally was viewed as a babysitting service by the psychodynamically oriented staff. The teachers were not considered part of the powerful

triumvirate composed of the psychiatrist, clinical psychologist, and psychiatric social worker. In time the educational staff began to see that their low status was caused by their failure to conceptualize their role in terms of its unique contribution to the overall treatment program. The school staff then formulated their concept of an educational program in this setting in terms of teaching the skills pupils needed in order to function in less restrictive environments, making them better able to communicate with other professionals and contribute to the overall NPI program. As this example suggests, you should not try to imitate other human service providers; instead you should provide educational services that are not available through any other professional group (instruction in social and academic skills).

If you are not working within an interdisciplinary facility, such as a hospital or residential treatment center, you will need to facilitate the student and family's access to services available from other agencies or persons (the question of whether these services are considered "related" under IDEA is not at issue here; assume, for the present, that your employing agency or the child's parents will pay for the service). Figure 12.7 is a checklist you may find useful in deciding whether to go outside your program for help with specific problems or to a different treatment program (remember that all decisions to move a student toward a more restrictive environment or to alter a student's IEP must follow due process). Use Figure 12.7 in conjunction with Figures 12.2, 12.3, and 12.4 to gain a comprehensive picture of the problem, the student, and the student's ecological settings when contemplating a referral decision. (Also use Figure 12.6 to guide the ARC's decisions about the need for related services.) The questions in Figure 12.7 are intended to be illustrative rather than exhaustive. Those behaviors encompassed in the first question suggest a request for related services, whereas subsequent questions imply difficulty in reaching educational objectives with the pupil.

If your decision involves seeking assistance from other providers, the questions of whose assistance you seek and for what services depend

Figure 12.7 Checklist to Identify Need for Collaborative Assistance

	Yes	Comments
1. Does the following apply to the pupil in any, in most, or all, of his ecological settings:		
Language disorder (echolalia, pronomial reversal, mutism, etc.)?	_____	
Self-stimulation, self-mutilation, hallucinations, catastrophic reactions?	_____	
Rumination?	_____	
Encopresis, enuresis, obsessive-compulsive behaviors (e.g., rituals, preoccupying thoughts?)	_____	
Chronic depression?	_____	
Phobias?	_____	
Generalized anxiety?	_____	
Suicidal behavior?	_____	
Sleep disorders?	_____	
Gang delinquency?	_____	
Interpersonal aggression?	_____	
Excessive masturbation?	_____	
Chemical intoxication?	_____	
Seizures?	_____	

2. Are you unable to control the consequences, or are unable to gain the cooperation of those who do control consequences affecting the pupil's target behaviors?   _____

3. Is (are) the pupil's problem behavior(s) not under the control of antecedent stimuli arranged by you?   _____

4. Does the pupil fail to respond (appropriately or inappropriately) to consequences administered by you?   _____

5. Are you unable to work with the parent?   _____

6. Are you unable to identify or control any of the pupil's reinforcers?   _____

7. Have you been ineffective in achieving meaningful gains with the pupil?   _____

Specify goals not met: _____

_____

_____

_____

_____

8. Are there other reasons why you cannot or will not work with the pupil and/or his caregivers?   _____

Note: If these problems are targeted on the student's IEP, you may be responsible as the primary treatment agent. However, you may also need to work with other agencies or professionals on these problems.

on the needs of the student (e.g., participation in an after-school therapeutic program) and the parents (e.g., respite care for their child). As indicated earlier, it is wise to maintain a log of your requests for collaborative assistance, with appropriate evaluative comments. Keep this log confidential unless there are compelling professional reasons for making portions of it public (e.g., being subpoenaed in litigation against a professional who has worked with some of your pupils).

Fortunately, as stressed throughout this text, the notion of education as a treatment agency operating in isolation is giving way to the concept of a system of care, in which education works collaboratively with other agencies and families to help students access a full range of services that meet their needs. Edgar and Siegel (1995) propose

> an adequately funded comprehensive social services system for all those with special needs (i.e., persons with disabilities, teen parents, drug-involved youth, sexual minority youth, adjudicated youth, youth in group and foster homes, dropouts, low-income youth, homeless youth, and newcomers) that asks a simple and direct question: Does the individual need services? If the answer is yes, the services (based on an empowerment dynamic, meaning that the recipient's needs will diminish over time) are provided, and no further questions need be asked. (p. 279)

Edgar and Siegel also argue that the role of education should be to prepare youth for a place in society, which includes helping them to cope with the inequities of our culture; collaborate with other agencies; provide a range of services and options; and advocate for change outside the education arena. They observe that educators should recognize that 25 to 30 percent of U. S. citizens are disenfranchised by poverty and lack of opportunity and that we cannot pretend to serve children if we remain silent on the issue of change.

Legal Constraints

Constraints on the Role of Teachers Today's newspapers contain numerous stories involving allegations of improper and illegal conduct by educators. The long-standing common law doctrine of *in-loco parentis,* giving teachers authority equivalent to that of parents, has been increasingly tested in the courts. As a teacher, you may be liable for injury sustained by a pupil as a result of negligence on your part or for defamatory material regarding students or fellow employees (contributory negligence must be ruled out in the case of older or more mature students). You or your agency also may be liable for negligence in depriving a student of appropriate treatment or due process (Weintraub & McCaffrey, 1976).

The Council for Exceptional Children (CEC) has developed a code of ethics and professional standards to guide practitioners and define their professional responsibilities (CEC Delegate Assembly, 1983). The introduction to these guidelines states that "special education professionals charge themselves with obligations to three parties: the exceptional student, the employer, and the profession" (p. 8). The CEC Code of Ethics consists of eight principles that form the basis for professional conduct.

I. Special education professionals are committed to developing the highest educational and quality of life potential of exceptional individuals.

II. Special education professionals promote and maintain a high level of competence and integrity in practicing their profession.

III. Special education professionals engage in professional activities which benefit exceptional individuals, their families, other colleagues, students, or research subjects.

IV. Special education professionals exercise objective professional judgment in the practice of their profession.

V. Special education professionals strive to advance their knowledge and skills regarding the education of exceptional individuals.

VI. Special education professionals work within the standards and policies of their profession.

VII. Special education professionals seek to uphold and improve where necessary the laws, regulations, and policies governing the delivery of special education and related services and the practice of their profession.

VIII.   Special education professionals do not condone or participate in unethical or illegal acts, nor violate professional standards adopted by the Delegate Assembly of CEC.

The professional standards derived from these principles are grouped into three categories: professionals in relation to exceptional persons and their families, professional employment, and professionals in relation to the profession and to other professionals. It is important to become familiar with these standards because they will affect your professional obligations and influence critical decisions. To obtain a free copy of the reprint entitled "Special Education and Professional Standards" (*Exceptional Children,* November 1983), Publications Sales, The Council for Exceptional Children, 1920 Association Drive, Reston, VA 22091.

As you study these standards, you will see the potential for conflict with your employing agency. Thus, in following them you may be on sensitive ground. In general, teachers' rights as private citizens (freedom of speech, right to action, right to due process) have been upheld by the courts. The chief reasons for the dismissal of a teacher have included insubordination, incompetence, neglect of duty, inappropriate conduct, subversive activity, or decreased need for the person's services (Weintraub & McCaffrey, 1976). If your behavior with respect to the above principles causes your employer to level charges against you, be prepared to seek legal counsel. You also may be named in a suit brought by a child's caregivers for failing to act in accordance with these principles. It is difficult to advocate for children while simultaneously maintaining allegiance to your employing agency.

Public Law 94–142 and its subsequent amendments address constraints on agencies providing educational services in that they declare and protect the civil rights of students with disabilities. The law guarantees these students the right to treatment, which encompasses procedural and substantive due process and equal protection, the right to equal educational opportunity, the right of access

to their records, and the right to an individualized education. In addition, the following provisions must be guaranteed by each state in their annual program plans (Thomas, 1979):

1. Extensive child-find or child identification procedures. (The first priority is to identify children who are not receiving any type of education. The second priority is to identify those who are receiving an inadequate education).
2. A full service goal and detailed timetable designed for the education of each child.
3. A guarantee of complete due process procedures.
4. The assurance of regular parent or guardian consultation.
5. Maintenance of programs and procedures for comprehensive personnel development, including inservice training.
6. Assurance of special education being provided to all children with disabilities in the least restrictive environment.
7. Assurance of nondiscriminatory testing and evaluation.
8. A guarantee of policies and procedures to protect the confidentiality of data and information.
9. Assurance of the maintenance of an individual program for all children with disabilities.
10. Assurance of an effective policy guaranteeing the right of all students with disabilities to a public education, at no cost to parents or guardians.
11. Assurance of a surrogate to act for any child when parents or guardians are either unknown or unavailable, or when the child is a ward of the state. (p. 10)

Your state department and employing agency are accountable for the implementation of policies, procedures, and safeguards. You are accountable for providing specific educational services in accordance with these guidelines. In the event that caregivers bring suit for failure to meet these provisions, you may be named as codefendant. If your professional behavior can be construed as negligent or unethical, you may be sued by the caregivers and not supported by your agency.

As a special educator, it also is necessary to have an understanding of IDEA and Section 504 of the Rehabilitation Act of 1973 (Yell, 1995). Most special education teacher preparation programs now include information concerning PL 101–476 as part of their curriculum.[5] Information regarding the legal requirements of Section 504 is offered less frequently; nevertheless, it is incumbent upon both general and special educators to know about the provisions and requirements of the latter legislation. Under Section 504, a student is considered to have a disability if he has a physical or mental impairment that substantially limits one or more major life activities, *or is regarded as having such an impairment.* Students eligible for services under Section 504 may be eligible for related services even if they do not need special education. This law provides due process and procedural requirements similar to IDEA; however, it is broader and it is administered by the U. S. Department of Education's Office of Civil Rights instead of the Office of Special Education and Rehabilitation Services (Fossey, Hosie, Soniat, & Zirkel, 1995). Consult Fossey et al. for a succinct discussion of Section 504 and its implications for educators.

Constraints on the Use of Behavioral Intervention
Legal constraints have been applied specifically to the use of aversive procedures in educational programs. (These issues were discussed at length in Chapter 4.) Although aversive procedures involve the presentation of a noxious stimulus or infringement of students' bodily or human rights, litigation generally has been restricted to corporal punishment in the form of spankings or beatings (Wood & Lakin, 1983). The school's right to use moderate corporal punishment has been upheld and is approved by most states. However, it has not been advocated in the special education literature (Wood, 1983b), and the American Federation of Teachers, the National Education Association, the

Council for Exceptional Children, and the American Psychological Association have issued statements opposing it (Wood, 1983a).

The use of seclusion timeout also has been argued in the courts, although until recently, litigation has involved mental health facilities rather than public schools (Gast & Nelson, 1977; Wood & Lakin, 1983). As indicated previously, a growing number of states and school districts are issuing policies regulating the use of behavioral interventions, particularly those involving restrictive or intrusive procedures.

Solutions to the problems posed by legal constraints are easier to suggest than to implement. With respect to your professional conduct, we suggest that you clarify your role and specific responsibilities and stay within them. By all means, follow the Code of Ethics and Professional Standards adopted by CEC (1983), but in so doing, make it clear that your goal is to improve pupil services, not to subvert the system or its administrators. Also carefully study IDEA, Section 504, and, particularly if you are working in settings that involve the employment of persons with disabilities, the Americans with Disabilities Act.

Guidelines for the use of aversive procedures are provided in Chapter 4, but here we emphasize that punishment is justified when the behavior it suppresses is more injurious to the individual or to others than the punishment itself and when no alternative exists (Wood, 1983b). Do not use corporal punishment; it is too subjective and is likely to have a long history of misapplication with your students. Instead, apply planned, objective, and systematic procedures such as extinction, verbal reprimands, response cost, or timeout in conjunction with positive reinforcement of incompatible behavior. If you must use a more extreme technique (overcorrection, aversive physical stimulation), see Wood's (1983b) suggestions:

1. All reasonable alternatives should be considered, if not tried, first. This consideration should be documented.

---

[5]Several excellent books are available on special education law. See, for example, Weber (1992).

2. Do not apply punishment of any type without first becoming thoroughly familiar with your state and local regulations.
3. The lines of authority for the punishment procedure should be clear.
4. Punishment should be adequately supervised, monitored, and externally reviewed.
5. All persons using punishment should understand its dynamics and complexities.

In addition, remember that prior parental consent to use punishment in an educational program is required by IDEA, and parents have the right to withdraw consent at any time.

INTERACTIVE TEAMING

Chapter 11 indicated that approaches based on school staff collaborations show great promise for delivering effective interventions for students who exhibit significant problem behavior. In this and previous chapters, we argued for a wraparound approach to service planning and delivery for students who present significant behavioral and emotional challenges to educators and other service providers. Interactive teaming (Thomas, Correa, & Morsink, 1995) is a process that structures the coordination of decision making among professionals who engage in collaborative planning and decision making on behalf of children and their families. An interactive teaming model is a new concept based on equal partnerships and shared decision making. Figure 12.8 illustrates the differences between the present system of serving students with special needs and this new model.

In a relatively short period of time, much has been learned about effective teamwork in educational decision making. Teaming greatly increases the ability to implement sound interventions on behalf of students and their families while at the same time providing support and technical assistance to teachers.

Team membership should be based on who can help meet the student's needs rather than on who occupies roles traditionally associated with decision making for students (e.g., building principal, guidance counselor, school psychologist). It is important to realize that merely requiring that persons function as members of teams will not ensure their effectiveness. In order for teams to be successful, ongoing, accountable training and technical assistance are required. Figure 12.9 contrasts the characteristics of effective and ineffective teams. Phillips and McCullough (1992) have developed an inservice curriculum for preparing both staff and parents to work as effective student/staff support teams. Thomas et al. (1995) provided thoughtful guidance for team development. Use these resources to increase the ability of school staff to form and maintain effective teams with parents and other providers on behalf of children and youth with emotional and behavioral needs. Recognize that teaming not only supports children and families, but also the professionals who work with them daily. Therefore, the presence of interactive teams in schools is an important benefit to you and your colleagues, and we strongly encourage you to seek training in this area and to take a leadership role in the formation of such teams.

STRESS AND BURNOUT

The many potential hazards of special education professional practice lay the groundwork for stress and burnout. Attrition among teachers of students with EBD is a major problem in the field. For example, Wrobel (1993) reports that 1,355 licensed EBD teachers in Minnesota chose not to work in programs for this population, despite 303 position vacancies. Burnout has been defined as "emotional exhaustion resulting from the stress of interpersonal contact" (Maslach, 1978, p. 56). How well you are able to maintain a healthy perspective of your job and your pupils in the face of stress depends on a number of factors. Researchers are just beginning to study and delineate these variables for educators working with children and youth with EBD. However, because a person's emotional reactions to job stresses are subjective and highly individualized, it is difficult to obtain reliable, objective data on the subject.

Figure 12.8　Contrasts between the current system and the proposed model for interactive teaming

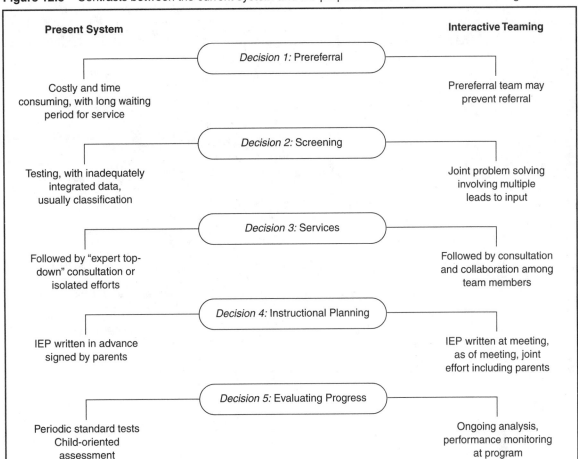

Present System　　　　　　　　　　　　　　　　　　　　　**Interactive Teaming**

Decision 1: Prereferral

Costly and time consuming, with long waiting period for service

Prereferral team may prevent referral

Decision 2: Screening

Testing, with inadequately integrated data, usually classification

Joint problem solving involving multiple leads to input

Decision 3: Services

Followed by "expert top-down" consultation or isolated efforts

Followed by consultation and collaboration among team members

Decision 4: Instructional Planning

IEP written in advance signed by parents

IEP written at meeting, as of meeting, joint effort including parents

Decision 5: Evaluating Progress

Periodic standard tests Child-oriented assessment

Ongoing analysis, performance monitoring at program

Source: Thomas, C. C., Correa, V. I., & Morsink, C. V. (1995). *Interactive teaming: Consultation and collaboration in special programs.* (2nd ed.). Copyright Prentice Hall. Used with permission.

Causes and Effects of Stress

Since stress is an integral part of working with pupils who exhibit behavioral disorders, be aware of other variables that can be emotionally and physically draining, for these may influence your decision to accept a job, change your place of employment, or leave the field entirely. Pullis (1992) administered a questionnaire to 244 teachers of students with EBD. His instrument, the Pullis Inventory of Teacher Stress (PITS), has three parts. Part I includes 29 items related to working conditions for teachers, including items

addressing pupil characteristics, workload issues, career issues, and school factors. Interestingly, the teachers rated school or setting factors, such as inadequate school discipline policy, attitudes and behavior of administrators, evaluation by administrators/supervisors, attitudes and behavior of other teachers/professionals, and too much work to do, as more stressful than pupil characteristics. Pullis observed that these results supported those of Schmid, Schatz, Walter, Shidla, Leone, and Trickett (1990), in that teachers reported feeling greater emotional exhaustion

Figure 12.9   Charicteristics of effective and ineffective teams

AN EFFECTIVE TEAM	AN INEFFECTIVE TEAM
A team is a unified group of people who join in a cooperative problem-solving process to reach a shared goal.	◆ Goals are unclear. ◆ Members are unprepared. ◆ Leadership is poor. ◆ Commitment to task is lacking.
EFFECTIVE	**INEFFECTIVE**
Participation and leadership are distributed among all members.	Participation is unequal, leadership is delegated and based on authority.
Goals are cooperatively formed to meet individual and group needs.	Members accept imposed goals.
Ability and information determine influence and power.	Position determines influence; obedience to authority is stressed.
Two-way communication.	Communication about ideas is one-way; feelings are ignored.
Decision-making steps are matched with situation: consensus is sought for important decisions.	Decisions are made by highest authority with minimal member involvement.
Conflict is brought out and resolved.	Conflict is ignored, avoided, or denied.

Source: Reprinted with permission from the publisher. Anderlini, L. S. (1983). An in-service program for improving team participation in educational decision-making. *School Psychology Review. 12,* 163.

and emotional distancing when they saw their program as not having adequate resources or support.

Part 2 of the PITS contains 18 items that evaluate the effects of stress. Pullis (1992) reported that his sample of teachers most frequently experienced exhaustion, frustration, feeling overwhelmed, carryover to outside life, guilt, and irritability. These effects were similar to those reported by learning disabilities resource teachers in an earlier study (Pullis, 1983), except that teachers of students with EBD reported carryover to life outside of school.

The causes of stress among teachers of students with behavioral challenges reflect conditions that occur frequently in their workplaces.

Trying to deal with the educational system; spending hours working outside the classroom; encountering nonsupportive school administrators and staff; and negative attitudes by professional colleagues can leave you feeling tired and defeated. What can you do? The first step is to recognize the symptoms of stress. Weiskopf (1980) described a continuum of signs of potential teacher stress. Initially, you may experience a vague feeling of personal distress, followed by irritability, fatigue, boredom, mild depression, or feelings of being overworked. These initial symptoms may be so subtle that you fail to notice them. Unless conditions improve, you may later find yourself increasingly resistant to change and less flexible, and you may tend to withdraw from social contact. Others may observe that you are becoming less effective. You may adhere rigidly to routines and rely excessively on manipulative controls to defend yourself from continued emotional stress. The later stages of burnout may involve more serious symptoms such as alcohol and drug abuse, marital conflict, absenteeism, chronic depression, and even mental illness. However, Weiskopf (1980) observes that these symptoms may be related to other personal problems and that precise data on burnout are not available. Therefore, do not expect to see all of these signs or to see them appear in this particular pattern. If you find yourself extremely dissatisfied with your work, find frequent reasons to be absent, or are unable to psychologically get away from your students' problems, you should do something about these signs.

Coping with Stress

Part 3 of the PITS consists of 15 strategies for coping with stress. Respondents to Pullis's (1992) study rated activities in the workplace (e.g., time management and discussions with colleagues), in addition to strategies used away from work (e.g., hobbies, nutrition, and exercise) as most effective. Interactions with other special education professionals was mentioned specifically as a factor contributing to job satisfaction. Respondents also indicated a desire for more courses and workshops to improve or update their skills. Unfortunately, substantial numbers of teachers reported using strategies that are not healthy coping mechanisms, including smoking, taking alcohol, drugs, or prescription medication, and excessive eating.

Many of the variables that should be changed to reduce stress are controlled by your employing agency, not by you. For example, Zabel and Zabel (1980) indicated that the probability of burnout may be reduced by lowering student-teacher ratio, reducing working hours, providing opportunities for time away from the job, sharing student loads through team teaching, and training in dealing with stress. All of these tactics require organizational change, which involves policy decisions at higher administrative levels. Wrobel

(1993) indicated that an important addition to the curriculum for teachers of children with EBD consists of skills in working effectively with the school administration.

Evidence that organizational variables affect teacher stress was provided by Bensky et al. (1980). One hundred fourteen teachers responded to a questionnaire evaluating stress and variables related to it. Those who had a clear perception of their jobs' expectations were under less stress. Also, teachers reported less stress if they perceived their school system as clearly either in compliance or not in compliance with IDEA. When they saw their school system as marginally in compliance, they reported greater stress. Apparently greater role clarity existed among these teachers when their district's status regarding the law was less ambiguous.

Although you can little effect such organizational changes as compliance with IDEA, reducing working hours, or training in stress management, you may be able to reduce the amount of stress that you experience personally. Weiskopf (1980) gave several suggestions:

1. Know in advance what the job requires in terms of emotional demands.
2. Set realistic goals for yourself and for your students.
3. Delegate routine work, such as paperwork, to aides or volunteers.
4. Avoid becoming isolated from other staff members.
5. Break up the amount of direct contact you have with students through team teaching, the use of learning centers, and so forth.
6. Remain intellectually active off the job.
7. Get physical exercise.
8. Interject newness and variety into your day to counterbalance routine.
9. Participate in hobbies and activities not related to your job.

However, keep in mind that there is no valid evidence that these methods reduce burnout (Weiskopf, 1980). The best deterrents are adequate professional and personal support and reinforcement. As Pullis (1992) observed, collaboration and communication skills are essential for teachers of students with EBD. Interactions with other professionals working with these students and their families through interactive teaming are as important for the support provided to you as they are for that given to the student. Eber et al. (1997) emphasized that a strength of the wraparound approach is the support it offers to teachers as well as to pupils and families. Wraparound planning also provides ongoing technical assistance, which leads to the development of new professional competencies and honing of existing skills. The potential of emerging distance communication and adult learning methodologies is just beginning to be appreciated as a strategy for providing resource support and technical assistance. As information technology improves, increasing access to and sharing of information, including linkages to other professionals, training programs, and resources will be possible, even for professionals working in relative geographic isolation.

It is true that while the skills needed to be effective with pupils who exhibit emotional and behavioral challenges can be learned, not everyone is cut out for this work. Effective teachers who remain in the field share a commitment to their students, and this is one of their major sources of satisfaction. Wood (1995) interviewed teachers about their profession. A few of their representative comments help to put our work in perspective:

"Most of my satisfaction comes from the kids— seeing them feel as if they belong, seeing them feel good doing something. I also love the freedom to try new, different things, figuring out how to do whatever it takes [to help someone learn]. Also I'm not stuck teaching boring subjects. My role affords me the opportunity to have fun and be a little bizarre myself from time to time."

"If you don't like these kinds of kids, then don't even consider teaching students with EBD. You'll know pretty quick if you like it. If you have a negative attitude about these kids, then forget it."

"They can drive you nuts, but they're never dull" (pp. 13–14).

As we have tried to demonstrate throughout this text, and especially in this chapter, working with problem students, their families, and their communities is difficult. Remaining psychologically fit and professionally effective requires that you know your role and its limitations. This is not sufficient, however. To be a successful educator who works with pupils with challenging behavior, regardless of whether they have been formally identified as having EBD, you also must be highly skilled. We hope this text has helped you acquire the skills you need to feel, and be, effective.

SUMMARY

The complexity and intensity of working with students exhibiting behavioral problems require high levels of dedication and expertise by professional educators. To function effectively, these persons need adequate support systems in their working and personal environments; they also must also recognize and work within the limitations of their roles. Optimal programming for children and youth with EBD should address their needs and the needs of other persons who care for and work with them across many different ecological settings. Our culture's practice of institutionalizing human services according to specific settings and agencies constrains those who must work within formal professional roles. This chapter has described some of these constraints and has suggested guidelines and strategies for working more effectively within them. Ultimately, the success of interventions on behalf of students with behavioral disorders will depend upon our ability to bridge professional and political boundaries. Our responsibility is to design strategies for students that provide meaningful habilitative or rehabilitative experiences to ensure the skills acquired in educational settings are retained and used to facilitate lifelong patterns of success.

CHRIS

Based on reports by Tina Harmon, Wraparound Facilitator LaGrange Area Department of Special Education, LaGrange, IL

The school-based portion[1] of the wraparound plan developed for Chris is presented in Figure 12.10. The form is designed to formalize a general plan; as in the case of IEPs, the specific implementation steps are designed by the providers who are responsible for each strategy. As Chris's wraparound facilitator, it was my job to contact the key stakeholders involved in planning for Chris, who are listed in Figure 12.11 (note that Chris also was included on the team).

The team met six times during the academic year to review Chris's progress and make adjustments in the plan.[2] The general format for each meeting is similar. First, the participants identify themselves in terms of their role and relationship to the student. Next, the facilitator describes the expectations for the products and outcomes to be developed in the meeting. Then the team discusses the strengths of team members and the resources available through them. We have found that beginning the planning discussion with a description of strengths leads to a more positive approach than when the conversation begins with a recitation of deficits (particularly the student's) and is more favorably received by stakeholders. It also provides a natural transition to the next step, goal setting and needs identification. This process involves first listing the performance levels of a "typical" student (not a "model" pupil) in the same settings as the target student. Then goals are set based on these performance levels, and stakeholders are asked to suggest specific strategies that should be developed to bring the student's functioning level to that defined for the typical student. Thus, the needs column of Chris's wraparound plan describes what the team must do to ensure that desired outcomes are achieved. These needs are then prioritized in terms of which should be addressed first. We limit the number of prioritized needs to no more than five per meeting to ensure that team planning will be in depth. Note that the first need identified for Chris's plan was for coordination among the team, and the desired outcome was consistent communication between home and school.

The next step is team brainstorming to generate strategies for meeting each prioritized need to be addressed. Using a flip chart, the facilitator then asks individual team members to commit to specific strategies. After these roles have been identified, a communication plan is developed so that team members will communicate regularly. The facilitator commits to contacting stakeholders regarding the student's progress. Finally, the team discusses their reactions to the team process and the plan, in terms of whether the meeting was productive and whether they feel the plan will be helpful. A follow-up meeting is scheduled within the next five weeks and procedures for calling an emergency meeting are identified.

At Chris's initial team meeting some of the participants found it difficult to identify any strengths. They insisted that he was "manipulative" and had a strong "need for control." My role in the iscussion was to help stakeholders reframe these characteristics as strengths. For example, we reframed his manipulativeness

---

Reprinted with permission from the author.

[1] Chris and his family had been nominated, and accepted, for integrated community-based wraparound services. His total wraparound plan addressed several life domains, including family, social, emotional/psychological, and legal, as well as educational. The school-based plan described here represent the wraparound goals, strengths, strategies, and needs for the educational domain. Space limitations do not permit an illustration of tina integration of Chris's school-based plan with those for other domains. However, wraparound plans must be integrated across domains, and this certainly was the case for Chris.

[2] Subsequent team meetings were attended by core team members, as well as other persons involved in implementation procedures. However, I made sure that all initial team members received updated plans.

(continued)

Figure 12.10   School-Based Wraparound Plan

Meeting Date _9/18/98_

Next Review _10/24/98_

Time _3:45 PM_

Student _Chris K._   Domain to Be Addressed _Education_

School Contact Person/Current Placement Contact Person _M. Annis_

LADSE Contact Person _Tina Harmon_

Desired Outcome	Strength	Need	Strategy: By Whom/When?
Consistent communication between home/school	Ms. K. very interested in Chris's school performance; wants to cooperate Ms. Annis willing to work with Chris in her class with help of the team	The team on the same wavelength —all team members informed —all team members current —messages received as intended —give definition of target behavior to all school personnel	—Tina will write up plan, share with all for input —team will informally check in daily to keep updated —Tina will circulate definitions of compliance, hands to self —Chris will give his moma note from Ms. Annis, summarizing her and Chris's evaluation of his performance each day
Chris will monitor himself re: compliance, aggression	Honest in reporting about self Great memory for details Responsible when he has a voice	Self-charting graph —prompt to self-evaluate —ensure accuracy —reinforce honest evaluations, even if negative behavior has occurred	—Tina and Ms. Annis will develop monitoring and checklist —Ms. Annis and Chris will evaluate independently each hour —compare evaluations every hour at first, less often if accurate (=/− one agreement) for 3 days
—Increase in compliance —Reduction in aggression, office referrals	Chris wants to improve, be part of the group Principal agreed not to use in-school suspension, will implement time-out for aggression in her office	Daily criteria for compliance 0 instances of aggression Peer buddy	Chris and Ms. Annis will take baseline on compliance for 3 days, negotiate criterion for acceptable daily performance, agree on reward if criterion is met Ms. Annis will tap her temple as a reminder to "stop, think, and act" Chris and Ms. Annis will recruit a peer buddy to hang with him during recess, lunch and bus waiting period; buddy will coach Chris in appropriate play and interaction skills

(continued)

Figure 12.10 *(continued)*

Same as above	Chris is willing to take his medicine; goes to nurse's office voluntarily	Nurse present when Chris comes to take his medicine Coordination of self-monitoring with pediatrician to evaluate continuing need for medicine	Chris will go to nurse's office each day at 12:30 (after lunch); Ms. Utley will have his pill ready Ms. C. will check with nurse weekly and will call Dr. McDowell's office every other week to report on Chris's performance Dr. McDowell will adjust dosage pending results of evaluations by Ms. Annis and Ms. Utley

as an indication of his social intelligence, and his need for control as evidence of leadership skills. This reframing helped us to generate acceptable strategies that took advantage of these strengths. Specifically, we put Chris in charge of monitoring his progress through a self-evaluation chart, and we established a contingency in which his teacher allowed him to have progressively more voice and choice in his daily school activities as he exhibited better self-control. His mother used a similar approach to establish a set of daily and weekly expectations, allowing Chris greater freedom and control in exchange for meeting these contingencies. Tommy, another sixth-grade student who is well-liked and respected by his classmates, agreed to serve as a peer buddy and to coach Chris regarding his interactions with peers during unstructured times.

Chris made steady progress throughout the school year. He enjoyed using the self-monitoring chart and became very accurate in evaluating his behavior. His teacher and his mother were pleased that he could be counted on to take responsibility for his own behavior, was able to accept responsibility for his actions, and was much more cooperative in complying with school and household routines and their requests. Chris reported that he had made many new friends within his class and the school and was very proud that he was able to succeed in a regular sixth-grade class. Because Chris still displayed impulsivity, hyperactivity, and distractability, it was decided to continue his medication (reduced to two times a day) throughout the summer, and to reconvene the wraparound team at the beginning of the next school year.

(continued)

Figure 12.11 Wraparound Confidentiality and Attendance Form

Date: __9/18/98__

I agree to honor the rights of privacy of any persons discussed in the wraparound meeting. I agree not to divulge any information regarding any family, person, or agency that may be referred to in the course of the meeting.

Name: (please print)	Role
Charlotte Orr	LADSE
Thelma Conroy	Monroe School Social Worker
Donna Jansen	District 181 Nurse
Mary Annis	Madison Grade 6 Teacher
LuAnn K.	Mom
Chris K.	Student
Albert Wooden	LADSE Psychologist
Julie Utley	Monroe Resource Teacher
MaryAnn McFadden	Monroe Principal
Annie Kringle	Teacher Consultant
Tina Harmon	LADSE Wraparound Facilitator

Crisis plan

Reschedule next meeting if a need is noted.
Per school plan—contact Tina at LADSE
Julie will intervene with safe physical management in case of physical aggression

Follow-up comments

Doing well at lunch; some problems at morning recess 9/26
Continue Chris's involvement in wraparound meetings

DISCUSSION QUESTIONS

1. What are the constraints that affect educators working in each of the following roles: special education resource teacher, special education self-contained classroom teacher, school psychologist, school social worker?

2. As a special education teacher, how would you deal with the problem of a regular classroom teacher who uses corporal punishment with one of your students?

3. How would you respond to parents who request your help in managing their child's behavior outside of school? (The student is being seen by a psychologist in private practice.)

4. The principal of your school wants to refer one of your pupils to a residential treatment program. You disagree with this action, but the principal insists. What should you do?

5. A psychiatrist has prescribed an antipsychotic drug for a pupil with EBD in your school. You have observed that the student is lethargic, withdrawn, and experiencing trouble concentrating. The parent, however, is pleased with the child's improved behavior at home and will not consider asking the psychiatrist to adjust the dosage. What course of action will you take?

6. You have been asked to participate in designing a study of burnout in your school district. How would you assess staff to identify signs of stress and burnout? What recommendations could you offer to reduce or prevent it?

REFERENCES

Anderlini, L. S. (1983). An inservice program for improving team participation in educational decision-making. *School Psychology Review, 12,* 160–167.

Bensky, J. M., Shaw, S. F., Gouse, A. S., Bates, H., Dixon, B., & Beane, W. E. (1980). Public Law 94–142 and stress: A problem for educators. *Exceptional Children, 47,* 24–29.

Bickel, W. E., & Bickel, D. D. (1986). Effective schools, classrooms, and instruction: Implications for special education. *Exceptional Children, 52,* 489–500.

Brophy, J., & Good, T. L. (1986). Teacher behavior and student achievement. In M. C. Wittrock (Ed.), *Handbook of Research on Teaching* (3rd ed.) (pp. 328–375). New York: Macmillan.

Burchard, J. D., Burchard, S. N., Sewall, R., & VanDenBerg, J. (1993). *One kid at a time: Evaluative case studies and description of the Alaska Youth Initiative demonstration project.* Department of Mental Health/Mental Retardation, State of Alaska, Center for Mental Health Services Substance Abuse and Mental Health Services Administration, U. S. Department of Health and Human Services.

Colvin, G., Kameenui, R. J., & Sugai, G. (1993). Reconceptualizing behavior management and school-wide discipline in general education. *Education and Treatment of Children, 16,* 361–381.

Council for Exceptional Children Delegate Assembly. (1983). Code of ethics and standards for professional practice. *Exceptional Children, 50,* 8–12.

Eber, L. (1996). Restructuring schools through the wraparound approach: The LADSE experience. In R. J. Illback & C. M. Nelson (Eds.). *Emerging school-based approaches for children with emotional and behavioral problems: Research and practice in service integration* (pp. 135–149). New York: Haworth Press.

Eber, L. (Fall, 1994). The wraparound approach: Toward effective school inclusion. *Claiming Children: The Nation's Mental Health Advocate for Children and Families.* Washington, DC: Federation of Families for Children's Mental Health.

Eber, L. Nelson, C. M., & Miles, P. (1997). School-based wraparound for students with emotional and behavioral challenges. *Exceptional Children, 63,* 539–555.

Eber, L., Osuch, R., & Redditt, C. A. (1996). School-based applications of the wraparound process: Early results on service provision and student outcomes. *Journal of Child and Family Studies, 5,* 83–89.

Edgar, E., & Siegel, S. (1995). Postsecondary scenarios for troubled and troubling youth. In J. M. Kauffman, J. W. Lloyd, D. P. Hallahan, & T. A. Astuto (Eds.), *Issues in educational placement: Students with emotional and behavioral disorders* (pp. 251–283). Hillsdale, NJ: Lawrence Erlbaum Associates.

Epstein, M. H., Nelson, C. M., Polsgrove, L., Coutinho, M., Cumblad, M., & Quinn, K. (1993). A comprehensive community-based approach to serving students with emotional and behavioral disorders. *Journal of Emotional and Behavioral Disorders, 1*(2), 127–135.

Federal Register (1977, Tuesday, August 23). Part II, 42 (163), 42474–42518.

Fossey, R., Hosie, T., Soniat, K., & Zirkel, P. (1995). Section 504 and "front line" educators: An expanded obligation to serve children with disabilities. *Preventing School Failure, 39*(2), 10–14.

Gast, D. L., & Nelson, C. M. (1977). Legal and ethical considerations for the use of timeout in special education settings. *Journal of Special Education, 11,* 457–467.

Gresham, F. M. (1991). Conceptualizing behavior disorders in terms of resistance to intervention. *School Psychology Review, 20,* 23–36.

Guthrie, P. (1991, November). *ARC determination of a related service.* Bowling Green, KY: Warren County Public Schools.

Hewett, F. M., & Taylor, F. D. (1980). *The emotionally disturbed child in the classroom: The orchestration of success* (2nd ed.). Boston: Allyn & Bacon.

Jones, V., & Jones, L. (1995). *Comprehensive classroom management* (4th ed). Boston: Allyn & Bacon.

Kauffman, J. M. (1993). *Characteristics of children's behavior disorders* (5th ed.). Upper Saddle River, NJ: Merrill/Prentice Hall.

Kauffman, J. M., Hallahan, D. P., Mostert, M. P., Trent, S. C. & Nuttycombe, D. G. (1993). *Managing classroom behavior: A reflective case-based approach.* Boston: Allyn & Bacon.

Kauffman, J. M., & Lewis, C. D. (Eds.). (1974). *Teaching children with behavior disorders: Personal perspectives.* Upper Saddle River, NJ: Merrill/Prentice Hall.

Malloy, M. (1995, April). *Mental illness and managed care: A primer for families and consumers.* Arlington, VA: National Alliancae for the Mentally Ill.

Maslach, C. (1978). Job burnout: How people cope. *Public Welfare, 36,* 56–58.

Phillips, V., & McCullough, L. L. (1992). *Student/staff support teams.* Longmont, CO: Sopris West.

Pullis, M. (1983). Stress as a way of life: Special challenges for the LD resource teacher. *Topics in Learning and Learning Disabilities, 3,* 24–36.

Pullis, M. (1992). An analysis of the occupational stress of teachers of the behaviorally disordered: Sources, effects, and strategies for coping. *Behavioral Disorders, 17,* 190–201.

Rivera, V. R., & Kutash, K. (1994). *Components of a system of care: What does the research say?* Tampa, FL: University of South Florida, Florida Mental Health Institute, Research and Training Center on Children's Mental Health.

Rosenshine, B., & Stevens, R. (1986). Teaching functions. In M. C. Wittrock (Ed.), *Handbook of research on teaching* (3rd ed.) (pp. 376–431). New York: Macmillan.

Schmid, K. D., Schatz, C. J., Walter, M. B., Shidla, M. C., Leone, P. E., & Trickett, E. J. (1990). Providing help: Characteristics and correlates of stress, burnout, and accomplishment across three groups of teachers. In R. B. Rutherford, Jr., & S. A. DiGangi (Eds.), *Severe behavior disorders of children and youth* (Vol. 13) (pp. 115–127). Reston, VA: Council for Children with Behavioral Disorders.

Skiba, R., & Polsgrove, L. (1996). *Developing a system of care: Interagency collaboration for students with emotional and behavioral disorders.* Reston, VA: Council for Exceptional Children.

Stroul, B. A. (1993). *Systems of care for children and adolescents with severe emotional disturbances: What are the results?* Washington, DC: CASSP Technical Assistance Center, Georgetown University Child Development Center.

Stroul, B. A., & Friedman, R. M. (1986). *A system of care for children and youth with severe emotional disturbances.* Washington, DC: Georgetown University Child Development Center, CASSP Technical Assistance Center.

Thomas, C. C. (1979). PL 94–142: An instructional module for inservice training. Frankfort, KY: Office of Education for Exceptional Children, Kentucky Department of Education.

Thomas, C. C., Correa, V. I., & Morsink, C. V. (1995). *Interactive teaming: Consultation and collaboration in special programs* (2nd ed.). Upper Saddle River, NJ: Merrill/Prentice Hall.

Wahler, R. G., & Cormier, W. H. (1970). The ecological interview: A first step in outpatient behavior therapy. *Journal of Behavior Therapy and Experimental Psychiatry, 1,* 279–289.

Weber, M. C. (1992). *Special education law and litigation treatise.* Horsham, PA: LPR Publications.

Weintraub, F. J., & McCaffrey, M. A. (1976). Professional rights and responsibilities. In F. J. Weintraub, A. Abeson, J. Ballard, & M. L. LaVor (Eds.). *Public policy and the education of exceptional children* (pp. 333–343). Reston, VA: Council for Exceptional Children.

Weiskopf, P. E. (1980). Burnout among teachers of exceptional children. *Exceptional Children, 47,* 18–23.

Wood, F. H. (1983a). The influence of public opinion and social custom on the use of corporal punishment in the schools. In F. H. Wood & K. C. Lakin (Eds.). *Punishment and aversive stimulation in special education: Legal, theoretical, and practical issues in their use with emotionally disturbed children and youth* (pp. 29–39). Reston, VA: Council for Exceptional Children.

Wood, F. H. (1983b). Punishment and special education: Some concluding comments. In F. H. Wood & K. C. Lakin (Eds.). *Punishment and aversive stimulation in special education: Legal, theoretical, and practical issues in their use with emotionally disturbed children and youth* (pp. 119–122). Reston, VA: Council for Exceptional Children.

Wood, F. H. (1995). Emotional/Behavioral disorders and the Zeigarnik Effect. *Education and Treatment of Children, 18,* 216–225.

Wood, F. H., & Lakin, K. C. (1983). The legal status of the use of corporal punishment and other aversive procedures in the schools. In F. H. Wood & K. C. Lakin (Eds.). *Punishment and aversive stimulation in special education: Legal, theoretical, and pracical issues in their use with emotionally disturbed children and youth* (pp. 3–27). Reston, VA: Council for Exceptional Children.

Wrobel, G. (1993). Preventing school failure for teachers: Training for a lifelong career in EBD. *Preventing School Failure, 37*(2), 16–20.

Yell, M. L. 1995). Editorial: The law and education of students with disabilities and those at risk for school failure. *Preventing School Failure, 39*(2), 4–5.

Zabel, R. H., & Zabel, M. K. (1980). Burnout: A critical issue for educators. *Education Unlimited, 2,* 23–25.

APPENDIX

INTERVENTION RESOURCES

Systematic Screening to Identify At-Risk Children and Youth

Walker, H. M., Severson, H., & Feil, E. G. (1995.) *Early screening project.* Longmont, CO: Sopris West.[1]

Walker, H. M., & Severson, H. (1990). *Systematic screening for behavior disorders.* Longmont, CO: Sopris West.

Universal Interventions

Alberg, J., Petry, C., & Eller, S. (1994). *A resource guide for social skills instruction.* Longmont, CO: Sopris West.

Beck, R., & Williamson, R. (1993). *Project RIDE for preschoolers.* Longmont, CO: Sopris West.

Black, D. D., & Downs, J. C. (1990). *Administrative intervention: A discipline handbook for effective school administration.* Longmont, CO: Sopris West.

Colvin, G., Sugai, G., & Kameenui, E. (1994). *Curriculum for establishing a school-wide discipline plan.* Eugene, OR: Project PREPARE, Behavioral Research and Teaching, College of Education, University of Oregon.[2]

Kameenui, E. J., & Darch, C. B. (1995). *Instructional classroom management: A proactive approach to behavior management.* Reston, VA: Council for Exceptional Children.[3]

Mayer, G. R., Butterworth, T. W., & Spaulding, H. L. (1989). *Constructive discipline: Building a climate for learning—A resource manual of programs and strategies.* Los Angeles: Los Angeles County Office of Education.[4]

Targeted Interventions

Algozzine, B. (1992). *Problem behavior management: Educator's resource service* (2nd ed.). Gaithersburg, MD: Aspen Publishers.[5]

Brown, W., Conroy, M. A., Fox, J. J., Wehby, J., Davis, C., & McEvoy, M. (1996). *Early intervention for young children at risk for emotional/behavioral disorders: Implications for policy and practice.* Reston, VA: Council for Exceptional Children.

Cipani, E. (1993). *Disruptive behavior: Three techniques to use in your classroom.* Reston, VA: Council for Exceptional Children.

Cipani, E. (1993). *Non-compliance: Four strategies that work.* Reston, VA: Council for Exceptional Children.

Hops, H. H., & Walker, H. M. (1988). *CLASS: Contingencies for learning academic and social skills.* Seattle, WA: Educational Achievement Systems.[6]

Hops, H. H., Walker, H. M., & Greenwood, C. R. (1988). *PEERS: Procedures for establishing relationship skills.* Seattle, WA: Educational Achievement Systems.

Mathur, S. R., Quinn, M. M., & Rutherford, R. B. Jr. (1996). *Teacher-mediated behavior management strategies for children with emotional/behavioral disorders.*

---

[1] Sopris West, 1140 Boston Avenue, Longmont, CO 80501. Phone: (303) 651-2829.

[2] For information concerning this curriculum, contact George Sugai, Project PREPARE, Behavioral Research and Teaching, Division of Learning and Instructional Leadership, Room 235 College of Education, University of Oregon, Eugene, OR 97403.

[3] Council for Exceptional Children, 1920 Association Drive, Reston, VA 20191-1589. Phone: (800) 232-7323.

[4] Division of Evaluation, Attendance, and Pupil Services, 9300 East Imperial Highway, Downey, CA 90242-2890. Phone: (310) 922-6381.

[5] Aspen Publishers, Inc., 200 Orchard Ridge Drive, Suite 200, Gaithersburg, MD 20878.

[6] Educational Achievement Systems, Inc., 319 Nickerson, Ste. 112, Seattle, WA 98109.

McIntyre, T. (1989). *A resource book for remediating common behavior and learning problems.* Boston: Allyn & Bacon.[7]

Phillips, V., & McCullough, L (1992). *Student/staff support teams.* Longmont, CO: Sopris West.

Polsgrove, L. (Ed.) (1991). *Reducing undesirable behavior.* Reston, VA: Council for Exceptional Children.

Rhode, G., Jenson, W. R., & Reavis, H. K. (1992). *The tough kid book.* Longmont, CO: Sopris West.

Rutherford, R. B. Jr., Quinn, M. M., & Mathur, S. R. (1996). *Effective strategies for teaching appropriate behaviors to children with emotional/behavioral disorders.* Reston, VA: Council for Exceptional Children.

Simpson, R. L., Myles, B. S., Walker, B. L., Ormsbee, C. K., & Downing, J. A. (1991). *Programming for aggressive and violent students.* Reston, VA: Council for Exceptional Children.

Sugai, G. M., & Tindal, G. A. (1993). *Effective school consultation: An interactive approach.* Pacific Grove, CA: Brooks/Cole.[8]

Walker, H. M. (1994). *The acting-out child: Coping with classroom disruption* (2nd ed.). Longmont, CO: Sopris West.

Walker, H. M., Colvin, G., & Ramsey, E. (1995). *Antisocial behavior in school: Strategies and best practices.* Pacific Grove, CA: Brooks/Cole.

Watson, R. S., Poda, J. H., Miller, C. T., Rice, E. S., & West, G. (1990). *Containing crisis: A guide to managing school emergencies.* Bloomington, IN: National Educational Service.[9]

School-Based Integrated Services

Illback, R. J., & Nelson, C. M. (Eds.) (1996). *Emerging school-based approaches for children with emotional and behavioral problems: Research and practice in service integration.* New York: Haworth Press.[10]

Skiba, R., Polsgrove, L., & Nasstrom, K. (1996). *Developing a system of care: Interagency collaboration for students with emotional/behavioral disorders.* Reston, VA: Council for Exceptional Children.

---

[7]Allyn and Bacon, A Division of Simon and Schuster, 160 Gould Street, Needham Heights, MA: 02194.

[8]Brooks/Cole Publishing Company, a Division of Wadsworth, Inc., Pacific Grove, CA 93950.

[9]National Educational Service, 1610 West Third Street, P.O. Box 8, Bloomington, IN 47402. Phone: (812) 336-733-6768. FAX: (812) 336-7790.

[10]The Haworth Press, Inc., 10 Alice Street, Binghamton, NY 13904-1580.

GLOSSARY

academic assessment Classroom-based component of comprehensive assessment; may include standardized academic achievement tests as well as curriculum-based measures

activity reinforcement Providing opportunities to engage in preferred or high-probability behaviors contingent upon completion of less preferred or low-probability behaviors

addiction Compulsive use of a drug, characterized by a behavior pattern that centers on drug use, procurement, and continued use. According to this definition, evidence of physical tolerance and dependence is not necessary for establishing that a person is addicted

admissions and release committee *See* child study team

advocacy To campaign for services your students need; to protect their legal rights

aggression A category of behavior that involves harm, injury, or damage to persons or property (e.g., kicking, pushing, throwing school books)

AIMS Assessment System Instruments used to evaluate the adequacy of students' classroom and peer social adjustments in less restrictive settings (Walker, 1986)

alcohol abuse The voluntary intake of alcohol in spite of adverse physical and social consequences

analogue measure A role-play or behavioral rehearsal in which an individual demonstrates how he or she would respond in a given social situation

anger control training An approach to help juveniles reduce aggressive behavior using modeling, role-playing, visual cues, and homework

anorexia nervosa Extreme self-starvation with no known physical cause brought about by an abnormal aversion to eating in which the weight of an individual with anorexia nervosa (usually an adolescent girl) falls at least 25 percent below normal

antecedent-behavior-consequence analysis (A-B-C analysis) A technique used to systematically identify functional relationships among behaviors and environmental variables

antecedent stimulus A stimulus that precedes a behavior; stimulus may or may not serve as a discriminative for a specific behavior

antisocial behavior Behavior that violates socially prescribed norms or patterns of behavior

applied behavior analysis A systematic, performance-based, self-evaluative technology for assessing and changing behavior

assessment The process of gathering data for the purpose of making educational decisions

assessment-based intervention (curriculum-based intervention) Systematic behavior change plan based on data provided by ongoing probes of a student's progress towards a specific goal or objective

417

attempted suicide   Includes some of the elements of completed suicide (i.e., having the conscious intent to die but not dying); attempters wish both to live and to die

autism   Condition characterized by extreme social withdrawal and communication skill deficits

aversive procedure   Any procedure involving the use of an aversive stimulus to modify behavior (e.g., lemon juice applied to a pupil's mouth following an episode of rumination)

aversive stimulus   A noxious stimulus having the effect of decreasing the rate or probability of a behavior when presented as a consequence (punishment); alternately, may have the effect of increasing the rate or probability of a behavior (negative reinforcement) when that behavior allows the student to escape or avoid contact with the stimulus

avoidant disorder   Experienced by children who go to great lengths to avoid contact with any strangers

back-up reinforcer   An object or event received in exchange for a specific number of tokens or points in a token economy

bar graph   A method of visually displaying data; may be used to show progress toward a specific goal or objective

baseline data   Data points that reflect an operant level (the level of natural occurrence of the target behavior before intervention); serve a purpose similar to a pretest; provide a level of behavior to which the results of an intervention procedure can be compared

behavioral contract   (behavior change contract, contingency contract) Written, signed agreement between the teacher, parent, therapist or other behavior change agent and the child, specifically and positively stating in an if-then format what consequence will result from the child's performance of the desired target behavior

behavioral-ecological assessment   The evaluation of observable student behaviors across the range of settings in which they occur

behavioral interview   An important part of the assessment process, interviewing students, their parents, and teachers to gather information about a student's strengths and needs

behaviorally disordered   Behavior characteristics that deviate from educators' standards of normality and impair the functioning of that student or others; manifested as environmental conflict or personal disturbances

behavioral momentum   Proactive strategy to promote compliance; involves a low-probability request preceded by a series of high-probability requests in the same or a similar response class

behavioral objective   A statement of the behavior to be achieved following intervention, the conditions under which the behavior will occur, and the criterion for acceptable performance

behavioral standard   An acceptable level of behavior based on the expectations of other persons

bulimia   An eating disorder in which eating binges are accompanied by vomiting, often self-induced

burnout   Emotional exhaustion (sometimes experienced by teachers)

caffeine   A stimulant drug found in some coffees, teas, and soft drinks; belongs in a chemical class named xanthines (pronounced "zanthenes") and is a methyl-xanthine compound

certification   A decision to classify a pupil for special education placement

changes in the environment   Environmental changes that can affect behavior, such as schedule changes, seating changes, changes in teaching staff or the class roll, changes in placement, and changes in the home environment

changing criterion design   A single-subject experimental design that involves successively or gradually changing the criterion for reinforcement, systematically increasing or decreasing in a step-wise manner

chart A method of visually displaying data using several to many data-representation symbols

checklist A quick, informal, yet systematic tool used to inventory behavior patterns and risk factors that may be associated with behavior disorders; a checklist may be completed by a parent, teacher, sibling, peer, or the target student

chemical abuse The self-administration of a psychoactive chemical that has not been prescribed by a physician; or the compulsive use of a chemical, persisting at a high level in spite of extreme disruption of physical well-being, psychological integrity, and/or social functioning

Child Behavior Checklist A checklist developed by Achenbach and Edelbrock (1980), used to screen children for psychiatric problems

childhood psychosis Term which denotes a wide range of severe and profound disorders in children, including autism, schizophrenia, and symbiotic psychosis

child study team A group of persons designated to oversee the assessment of a student with a disability, as well as the implementation and evaluation of the student's IEP

classroom adjustment code (CAC) A five-second interval recording system that measures three categories of pupil and teacher behavior; used to evaluate the adequacy of students' classroom and peer social adjustments in less restrictive settings

classroom density The number of students per amount of classroom space

clinical syndrome *DSM-IV* classifies psychological disorders along five axes, or dimensions; Axis I consists of the major pattern of symptoms or clinical syndrome that the student exhibits

clock light An environmental intervention that signals on- and off-task behavior

cocaine A mood-altering drug, originally prescribed as a topical anesthetic, now widely abused; the physiological effects of cocaine use are very similar to that of amphetamines

cognitive behavior modification An approach that involves teaching students to apply cognitive strategies in interpersonal problem solving

collaborative approach A transdiciplinary team approach to assisting a student in self-management of problem behaviors

collaborative consultation An interactive process involving a team of persons who jointly address mutually defined problems

collateral effect One intervention affecting several target behaviors

communicative function Maladaptive behaviors can occur because students lack or do not use more effective means of communicating their needs or obtaining reinforcement; replacement behaviors which serve the same communicative function must be taught

community-based training Behavioral interventions implemented in natural settings rather than in the classroom in order to promote skill transfer

competing explanations In single-subject design, the uncontrolled factors that influence the behavior simultaneously with the intervention; confounding variables

compliance training Reducing oppositional behavior and training students to respond quickly to adult directions

conditioned reinforcer (secondary or learned reinforcer) A stimulus that has acquired a reinforcing function through pairing with a previously established reinforcer; most social, activity, and generalized reinforcers are conditioned

conditions Within a behavioral objective, the part that specifies where, when, and with whom a target behavior will occur; description of the antecedents, including prompts and setting events, that will signal the behavior to occur

consensual observer drift Two observers gradually changing their response definitions while recording data

consequence Any stimulus that is presented contingently following a particular response

constructs Theoretical assumptions based on available data

consultation Providing indirect services to pupils by helping their teachers or parents directly

contiguity The timing of reinforcement or punishment immediately contingent upon the target behavior, so that a connection between the behavior and its consequence is readily apparent

contingency The relationship between behavior and its consequences; contingencies are often stated in the form "if-then"

contingency contracting Placing contingencies for reinforcement (if-then statements) into a written document; creates a permanent product that can be referred to by both teacher and student

contingent observation A form of timeout in which a child is removed from reinforcement while observing others receiving reinforcement

contingent teacher attention A type of social reinforcer in which the teacher responds with smiles, praise, attention, and physical proximity when a student performs a desired behavior

continuous measurement Continuous data collection for the purpose of monitoring and evaluating student progress

continuum of services A range of special education service options with consideration given to more restrictive educational placements only after interventions have proven unsuccessful in less restrictive settings

contracting *See* contingency contracting

coprophagia The eating of feces

controlled procedures Disciplinary interventions permitted by the courts only in accordance with specific legal guidelines

Council for Children with Behavioral Disorders (CCBD) Major professional organization for special educators serving students with emotional and behavioral disorders

criteria The part of an instructional objective that specifies the requirements for acceptable performance of the target behavior

criterion-based assessment (CBA) Assessment of a pupil's status with regard to specific curriculum content and objectives

criterion of functioning in the next environment Identifying the skill requirements and expectations of less restrictive environments and teaching these in order to increase students' chances of successful participation

criterion of the least dangerous assumption When conclusive data are not available regarding the effectiveness of an intervention, educational decisions should be based on assumptions that, if incorrect, will have the least dangerous effect on the student

criterion of ultimate functioning The functional skills needed by adults to participate freely in community environments

cubicle *See* study carrels

cumulative graph A graphic presentation of successive summed numbers (rate, frequency, percentage, duration) that represent behavioral occurrences

curriculum-based assessment (CBA) Informal, teacher-made tests used to measure progress towards IEP and other classroom goals and objectives

curriculum modification Revision or change in curriculum to provide appropriate instruction based on individual needs

data-based decision making Using direct and frequent measures of a behavior as a basis for comparing student performance to a desired level and making adjustments in the student's educational program based on these comparisons

data decision rules Rules that suggest how to respond to patterns in student performance; developed by the teacher to facilitate the efficient and effective evaluation of instructional and behavior management programs

data level change   The amount of relative change in the data within or between conditions

data stability   The degree of variability of individual data points above and below the trend line

data trend   The general path of graphed data. A trend line often must be interpolated by the teacher, since data paths seldom follow straight lines, nor do they increase or decrease in even increments

decertification criteria   The goals and objectives for a student's special education program; when goals are met, the student should be returned to regular education

dependence   Compulsive drug use to ward off physical or emotional discomfort; the person depends on the drug to prevent withdrawal or abstinence-related distress; physical and psychological dependence are determined on the basis of overt and predictable withdrawal symptoms

dependency   The need for maximum adult support, accompanied by minimal independent skills

dependent group-oriented contingency   The performance of certain group members that determines the consequence received by the entire group

dependent measure   A variable that is measured while another variable (the independent variable) is changed in a systematic way, with the goal of establishing a relationship between the two variables

dependent variable   The behavior that is changed by intervention, through manipulation of an independent variable

depressants   Drugs belonging to the classes of barbiturates (phenobarbital, hexobarbital), benzodiazepine and propanediol minor tranquilizers (Librium, Valium, meprobamate), and antihistaminic sedatives. Barbiturates are commonly prescribed for sleep facilitation and for control of seizures. Benzodiazepines and propanediols are anti-anxiety agents. Benzodiazepines are also used to control seizures and promote muscle relaxation.

Antihistamines are used to control allergies and respiratory ailments.

depression   A behavioral disorder characterized by prolonged feelings of sadness, hopelessness, emptiness, or discouragement that are out of proportion to reality; physical symptoms may include eating, sleeping, or sexual excesses or deficits; affect can range widely from listless apathy to suicidal recklessness

detention   A behavioral correction intervention in which a student must stay for 30 to 90 minutes before or after school to complete assignments

developmental regression   A temporary lapse in an individual's social skills

differential reinforcement   Four strategies that involve reinforcement applied differentially to reduce undesired behaviors while increasing desired behaviors; see DRL, DRO, DRI, and DRA

direction/adult involvement   Leadership, structure, and quality of interactions provided by a teacher, parent, or other significant adult in a child's life

direct observation   Observation of a student in those settings in which the target behavior occurs

discrete learning trial   A learning trial that has a discriminable beginning and end; involves the presentation of a prompt or discriminative stimulus, a pupil response, and subsequent teacher feedback

discrimination   Demonstration of the ability to differentiate among stimuli or environmental events

discriminative stimulus   (S^D) An antecedent stimulus that is likely to occasion a particular response because it signals the probability that reinforcement will follow the response

differential reinforcement of alternative behaviors   (DRA) A procedure in which reinforcement is delivered for behaviors that are alternatives to the target behavior

differential reinforcement of incompatible behaviors   (DRI) Systematically reinforcing a response that is topographically incompatible with a behavior targeted for reduction

differential reinforcement of low rates of behavior (DRL)   A procedure in which reinforcement is delivered when the number of responses in a specified period of time is less than or equal to a prescribed limit; encourages maintenance of a behavior at a predetermined rate lower than the baseline or naturally occurring rate

differential reinforcement of the omission of behavior (DRO)   A procedure in which reinforcement is delivered when the target behavior is not emitted for a specified period of time; behaviors other than the target behaviors are specifically reinforced

drug   Any chemical that is consumed and is present in abnormal concentration in the body; includes substances such as insulin or other hormones found naturally within the body, which can dramatically influence emotion and behavior if their concentrations are not kept within normal limits

drug abuse   The voluntary intake of a chemical in spite of adverse physical and social consequences

drug tolerance   Physical adaptation to the effects of a drug so that more of the drug is necessary to produce the same effect with repeated use

Diagnostic and Statistical Manual of Mental Disorders, 4th edition *(DSM-IV)*   A manual that defines and classifies mental disorders according to American Psychiatric Association guidelines (APA, 1994)

due process   Procedural safeguards established to ensure the rights of exceptional students and their parents

duration recording   Recording the amount of time between the initiation of a response and its conclusion; total duration recording is recording cumulative time between the initiation of a response and its final conclusion (e.g., one may record cumulative time out-of-seat across several instances); duration per occurrence is recording each behavioral event and its duration

dysphoria   Sadness, a symptom of depression

dysthymia   A persistent mood of depression or irritability, more days than not, for most of the day, for at least a year

eating disorders   Maladaptive, health-threatening behaviors that involve food; *see* anorexia nervosa, bulimia

echolalia   Parroting repetition of words or phrases; observed in children with autism, schizophrenia or psychosis

ecological approach   An approach to assessment that focuses on the student's interactions with the environment rather than on the deficits of the student

ecological ceiling   Acknowledgment that it is unrealistic to expect target behaviors to increase or decrease to rates above or below those of peers in the same settings

ecological model   Assumption that behavior disorders primarily result from flaws in a complex social system in which various elements of the system (e.g., child, school, family, church, community) are highly interdependent, and that the most effective preventative actions and therapeutic interventions will involve changes in the entire social system

ecological settings   Various subsettings in which a student's behavior occurs

edible reinforcement   Providing edible items that are reinforcing for the student, contingent upon the performance of desired behavior

Education of the Handicapped Act   (PL 94–142) The public law that guarantees appropriate educational experiences for children and youth with disabilities

effective behavior support   Behavior change strategies which involve the teaching of appropriate alternative behavior that serves the same communicative function as the undesirable target behavior

elective mutism   Refusal to talk by an individual who is able to talk; may occur in one setting and not in others

emphysema   A disease in which the alveoli or air sacs of the lung are destroyed, thus preventing the normal exchange of oxygen and carbon dioxide; resulting in breathlessness, expansion of the rib cage, and possible heart impairment

environmental analysis   A technique used to provide the intervention team with information on specific settings, times, and adult actions for further examination

environmentally mediated strategy   Changing of some aspect of the environment to prevent or manage behavioral problems

equal interval graph paper   A form for presenting behavioral data: vertical lines represent training sessions or calendar days, and horizontal lines may represent number, percentage, or rate (frequency); emphasizes absolute differences among data points

equal ratio graph paper   A form for presenting behavioral data in terms of rate per minute or percent; semilogarithmic rather than additive, therefore changes in rate of performance that are proportionately equal are visually presented as equal

event recording   Recording a tally or frequency count of behavior as it occurs within an observation period; an observational recording procedure

expulsion   A disciplinary consequence that involves exclusion from school

externalizing   A pattern of behavior characterized by acting out against persons or objects in the environment

extinction   Systematic withholding of reinforcement for a previously reinforced behavior in order to reduce or eliminate the occurrence of the behavior

facial screening   A procedure for reducing stereotypic behaviors by covering the student's face with a hand or a cloth bib when the student engages in the target behavior

fair pair rule   Teach and/or positively reinforce a desired social behavior to replace the behavior to be reduced

feedback   Providing the student with descriptive information regarding his or her behavior; includes specific praise as well as specific error correction

follow-up assessment   Evaluating the student's current status with regard to lEP or intervention objectives, and evaluating the effectiveness of the educational program

formative evaluation   Evaluation that occurs as skills are being developed

frequency (rate)   The number of times a behavior occurs during an observation period

frequency polygon   A noncumulative frequency graph; may be used to report frequency, rate, or percent data

functional analysis   A technique used to systematically identify functional relationships between behaviors and environmental variables

functional mediation   A strategy that takes advantage of potential discriminative stimuli common to acquisition, fluency, and generalization training

functional relationship   In applied behavior analysis, demonstrated when a behavior varies systematically with the application of an intervention procedure; sometimes called *a cause-and-effect relationship;* change in a dependent variable due to a change in an independent variable

functional response class   Behaviors grouped because they have the same effect on the environment (e.g., attention-seeking behaviors)

generalization   Expansion of a student's capability of performance beyond those conditions set for initial acquisition; *stimulus generalization* refers to performance under conditions—that is, cues, materials, trainers, and environments—other than those present during acquisition; *maintenance generalization* refers to continued performance of learned behavior after contingencies have been withdrawn; *response generalization* refers to changes in behaviors similar to those directly treated

generalization training   Intervention specifically directed at achieving generalization across settings, time, or responses

good behavior game   An independent, group-oriented contingency that applies consequences to a group, contingent upon each member reaching a specified level of performance

Grandma's Law   *See* Premack Principle

graph   A method of visually displaying data; typically uses only one or two symbols to represent data

group contingency   A peer-mediated strategy in which several peers and the target student work with the teacher to modify behaviors; behavioral consequences are applied to all group members according to teacher-made rules

group goal setting   An intervention that consists of two major components: 1) the teacher assists each student in establishing a social behavior goal; and 2) each student receives teacher and peer feedback on progress toward that goal during highly structured group discussions

group-oriented contingency   Contingencies related to the behavior of groups of persons

hallucinogens   A chemically heterogeneous group of drugs with the common property of altering sensory experiences and mood; marijuana, LSD, PCP and psilocybin are hallucinogens

hashish   A purified resin of the marijuana plant

heroin   Ciadetylmorphine; an addictive narcotic opiate

high-probability behavior   Behavior that has a high likelihood of occurrence; preferred activity

home-based contract   Written contingencies for reinforcement in which parents have agreed to participate

ignoring   Withdrawing social attention in response to an undesired behavior

independent group-oriented contingency   Group behavior management strategy in which the same response contingency is in effect for all group members, but is applied to each student's performance on an individual basis

independent variable   The treatment or intervention under experimenter control that is being manipulated in order to change a behavior

indiscriminable contingencies   Consequences that are made less predictable, more natural, and less teacher-controlled through the use of intermittent, gradually thinned schedules of reinforcement

individualized education program (IEP)   A written educational plan developed for each student eligible for special education

inhalants and volatile solvents   Chemicals that mix easily with air and can be inhaled, includes hydrocarbons (benzene, carbon tetrachloride), freons (trichlorofloromethane), ketones (acetone), esters (ethylacetate), alcohols (methyl alcohol), glycols (etylene glycol), and gasoline; common sources of these chemicals are aerosols, fingernail polish, household cements, lacquer thinner, lighter fluid, cleaning fluid, and model cement

in loco parentis   Legal doctrine giving the school parental authority over and responsibility for students during school hours

in-school suspension   A school intervention that includes a reinforcing setting from which the student is removed, a non-reinforcing environment to which the student goes, and contingencies that govern the student's passage from one environment to the other

instructional dimensions of the environment   Variables such as the type and sequence of instructional methods, materials, and activities

instructional time   The amount of time that students are engaged in active learning and instruction

integrated service plan   *See* wraparound plan

intellectual assessment   The process of gathering data through IQ testing and adaptive behavior measurement to see if a behavior problem may be due to a cognitive impairment

intensity   A measure of behavior that involves recording both its frequency and its duration

interactive teaming models   Collaborative intervention methods such as the use of teacher assistance teams to promote the effective education of students with behavior problems in the least restrictive environment

interdependent group-oriented contingency   Group behavioral intervention in which each student must reach a prescribed level of behavior before the entire group may receive positive reinforcement for that behavior

intermittent schedules of reinforcement   Schedules in which reinforcement follows some, but not all, correct or appropriate responses, or follows when a period of appropriate behavior has elapsed; these include ratio, interval, and response-duration schedules of reinforcement

interobserver agreement   Comparison of observation data between two or more observers to check reliability

interval recording   An observational recording system in which an observation period is divided into a number of short intervals, and the observer counts the number of intervals during which the behavior occurs rather than instances of the behavior

interval schedule of reinforcement   A schedule for the delivery of reinforcers contingent upon the occurrence of a behavior following a specified period of time; in a fixed interval (FI) schedule, the interval of time is standard (e.g., FI5/min indicates the delivery of reinforcement for the first occurrence of behavior following each five-minute interval of the observation period); in a variable interval (VI) schedule, the interval of time varies (e.g., VI5/min indicates the delivery of reinforcement for the first response that occurs after intervals averaging five minutes in length)

intervention   Systematic involvement with a student in order to improve his or her performance socially, emotionally, or academically

intervention plan   The components include a behavioral objective, what will be done, who will do it, how it will be done, when it will be done, when it will be reviewed, who will review it, and what will happen if the plan is ineffective or if undesired side effects occur

interview   Informal method for obtaining assessment data from both children and adults

intrusiveness   The extent to which interventions impinge or encroach on students' bodies or personal rights

juvenile delinquency   Pattern of illegal activities exhibited by a youth

latency recording   Recording the amount of time between the presentation of the S^D (discriminative stimulus) and the initiation of a response

learned helplessness   Passivity, a lack of drive or initiative to problem-solve which may result from fears of failure or success, or from a lack of trust, habitual put-downs (verbal abuse), or patterns of overprotectiveness by adult caregivers which can lower a child's self-confidence

least intrusive alternative   *See* least restrictive alternative

least restrictive alternative   Using the simplest yet most effective intervention based on available data regarding the effectiveness of a procedure

least restrictive placement   The placement imposing the fewest restrictions on a student's normal academic or social functioning

level   Quantity of behavior as represented on a graph

levels system   A method of differentiating hierarchically any aspect of an individual's performance (e.g., in a token economy or for assessment purposes); also referred to as *phase system*

limiting behaviors   Behaviors that limit the student's access to regular education programs or other less restrictive settings

line of desired progress (aim line)   A line drawn on a behavior graph to depict the desired rate of pupil progress toward a terminal goal

low-probability behavior   Less preferred behavior; unlikely to occur without contingent reinforcement

lysergic acid diethylamide (LSD)   The prototypical hallucinogen

magnitude of behavior change   The quantity by which a behavior increases or decreases with respect to some prior amount of behavior

mainstreaming   The integration of exceptional children with typical peers

manipulating antecedent stimuli   Strategic control of setting events such as classroom physical arrangement, teacher proximity, and scheduling in order to facilitate desirable behavior

marijuana   The dried leaves and flowers of the hemp plant (genus cannabis, cannabis sativa)

measurement probes   Periodic data samples used in making intervention decisions

mediator   Parent, teacher, or other person who provides direct services to a child with the support of a consultant

medical model   An assessment and intervention model used by mental health professionals; based on the identification of physiological, emotional or cognitive pathology that is presumed to underlie the student's behavior problems

memoranda of agreement   Documents produced at interdisciplinary team meetings that specify what services are to be provided, when, where, and by whom; signed by all team members

mental health assessment   The identification of emotional or cognitive pathology that is presumed to underlie a student's behavior problems

modeling   An instructional procedure by which demonstrations of a desired behavior are presented in order to prompt an imitative response

momentary time sampling procedure   Recording the occurrence or nonoccurrence of a behavior immediately following a specified interval of time

monitoring teacher verbal behavior   A teacher's self-monitoring to gain awareness and increased control of verbal messages

movement suppression procedure   A variation of timeout from reinforcement in which the student is punished for any movement or verbalization while in a timeout area

multiple baseline design   A single-subject experimental design in which a treatment is replicated across (1) two or more students, (2) two or more behaviors, or (3) two or more settings; functional relationships may be demonstrated as changes in the dependent variables occur with the systematic and sequenced introduction of the independent variable

multiple probe design   A variation of the multiple baseline design in which data are collected periodically rather than continuously across settings, behaviors, or students

narcotics   Drugs which dull the senses, block painful sensations, and induce sleep

natural community of reinforcement   A child's family and peers who provide reinforcement that maintains his or her behavior

negative reinforcement   The increase in rate or future probability of a behavior that occurs when the behavior successfully avoids or terminates contact with an aversive stimulus

nicotine   A habit-forming drug found in tobacco; nicotine is chemically classified as an alkaloid and is physically toxic, causing nausea, salivation, abdominal pain, vomiting, diarrhea, cold sweat, headache, dizziness, confusion, convulsions, and respiratory failure at high doses; a common active ingredient in several insecticides

noncompliance   Refusal to obey teacher directions; behavior that is not under the verbal stimulus control of an adult

norm-referenced standardized test   A test that compares a student's performance to that of the students in a norm group; standard scores are identified on the basis of this group's performance

observer drift A change in the observer's response definition while observing behavior and recording data

off-task behavior Behavior exhibited by a student who is not attending to or participating in a classroom activity; not working on an assignment

on-task behavior Behavior exhibited by a student who is working on an assignment or paying attention during a classroom activity

operational definition Describing a behavior in terms of its observable and measurable component parts

oppositional behavior A pattern of refusal to follow directions, even when the refusal is destructive to the interests and well-being of the oppositional individual

organized games Structured play directed by the teacher; an intervention intended to reduce aggression during recess

overanxious disorder Experienced by children who are chronically fearful or worried about future events, demands made of them, their health, or their social and academic skills

overcorrection A procedure used to reduce the occurrence of an inappropriate behavior; the student is taught the appropriate behavior in which to engage through an exaggeration of experience; in *restitutional overcorrection* students must restore or correct an environment they have disturbed to its condition before the disturbance and must then improve it beyond its original condition, thereby overcorrecting the environment; in *positive practice overcorrection* students, having engaged in an inappropriate behavior, are required to engage in exaggerated practice of appropriate behaviors

parent surrogate An adult appointed to take the role of the parent and to make decisions regarding the most appropriate educational program and placement

peer coaching A procedure involving peers and adults who provide instruction to train social isolate pupils in social skills

peer imitation training An intervention that requires an isolate child's classmate to model social behaviors and encourages imitation

peer manager strategy Young socially withdrawn students being trained to play "class manager" to increase their social interactions and sociometric ratings

peer-mediated intervention An intervention that requires a member of the individual's peer group, rather than an adult, to take the primary role as the agent of behavior change

peer modeling Having the student model or imitate the behavior exhibited by peers

peer monitoring Having students observe and record the behavior of a classmate

peer-rating method Sociometric screening method in which students rank one another in terms of popularity or other perceived social attributes

peer reporting An intervention designed to help students improve their social interactions and reduce aggression

peer social initiation An intervention strategy to improve the social skills of withdrawn children

peer tutoring Formal instruction of one child by another

percent of interobserver agreement Measure of the reliability or consistency of data collection across two observers, calculated as

$$\frac{\text{agreements}}{(\text{agreements} + \text{disagreements})} \times 100$$

perceptual reinforcement Reinforcement by engaging in particular perceptual experiences; a key to understanding self-stimulatory behaviors is to view them as a form of perceptual self-reinforcement

performance deficit A skill that a student can perform but does not because of a lack of motivation

performance feedback Providing the student with descriptive information regarding role-playing activities or academic performance

performance graph   A graph that plots a change in a single task or behavior

permanent product recording   A measurement strategy based on tangible evidence of behavior (e.g., written work, numerical count, videotape, physical injury or property damage)

permitted procedures   Disciplinary measures included in a school district's discipline plan for use with all students

phase line   Vertical lines drawn on a behavior graph to designate where program changes have been made

phencyclidine (PCP)   Frequently abused hallucinogen likely to promote aggressive behavior with concurrent increased physical vigor and lack of response to pain

phenobarbital   A barbiturate sedative hypnotic; also used as anti-seizure medication in children; it and other types of anti-epileptic medication such as phenytoin (diphenylhydantoin), Cylert (pemoline) and Tegretol (carbamazepine) also have potentially negative side effects (e.g., depression, insomnia, weight loss, confusion, hallucinations)

phobia   An abnormally intense dread of certain objects or specific situations which may severely limit activities related to the fear reaction

physical aversives   Unpleasant or painful physical stimuli, such as foul tastes and odors, electric shock, slaps, and pinches, used to punish dangerous maladaptive behaviors (such as SIB) when less intrusive methods have failed

physical dimensions of the environment   Variables such as lighting, temperature, seating arrangement, noise level, and time of day that can affect behavior

pica   The persistent eating of nonfood substances (i.e. paper, paint, dirt, etc.)

pinpointing   Specifying in measurable, observable terms a behavior targeted for change

placheck   Recording which students are engaged in a particular activity at the end of specified intervals

planned ignoring   A variation of timeout in which social proximity and attention are consistently withheld for a specific length of time immediately contingent on a pupil's undesirable behavior

point-by-point reliability   A method used to assess the agreement between two observers when discrete units of observation are compared
Formula:

$$\frac{\text{number of agreements}}{\text{number of agreements plus disagreements}} \times 100$$

portfolio   Collection of representative samples of a student's work used to measure proficiency, rate of skill development, and effectiveness of teaching methods

positive practice overcorrection   A procedure in which the student is required to engage in a period of exaggerated alternative behaviors (e.g., exercises) after an episode of an unwanted behavior

positive reinforcement   The presentation of a stimulus contingent on the occurrence of a behavior that results in an increase in the rate or future probability of that behavior over time

postvention   Actions taken by school psychologists, counselors, administrators, and educators to prevent contagion after a suicide and to help students and staff deal with bereavement

praise   Giving positive verbal attention contingent upon appropriate behavior

pre-correction   Adjustment in academic instruction based on the teacher's anticipation of student error and intended to prevent errors by providing supportive prompts

predictability   Familiar daily classroom routines and a teacher's consistency in applying consequences can help students gain stability by letting them know what to expect

Premack Principle   An empirical observation that, when access to a high-probability activity (behavior that occurs at a higher rate in the natural environment) is made contingent upon the exhibition of a low probability behavior (one that occurs at a lower rate in the natural environment), the latter will increase in rate (also called *activity reinforcement* and *Grandma's Law*)

prereferral interventions Straightforward and relatively easy program modifications implemented by the regular classroom teacher to see if behavior problems can be solved without referring the student for formal evaluation for special education placement

primary treatment setting The setting in which the intervention is applied directly

principle of hierarchical application Educational tenet stating that more intrusive and restrictive discipline procedures may be used only after less intrusive and restrictive procedures have been applied and have been unsuccessful in promoting student compliance

procedural reliability The extent to which intervention procedures are being consistently followed

progress graph A graph that shows progress toward mastery of a set of objectives

prohibited procedures Unlawful disciplinary actions, such as a unilateral change in the placement of a special education student

projective technique A psychological assessment procedure in which the client "projects" thoughts and feelings through responses to ambiguous stimuli such as pictures or ink blots

prompt An added stimulus that increases the probability that the S^D (discriminative stimulus) will occasion the desired response

psychological problems Problems characterized by sudden changes in behavior or mood; feelings of sadness, fatigue, anhedonia; changes in appetite and sleeping habits, feelings of worthlessness

psychopathology Mental illness; in psychiatry, the study of significant causes and development of mental illness; more generally, behavior disorder

psychosis Behavior disorder characterized by a major departure from normal patterns of acting, thinking, and feeling

public posting Publicly listing the names of persons who have (or have not) engaged in a target behavior

punisher A consequent stimulus that decreases the future rate or probability of a behavior

punishment Presentation of an aversive stimulus, or the removal of a positive reinforcer (response cost) as a consequence for behavior which reduces the future rate of the behavior

rate The frequency of a behavior during a defined time period
Formula:

$$\frac{\text{frequency}}{\text{time}} = \text{rate}$$

rating scale A scale using information supplied by a teacher, parent, sibling, peer, or the target student to describe the child's behavior

ratio schedule of reinforcement A schedule for the delivery of reinforcers contingent upon the number of correct responses; in a fixed ratio (FR) schedule, the number of appropriate responses required for reinforcement is held constant (e.g., FR5 indicates the delivery of reinforcement following every fifth appropriate response); in a variable ratio (VR) schedule, the number of appropriate responses required for reinforcement varies (e.g., VR5 indicates that reinforcement is delivered on the average of every fifth appropriate response)

reduction of response maintenance stimuli Prompts are faded and reinforcement is thinned, so that natural antecedents and consequences can "trap" the behavior in the natural environment

reinforcement Provision of a reinforcing consequence or removal of an aversive stimulus contingent upon the occurrence of a behavior, resulting in an increased or maintained rate of the behavior in the future

reinforcer sampling   Prior to the start of a behavioral intervention, the student is provided with samples of reinforcers which may be earned during the intervention

reinforcing event menu (RE menu)   A pictorial or verbal list of a variety of reinforcing events

relevant behaviors   Student's social repertoire behaviors that are likely to evoke reciprocal social interactions that strengthen further social initiations on the student's part

reliability   Consistency of measurement; the extent to which an observation holds true across time and observations; types of reliability include test-retest, alternate form, split-half, and interrater

replacement behaviors   Desirable skills that are strengthened as undesirable maladaptive behaviors are reduced; often replacement behaviors serve the same communicative function as the maladaptive behavior

reprimand   A verbal aversive used by adults to influence children's behavior by telling them their behavior is inappropriate

response class   Behavior definitions including several related responses which serve the same or similar functions

response cost   A procedure for the reduction of inappropriate behavior through withdrawal of specific amounts of reinforcers contingent upon the behavior's occurrence; fine or penalty

response definition   The definition or description of a behavior in observable, measurable terms

response generalization   Changes in untreated behaviors related to those behaviors targeted for intervention

response latency   Time that elapses between the presentation of a discriminative stimulus and the initiation of the desired response

response latency recording   A measurement strategy in which a timer is started when a task request

is given and stopped when the pupil begins to comply with the request

response maintenance   The continuation or durability of behavior on a naturally occurring reinforcement schedule after an intervention has been withdrawn

response-reinforcer procedure   An intervention in which the immediate environment is manipulated so that the student, as a result of completing a task, has immediate access to a reinforcer physically imbedded within the task

restitutional overcorrection   The student must restore an environment which he or she has disturbed to its condition before the disturbance and must then improve it beyond its original condition, thereby overcorrecting the environment

restraint   Limiting physical movement to prevent injury to self or others

restrictiveness   The extent to which an intervention inhibits a student's freedom to live like other students

reversal design (ABAB design, similar to withdrawal design)   A single-subject research design in which an intervention condition is reversed in order to verify the existence of a functional relationship; its four phases include baseline (A), intervention (B), contratherapeutic reversal of intervention, which may be similar but is not identical to baseline (C), and reinstatement of intervention (B)

reverse tolerance   Increased sensitivity to a drug; may be the result of metabolic factors that produce a build-up in the body over time with regular use

ripple/spillover effect   A spreading effect in which an intervention with one student, one behavior, or in one setting influences change in another student, behavior, or setting; *see* generalization

ritualistic behaviors   Repetitive, stereotypic acts that appear to have no function in the environment

role-playing   A therapeutic procedure that helps introduce new behaviors to enhance social relationships (the adult attempts to recreate certain situations for the student in an effort to help that student practice skills that have been difficult)

rule   A basic component of a school's discipline code, communicating student and teacher expectations; rules should be few, clear, and stated positively

rumination   Self-induced regurgitation and re-chewing of food with loss of weight or failure to thrive

SBS Checklist of Correlates of Child Handicapping Conditions   A checklist by Walker and Rankin (1980) describing conditions and characteristics commonly associated with disabilities in children

SBS Inventory of Teacher Social Behavior Standards and Expectations   A rating scale by Walker and Rankin (1980) describing adaptive and maladaptive student classroom behavior

scatter plot   A type of graphing used to determine if there is a significant relationship between two variables

schedule of reinforcement   A schedule for the delivery of reinforcers for the purpose of increasing or maintaining behavior

scheduling   Posting daily activities in a clear schedule that reflects how students should spend their time

schizophrenia   A psychotic disorder characterized by distortion of thinking, abnormal perception, and bizarre behavior and emotions

school phobia   Fear of going to school, usually accompanied by indications of anxiety about attendance (abdominal pain, nausea, or other physical complaints) just before leaving for school in the morning

school records   Archival information helpful in assessing social skills and problem areas

school survival skills   Skills necessary to do well in school, such as classroom deportment and time-management strategies

school-wide intervention   Universal intervention in which a behavior management system is applied consistently across the student population

scopolamine   One of a class of drugs known as anticholinergics, because they inhibit the activity of the brain chemical acetylcholine, which is considered important for mood and sensory regulation; scopolamine is derived from plants in the nightshade family; has been used as a sedative and a truth serum

screening   Identification of students at risk for behavioral problems

selected intervention   Behavioral change procedure chosen to suit the needs of a particular student

self-evaluation   A procedure in which student assesses his or her own behavior by rating

self-injurious behaviors (SIB)   Behaviors that hurt the person exhibiting them; also referred to as "self-mutilating" or "self-destructive" behaviors

self-instruction   A procedure in which students use self-talk in the form of "coping statements" as an aid to problem-solving

self-management   An intervention in which the target individual plays the primary role in changing her or his own behavior

self-mediated stimuli   A strategy that involves having the student carry or deliver stimuli discriminative of appropriate responding

self-mediated strategies   Strategies for behavior management in which the student controls his or her own planned intervention

self-monitoring   Recording one's own behavior to increase one's time on task, academic productivity, or appropriate social interactions

self-mutilation   Self-injurious behavior that results in tissue damage

self-recording   Students recording data on their own performance

self-regulation A range of procedures (e.g., self-monitoring, self-evaluation, and self-reinforcement) in which the student acts as his or her own behavior change agent; self-regulation is relatively non-intrusive, nonrestrictive, and allows classroom activities to proceed with a minimum of interruptions

self-reinforcement A procedure whereby students reinforce their own behavior

self-report A procedure whereby students report their own performance

self-stimulatory behavior Any repetitive, stereotypic activity that appears to serve no purpose other than to provide sensory feedback

self-verbalization A strategy used with socially immature and impulsive students to improve their academic performance by self-instruction or verbalization

sensory extinction A procedure designed to eliminate a particular sensory consequence of a given behavior; based on the hypothesis that certain individuals have a strong preference for one aspect of sensory input (e.g., tactile, proprioceptive, visual, or auditory) and engage in self-stimulatory behaviors to increase this sensory input

sensory preferences Sensory experiences that are desirable to the child

sensory reinforcement Providing the child with preferred sensory experiences contingent on behavior

separation anxiety Intense fear and worry when separated from significant others or familiar surroundings; separation anxiety is typical of a developmental stage in toddlers, but is of concern when it persists or occurs in older students

sequential modification Replicating intervention procedures in other settings in which the desired behavior change is relevant without systematically programming for the durability of treatment effects once intervention is withdrawn

serious emotional disturbance Exhibiting one or more characteristics over a long period of time

and to a marked degree which adversely affects educational performance: (1) an inability to learn that cannot be explained by intellectual, sensory, or health factors, (2) an inability to build or maintain satisfactory interpersonal relationships with peers and teachers, (3) inappropriate behavior or feelings under normal circumstances, (4) a general pervasive mood of unhappiness or depression, or (5) a tendency to develop physical symptoms or fears associated with personal or school problems

setting events Antecedent stimuli such as the time of day, transition periods, or the behaviors of peers and teachers that set the occasion for certain behaviors

shaping Behavior change process in which a new or unfamiliar behavior is taught through rewarding successive approximations of the behavior, progressing step-by-step toward a terminal objective

single-subject research design Experiment intended to establish a functional relationship between dependent and independent variables; in a single-subject design the target individual serves as his or her own control

skill deficit A target behavior that cannot be performed due to a lack of appropriate skills

social dimensions of the environment Variables such as the number of peers and adults in the classroom, proximity to others, and frequency and types of social interactions

social competence An ability to establish satisfactory social relationships

social interaction code (SIC) Assessment of three major classes of events associated with a student's peer interactions

social isolation Behavior of individuals who seldom interact with their peers or with adults

social learning theory Assumption that antecedent or setting events (e.g., models, prompts, instructions), consequences (rewards and punishments), and cognitive processes (perceptions, thoughts, feelings) combine to influence behavior; includes features of applied behavior analysis with additional emphasis on cognitive factors

social maladjustment Predelinquent or delinquent behavior patterns which may indicate the existence of an emotional or behavioral disorder

social performance deficit Refers to a student's knowing how to perform a specific social skill while being unmotivated to do so

social reinforcement Teacher or peer attention (feedback, attention, and approval) given contingent on behavior which maintains or increases the behavior

social skills Specific social behaviors (e.g., a greeting, a nod during a conversation, a handshake) that facilitate interpersonal interactions

social skills deficit Inability to perform a particular social skill

social validation Degree to which significant others agree that a behavior should be changed, approve of a particular behavioral intervention, or concur that intervention has been effective

social withdrawal A cluster of behaviors that result in an individual's escaping or avoiding social contact

sociometric procedure A technique used to evaluate the social status or position of individuals in a particular social reference group

special education admissions and release committee (ARC) A team that decides when assessment information indicates a need for special education placement; the team also decides if goals have been met and a student should be decertified

standardized test A formal assessment instrument in which a student's score may be compared to scores of a norm group

static measures Assessments that provide a report of progress at discrete points in time (e.g., annual or semiannual reassessments)

stereotypic behaviors Repetitive, apparently nonfunctional movements (e.g., rocking, hand-flapping) characteristic of autism and other severe behavior disorders

stimulants Drugs which accelerate pulse and respiration, such as amphetamines, (speed), cocaine, caffeine, nicotine, phenylpropanolamine, methylphenidate, and pemoline

stimulus change Altering the discriminative stimuli for a particular response

stimulus control The relationship between behavior and its antecedent in which the antecedent occasions the behavior; repeated occurrences of the behavior are dependent upon its being reinforced; an antecedent that occasions a response and therefore results in reinforcement is known as a discriminative stimulus (S^D); an antecedent that does not occasion a response and therefore does not result in reinforcement is known as an S-delta (S^D)

stimulus fading The gradual removal of discriminative stimuli

stimulus generalization The transfer of behaviors that have been trained in one setting or in the presence of specific discriminative stimuli to new settings or the presence of stimuli for which they have not been taught

stimulus variation A procedure to increase social responsiveness in a student who habitually engages in self-stimulatory behavior

stress Real or imagined physiological, mental, or emotional strain or pressure which is a typical aspect of everyday life; each individual must develop his or her own personal repertoire of coping skills to deal with stress. Development of optimistic yet realistic expectations, good health habits, organization and time-management skills, humor, religious faith, and a network of social support are a few of the ways people cope well with stress. Overwork, overeating, and abuse of alcohol, tobacco and other drugs are a few of the maladaptive ways people react to stress. Depression, anxiety attacks, displaced hostility, physical ailments, and burnout are some of the negative outcomes which can occur when stress exceeds an individual's ability to cope.

structured learning   Approach to teaching prosocial behaviors to students using modeling, role-playing, performance feedback and transfer of learning

structuring   Clarifying the relationship between a behavior and its consequences

student prompting of teacher praise   Students solicit praise contingent upon their own behavior

study carrels or cubicles   A study area for isolating easily distracted pupils so they can concentrate better

sufficient stimulus exemplars   A strategy that involves arranging for more than one, or for a small set of, discriminative stimuli to control the target behavior

suicidal ideation   Having thoughts about killing oneself

suicide   When someone takes his or her life with conscious intent

summative evaluation   Evaluation done at the end of a program

suspension   A temporary exclusion from school to manage behavior

syndrome   Recurring actions or symptoms that combine to form a disordered pattern

system of care   Multidisciplinary approach to meeting the needs of a child with a behavior disorder in which several agencies collaborate to provide individualized services that wrap around the child and family

systematic desensitization   A systematic procedure to help a person relax when engaging in activities that previously were anxiety-provoking; involves gradual, controlled exposure to the anxiety-producing stimulus accompanied by positive reinforcement

tactile (sensory) reinforcement   The application of tactile or sensory consequences to reinforce behavior; used primarily with students with severe and profound disabilities

tangible reinforcement   Contingent provision of non-edible items to reinforce behavior

target behavior   A behavior identified for change that is observable, measurable, defined so that two persons can agree as to its occurrence, and stated so that a criterion can be set for a desired level of performance

task analysis   The process of breaking down a complex behavior into its component parts so that it can be taught in small, easy steps

teacher assistance team   Staff who assist the regular educator with prereferral interventions; the team may also assist teachers with behavior management problems involving special education students

teacher expectations   The rating of important adaptive behaviors and teachers' tolerance for maladaptive behaviors in terms of how they affect their willingness to work with students in their classroom; a vital consideration for the mainstreaming and inclusion of special education students

Teacher Interview for Psychiatric Symptoms (TIPS)   Instrument for identifying psychiatric problems in children (Kerr & Schaeffer, 1987)

teacher interview   An informal method for screening and identification of students with behavior problems

teacher-mediated strategy   Behavior management strategy that involves a teacher's direct interaction with students

teacher ranking   Sociometric screening procedure in which the classroom teacher generates an ordered list representing his or her perceptions of students from lowest to highest risk of either internalizing or externalizing behavior problems

terminal behavior   The desired end product or goal for change in a student's behavior

therapy   A procedure for bringing about positive social adjustment

time delay   An errorless teaching procedure in which the time interval between a task request and an instructional prompt is systematically increased until the pupil emits the correct response before the prompt is given

time management   The organization of time for school tasks; a key to stress management and academic success for both students and teachers

timeout   A procedure for the reduction of inappropriate behavior whereby the student is denied access, for a fixed period of time, to the opportunity to receive reinforcement

timer game   Using a kitchen timer to shape pupil behavior and train teachers to use tokens and praise

time sampling   Observational recording system in which behavior is observed for a limited time period (e.g., 5 minutes of a 60-minute period)

token economy   A system of behavior modification in which tangible or token reinforcers such as points, plastic chips, metal washers, poker chips, or play money are given as rewards and later exchanged for back-up reinforcers that have value in themselves (e.g., food, trinkets, play time, books); a miniature economic system used to foster desirable behavior

topographic response class   A class of behaviors that are related in terms of their form, or the movements comprising the response (e.g., handraising)

topography   The physical form or description of a motor behavior

total reliability   A method used to assess the agreement between the total numerical counts of behaviors obtained by two independent observers Formula:

$$\frac{\text{smaller frequency}}{\text{larger frequency}} \times 100$$

train-and-hope programming   Assessment probes conducted in generalization settings in which generalization is not specifically programmed

train loosely   Teaching principle for generalization in which trainers, settings, situations, prompts, and so on are varied across all phases of the learning process

transenvironmental programming   A strategy consisting of four components: (1) assessing the behavioral expectations of specific generalization settings, (2) competency training in the special education environments, (3) selection and use of techniques for promoting the transfer of skills across settings, and (4) monitoring and evaluating student performance in generalization settings

transfer of training   See *stimulus generalization*

transition plan   A program designed to help students cope with the move from one setting to the next, usually including annual goals and short- and long-term plans

transition services   Services and agencies designed to aid students in the move from one setting to another, including helping the individual make work and social contacts, helping him or her become established, and following up with the individual and his or her progress in the new environment

transition strategies   Strategies that involve transferring students and their entire repertoires of behavior to new settings

trapping effect   Behavior is "trapped" in the natural environment when it is relevant to the student's lifestyle and needs and is reinforced by naturally occurring schedules of reinforcement, usually in the form of social attention

trend   Data points on a graph which show whether a behavior is increasing, decreasing, or remaining stable (an ascending or descending trend is defined as three consecutive data points in a single direction)

trend lines   Lines of "best fit" that are drawn to represent the path shown by graphed data—increasing, decreasing, or level

triadic model   A description of the relationship between a behavioral consultant, a mediator (primary intervention agent), and the target pupil

trial-by-trial recording   Recording student responses to individual prompts given by the teacher over a set of discrete trials

trials to criterion recording   A measurement strategy for monitoring progress through a task-analyzed sequence or for measuring skill generalization

universal intervention   Behavior change procedure applied to an entire class or school

unprompted generalization   A strategy that involves monitoring in generalization settings and reinforcing spontaneous generalization

validity   The degree to which a test measures what it purports to measure; types of validity include content, criterion-referenced (predictive and concurrent), and construct validity

variable reinforcement   Observing and reinforcing students after varying time intervals, which average a designated time interval

verbal aversive   Unpleasant verbal behavior (i.e., yelling, scolding, whining) that may serve as aversive stimulus

vicarious reinforcement   Reinforcement of a student for appropriate behavior so that observing students will imitate the behavior

visual analysis   Evaluating the significance of behavior change through visual inspection of a behavior graph

visual screening   A procedure for reducing stereotypic behaviors in which the teacher covers the student's eyes with his or her hand when the student engages in the target behavior

volatility   Drug inhalants mixing readily with air in high concentrations

Walker-Rankin Child Behavior Rating Scale   A criterion-referenced scale on which the teacher in the sending setting assesses the target student's behavioral status on the items designated as critical or unacceptable (Walker, 1986)

window of variance   The amount of desired stability around the trend; found by drawing parallel dotted lines representing a 15-percent range above and below the trend line

withdrawal design   (ABAB or ABA design, similar to reversal design)   A single-subject research design that involves collecting baseline data (A), followed by an intervention condition (B), a withdrawal of intervention procedures, or return to baseline conditions (A) and a reinstatement of the intervention (B)

wraparound plan   (integrated service plan)   A multi-agency plan of care designed to meet the individual needs of a youth with an emotional or behavioral disorder and his or her family

INDEX